A NATION
AND NOT A
RABBLE

ALSO BY DIARMAID FERRITER

The Transformation of Ireland 1900–2000
Judging Dev: A reassessment of the life and legacy of Éamon de Valera
Occasions of Sin: Sex and Society in Modern Ireland
Ambiguous Republic: Ireland in the 1970s

A NATION
AND NOT A
RABBLE

THE IRISH REVOLUTION 1913–1923

DIARMAID FERRITER

P

PROFILE BOOKS

First published in Great Britain in 2015 by
PROFILE BOOKS LTD
3 Holford Yard
Bevin Way
London WC1X 9HD

www.profilebooks.com

1 3 5 7 9 10 8 6 4 2

Typeset in Garamond by MacGuru Ltd
info@macguru.org.uk

Printed and bound in Great Britain by
Clays, Bungay, Suffolk

A CIP catalogue record for this book is available from the British Library.

ISBN 978 1 78125 041 9
eISBN 978 1 84765 882 1

The paper this book is printed on is certified by the © 1996 Forest Stewardship
Council A.C. (FSC). It is ancient-forest friendly. The printer
holds FSC chain of custody SGS-COC-2061

FSC
www.fsc.org
MIX
Paper from
responsible sources
FSC® C018072

For Carmel Furlong

CONTENTS

ACKNOWLEDGEMENTS

Taking the long view, work on this book began nearly twenty years ago when, with Paul Rouse and Catríona Crowe, I was involved in the research of a National Archives of Ireland (NAI) exhibition to mark the seventy-fifth anniversary of the foundation of the Irish Free State in 1922. That research introduced me to the Dáil Éireann files and other collections in the NAI and the documents led to much reflection then and in subsequent years on the nature and experience of the Irish revolution and its various layers. More research in the NAI as well as trawls through the extensive collections in the University College Dublin (UCD) archives, along with the UK National Archives in Kew, London, and the Public Record Office of Northern Ireland in Belfast, brought me to a deeper awareness of this period, an appreciation of its complexity and the reasons so many become absorbed in it. I am grateful to the staff of all these archives and the staff of the UCD library, which also houses valuable primary source material for the revolutionary decade this book assesses. My colleagues in the School of History and Archives at UCD deserve my deep gratitude for support and collegiality, especially Kate Breslin, as do friends for offering warmth and great company, including the Briggs family, Aisling Caden, Stephen Cullinane, Mark Duncan, Adrienne Egan, Liza Finnegan, Ronan and Karen Furlong, Ambo Kearney, Seán Kearns, James Kelly, Philip King, Cormac Kinsella, Pat Leahy, Anne, Tom, Catherine, Lucy, Rose and Kevin Maher, Peter Mooney, Deirdre

Mulligan, Paul Murphy, Margaret Mac Curtain, Nuala O'Connor, Greg Prendergast, Antoinette Prout, Yetti Redmond, Paul Rouse, Martin Walsh and David Whelan. Profile Books, yet again, have been generous and patient and provided unstinting support; thank you to the late Peter Carson as well as Andrew Franklin and Penny Daniel. I am particularly grateful to Trevor Horwood for his skilful copy-editing, and to Deirdre McMahon and Catríona Crowe for comments on earlier drafts of this book and for the conversations Catríona and I have had about this period and much else over many years of treasured friendship. As always, my greatest debts are to those closer to home; to my cherished parents, Nollaig and Vera, sublime siblings Cian, Tríona and Muireann, and those we are lucky enough to have as long-standing, close and loyal friends, including the wonderful Carmel Furlong to whom this book is dedicated. I am also beyond fortunate to be surrounded by three beguiling, inspiring, intensely loveable and infuriating daughters, Enya, Ríona and Saorla, and the adorable, formidable, insightful, sceptical, funny and generous Sheila Maher, whose support and love have helped this book, like the others, move from abstract to real.

INTRODUCTION

In January 1922, George Gavan Duffy, a barrister and Sinn Féin TD who had served as an envoy for the Irish republican movement in Paris during the War of Independence, was appointed Minister for Foreign Affairs in the southern Irish provisional government, formed after the Anglo-Irish Treaty had been ratified to bring an end to that war. The Treaty offered, not the Irish Republic Sinn Féin had sought, but an Irish Free State as a self-governing dominion within the British Commonwealth, with continued subordination to the British Crown represented by an oath of allegiance to that crown. In April of that year, Gavan Duffy articulated a fear that the looming civil war had the potential to do lasting damage to Ireland's reputation abroad and the fledging Free State's dignity. He concluded there was urgency that those on both sides of the Treaty debate should ensure Ireland was seen 'as a nation and not a rabble'.[1]

That particular word – 'rabble' – and other versions of it, frequently surfaced in assessments of the breakdown of the established order and the mayhem often apparent in the period of the Irish revolution from 1913 to 1923 that ultimately led to the creation of the state of Northern Ireland in 1920 and the Irish Free State in 1922, subsequently the Irish Republic. A horrified unionist, writing to her friend at the end of 1918, remarked: 'This is a very unpleasant country to live in now. We are going through so many changes. The democracy in Ireland are a very bad lot, they are so low and uneducated, only a rabble led by the priests.'[2] Likewise, the diaries of Elsie

Henry, who worked with the Red Cross charity in Dublin and had friends and brothers fighting in the First World War, include a letter written by a contemporary in April 1918 about growing tension over possible conscription of Irish men into the British army. It included the observation 'the peasants and labourers of Ireland are inflammable material, who are now led by skilful leaders, backed up by the late insurrection, by song, ballads and what passes for history and by a literature; and they are out or will be out soon – if conscription is imposed'.[3]

The playwright and Abbey Theatre director Lady Augusta Gregory, when corresponding from her home in Galway with poet W. B. Yeats in the immediate aftermath of the 1916 Rising, commented: 'It is terrible to think of the executions and killings that are sure to come ... yet it must be so – we had been at the mercy of a rabble for a long time, both here and in Dublin, with no apparent policy.' And yet, as the executions of the Rising's leaders were carried out, she changed her tone. Her mind was now 'filled with sorrow at the Dublin tragedy'; the execution of John Mac-Bride, a long-standing republican activist and Boer War veteran, who was not involved in the planning of the Rising but who joined the fighting at its commencement, was 'the best event that could come to him, giving him dignity'. The leaders, she concluded, were 'enthusiastic ... and I keep wondering whether we could not have brought them into the intellectual movement'.[4]

This concern with and admiration for dignity was partly what propelled Lady Gregory and other cultural nationalists to do what they did for Ireland, but it also left them feeling uncertain and ambiguous in their responses to the Irish revolution. Gregory had different views of what was happening at different stages. So did many. The idea of the 'rabble' and the fear of it also reflected class divisions and the threat of class conflict, so obviously manifest in the Dublin Lockout of 1913, when employers refused to recognise the right of unskilled labourers to be members of the Irish Transport and General Workers Union (ITGWU): 'This is why the ITGWU was seen as such a threat. It organised outside of the craft unions, and brought together as a powerful industrial force the workers who were dismissed as rabble.'[5] With a home rule Ireland on the horizon, the 1913 Lockout was also a power struggle in relation to who would control a self-governing Ireland.

The militancy of the marginalised was feared, and the adoption of their cause by some of Ireland's elite was abhorred by others of the same ilk. Elsie Mahaffy, daughter of the Provost of Trinity College Dublin, for example, wrote about the involvement of Constance Markievicz in Irish republicanism in 1916, to the effect that she was 'the one woman amongst them of high birth and therefore the most depraved ... she took to politics and left our class'.[6] But Markievicz, a member of an Anglo-Irish aristocratic family, despite her reputation for radicalism, hardly exhibited much solidarity with those less well off who were with her in Aylesbury prison after the 1916 Rising, and later complained to her sister that she had been imprisoned with 'the dregs of the population'.[7] (Yeats was later to complain that Markievicz, who died at the age of fifty-nine, had sacrificed her beauty and burned herself out campaigning on behalf of those who were 'ignorant' – another rebuke of the 'rabble'.)[8]

Some of the correspondence highlighted above underlines the danger of generalising about the Irish revolutionary period and the inadequacy of its traditional narratives, reflected in the recent observation of Roy Foster that 'we search now, instead, to find clarification through terms of paradox and nuance; we have become interested in what does not change during revolutions as much as what does'.[9] This is partly due to the abundance of new source material that throws up such a variety of perspectives, admissions and ambiguities. These sources, discussed in Part I of this book, challenge the following notion, articulated by Irish novelist Colm Tóibín in his introduction to a collection of Irish fiction:

> Those central moments in French history are communal and urban,
> but the critical moments in Irish history seem more like a nineteenth-
> century novel in which the individual, tragic hero is burdened by the
> society he lives in. We have no communards, no rabble in the streets.
> Instead, we have personal sacrifice as a metaphor for general sacrifice.[10]

Likewise, it has long been contended that while the revolution transformed Anglo-Irish relations, 'it did not change the relationship between one class of Irishmen and another. Its impact was nationalist and political, not social and economic.'[11] That assertion about a primarily political revolution, however, is also problematic; more probing of sources that highlight the 'history from below' of the period suggest that social and economic forces did have an impact; while radical impulses may have been resisted, they had an ongoing presence, and the fear of the 'rabble' and its potential to destabilise the 'political' revolution was often apparent.

Concerns and disputes over land – a central theme throughout the revolutionary period and discussed in Part II of this book – the cost of living, unemployment and victimisation abounded. There were also difficulties in reconciling the priorities of the Sinn Féin and labour movements, and local feuds simmered both during the revolution and in its aftermath. As a result of the revolution, some clearly fared better than others, which underlines the fact that the revolution *did* 'change the relationship between one class of Irishmen and another', not through the creation of a new socialist regime, but through the existence a hierarchy of benefit. As the writer Francis Stuart, interned during the civil war, saw it, 'we fought to stop Ireland falling into the hands of publicans and shopkeepers and she had fallen into their hands'.[12]

During the revolution and after it, there were many groups that could be and were identified as 'rabble', including those who took up arms and were wary of centralised control, in both Ulster and southern Ireland; those suspicious of constitutional politics and its practitioners, women demanding the vote, and those who laboured in the city and rural areas and agitated for greater status and wages. Other relevant groups included those who volunteered for service in the British army during the war, the 'separation allowance women' they left behind, and those who rejected the Anglo-Irish Treaty and took up arms against it. All, in their own ways, created difficulties for those seeking to control and direct the revolution, and their experiences involved a multitude of personal motivations and expectations.

If it is true that events of this period in Ireland, especially the 1916 Rising, amounted to 'Ireland's 1789',[13] how relevant are international studies of the 'rabble' or 'crowd' to the Irish situation? George Rudé's work on this theme from the 1960s in relation to popular disturbances in England and France in the eighteenth and nineteenth centuries was influential and pioneering. Using Marx's description, he was interested in the ideas that 'grip the masses' and the role they play in the peaks and troughs of a popular movement. Rudé was praised for 'putting mind back into history', as he looked at leaders but especially followers, at whether their motivations could be seen as involving 'backward' or 'forward looking' concepts, and whether the crowds could develop a distinctive sociopolitical movement of their own.[14] Rudé focused on the needs of the groups and classes that absorbed ideas, the social context in which these ideas germinated and 'the uses to which they put them'.[15] His framework of inquiry was further developed and challenged in subsequent decades by the study of different types of crowds; those who assembled for religious reasons, or on state occasions or for funerals; not necessarily 'the masses', but different groups of various sizes that assembled, influenced each other's behaviour and who could be marshalled by elite factions.[16]

There were a number of traditions in Ireland well before the early twentieth century that were relevant to 'crowd' themes; the proliferation of crowd activity during the era of Daniel O'Connell, leader of the successful movement for Catholic emancipation in the 1820s and the unsuccessful subsequent movement for repeal of the Act of Union in the 1840s, agrarian unrest, the Land War of the 1870s and 1880s and the attendant mass meetings organised by the Land League, Fenian uprisings, commemorations, funerals and election rallies. Ulster also had its own traditions of agrarian and urban mobilisation to draw on, including campaigns against home rule in the late nineteenth century. Developments in communications, the use of partisan newspapers, increased literacy, the priorities of a younger generation and greater public prominence for women all played their part in mobilising groups.

The important point is that increasingly in nineteenth-century Ireland, various groups 'saw crowd strength as a sign of the seriousness of their intent', and there is no doubt that this impulse gathered momentum in the 1913–23 period; mass rallies, funerals, election meetings, military drilling and protests were paramount. Crucially, these assemblies heightened the sense of 'the other' or being on the 'right' or the 'wrong' side, and increasing invective was employed in relation to how those deemed to be on the 'wrong' side could be described. During the Irish revolutionary period militia forces were established, most notably the Ulster Volunteers and Irish Volunteers (subsequently the IRA) in 1913; for their members and those they declared to be defending they were noble and courageous, to their opponents they were an ignorant rabble being duped or used by corrupt leaders.

A growing scepticism about constitutional politics was also relevant here; as was recalled by IRA member Christopher ('Todd') Andrews, the Irish Parliamentary Party (IPP) that took its seats in the Westminster Parliament, and fought for home rule rather than an Irish Republic, became discredited to the point that 'the word "politician" was never applied to a member of the [republican] Movement. It was a word of ill-repute.'[17] In retaliation, some of those IPP politicians, particularly as a new Sinn Féin political mass movement began to threaten the IPP's very survival, turned on the 'rabble' with a panicked snobbery. This was particularly apparent in one of the last letters written by IPP leader John Redmond, who in criticising his own party for not uniting around him in early 1918 suggested the result of such disloyalty in Ireland would be 'universal anarchy, and, I am greatly afraid, the spread of violence and crime of all sorts, when every blackguard who wants to commit an outrage will simply call himself a Sinn Féiner and thereby get the sympathy of the unthinking crowd'.[18]

The mistake here was in asserting that those embracing the new politics and resistance were dupes; they were in fact far from 'unthinking'; they were young and determined to reject Redmond's generation, and with confidence and purpose, 'knew that they were different from their parents'.[19] But their revolution was, in turn, while propelled by much idealism and courage, also multi-layered, complicated, messy, brutal and sometimes compromised as a result of competing impulses at national but also local level, as smaller 'crowds' or independent-minded 'rabbles' pursued their own agendas. The revolution could serve as a useful cloak for the settling of scores that had little to do with ideas of nationalism or 'the nation'.

The fear political leaders had was that they would not be able to control these movements; that the 'rabble' might go its own way. There were strong tensions in relation to centralisation and local initiative in both the unionist and republican movements that were at odds with the images these groups wanted to portray of themselves, and attempted to portray in earlier partisan accounts of the revolution, as united and monolithic. Tensions between different social classes always bubbled beneath the surface and sometimes boiled over. For those who wanted to defend the union with Great Britain and those who wanted to break it, mobilisation was deemed imperative to pressurise British governments, but such activity could not completely mask internal fractiousness: 'although such mobilisations were portrayed by the media as highly disciplined non-violent affairs, there was always an underlying element of threat, namely, that the leadership could not hold the masses in line indefinitely'.[20] This was even more complicated during the War of Independence from 1919–21, when republicans fought a guerrilla campaign, and before that, many UVF members had found themselves in a different theatre of war altogether as soldiers in the trenches of the First World War, as did thousands of recruits from southern Ireland. The difficulties of control also became acutely apparent during the civil war in the south from 1922–3, but also in the new state in Northern Ireland from 1920.

The labour movement was also relevant here, as part of a broader development in the UK of conflict between the 'socialist' and the 'national' interest, creating obvious class divisions that British liberals struggled with. Labour unrest, combined with tension over home rule, armed resistance in 1916, suffragism, as well as the rising cost of living, complicated British rule in Ireland.[21] In responding, British governments struggled with their Irish policy, initially granting concessions through, for example, land reform and the expansion of access to education and local government, and increased welfare provision for the 'rabble', but preoccupied with so much else, they also turned a blind eye to growing militancy and gunrunning. Their perspective was also undermined by lazy racial stereotyping about a 'peculiar kind of [Irish] patriotic impulse', and by applying different standards to the threat of Ulster violence and the threat of southern Irish republican force.[22]

And what of ideas of 'the nation' during the revolution, the term that, along with the 'rabble', so preoccupied George Gavan Duffy? Ten years previously, Tom Kettle, who had been elected an MP for the IPP in 1906 but at the end of 1910 left Parliament to pursue his writing, in *The Open Secret of Ireland* (1912), declared: 'the open secret of Ireland is that Ireland is a nation'. This had earlier been given credence by Alice Stopford Green in *Irish Nationality* (1911) and *The Making of Ireland and Its Undoing* (1908), books that insisted on the unbroken continuity of a national tradition in Irish history. Green was the wealthy daughter of a Protestant archdeacon and married the social historian John Richard Green; financial security allowed her to develop her own interest in history, and in the 1890s she was converted to Irish home rule through a growing distaste for British imperialism:

> She contended that pre-Norman Ireland [before the twelfth-century invasion] was not a home to barbarians but to an admirable civilisation, which, she insisted, was marked by an attachment to spiritual rather than material values. This argument was clearly motivated by, and had implications for, contemporary politics. She sought to prove that, before interference from England, the Irish had successfully governed themselves and should be allowed to do so again.[23]

But that did not mean that Green was comfortable with the violence of the Irish revolution; it troubled her greatly.

Tom Kettle, killed in action with the British army at the Battle of the Somme in 1916, exemplified some of the dilemmas for those who resisted narrow definitions of nationalism. While he had maintained the moral right of Ireland to rebel 'if it were possible', he did not think it wise to build 'an impossible future on an imaginary past', an approach that, historically, had led English parties to wipe Ireland 'off the slate of popular politics'. A liberal Catholic, he also admired European civilisation, and regarded it as a greater cause than Ireland's.[24] Such perspectives came under increased pressure in Ireland during the First World War, but what linked many of the militant or military-minded who went in different directions were similar ideas: 'militarism, honour, patriotism, self-sacrifice, manhood, adventure ... spiritual yearnings defying the grey calculations of a secure and cautious life'.[25]

Also in 1912, librarian and Jesuit Stephen Brown, in the Jesuit-published journal *Studies*, maintained that the word 'nation' was too glibly used and that its uses were 'untroubled by any consciousness that the idea which this word claims to express presents special difficulties of definition'.[26] It could be defined, he suggested, according to race, language, customs, religion, history, a national government or just common interests, or to those living in a common territory in organised social relations 'held together in a peculiar kind of spiritual oneness'. This definition was certainly relevant to those who proclaimed a republic at the outset of the Easter Rising in 1916; after all, Patrick Pearse, chosen as president of that republic by the rebels, wrote an article two months before the Rising entitled 'The Spiritual Nation'. But Brown suggested 'there can be no precise or final formula'.[27]

This absence of an accepted definition was in itself significant in the decade of revolution; notions of the nation became divisive in what was a plural as opposed to a unitary society, as represented by the experiences and allegiances of the majority in Ulster who claimed to be part of another nation, in contrast to southern Ireland. Conflicting definitions led to aggressive exclusion, or as the historian Nicholas Mansergh put it: 'The greater the success in translating the inner feelings of a community into language, almost inevitably to be communicated in part in emotional imagery, the more likely it is for those who are not members of that community to have a feeling of alienation.'[28] These feelings of alienation, when combined with other tensions, developed a momentum of their own which could also exacerbate the sense of a 'rabble' that needed to be contained or resisted.

For some, nationalism was about will and spirit and antiquity, an appeal to the dead generations; for others it was something that needed to be called into being and could include social aims, an obvious priority for the leading Labour intellectual of this era, James Connolly, for whom 'the Irish question' was 'a social question'.[29] Small radical groups and wordy polemical journalists who fuelled 'the little newspapers and magazines of the nationalist fringe'[30] went to great lengths to excoriate what they regarded as the failures of the contemporary order, but what they wanted to see it replaced with depended on perspectives that could be informed by many things, including age, class, gender and political inheritance.

It was also the case that separatist language and sentiment would only gain a broader acceptance when linked to grievances such as urban poverty, rising food prices and taxes, cessation of land distribution and emigration.[31] As a result, the balance to be struck between political separatism and social advance was delicate and rarely satisfactorily achieved. These material questions also pervaded the process after the revolution of compensation and the quest for military service pensions and recognition, discussed in Part III of this book.

Those looking for evidence of broad, sophisticated ideological debate during the decade may be disappointed, but perhaps in that search, they are misguided in projecting later preoccupations on to a generation that were not republican theorists and saw no reason to be. Those who propelled the republican revolution were more focused on the idea of separation from Britain 'rather than implementing any concrete political programme'. Ideology does not feature strongly in most accounts of the revolution and, in the words of Charles Townshend, 'the new nationalist leaders did not see it as necessary to analyse the "self" that was to exercise self-determination', or as Mansergh had asserted at a much earlier stage, the republican leaders 'do not appear to have debated what may have appeared to be potentially dividing abstractions'.[32] Political scientist Tom Garvin's estimation was that 'Irish republicanism was not a political theory but a secular religion'.[33] So too was Irish unionism, but for British politicians dealing with both perspectives, any theories of nationalism were unwelcome intrusions, 'because at almost every point behind the argument lay the deeper question: were there in Ireland two nations? Or two communities? Or only contrived divisions?'[34] When asked by the founder of Sinn Féin, Arthur Griffith, why the British government had abandoned the idea of 'Irish oneness' or treating the island as an entity, British prime minister David Lloyd George replied: 'we could not coerce Ulster'.

But alongside pragmatism, such assertions also hid double-dealing, false promises and inconsistency in relation to what Britain would decide merited coercion. The Irish revolution threw up obvious dilemmas: what rights do majorities and minorities have and how can they be asserted or vindicated? Such questions were never resolved to the satisfaction of most during the revolutionary period and remained unresolved long after it. They were also relevant to how the revolution was remembered and commemorated, who should control that process and who the 'true' inheritors of its legacy were, as also discussed in Part III of this book.

There is little doubt that in its aftermath, a social analysis of the revolution struggled to find space on the crowded canvas of political and military writing on the period. This has been somewhat countered in recent times and has included an increased focus on regional and micro studies, as well as a probing of the social composition of those involved.[35] The Canadian historian Peter Hart has made the point that, because of the range of source material available, Ireland is a great laboratory for the study of revolution:

> Ireland's is quite possibly the best documented revolution in modern history. For "a secret army", the guerrillas left an extraordinary paper trail through their own and their opponents' records as well as in the daily and weekly press. This continued long after the war was over, as gunmen claimed pensions, wrote memoirs and commemorated themselves and their comrades.[36]

Hart also suggested in 2002 that, as a result of such archival riches, the revolution 'needs to be re-conceptualised and to have all the myriad assumptions underlying its standard narratives interrogated', to include examinations of 'gender, class, community, elites and masses, religion and ethnicity, the nature of violence and power'.[37] There is now also much more focus on the key role women played in cultural, political and military awakenings and finding new outlets, and what they suffered on account of their gender; no longer is their documented involvement just a case of 'fleeting glances of these shadowy female characters'.[38]

Rectifying the imbalances that affected more traditional accounts of the revolution is not just about new sources (discussed in Part I); giving the social history of this period a new prominence is also about using long-opened but neglected collections, or indeed, looking at 'political' sources in a different way. As the renowned historian of twentieth-century Ireland Joe Lee suggested, 'it is often overlooked how much social history can be found in the accounts of political events'.[39] The National Archives of Ireland collections for this period, for example, include the Dáil Éireann records, used extensively in Part II of this book, which give a detailed overview of the administration of various underground republican government departments and the problems they confronted. The records of the Ministry of Local Government and accounts of the proceedings of local authorities transmitted to central government also give an insight into a multitude of regional social and economic problems. The same is true of the records of the Dáil Éireann Land Settlement Commission, which document the attempts to arbitrate on the claims of individuals to land from which they had been evicted.

The collections of the British National Archives in London also contain numerous reports of what was going on in Ireland at local and national level and the collections in the Public Record Office of Northern Ireland (PRONI) illustrate aspects of the internal dynamics of the Ulster movement and political, religious and military strife. Other documents compiled in the 1920s offer a perspective on the social legacy of the revolutionary period, including the papers of the Committee on Claims of British Ex-servicemen, established in 1927 to look into the plight of Irishmen who had fought with the British army in the First World War. As one witness insisted, in outlining their social and economic grievances, 'it is about time the promises made to them in 1914 were carried out. The men are not getting younger and they are not getting stronger.'[40] Many in the revolution's aftermath found themselves living as mental 'internees' (a word used by nationalist and writer Alice Milligan), disappointed by the new states created as a result of the revolutions and feeling at home 'nowhere'.[41] What transpired after the revolution also bred new dismissals of the 'rabble', involving cynicism and snobbery on the part of some about democracy itself. Mabel FitzGerald, for example, a 1916 Rising participant, and wife of Desmond, War of Independence veteran and pro-Treaty minister in the 1920s, wrote in a personal letter in 1944: 'I find the masses are always wrong, they seem to stand for the worst in man ... adult suffrage seems to have led only to the supremacy of people without standards and values and of the half-baked educationally ... they already dominate everything here [in Ireland].'[42]

For all those who were celebrated, honoured and feted, or who forged rewarding political careers in the aftermath, many more were left wounded and impoverished despite their military, political or intellectual contribution to the decade, and even for victims there was an obvious hierarchy. The most recent opening of new archives, especially the Bureau of Military History statements collected from veterans of the revolution in the 1940s and 1950s and locked up until 2003, and the Military Service Pensions Collection, documenting the applications of those who applied for recognition of their military service during the revolution, the first batch of which was released in 2014, discussed in Parts I and III of this book, has been part of another broadening of the parameters of historical inquiry into the revolutionary period. Collectively, these various records reveal a fascinating web of different Irish experiences, including understandable feelings of despair and resentment and the search for stability in the midst of mayhem, but also humanity and humour as people reacted to issues of law and order, economics, land, class struggle, violence and the dominant political questions.

There is now more interest in the experiences of those who would not have been mentioned or considered to the same extent in earlier decades. Alongside a continuity of interest in high politics, Anglo-Irish relations and the 'leading personalities' of the era, new questions have emerged in relation to the revolution, prompted by this new archival material: how did the revolution affect the people of this era, combatants and non-combatants, male and female? What information do we have of 'people getting on with their lives through periods of national trauma'?

This was a description used in relation to a project launched by Trinity College Dublin in 2013 to encourage those who might have family archival material relating to the period. One example given was that of two lovers corresponding in 1915; when their son was asked in 2013 what 'side' they were on in 1916 during the Easter Rising, his response was 'They were not on any side ... they were on the getting on with life side.'[43] What did 'getting on with life' involve for those who lived through the revolutionary period? How did contemporaries make sense of it and its aftermath and legacy? This book, in examining aspects of the Irish interior of the revolution, seeks to underline the significance of those questions, highlight some of the archival material available in attempting to answer them, and to look generally at the evolution in the understanding and perception of the revolution since the 1920s; to consider how we came to know what we know about the period, who told us and why; its impact, legacy and how it has been remembered.

The first part looks at how the revolution was framed by those writing about the subject, including veterans and later professional historians; what agendas they followed, the sources they used, the controversies they engendered and how the growing importance of archival material expanded the range and scope of historical inquiry. The second part offers an analytic narrative of the revolution, largely driven by recent sources, which, while acknowledging the significance and contribution of well-known political and military leaders and the Anglo-Irish high politics that bordered the revolution, also provides a detailed focus on the social forces and human impulses that predominated, the tension between central control and local dynamics, between notions of 'the nation' and the concerns of 'the rabble', and the gulf between rhetoric and reality. The third part assesses the detritus of the revolution, the legacy for some of those directly affected, their quest for recognition of their service, how commemoration of the period presented challenges for both state and society from the 1920s onwards, and where we are now in relation to understanding and remembering the revolution during its centenary.

PART I

IN SEARCH OF
THE RABBLE

ONE

OPENING THE
WITNESS ACCOUNTS

On the evening of 11 March 2003, state cars began to arrive at the
Cathal Brugha military barracks in Dublin, home of the Irish Military Archives. The Taoiseach, Bertie Ahern and the Minister for Defence,
Michael Smith were in attendance, as was the former Taoiseach Liam Cosgrave. His father, William T. Cosgrave, was one of the Sinn Féin ministers
during the Irish War of Independence and went on to become president
of the Executive Council (prime minister) of the new Free State in 1922.
Gathered there also was a group of Irish historians, some of whom had
been waiting for this occasion for many years. An archive was about to be
opened, after a half-century under lock and key, that would shed light on
a period still much disputed in Irish history, the revolutionary period of
1913–23.

The historians who were present that day represented two different
generations; those who had come to prominence from the late 1960s to
the 1980s during the most intense periods of the Troubles of Northern
Ireland that began in 1969, and a younger generation who began studying
history at university in the late 1980s and early 1990s and had established
themselves as professional historians during the peace process that brought
the Troubles to an end in the late 1990s. The politicians who attended
included those politically active in the 1960s and 1970s as the offspring
of the revolutionary generation, and their successors who governed in the
1980s and beyond, while the ghosts of those who fought in the War of

Independence and the civil war loomed large; the barracks itself is named after Sinn Féin's Minister for Defence during the War of Independence.

The archive unveiled and formally launched that day was that of the Bureau of Military History (BMH), which included over 1,700 statements taken from 1916 Rising and War of Independence veterans in the 1940s and 1950s, whose witness accounts of their role in the conflict were impounded in the late 1950s, with no agreement as to when they might be opened, but with a consensus that it would not be for at least another generation. That was hardly surprising; many of the events, individuals and legacies of the revolutionary era were still raw and divisive in mid-twentieth-century Ireland, and there was concern about allegations and accusations that might be contained in the statements with no right of redress. Those involved in collecting the statements, however, had been adamant about their neutrality, and had held firm to their independence; when the old IRA organisation in Limerick city insisted that all potential statements for the BMH had to be submitted to it before being given to J. J. Daly, the Bureau's investigator for Limerick, for example, Daly refused to accept this and the delays caused by his refusal 'were surely worthwhile'.[1]

While there was much agreement in 2003 as to the potential value of the BMH statements for professional historians and those interested in history generally, a committee of historians and experts that had been asked to advise the government on the BMH process in the 1940s was not united in its attitude to the value of the collection, when it might be released and the probable verdict of posterity. Richard Hayes, chairman of the Bureau's advisory committee, and director of the National Library of Ireland, wrote to fellow committee member Robert Dudley Edwards, Professor of Modern Irish History at UCD, in February 1958, in relation to disagreement as to when the material should be opened to researchers: 'I think we can do nothing and I have no time to bang my head against a blank wall. Incidentally, the material collected seems to me to be of so little value that I do not mourn the loss.'[2]

Florence O'Donoghue, another committee member and a War of Independence veteran and keen historian, was adamant that there was no justification for impounding original documents 'which would be available if they had not been given to the Bureau. I put in a number of original documents, some my own, some I had got from friends. I would never have done so if I knew they were going to be inaccessible for a very long period.' In the 1940s and 1950s part of the government's mission in relation to the BMH, it appeared, was 'to keep the documents out of the historians' hands'; they were there to advise, not supervise.[3] Dudley Edwards scribbled a note after a meeting with another of the members of the advisory committee, Sheila Kennedy, a lecturer in history in Galway, to the effect that 'she is fed up with the Bureau, feels it is a dreadful waste of money which could be put to much better historical uses' and that the work 'could well have been done in a university'. This reflected resentment that the work was being carried out by people who were not professional historians, but public servants employed by the Department of Defence.[4] Furthermore, Hayes had severe doubts about the statements being made available to the general public: 'If every Seán and Seamus from Ballythis and Ballythat who took major or minor or no part at all in the national movement from 1916 to 1921 has free access to the material it may result in local civil warfare in every second town and village in the country.'[5]

Five decades later, this assertion by Hayes might be seen as delightful exaggeration underpinned by a good deal of snobbery. It was an interesting stance, not just in relation to the sensitivities and divisions of the era, but also on the question of to whom the story of the revolution belonged and who should be in a position to research and document it. One of the most notable developments in recent years in Ireland in relation to the history of this period and access to its documentation has been its democratisation, including the opening up of archival material, a lot of it online, to much bigger audiences than was previously the case. It is no longer the preserve of state or an academic elite; much of it is now open to anyone with an Internet connection.

What have such developments meant in relation to an understanding of the revolutionary period? In some respects it was about building on the information contained in valuable collections of source material that had been available for decades. Before the opening of the BMH, historians had access to accounts of life in IRA flying columns and the day-to-day activities and operations of the republican movement during the period 1913–21. The huge archive of Richard Mulcahy, for example, who was chief of staff of the IRA during the War of Independence and whose papers were deposited in the UCD archives in the 1970s, shed much light on the internal dynamics and difficulties of the republican movement. After retiring from politics in 1961 Mulcahy spent much of that decade collating his papers and complementing them with voice recordings of contemporaries, and 'his pioneering decision, under the terms of the Mulcahy Trust established in December 1970, to make permanent arrangements for depositing his papers in the archives department of UCD, made him an exemplar for other leading politicians from both sides of the treaty divide'.[6]

Likewise, Ernie O'Malley, a leading figure in the IRA who had the distinction of writing the best literary accounts of the revolution, had earlier amassed more than 450 handwritten interviews of veterans of the War of Independence and civil war. A native of Castlebar in County Mayo born into comfortable middle-class circumstances, O'Malley was active as an IRA organiser and was appointed commander of the IRA's 2nd Southern Division in 1921. He opposed the Treaty and played a leading role in the anti-Treaty IRA campaign. He conducted the interviews himself; for six years he 'criss-crossed Ireland in his old Ford, driving up boreens and searching out old companions in order to record, and in a sense relive, the glory days of the revolution'. What had begun in the late 1930s 'as an effort to supplement his own knowledge had developed by 1948 into a full-blown enterprise to record the voices, mostly republican, of the survivors of the 1916–23 struggle for independence', with his material eventually deposited in UCD.[7] O'Malley was therefore conducting his own oral history in tandem with the state's BMH project, but the BMH project was larger and broader in relation to the number and mix of witnesses and the statements were recorded in typescript, unlike O'Malley's, whose handwritten accounts of interviews created significant obstacles for historians because his writing was so difficult to decipher.

After the opening of the BMH in 2003, those seeking to reconstruct events in a particular part of the country now had new opportunities to consult a concentrated body of statements from that region and weigh them alongside information already in the public domain. The mass of statements also enabled historians to reconsider an issue that had not been in any sense settled – the degree to which IRA activities were subject to centralised control. The statements also invited reassessment of such themes as the organisation of the Easter Rising of 1916, the role of women in the conflict, the impact of the First World War and the conscription crisis of 1918, as well as the influence of cultural organisations in the opening years of the century. Many of the contributors placed their statements in the wider context of the social, economic and cultural upheavals of these years.

The BMH statements suggest the resourcefulness and commitment of this generation were exceptional. Theirs was overwhelmingly a revolution of the young; they were physically fit (they thought nothing of cycling from county to county) and, in the main, politically disciplined. Those looking for evidence of intense ideological debate may be disappointed, but the Bureau files contain much material of interest to the social historian. For Elizabeth Bloxham, flirting and youthful exuberance were part of her membership in Cumann na mBan (CnB) the female auxiliary of the IRA established in 1914, but her statement, like many others, also underlined the seriousness of their mission: 'I have sometimes wondered if an invisible onlooker could have realised underneath our gaiety we were all in such deadly earnest.' Bridget O'Mullane, organising branches of CnB, recalled that

> the life was strenuous, as I generally worked in three meetings a day to cover the various activities of each branch. My meals were, of course, very irregular, and the result of this sort of life, which I led for three years ... was that my weight was reduced to 6 stone. I got many severe wettings and consequent colds, which I was unable to attend to. The reaction to this came during the truce [July 1921] when I broke down and had to get medical attention.[8]

Just over ten years after the opening of the BMH archive, a more significant, indeed monumental, archive was in the process of being gradually released to the public; the Military Service Pensions Collection (MSPC), a voluminous collection of nearly 300,000 files relating to the processes involved in the award of pensions for military service during the 1916 Rising, War of Independence and civil war period and for compensating those who suffered loss and injury. Launched by the Taoiseach Enda Kenny in January 2014 as part of a phased programme of the online release of the documents, this archive opens many other doors to an understanding of the role of the ordinary Volunteer from 1916–23 as pension applicants, under a string of legislation from the 1920s to the 1950s, had to provide detailed accounts of their activities to make a case as to why they were deserving of a pension. Their accounts needed to be verified by referees and the administrative process involved the creation of an enormous body of supporting documentation.[9]

What was apparent during the administrative process from the 1920s onwards was that the bar would be set very high in relation to qualifying for a pension; in the words of William T. Cosgrave in 1924, the definition of active service made it clear the government 'does not intend there should be any soft pensions'.[10] This was, and remained, the case. The archive is, as a result, also a chronicle of great disappointment; the vast majority of those who applied for these pensions were not awarded them. A government memorandum from May 1957 revealed that 82,000 people applied for pensions under the main Pensions Acts of 1924 and 1934; of these, 15,700 were successful and 66,300 were rejected.[11] The archive contains an extraordinary level of testimony and detail about individual and collective republican military endeavour, but it is also an archive that reveals much about frustrated expectations, concern about status and reputation and difficulties of verification; it does much to illuminate aspects of the afterlife of the revolution.

While the list of those awarded military service pensions at the highest grade under the 1924 and 1934 Acts reads like a roll call of some of the best known gunmen and later politicians of that era, the bulk of the MSPC archive is filled with the accounts of those who were not household names, and includes many voices of desperation and urgent pleas for pensions due to the abject circumstances of a host of War of Independence and civil war veterans.[12]

Close association with the Irish revolution and its architects was no guarantee of a comfortable life. In July 1941, Nora Connolly O'Brien, a daughter of the labour leader James Connolly, executed after the 1916 Rising, and who herself had been an active member of CnB, wrote to a confidant that she had not

> heard a word yet from the Pensions Board, so don't know what is going to happen in my case ... I am at my wits end. We are absolutely on the racks. This week will see the end of us unless I have something definite to count upon. Seámus [her husband] has had no luck in finding any kind of a job. I was hoping that the pension business could be hurried up and what I could get might tide us over this bad spell. There seems no prospect of anything here so we have written to England applying for jobs. I'm absolutely blue, despondent, down and out, hopeless and at the end of my tether ...[13]

In contrast, Tom Barry, one of the best known and most admired of the flying column leaders during the War of Independence, as a result of the Kilmichael ambush of 28 November 1920, when he led an attack on a patrol of Auxiliaries, seventeen of whom were killed, was primarily concerned about status and reputation rather than material survival in relation to his pension. In January 1940 he received his military service pension award of Rank B rather than Rank A, which 'I reject ... on the grounds of both length of service and of rank'. He was livid that the Board had disallowed him full-time active service on certain key dates: 'It is sufficient to state that my award was humiliating to a degree ... I do ask the Board now to understand that I am feeling ashamed and ridiculous at the award and that I am entitled at least to have this humiliation removed from me.' He insisted on his appeal being heard in person and maintained that he had many former IRA officers who were prepared to verbally testify on his behalf. He successfully appealed his decision and was awarded Rank A.[14] The multitude of narratives in the MSPC archive contain a variety of sentiments and tones; pride, arrogance, anger, self-belief, righteousness and, more often than not, dignity (see Part III). These were also sentiments that strongly influenced written accounts of the revolution in its aftermath.

TWO

WHO OWNED THE REVOLUTION?

The question of ownership of the revolution and its legacy was apparent from a very early stage, as was fear about the consequences of some of the radical sentiments it had engendered. Consequently, it was frequently deemed necessary to rein in lawlessness and affirm the need for malcontents to know their place and their status. A struggle to reconcile rhetoric and reality was also relevant to the contested legacy of the period and how it was written about. Adaptation was not easy for many, perhaps because, as was recalled by Ernie O'Malley, 'we had built a world of our own, an emotional life but with no philosophy or economic framework'.[1] For many, the easiest way to deal with the legacy was to remain silent. When he spoke to the BMH in 1951, George Gavan Duffy, by that stage President of the High Court, began starkly:

> I hark back to the aftermath of the Treaty with reluctance and distaste, for the memory is painful and a country so bitterly divided, nearly half and half, on so vital an issue presents a sorry spectacle. The next generation took the measure of the shortcomings of the two parties for and against the Treaty; and perhaps the most disturbing feature in Irish life during the past 30 years has been the detachment of the bulk of the younger people from public affairs; I attribute that stolid indifference largely to disgust at the rancour permeating our public life for many years after the Treaty. The resort of the bellicose Republicans to civil

war was inexcusable, but the personal acrimony that infected several of the leaders on both sides was of more lasting effect.[2]

When, in 2014, the seventy-two-year-old president of Ireland, Michael D. Higgins, made the first state visit to Britain of an Irish head of state, he referred to his own father's involvement in the War of Independence and the internal divisions it created, but also quoted the constitutional nationalist Stephen Gwynn, who referred to the damage it did to Anglo-Irish relations, causing British and Irish to 'look at each other with doubtful eyes'. Higgins's own father, John, was imprisoned in Kildare during the civil war, lost his job, and the financial strain fractured the family; according to the president's brother, their father 'never spoke very much about it all actually. They just didn't.'[3]

When he was interviewed in 2012 about commemorating the events of this period, artist Robert Ballagh offered a personal anecdote that was by no means unique:

> Politics were never discussed in my home, and much later on I discovered one of the possible reasons why. On my mother's side, during the Civil War, my grandmother and my grandfather were on opposite sides and ended up, I think, not talking for about a decade. So I can appreciate why my mother felt that politics was not a proper subject.[4]

In the immediate aftermath of the revolution, for some of the participants it was difficult to let go; others slotted comfortably into the new order and began to fashion self-serving narratives of the period. By 1924, when Kevin O'Higgins, the new Free State's Minister for Home Affairs, later Justice, who was assassinated by republicans in 1927, addressed the Irish Society of Oxford University, he suggested that 'to form a just appreciation of developments in Ireland in 1922 it is necessary to remember that the country had come through a revolution and to remember what a weird composite of idealism, neurosis, megalomania and criminality is apt to be thrown to the surface in even the best regulated revolution'.[5] Most of these words, of course, did not, as far as he was concerned, apply to the 'eight young men in city hall standing amidst the ruins of one administration with the foundations of another not yet built and with wild men screaming through the keyholes', his description of the beginning of the civil war from the perspective of the pro-Treaty provisional government.[6]

The reference to the screaming wild men was another version of the 'nation and rabble' thesis; pro-Treaty state builders had their eyes fixed on the prize of a successfully built nation state, and a rabble was out to undermine them viciously: 'an ebullition of the savage primitive passion to wreck and loot and level when an opportunity seemed to offer of doing so with impunity'. Simply translated, there was no idealism on the republican side; the eloquence of Éamon de Valera, political leader of the anti-Treaty republicans, was 'frenzied', but Michael Collins, the former director of intelligence for the IRA and then pro-Treaty leader killed during the civil war, was someone who was 'sprung from the loins of the people, his love for the people was too big, too real, to allow his nationalism to become a thing of dry formulae or doctrinaire theories'.[7]

The year the civil war ended, writer George Russell (AE), who had been identified publicly with revolutionary nationalism by Hamar Greenwood, chief secretary for Ireland, in a speech to the House of Commons in 1920, but who became more detached from the republicans' dreams and preferred to focus on the practical social and economic possibilities of independence, wrote an article lamenting that the champions of physical force had squandered the spirit created by poets and scholars. Free State Ireland, he maintained, had 'hardly deflected a hair's breadth from the old cultural lines'.[8]

But had the revolution ever really been about creating and nurturing a free spirit? And how else did those who wrote about the revolution frame these issues? According to renowned author and former IRA Volunteer Seán O'Faoláin, the civil war 'woke us up from the mesmerism of the romantic dream. It set us asking questions ... about the pre-sanctified dogmas of our history. We were blessed by a series of writers who ... had the courage to face experience and record it.' This was certainly what playwright Seán O'Casey did in his three Dublin plays in the 1920s: *The Shadow of a Gunman* (1923), *Juno and the Paycock* (1924) and *The Plough and the Stars* (1926). O'Casey, secretary of the Irish Citizen Army (ICA) in 1914, the workers' militia formed as a result of the 1913 Lockout and whose members played a prominent role in the 1916 Rising, was sceptical about the Rising, and caustic about the marginalisation of the labour movement. He complained that James Connolly, who led the ICA to battle, on his way to being a republican martyr, 'saw red no longer, but stared into the sky for a green dawn'.[9]

O'Casey, as well as settling scores and trouncing his enemies in his vivid but sometimes unreliable autobiographies, was determined to confront the founding myths of the state and show them as a false dawn by highlighting the consequences of personal idealism, however noble, at the expense of preoccupation with the welfare of those on whose behalf battles were supposedly being fought. He also used the plays to reflect his disillusionment with the labour movement and its complicity in its own marginalisation.[10] In a letter he wrote in the same year he was working on *The Plough and the Stars*, he was adamant that the creation of the Free State had made little difference to urban squalor: 'It isn't a question of English or Irish culture with the inanimate patsies of the tenements but a question of life for the few and death for the many. Irish-speaking or English-speaking, they are all what they are; convalescent homes of plague, pestilence or death.'[11] Hanna Sheehy-Skeffington, an active suffragette and republican during the revolutionary era, whose husband had been killed in 1916, was one of the most vocal critics during the disturbances the play generated, and accused O'Casey of 'making a mockery and a byword of a revolutionary movement'. She went further by describing the protests as between 'the Ireland that remembers with tear-dimmed eyes all that Easter week stands for' and 'the Ireland that forgets, that never knew'.[12]

O'Casey had done nothing of the sort; he had, instead, depicted with a searing accuracy some unpalatable aspects of the interior and the reality of the Irish rebellion, which was complicated and difficult, and the certainty expressed by so many in its aftermath was rarely evident at the time. Through drama, O'Casey became one of the first critical historians of the revolution by challenging the heroic narrative.

In contrast, when the recollections of Máire Nic Shiubhlaigh, a renowned actress who had been present in Jacob's biscuit factory during the 1916 Rising, and was a very focused senior member of CnB, were published, based on a lecture given to the Galway branch of the Women Graduates Association in 1948, what was notable was that her memory of the dedication and politicisation experienced by her and her circle became a more general assertion that Dublin at that time was 'full of earnest young people, all of them anxious to do something useful for Ireland'. This was a convenient transference of the personal to the general, but also selective; what were difficult and contested years (reflected in her own theatre career and the intrusion of politics) became instead *The Splendid Years*.[13]

THREE

THE HISTORY WARS

Whatever about the initial view of politicians and artists and the great silence that affected many families, how would the historians tackle these questions and come up with new ones? When did an interest develop in creating a framework for historical interpretations of the Irish revolution; who was prominent in that regard and what tools did they have at their disposal? In August 1922, less than a week after the death of Arthur Griffith, founder of the original Sinn Féin, one of the chief negotiators of the Anglo-Irish Treaty and president of the Dáil, a hardly sensitive Darrell Figgis, a self-regarding propagandist and independent pro-Treaty TD, wrote to Griffith's widow Maud expressing condolences but also asking to write his official biography as he believed Griffith had wished him to do. Maud replied that she was 'making other arrangements' for such a biography.[1] No serious biography of Griffith, however, was to appear for three decades, as after the civil war 'he was almost forgotten by his ungrateful pro-treaty colleagues', a reminder that a central role in the torrid years was no guarantee of prominence in the histories of the period, particularly for those who were – and this is debatable – deemed to have represented the 'passive resistance tradition'.[2]

Walter Alison Phillips came to the task of writing his history early in producing *The Revolution in Ireland, 1906–23* (1923), in his own words, 'as the embers of civil war were still glowing in Southern Ireland'.[3] He obtained privileged access to some of the records at Dublin Castle (the headquarters of British government in Ireland), including county inspector reports from the Royal Irish Constabulary (RIC), the main Irish police force during the era, but most of his information and 'often the most valuable, was obtained in conversation with men in responsible positions ... whom I had every reason to trust', though he could not identify them.

In a subsequent edition in 1926 he also referred to the 'avalanche of abuse' he was subjected to after the first edition, and dismissed all the criticism – including the contentions that his book was an attack on the Irish Free State, that it had unduly harsh things to say about 'the decline of the moral authority of the church in Ireland' and that it was biased in relation to Ulster – as 'nonsense'. His defence of his stance on Ulster however, was hardly a ringing declaration of objectivity: 'If there is no admission on my part that Ulster ever did wrong, there is equally no statement of mine that she did right.'[4] He did, however, acknowledge that the arming of the Ulster Volunteer Force (UVF) in 1913, to resist the implementation of home rule with force, had led to the arming of the southern Irish Volunteers (established at the end of the same year) to ensure home rule was implemented. There was no disguising, however, Phillips's appalled unionist tone: the 'Sinn Féin terror' was a 'moral disintegration' underpinned by a 'crude idealism', and with regard to the IRA, 'the great majority of this army consisted of shop assistants and town labourers'.[5] He made no bones about his unionism; he regarded the 1916 Rising as treason, supported the execution of its leaders and considered the national myth around 1916 distasteful.

In 1926, the unionist *Irish Times* newspaper referred to the second edition as a 'well weighed study ... an example of how contemporary history should be written' and there was admiration for 'the sureness with which he picks out those events and sayings which are certain to have a lasting significance'.[6] It also noted the book was 'severely' critical of the policy of the British government; Phillips had lambasted the decision to cut a deal with republicans in 1921 as the 'great surrender' but an article on the book in the same newspaper when the first edition was published in 1923 underlined the perils of contemporary history: 'That Professor Phillips should be wholly free from political bias would be too much to expect ... no man who sits down to write a history of his own time, especially if it is a time of passion and conflict, can escape from himself or reduce his mind to an Olympian neutrality.'[7]

Phillips's book prompted some Irish republicans in government in the 1930s to express a desire for an account of the revolution to counteract

Phillips's bias, and this ultimately played a part in the establishment of the BMH. In 1933, the Minister for Education Tomás Derrig had referred to 'the necessity for taking steps to collect and preserve the records of the Black and Tan period' and he was influenced also by 'General Brennan [Michael Brennan, chief of staff of the Irish army who had been the only commander of a western or southern division to accept the Treaty] [who] has been speaking to me about the lack of knowledge of the 1916 leaders and of the events subsequent to 1916 displayed by boys with the Leaving Cert' (the state's senior school exam).[8] What was needed, it was believed, was a 'record of facts' from 'the Irish point of view'.[9]

Nor was this just the concern of those presiding over the education system. In August 1927 the Cork City Branch of Cumann na nGaedheal (the name adopted by pro-Treaty Sinn Féin after 1923) met to consider potential candidates for a by-election; one member inquired about the possibility of inviting Diarmuid Lynch home from the US to contest the election, which was met with a query from one of the assembled: 'Who is Diarmuid Lynch?' There was a wrathful response to this from Bean Mhic Giolla Phóil, a sister of Michael Collins: '1916 is of course forgotten and so are all those who ever did anything in the fighting days'.[10] Lynch, a member of the supreme council of the Irish Republican Brotherhood (IRB), which secretly planned the 1916 Rising, had served in the GPO in 1916 and was elected a Sinn Féin TD in 1918 but had resigned in 1920 and emigrated to the US before returning in 1932.

Dan Breen, a renowned Tipperary IRA veteran who after the war struggled with its legacy and a drink problem, had no desire for any attempt at 'Olympian neutrality'. His ghostwritten book, *My Fight for Irish freedom* (1924), sold a lot (an estimated 20,000 copies) but served more to popularise him than to provide any real insights or detached analysis. The publishers' advertisement for Breen's effort billed it as 'a most astounding book' with 'the inner secrets of the Irish campaign revealed for the first time' and 'full of thrilling adventures'.[11] For young republicans of that era being 'as good as Dan Breen' was the benchmark.[12] Breen generated renown for the laconic if not chilling observation in relation to the opening shots of the War of Independence (when his brigade ambushed and killed two RIC men escorting gelignite to Soloheadbeg quarry in January 1919) that 'our only regret was that the police escort had consisted of only two peelers instead of six. If there had to be dead peelers at all, six would have created a better impression than a mere two.'[13] Breen lived until 1969, and got to make quite an impression on television with his War of Independence reminiscences.

The history books of the post-revolutionary period included no shortage of apologias and cementing of civil war divisions, as well as determination to propagate an afterlife for some of its victims, grounded in an insistence on their importance as thinkers that was hardly merited by what they had left behind. Liam Mellows, for example, became the poster boy for republican socialists, having done little to justify such elevation. Mellows, under Rory O'Connor, was one of the leaders of the anti-Treaty IRA garrison in Ireland's main judicial building, the Four Courts in Dublin, at the outset of the civil war in defiance of the pro-Treaty provisional government, and after surrendering was imprisoned in Mountjoy, where he was something of a tutor to young left-wing republicans, including Peadar O'Donnell, later a renowned writer. Some details of his programme for a new socialist Ireland were published as 'Notes from Mountjoy', and reflected the influence of James Connolly. On 8 December 1922 he was executed by firing squad. But was he really the great lost socialist leader? O'Donnell used his civil war diary, *The Gates Flew Open* (1932) to insist that Mellows 'will grow in influence and stature' and by extension asserted 'it is no longer of any importance who took what side in that period ... the interest should shift towards the study of the play of social forces that went into the making of the crisis of the Treaty', an invitation historians were slow to embrace.[14]

O'Donnell was determined to propagate Mellows's memory despite the scant body of material Mellows left behind. What Mellows had insisted on in prison was that the Democratic Programme of January 1919, setting out the social aspirations and promises of equality of the new republican parliament as it met in Dublin after the December 1918 general election, should become 'something definite'. The 'gombeen men' were on the side of the Treaty and the republicans were 'back to [Wolfe] Tone – and it is just as well – relying on that great body, "the men of no property". The "stake in the country" people were never with the Republic.' He was also critical of the pro-Treaty Catholic bishops ('their exaltation of deceit and hypocrisy').[15] Liam Lynch, chief of staff of the IRA, was certainly not moved, writing to colleague Liam Deasy that the need for implementation of the Democratic Programme was 'not urgent at the moment'.[16] The historian of Sinn Féin, Michael Laffan, has suggested that when some of Mellows's ideas were leaked, de Valera was embarrassed by them as 'he had no wish to see the emergence of a new Republican political party whose policies or rhetoric would further alienate the dominant conservative elements in Irish society'.[17]

And what of de Valera as keeper of his own flame? Historian Patrick Murray has detailed de Valera's constant preoccupation with the verdict of history and his need

> to keep his reputation in constant repair and an anxiety to influence the interpretation of his political activity and discourse. His effort to police the evolving public presentation of his career was not a foible of old age but the settled practice of a lifetime. He consciously developed the mythopoeic significance of his career in order to emphasise his unique contribution to history along with his probity, consistency and sound judgement. There was also the obsessive, recurring focus upon a particular set of episodes in which he was the central participant.[18]

In this, he actively engaged in 'his parallel role as supervisor of those accommodating historians whose function it was to interpret this history in terms favourable to him'. Practical politics meant that de Valera, like many other successful politicians, had to effectively exploit history 'while being determined not to become its captive', and had to be careful, as one of the beneficiaries of the cult of 1916, and the sole surviving battalion commander of Easter Week, to qualify references to the necessity and legitimacy of bloodshed in the pursuit of independence.[19]

Murray's observations need to be placed in the context of the 'history wars' which began in the early 1920s when the Free State government commissioned Piaras Béaslaí, who had served as publicity officer for the Dáil during the War of Independence, and who was close to Michael Collins, to write the life of Collins. The government gave him access to files (which was not to happen again until forty years later) and it was part of its attempt to authorise an official version of its own contested recent history, by 'drawing a line of apostolic succession from 1916 and by analogy, justifying its actions in the civil war'.[20] There is little evidence that Béaslaí engaged with the anti-Treaty side, and the book was hostile to de Valera.

It was published in 1926 and marked, in the words of Deirdre McMahon, 'the opening shots of a hard-fought historical war. The civil war may have ended militarily ... but some of the combatants simply moved the field of battle to the history books.'[21] The prolific P. S. O'Hegarty, the writer and civil servant who had been a member of the IRB but who grew disillusioned with physical force republicanism, had also been quick to take up pen on behalf of the Free State by publishing the polemical *Victory of Sinn Féin* in 1924 (in which de Valera and his supporters were classed as 'irresponsibles', 'slanderers', 'poison tongues', with the contention 'they went like so many devils doing the devil's work everywhere').[22] He later published *A History of Ireland Under the Union* (1951), which was more measured in tone and not quite as ferocious in its denunciation of the republicans, though, as with the earlier book, de Valera was identified as the prime cause of the civil war. Its overall nationalist thrust appealed to many and it garnered a wide audience.

Not all the authors, however, had been combatants, as seen with the publication of Frank Pakenham's *Peace by Ordeal* (1936), an account of the Treaty negotiations which was regarded as a cut above many; Pakenham, the 7th Earl of Longford, who had a strong emotional attachment to Ireland and formed what became a lifelong friendship with de Valera, had the advantage of being able to talk to key participants on both sides and managed, with verve, to produce a balanced assessment, at a time when the issues were still raw and emotive. He included vivid portraits of the participants, underlined the consequences of the tensions and distance between the Irish negotiators in London and their colleagues who remained in Dublin, and the extent to which the Irish delegation was outmanoeuvred by the British. Despite the book's obvious merits, it was, inevitably given recent divisions, also contested; George Gavan Duffy, one of the signatories of the Treaty, objected to *Peace by Ordeal*'s 'colouring rather than the narrative'.[23]

Ernie O'Malley's *On Another Man's Wound* (1936), Desmond Ryan's *Unique Dictator* (1936), Frank O'Connor's *The Big Fellow* (1937), Dorothy Macardle's *The Irish Republic* (1937), and a second edition of the Béaslaí biography of Collins also appeared in this decade. In this light, de Valera's historical policing did not occur in an 'obsessive' vacuum, and is understandable when considered as part of a long process of action and reaction. De Valera had suggested to his secretary Kathleen O'Connell as early as January 1924: 'I think we ought to prepare for publication a documentary history of the period Easter 1916 to Easter 1923.'[24]

Ernie O'Malley's account was unique, for both its evocativeness and literary achievement, and was penned in New Mexico, Mexico and Peru from 1929–32. The initial draft of the book ran to thirty-nine chapters and his son Cormac observed that when he returned to Ireland in 1935, Peadar O'Donnell helped persuade the London firm Rich and Cowan to publish the first twenty-two chapters in 1936 as *On Another Man's Wound* (the remaining chapters covering the civil war lay undiscovered for years until they were published by Anvil Books in 1978 as *The Singing Flame*); in Dublin it was published by the Sign of the Three Candles Press.

An American edition of *On Another Man's Wound* was published in 1937 and received impressive reviews; the *New York Times* referred to it as 'a stirring and beautiful account of a deeply felt experience'.[25] Accounts of torture removed from the English edition were included in the US version. Cormac O'Malley was able to keep it in print in England in the 1960s 'but could not persuade an Irish publisher to reprint the memoir'.[26] When challenged by some contemporaries in the 1930s about its content, O'Malley's defence was, 'I had to stand over what I had honestly remembered and sincerely written.'[27]

He was uncompromising, single-minded, courageous and both inflicted and suffered pain; he was subtle but self-conscious and literary, and willing to write about motives, which made his account distinctive.[28] He also held democracy in contempt and believed that people should be coerced if necessary, or in his words, 'clear out and support the Empire'. The revolution was the most intense experience of his life; several times he mentions that he did not expect to live through it. He had absorbed a myth in youth and was 'prepared to follow it, like a single flame, no matter what the cost was to himself or others'. One glowing assessment included the assertion that there was 'no work that captures better the spirit that turns into revolution, to prevail over almost impossible odds and superior military force'.[29]

Dorothy Macardle, daughter of a unionist mother and home rule supporting father, reacted against her mother's idealisation of the British Empire and absorbed cultural nationalism at secondary school in Dublin in the first decade of the century before attending university and qualifying as a teacher. Converted to Irish republicanism early in the War of Independence, when she was introduced to de Valera, she was an able writer for the republican side and knew many of them well; she had been arrested and interned during the civil war, was deeply affected by the death and executions of republican friends and furious with the Catholic Church for its support of the provisional government. She also began to collect witness accounts of those involved in the revolution; in 1924 her *Tragedies of Kerry* was published, an exposé of atrocities committed by Free State troops in Kerry during the civil war, based on eyewitness accounts. She began to assemble further material and in 1937 published *The Irish Republic*, essentially the story of the revolution from the anti-Treaty (and especially de Valera's) perspective. Macardle stressed that contemporary documents rather than the witnesses were the most significant part of the book. The first edition was published by the London publisher Victor Gollancz, whose Left Book Club made it a book choice. It generated considerable controversy, as de Valera's rationalisations and interpretation were followed faithfully without challenge. Patrick Maume makes the point that the book 'is now prized more for the insights it provides into the ideological disputes of its time than as a historical work in its own right'. This is a reminder of the way in which 'history' was being used for party political purposes. But Macardle was no poodle of de Valera's; she had a strong liberal streak and an independent mind, though it is clear from de Valera's correspondence that he saw her as one to do his bidding, writing to Kathleen O'Connell in 1935 'I am getting Dorothy to write an article for the *Irish Press*' (the newspaper he established in 1931).[30]

Frank O'Connor's *The Big Fellow* (1937), his eulogy for Michael Collins, was an interesting illustration of the changed political sympathies of a writer who had been interned as a republican in 1922. Many others had an equally high opinion of Collins and their commitment to him endured. His contemporary Richard Mulcahy, chief of staff of the IRA during the War of Independence who also commanded the military forces of the provisional government during the civil war, was so incensed by a novel of Constantine Fitzgibbon in the 1960s – *High Heroic* – in which Collins, on page one, was featured getting out of bed with a prostitute, that he pressed the Minister for Justice to refuse Fitzgibbon his naturalisation papers, denouncing the author's 'foul penmanship'.[31]

Desmond Ryan's *Unique Dictator: A Study of Éamon de Valera* (1936) was another pointed contribution; Ryan had served in the GPO under Patrick Pearse and in 1919 did much to solidify the reputation of Pearse as the most significant leader of the Rising, by publishing *The Man Called Pearse* (1919), whom Ryan, shamelessly, referred to as 'a perfect man'.[32] Ryan's diaries reveal a man often plagued by self-doubt and a 'want of self confidence, a very ugly, provoking and dangerous beast'.[33] But he expressed certainty about many things, particularly the virtue of Pearse, the Rising and the quest for political independence (despite getting temporarily 'fed up with demonstrations and meetings').[34] But it was an appreciation of these agonies that made his writings valuable; *Unique Dictator* was no hatchet job. Ryan was interested in the style of political leadership that de Valera practised and was able to identify both his flaws and achievements; given the era during which it was written, it was admirable that he could attempt such objectivity. No such nuance was to be found in the offerings of some of his contemporaries, who sermonised, not through biography, but in pamphlet form. One such offering was published in 1938 under the title *Towards Irish Nationalism: A Tract: Offered in Awe and Reverence to the Sublime Patience and Agonised Endurance of the Exploited People of Ireland.*[35]

FOUR

THE FIGHTING STORIES

In the 1940s there was a determination to ensure that accounts of the revolution were published to honour the memory of not just the leaders and politicians, but the grassroots volunteers who had fought, as reflected in the *Fighting Story* series, 'told by the men who made it'. The books were initially published by *The Kerryman* newspaper in Christmas and special editions in the years before the Second World War, and subsequently republished by Anvil Books. Dan Nolan, the managing director of *The Kerryman*, who was related to the founders of the newspaper and who during his youth had witnessed their harassment by British forces during the War of Independence, made the paper very successful commercially, and was one of the co-directors of Anvil Books, which established itself as 'the pre-eminent' publisher of memoirs and accounts of the War of Independence period.[1]

Four books appeared between 1947 and 1949: *Rebel Cork's Fighting Story*, *Kerry's Fighting Story*, *Limerick's Fighting Story* and *Dublin's Fighting Story*. These accounts dwelt on the experiences of some of the counties most active in the republican campaign and were dramatically described as 'gripping episodes' and 'more graphic than anything written of the late war zones'.[2] They were valuable contemporary accounts, and also designed, as was stated in the preface to *Dublin's Fighting Story*, to 'preserve in the hearts of the younger generation that love of country and devotion to its interests which distinguished the men whose doings are related within'. It was also clear that there was no question of straying beyond 1921 to coverage of the civil war; it was simply still too soon for any attempt at a public memory of that event.[3]

There was much defiance and resoluteness on display in these books. There was a temptation after the events to simplify or romanticise what was a painful period for many, marked by pride, but also by suffering and conflicting allegiances. The books humanised the period and underlined the bravery and idealism that was evident and the members of CnB received due recognition as women who 'left their names indelibly' on the story of the revolution.

The Fighting Story series captured the excitement and the immediacy of the Irish War of Independence and the belief that the leaders of the revolution did not urge people to take dangerous courses they were not themselves prepared to take. Many of their tragic ends were documented, and the books were a reminder of how some leaders were better remembered than others. Arthur Griffith, for example, was recalled by Liam O'Briain, the language scholar and 1916 Rising veteran, as 'the profoundest thinker of them all and one of the greatest men that Ireland ever produced'.[4]

There was also concern expressed about what Seán McGarry, who served on the headquarter staff in the GPO in 1916, referred to as 'a generation so lamentably ignorant' of the achievements of Michael Collins. The certainties and emphatic assertions in the books about 'the destiny of an ancient people' and the righteousness of their course of action were exaggerated, simplistic and even disingenuous; the contention that the source of their strength during the years 1916–21 'lay in their faith in their cause' may have been accurate, but the contentions in the books about 'the unflinching support of a civilian population', and IRA Volunteers coming through the ordeal 'with immaculate hands' were fallacious and made plaster saints of them.[5]

Tom Barry's book *Guerrilla Days in Ireland* was published in 1949, became a bestseller and was frequently reprinted. A better written, more forceful and direct book than Dan Breen's, it did not suffer from the ghost-written curse, but it did perpetuate the heroic, unquestioning narrative. Barry had joined the British army in 1915 and subsequently adapted his military experience to the operation of IRA guerrilla warfare in Tipperary, becoming one of the most famed of column leaders. Other veterans used newspaper columns to share their memories and develop a popular nostalgia, including Cathal O'Shannon – one of approximately one hundred

Irish Volunteers who assembled in County Tyrone at Easter 1916 and who was subsequently imprisoned and then played a leading part in the labour movement during the War of Independence – in the *Evening Press* in the 1950s, and Piaras Béaslaí in his 'moods and memories' pieces in the *Irish Independent* in the early 1960s.

The *Capuchin Annual*, a periodical published by the Order of Friars Minor Capuchin in Dublin from 1930 to 1977, which Tom Garvin described as 'a useful and surprisingly little-used preliminary sampling of Irish clerical nationalist outlooks',[6] was often focused on high culture. It was a conservative voice that could also be dissenting but afforded much space to the nationalist interpretation of the revolution. One of the *Annual*'s most prolific contributors on history was Aodh de Blácam who had authored two political manifestoes, *Towards the Republic* (1919) and *What Sinn Féin Stands For* (1921) during the War of Independence, arguing that Ireland, having had feudalism and capitalism imposed on it only as impositions by external forces, could transform itself into a decentralised, rural, cooperative commonwealth by reviving its Gaelic traditions. He excelled as a propagandist and was at home in the pages of the *Capuchin Annual*, where he could balance historical fact with romance while relating past and present events.

Likewise, Diarmuid Breathnach, a civil servant who regularly contributed to the annual, declared in 1952 that

> the Ireland of history adhered with dogged determination to a concept which sustained it during the ensuing struggle. That concept embraced four freedoms – loyalty to the faith, to history, to the ideal of independence, and to the native language. Whether passive or active in her resistance Ireland always held those four loyalties to her heart ... it is far better for us to remain clad in the homespun of our racial thinking. Only then shall we prove true to the toiling generations of our fathers all down the bitter years.

The triumph of the War of Independence was celebrated without nuance: 'Anglo-Ireland was dead!'[7]

Not all nationalists were willing to tolerate such simplistic defiance. In a withering editorial to mark the twenty-fifth anniversary of the 1916 Rising in 1941 in *The Bell*, the literary and social periodical he had established in 1940, Seán O'Faoláin crafted a critique of the failures of Irish independence and the failure to honour the promises of 1916 under the title 'Ireland 1916–1941: tradition and creation'. He posed many questions and wondered whether James Connolly, the labour leader executed for his part in the Rising, would be satisfied with the Ireland of 1941:

> Here, we know better than most how much a man's emotional blood-stream is made up of memories ... If there is any distinct cleavage among us today it is between those who feel that tradition can explain everything and those who think that it can explain nothing ... we are living in a period of conflict between the definite principles of past achievement and the undefined principles of present ambition ... con-tradiction is everywhere ... of all our antique symbols there remain only two – the official harp, and a design on the half-penny stamp, which not one person out of a thousand understands.[8]

But, aside from minority crusades exemplified by the work of O'Faoláin, to what extent would the self-serving 'Four Freedoms' accounts of the revolutionary years dry up? The *Capuchin Annual* did much to con-tinue to propagate the memory of 1916 and the War of Independence; in 1942 the danger of forgetting was also highlighted in the *Father Matthew Record*, and an urgency expressed about 'gathering up the fragments while they remain'.[9] There was even more of an urgency about this by 1966, with contributor Fr Henry Anglin insisting in the *Capuchin Annual*:

> Fifty years have passed since the pulses of young Irish men and women beat fast with secret hope and urgent preparation for a rendezvous with honour. Ireland's intellectual elite insisted again that our country is an independent nation and not a province of England; that every true Irishman must assert this and prepare himself for a noble encoun-ter to establish the Irish nation's independence ... what young men and women they were! Only then has the nation had soldiers individually inspired with so selfless a spirit, so loyal a heart. Only one who has lived when they lived, who heard them talk, who knew their thoughts would believe that men and women such as they lived in this world ... we have sought men who manned the posts during Easter week to relate their memories of the stirring encounters. Their articles may suffer a trifle because of the vagaries of human memory but they make up for this in being warm, story-teller accounts, companionable, flesh and blood.[10]

Inevitably, some grew tired of this bombast. Nor could it withstand new contemporary political priorities, changed environments and more extensive research; none of that, however, meant the popular appetite for it completely diminished. Seán O'Faoláin, in another edition of *The Bell* magazine had insisted: 'It is essential for the mental health of Ireland that we should as quickly as possible get to the stage where we do not give a damn about Britain.'[11]

That was not to happen with anything like the speed O'Faoláin desired, and what was also notable was the fascination the revolution continued to exercise over English writers, including Edgar Holt in *Protest in Arms: The Irish Struggles, 1916–23* (1960). Holt found in the Irish struggle, according to F. X. Martin, the Augustinian priest who joined the UCD history department in 1959, 'the mixture of realism, paradox, humour, individuality and stark reality which contrasted favourably with the impersonal character of armed strife elsewhere'.[12]

Unionists were also quick to write the narratives of heroic Ulster resistance during the revolutionary period. The First World War, and especially the Battle of the Somme, during which there were 5,500 Ulster Volunteer casualties and almost 3,000 fatalities, dominated much unionist writing in the 1920s and included Cyril Falls's *History of the 36th (Ulster) Division* (1922) and *History of the Royal Irish Rifles* (1925), while events leading up to the foundation of the state were interpreted with a 'piety worthy of a P. S. O'Hegarty' by Ulster Unionist MP Roland McNeill in *Ulster's Stand for Union* (1922).[13] The book closed with the inauguration of the Northern Ireland parliament in June 1921, presented as the unionists' valediction accompanied by a solid majority (the party won forty out of fifty-two seats). McNeill's first book, *Home Rule: Its History and Danger* (1907), was a polemical attack on Irish nationalism and he became friendly with Edward Carson, who became leader of the Unionist Party in 1910, which facilitated 'unrivalled access to the inner workings of the party' for the 1922 book, allowing it to become the first weighty documented account of organised unionism.[14]

In the 1930s there was a mixture of defiance and acknowledgement that partition was as good an outcome as could have been achieved, given Britain's growing disenchantment with Ireland, or as Henry Maxwell acknowledged in *Ulster Was Right* (1934) 'it was like nothing but a sinking ship whose only chance of safety lies in the immediate closing of the watertight doors'.[15] But there was also a recognition from Henry Harrison, a veteran Parnellite and later confidant of John Redmond and supporter of de Valera, in his *Ulster and the British Empire: Help or Hindrance?* (1939), that partition was 'a word of evil omen' implying something 'resembling the surgical division of a living organism – a lopping off of limbs'.[16]

The contrast to that assertion was found in St John Ervine's biography of Carson's fellow unionist warrior and successor, the first prime minister of Northern Ireland, James Craig, in *Craigavon: Ulsterman* (1949). Ervine's stance was that during the years of upheaval unionists in Ulster had increased their profile and relevance and had gone from being a small minority in Ireland to a 'self-contained, self-governing Ulster – practically out of danger'. Ervine, also well known as a playwright, had been an advocate of home rule and critic of Ulster unionism in earlier years. He served in the British army and lost a leg in the First World War, then became increasingly critical of IRA and British atrocities and reverted to unionism. Sympathetic and celebratory biographies of Carson and Craig were also written by Edward Marjoribanks and Ian Colvin, and later Montgomery Hyde's *Carson* (1953) appeared. Hyde was another Unionist MP and depicted Carson's opponents as 'notorious', 'excitable' and 'irresponsible ... wild men', while Hugh Shearman's *Not an Inch: A Study of Northern Ireland and Lord Craigavon* (1942) was introduced as a 'non-party account' and at least acknowledged tactical mistakes by unionists, but also exaggerated the notion of there being, in 1910, two 'distinct kinds of unionism', Ulster and Irish.[17] This was a revision too far given that, even in 1912, the southern unionists were being heralded by their Ulster counterparts as joint crusaders for maintaining the whole of Ireland in the Union.[18]

This was a revealing Ulsterisation of unionism which marginalised the tradition of Irish, as distinct from Ulster, Protestantism championed by William Armour, the Antrim journalist, liberal Presbyterian and Oxford educated author and later editor of the *Northern Whig* newspaper. After returning to London he authored *Facing the Irish Question* (1935) and *Ulster, Ireland, Britain: A Forgotten Trust* (1938) as well as *Armour of Ballymoney* (1934), a biography of his father, James Brown Armour, who had famously asserted in the 1890s that 'the principle of home rule is a Presbyterian principle'; he stuck to that belief despite opposition from his peers. He later opposed partition and the establishment of the northern parliament, insisting in 1923 that northern unionists had had to accept a form of home rule that 'the devil himself could never have imagined'.[19]

In 1967 A. T. Q. Stewart's *The Ulster Crisis* (1967) was among the last books 'which cast the founders of Northern Ireland in a heroic mode' and, although criticised by historian F. X. Martin for being written in such an 'urbane fashion' that it 'turns a blind eye on the repellent Orange bigotry', it was still an acclaimed work of professional scholarship.[20] Stewart, though elegant and reserved, with a dislike of polemic, became one of the leading historians and public intellectuals in Northern Ireland during the Troubles and was regarded as being particularly insightful about Northern Irish mindsets. By 1969, and under pressure, prime minister of Northern Ireland Terence O'Neill, in *Ulster at the Crossroads*, had to defensively insist that just because there was talk of a new Ulster did not mean 'that the Ulster of Carson and Craig is dead'. But this was precisely what more fundamentalist unionists like Ian Paisley decided was the case, and that contention formed one of the blocks of their appeal in resisting change as the outbreak of the modern Troubles loomed.[21]

FIVE

CLOSING YOUNG MINDS?

Stirring accounts of the revolutionary period were invariably selective and this was particularly relevant to the issue of how this era was taught in schools. In Northern Ireland in the state schools and the mainly Protestant voluntary grammar schools, the attitude was that Irish history should be ignored; in 1931, Ulster Presbyterian William Corkery, who had authored the propagandist *The Church of Rome and Irish Unrest: How Hatred of Britain is Taught in Irish Schools* in 1918, was anxious that there would be no history teaching that would 'weaken or undermine the loyalty ... to those ideals for which the Protestant people of Ulster had stood in the past'.[1] In Northern Ireland's Catholic schools, Irish history was relegated behind world and British history. David Chart, who had worked as an archivist in Dublin in the first two decades of the twentieth century and joined the Northern Irish civil service after 1921, where he spent almost twenty-five years working in the Public Record Office of Northern Ireland, authored *A Short History of Northern Ireland* (1927), which omitted all references to 'recent controversies' and all political events since the Act of Union in 1801.[2] What there was of Irish history was nationalist, with the unionist contribution ignored: 'It was only at A level that any significant study of Irish history was undertaken and by then it could be argued, many young adult minds had already begun to close.'[3]

When, in the south, Pádraig Ó Brolcháin was appointed in 1922 to take over the functions of the Board of National Education he emphasised that teachers in the Free State were to work 'for the strengthening of national fibre by giving the language, history, music and tradition of Ireland their natural place in the life of Irish schools'. This, it appeared, was also about rationalising the existence of the new state and demonstrating that the Irish race 'had fulfilled a great mission in the advancement of civilisation'.[4] By 1926 change to the curriculum 'lightened the requirements in history' as it had been deemed to overburden minds too young; formal teaching of history as an obligatory subject would not now begin until fifth class, and they and sixth class would be taught history up to the Treaty of 1921. But in 1932 new Minister for Education Tomás Derrig insisted teachers were not making sufficient use of history to cultivate patriotism. A school inspector in the south-eastern division in 1930 was equally unimpressed and his comments suggested there was little intense indoctrination at work: 'Many teachers are not greatly interested in history and as a consequence, their teaching of it is dry, without life or power ... it is surprising how little knowledge the senior pupils in many schools have of the history of their own times; one would imagine that they had never heard of Arthur Griffith, for example, or of Easter week.'[5]

At second level, the outline of history deliberately excluded recognition of British and Empire history. Fr Timothy Corcoran, the Jesuit Professor of Education at UCD, who was a key adviser on school curricula, saw history as a 'branch of religious instruction', linked with moral principles and moral action.[6] This underlined the belief in the superior spirituality of the Irish people, a fidelity to Catholicism that underpinned conceptions of freedom, it being maintained that during the '5 glorious years', 1916–21, the republican movement was 'not a military movement, but the movement of a people whose power of progress and resistance had become spiritual'.[7] The message was clear; religion was the foremost influence on Irish identity with roots that were deeper than any political movement, a message unsubtly imparted in relation to an earlier era of history in Helena Concannon's *Irish History for the Junior Grade Classes: The Defence of our Gaelic Civilisation, 1460–1660* (1921). Here, Concannon, an advanced nationalist and future TD, emphasised the exclusivity of the Irish race and the English attempt to undermine it through 'radical and cultural assimilation', religious persecution and 'all conceivable' forms of aggression, countered and overcome by a national tradition of resistance, and spiritual and moral courage.[8]

Another of the standard history texts of this era, but one that touched on more recent history, was Mary Hayden and George Moonan's *A Short*

History of the Irish People, 1603–1924 (1927); the authors – Hayden was the first Professor of Modern Irish History at UCD and Moonan was a barrister – introduced it by stating that, 'while writing from a frankly national standpoint, the authors have made every effort to attain accuracy and avoid prejudice. Events are dealt with, as far as possible, in the spirit and atmosphere of their own times, but are judged by their final effects upon the destinies of the nation.'[9] The commentary on the 1916 Rising was brief and sober; there is reference to the 'real greatness' of Michael Collins; reprisals by Black and Tans during the War of Independence take up more space than the operations of the IRA (which just 'paid back in ambushes, by single shootings and by the destruction of police or military barracks'), but the strife, it is asserted, 'was ruining Ireland morally and materially'. Anti-Treaty republicans during the civil war are referred to as 'The Irregulars', a derogatory label used by the pro-Treaty side during the civil war to deny their opponents military legitimacy.[10]

The tone here could hardly be described as bombastic or triumphalist, which is not surprising given how recently the civil war had been fought, but some of Hayden's sympathies are apparent. Hayden had been politically active during the revolution, but was more associated with suffragism than nationalism, and in her own words 'could not in conscience help' the 1916 rebels, despite her friendship with Patrick Pearse.[11] James Carty's *A Junior History of Ireland* (1932) was also widely used as a textbook. Carty was a librarian who had been employed by Dáil Éireann during the War of Independence but was later expelled from the civil service because he took the anti-Treaty side, and did not rejoin it until 1932, but his textbooks have been praised as 'judicious'.[12] Significantly, his history commenced with the Stone Age and went up to 1921, thus avoiding the civil war. Nonetheless, some teachers were frustrated with what one of them described in *The Bell* in 1943 as 'the biased, propagandist attitude of so many Irish history textbooks' (every villain 'is a foreigner, every hero, an Irishman ... the choice of Irish history is very limited, only a few of them are published and none is really good'). The writer suggested that students needed exposure to modern British history to learn about 'democratic heritage', but more criticism was devoted to the crowded curriculum in the first few years of secondary school: 'The unfortunate pupils are supposed to learn European and Irish history from 1000AD to 1920!'; history exams became, as a result, 'a breathless race against time'.[13] Notwithstanding such criticisms, the proponents of nationalist history still had much fuel left in their tanks, including P. S. O'Hegarty, whose *Ireland Under the Union* (1951), as seen earlier, became a standard popular history of the period 1800–1921 and was used by some teachers; it was a book, suggested O'Hegarty, that was 'the story of a people coming out of captivity, out of the underground ... coming out at last in to the full blaze of the sun'.[14]

Montgomery Hyde, as Ulster Unionist MP for Belfast North in 1958, declared in the House of Commons that the version of Irish history taught in schools in the Republic tended to 'glorify assassination', suggesting those members of the IRA engaged in the Border Campaign in the late 1950s had been unduly influenced by such history. But a memorandum by G. D. Anderson, from the British embassy in Dublin, suggested not all history books were that bad; the real problem 'is the manner in which the background to the written history is given orally by the teacher and by the glosses and emphases which he gives. Having read a selection of school history books I still find it difficult to believe that they could by themselves be capable of producing the obsessive hatred of England.'[15] But a week later J. Chadwick in the Commonwealth Relations Office (CRO) in Downing Street, in a letter to T. Green in the Home Office, insisted:

> The fact remains that teaching – at least in the better type of school – is quite objective ... my own feeling for what it's worth is that such present-day hatred as finds its outlet in the IRA and its splinter groups is due as much to frustration and lack of employment prospects in the country areas as it is to any crusading spirit based on Anglophobia. In a nut shell, much of the alleged hatred could really be translated as the Irish love of a fight to relieve the monotony of the daily round.[16]

In a further letter from the Dublin embassy to the CRO in April 1959 Anderson described this history issue as 'one of the least promising of the many problems that impinge on Anglo-Irish relations', as it was 'virtually impossible, given the dogmatism of the Irish temperament to undo all that has been deliberately done since 1922 to inflate the nationalist ego by the rewriting of history from a nationalistic point of view'. He did single out for praise, however, Fine Gael TDs James Dillon and Oliver J. Flanagan, for criticising such teaching, suggesting the Minister for Education Jack Lynch had studiously ignored their observations, 'no doubt under the watchful eye of Mr [Frank] Aiken [IRA veteran and senior government minister] and other old stagers on the government front bench'. Flanagan had indeed been vocal on this question; when addressing the Tullamore local branch of the Irish National Teachers Organisation in 1957, he had insisted 'hatred should not be taught in our schools as is evident in our teaching of history. In many schools and by many teachers are children taught to hate England.'[17]

But revealingly, for many students of this era the story of Ireland ended with the 1916 Rising. Tom Garvin notes that in an Irish-language comic book for children from 1950, the civil war, very much in living memory at that time, 'was more or less skipped'.[18] In his memoir of growing up in 1950s and early 1960s Dublin, Gene Kerrigan, who earned a reputation as an exemplary investigative journalist in current affairs in Ireland in the 1980s, recalled his first introduction to the civil war. His recollection was framed in disillusionment and some cynicism. It was November 1968:

> I didn't know about the civil war until I was nineteen. I found out about it watching the *Late Late Show* [Ireland's most popular television chat show] ... one of the guests that evening was an Australian writer named Calton Younger. He was there to discuss his book, titled *The Irish Civil War*. I watched, slightly puzzled at first, then more than a little agitated.
>
> What civil war?
>
> I had lately turned nineteen, five years out of school, making my way in the world, and I'd just discovered that there had been a civil war in my country only twenty-six years before I was born. What's more, the people on the TV seemed to be discussing the Irish Civil War as though it was a matter of common knowledge ... how could it have escaped my attention?

It prompted him to dig out his old primary school history textbook, James Carty's *Junior History of Ireland*, the version published in 1959, which had lauded the 1916 martyrs and then proceeded to the Treaty negotiated between Britain and Irish republicans at the end of 1921. That was it: 'there endeth the lesson' as Kerrigan recalled.

> There wasn't a single word in the book or in my schooling about the bloodshed that led from the Treaty and the split which created the dominant political culture of the decades that followed ... since discovering the missing civil war I have never totally believed the official version of anything.[19]

But by the 1960s changes were afoot; the Institute of Irish Studies established in Belfast in 1965 sought to coordinate research in different disciplines and undermine the idea of history as a morality tale, while during this era of transition in the Irish Republic, the nationalist bias in teaching was coming under critical scrutiny. Leading educationalists Mark Tierney and Margaret Mac Curtain authored a textbook, *The Birth of Modern Ireland* (1969), in which they asserted that the modern IRA should 'not be confused with the old IRA' of 1916–23.[20] Significantly, Mac Curtain, a well known Dominican nun and active feminist who taught history at UCD, had also served on a committee of seven which included other historians, teachers and a psychologist, who first met in January 1966 to discuss the teaching of Irish history. It suggested that 'factual content may be more profitably weighted in terms of the recent past of our country'. While still interested in history to showcase 'heightened feelings of morale' and 'those who have served Ireland in a patriotic way', the committee was also anxious about respect for diversity; that history would be taught in order to 'broaden and humanise education' leading to 'better citizens'; that 'no child should leave school in ignorance of the formation of the state'; and that 'a general public outlook which is not susceptible to propaganda' be facilitated.[21] This was a clear criticism of the tendency to 'lean very heavily on the restricted "Ireland versus England" theme up to 1916 and stopping there'. Knowledge of the divisive revolution should not be suppressed by 'drawing a curtain over the events of 1916–21 and over the subsequent tragic civil war'. It also noted that one-third of all teaching time given to history in 1961/2 was delivered by teachers 'who at no time studied history in their university courses' and pleaded for more social history: 'people should emerge. Many textbooks are deplorably dull from this viewpoint.'[22]

The primary education system generally in the 1950s and 1960s remained an area of concern, because as was clear from an OECD report initiated by the Department of Education in 1962, *Investment in Education* (1966), the majority of pupils in that era 'completed their schooling at that level'.[23] A Council of Education report in the early 1950s listed a range of landmarks in Irish history that should be taught in fifth and sixth class: St Patrick, the Plantations, the Land War and the War of Independence; partition was not even mentioned, 'nor are the unionists whose existence on the island is totally ignored'. The emphasis was on what the nation lost 'through its subjugation and why and at what cost it persevered in asserting its right to run its own affairs', an approach conducive to a simplistic nationalism, or in the words of Dominic Behan's song about the Border Campaign (1956–62):

> I was taught all my life cruel England to blame
> So now I'm part of the patriot game.[24]

Such an interpretation, however, was being countered by new initiatives, including a revised programme for history in national schools in 1962, and was less relevant to the secondary school system, which had a more balanced curriculum that included British, though not European, history, but it was still the case that its teaching also finished in 1916. The History Teachers' Association of Ireland emerged in 1963 for those teaching history in secondary schools. G. A. Hayes McCoy, a history professor in UCG, described Irish-produced school history books in 1962 as 'unimaginative, unattractive, dull, biased and tendentious'. A secondary school history teacher in Cork wrote to a colleague in 1967:

> You would be amazed at the number of schools down in this direction where history is no longer taught in the higher classes. The reasons given are:
>
> No proper texts.
> Unfulfilled promises.
> An impossible course for the Inter Cert.
> No interest shown by the department [of Education].

These complaints were made during a decade of reform in education and the announcement in 1966 of the introduction of free secondary education, because of the *Investment in Education* report with its preoccupation with skills required for economic growth and educational inequalities. A new curriculum was introduced for the Intermediate Certificate the same year and a new Leaving Cert curriculum to be examined in 1971, which taught history up to the mid twentieth century. Elma Collins has suggested that by the 1970s, 'Irish history textbooks were on a par with the best produced anywhere in Europe'.[25] As Minister for Education in the coalition government of 1973–7, Richard Burke was also vocal about the need to challenge nationalist bias in the teaching of Irish history, described as a requirement for 'a new perspective on the past'.[26]

SIX

KEEPERS OF THE REVOLUTIONARY FLAME

Whatever about changes in the education system, there was still the unfinished business of the political history and propaganda promoted by the keepers of the flame who were in a position to write about it or react to each other's accounts or rehabilitate those they felt had been wronged or neglected. There were also nascent books that were researched and partly drafted but never published: a proposed volume by Michael Hayes, for example, the UCD academic and Sinn Féin TD who was interned during the War of Independence, and subsequently supported the Treaty, was provisionally titled 'Successful Irish Revolt – The story of Dáil Éireann'. Those who read drafts included historians Nicholas Mansergh and F. X. Martin. Hayes had originally been approached by an Irish publisher who highlighted what he regarded as a failure of pro-Treaty politicians to defend their position historically.[1] This led to some interesting conversations between the pro-Treaty survivors of that era in the 1960s. Hayes kept notes of a conversation he had with Richard Mulcahy on 'the difficulties of disentangling relationships and status between 1919 and 1922'.[2] The following year he also had conversations with Cecil Lavery, the Supreme Court Judge and former Fine Gael TD, who was also urging William T. Cosgrave to record his contribution for posterity. Cosgrave had brought him to his house and showed him rows of boxes and files and suggested, 'It's all there, but there is nothing important.'[3] Cosgrave died suddenly that very month.

Ernest Blythe, an Ulster Protestant nationalist who lived until 1975 and wore many hats – revolutionary, politician, pro-Treaty government minister (who then drifted out of active politics in the 1930s), managing director of the Abbey Theatre, and Irish-language revivalist – was vocal in the 1960s about some of the key controversies of the revolutionary era. Conscious of northern unionist sensibilities, Blythe believed the abandonment of the Irish language by most Irish nationalists left them without a defining characteristic other than their Catholicism. This was distasteful to Protestant Ulster, and he queried the case against partition and the rhetoric underpinning it, which he suggested had been a counterproductive stance by nationalists. Blythe had a confrontational, aggressive style and was memorably described by a former editor of the *Irish Times* as 'the most reasonable unreasonable man in Ireland'.[4]

While newspapers and political scientists were keen to use his contributions as he was one of the few vocal veterans by the 1960s (Basil Chubb, the leading political scientist of his era, informed him in 1960 that 'anything you say about this period is interesting and important'), he was not good at making his case succinctly and editors had to frequently tell him that his articles were simply far too long.[5]

Blythe had no intention of remaining quiet about some of the most emotive episodes of the Treaty era and was also keen to offer 'some sort of an inside view' – and that in itself was an interesting choice of phrase, as Blythe if anything was a sort of detached insider.[6] He jumped into the fray after the publication of Frank Gallagher's *The Anglo-Irish Treaty* in 1965. Gallagher had served in the Dublin Brigade of the IRA during the War of Independence, but his real influence was as an exceptionally good propagandist. Resolutely opposed to the Treaty, he remained convinced of the righteousness of the anti-Treaty position and the moral purity of the revolution.[7] Gallagher's book was an unoriginal part of an incomplete biography of de Valera and was published three years after his death; in reviewing it under the heading 'Negotiations ... a maze of pretence', Blythe began with the assertion that Gallagher was a propagandist during the revolution and 'that could almost be said to have precluded him from writing anything that would be of value as history ... he could be very reticent about things of which he was aware, but which did not suit his argument.'[8]

Blythe was unusual in asserting 'the role of fair and friendly British opinion' in bringing about the truce in 1921 and was scathing of Gallagher's contention that Irish republican strength was 'unbreakable' as long as unity was maintained, adding the spiky put-down that 'after an interval of 30 or 35 years he might have been expected to do a little thinking about the critical decisions of the period'. The British government, he suggested 'behaved with great patience' in 1921 and 'showed reasonable generosity'. Gallagher's mind, he maintained, 'did not broaden with the passage of the decades' though his book 'may, however, be prized in future as a curious memento of an ideology'.[9]

Blythe was lauded for his efforts ('masterly') by Seán MacEoin, who had commanded the North Longford Flying Column of the IRA during the War of Independence, supported the Treaty and was now a veteran Fine Gael TD who was to live until 1973.[10] Blythe was hailed too by J. J. McElligott ('splendid ... it puts Treaty history in its proper historical perspective').[11] McElligott, who lived until 1974, had participated in the 1916 Rising and had helped to establish the Department of Finance.

Blythe was also on hand to review Eoin Neeson's *The Civil War in Ireland* in 1966 and had a lot to reflect on; he could not manage the review in one article and it was spread over separate days in the *Irish Times* – the 'Book of the Day' instead became the book of four days – but once again, from an editor's perspective, there was an advantage in having a player from that era when, over forty years after its end, the civil war legacy still generated heat and vitriol.[12] Blythe maintained in relation to Neeson, a journalist and former director of the Government Information Bureau, that 'the sympathies of the writer of this book are all with those who opposed the Anglo-Irish Treaty ... he has been thoroughly soaked in hectic and unreliable propaganda'. But at the same time, he thought his account of the actual warfare in 1922 was 'astonishingly objective and impartial and seems to me to represent an outstanding feat of mental self-discipline'.

Blythe repeatedly used the word 'hysteria' (or sometimes 'mob hysteria', a telling description) in relation to the 'mystic' republican exercise; he was also once again laudatory of Britain's 'magnanimity' and downplayed the excesses of the Black and Tans, recruited to thwart the IRA during the War of Independence, as 'merely the kind of thing that always occurs when troops or police anywhere are subjected to persistent guerrilla attack'.[13] He also maintained that 'Mr Neeson writes as if he were still in the early 'twenties when he denounces the decision of the government, delayed for months after the outbreak of [civil war] hostilities, to execute men caught in possession of arms and ammunition'.[14] Blythe was also impressed with the rabble; public opinion, he insisted, was with them: 'the summary executions provided a notable immediate increase in confidence in the government. That was, I think, very remarkable in a country like ours in which by tradition people were anti-government.' Control over Irish destiny, he maintained, had 'effected a transformation in public attitudes', and he finished by noting that 'the author says more than once that nothing was achieved by the civil war which could not have been achieved by negotiations. Actually, as is surely obvious, the civil war gave us stable democracy, a great achievement.'[15]

Books on the revolution continued to appear in the 1960s and 1970s, inevitably to mixed receptions. Leon O'Broin, a senior civil servant and noted historian, wrote extensively and became preoccupied with the relationship between British figures and Irish nationalism, and the perspectives of civil servants in the British administration formed the basis for *Dublin Castle and the 1916 Rising* (1966). After his retirement in 1967 he had more time to devote to research and critiques; he was unimpressed with Eoin Neeson's *The Life and Death of Michael Collins* (1968), which was undermined, he felt, by not making use of survivors of the early Free State governments and his use of sources from 'the other side' whose names were not given 'for obvious reasons'. He also raised an eyebrow about assertions concerning Collins's relationship with Griffith that were 'extravagantly speculative'.[16] Interestingly, he suggested that a work of fiction by Desmond Ryan, *Michael Collins and the Invisible Army*, originally published in 1932 and reissued in 1968, was more authentic because, despite most of the characters being fictitious, 'Ryan wrote out of firsthand experience; he was a primary source in himself'.[17]

Calton Younger's *Ireland's Civil War*, published in 1968, was another significant publication. It appeared to somewhat romanticise the violence of the War of Independence as being necessary 'to acquire the kind of mentality that men must acquire to win freedom ... It is not often that a country produces a generation of men and women fanatical enough and ruthless enough to carry through a revolution, a generation of poets and propagandists and political idealists, dedicated fighting leaders, brave men to follow them and a civilian population ready to shelter, feed and protect them.'[18] Younger, however, was a gifted writer and was no misty-eyed, naïve chronicler of conflict. A native of Victoria, he was educated in Melbourne and served as an observer for the RAAF during the Second World War. He spent three years as a prisoner of war and his experiences left him with 'an abhorrence of oppression', an 'understanding of freedom' and an 'unsentimental compassion for those in difficulties'.[19]

Michael Hayes was determined to respond to Younger and give his interpretation of the debates of that era 'as a participant in them at cabinet level'. He made the point, 'Curiously, one of the prime sources, as well as the most informative, for any history of the Civil War has long been available, and equally long neglected. Too few people read the three volumes of the Dáil debates from January 1919 to June 1922.'[20] They included de Valera's infamous assertion: 'I have been brought up amongst the Irish people ... and whenever I wanted to know what the Irish people wanted I had only to examine my own heart and it told me straight off what the Irish people wanted.'[21] The debate on the Treaty itself had been published by Talbot Press in 1923 even before the government's use of the Stationery Office as a publication bureau; Gerard O'Brien points out that 'the final chapter in the development of the Dáil debates into a historical source came in 1972, when a number of private sessions of August and September 1921 and debates held in camera in December 1921 and January 1922 were published in one volume'.[22] Hayes also insisted, in relation to the civil war legacy:

> The bitterness engendered was great but it has been exaggerated both as to depth and duration. Many of those who were together in the Rising of 1916 but were divided in 1922 preserved their friendships. In University College [Dublin] after 1932 I often saw groups of students in earnest conversation and including the sons of opponents in the civil war.[23]

What did endure, however, was a reluctance to forgive on the part of some of that younger generation's parents. Richard Mulcahy, for example, became almost obsessively resentful at the success of Fianna Fáil and the status of de Valera, who served as president of Ireland from 1959 to 1973 after dominating politics from the 1930s to the 1950s. As far as Mulcahy was concerned de Valera had been primarily responsible for the civil war and he could not forgive what he regarded as a monumental betrayal.[24] But Mulcahy was also despised by many anti-Treaty republicans because when he was commander-in-chief of the National Army during the civil war he backed the establishment of military courts with the power to impose the death penalty, which led to the execution of over seventy-five republicans.

SEVEN

BROADENING THE INTERPRETATIONS AND THE SOURCES

F. S. L. Lyons's book *Ireland Since the Famine* (1971) was a landmark and is still widely used today. Historian Roy Foster makes the point that the book, published when Lyons was a historian at the University of Kent (after which he moved to Trinity College Dublin; he was very comfortable in both countries) was 'generally seen as the defining work of what had come to be called "revisionism", querying some of the accepted verities of the old-style nationalist view of Ireland's struggle for freedom. This is not, in fact, an altogether convincing analysis; much in Lyons's vast synthesis is perfectly in tune with the "heroic" version of Irish history'.[1] Perhaps it was this element of balance that allowed it to successfully stand the test of time. Reviewing the book in 1971, Terence de Vere White, a writer and solicitor brought up in a religiously divided house, who was sympathetic to Fine Gael and a critic of political violence and who had written a biography of Kevin O'Higgins in 1948 (which was undermined by lack of evidence for some of the assertions he made and which was greeted with silence from O'Higgins's former cabinet colleagues)[2], found Lyons's book 'monumental' and the tone 'admirable ... he never makes propaganda. He is invariably polite. So a scholar should be.'

But significantly, he also wrote:

I am not sure where Dr Lyons stands on what seems to me the most vital issue in Irish historical controversy – the use of force. I seem to scent approval of it until it became effective. Then he finds Mr Blythe's prescription for treating anyone who had any truck with Conscription 'cold savagery'. He does not hesitate to use the word 'murderers' for Wilson's slayers [Henry Wilson, security adviser to the Northern Ireland government, assassinated by two IRA men in London in 1922] The Soloheadbeg ambush, which is usually a matter for glory, he excuses on the grounds that it was not intended that the two policemen be killed and the gunmen were 'young, impetuous and perhaps nervous'. No account by the ambushers or their admirers bears this out ... this gentle handling of legend is also apparent where Pearse is concerned.

But he insisted Lyons was always 'scrupulously fair', supported the view that British mismanagement of Ireland was not, at government level, vindictive, 'and I had never realised before that the vote for Sinn Féin in 1918 was less than 48 per cent of the electorate'.[3]

Lyons's work was also important because of a shift in emphasis that recognised the importance of social and economic themes and he later turned his attention to the collision of different cultures in *Culture and Anarchy in Ireland* (1979). The 'pessimistic and slightly sardonic tone' of such work was also a new departure. Lyons maintained in 1976, in rejecting the idea that a sense of patriotism and love of country united those of different creeds, that what was felt in the 1970s for the early part of the twentieth century was 'nostalgia rather than embarrassment and if we feel nostalgia it is, ironically, because perhaps we still do not sufficiently realise the depths and intensity of the feelings by which, already at that date, men were divided rather than united'.[4]

Lyons was not the only eminent historian in the 1970s grappling with how to assess violence and constitutionalism during the revolutionary era. Nicholas Mansergh, who was central to the establishment of courses in twentieth-century Irish history at Cambridge University, and whose childhood in Tipperary coincided with the War of Independence, did not shirk from facing these challenges in *The Irish Question: 1840–1921* (1975), suggesting that constitutionalism during this period 'was not enough' and that violence was inevitable. This was partly a reaction to the assertion of Lyons in *John Dillon, a Biography* (1968), an account of the life of one of the leading nationalist parliamentarians of that era, that Dillon had learned from harsh experience that 'patriotism was not enough'. Mansergh concluded that 'force, or the threat of it, delivered the goods, or most of them, where constitutionalism, after long trial, had not'.[5]

By the end of the 1970s, while welcoming the quality and quantity of the books being published on revolutionary Ireland, Michael Laffan wondered if there were 'perhaps too [many], since energy and ideas are devoted to them at the expense of other, more neglected aspects of Irish history'. He welcomed those books that 'superseded' the nationalist propaganda of Macardle's *The Irish Republic*, and while he suggested the tone of most of the books was still nationalist in sympathy, it was 'sceptical and unideological' in contrast to much that was written before the 1960s. In particular he welcomed the publication of the Ruth Dudley Edwards biography of Patrick Pearse, *The Triumph of Failure* (1977), which challenged the traditional hagiography, 'summed up so tastelessly by the Galway Cathedral fresco in which Pearse faces his fellow Irish saint and martyr John F. Kennedy'.[6] This was the Pearse who evolved, in Laffan's words, 'from tiresome prig through tolerant idealist to revolutionary zealot', precisely the kind of tone that irritated the traditionalists. Journalist, former politician and historian Conor Cruise O'Brien was even more scathing about Pearse, though Laffan suggested O'Brien's 'doubts and hesitations' about physical force, though more forcefully expressed, were shared by many historians; he also suggested '[John] Redmond remains strangely neglected'.[7]

This was to remain for decades the fate of the leader of the Irish Parliamentary Party and indeed the whole constitutional nationalist movement which had been eclipsed by Sinn Féin in 1918, the same year Redmond died. Redmond's colleague Stephen Gwynn noted in 1919 that after failure to reach an agreement with southern unionists, Redmond's feeling was that 'everything ... was wrecked; he saw nothing ahead for his country but ruin and chaos'.[8] The question for historians subsequently was the extent to which Redmond was responsible for that, but there appeared little appetite to tackle it at this stage. Gwynn's son Denis published a biography of Redmond in 1932, a last blast defence of Redmondism in the same year Fianna Fáil came to power, marking the beginning of an era when the history of Redmond and the IPP became increasingly marginalised. Redmond's political principles, according to Paul Bew, came to be regarded as 'those of a weak-kneed and ineffectual constitutionalism' and in relation to political biography it would be decades before he was rehabilitated (see Part III).[9]

But it would be erroneous to suggest that Redmond was entirely forgotten; de Valera, for example, paid him a generous tribute in 1956, the centenary of his birth, describing him as part 'of the fight made for our nationality ... a great Wexford man to whom we are quite ready to give credit for having worked unselfishly according to his views for the welfare of this country. We will give credit to those who oppose us for being as honest in their views as we are in ours.'[10]

Political and generational change also impacted on historical research into Ulster unionism: of particular note was that those writing on unionism in the 1970s were not necessarily themselves unionists or insiders; unionist history was no longer 'the preserve of unionist principle'.[11] Michael Farrell's *Northern Ireland: The Orange State* (1976) was an indictment of the injustices experienced by the Catholic minority but also a call for political action to remedy them; Farrell was a prominent activist in the civil rights movement. Marxist analysis also grew wings and a new form which was not predicated on subordinating its analysis to the Protestant tradition, with Paul Bew, Peter Gibbon and Henry Patterson looking at the internal machinations of unionism and the varieties of social and economic tensions in rural and urban unionism and among the Protestant working class, and the power shift away from the landed elite to the merchant princes.

This was apparent in Gibbon's *The Origins of Ulster Unionism* (1975) and Patterson's *Class, Conflict and Sectarianism* (1980). As Alvin Jackson characterised it, the significance of such work was that 'the nature of the partition question is much less important than the nature of the partitionists themselves; qualitative distinctions between unionism and nationalism are much less important than qualitative distinctions *within* unionism'.[12] Patterson quoted James Connolly on the dynamics within the Ulster protestant community – 'we do not care so much what a few men did as what the vast mass of their co-religionists do' – as Connolly highlighted how 'the sturdy Protestant democracy' had elected landlords and nominees of landlords during the nationalist land league struggle of the 1870s and 1880s to transfer land from the landed elite to tenants.[13] The Protestant working class was not simply a tool in the hands of the bourgeoisie, or duped, it was further maintained, but had independence of mind. It was also apparent that the heroic narrative of the doughty fights of the unionist leadership were being revealed as less than selfless, but riven with an arrogant righteousness, Patrick Buckland revealing in *James Craig* (1980) that his 'longest and most passionate letters to the cabinet secretariat related to the design of concrete fencing posts to the Stormont estate', the grounds that contained the Northern Ireland parliament.[14]

Southern unionism also received fresh attention in the 1970s, most obviously with Patrick Buckland's *Irish Unionism I: The Anglo-Irish and the New Ireland* (1972) which was bolstered by J. C. Beckett's *The Anglo-Irish Tradition* (1976) as Beckett's personal commitment to his Church of Ireland identity found an outlet in his scholarship. A native of Belfast and an evangelical Protestant by background, Beckett, who as a historian was lucid and stylistic, had a far from a privileged upbringing; his family 'occupied a marchland, both socially and physically, between working-class Belfast and the affluent Presbyterian suburbs'; but he was something of a 'muted' snob.[15] This book was, in his words, 'a work of reflection rather than research' and was in essence an emotional obituary for an Anglo-Irish tradition which he believed was 'essentially an Irish view'. He pointed to all they had achieved in literature and public life (the eighteenth century is particularly celebrated) and how they could, if allowed, have achieved much more. While he acknowledged arrogance and a sense of entitlement, there is also a mist of nostalgia for the landlord days and too great a tendency to depict Irish nationalism as narrow-minded.[16]

A crucial issue in the midst of all this, and referred to by Leon O'Broin when he was reviewing Eoin Neeson's work on the civil war in the late 1960s, was the release of British state papers, without 'anything from the Irish side to enable us properly to evaluate them'. Calton Younger had also made use of the recently released British papers. From the 1930s to the 1960s 'exceptional' access facilities to Irish state papers were operated on an erratic basis; the view had been expressed by a senior civil servant in 1944 that it was better to 'go slow' in relation to the records of the revolutionary period, and in the 1950s there was frustration for biographers trying to circumvent restrictions. Even in the 1960s the fear was of 'denigratory revelation' from state files.[17]

Whatever about documented reminiscences in the 1940s and 1950s, and the existence of personal and private collections – the very extensive David Lloyd George papers, for example, were released in the late 1960s, and he was a crucial figure in Anglo-Irish relations during the War of Independence as prime minister – the issue in subsequent decades was largely about the release of these 'official' papers in relation to the revolutionary period on both sides. Irish historians had to wait until 1986 before a National Archives Act with a thirty-year rule for the release of state papers was agreed. By the late 1960s the State Paper Office (SPO) in Dublin was operating a seventy-year rule, but the British Public Record Office (PRO) a fifty-year rule; access to 1922 papers in Dublin, it was feared by the Irish government, could result in 'injury ... to national unity and harmony'.[18] But prior to these assertions, correspondence in 1963 between the PRO in London and the British Cabinet Office dealt with the question of the publication of official records concerning the negotiation of the Anglo-Irish Treaty in 1921, which was desired by the Irish government. The PRO noted that 'there is always some difficulty in tracing the records of the former Irish Office and the Colonial Office about the events leading up to and following upon the signature of the Treaty'.[19] J. D. Woods in the Cabinet Office did not want the 'Irish side' giving access to cabinet documents, preferring that both countries would adopt a fifty-year rule in this matter: 'Is there any hope of persuading the Dublin people to drop the idea?' He did not want 'pressure for the amendment of the 50-year rule which has so far been resisted'. But what was also interesting was the notion of select or privileged access: Woods said he would meet the request as long as there was no commitment to allow general access; if they would 'confine the facilities to a very small number of reliable and responsible historical writers of first class eminence'.[20]

The previous year, the British ambassador in Dublin had suggested the issue was not urgent, and 'the longer the subject remains dormant the better from our point of view'. The ambassador was able to stall the Irish, who did not seem to want to push it much anyway, but the notion of an initial gesture that would lead to demands for further access was something that was causing anxiety, as again was the issue of what constituted a historian. Access being allowed by an Irish government 'could well cause difficulties, the first being the problem of defining the term "bona fide historian". There is no strict definition that could be used and it is surely possible for any writer to talk himself into the character of a bona fide historian.'[21] The issue was left in abeyance, but Britain subsequently moved towards a fifty-year rule. Staff of the SPO had been successful in 1967 in persuading the Irish government to lift restrictions on pre-1916 material but 1922 was still a no-go area, or as Taoiseach Jack Lynch told Eoin Neeson, even if Britain opened papers of that era, the Irish government would not, as access 'might well stir domestic controversies that best lie buried'.[22]

In March 1970, a deputation from the Irish Manuscripts Commission (IMC), originally established in 1928 to promote the preservation and promotion of historical documents, met the Minister for Education, Pádraig Faulkner, to press for the introduction of archives legislation that one of his predecessors Donogh O'Malley had promised in 1967 but to no avail. The IMC, historian Robert Dudley Edwards in UCD and his colleagues faced 'persistent official apathy towards archival preservation, access and administration'.[23] This was the same year the Irish Society for Archives (ISA) was formed and Dudley Edwards was adamant that what was needed in Ireland was a determination to learn from abroad; as he articulated in a private letter after a lecture given by a German expert, what was required was a 'Teutonic determination to build up the movement' and he even wondered 'should we organise an archival students revolt?'[24] But the attitude in the Department of the Taoiseach to the idea of getting outside experts to help regarding legislation was characterised by 'innate capriciousness, sheer indifference to the future of Irish archives or a paranoia born of self-delusion'.[25]

There had certainly been consistency in this regard, despite individual politicians who were well disposed: wilful neglect and restricted access were dominant themes in relation to archival material, along with a determination to 'delay almost indefinitely the development of an objective academic appraisal of many aspects of Irish history'.[26] The Department of Finance, for example, was not impressed that archival and history projects promoted by the IMC were 'absorbing public money that might be put to better use'; bureaucrats in Finance had their own preferred solution – the abolition of the IMC. That Finance did not succeed was partly because both William T. Cosgrave and Éamon de Valera gave the IMC strong support; despite the dismissive tone of Finance mandarins – 'Historians, the officials quickly came to believe, did not understand the value of money' – and the determination of Finance Minister Seán MacEntee to micromanage every aspect of its work in the 1930s, the IMC prevailed.[27]

Both the IMC and the ISA were vocal in the 1970s in reminding the state of its failure to preserve its own records at national and local level; Liam Cosgrave, son of William T. and Taoiseach from 1973–7, acted quickly in ensuring archives were a priority, and Garret FitzGerald, Minister for Foreign Affairs in the same period, and like Cosgrave, the son of parents involved in the revolution, was also proactive and supportive.

It had also been highlighted that when Jack Lynch was Taoiseach in 1971, he asserted that, 'contrary to what appears to be a widely held belief that there is a fifty-year rule here governing access to departmental records, there is, in fact, no rule', and it was further asserted in 1971 that, despite an announcement in 1967 that papers relating to the Anglo-Irish Treaty would be made available to 'bona fide' historians, 'not a single application has been received for access to the Treaty papers'.[28]

But there was still criticism that nothing was available beyond 1922. Garret FitzGerald suggested in 1971 that the country was now mature enough 'to absorb whatever there is to absorb in an adult manner ... this country will look very odd indeed in international eyes if Britain continues to release information about Irish matters before we do – as has already happened. We will have to stop being afraid of our own history.' Meanwhile, Lynch informed Cosgrave that he was examining the option of a thirty-year rule governing access to state papers.[29] The first release of post-independence official archives followed in 1976. Cosgrave announced in the Dáil in December 1975 that he had decided to make available for access the government and cabinet minutes down to June 1944 (with it being noted in the Department of the Taoiseach that the material would first have to be read individually 'to ensure that no seriously embarrassing material was released').

In September 1977, Dan O'Sullivan, secretary of the Department of the Taoiseach, was appalled at the conditions in which materials were being held at the SPO: 'I would describe the situation in relation to the custody of files, books and index records as chaotic and wonder how the system survives or how the staff can find anything.' He pointed out that three years had passed since an interdepartmental committee on the archives had reported to the Minister for the Public Service on a general scheme of an archives bill operating with a thirty-year rule, but it had still not been submitted to the government; there were predictions that it would be enacted in 1981.[30] No bill was actually enacted until May 1986.

The significant legacy of the initiatives undertaken by Dudley Edwards in the 1960s and 1970s was also reflected in the abundant papers in the UCD archives relating to the revolutionary period. Building on the initial deposit of the Richard Mulcahy papers in the 1970s, it grew in subsequent decades to house an unrivalled collection of the private papers of key individuals and organisations involved in the revolutionary era and the evolution of the southern state, on both sides of the civil war divide, including Frank Aiken, Todd Andrews, Cathal Brugha, Desmond FitzGerald, Ernie O'Malley, Ernest Blythe, Patrick McGilligan, the MacSwiney family, Eoin MacNeill, Seán MacEntee, Sighle Humphreys,

Desmond Ryan, the IRB, Irish Volunteers and eventually, Éamon de Valera. Many politicians and officials had connections with UCD and responded positively to requests from Dudley Edwards to deposit their papers, requests which 'had all the force of a royal command'.[31] It became 'a cardinal principle' that depositors had a right to impose 'reasonable' access conditions to their papers but Dudley Edwards also insisted that, while depositors had rights, researchers had responsibilities.[32]

The National Library of Ireland, which dates back to 1877, has custody of significant Irish literary and estate manuscript collections, and is an institution with links to James Joyce, W. B. Yeats and many other writers and scholars who used its majestic reading room and often donated valuable manuscript collections to its care. It also became a crucial repository for the papers of the revolutionary generation, especially those immersed in the cultural nationalism of the early twentieth century, including Stephen Gwynn, Bulmer Hobson, Rosamund Jacob, Piaras Béaslaí, Thomas MacDonagh and Liam de Róiste, their papers facilitating an insight into the motivations that propelled them – their 'revolutionary mentalities' – and the extent to which they were alienated, not just from British rule, but from 'the values and ambitions of their parents'.[33]

EIGHT

NEW SCEPTICISMS, NEW REVISIONS AND THE SHADOW OF THE TROUBLES

The changes highlighted above by Laffan in relation to the writing of the history of the revolution in the 1970s came during a decade when the primary school curriculum was seriously revised (in 1971). It was revised again in 1999 and 'the almost 30-year gap between the two curriculum statements means that changes in the way in which Irishness is articulated are shown very starkly.'[1] In 1971 there was still emphasis on the notion that one of the aims of history was that 'the child's imagination may be forced by the habitual vision of greatness [which] should lead to a greater understanding of historical and cultural heritage' but that there should also be an attempt to 'foster a proper appreciation for those who served Ireland in humbler ways', as everyday lives offered 'opportunities for the exercise of important civic virtues', but the real lesson 'to be learnt is one of moral and patriotic virtue rather than exaggerated nationalism'.[2] Furthermore, 'the sympathy of the generous young mind will naturally lie with the oppressed and all the more so when, in the main, its own people were the sufferers', which could be seen as an invitation to propagate the MOPE syndrome (the Irish as the Most Oppressed People Ever).

But the 1971 curriculum also referenced Christianity rather than Catholicism and the contribution of all creeds to Ireland, and specified that history should be 'true to the facts and unspoiled by special pleading of any kind'. The reading material recommended, however – copious lives of Irish saints – made clear the Catholic heritage was still a dominant focus and the suggestion that a variety of sources be used rather than reliance on a textbook was largely ignored in practice.[3] By 1999, there was an increased focus on 'global', 'local' and 'European'; the lexicon of patriotism and virtue was excised in favour of diversity; the 'Irish experience' was about the child's right to 'understand and participate in the diverse cultural, social and artistic expression of that experience' along with the 'European heritage and sense of citizenship'. History was now more, it seemed, about interpretation – 'the central aim of the lesson should be to enable the child to ... examine how people today can interpret incidents in the past in different ways' – and developing the skills of empathy.

The period between the two curricula witnessed the worst of the Northern Irish Troubles; at the height of this conflict, there was some reflection on the function of professional historians in the development of a 'shared' history. Historian David Harkness was very explicit in 1976 about 'the peculiar obligation which lies upon the people of Ireland and of Northern Ireland in particular, to know their history and to know it for the community's sake ... it is my belief that ... history can still serve to reconcile.'[4] Others would have baulked at that contention as a contrivance too far and beyond the remit of historians.

A common history curriculum was introduced in Northern Irish schools for the first time in 1991, attempting to bridge a gap between state and Catholic schools; it has been argued that the key roles played by historians in this, especially those from Queen's University Belfast, 'above and beyond their work as researchers, shows that they tried to reconcile their scientific work as academics with a recognition of their social role, thus providing a good illustration of the ambiguous nature of the social function of historians in contemporary democracies'.[5] This was facilitated by growing interest in social and economic history, the impact of the Troubles and the growing tendency of academic historians and history teachers to meet to discuss the teaching of history. It also led to historians questioning their own social function, some believing that a social and moral dimension to their profession was demanded while 'remaining true to their scientific responsibility'.[6]

In the Republic, a revision of traditional interpretations of the revolutionary period coincided with the release of an abundance of new archival material. F. X. Martin, the UCD historian, while holding the chair of medieval history, created more of a stir with his work on the 1916 Rising and the lead up to it than he did with his medieval history research. His output included *The Irish Volunteers, 1913–15: Recollections and Documents* (1963), *The Howth Gun-Running, 1914* (1964), and an article in 1967 – '1916 – myth, fact, and mystery' – which although published in a somewhat rarefied journal, was a 100-page challenging and insightful overview and a precursor to some of the later revising of accepted wisdoms. In it, Martin criticised the neglect by historians of John Redmond, rehabilitated Eoin MacNeill, who as chief of staff of the Irish Volunteers had tried to prevent the 1916 Rising, and in relation to whether the Rising was morally justified, asserted 'the democrat and the theologian may question the means they [the rebels] used'.[7]

A strongly revisionist article was published in the Jesuit publication *Studies* in 1972 by Fr Francis Shaw SJ, who had studied at UCD under Eoin MacNeill, in his position as chair of Early Irish History. Shaw, whose father had been a Cumann na nGaedheal (the new name for pro-Treaty Sinn Féin from 1923) TD in the 1920s, had spent time in Germany during the seizure of power by the Nazis and despised racial hatreds and destructive ideologues.[8] His article, originally entitled 'Cast a cold eye: prelude to a commemoration of 1916', had been intended for publication in 1966, the fiftieth anniversary of the Rising, but because of its perceived attack on the legacy of 1916 was delayed (and its original title rejected). Newly titled 'The canon of Irish history: a challenge', it maintained that 'Pearse, one feels, would not have been satisfied to attain independence by peaceful means'. It criticised the way Pearse 'consistently and deliberately and without reservation' equated 'the patriot and the patriot people with Christ', which Shaw argued was in conflict with Christian tradition.[9]

In tandem, some of the old men of the revolutionary era began to cast cold eyes on the years of militancy. Seán O'Faoláin, for example, when asked to pen a self-portrait in 1976 noted that he was born in 1900

in a place that did not exist. That is to say I was born in Ireland, which then was, politically, culturally and psychologically just not there. All that was there was a bastard piece of the British Empire ... not that this bothered me in the least. On the contrary I was tremendously proud of belonging to the Empire, as were at that time most Irishmen ... and then, in the April of 1916, the date of the last Irish rebellion, I suffered the greatest trauma of my entire life. I had the upsetting experience of being suddenly presented with a country whose birth was supposed to wipe out all those social values that I had so contentedly lived by for my first sixteen years.

In the IRA from 1918–24 –'one of the most ecstatic periods of my life' – he found

> all moral problems vanished in the fire of patriotism and death and destruction ... during those heavenly years I dreamed of liberty, equality, fraternity. I adored without reservation the risen people. Every month I discovered a new Napoleon in yet another political or military leader.

At the age of twenty-four, however, O'Faoláin was 'awakened from my feelings of rapture' with the problem of

> practical politics intruding on political theory ... In Ireland I had thought in my innocence that a republic meant equality as well as liberty and fraternity. Thereafter I knew that a republic always means not a state of government but a state of mind and that it is for that reason as indefinable as such forces as love or truth.

By 1976, he had 'no last speck of patriotism left in me'.[10]

With the backdrop of the Troubles in Northern Ireland from the 1970s to the 1990s, 1916 was more of a target for ire than the period 1919–23. For historian and Labour Party politician Conor Cruise O'Brien, for example, whose grandfather was David Sheehy, a nationalist MP who was embittered at the defeat of the constitutional nationalists in 1918 and very hostile to Sinn Féin, was the origin of all later ills. O'Brien described Pearse as 'a manic, mystic nationalist with a cult of blood sacrifice and a strong personal motivation towards death. A nation which pretends to take a personality of that type as its mentor, without really meaning it, is already involved in a disaster, a disaster of intellectual dishonesty and moral obliquity.'[11] O'Brien's influential *States of Ireland* (1972) provocatively questioned the implications of the strength and dominance of the Catholic Church for the political and cultural ethos of the generation that came to adulthood during the revolution, and its long-term legacy. For others, such disparagement was about an official, ignorant denigration of a legitimate revolutionary impulse that had become an embarrassment; for others still, this was all a sideshow under the misused term 'revisionism'. Was there a particular reason, wondered Michael Laffan, why 1916 should remain beyond revision and the uncovering of myths?[12]

Undoubtedly some historians and political scientists, in response to the Troubles, began to paint their history in black and white instead of grey, absorbing messy reality into a neat narrative of constitutional progress. John Regan points out that political scientist and leading broadcaster Brian Farrell falsely insisted in 1971 that those who resorted to arms after 1922 'found themselves on the periphery of Irish political life'. This was fallacious; Éamon de Valera, notes Regan, joined the anti-Treaty IRA at the outbreak of civil war and was president of Ireland while Farrell was writing. Certainly, it can be concluded that Farrell's focus was influenced by contemporary events; as Ronan Fanning has much more recently asserted, during the Troubles 'political imperatives prevailed over historical truth'. Reordering the revolutionary generation as pro-state democrats or anti-state dictators was common, as numerous scholars felt it vital to define the IRA in 1922 as anti-democratic in order to undermine the Provisional IRA during the Troubles; a manifestation of southern twenty-six-county nationalism.[13]

Some of Regan's declarations, however, such as 'we must begin anew to part historical research from its impostors', have been rebutted by David Fitzpatrick, author of the first major regional study of the Irish revolution published as *Politics and Irish Life: Provincial Experience of War and Revolution* (1977), who rejects the notion of the 'insidious influence of Irish public histories presented as objective historical evidence'. True, many historians had a strong distaste for paramilitaries; some did feel a moral obligation to draw lessons of contemporary relevance from revolutionary history, sometimes before non-academic audiences, as an exercise in 'public history'. This was 'widely regarded as a civic duty for near contemporary historians in a country, like Ireland, saturated with history and pseudo-histories', but there is no justification for the suggestion that this led to endemic distortion or falsification of history. It was often about legitimately challenging those who were abusing history and falsifying the past for their own ends. Some of those who had proclaimed the perils of contemporary history, or had been taught by those who wanted to avoid looking at the twentieth century – Robert Dudley Edwards had been adamant in the 1940s that it was the function of the historian not just to interpret the past but to preserve the records for the present, but added 'we are far too near the period of 1921 to do more than collecting'[14] – towards the end of their careers found themselves addressing that very period, supposedly to prevent it being hijacked for propagandist purposes and to stop the abuse of history.[15] But overall, as Fitzpatrick pointed out, 'Historians differed'.[16]

Other historians of that era were also critical of simplistic labels and were 'too individualistic to enjoy being corralled into membership of a school'. Michael Laffan, for example,

> felt that he was a member of a generation which had benefited from the professionalisation of history ... he had been trained to be suspicious of the nationalist version of Irish history, just as he had been trained to be suspicious of the unionist version ... In adopting new perspectives on such fundamental parts of modern Irish history as the Rising, historians were simply being true to their professional responsibilities, doing no more for Irish history than American and French scholars when they revised long-standing accounts of the revolutions which had transformed their own societies. Not to do this would be the real betrayal.[17]

There was also more focus on the less than straightforward relationship between the British government and unionists in Andrew Gailey's *Ireland and the Death of Kindness* (1987), which challenged the idea that the British government had a coherent approach to killing home rule with kindness by addressing Irish grievances in relation to land, religion and education. The same year Clare O'Halloran's *Partition and the Limits of Nationalism* (1987) shed new light on nationalist attitudes towards Ulster Unionism, highlighting the failure of nationalists to adapt their ideology to acknowledgement of partition, with a resultant ambivalence about the need to understand northern nationalist and unionist mentalities in favour of its preferred focus on British culpability. Partition, it seemed, was not just political but psychological. This was also relevant to John Bowman's *De Valera and the Ulster Question, 1917–73* (1982), where de Valera is depicted as a pragmatist under pressure from ideological republicans but also oscillating regarding his thoughts on partition from 1917–21 and naïvely believing partition 'could be solved by logical argument'.[18]

Other controversial questions were a part of that period of historical scholarship and polemic; was it any longer accepted that there was a symbiotic relationship between the IRA and the people during the War of Independence? Was there a need to challenge the 'assumption of inevitability' regarding the level of violence and the establishment of partition?

Was the idea that the IRA had a mandate for violence flawed? Had it been underestimated 'how near a negotiated settlement was in December 1920'?[19] Was the question of Roy Foster – 'Whether the bloody catalogue of assassination and war from 1919–21 was necessary in order to negotiate thus far' – answered or avoided?[20] Was there a need to focus more on the part that political and passive resistance played in gaining independence? Arthur Mitchell's *Revolutionary Government in Ireland: Dáil Éireann, 1919–22* (1995) meticulously underlined the extent to which 'to tie the whole campaign together there was the political leadership which created an alternative government', and he saw in the creation of a counter state and the replacement of a monarchy with the structures of a republic, evidence of 'the essentially progressive and democratic nature of the Irish independence movement', although 'in social and economic matters the party [Sinn Féin] generally was cautious and conservative'.[21]

In relation to tone, style and approach, underpinning some of these controversies was the lingering scent of scholarly regret at what had happened as opposed to what some wished would or should have happened. Literary historian and critic Terence Brown has suggested that much of the revisionism propounded by Conor Cruise O'Brien was 'intellectually depressing' because it was 'unhistorical' speculation and an assumption that Irish independence would have occurred without the 1916 Rising.[22] UCD historian Mary Daly was later to suggest that the debate about revising historical interpretations during this era prompted a degree of 'armchair history'; prolonged and tendentious discussions about 1916 and its legacy were too often 'conducted without the benefit of any new research' and 'became a comfortable alternative to long hours spent in the archives'.[23] As summarised by Tom Garvin:

> There is a common argument to the effect that the violent birth of modern Independent Ireland was in some way foolish and unnecessary, because the democratic politics of consensus, reasoning and bargaining would have achieved independence more easily and without bloodshed. Let me speculate briefly on what might have happened had the Rising not taken place. With the arrival home of the [First World War] veterans in 1919, and with the discredited Redmondites still holding on in Westminster, armed nationalism (which would have returned from the trenches with rather pronounced opinions about the British establishment and its right to rule anybody) would

have been alienated fatally from constitutional nationalism. An incoherent but vicious sectarian war between North and South, with no new generation of political leaders in place, could easily have occurred. The Rising redefined the quarrel as one between two vaguely defined entities, England and Ireland rather than one between Catholics and Protestants.[24]

In other words, Ireland could have been even worse off. Home rule as a solution had been legislated for but had been suspended for the duration of the war without a solution to the dilemma of unionist resistance in Ulster; is it possible that a compromise could have been reached with the unionists? The renowned historian of Ulster unionism, Alvin Jackson, contributed an essay of over fifty pages to Niall Ferguson's *Virtual Histories: Alternatives and Counterfactuals* (1997) speculating on what would have happened if home rule had been imposed on Ireland in 1912, noting that 'the 1912 Bill, suitably presented had a greater chance of success than its predecessors [in 1886 and 1893], and is therefore an intellectually more valuable focus for counterfactual speculation'. He concluded that

> the price paid by all the Irish for a unitary state might well have been higher than the price paid for partition; an unstable thirty-two county Ireland, as opposed to an unstable six-county Northern Ireland ... had Ulster Unionists been eased into a home rule Ireland, then it is just conceivable that a stable pluralist democracy might have swiftly emerged. But it would have been a high risk strategy, with every possibility that a short-term political triumph for Liberal statesmanship might have been bought at the price of a delayed apocalypse.[25]

UCD Historian Ronan Fanning, who specialised in the history of Anglo-Irish relations, maintained in the mid 1980s that

> although the aims of the constitutional politician committed to the idea that nothing can be gained by violence are diametrically opposed to the aims of the paramilitary spokesman convinced that his organisation's objectives can only be gained by physical force, both are anxious to plunder and to prostitute the past for their purposes in the present. The more intense the contemporary conflict between such competing legitimacies, the greater the temptation.[26]

Because of the slowness of the release of archival material, a political stability which fostered the idea that violence was historical and not contemporary, and the determination of the guardians of the 'new histories' from the 1930s not to engage with twentieth-century history and the new popularity of social and economic history, there was also the problem that 'there was no time for historians to produce anything approximating to a definitive history of the Irish revolution before old mythologies were revived and new mythologies created by the eruption of violence after 1968'. This added to a profound pessimism on the part of historians like Leland Lyons: 'I would really find it hard to be both a conscientious historian and an optimist.'[27]

Fanning also quoted historian Bernard Lewis from the mid 1970s as a way of offering a succinct summary of what motivated the Irish political establishment after 1969 to be revisionist: 'those who are in power control to a large extent the presentation of the past and seek to make sure that it is presented in such a way as to buttress and legitimise their own authority, and to affirm the rights and merits of the group which they lead'. Equally, those who used the term 'revisionist' as a pejorative epithet were just 'desperately determined to preserve their ideology intact'; it was thus necessary for historians to write about recent political history to save it being hijacked by ideologists.[28]

In relation to British–Irish relations at a time when the Troubles were raging, Fanning also underlined the endurance of the 'bland indifference with which the British react to events in Ireland which we, the Irish, immediately recognise as historically important'. There was the perennial difficulty of commanding British attention when it had much more important foreign policy considerations (especially the Anglo-US relationship), as well as the ambiguities that clouded the relationship: 'the basic ambiguity arises from our insistence that the Northern Ireland problem is a British responsibility to which there is only an Irish solution'.[29]

Brendan Bradshaw, who lectured in Irish history at Cambridge University, insisted that some historians were deliberately engaging in 'sins of omission' in relation to traumatic events which were becoming marginalised in the writing of modern Irish history.[30] Bradshaw, writing on the 'scientific' approach to history, an unsatisfactory label often applied to new professional standards, rules and discipline promoted by Dudley Edwards and Theo Moody for Irish historical writing from the 1930s and exemplified in the launch of the academic history journal *Irish Historical*

Studies in 1938, attacked the 'revisionists' in 1989. There was, he insisted, a 'credibility gap' between academic history and the Irish reading public, and the detached 'scientific' historians had failed to see how 'the bitter reality, recalled in song and story, continues to haunt the popular memory'. Irish historians, he insisted, had an obligation to mediate by 'acknowledging the burden of the past'.[31] He also accused them of bringing a 'corrosive cynicism' in their approach to the heroes of the past. This was an insistence that what people deserved was a 'public history' and not a past-centred, value-free and objective approach. The preoccupation with liberty, as reflected in songs and folk memory, if so derided and mocked by revisionists, would leave that strand of the Irish political tradition to the contemporary men of violence. Bradshaw's piece was presented as a plea for both empathy and imagination but his critics doubted his contention that his was not 'a plea for green history', and saw it as a demand for unashamedly nationalist history.

Surely, however, one of Bradshaw's contentions was correct: that historians 'should provide contemporary society with the means of self-understanding by enabling it to understand the historical process which brought it into being'. He believed it was necessary for them to have an empathy defined as 'a quality of imaginative sympathy, which enables the historian to experience the external content of the historical process as it was experienced by contemporaries – a kind of intuitive leap – into the past' – surely a noble aspiration? He denied that empathy and objectivity were incompatible and also maintained it was possible to admire both Pearse and Daniel O'Connell, the iconic constitutional nationalist of the nineteenth century.[32]

Others were also critical of the 'scientific, value free' approach to history which was, Tom Bartlett insists, 'emotionally sterile, morally dubious and utterly boring'.[33] A member of an audience at a lecture by UCD historians on the Flight of the Earls in London in the late 1980s is said to have called out, in reacting to the revisionist tone of the lecture: 'For God's sake, leave us our heroes.'[34]

The year 1922 also became much debated and much simplified, including by those who had appealed for 1916 not to be distorted. In relation to the Anglo-Irish Treaty that created the Irish Free State, by the time of the seventy-fifth anniversary in 1996, Tom Garvin took Leland Lyons's 1970s arguments further, by distinguishing between those who in 1922 saw the abstract republic as 'a moral and transcendental entity' and those who, more sensibly in his view, and with more legitimacy, saw it as a 'bargaining device in achieving rational, legal self-government for as much of Ireland as possible'. While in *1922: The Birth of Irish Democracy* (1996) Garvin acknowledged there were those who had sympathised with both perspectives, he emphasised how important it was that the moderates triumphed.[35] There is little doubt that the shadow of the Troubles was relevant here also, prompting a desire to emphasise that, whatever the difficulties of the Republic, it was a remarkably stable and peaceful entity compared to the North. Reducing the civil war divide to pro-Treaty political 'democrats' and anti-Treaty military 'dictators' did no justice to the complexity of the dilemmas and views of 1922; neither side during this conflict had a monopoly on virtue or democratic sentiment and a history 'insisting on the fidelity of the state's constitutionalism from 1922', was a selective history.[36] But neither was it realistic to expect that Irish historians would be unique in completely preventing politics or contemporary environments from intruding on their writings.

Ciaran Brady, a historian at Trinity College Dublin, brought together some of the contributions to the revisionist debate in the stylish and lively *Interpreting Irish History: The Debate on Historical Revisionism, 1938–1994* (1994) and summarised the evolution of Irish history as a professional discipline, its character and purpose, and the degree to which the recent debates had focused minds on whether there was a necessity to abandon or undermine the telling of Irish history as a 'morality tale', but also if it was possible to have a professional history which would not 'filter out the trauma of the national past' (perhaps through more humility and less 'ironic detachment'). There were no clear-cut answers; Brady also made the fair point that 'value free' history had never, in any case, been clearly defined.[37]

NINE

LABOUR, GENDER AND THE SOCIAL PERSPECTIVE

In 1966, at the time of the fiftieth anniversary of the Easter Rising, there was a determined attempt to sideline the labour movement in promoting the nationalist narrative. While James Connolly's was the main name invoked by champions of the labour interest, and there was a challenge to the notion of 'five glorious years' (1916–21), with the labour movement instead using its starting point as 1913 and presenting the 1913 Lockout and the 1916 Rising as closely bound, the labour perspective was still 'assumed into the broader nationalist story'.[1]

Those on the left remained determined to reassert their place in the nationalist canon; in this sense 1916 could not be depicted as an end point. George Gilmore, who had opposed the Anglo-Irish Treaty, commencing a decade in which he spent much time in prison, insisted, 'Labour waited, and that was the great failure of our generation.' Little was heard from Gilmore and his associates in the 1940s and 1950s after their attempt to socialise the republican movement in the 1930s fell flat, but after the formation of the Wolfe Tone Society (1964), which had evolved from the republican commemorative groups established in 1963 to mark the bicentenary of Wolfe Tone's birth (he is regarded as the ideological founding father of modern Irish republicanism) and included intellectuals such as Roy Johnston, a Protestant republican with influence over the IRA, and who were committed to hosting debates and discussion groups and a united Ireland, Gilmore began to speak to a new generation of republicans. In 1966, in a pamphlet on 'Labour and the republican movement' he espoused the principles of James Connolly and appealed to younger republicans not to repeat the mistakes of their predecessors by being rich in principle but disastrously short on policy. In tandem, leading labour historian Desmond Greaves asserted that the bourgeoisie had stayed aloof in 1916 and had been on the sidelines during the revolution but had been its ultimate beneficiaries.

Greaves also wrote *Liam Mellows and the Irish Revolution* (1971), which focused on class relations during the revolutionary period 1916–23, but did not reveal his sources; an obituary essay written by one of his fellow socialists suggested he deliberately excluded his sources by remarking 'let the academics do their own work'.[2] Greaves also justified this on the grounds that he believed history books should be conceived aesthetically; 'Thus,' he said, 'In the Mellows book I deliberately highlighted the events before Mellows' death, when his fortunes seemed to be improving, in order to make more vivid the contrast with his death sentence. That would be impermissible in an academic thesis, where all facts are equally important, so the overall result is formless.'[3]

In 1969 the Wolfe Tone Society convened a symposium on an agenda for Irish historians and wondered not only 'What is the situation of our national archives?' but also 'What should be the response of historians, as historians, to the problems and challenges facing Irish people and the Irish nation today?'[4] Labour activist John de Courcey Ireland had his own answer to that at an anti-imperialist festival in 1974 – the need to think and act within a broader international context:

> There is probably no country in the world that has had its history so distorted into myth as ours. The now traditional myth, of course, is that the Irish people are in no sense as other men are, but a mighty company of slumbering saints, pure Gaels by blood and temperament awaiting the leadership of a heaven-sent elite to a pinnacle of political or ideological greatness (in some versions both) which will astonish the world.[5]

He also engaged in debate with historian, political scientist and Labour Party TD David Thornley (who liked to cast himself in the mould of James Connolly, as a practising Catholic, Marxist socialist and republican) about the principles and legacy of Connolly: 'We've got to face the fact that our best leaders do make errors.'[6]

Another labour historian, Arthur Mitchell, had insisted in 1971 that 'opportunities for fostering social and economic revolution were ever present during the period 1919–23', but that 'moderate' leadership had prevented the labour movement from taking those opportunities forward.[7] This was an issue that was to continue to exercise historians; significantly, the Irish Labour History Society was established in 1973. The early editions of its journal, *Saothar*, provided a platform to broaden the parameters of labour history, Emmet O'Connor pointing out in 1983 that 'an age of agitation' could not be reduced to looking just at James Larkin, who led the 1913 Lockout, and Connolly. Larkin, he maintained 'had a coherent, radical vision of trade unionism that is of relevance both historically and politically. It is only when we reduce the legacy to a lone star legend that it becomes deceptive and disturbing ... Connolly too has been fetishised and then buffeted between iconography and iconoclasm'.[8] Connolly, he insisted, should not be defined solely in terms of his anti-imperialism, and 'the assumption that the labour revival after 1917 was inspired by resurgent separatism' was 'a misconception in labour history'; it was, in reality, built up from the base, with rapid enrolment of unskilled labourers into a pioneering movement at a time of social change.[9]

In 1974 Mitchell produced his seminal *Labour in Irish Politics, 1890–1930* which drew heavily on periodicals, labour reports and interviews with those who had been involved, and underlined how narrowly based the Labour Party, formed in 1912, had been. It had not sufficiently appealed to small farmers or labourers, did not become the focus of radical activity and lacked an industrial base.[10] But where would the labour focus on the revolution move thereafter? In 1995, a review of labour history up to that point suggested, 'Before the 1970s, the bibliography comprised a few books written mainly by authors based abroad, a handful of home produced theses and articles, occasional trade union publications, and a trickle of left-wing historical pamphlets.' But change was evident: the notion of the forward march of labour 'crippled by the priest, the peasant, and the patriot, and the near apologetic view of Irish labour as a pale imitation of its British counterpart is yielding to a more objective awareness of Irish exceptionality'.[11]

Emmet O'Connor's *Syndicalism in Ireland, 1917–23* (1988) was seen as demonstrating that the revolutionary period was the 'one period in modern trade union history where the rank and file thrust themselves into the picture'.[12] Also significant here was Liam Cahill's *Forgotten Revolution:*

The Limerick Soviet, 1919 – A Threat to British Power in Ireland (1990), detailing a general strike that paralysed the city for two weeks, invoked the example of Russia and even produced its own currency. But it was still framed by the wider republican struggle – it was the death of an IRA trade unionist that prompted it – and initial support by Sinn Féin and the Church dissipated when it threatened to become too autonomous. In any case, the labour movement behind it demonstrated 'an extremely hazy concept of socialism'.[13]

The point was also made in 1995 that 'there is no shortage of left-wing opinion on why labour solidarity disintegrated in 1921–23 – leadership betrayal being a common theme; it would be nice to know more on how it happened'.[14] There was also an interesting Ulster dimension to this, elaborated on in Henry Patterson's *Class, Conflict and Sectarianism: The Protestant Working Class and the Belfast Labour Movement, 1868–1920* (1980) and Austen Morgan's *Labour and Partition: The Belfast Working Class, 1905–23* (London, 1991). These books challenged the idea of sectarianism as endemic in these labour movements and 'laid emphasis on the radical element in Protestant labour politics'.[15] There have been challenging assertions about the perceived labour failures of the Irish revolutionary period, particularly 1917–1923, as examined by Conor Kostick in *Revolution in Ireland: Popular Militancy, 1917–23* (1996); he concluded that the workers were defeated during that period because they were betrayed by their leaders. Arthur Mitchell rejected this by arguing that it is situations that create leaders rather than the reverse.[16]

Labour history also began to move beyond hagiography and demagoguery to restore the complexity of individuals who were prominent. Accounts of James Connolly included observations of his darker side and frequent displays of volatility and the confusing and ambiguous relationship he had with Ireland and his contemporaries. In 2005 Donal Nevin, a well-known trade unionist and tireless chronicler of labour history, quoted extensively from 200 letters that revealed aspects of Connolly's relationship with his colleagues.[17] Nevin maintained that,

> at the remove of a hundred years it is difficult to comprehend the messianic fervour that motivated left-wing socialists in the first years of the twentieth century as they assumed the imminent collapse of bourgeois capitalism and its replacement by a co-operative organisation of industry and the building of a Commonwealth that would replace the

exploitation of Labour and lead to the emancipation of the workers ...
The time span envisaged for the coming of the social revolution was a
short one ... Connolly's writings in the years 1896 to 1903 must be seen
in this light.[18]

Connolly's acute disappointment at the reception he received in
these early years is also recorded: following the failure of the tiny Irish
Socialist Republican Party and the *Worker's Republic* newspaper in 1903,
he wrote: 'I regard Ireland, or at least the socialist part of Ireland which
is all I care for, as having thrown me out and I do not wish to return like a
dog to his vomit.'[19]

Larkin was written about as a leader who was inspirational but difficult to collaborate with, and he shamelessly encouraged an unhealthy
cult of personality. He revolutionised Irish trade unionism by lessening
dependence on the British labour movement, and in doing so laid the basis
of the modern Irish labour movement, but was also largely remembered
not especially for what he did, 'but in image and idea; in the image of
Dublin workers as a "risen people" in 1913, and the idea of workers' solidarity as a code of honour. Significantly, he has been celebrated more in art
and literature than in historical scholarship.'[20] One such example was the
epic historical novel by James Plunkett, *Strumpet City*, published in 1969,
which illuminated the city of the period in all its glory and grime through
a host of characters covering different social spectrums and allegiances.
Plunkett was himself an active trade unionist and worked briefly with Larkin towards the very end of his life, though Larkin remains a force rather
than a rigorously dissected character in his book. While there is no doubt-
ing where Plunkett's sympathies lay in the period he covers (1907–13), he
avoided a sentimental or propagandist approach and took his historical
research very seriously. The achievement lay in the depiction, not of militant nationalism, but of 'ordinary nobility' and a refusal to romanticise the
city which had a death rate of 22 per 1,000 people in contrast to London's
16. Asked to explain the book's success, Plunkett replied simply: 'I didn't
take my eye away from the people at any stage ... the duty of a good writer
of fiction or drama is not to preach. It is to absorb, to observe, to distil and
to reveal – gently.'[21]

But Larkin and the Lockout were to receive more comprehensive
treatment from future historians, journalists and trade union activists,
including Pádraig Yeates (who was all three) in the weighty *Lockout:*

Dublin, 1913 (2000) which provided a detailed corrective to the problem that prior to his book, there was 'no basic record of what happened. The Lockout is frequently referred to, often analysed – usually as a prelude to 1916 and all that – but never described.' He not only convincingly argued that the traditional 'prelude to 1916' narrative of the Lockout was unwarranted, but also gave comprehensive treatment to the character of Larkin, warts and all, noting that his comrade James Connolly observed that Larkin was 'consumed with jealousy and hatred of anyone who did not cringe to him'.[22] Emmet O'Connor also provided a master class in dissecting the complex Larkin in the concise biography *James Larkin* (2002); the labour leader here is a man who could be both 'hero' and 'wrecker'.[23]

The social and cultural factors that propelled the revolutionary generation and the extent of their conservativeness also began to receive more attention. In 1986, Tom Garvin maintained that Irish socialism as well as nationalism was imbued with a nostalgia for the 'Gaelic tradition' through which separatism could endure: 'James Connolly saw the Irish bourgeoisie as usurpers, much as Pearse saw the English as usurpers. The great farmers had arrogated to themselves the land that, under the medieval Gaelic system, had belonged to the kin, or people as a group.'[24] The Fenian leaders were 'upwardly mobile' and the later Sinn Féin revolution was dominated by young Catholic men who could be considered middle-class, but its leadership was non-agrarian and well educated. Of the 124 TDs in the 1921 Dáil, 84 were born outside of a large city or town, and of that number, half were rural. There is a similar pattern of a rising political class originating among the rural and small-town petite bourgeoisie. One pro-Treaty TD, when debating its merits in January 1922, observed impatiently that the sons of rich farmers had been as patriotic as any during the struggle, and that virtue was not a monopoly of the poor: 'You may as well say it is essential to reduce one's body to poverty to save one's soul.'[25]

But what of the observation of Ernie O'Malley to the effect that, 'In the country the small farmers and labourers were our main support and in the cities the workers with a middle-class sprinkling; towns we could not rely on.'[26] More recent scholars have been conscious of examining this question of class basis for support; in Cork by the end of 1915 the Cork City Volunteers were 'primarily working and lower middle class', though its CnB leadership indicated the dominance of 'respectable' women from the Catholic lower middle class and the Sinn Féin leadership was dominated by members of the lower middle class, a 'social step below the Irish party elite', challenging David Fitzpatrick's 1977 thesis that they were of the same ilk.[27] Fergus Campbell found the same in Galway.[28] But did the IRA really regard itself as part of the rural poor? Marie Coleman, in looking at Longford, also observed 'arguments which suggest the less prosperous were more likely to engage in revolutionary activity are given added weight by the evidence of this county'.[29] In Limerick, however, it was maintained that there was no big cleavage; that the SF leadership was built on 'the bones' of the IPP one.[30] What was clear, however, was that Sinn Féin leaders were not going to give hostages to fortune in class terms if they were to generate the support they needed; they were anxious about land agitation and wedded to the primacy of private property; de Valera and others insisted that patriotism had to rise above all class interests. But the reality underlined by the new perspectives is that the independence movement garnered support from many interests across the social spectrum.

Heightened interest in the social and economic context led to a very productive investigation of a variety of social history sources. Pádraig Yeates, looking at Dublin in *A City in Wartime, 1914–18* (2011) and *A City in Turmoil 1919–21* (2012) filled his books with the struggles of ordinary people living their lives during extraordinary political and economic upheaval, reminding readers that for all the headline-grabbing events, putting bread on the table was still the most important priority for most. The author's research of contemporary newspapers, local authority and private archives succeeded in offering a multitude of perspectives on the political, military and administrative concerns of an elite involved in governance, but also the personal individual preoccupations with light, heat, fuel, food, housing and survival in the trenches of the Western Front.[31]

Many of the revolutionary women who had been 'lost to history' were also afforded a new place in the narrative. As the pioneer of women's history in Ireland, Margaret Mac Curtain, noted, the Report of the Commission on the Status of Women in 1972 expressed the aspiration that women would retrieve their own history, and she and others embraced this challenge with gusto, despite the fact that, as she recalled, 'writing women into Irish history became a subversive activity for women historians in the 1970s. The universities were not ready for an innovation which, in the opinion of the historical establishment, possessed neither a sound methodology nor reliable sources.'[32] Brian Moore's poem *Invisible Women* provocatively challenged the male narrative:

Ireland, Mother Ireland, with your freedom-loving sons,
Did your daughters run and hide at the sounds of guns?
Or did they have some part in the fight
And why does everybody try to keep them out of sight?[33]

Some men, of course, had also been determined at the time of the revolution to keep them out of sight, or certainly, Margaret Ward noted in *Unmanageable Revolutionaries: Women and Irish Nationalism* (1983), out of the fighting: 'at no stage were [women] accepted as equal members', though she acknowledged there was greater gender equality in the Irish Citizen Army.[34] Those who came to prominence in accounts of the revolution in the 1970s and 1980s were those, such as Constance Markievicz, who 'assumed male dress and roles during revolutionary times'.[35] Thirty years later there was much interest in the fate and correspondence of interned and imprisoned women, seen in Ann Matthews's *Dissidents* (2012), but preceding that had been numerous accounts of the broader social, cultural, educational and religious contexts relating to the status of women, for example in Senia Paseta's *Before the Revolution: Nationalism, Social Change and Ireland's Catholic Elite, 1872–1922* (1999) and a determination by Ward and others to document the women's own voices, as seen with *In Their Own Voice: Women and Irish Nationalism* (1995).

Female activists also focused on improving the health and welfare of their fellow citizens, an example being Dr Ada English who as an academic, doctor and nationalist worked and campaigned in a male-dominated environment that was often hostile to female independence. A staunch opponent of the Anglo-Irish Treaty of 1921, she did not voice her opposition to it as the relative of a dead male patriot, declaring: 'I have no dead men to throw in my teeth as a reason for holding the opinions I hold.' She believed it was a fatal spiritual surrender and she paid the price, losing her Dáil seat. But she devoted her life's professional work to Ballinasloe District Asylum.[36] Kathleen Lynn was another crucial reformer in medicine, but also a significant presence in the revolution: a doctor who was active in the suffrage movement, vice president of the Irish Women Workers' Union and medical director of the Irish Citizen Army, and who was elected to the executive of Sinn Féin in 1917. She established St Ultan's hospital for children in Dublin in 1919 with Madeleine ffrench-Mullan, with whom she shared her political work and her personal life.

Lynn and ffrench-Mullan were just one of a number of female couples involved in the political and social movements of early twentieth century Ireland who established a 'lasting, committed political and domestic relationship with another woman', such as Eva Gore Booth (sister of Constance Markievicz) and Esther Roper, Louie Bennett of the Irish Women Workers' Union and Helen Chenevix, trade unionist and pacifist.[37] Gore Booth, who 'despised her aristocratic heritage', was an influential labour and suffrage campaigner in Britain. She gave poetic expression to her opposition to conscription in 1918, wrote powerfully about the Rising, made common cause with Roger Casement and was a lot more than just 'the sister of Markievicz'.[38]

Others felt themselves marginalised at the time, as is clear in Leeann Lane's *Rosamund Jacob* (2010); Jacob, a suffragette and nationalist, was conversant from 1909 with practically all those involved in radical politics but lamented her lack of influence or status. After 1916 she complained she was 'all the time suffering from envy and jealousy of the people I met who had been out in the Rising. It seems as if I was destined to be an outsider and a looker-on in everything all my life; never to be in it.'[39] In contrast, Annie Ryan's *Witnesses: Inside the Easter Rising* (2005) sought to make the most of the BMH statements to underline her view that women were 'the really outstanding Citizen Army people'. What was involved in non-combat work was not necessarily genteel or light on effort; there were many resourceful women in CnB whose structures proved efficient and reliable and whose role in transporting dispatches was indispensable. As Leslie Price discovered, the safest way for these messages to get to Cork was through Celbridge (in Kildare) and 'to test its efficiency she cycled every yard of it herself as far as Cork' (a distance of 150 miles).[40]

In 2002, volumes 4 and 5 of *The Field Day Anthology of Irish Women's Writing*, in the words of its editors, provided a 'set of contexts for understanding how women lived in Ireland'.[41] Catríona Crowe, in heralding its publication and celebrating it as 'almost overwhelming', highlighted one of its sections edited by Maria Luddy under the title 'Women and Politics in Ireland, 1860–1918'. This gave an indication of how widely the issues of power, and lack of it, and the variety of women's voices in the revolutionary period, could be framed. Luddy examined 'informal political activity by women – membership of secret societies, mob violence – as well as female philanthropy as a political force. She also deals with the suffrage movement and women's involvement in the nationalist revolutionary period.

Her selection includes Isabella Tod's stern Puritanism as well as Maud Gonne's whimsical egotism, Anna Parnell's reflections on the Ladies' Land League, Hanna Sheehy Skeffington on the suffrage movement, Cumann na mBan's manifesto, and Nora Connolly's heartbreaking account of her last meeting with her father on the night before he was executed ... Mary MacSwiney's 1914 piece from the *Irish Citizen* outlines the nationalist/feminist dilemma: "The women of Ireland want the Vote, but they do not want it ... at the expense of Home Rule".[42] It also became apparent that it was incumbent upon historians to document 'more obscure personalities', including 'the shrewd newsagent Nora Wallace' and others previously 'lost to history'; Wallace was active in Cork in forming a city branch of the Irish Citizen Army girl scouts.[43] Women were also afforded opportunities in journalism, the writing of pamphlets and journal articles, whose authors included Alice Milligan who also wrote plays to hone her preoccupation with 'the memory of the dead'; these publications provided opportunities to women sometimes 'denied a role elsewhere'.[44]

The new sources have also allowed a more nuanced approach that allows the women to be seen through the lens of their times and the prejudices that existed against them but also among them; the contrasting assessments of what constituted activism and dignity; and the extent to which social and geographical circumstances could limit or broaden their horizons and opportunities. This approach has ensured that there is no easy answer to the question of what characterised *Irish Nationalist Women, 1900–1918*, the title of Senia Paseta's book in 2014, but it is a book that evaluates the women's contribution on their own terms, and the author was moved to declare that 'this is emphatically a work of women's history'.[45]

TEN

THE POLITICS OF PEACE AND THE TWENTY-FIRST-CENTURY PERSPECTIVE

In tandem with the peace process of the 1990s and early twenty-first century, the First World War and Irish revolution were no longer confined to their own spheres in historical analysis as it was deemed necessary to 'discard the prism of political allegiance' when looking at Ireland during the war years: 'The Easter Rising and the conscription crisis are as important to Ireland's First World War experience as Gallipoli and the Somme.' There were explorations of collective pressures for enlistment that existed outside of politics; there even developed a notion of the First World War as 'Our War'.[1] More than 200,000 Irishmen fought in the war with roughly 40,000 of them killed; service in the British army was a common family tradition, and was not seen by many of them as involving either a pro-British or anti-Irish stance. Such nuanced identities, however, were, until recently, conveniently ignored. Keith Jeffery in *Ireland and the Great War* (2000) focused on four threads of the Irish relationship with the war – obligations, participation, imagination and commemoration – and linked the Irish experience in the Battle of the Somme with the experience of the 1916 Rising, but the distance between the two sides was already so large it was hardly going to be bridged by a common war experience.

John Horne identified the features that emerged in the midst of the war; the intensity with which societies engaged with it, the mass deaths caused in combat and then, after it, 'remembrance: how people came to understand an event whose trauma none had anticipated'.[2] At approximately 40,000, the number of Irish soldiers who died in that war was in stark contrast to the roughly 7,500 fatalities in Ireland during the revolutionary period. Horne and others were also making an appeal for the Irish experience of this war to be seen in its European and international context, another of the ways in which perspectives on the Irish revolution have changed.[3] At the time of the formation of the Ulster and Irish Volunteers in 1913, Europe was riven with conflict and labour unrest; militarism on the part of civilians was evident in Germany, Britain and Poland, and independent military action of smaller nations was evident in the Balkan wars of 1911 and 1912 and the emerging nation states of Serbia, Bulgaria and Greece, developments that did not go unrecorded in Ireland. The formation of the Volunteers was an Irish manifestation of the rise of the 'generation of 1914' whose rhetoric embraced the prospect of heroic conflict; it was a time of transition and dislocation, predictions of the end of empire, the promotion of the cult of manliness as the gateway to public virtue, and demands for suffrage and equality for women.[4]

How and where the Catholic Church positioned itself during these years was the focus of David Miller's *Church, State and Nation in Ireland, 1898–1921* (1973), which placed the Church centre stage in relation to the political upheavals of that era as 'a central fact of Irish life'. Whatever divided the constitutionalists and supporters of violent upheaval, they had their religious affiliation in common, and Sinn Féin was in some ways in a more advantageous position in soliciting clerical support as it was not compromised in the way some Church personnel felt the IPP was by reliance on a Liberal Party that had significant support from nonconformists. But the availability of more archival material ensured that subsequent appraisals included more caveats and less of an acceptance of Miller's highlighting of the 'Orange bigotry' of Irish Protestants by ignoring Catholic bigotry.[5] Jérôme aan de Wiel's *The Catholic Church in Ireland, 1914–18: War and Politics* (2003) charted the transition within its ranks of support for home rule to support for Sinn Féin and suggested that it was following as much as leading opinion; it simply could not, for example, 'run the risk of forcing Irishmen to join the army'.[6] How was the balance to be struck for the Church after the First World War? Enda McDonagh, a leading moral theologian, made the point in 1976 that Irish revolutionaries had 'always been able to distinguish their patriotism and their religion'.[7] This undoubtedly caused tension at the time; during the War of Independence, the Sinn Féin government drafted a letter to the Irish bishops heralding their role in the history of Irish republicanism ('800 years') and the after-math of the 1916 Rising, asking them to recognise the legitimacy of the Dáil, with this wording: 'we ask you to distinguish between our pos-ition and our actions'.[8] Many did, some did not, but there was deliberate vagueness at play, and private and public utterances and correspondence recently unearthed have underlined the consequences of such ambiguity and its abandonment at the outbreak of the civil war, as well as the intri-cacies of ham-fisted and naïve Vatican interventions in Irish politics dur-ing this period.[9]

A major focus on the sources for diplomatic history has also been reflected in the *Documents on Irish Foreign Policy* series, a partnership between the Irish state, national archives and Royal Irish Academy, the first volume of which covered the years 1919–22, beginning with the Dec-laration of Irish Independence in January 1919. As well as making use of the considerable holdings of the state archive, its compilers were able to draw on the UCD archives, including the papers of Éamon de Valera and Des-mond FitzGerald. Rather than building on an established historiography, it forged a new departure in relation to areas that have been neglected; significantly, much more material than expected was discovered for the years 1919–22 underlining the seriousness with which presenting the Irish republican case abroad was taken.[10]

The dynamics, personalities and wrangling underpinning the Sinn Féin Party were finally given the textured assessment they warranted with Michael Laffan's authoritative *The Resurrection of Ireland: The Sinn Féin Party, 1916–1923* (1999), which was the culmination of thirty years' research, and remarkably polished as it documented 'the democratic face of the Irish revolution'. While Sinn Féin 'faltered' in 1922 (and split into what ultimately became Fine Gael and Fianna Fáil), it still remained 'the principal means whereby Ireland's constitutional tradition was transmitted through years of turbulence, and it played an important role in ensuring that governments of independent Ireland would be responsible to the people'.[11] Historians were also in the business during this era of challeng-ing exaggerated, bombastic references made by some of the revolution's participants to their own roles; Canadian historian Peter Hart's *The IRA and Its Enemies: Violence and Community in Cork, 1916–23* (1998) was a notable and controversial example. For some, Hart (the detached Canad-ian 'outsider' and upstart) had a deliberately anti-republican agenda; for others he was simply being excoriated as the messenger who, through forensic research, found it necessary to remove the halos from some of Ireland's revered patriots. Given a new focus on silences, disappearances and killing of informants during the revolutionary era and a contemporary current affairs focus on victims of the modern Troubles in Northern Ireland, this was also about the extent to which differences between the old and new IRA 'becomes more and more difficult to outline'.[12]

Hart's trenchant critics raised legitimate questions which Hart did not adequately address and his responses were too often acerbic and intemperate (as has been some, though not all, of the criticism of his work); he accused his critics of practising a 'faith-based or creationist history'.[13] The reality is that the contradictory evidence over what happened during seminal moments, battles or exchanges during the revolution do not merit emphatic conclusions, but what Hart did succeed in doing was to subject the ideology of early twentieth-century republicanism to serious scrutiny, revealing a revolution that was often noble but frequently brutal. His work also revealed much about the social composition of the IRA in Cork, the most violent county in Ireland during this period, where 700 died during the struggle for independence, and the manner in which they dealt with internal opposition, uncomfortable questions that had hitherto not been seriously addressed by historians; the book thus succeeded in reopening debate about the meaning and methods of the War of Independence.[14]

The status of the constitutional tradition also remained contested. Paul Bew, the historian who also advised unionists during the peace process, produced his mammoth *Ireland: The Politics of Enmity, 1789–2006* in 2007 and suggested that the British reaction to the Rising in 1916 did much to create the 'politics of the gun' between 1919 and 1923, which was a manifestation of 'an emotional hardening' taking place. He quoted Stephen Gwynn at length, including his 1922 assertion, doubtless shared by Bew, that 'generous recognition for differing interests without regard to their numerical strength is the saving formula for Ireland'.[15] Gwynn, from a unionist background, was convinced by Irish nationalists' arguments. A Protestant intellectual, he was active in the Gaelic League, served as a Redmondite MP and enlisted in the British army during the Great War, but he also believed that nationalist Ireland still had much to gain from unionist culture and its adherents' skills. By 2014 historian Dermot Meleady encouraged a reading of Redmond as Ireland's 'national leader'; one who had been so 'comprehensively erased by history' but who, while making mistakes, was still astute, kept his party together when a lesser leader would have allowed it to disintegrate, and had 'prudence, vision and far-sightedness' as well as 'self-sacrificing dedication to his nation's independence'.[16] Ronan Fanning, however, suggested in *Fatal Path* (2013) that 'there is not a shred of evidence that Lloyd George's Tory dominated government would have moved from the 1914-style niggardliness of the Government of Ireland Act to the larger, if imperfect generosity of the Treaty, if they had not been impelled to do so by Michael [Collins] and his assassins'; the Redmond in Fanning's book is naïve and delusional.[17]

The voluminous and far-reaching *Dictionary of Irish Biography*, published in nine volumes in 2009, is now an indispensable guide to many of the revolutionary era's personalities, including Redmond: Michael Laffan concluded that he

> was spectacularly unlucky in the timing of the First World War and – like very many others – he miscalculated its duration. Ultimately he and his party fell victim to the rival extremes of Ulster unionism and Irish republicanism. Nonetheless he was a worthy and noble representative of the Irish political tradition, he proved that patience, negotiation and compromise could bring about important reforms, he helped to embed parliamentary procedures in the habits and instincts of Irish nationalists, and he played a significant role in transforming Ireland in the decades before the First World War. The miscalculations and failures of his later years have obscured his many achievements.[18]

Michael Collins continued to fascinate Peter Hart and others. While Collins was popularly remembered as a martyred and effective soldier, his skills actually lay in other areas ('maybe he just always wanted to be an accountant').[19] The secret of his success, according to Hart in *Mick: The Real Michael Collins* (2005), was that he simply worked harder than anyone else; de Valera had to remind him at one stage that 'The Almighty did not give everybody the ordered mind he gave you.'[20] Nor was he too preoccupied with what republic was being fought for; in Collins's own words in 1920, 'no-one has ever defined it'.[21] Curiously and unfortunately, Hart also decided to bring far too much of himself into his repackaging of Collins, undermining his original research with unnecessary hagiographical interludes, suggesting, for example, that 'he must have been a wonderful person to have a drink with, and one of the most exciting friends you could ever imagine'.[22]

Some have been driven to remembrance by an uncritical devotion with little space for objectivity; a version of Michael Collins's speeches was republished, for example, in 2010 and the dedication was 'in loving memory of Michael Collins'. In her foreword, Mary Kenny gushed about the 'magnificently eloquent' Collins, whose 'overall vision is still inspiring ... he wants the arts and music to belong to all of the people and not just an elite'.[23] Here, Collins was being repackaged as the great champion of cultural democracy. Kenny's tone was not far off that reached by Napoli McKenna, who provided secretarial assistance during the Treaty negotiations in London in 1921 and whose recollections were published in the *Capuchin Annual* in 1971. She recalled, in relation to 5 December 1921, the day before the Treaty was signed:

> What this man's mental torture must be. I realised fully the weight of responsibility placed by events upon his young generous shoulders with the tenderness with which a mother watches her fever-stricken child. I gazed on his pale face, now relaxed and calm and wanted to push gently away the rebellious lock hanging on his forehead.[24]

It was clear that a dominant impulse in relation to documenting the life of Collins continued to be the life that was not; Collins, had he lived, the argument goes, would have changed everything. Margery Forester insisted in *Michael Collins: Lost Leader* (1971), 'There would have been no firing squads [during the civil war] because the power of his humanity would have found the solution which those who followed him sought desperately in vain.'[25] Thirty years on, there was still much perpetuation of the cult of Collins, the 'James Dean of Irish history',[26] and exaggeration of his vision. The book of his collected speeches, *The Path to Freedom* (1922) suggested he had no sympathy for social radicalism and embraced a limited Gaelic revivalist philosophy. In addition, as Minister for Finance, 'he allowed his civil service to achieve a control that resembled that of the Whitehall Treasury. The bureaucratic conservatism of the Free State, therefore, owed arguably much to Collins.'[27]

Éamon de Valera, on the opposite side of the civil war divide to Collins, and who outlived him by more than fifty years, came to dominate Irish politics from the 1930s to the 1950s and attracted adulation, but also venom, due not just to his role in the revolutionary period, and especially the civil war, but also because of his governance during difficult and contested post-state-formation decades, politically and economically. Five years before he died in 1975 his officially approved biography, by Lord Longford (Frank Pakenham) and Thomas P. O'Neill, had insisted he was a creator of Ireland's destiny, and that it is 'impossible to exaggerate the extent to which de Valera submitted all his actions to a criterion which was at once intellectual and moral'.[28] Other writers developed anything but a laudatory assessment during subsequent decades, most notably in 1993, when a biography by Tim Pat Coogan, *Long Fellow, Long Shadow*, concluded that de Valera's career was a triumph of rhetoric over reality; that he did 'little that was useful and much that was harmful'.[29] But in recent years a revision of such a damning judgement has emerged, part of a discomfort with the extent to which the phrase 'de Valera's Ireland' became shorthand for all the shortcomings of twentieth-century Ireland.[30]

As well as Charles Townshend's *Easter 1916: The Irish Rebellion* (2005), which succeeded in presenting a much broader and more textured analysis of the Rising, including the view from the British side – Townshend, based at Keele University, has been writing on the Anglo-Irish conflict since the 1970s and also authored *The Republic: The Fight for Irish Independence, 1918–23* (2013), which includes a detailed overview of the way in which the IRA was organised throughout the country and the extent of local nuances, feuds, resilience and weaknesses – new lives of the 1916 leaders have also appeared, such as Gerard MacAtasney's *Tom Clarke: Life, Liberty and Revolution* (2012). These serve a dual purpose: to update biographical studies that are decades old (the 2012 biography of Clarke is the first since Louis Le Roux's in 1936) but also to showcase some of the archival gems that should inform new perspectives as the centenary of the Rising looms; the lengthy letters penned by Clarke were purchased by the National Library of Ireland in 2006.[31] Such correspondence is central to underlining numerous identities and layers and tensions, which contrast sharply with the simplistic assertions of contemporary politicians that 'in 1916, we were all one, before there were any splits'.[32]

Chroniclers were also determined to document those deemed to be unjustly neglected or forgotten and introduce them 'to a new generation'; deserving of this because they 'sacrificed ... health, career, comfort and financial security to further one cause'.[33] Others sought to document the lives of their relatives because of a refusal of the participants to speak about their involvement, one grandson referring to his grandfather's efforts 'in later years to avoid any mention of his past', details of which he 'steadfastly refused to divulge'.[34]

But there is also now much more of an interest in uncovering those who were not well-known leaders, or who were prominent at the time and were subsequently marginalised, such as the anarchic Jack White, who first published his autobiography *Misfit* in 1930. He was interesting as one who was born into a loyalist and middle-class family but became the co-founder of the Irish Citizen Army. His book was republished in 2005 and his son Derrick, who was four years old when his father died in 1946, admitted 'I am not convinced I would have liked the man'. White was described in 2014 as 'a man who has fallen through the cracks of history'.[35]

Some recent books have sought to challenge the notion of the 'unflinching patriotism' of local communities; just how far-fetched, for example, was the idea, as enunciated by an Australian priest, of ageing mothers with 'their heads bowed in sorrow over a murdered son, but whose hearts are throbbing with pride at the thought that their loved ones have died for Ireland'?[36] In truth, the lesson is that there is no one-size-fits-all scenario for the regions; in Kerry 'personalities and personal agendas often dominated' and 'for a good part of the war the Kerry men were badly organised'; there were communal networks but also rifts between officers and fighters who 'effectively renounced brigade control' and were operating independently.[37] Another historian of a county's experience, in this case Limerick, noted that 'even the most benign questioning of popular myths, or indeed prevailing academic attitudes, can prick acute and sometimes malignant sensitivities'.[38]

There is also a pronounced emphasis on the witness account – 'every effort has been made to allow the people who lived through Mayo's turbulent history between 1919–24 to speak for themselves through the use of their letters, diaries and speeches. This is Mayo's story' – with a consequent desire to 'dispel the myth' that a particular county was quiet during the revolution, an assertion of wounded pride not just prompted by new research but also underpinned by a more traditional attitude and the heroic narrative.[39]

In Daniel Corkery's foreword to Micheál Ó Súilleabháin's *Where Mountainy Men Have Sown: War and Peace in Rebel Cork in the Turbulent Years, 1916–21* (1965), Corkery was adamant 'People did not want to see books written ... in an official report style'; they did not need 'specimens of dried out expertness'. This, essentially, was about giving the story back to the 'rabble'. The Ó Súilleabháin book, Corkery maintained, 'the man in the street and in the haggard will be glad to know. For it goes its own neighbourly way. It is nothing but itself.'[40] It is significant that this book was reissued in 2013 at a time when there was much interest in the witness account, particularly due to the opening of the BMH and MSPC archives.

A pride somewhat submerged during the worst of the modern Troubles also emerged in other accounts. In relation to the civil war, at the time of its eightieth anniversary in 2003, Eoin Neeson lamented 'mendacious Free State propaganda still being peddled' and 'unfortunately, younger generations tend to see such dissembling as fact',[41] a curious lack of confidence in the intelligence of younger people. Neeson was correct about the dominance of the Free State viewpoint, but what of his own assertion in *Birth of a Republic*, published in 1998, that

> there is no right and wrong (though one must exclude some individual acts which occurred in the course of events). To believe otherwise is to believe that the honourable were dishonourable, that the dedicated were unpatriotic and that those who had fought as companions-in-arms for justice and liberty were no more than time-serving opportunists.[42]

What is striking about this is not just the pious tone, but also the determination to close down any possibility that there might have been grey areas. Such black-and-white moralising is hardly conducive to making sense of a conflict that was complicated and messy. In contrast, the scholarship of Fearghal McGarry, including *Rebels* (2011), offered a textured attempt, through extensive use of the BMH statements, to understand the 'motivations, mentality and experience' of the 1916 insurgents, and as he elaborated elsewhere, there was a diverse range of factors that influenced the political formation of the Volunteer generation. They included 'family background and childhood influences, local and communal influences, intergenerational tensions, education, popular traditions of Irish history, print culture and associational culture. But there is little discussion of ideology in the statements ... Volunteering did not popularise republicanism.' They saw themselves as existing to counter the unionist threat to home rule, not to fight for Irish independence: 'The Volunteer movement had not built its base on the back of the ideology of the IRB, and even within the much smaller Irish Volunteers group after the split, there was considerable opposition to the IRB.'[43]

Anne Dolan suggested in 2010 that 'we know the War of Independence almost like a series of snapshots. Familiar images, incidents and individuals map out the two and a half years of ambush and execution, of reprisal and assassination, of fear, terror, curfew and martial law. Its chronology is almost plotted out with a sequence of iconic moments.'[44] But the well-known events were played out 'against the background of other small local wars': quiet and noisy counties, the dominance and influence of local individuals and traditions, quiet and loud intimidations and fluctuating levels of violence. But who bore the heaviest cost? Dolan makes the point that 'the civilian experience is possibly the most overlooked aspect of the war. It gets lost in the eagerness to examine the combatants.'[45]

The new archival material offers a chance to bring more clarity to these and other issues; it also underlines the difficulty of the assertion of Seán O'Faoláin in 1976, mentioned above, that 'all moral problems vanished in the fire of patriotism and death and destruction'. They did not; if anything they were compounded by it and created a dilemma about how to make the transition from the military to the political. As Ernie O'Malley saw it, 'fighting was so easy compared with that soul-numbing, uphill fight against one people's ignorance and prejudice', his tortured description of politics.[46] Nor should it be believed that the witness accounts contain all the answers or do not have to be treated with caution; memories could be faulty, prejudices could be at work as scores were settled and some may have had reason to either exaggerate or be overly reticent.

Debates will also continue about the extent of sectarian impulses, how to define democracy during this period and the degree to which historians deliberately avoided or embraced certain evidence or perspectives, a theme that has exercised John Regan, elaborated on in the book *Myth and the Irish State* (2014). His own reference to 'more acceptable sources' than those used by historians whose accounts he disputes highlights the danger of the high moral historical ground; it is hardly surprising and hardly troubling that different historians focus on different collections of documents or will interpret the same source material in different ways.[47]

What we do need to look for, however, is honesty as opposed to myth and simplicity and there is much food for thought for the historian in the reasons Seán O'Faoláin put forward for establishing *The Bell* magazine in 1940: the need to search for the 'bits of individual veracity hidden amidst the dust heaps of convention and tradition'. This was a version of Marc Bloch's 1944 definition of 'the good historian [who] is like the ogres of legend: wherever he sniffs out human flesh, there he knows he has found his prey'.[48] A similar approach would serve new histories of the Irish revolution well.

There would also be much to gain from thinking in a more layered and nuanced way about identity during the revolution, and trying to understand the participants through the prism of their era, as expressed simply by the novelist Roddy Doyle in 2012: 'there are more layers to being Irish' than his generation, born in the 1950s, were led to believe, but also that 'there should be questions so that we give back these people their humanity. Let's see human beings making these decisions, flawed and all as they are.'[49] That amounts to wise advice and something it is possible to aspire to, given the range of sources now available. When the Irish playwright Seán O'Casey died in September 1964, an obituary pointed out that even at the end of his life he was calling out for younger writers to not be 'afraid of life's full-throated shouting, afraid of its venom, suspicious of its gentleness, its valour, its pain and its rowdiness'.[50] The same call can now be made of historians of the Irish revolution.

PART II

REVOLUTIONARY IRELAND: 1913–23

ELEVEN

AN EVOLVING
NATIONALISM

For all the intense political awakening in early twentieth-century Ireland that prompted a variety of activists, radicals and conservatives to mobilise, agitate, demand change or resistance to change and plan for a new type of Ireland or defend it as it was, others found themselves getting on with their personal lives, jobs or ambitions and negotiating a variety of opportunities and inconveniences. As David Fitzpatrick remarked in looking at the revolutionary years in Clare, there was still 'hay to save, cows to milk and women to order about'.[1] Not all were consumed with the idea, articulated by Belfast native and nationalist Bulmer Hobson, that 'Young Ireland had come alive again'. That was Hobson's conclusion about the immersion of many in the Gaelic League, established to revive the Irish language in 1893, the Gaelic Athletic Association (GAA), established in 1884 to promote native sports, the literary and dramatic revivals, and 'the young Sinn Féin movement ... taking shape'.[2]

By the 1870s, just over one million students had enrolled in over 7,000 national schools that provided a foundation-level education, though only one-third attended 100 days, at a time when schools were open a minimum of 200 days; fifty years later, following a fall of over one million in the overall Irish population, about 670,000 students were enrolled.[3] The establishment of the intermediate education system in 1878 and a four-year course at secondary schools resulted in an enrolment of 20,000 students in 1880, rising to roughly 27,000 in 356 'superior' schools by 1920. For those with access to even further education, there was much idealism and attachment to the notion that the early twentieth-century generation of students needed to apply itself to the promotion of Irish nationalism and the building of a new, home rule Ireland. Critic and teacher Mary Colum, active in the literary revival while at university in Dublin, recalled in the 1940s in relation to the early twentieth century, 'almost everything significant in the Dublin of that period was run by the young; youth, eagerness, brains, imagination are what I remember of everybody. There was something else that was in all of them; a desire for self-sacrifice, a devotion to causes; everyone was working for a cause, for practically everything was a cause.'[4] Such sentiments were also on display in the *National Student* magazine, which was first published in May 1910. Contributors argued that students in University College Dublin (UCD) needed to prize their status as university students and direct their energies towards the regeneration of the country; that they were, in effect, home rule leaders in waiting. But they were an elite group; the total number of students in UCD in 1910/11 was 695.[5]

There were in the region of 25,000 civil servants in 1912, the vast majority of them working for the Post Office; civil servants were convenient targets for those who sought to decry overstaffing, overspending and inefficiency in the Dublin Castle regime, 'a labyrinth' of dispersed authority. The idea that it was ripe for serious trimming gained much currency in the context of an imagined home rule Ireland. The difficulty for civil servants was that despite the considerable concerns they had over tenure, remuneration, promotion and pension rights, they had no legal rights arguable in a court of law. They formed a general committee to respond to the political upheaval of this era and highlighted many of their grievances, and in doing so developed a trade union consciousness. What most observers agreed on was that the main weakness in Irish administration was 'the quasi independence of many of the Boards and the lack of any clear line of responsibility binding politicians and civil servants'. Dublin Castle lurched from crisis to crisis; there was no real engagement with the problems of Irish administration, and political disloyalty in the civil service was treated with considerable leniency.[6]

A career as a policeman was regarded as respectable employment for a farmer's son. What was also notable was the big increase in the proportion of Catholics in the professions; in 1861, for example, 28 per cent of barristers were Catholics; by 1911 the figure was 44 per cent.[7] The greater prosperity of Catholic communities (who in 1912 comprised 89.6 per cent of the population of the twenty-six counties of what later constituted the Republic) was also reflected in the vast increase in the number of priests: in 1840 there had been an estimated 2,200 and by 1911 the figure was 4,000, despite a halving of the population as a result of the Great Famine (1845–9) and emigration. Even more striking was the increase in the number of nuns from 2,000 in 1861 to 8,800 in 1911; the number of nuns 'never stopped growing' throughout the nineteenth century, while the population fell. Nursing and teaching were their two most common occupations and they held considerable power in society while being simultaneously 'the least powerful of all those who took vows in the Roman Catholic Church, being irrevocably barred from ordination'.[8] Catholicism was increasingly asserting itself vigorously and sometimes aggressively in the public and private spheres; Catholic associations, sodalities and publications were thriving and confident.

Most Irish farmers owned their own land, some 11 million acres having been purchased as a result of the Land Acts of the late nineteenth and early twentieth century. The underlying strength of the farming community was reflected by the stability in the number of farms over fifteen acres and a decline in agrarian unrest: 48 per cent of all holdings in 1910 were between five and twenty-nine acres, and those who worked them were still vulnerable to market vagaries, weather and moneylenders, but there had been a significant increase in the number of strong farmers and graziers who worked holdings of thirty acres and over. By 1912, Irish agriculture was producing nearly 50 per cent more than it had in the 1840s, and this production was divided among a smaller group.[9] While the standard of living of farm labourers had improved in contrast to the 'harrowing' post-famine standard, they were still alienated as living and working conditions lagged so far behind aspirations. Numerical weakness and unemployment hindered agricultural workers' capacity to organise and agitate, but Labourers' Acts also facilitated cottage building.[10]

Significantly, in 1861, one rural family in ten still lived in what was termed 'fourth class' accommodation (one room per family), but by 1911 only one in a hundred did. Michael Davitt, an iconic figure in the Land War of the 1870s and 1880s, had predicted that this war would trade one inequality for another and create new social tensions and he was correct.[11] Increased commercialisation of the economy created outsiders and larger holdings organised to reflect market demand, facilitated by the growth of banking and transport infrastructure. By the early twentieth century the farmer had a level of security far removed from the mid-nineteenth-century experience. But those labouring on behalf of the farmers did not feel so fortunate; by the summer of 1913, trade unionist James Larkin found that 'the harshness and misery of the agricultural labourer's lot rivalled in intensity the worst experiences of his inner-city colleague'.[12] As a result, the trade union movement was beginning to make its voice heard and there were lively debates about government and politics, law and order and health, welfare and gender.

While emigration from Ireland in the period 1901–10 was a substantial 346,000, this was considerably less than the figure for 1891–1900, which was 434,000. There was still discontent with economic policies and nationalists often insisted that a home rule Ireland would strive to achieve a fairer distribution of the tax burden. British government expenditure on Ireland exceeded revenue, but taxation was higher in Ireland than in Britain in relation to income, particularly as a result of indirect taxes on consumer goods such as tea, tobacco and whiskey. As the poor consumed relatively large quantities of these, a contemporary observation, quoted by economic historian Louis Cullen, was that 'Ireland was not poor because she was overtaxed but overtaxed because she was poor'.[13]

One of the notable trends in post-famine Ireland was the increase in the proportion of women who were single, from 43.3 per cent in 1861 to 48.26 per cent in 1911, and women were more visible in social and political life at this time. Trade unionist Louie Bennett of the Irish Women Workers' Union inaugurated the Irish Women's Suffrage Federation in 1911. There was a variety of small suffrage societies in Ireland dating back to the late nineteenth century, some relatively genteel, but the formation of the nationalist leaning Irish Women's Franchise League (IWFL) in 1908 by Hanna Sheehy-Skeffington and Margaret Cousins indicated a new militancy. In 1912 the first edition of the *Irish Citizen*, a weekly suffrage newspaper, appeared, and its motto drew on the words of Isabella Tod, who had founded the Northern Ireland Women's Suffrage Society in 1872–3: 'For men and women equally the rights of citizenship; from men and women equally the duties of citizenship'; its editors pleaded that 'those who have the power of expression will send us articles, notes and letters'.[14] But the tactics had evolved. With home rule on the horizon, the IWFL insistence was that any future Irish parliament would grant votes to women; the IPP refused to support this demand and some of the responses included the breaking of windows in government buildings.

Feminist and suffrage campaigners also interacted with the labour movement: 'The poorest and meanest woman anywhere who is revolting against the conditions of her life and longing for a chance to relieve its monotony – all these are part and parcel of the great uprising amongst women.'[15] Articulate, politicised women were unusually busy; as Helena Molony recalled, she was 'in great demand because I happened to have the misfortune to be able to speak. On any pretence we would hold a meeting – probably because it was forbidden.'[16] Significantly, Molony became the first female political prisoner of her era after she smashed a portrait of King George V when the monarch visited Ireland in 1911, a reminder that for some of the women, nationalism took precedence over the suffrage question. Molony was also conscious of social standing: 'At the time it was terribly humiliating. No one but rowdies went to the police station ... We held that an agitation for votes for women inferred claiming British citizenship and consequently was inconsistent with Irish republicanism.'[17]

As a result of her militancy, Hanna Sheehy-Skeffington was imprisoned, as were twenty-six other suffragettes in Ireland from 1912–14. Skeffington went on hunger strike in sympathy with members of the British Women's Social and Political Union who intervened in Ireland, and threw a hatchet at visiting British prime minister Herbert Asquith in 1912, and her prison diary recalls that some of the male nationalists of that era disapproved of such a 'womanly' action (believing that the women should 'take their medicine'[18]). Therein lies one of the great ironies of Irish political and penal history, as it was precisely the hunger strike tactic that would bring the male republican movement considerable profile, sympathy and value in the following decade. James Connolly was less reticent about using the women's example when he was imprisoned as a result of his labour activities: 'What was good enough for the suffragettes to use ... is good enough for us'. As his daughter recorded, 'He was never ashamed or afraid to admit from what source he took his methods or his stance.' Later, the wife of a prominent republican in the War of Independence acknowledged that the hunger strike 'was completely novel in the men's case'.[19]

But the Irish suffragettes also prized their independence from their British counterparts and their self-reliance was a considerable achievement, given the hostility directed towards them.

Women's 'intrusion' into the public sphere brought a ferocious reaction from Lambert McKenna, a Jesuit ordained in 1905 who taught at Belvedere College in Dublin and who maintained that 'in pressing women into the rough and tumble fight for existence, in putting before her, as her ideal, the modern Virago instead of the gentle maid of Nazareth, in setting her up not as a help but as a rival of man, the modern world is working its ruin.[20] But most women were more focused on work than politics. In 1911, for example, there were 125,783 female indoor servants in Ireland, of whom 47 per cent were under the age of twenty-five, and 92 per cent were unmarried; domestic servants were the largest group of employed women outside of the manufacturing sector. They usually worked sixteen-hour days with just one half-day per week off.[21]

The commercial importance of towns had been enhanced by better communications and between 1891 and 1911, Belfast's population had risen by half, an indication of the striking success of the city's shipyards. In Dublin, there were 350 trams operating on lines that ran for sixty miles around the city, part of a public transport system that was one of the most impressive of any city in the world, and bicycles had become a very popular mode of transport.[22] Social life was vibrant and varied, with a great interest in sport, music, dance, conversation, theatre and language. The first Irish cinema had opened in Dublin in 1909 when writer James Joyce, having persuaded wealthy Triestines to back it financially, unsuccessfully sought to make it commercially feasible; music-hall comedy and pantomime were also popular. Fair days, race meetings and religious holidays were honoured traditions. In rural areas, house visiting was the most common form of social interaction and match-making was a priority in January and February as there was little work to be done in the fields during winter.[23]

But information gleaned from the census returns of 1911 is also a reminder of the extent of poverty and premature death in the larger cities. Overall, the death rate in Dublin in 1911 per 1,000 people was 22.3. In London it was 15.6. In Dublin in 1911, 26,000 families – roughly one-third of the city's population, amounting to over 87,000 individuals – lived in one-room dwellings. In 1913 there were 1,444 deaths from TB in the city and thirteen from typhus. Of tenement 'heads of household', 26 per cent earned less than 15s a week. The decay of the city was epitomised by Henrietta Street, on the north side of the city, where an astonishing 835 people lived in just fifteen houses. At number 10 Henrietta Street, the Sisters of Charity ran a laundry with more than fifty single women living in the house.[24]

Kevin O'Shiel, at this stage a law student in Trinity College Dublin, later reflected on this slum living, emphasising that there were those who benefited:

It is still more to be wondered at how any so called Christian could make money with an easy conscience, on such human misery, indeed, depravity. And make money and flourish those slum owners did. Numbers of them got elected to the Corporation; in some cases by their grateful 'tenantry' and were looked up to as highly respectable and worthy citizens of 'no mean city'.

What remained in his memory was the smell: 'There was never, by any chance, water laid on and of course, no flush lavatories; the result was an indescribable accumulation of filth ... [It] often took me all I could do not to be overcome with the all pervading stench of human odour.'[25]

D. A. Chart, an archivist and civil servant with a great sympathy for the poor, produced a paper on housing conditions in 1914: 'In some tenement rooms, the bedstead is not to be seen in its usual place in the corner, but in its stead, there is spread on the floor a mysterious and repellent assortment of rags which few inquiries have had the hardihood to investigate and which is believed to serve as a bed.'[26]

Observers also noted the strong sense of community and resilience of the inhabitants ('no gayer, brighter or wittier crowd of youngsters to be found anywhere') but the tone of 'outrage' in relation to the slums was common in the first two decades of the twentieth century, not just because slum living conditions were still the lot of so many, 'but that such side-stepping and hesitancy should characterise the activities of the elected authorities responsible for the public well-being'. By 1918 a member of the Local Government Board, which had conducted an inquiry into Dublin housing conditions in 1913 and 1914, believed improved housing was needed for at least 41 per cent of the city's population.[27] The housing inquiry estimated that 14,000 new dwellings were needed and a further survey in 1919 estimated a figure of 22,700. The warped relationship between the ownership of property and land and municipal politics meant that housing conditions remained neglected.

The welfare of children was also receiving more attention; the first Irish branch of the Society for the Prevention of Cruelty to Children had been established in 1889. Patrick MacGill's *Children of the Dead End* (1914) deals with a bleak childhood in Edwardian Donegal. Like so many others, MacGill was brought to a hiring fair at the age of twelve, because, as the traditional verse went, 'there's hope beyond the mountains for a little boy of twelve'. His depiction of the fairs and his subsequent treatment at the hands of rapacious employers is encapsulated in the observation that for these employers 'I was not a human being, a boy with an appetite and a soul. I was merely a ware purchased in the market place, something of less value than a plough and of no more account than a barrow.' The money he earned as a result of this slave market was, of course, sent home. MacGill's reflections on this cruel economy were equally revealing about parental attitudes to children in families struggling for basic subsistence: 'I was born and bred merely to support my parents and great care had been taken to drive this fact into my mind from infancy. I was merely brought into the world to support those who were responsible for my existence.'[28]

On the surface however, despite obvious inequalities, the early twentieth century seemed a relatively peaceful phase of Ireland's history. In many respects, it is necessary to go below the surface in order to locate the sentiments that fuelled movements that gradually hardened into a more focused determination to forge change and resistance. Extensive rail travel facilitated the development of national GAA competitions and the bedding down of the organisational structures of the association. It had also got stricter; in 1911 it made ineligible for membership 'all who participate in dances or similar entertainments got up by or under the patronage of soldiers or policemen'.[29]

Whatever about its relative stability, and the determination of most to take advantage of the opportunities provided by their citizenship of the UK – defenders of this connection pointed to Land Acts that facilitated increased ownership of land by former tenants, the introduction of local government, an expanding education infrastructure and the introduction of old age pensions in 1909 – early twentieth-century Ireland also had its full share of resentments, snobberies, hypocrisies and frustrated expectations. Class divides were relevant to the development of a new nationalist self-image by those outside the existing patronage networks. In 1979, in his memoir of growing up in Dublin in the early twentieth century, *Dublin Made Me*, veteran Irish republican and public servant Todd Andrews, born in 1901, recalled in vivid detail his childhood in the city, a time when Catholics 'varied socially among ourselves but all had the common bond, whatever our economic condition, of being second class citizens'. But those 'at the top of the Catholic heap', such as doctors, solicitors and merchants, were thriving, as were the Catholic middle class, including civil servants, publicans, journalists and bank managers. In contrast, there existed

at the bottom of the heap, the have-nots of the city, consisting of
labourers, dockers, coal heavers, shop attendants, messenger boys and
domestic servants. Even those who had regular work were seldom far
above the poverty line and very many were below it ... when I was a
child, every mother of young children lived in constant dread and
sometimes real terror of sickness.[30]

Many felt excluded from the prevailing political establishment but
also from those seeking to replace them. Helena Molony was one of them,
and she recalled resentment at Arthur Griffith's Sinn Féin movement,
established in 1905, with its emphasis on passive resistance, and the sort of
home rule Ireland envisaged by its proponents: 'The social ideas of Sinn
Féin did not appeal to us. They wished to see in Irish society (as their official organ once expressed it) "a progressive and enlightened aristocracy,
a prosperous middle class, and a happy and contented working-class". It
all sounded dull, and a little bit vulgar to us.'[31] In any case, Griffith, advo-
cating that Irish MPs should abstain from Westminster, was struggling
to make his new movement challenge the dominance of the Irish Parliamentary Party, which by then had dominated nationalist politics for three
decades through its home rule campaigns, with the aim – soon, it seemed,
to be realised – of creating an Irish parliament for purely domestic affairs
while remaining part of the British Empire and retaining representation at
Westminster. But John Redmond, as leader of that party, while exhibiting
noble traits, also represented a generation of Irish nationalists who were
arrogant and removed from the concerns of those who felt aggrieved. The
IPP tended to rely on pliant henchmen and its representatives rarely had
to contest hard-fought elections, many MPs being returned unopposed
for decades. In the late nineteenth century most of those MPs had been
young and quite militant, with an average age of forty; but by 1918 their
average age was fifty-five.[32]

The members of the many small organisations and agitators, including the disgruntled working-class victims of the 1913 Lockout who formed
the Irish Citizen Army, the women demanding the vote and a role in
Irish nationalism, and those in the Irish Republican Brotherhood (IRB)
intent on reviving the tradition of Irish defiance of British rule, were much
younger, and this gulf between the generations was a crucial part of a growing militancy. The IRB, dedicated to achieving its aims through rebellion,
and in existence as a clandestine oath-bound organisation since 1858, had

been revitalised in the early twentieth century by a new generation, with the help of the older Thomas Clarke, imprisoned in England after a bombing campaign in the 1880s, and determined since his return to Dublin in 1907 to see a rebellion launched in his lifetime. Denis McCullough, a future president of the IRB Supreme Council, put it bluntly: 'I cleared out most of the older men (including my father) most of whom I considered of no further use to us.'[33] They were working hard to undermine what they identified as a prevailing smugness within the status quo, but the odds against their success were formidable.

Culturally, the early twentieth century witnessed considerable vibrancy, predicated on the notion of a resurgence of national spirit. The Gaelic League was significant culturally, socially and ultimately politically. It represented, according to Arthur Clery, a lawyer and nationalist, 'the new spirit' for a native population 'anxious to *be native*' as organisers and travelling teachers toured the country giving classes 'usually mixed as regards sex', and 'in the flat dullness of an Irish village, or, worse still, an Irish country town, a Gaelic League class is to the ranks who avail of it an unexpected source of light and gaiety. Only those who aspire to an upper middle class position fight shy of it, lest they be compromised.'[34] A member of the Supreme Council of the IRB, P. S. O'Hegarty, referred to his experience of the League at the Munster Féis (singing competition) in 1902: 'Something in the songs ... something in the music ... something in the atmosphere gripped me and I seemed to be put in touch with something far back in the race ... for the first time I saw the whole of Ireland.'[35]

D. P. Moran, the influential nationalist journalist, and author of *The Philosophy of Irish Ireland* (1905), who became a champion of the Gaelic League and established the vibrant newspaper *The Leader* in 1900, had insisted in 1898 that if Irish people learned that 'we are getting parlously near that time when we shouldn't be a distinctive people at all, we might then mend our ways and so something masculine'.[36] This was one of many assertions about the necessity of Irish manliness. Joe Nugent points out that in 1898, 600 future priests in St Patrick's seminary in Maynooth sang a rallying song 'with the duty to marshal the manhood of Ireland'. The words of the song included

Gather in the name of Columb, sons of Erinn, priests of Erinn
Gather, and clasp all hands in a vow for her regeneration
Gather, the call is great – to strengthen the soul of a nation.

Is he a priest who would mock or shirk the work that is therein?
Gather, fast gather, and link in a brotherhood all.[37]

This was the occasion of the inauguration of the League of St Columb, the sixth-century Irish warrior-become-saint, its objective being to shape an Irish identity, in its own words, through 'the actualisation of the authentic Irishman'. Nugent suggests that 'by socialising the discourse of Irish nationalism ... the clergy deeply inflected the trajectory of Irish manly development'.[38] Cultural nationalists needed to fashion a set of images and icons that would invoke a glorious past on the journey to the future and this became an 'insistent question' in the 1890s. Likewise Standish O'Grady, one of the fathers of the Irish literary revival, who produced two volumes of Irish history in 1878 and 1880, used the legendary figure of Cúchulainn 'to galvanise the weakened generations of Ireland into an awareness of their heroic masculinity' and the Anglo-Irish Ascendancy active in the revival also embraced this as they were enchanted by the notion of a vigorous but lost Irish aristocracy.[39]

Cúchulainn was also pivotal in Cork journalist and nationalist A. M. Sullivan's *The Story of Ireland* (1867), written as a patriotic, popular history for children, but the Church was also quick to carve out its claim on the heroic ideal, as 'it too had a stake – the control of its subjects – in the estate of manhood'. God's saints, as was expressed in the *Irish Ecclesiastical Record* in 1890, 'are our models and examples. These alone are worthy of our imitation.'[40] Initially the Catholic Church was wary about the IRB in this regard, but this suspicion waned and by the early twentieth century priests were visible and audible at some demonstrations and mirrored the political sentiments about the examples these dead martyrs gave in terms of national redemption and early Christian martyrs; a parish priest in Tipperary, Fr Arthur Ryan, for example, was reported as saying in 1911:

When it comes to the duty of dying for our country, we must all be extremists. Death is the last extremity – an extremity, remember, demanded in the last resort by every nation from its sons. No man, whether he be Englishman, Frenchman, German or Irishman, is worthy of his country until he is ready to be an extremist in her cause and ready to die for her at her call.[41]

Thomas Brophy has pointed out that 'for much of the nineteenth and the early twentieth centuries dead patriots proved effective instruments for European nationalists. Irish political funerals had much in common with counterparts in Poland who resisted Russian rule and in Hungary who chafed under Viennese domination.'[42]

But that did not mean that Church ownership and control was guaranteed, which would explain the somewhat defensive tone of popular novelist Canon Sheehan's lecture at Maynooth in 1903, entitled 'The Dawn of the Century': he insisted that 'the priests have the lead and they must keep it'.[43] Sheehan's first novel had been published in 1895 but by now he was internationally renowned as author of *My New Curate* and *Luke Delmege*. What was interesting about him, particularly as revealed in the posthumously published *The Graves at Kilmorna* (1915), was the sense of someone torn between conflicting stances regarding the plights of his time and his history; he had a certain nostalgia for the Fenians of his youth but was anxious about the direction of contemporary politics.[44]

Some were wary of the Church having undue influence in political affairs; P. S. O'Hegarty and Terence MacSwiney, who went on to play prominent roles in the revolutionary period, had been at school together in Cork and corresponded regularly thereafter and frequently argued about their attitudes to the relationship between Church and State. O'Hegarty argued the Fenian position of old in relation to separation of both whereas the more devout MacSwiney was warier and refused on religious grounds to join the IRB. O'Hegarty denounced clerical interference in nationalist politics and had written to MacSwiney as early as 1904 insisting he was anti-clerical because the clergy in Ireland 'ruined every movement – directly or indirectly – since the passing of the Maynooth grant in 1795' (when the British government supported the founding of the Catholic seminary at Maynooth in Kildare).[45]

Those sympathetic to Irish nationalist versions of history could also fashion their own narratives and books. The Christian Brothers, a teaching order that played a dominant role in the revitalisation of Irish Catholicism from the early nineteenth century, in their *Irish History Reader* (1905) proclaimed that 'a nation's school books wield a great power' and the need for 'glowing words on Ireland's glorious past', a continuation of the theme of their 1874 book *Outlines of Irish History for the Use of Children in Primary Schools*, where teachers were 'admonished to dwell with pride' on 'great men and their great deeds, and on her devotion through all the centuries to the faith'. Historian Peter Hart has suggested that 'in teaching patriotism, the Brothers created gunmen'.[46] This may be an unproven sound bite; after all, another very popular textbook was P. W. Joyce's *A Child's History of Ireland* (1897), which was regularly updated thereafter and according to Joyce himself, who was also a teacher and respected Irish language scholar, his book was written 'soberly and moderately … pointing out extenuating circumstances when it was just and right to do so'. While by 1908 history had become a 'definite course of instruction' (and therefore an independent and compulsory subject) and the *Irish School Weekly* began to publish a regular column on Irish history to assist teachers, it was hardly something that overwhelmed Irish nationalists in the broader sense. Douglas Hyde, for example, founder of the Gaelic League and the first Professor of Irish at UCD, in 1911 'remained unaware that Irish history had become a specific subject'.[47] In contrast, the Provost of Trinity College Dublin, John Mahaffy, a committed unionist and long-time enemy of nationalists (he had attempted to have Irish removed from the intermediate curriculum on the grounds that the language contained no literature that was not 'religious, immoral or indecent'), blamed teachers for transmitting the events 'of long past history calculated to make rebels of those who in the present have no reasonable basis for disloyalty'.[48] But this may have been deliberate exaggeration, as the reports of the inspectors of primary schools between 1902 and 1914 were very negative about history, focusing on the dullness and lifelessness of the approach and the inadequacy of teachers.[49]

For some, an interest in history was a reaction to contemporary happenings outside school, Todd Andrews recalling that after 1916 'we read Irish history no longer as a school subject but as something we wanted to know and understand'. But he also maintained that his revolutionary fervour was 'based mainly on emotionalism and enthusiasm. I rarely thought; I felt.'[50]

This did not mean that individuals who played a key role in the revolution were not influenced by avid reading or nationalist interpretations of Irish history. Robert Holland, who fought in the 1916 Rising, found himself during that week 'thinking all about my school days, the lectures that the Christian Brothers gave us', and Patrick McCartan, a medical student and Sinn Féin member elected to Dublin Corporation in 1909 and later a member of the IRB Supreme Council, recalled in 1924 that 'we separatists saturated ourselves with writings by and about the men of 1798, 1848 and 1867', the respective dates of the United Irishmen, Young Ireland and Fenian rebellions.[51] Periodicals that specifically targeted young readers and were packed with popular Irish history included *Shan Van Vocht* and the Christian Brothers' *Our Boys*, first published in 1914. But was there something more stirring instilled in young people outside of school, books and magazines? In 1911, Fr Edward Gaynor, a curate in Cork, wrote a rare account of how music as an oral tradition was passed on to the younger generation in his locality during the post-famine years:

> I grew up surrounded by a group of absolutely illiterate farm labourers and their families in a district that was then very remote from outside influences. These people had amongst them a number of simple airs to which they sang crude [nationalist] ballads of their own making. From earliest childhood, these were always in my ears.[52]

Likewise, Liam Deasy, who was regularly a part of Tom Barry's flying column during the War of Independence, remembered from his youth the emphasis on the continuity of the separatist endeavour: 'The Battle of Kinsale was often discussed on a winter's night. The fearsome massacres of Cromwell were known to us from local tradition, as indeed were the Rising of 1798, the ill-fated Insurrection of 1848 and above all the Fenian Rebellion from 1867'. This was all highly romanticised, with the result that the contemporary activities 'were to me and my companions like signs of the return of the Golden Age of Ireland's ancient chivalry'.[53] It is also the case, however, that English adventure literature and comic books that were essentially a celebration of British imperialism were also being consumed with relish by Irish republicans of that generation.[54] Some of the British textbooks in use in some Irish schools were unashamedly bombastic and jingoistic in their celebrations of a perceived civilising imperialism, such as C. R. L. Fletcher and Rudyard Kipling's *A School History of England* (1911). Englishness was associated with courage, manliness and self-denial; in India 'our rule has been infinitely to the good of all the three hundred millions of the different races who inhabit that richly peopled land', and eighteenth-century Irish nationalists had shown 'little gratitude' for the 'removal of grievances'.[55]

Another of the notable developments of the era was the expansion of the media and the importance of the communications revolution, manifested in the increase in the number of short-lived polemical newspapers but also more enduring nationalist provincial newspapers which were indicative of the late nineteenth-century campaign of displacing or co-opting the professional and commercial elites that dominated contemporary Catholic society, and an instructive barometer of local political and social temperatures.[56] The abolition of taxes on the press after 1855 was crucial for the growth and availability of cheaper news media, which coincided with the evolution of nationalism: 'The size of the feast in terms of material is demonstrated by the sheer bulk of Irish newsprint available between 1850 and 1892 when about 218 provincial papers appear to have been in print.' Illiteracy also continued to fall, from 47 per cent in 1851 to 33 per cent in 1871 to 25 per cent in 1881.[57] It is estimated there were 332 newspapers circulating in Ireland from 1900 to 1922, not including those that originated in Britain. While many were fringe publications and had content that was banal and full of bathos there were also more successful titles like *United Irishman* and *Sinn Féin*, largely written by the exceptionally prolific Arthur Griffith in a style that was strident, scornful, funny and 'uncompromisingly modern'; *Sinn Féin* had a print run of 8,000 copies a month by 1911.[58]

In relation to national daily newspapers, in 1900 William Martin Murphy, a giant of Irish entrepreneurship, bought the struggling Parnellite *Irish Daily Independent* and merged it with the also long-suffering *Daily Nation*. In 1904 he relaunched the *Irish Independent* as a halfpenny paper modelled on the 'new journalism' pioneered by Lord Northcliffe (who launched the *Daily Mail* in London in 1896) and his willingness to invest large sums and experiment with new journalistic techniques created a successful, profitable paper. It is estimated that total sales of Irish newspapers in Ireland grew by a factor of seven between the early 1880s and the 1920s, from 75,000 copies per day to over half a million, but one of the victims of Murphy's success was *The Freeman's Journal*, which supported the constitutional nationalists, circulation of which remained at about 35,000, while circulation of the *Irish Independent* grew to about 100,000 daily by 1915.[59]

Political demonstrations, funerals, marches for dead patriots and commemorative events such as those for the 1798 rebellion also played their part in cultivating nationalism. One particularly enduring commemorative impulse was that for the Manchester Martyrs, marking the execution of three Irishmen, William Philip Allen, Michael Larkin and Michael O'Brien, in Manchester in 1867, after they had been found guilty of killing a policeman during the rescue of two Fenian prisoners from a police van. Political ballads and songs also assumed a role; the execution of the men had inspired the composition of the commemorative song 'God Save Ireland' that was sung at many nationalist meetings. There was also the phenomenon of the Wolfe Tone demonstrations and 'Decoration Day', which had begun in 1892, following the death of Parnell in 1891, which though falling usually on the anniversary of the Manchester Martyrs, became focused on all the patriot dead, including those from 1798 and 1867, and laid the groundwork for the 1798 centenary celebrations in 1898 which were dominated by IRB men. The Manchester commemorations were also notable for the extent of working-class mobilisation, and 'although the police denied much political weight to those who took part in the demonstrations, they were cautious about the fact that the IRB could exert a significant influence upon lower class community life in Dublin'.[60]

These commemorations were, by the early twentieth century, able to incorporate a whole range of groups and gave much oxygen to the IRB and allowed for speeches that were critical of the IPP, though neither Sinn Féin nor the Gaelic League showed much interest in the commemorations of the early years. By 1913, however, the Manchester Martyrs demonstration in Dublin was the largest held for over twenty-five years, with an estimated 12–15,000 participating, marshalled by veteran Fenian Tom Clarke of the IRB and Sinn Féin councillors; trade unionists led by James Connolly and Delia Larkin also played a prominent part. Clarke was intoxicated with its success and size. He wrote to Joseph McGarrity, leader of the Irish American Clan na Gael (the American wing of the Fenians):

> Joe, it is worth living in Ireland these times – there is an awakening – the slow, silent prodding and the open preaching is at last showing results ... we are breathing air that compels one to fling up his head and stand more erect ... it was a magnificent demonstration – the finest thing of its kind I ever witnessed in Dublin or anywhere else – and let me tell you, no other party in Ireland today could have brought the people together – so many different and opposing sections for any purpose – except ourselves.[61]

Overseas correspondence was unsurprising, given the wide-scale emigration to North America and Australia (between 1846 and 1855, 1.8 million Irish people emigrated to the US, and 86 per cent of those who emigrated between 1901 and 1910 also went to America), although the exodus had slowed by the time of Clarke's letter: by 1910, less than 1.5 per cent of the US population were of Irish birth; the figure for Australia in 1911 was 3 per cent. But that still meant many in those countries were of Irish descent, and 'concern with Irish affairs reached new levels of intensity in the US and Australia between 1914 and 1921'. Such vocal support 'was not without its own cost'; the status of immigrants became more precarious as both nations preferred isolationism and exhibited more hostility towards immigrants and, ultimately, a certain disengagement with Irish affairs.[62]

As well as generational change in relation to the IRB, there was also the specific targeting of children and teenagers, as seen in the formation of the Irish National Boy Scouts, Na Fianna Éireann, opened to eight- to eighteen-year-olds and founded by Bulmer Hobson and Countess Markievicz in 1909. It developed branches in nineteen counties in Ireland as well as in Glasgow and Liverpool and some of its members went on to participate in the 1916 Rising. As with Baden Powell's Boy Scouts, whose influence it was set up to counteract, Na Fianna,

> was one of the many 'pseudo-military youth groups' that proliferated in Europe in the late nineteenth and early twentieth centuries. These organisations were not only a manifestation of the cult of discipline, training and manliness that grew out of the menace of the coming war but also perhaps, a reaction to the widely perceived *fin-de-siècle* 'decadence'.[63]

Those championing socialism and a determination to employ the words 'republic' and 'socialist' in the same context were a minuscule group, but refused to await the endorsement of middle-class Ireland. The appearance of Ireland's first regular socialist newspaper – the *Worker's Republic* – was one of their notable achievements. James Connolly was a towering presence, but there were other young and bohemian characters who added left-wing colour and passion to Dublin and Cork through membership of the Irish Socialist Republican Party (ISRP), which was established in 1896 and lasted until 1904. At one of the earlier ISRP meetings, one of the questions discussed was 'Are we Utopians?'[64] Perhaps they were, but what is striking is how social democratic and far-sighted the party's programme was, including free education, child welfare support, legislative restrictions on the hours of labour, a minimum wage and the modernisation of agriculture. Connolly maintained, with a measure of truth, that the votes they received 'were cast for socialism in spite of a campaign of calumny unequalled in its infamy'. But there was also a tendency continually to blame their opponents at the expense of self-critical analysis, an over-reliance on propaganda, a naïve belief that republicans would eventually be won over to a socialist philosophy, and a neglect of the Protestant loyalist working class. Connolly's censorship of any discussion of religion was also counterproductive and unreasonable.[65]

At Clonmel in Tipperary in May 1912 the Irish Congress of Trade Unions (ICTU, established in 1894) decided 'that the independent representation of Labour upon all public boards' should be one if its objectives, signalling the birth of the Labour Party, a product, it seemed, of the 'prevailing sense of possibility' and a declaration by the labour movement 'that they intended to influence the shape of Irish society using district council room, city hall, and most importantly, the anticipated home rule parliament'.

The early years of the party's existence, however, 'were more faltering than dynamic', or in Michael Laffan's phrase, for a long time it would remain 'more an aspiration than an organisation'.[66] The 'shadow of the national question' was relevant here, but so too was religion. There is little doubt that from its earliest days the Labour Party was targeted specifically on the question of the religious faith of its leaders and members locally and nationally. Arthur Mitchell maintained 'the lack of support for the party made it clear that a majority of Dubliners accepted the image of Larkin, Connolly and the other leaders as anti-clerical, socialist revolutionaries', a picture painted by nationalist politicians, the press and the Church.[67]

It was inevitable that the Church would be so vocal, given the ambitions of its personnel. As soon as he was elevated to the rank of Catholic Archbishop of Dublin in 1885, for example, William Walsh made it quite clear that politics was as much his business as religion – indeed, the reason he eventually allowed his name to go forward for the position was what he called 'the political side of the case'.[68] It is tempting to conclude that religion was very low on his list of priorities and in time he was to devote much attention to the university question, constitutional nationalism and labour issues, matched by a determination to oversee the building of orphanages and hostels, though he shared the middle-class fear of socialism as a threat to the moral welfare of the working class.

The Catholic Hierarchy was not unanimous on these issues; although he was highly regarded nationwide, Walsh's tactics did not always sit comfortably with his colleagues, some of whom became irked with his ubiquitous newspaper articles. An indication of his tactical approach was contained in a letter he sent to Bishop O'Dwyer of Limerick on the university question, when he wrote: 'We must keep hammering away at the grievance and insisting on it being dealt with. If we propose anything definite, they will simply fall back on a criticism of details. Just now it will be easy to force them to take the initiative in proposing, then we can criticise from our side with a much better chance of results.' It was this robust confidence that was the hallmark of a Church determined to play a central part in laying the foundations of a future home rule state.[69]

Whatever about leadership of an elite, what of the Catholic grassroots? The Ancient Order of Hibernians (AOH), established as an Irish-American benevolent society in New York in 1836, was particularly visible and aggressive when its Irish wing was energised and expanded under national president Joseph Devlin, a Belfast nationalist MP, from 1905. It was a specifically Catholic body which Devlin marshalled as an organisational arm of the IPP:

> Under his tutelage the AOH expanded from 10,000 members in 1905 to 60,000 in 1909, despite opposition from some Catholic bishops (notably Cardinal Michael Logue, the Archbishop of Armagh) who distrusted it because of its close affiliation to Dillonism [the faction of the IPP led by John Dillon], its secrecy, and its habit of staging dances and other entertainments without paying what they regarded as due deference to local priests.[70]

In 1911 one observer suggested, 'if anyone cared to prophesy the coming nationalist organisation he would certainly be safer in indicating the Hibernians than any other'.[71] The AOH excelled at machine politics and certainly delivered votes by disreputable methods and was also depicted, not without accuracy, as an aggressive manifestation of 'Green Orangemen', to be for the Catholic community what the Orange Order was for Protestants. In 1909 Logue had described it as a 'pest, a cruel tyranny and an organised system of blackguardism'.[72]

William O'Brien, a nationalist leader and agrarian campaigner, was also markedly hostile to the AOH; he had formed the United Irish League

(UIL) in 1898, believing that agitation outside of Parliament was essential to further the nationalist cause, winning the support of both anti- and pro-Parnellites and some Fenians, and the formation of the UIL encouraged a defensive reunification of the IPP, which had been riven with splits after the demise of Parnell. The UIL, in O'Brien's words, would draw 'an irresistible strength and reality from conditions in the west, [and] ... throw open to the free air of a new national spirit those caverns and tabernacles of faction in which good men ... had been suffocating'.[73] But O'Brien fell out with the IPP, forming the dissident All for Ireland League in 1909.

There was also ferocious infighting, and personal antagonisms, both of which characterised the politics of the period. While the IPP had succeeded in getting the British Liberal Party to back home rule by 1912, Patrick Maume suggested that 'the central problem of the Irish Party was that it was not an ordinary party. It was often compared to an army, depending on unconditional obedience; but could it maintain discipline with no prospect of victory and with its officers quarrelling?'[74] The answer seems to have been a resounding no, as local government reform was pivotal in strengthening intermediate organisation at the expense of centralised leadership, and grassroots organisations, most obviously the UIL, disrupted the prospect of an Ireland managed by brokerage between the British government and Catholic lay and clerical elites.

The 1898 Local Government Act provided another stimulation to nationalism, but in the early days, the profound conservatism of the membership and indeed aims of the local authorities betrayed any idea of the introduction of local government heralding a revolutionary new dispensation in Ireland. For all the talk of the abolition of the old Boards of Guardians and the disappearance of the landlord class from the administration of local affairs, there is much validity in the argument that one oligarchy was merely replaced by another – that of the substantial farmer, and with him, an attendant mindset which was slow to embrace change and reluctant to spend money. The first parliamentary leader of the Ulster Unionists, Edward Saunderson, was accurate indeed when he noted, 'When an Irishman ... is confined within the lines of common sense and shown that if he chooses to indulge in eccentricity he will find it an expensive enjoyment, that Irishman is seen to be as sensible as any other man ...'[75]

Did the leadership of the Irish nationalists understand Westminster better than they understood the grassroots and were IPP members quality public representatives (unpaid until 1911)? The role of small groups of advisers, and distance from Dublin due to presence in the Westminster Parliament, were problematic for John Redmond's leadership. While the IPP dominated more than three-quarters of the constituencies in the country, in the December 1910 general election, fifty-three of the eighty-four seats it won were filled by unopposed candidates, at a time when the Irish electorate was just 700,000, making it 'well-nigh impossible to calculate the popular support' enjoyed by the IPP, and socially, there was an increasing gap between the middle-class leadership of the party and its MPs from humbler stock. Redmond may have been honourable in his quest for conciliation but with increased unionist militancy and Liberal duplicity he also could appear weak and naïve.[76] It may have been assumed the measures of reform in land, education and welfare provision enacted in the decade prior to 1916 would cool ardour, and they did to an extent, but that did not mean there was not a determined minority appetite for alternatives. The interest of a younger generation in Sinn Féin was certainly vital: P. S. O'Hegarty wrote to Terence MacSwiney in 1907 urging him to rejoin the Cork Branch of Sinn Féin: 'it's rotting for want of a man with passion in him'; MacSwiney, however, believed the 'Hungarian' policy compromised republicanism (Arthur Griffith cited the revival of Hungary after defeat by Habsburg forces in 1849, and its achievement, peacefully, of equal status with Austria in the *Ausgleich* of 1867), but Griffith was also pragmatic and wanted to prioritise the importance of economic nationalism, taxation and industrial development rather than dwelling on republicanism, and he was moderate enough to feel it necessary to leave the IRB.[77]

But social and economic priorities meant that separatist language would gain acceptance only when linked to grievances such as urban poverty, rising food prices and taxes, cessation of land distribution and emigration. Political capital was being made out of a long-standing separatist subculture which was given credibility by the corruptions of early twentieth-century Ireland. The exchange of letters between brothers Michael and John Moynihan, from a prominent Tralee family, give some sense of the disillusionment. As Michael saw it in November 1912, when he was working as a civil servant, the Home Rule Bill was 'calculated to push the power into the hands of the most dangerous and inefficient class in the country. All the indicators are that the Irish parliament will be similar in character to the present Dublin Corporation, which is shunned by all decent men and instead of being an object of pride is an object of contempt to the citizens.'[78] A year later, he complained of there being not a 'shred of principle' left in any of the political parties, with cynical Liberal ministers and Tory newspapers, which 'in a gingerly fashion try to use the Dublin labour movement as a stalking horse against nationalism. Add to this the criminal hypocrisy of both parties (of all indeed) towards the "Ulster Question" and one gets a vision of political depravity far lower than any that existed in the days of open bribery.'[79]

This raises the interesting question of attitudes to the Irish establishment during this period, particularly in relation to the question of the 'greening of the Irish administration', measured by the extent to which educated Catholics were assuming positions at senior levels of the Irish establishment and displacing Protestants, only for their advancement and hopes of long-term power to be scuppered by the revolution after 1916, and the triumph of Sinn Féin representing a different milieu altogether. Fergus Campbell has challenged such a narrative by examining landed, political, administrative, police and economic elites from the 1870s to the time of the First World War, based on 1,200 biographies of influential figures in the establishment. Promotional practices in the civil service, for example, did not favour educated Catholics and such appointments remained nepotistic and corrupt (the British civil service was more meritocratic and offered more opportunities than did the Irish). This was also relevant in the senior ranks of the Royal Irish Constabulary (RIC) which had policed Ireland since 1814. A volunteer in the 1916 Rising referred to a contemporary of his in the RIC who 'was one of those, I think, who, finding himself at middle age in the service of his enemy now at war with his countrymen, was seriously disturbed by his latent sympathy for their efforts, yet felt bound by his contract of service as well as his dependence on it for the welfare of his family'.[80]

There was still a strong sense of a closed elitism in relation to Protestant Ireland, and belittling of Catholics, despite their wealth or education, and such structural inequalities were an important factor in the revolution.[81] This complicates the arguments put forward by Senia Paseta, that the university students supporting the IPP and preparing for home rule were more 'nationally minded' than later republican propaganda allowed. Some of them were in reality unashamedly elitist and conservative. Economist George O'Brien, for example, recalled the atmosphere at King's Inns, where he was a law student:

The Buildings dated back to the eighteenth century and had that air of aristocratic dignity which appealed to me so strongly. The ceremonial procedure at dinner, the elaborate uniforms of the servants, the procession of the benchers, the gallery of portraits of judges in the dining hall – all these things satisfied some sense of order and security.[82]

Did such fawning exist because of the desire of the Catholics to get their toe in the door behind which were protected elites? O'Brien was born in 1892, and his father was a self-made businessman and hotelier; George was educated at Belvedere and UCD before the King's Inns. Sustained by a private income he was able, after he abandoned practising law, to pursue other interests and studies in economics, before becoming a stalwart of government committees and a UCD professor, his economic thinking very much dominated by the tradition of nineteenth-century liberalism.[83]

TWELVE

ULSTER PREPARED WITH ONE VOICE? 1910–14

It was also the case that nationalist organisation was further fuelled by the extraordinary example given by unionists in their resistance to the introduction of the third Home Rule Bill in 1912. The 'Ulster Crisis' was not just one for Irish unionists, but for Irish nationalists and British Conservatives and Liberals, and raised fundamental questions about constitutionalism, the nature of the state, nationhood and empire, Edwardian militarism and the extent to which such militancy would be controlled from the top or the bottom.[1] For unionists there was one towering question, articulated clearly by British MP Harry Lawson to underline the dilemma of the 'Liberal' era: 'How are you in these days, these democratic days, in this democratic age, in this democratic country, to force a million men into a system which they refuse to join ... how are you going to expel the Irish minority from citizenship of the UK?'[2] The 1912 resistance also marked a new departure; opposition to home rule in 1885 and 1892 was organised on an all-Ireland basis but it was the 'Ulsterisation' of the issue from 1912–14 that prompted a new sense of a dominant 'Ulster crisis'.

The distinctiveness of Ulster from the rest of the island was obvious in terms of its religious make-up (by 1911, Protestants in Ulster accounted for 56.3 per cent of the population, but only 10 per cent of the other provinces were non-Catholic), industry (Belfast had the world's largest shipping yard), connections (Belfast was frequently likened to English rather than Irish cities), and a civic pride born of commercial success, seen for example in the opening of the new Belfast City Hall in 1906. Shipyard workers, the 'autocracy of labour', could earn £2 per week by 1914. Belfast also, however, lagged behind many English local authorities in educational provision, and was afflicted by a serious typhoid problem; TB was responsible for one in every six deaths notified in Belfast, and the sectarian divide was reflected in the fact that in 1901, only one in sixteen Catholic families had fixed baths, compared to one in six Protestant families.[3]

The Orange Order, originally established in 1795 and 'conceived and brought forth by humble men',[4] began to revive in face of the threat posed by home rule from the mid 1880s and although the Home Rule Bills of 1886 and 1893 were defeated there was a recognition by 1912 that the opposition to the new threat would have to be on a much grander scale. There had also been a growing awareness of the threat to internal unionist cohesion, and accusations that the landed leadership of the unionist parliamentary party under Edward Saunderson was not adequately protecting the interests of the grassroots. The formation of the Ulster Unionist Council (UUC) in 1905 as an umbrella group to make the parliamentary party accountable was one response to such schisms, while the formation of the Joint Committee of the Unionist Associations of Ireland in 1908, the revival of the nineteenth-century unionist club movement, and the creation of the Ulster Women's Unionist Council were others. Lawyer Edward Carson taking over the leadership of the Unionist Party in 1910 signalled a new direction, as the Liberal Party maintained power under Herbert Asquith, while the following year Andrew Bonar Law was elected leader of Britain's Conservative Party and pledged support for the Ulster Unionists, and the very label 'Ulster Unionists' spoke volumes about the way in which perspectives had changed.

Those directing unionist opposition had, in the first decade, become concerned with the 'splintering impact of Protestant populism' as represented by T. H. Sloan, a labourer at Harland and Wolff's ship factory and champion of the working-class Orangemen, who was elected an MP for Belfast South in 1903 and established the Independent Orange Order which had sixty-eight lodges by 1906. Saunderson, the recognised leader of the Irish unionists in Parliament since the mid 1880s, insisted 'any Orangeman who votes for Sloan is voting for the destruction of the machinery of the Orange institution which is absolutely necessary to its continued existence'.[5] Revd James Hannay, Church of Ireland rector in Westport, County Mayo, likened the IOO to the Gaelic League: 'Both are profoundly democratic in spirit. Both demand in their members and tend to create in them, a vigorous independence of thought and action. Neither body relies on or receives the help of the rich or the patronage of the great.'[6]

But both also fell victim to those intent on swallowing them for other purposes. The key issue for the unionist elite now was the speed with which such threats 'could be absorbed and defused'.[7] Contemporary Ulster unionism was moving on from the leadership of Saunderson, and the landlord interest and background he represented, but it shared a new manifestation of his expressed concern in 1882:

> I have become an Orangeman because the state of the country for the past two years had been simply unbearable. The very foundations of society were shaken and about to crumble almost into the dust ... every Protestant deserving the name is as ready to fight today as his ancestors were 200 years ago ... that we are prepared with one voice ... and at all hazards to show that we will not have these men reign over us.[8]

A new version of this sentiment involved the sharpening of the unionist antennae, but initially, it was still an Irish as opposed to an Ulster unionism, as was apparent at a meeting in Portadown in 1906, for example, when Saunderson said 'he did not come as a Tory, for he never was a Tory, nor as a conservative because he never was one. Nor as a liberal, because the word had no meaning for him. He came there as a unionist.'[9] His successor, Carson, now had to bring a new focus and definition to such unionism and bring different groups into a united campaign as home rule threatened. In relation to the possible fracturing of that campaign, Ruth Dudley Edwards suggests of the Orange Order that, as was frequently its fate, 'it was in many respects an embarrassment to its allies' because it challenged the desire for unionists to claim they were such a broad church.[10] This was underlined not just by Sloan but also the independent unionist farmers led by T. W. Russell – he was the grandson of an evicted crofter and obsessed with the land question, and crucially, not averse to cooperating with nationalists on matters of mutual interest – revealing the extent to which unionism was an alliance of different forces and factions. What was also striking in the first decade of the century was the degree to which focus was shifting away from Parliament and towards grassroots organisations demanding control. While the emergence of Carson as the new

leader was a turning point, according to Alvin Jackson, while being associated with some of the most controversial issues arising from the Ulster
unionist campaign, including militancy – or the threat of militancy – and
the demand for partition, he 'should not be seen as either an uncomplicated partitionist or an untrammelled militant. He was an Irish unionist,
who supported the constitutional union between Great Britain and all of
Ireland, but he was also an essentially pragmatic politician who by October 1913 (if not earlier) had come to realise that southern unionism was a
forlorn hope.'[11]

Given the Parliament Act of 1911, which curtailed the legislative veto
of the House of Lords, and thus a veto on a House of Commons-sup-
ported Home Rule Bill, the Irish question was clearly going to complicate
British politics greatly. Simultaneously, the Orange Order began to drill
under the auspices of Fred Crawford and Robert Wallace. Crawford was a
member of the Ulster Unionist Council and from 1911 was a key figure on
its secret military committee. Over the next few years he attempted various schemes to import arms into Ulster and was thus a central figure in the
emergence of the gun into Irish politics at this juncture.[12]

Ulster Day in September 1912 was planned with great precision,
preceded by rolling public meetings and culminating in the signature of a
covenant, a pact with God, pledging resistance to home rule. The crowd
were addressed by a former Presbyterian Moderator, Dr William McK-
ean, who declared: 'we are plain blunt men who love peace and industry ...
the Irish question is at bottom a war against Protestantism'. Crucially,
the wording of the covenant was that those signing would use 'all means
which may be found necessary to defeat the present conspiracy to set up
a home rule parliament in Ireland'. Women separately signed their own
covenant and, in total, about 470,000 people signed. This was a pledge
to resist home rule for all of Ireland, but the association of unionism with
Ulster was becoming more apparent. Joseph Peacocke, the Church of Ireland Archbishop of Dublin, for example, was concerned that if southern
members of the Church of Ireland were associated with it, nationalists
might 'raise hostility against them throughout the other provinces' and his
fellow bishop in Cork thought that the great majority of the laity in the
south 'object to being in any way identified with the Ulster movement'.[13]

The propensity to militancy was being commented on at various
stages during this era. In 1911 and 1912 there were reports coming in to the
Chief Secretary's Office (CSO – under British rule, the Irish executive

government based at Dublin Castle was led by the Lord Lieutenant, or viceroy, the king's representative in Ireland, and his immediate subordinate was the chief secretary) of the growing penchant for bearing arms and dummy arms. In Fermanagh in April 1911, for example, one report read: 'alleged illegal training of Orangemen ... about 40 men assembled and went into a course of rifle practice', and the following year in the same place 'about 20 young men being present with dummy guns'.[14] A letter from the CSO to the undersecretary in February 1912 ruminated that

> as there is at present no law dealing with possession and carrying of arms in Ireland other than the Gun Licensing Act of 1870 and as reports received from time to time from the police go to show that unfortunately arms, especially revolvers are at present in the possession of persons likely to use them for unlawful purposes, it is submitted for consideration whether instructions should not be issued to the police to bring before the RM [Resident Magistrates] or other JPs all persons of bad or indifferent character whom they may detect in the possession of arms, especially revolvers with a view of requiring them as 'persons of evil fame' to find sureties to be of good behaviour.[15]

The same year, W. C. Trimble, a magistrate for the county of Armagh, was active in organising an escort for Carson in Enniskillen ('it is a time for exhibition of welcome; each rider is requested to come in riding breeches and putties if he has them or tight trousers and leggings and spurs'), but a memorandum from the Attorney General the following year took issue with him masquerading as leader of a band of merry horsemen:

> The idea seems to have occurred to him to create a permanent drilled force without lawful authority and it has culminated in what is obviously a mere pretence that this Enniskillen Horse is a troop trained with lawful intentions and loyalty to his majesty. The position of Mr Trimble and his character are such that it has not been considered desirable, up to the present, to take his actions seriously. I should regard any recognition of this so-called Enniskillen Horse as calculated to create further difficulty in dealing with practices which are on the borderline of illegality and which are carried out in some parts of the North of Ireland.[16]

Carson sanctioned the formation of the Ulster Volunteer Force (UVF) in January 1913, and while some contemporary nationalists saw this 'as a game of political bluff',[17] Fred Crawford thought differently, and throughout 1913 imported thousands of rifles, some machine guns, and a large quantity of ammunition into the north. In December 1913 a royal proclamation prohibited the importation of arms into Ireland. The UVF claimed a membership of 100,000 and despite a class-bound officers corps, it has been described by its historian Tim Bowman as 'the real "people's army"' of the Irish revolution, and not a landlord-led militia bankrolled by the establishment. But despite the image its leaders sought to portray of it – a monolithic, united force – it was, in reality, socially and regionally diverse, contained many middle-aged recruits (unlike its soon to be organised southern counterpart), inconsistently organised, and impeded by lack of funds and disputes between local units and headquarters. Carson did not want any militant rabble taking the initiative and his key message to it was one of caution: 'restrain your men to the utmost'.[18] Sanctioning the formation of the UVF (and gunrunning) was daring, but it was also imperative for Carson to control it, while ultimately hoping it would not have to fight, and he worried about his ability to do that. What was relevant here, in the words of A. T. Q. Stewart, was 'the permanent duality of the Protestant defence'; those who wanted to avoid confrontation and 'others to resist to the last'.[19]

In April 1913 the CSO was also made aware, under the label 'Crime Special', of 'the forward movement, soon to be outlined by the unionist leaders ... the principal item in this movement will be the arming of members of the UVF, the unionist clubs and also all Orangemen'.[20] Weekly reports were being sent to the CSO on 'Unionist Movement versus Home Rule'; a typical entry for 1914 read 'Lurgan District – 200 Italian, 100 Martini Henri and 500 Lee Enfield rifles are stated to be in the old Brewery and in the Orange Hall, Lurgan'.[21]

Women were also being mobilised in unprecedented numbers. According to the Marchioness of Londonderry, Edith Stewart, in 1909:

It is conceded how much influence women possess in these days and they are encouraged in their political efforts by the men, their help is sought in elections, in canvassing and in forming various political leagues and societies ... now, if women are allowed to exercise any influence at all, why in ordinary justice should they always be subject to indirect methods?[22]

She was a supporter of women's suffrage but campaigning on that question was complicated in Ulster, which was home 'to an array of suffrage movements' – about twenty suffrage associations by 1914 – incorporating 1,000 women. This was largely a middle-class affair, and inevitably it was difficult for the women to find space on the political spectrum, the Irish Women's Suffrage Society noting, 'In Belfast, nothing will be entertained but home rule struggling with Unionism.'

Carson suggested that suffrage would be granted under an Ulster provisional government, one of the contingency plans to resist home rule; he did not follow this gesture of equality through, but there was to be no war declared by the Ulster Women's Unionist Council (UWUC), which was established in January 1911 and evolved into the largest women's movement in Ireland. It claimed a membership of over 100,000 and was formed, in the words of the Marchioness of Londonderry,

> to express the feelings of the people of Ulster, who have fought with every means in their power to remain associated with England ... We banded ourselves together to see how we might best organise ourselves to impress our fellow-countrymen in England with the fact that Ulster will not consent to the tearing asunder of this country.[23]

The UWUC, however, declined to nominate women for Parliament as 'the time was not yet ripe for this and the essential thing in the first parliament was to preserve the safety of the unionist cause, that much organisation and construction work would be necessary for which perhaps women had not the necessary experience.'[24]

Historians, including David Fitzpatrick, have underlined the extent to which the social and cultural organisations underpinning formal unionist party politics were by no means always united. Fitzpatrick pointed to the tensions between the 'gentle old guard of rural Orangeism' with the more aggressive, bullying Belfast members as well as highlighting the ambiguous relationship between social, political and religious identity, concluding that during the revolution 'the line between sectarian and social conflict was always indistinct'.[25] Such difficulties were also relevant to the minority nationalist population; Belfast MP Joe Devlin found himself immersed in the 'local and sometimes grubby negotiations' which his party leader John Redmond found 'repugnant'. Although Devlin had entered politics as a campaigner for independent lay leadership, he became increasingly devoted to the defence of Catholic Church interests, and while he was a proponent of greater cooperation between the Catholic and Protestant working class, his political machine was an exclusively Catholic organisation, the AOH. He may have championed the working class, but the ethos of the groups he associated with was 'characterised by an essentially individualist drive for upward social mobility'.[26]

But how was the new dawn of unionist resistance to play out, given that the threat of home rule was now much more real than in the late nineteenth century? The Unionist Club Council minute book recorded that in May 1896 Lord Templetown had been presented with a 'set of the most artistic and truly beautiful silver cups' alongside verbal tributes 'overflowing with the kindest sympathies of warm, true Irish hearts'.[27] That was the end of that phase of the battle (both the 1886 and 1893 Home Rule Bills were defeated) and the interesting thing was that the hearts were Irish, not Ulster hearts. The next entry in the minute book was in January 1911 where it was deemed time to be once more 'called into activity', again with Lord Templetown as president. A representative from County Clare hailed the unionist clubs as 'they rallied all the scattered unionists together'; he also believed Templetown was 'a true patriot and nationalist' and in this the survival of the nineteenth-century approach and terminology can be seen, but it was not to last long.[28] There were already indications of the gulf between Ulster and southern unionists. It was insisted that '80 to 90 per cent of the people in this county [Clare] were hostile to that detestable project of home rule. But they dare not speak out and Ulstermen could hardly realise how they were dragooned by the vilest system of intimidation ever known in a civilised country.'[29] Such declarations and 'statistics' about Clare were highly delusional; its premier newspaper, the *Clare Champion*, made much of the county's loyalty to John Redmond and John's brother Willie represented the East Clare constituency as a home rule MP.[30]

By February the following year it was recorded that 232 unionist clubs had been formed to date and they faced the task of 'informing the British electorate as to the real meaning of home rule'.[31] The determination to influence English public opinion was not just rhetorical. The UWUC executive minutes for May 1914 recorded that from June 1913 to March 1914, literature was sent to 14,902 electors in sixty-five English and Scottish constituencies; such communication was based on the Council's maxim that 'prevention is better than cure' when it came to home rule.[32] By August 1913 the number of clubs formed had risen to 316 and the Bangor Unionist Club won 'the miniature rifle competition'. It was also highlighted that the clubs had financed trips from 'radicals from across the Channel who have come over and investigated the Irish question for themselves ... in every case such visits have proved to be of the very greatest advantage and have considerably modified the views of those who had previously been among our bitterest opponents', but it also recognised the problem of there being many clubs 'so scattered'.[33] Inevitably, by the following year sentiment had hardened and a delegate from Clones 'suggested the advisability of distributing six rifles to each club for instructional purposes'.

The UUC was also tactically shrewd in creating its own labour organisations in 1918 in order to give them some voice but also to absorb them so as to prevent a re-run of the Independent Orange Order debacle of 1903.[34] What it was reacting to was not liberalism among Presbyterians, 'but the much stronger tradition of autonomous political activity by the Protestant Labour aristocracy, shopkeepers and small employers' dating back to the late 1860s, complex in its origins but combining anti-Catholicism with 'anti-Landlord and anti-oligarchic sentiment'.[35] The four-month Belfast Dock strike of 1907, which had united Protestant and Catholic dockers against Belfast's leading capitalist Thomas Gallaher, had resulted in defeat of the workers and 'played into the hands of resurgent unionism'; the strikers had been led by James Larkin, but he 'left no coherent rearguard armed either with theory or rhetoric with which to resist Belfast's counter revolution'.[36]

James Connolly tried in 1911 to rouse the Belfast labourers again, telling them the majority of the 'poor slaves' of the Protestant working class were 'descendants of the men who fought for civil and religious liberty at Derry, Aughrim and the Boyne', landmark battles of the Williamite war of the seventeenth century that confirmed the Protestant dominance of Ireland, and that 'if these poor sweated descendants of Protestant rebels against a king had today one hundreth part of the spirit of their ancestors in question, the reconquest of Ireland by the working class would be a much easier task than it is likely to prove'.[37] The stranglehold of sectarianism, however, was very difficult to overcome. By 1914, Protestant trade unionists in Belfast rejected the claim of British labour leader Ramsay MacDonald that they had been 'led away by the crooked news of the Tory press' and business interests; a manifesto signed by 2,000 of those

trade unionists rejected home rule 'as freemen and members of the greatest democracy in Great Britain and Ireland'.[38] But the demise of independent Orangeism also stripped the ideology of the Protestant working class
of some of its more 'progressive elements'.[39] It became more difficult to
emphasise what the Protestant and Catholic working class had in common. Frederick McGinley, a Catholic born in 1894 who grew up in the
Ardoyne area of Belfast, was adamant that as he was growing up before
intense conflict, the people of the Ardoyne 'were working class' and were
united about their status in a way that transcended religion: 'In no way
could they be called lower class ... labour was producing its own intelli-
gentsia ... the hand loom weavers were well read and deep thinking men.'[40]

Money and business interests were also essential to the unionist campaign – nationalists were at pains to counteract what was labelled 'the
Orange movement of organised force ... financed by all wealthy and aristocratic enemies of popular liberties'[41] – as underlined by the role played
by stockbroking magnate James Craig. According to Alvin Jackson,

> Craig helped to create the means by which Ulster unionism, that most
> fissile of movements, sustained a unity and discipline in the face of
> grinding pressures. Craig, rooted in eastern Ulster, helped to popular-
> ise the advocacy of six-county exclusion among northern unionists.
> Craig, much more than Carson, may thus be seen as an architect of
> the partition settlement that evolved between 1912 and 1920.[42]

Craig, in an illustration of the way unionists were able to mix arrogance and vanity with victimhood, was later to declare in 1918 that,
'if they could not save the whole country for the Empire, they could at
least save themselves'.[43] Propaganda – and specifically, modern market-
ing techniques – also continued to be vital; 1912–14 involved a two-year
advertising campaign, including those run by agencies in London, and
Craig, due to his business interests, was well alert to this.[44] Economic questions were relentlessly focused on ('What is home rule to be? TAXES!
TAXES!! TAXES!!! ... Irishmen under home rule will be twice taxed') by
both Britain and Ireland.[45]

Under the auspices of the Joint Committee of Unionist Associations
of Ireland, southern unionists bore 'the greatest burden' in supervising
work in England and Wales, but by 1912 and 1913, in the words of Patrick
Buckland, 'the concept of Ulster had, to Ulstermen, achieved an almost

mystical significance'.[46] The Irish Unionist Alliance, the southern unionists' political organisation, had only 683 members by 1913 and its members' main challenge was 'to prove to the outside world that they existed'.[47] As David Miller characterised it, by 1912, northern unionists would 'vote against home rule for Ireland to the end of time, but they would only fight for the exclusion of Ulster'.[48] When Carson was speaking at the Theatre Royal in Dublin in 1913, Andrew Bonar Law is reputed to have asked him in hushed tones to 'say something about themselves'. Carson snapped back, 'What is there I can say?' Some of the audience whispered the word 'betrayal' to each other.[49]

One could justifiably assert, however, that southern unionists were doomed from the outset. Not only had electoral and land reform weakened the strength of the most influential of their number, but from the beginning, like their nationalist counterparts, they were by no means a homogeneous group, and this was always to remain evident. In Cork, for example, there were gulfs between the city and county brands of unionism, with city unionists less isolated and more integrated.[50] By the time of the First World War, Lord Middleton, leader of the Irish unionist peers and chairman of the Irish Unionist Alliance, was suggesting that what energy was left 'should be devoted to the furtherance of the war' and by the time of the War of Independence was pursuing a strategy that was based on him and the Anti-partition League 'gradually feeling their way towards a political settlement based on dominion status'.[51]

And what of the relationship between the British Conservatives and Ulster during the home rule crisis in the years before the Great War? Did they believe that the most salient aspect of unionism was an expression of pride in imperial citizenship, which, according to Paul Bew obscured its real dimensions?[52] Walter Long, who had succeeded Saunderson as leader of the Irish Unionist MPs in 1906 but then became a Conservative MP backing the unionists, had strong personal and political connections with southern Ireland and initially believed that English Tories needed to stand firmly behind *all* Irish unionists in resisting the Liberals, but how was a balance to be struck in this regard? And what impact would such a stance have on a Tory Party that was already factionalised, demoralised and preoccupied with tariff, tax and class issues in British politics? Put another way, was Ireland 'really the most advantageous arena in which the Tories could carry on the political struggle? The responses of contemporary commentators to this question differed substantially.'[53]

Another dilemma for the Tories was the extent to which they could endorse the growing militancy of unionist soldiers, including the Curragh Mutiny of March 1914: after meetings in London with the army council and a special cabinet committee on Ulster, Sir Arthur Paget, commander-in-chief of the British forces in Ireland, made an exceptionally intemperate speech to officers at the Curragh military camp in Kildare on 20 March 1914. He informed them that extensive operations in Ulster were imminent, that the country 'would be in a blaze' within a day, and that while officers resident in Ulster would not be compelled to take any action against unionists, other officers who were unwilling to participate would be dismissed.[54] Hubert Gough, brigadier general commanding the 3rd cavalry brigade of the British army stationed at the Curragh, was infuriated, and tendered his resignation, as he was unwilling to initiate military action in Ulster. A further meeting called by Paget on 21 March to clarify the orders did nothing to mollify those concerned. Following Gough's lead, fifty-nine fellow officers (out of seventy) insisted they would resign if ordered north and all were summoned to London.

Gough wanted a written assurance that the army would not be compelled to force Ulster to accept home rule. This was provided on 23 March by the Secretary of State for War, J. E. B. Seely, but his assurance was repudiated by the government, as the full terms of the guarantee had exceeded those given by cabinet, and British prime minister Herbert Asquith was forced to intervene to end the confusion and uncertainty. Seely subsequently had to resign, as did military chief of staff John French. Paget's offer of resignation was not accepted, although his actions certainly prevented him obtaining a field command during the First World War. The revelation of the army's desire to interfere in politics was a great embarrassment to the government, which was humiliated by being forced into a denial of any intention to use force against Ulster.

Gough worked in cahoots with senior military supporters, unionists and Conservative Party politicians and journalists in obtaining his written assurance, highlighting the close relationship between some Anglo-Irish officers, the UVF and its political sympathisers. Blatantly partisan newspapers also played a role in igniting and stoking the flames of the controversy. In London, the *Pall Mall Gazette* published a dramatic editorial on 21 March: 'The latest news from Ireland is the most serious yet received. Its gravity cannot be overestimated. We are on the verge of civil war.'[55] Gough and his fellow officers, the unionist press subsequently declared, had saved the country by refusing to allow an unscrupulous government to make the army a pawn in a political plot, while the liberal and labour press expressed disgust at the hypocrisy of a unionist press praising the defiance of officers of an imperial army, and depicted Gough and the others as seditious. Henry Wilson, another Anglo-Irish officer and director of military operations at the War Office, also blatantly interfered in political affairs (he declared that the army had 'done what the Opposition failed to do'[56]), but the government was afraid to dismiss him.

Inevitably, anger felt by Irish nationalists about the Curragh debacle increased the momentum behind the Irish Volunteers, which had been established in November 1913 (see chapter 13). In the 1950s the Cork nationalist and War of Independence veteran Florence O'Donoghue asked this question of Asquith's government in 1914: 'Why did it surrender its authority and capitulate to the dictation of a group of serving officers and the unseen powers behind them?'[57] Other questions the crisis raised included whether Carson had control over the militancy he had inspired (privately, he was nervous about this) and in what direction this militancy was taking the British Conservative Party under Bonar Law which, although revelling in the Liberal Party's discomfort, was clearly reacting to rather than controlling events.

It also led to renewed urgency about the need to exclude all or part of Ulster from the provisions of the Home Rule Bill. This had serious implications for the status of John Redmond, out of whom Asquith became even more determined to wring concessions. The outbreak of the First World War later that year postponed these crucial questions, but they were to fester, and much damage had been done to the British government's authority and the idea of the army as above politics.

Although a temporary calm was apparent in the immediate aftermath of the Curragh crisis, it had exposed much that was to remain uncertain, most obviously an army divided on the question of its attitude to the UVF, and the army did nothing to stop the UVF when it landed guns at Larne a few weeks later on 24 April. By using a defence fund subscribed to by British and Irish unionists, Fred Crawford bought 20,000 rifles and 2,000,000 rounds of ammunition in Hamburg and spent two months arranging their shipment to Ulster. From aboard a Norwegian collier, they were eventually landed at Larne, Bangor, and Donaghadee on the night of 24–25 April 1914 and distributed to UVF units throughout Ulster. The landing and quick distribution of the arms boosted the morale of the UVF. Crawford revelled in giving his embellished version of the events, noting in his diary, 'I shall endeavour from memory to give a full account'; what this amounted to at the outset was the following, typically messianic assertion:

'It is a great honour, but I feel it is also a terrible responsibility, for on the success of my venture depends the whole of the Ulster question. If I fail Ulster is lost and God help her. If I succeed then Ulster will be free forever from home rule. No government could coerce her with the arms and ammunition behind her that I shall bring in.' During times when it seemed the mission was imperilled, 'I could never face the heartbroken wail of disappointment the people of Ulster would put up when they heard the loss of their hopes.'[58]

There was also an important continental context to this gunrunning bravado, or what amounted to an 'Irish factor' in the build-up to the First World War. Two 'hotspots' were developing simultaneously in Europe: Serbia in central Europe and Ireland in western Europe. Since its improved relations with Britain in the first decade of the century, France had lost interest in liaising with Irish militants, but for Germany, providing arms to Irish groups to destabilise Britain was an attractive option, though it remains difficult to document the full extent of its appeal.[59]

Amidst all the Ulster militancy and brinkmanship many concrete and practical plans were being laid. In September 1913 the UUC and the Ulster Union of Constitutional Associations held a special meeting in Belfast and laid plans for a provisional government, with an Ulster Military Committee as well as personnel, finance, supply, railway and medical boards, along with a Finance and Business Committee and a Legal and Customs and Excise Committee. There was also a declaration that they would indemnify 'all members of the UVF in respect of any personal injury, or loss of life which shall be sustained by them in the execution of their duty as such members or in the execution of any order of the provisional government'.[60] But that summer, all did not seem rosy as far as Carson was concerned: at a private meeting of 150 businessmen in the old Town Hall in Belfast he made it clear he was 'not very pleased with the response to "the Carson fund", not happy with the low turnout at the meeting', and regarding Catholics in mixed workplaces, 'he strongly advised every precaution to be taken to secure that such workers would not be interfered with'. Another contributor insisted 'a great amount of harm was done to the case in the past by neglect of this'.[61]

Inevitably, much was overshadowed by the outbreak of the European war in 1914; in May 1915, Edward Carson wrote to General George Richardson in relation to Richardson's planned meetings with divisional and battalion commanders of the UVF and wanted to convey the urgency of

> the absolute necessity of keeping our Ulster Volunteers, so far as organisation is concerned, as perfect as possible ... as the home rule bill has been placed on the statute books and will come into operation the moment the war is over we must be in such a position as in a very brief time, to render ourselves effective against all attempts to force the bill upon us.[62]

They were certainly effective in that regard. In 1918, Thomas Johnson, leader of the Irish Labour Party, compiled *A Handbook for Rebels: A Guide to Successful Defiance of the British Government*, containing extracts from speeches by Carson, Andrew Bonar Law, and Tory and Attorney General F. E. Smith, who 'with complete success by a display of armed force challenged the might of the Empire and were afterwards honoured and rewarded by the government they defied'; it contained 'some useful hints on the science of bloodless rebellion'.[63]

THIRTEEN

LABOUR, NATIONALISM AND WAR: 1913–16

The formation of the UVF had profound consequences for Irish nationalists. London-based Irish journalist Robert Lynd maintained that the UVF 'burst open the gates through which a flood of arms began to pour into the country'.[1] In their coverage of the launch of the Irish Volunteers organisation in Dublin on 25 November 1913, contemporary newspapers suggested attendance was over 5,000. The *Freeman's Journal* reported that the attendees were shepherded by 'a big brigade of stewards ... wearing green and orange badges' and 'the St James's Brass and Reed Band discoursed a selection of national airs, the refrains of which were joined in by many in the assemblage. By far the greatest numbers of those in attendance were young men.'[2] But when Laurence Kettle, a moderate nationalist who became joint secretary of the Volunteers' provisional committee, rose to read the manifesto of the new organisation, a call of 'Cheers for Larkin' was raised by a small section of the crowd and 'Mr Kettle's voice was completely drowned'.[3]

This was a reminder that the launch occurred in the midst of the long drawn-out Dublin Lockout, after 400 employers locked out over 20,000 workers for belonging to, or supporting, the Irish Transport and General Workers Union (ITGWU) led by James Larkin. Two weeks before the formation of the Irish Volunteers the Irish Citizen Army (ICA) had been established as a militia to protect the workers. At the turn of the century there were a million employees and 70,000 trade unionists in Ireland, three-quarters of whom were in British societies; the challenges for Larkin were 'how to build bargaining power in an economy where 7 out of every 9 employees were unskilled and easily replaced' and to move away from reliance on British unions, and sympathetic action was deemed to be the answer: 'The slums had nothing to do with it, to begin with at least, though when the propaganda war began in September, Larkin made sure the slums were in the picture.'[4]

Despite the boast of the IPP in 1910 that well before the establishment of the Labour Party it had championed the cause of workers and 'was essentially a Labour Party', muteness or sometimes hostility was evident in its reaction to the Lockout. The party had backed welfare reforms and recognition of trade unions, but as one activist put it during the Lockout, the party's MPs were mostly 'employers and capitalists'. What it was, rather, was petit bourgeois in character: 'F. S. L. Lyons has shown that although by 1910, 54.2 per cent of the party had upper middle class occupational backgrounds, the number of large farmers, provincial newspaper proprietors and prosperous shopkeepers was growing.'[5] IPP members were most likely to advocate industrial arbitration rather than intervention, but they were reluctant in this and denounced the 'sympathetic strike'; tackling working conditions and industrial relations 'could wait until the foundation of the nation-state, for however hollow it rang for some, the party insisted that it represented "not a class but a nation"'. By the time of the Lockout, Larkin's newspaper the *Irish Worker* was referring to the 'utter indifference' of the IPP.[6]

The *Irish Worker* also attacked the AOH, accusing it of assisting the employers; John D. Nugent, its president, in turn castigated Larkin and his 'syndicalist madness'.[7] IPP members targeted Larkin as a despot and autocrat. IPP MP T. M. Healy defended the employers, whom he described as 'harried ... like men in a besieged city ... all of them were friendly to trade unions'.[8] The Catholic Church echoed such rhetoric and opposition, to which Larkin replied that the 'influence of the Church ... has been induced to use men to betray their own class ... I am told I am an Atheist. Why, it is the Clergy who are making people Atheists.'[9]

There were also fierce media battles waged throughout the Lockout's duration. The *Freeman's Journal* during its early stages was neutral, 'critical of all the participants', but its coverage evolved into strident criticism of Larkin, distinguishing between trade unionism ('a very good thing') and Larkin syndicalism, 'a very different thing, a very bad thing and leads not to progress but chaos'.[10] The *Irish Times* had a very anti-Larkin line in 1913 but nonetheless was prepared to publish W. B. Yeats's poem 'September 1913' and George Russell's (AE's) 'Open Letter to the Masters of Dublin'; their offerings underlined a palpable sense of urgency and crisis, but also a sense of people meaningfully engaged with the society around them. Dermot Keogh has argued that 1913 was important because of its contribution to that process, but that such a consciousness was not necessarily socialist, let alone revolutionary.[11]

James Larkin's sister Delia also had a key role to play in Labour affairs during this era and had a close association with James during the Lockout. She was prolific in her contributions to the *Irish Worker* from 1911 to 1914, and her brother's ITGWU rival, William O'Brien, later described her, as like Larkin himself: 'very difficult to get on with'. She served four years as general secretary of the Irish Women Workers' Union (IWWU) and an *Irish Times* obituary of her in 1949 was kind and accurate:

> When her brother set out to organise the unskilled and semi-skilled workers of Dublin – a hopeless task in those days – Delia took on something even tougher; she would organise the women. People just sat back and laughed, but Delia fought on and won. It is largely owing to her tenacity and courage that women in Ireland are industrially organised today.[12]

She also did it facing hostility from Liberty Hall (the headquarters of the ITGWU); running soup kitchens during the Lockout, she became the 'public face' of the Hall, catering for over 2,000 Dublin children every day. Paradoxically, however, it was the Lockout that also did damage to her public career; the IWWU's membership was decimated in 1913 and she was left vulnerable after James left for America in 1914. When she had launched the IWWU – championing the cause of domestic and factory workers, waitresses, printers, and dress makers – in 1911 she insisted that female employees enduring poor pay and conditions were 'weary of being white slaves who pass their lives away toiling to fill the pockets of unscrupulous employers'.[13] By 1913 she had recruited many of the women employed in the Jacob's biscuit factory in Dublin, who were subsequently locked out by their employers; at the end of the Lockout in January 1914, 400 members of the IWWU were not reinstated. Rosie Hackett was one of them and went on to become a key figure in the IWWU for the next four decades.

One of the iconic events of the dispute became known as Bloody Sunday, after the police baton charged a large crowd in O'Connell Street:

> Individuals fled in all directions in their attempt to escape the blows which were dealt with fierce intensity by the infuriated members of the police force ... the scene of the disturbances was strewn like a battlefield with the bodies of injured people, many of them with their faces covered with blood and with their bodies writhing in agony. The whole episode lasted only a few minutes, but in that brief space of time hundreds were injured, some seriously.[14]

On 2 September, the *Freeman's Journal* reported that 400 had been injured over two days of rioting and two, James Nolan and James Byrne, were killed. James Connolly's daughter Ina recalled 'there were baton charges with a savagery that brought forth denunciation even from those who had no sympathy with the strike. Many had their heads broken; in fact, some who were beaten never recovered.'[15]

The 'Dublin Labour Troubles Report' compiled for the British government responded to allegations of police brutality by dismissing contentions that police 'were placed at the disposal of the employers to crush out the strikers', insisting their actions were

> solely for the protection of property ... the numbers of unemployed on the streets rendered the task of preserving the peace difficult and taxed the resources of the police to the utmost. From time to time processions of the strikers and unemployed through the streets led to scenes of disorder, tramcars being specially singled out for attack. In the country practically all work was stopped on the night of 16th September. Serious rioting occurred in the village of Finglas close to Dublin. A public house was attacked and a constable drew his revolver and fired several shots wounding a youth named Patrick Duffy in the back. The police force of the city was augmented during the strike by a force of 5 district inspectors, 13 head constables and 488 men.

Reference was also made to an allegation by Larkin that one of the young female strikers at Jacob's factory had been sent 'to a home for fallen women' for assaulting one of her colleagues who refused to strike; it was pointed out that as she was under sixteen years of age she had been sent instead to the reformatory school at High Park.

There was further violence on 21 September: 'tramcars were wrecked and the police had to make a number of baton charges before the mobs could be dispersed. Thirty-five civilians and several policemen were injured.'[16] In the midst of all this, a few nights later, two tenement houses collapsed in Church Street, causing the deaths of seven people. Hugh Sammon, aged seventeen, died with his four-year-old sister Elisabeth in his arms after repeatedly re-entering the building to save the occupants; the previous day he had been laid off by his employer, Jacob's, for refusing to repudiate his trade union.[17]

On 13 November, at a meeting to celebrate Larkin's release from jail, Connolly announced the formation of the Irish Citizen Army and again, it is significant that the Ulster influence was cited: 'Listen to me, I am going to talk sedition. The next time we are out for a march I want them to come with their corporals, sergeants and people to form fours. Why should we not drill and train our men as they are doing in Ulster?'[18] Later, Seán O'Casey was keen to contrast the ICA with the Irish Volunteers:

> Now there were two Cathleen ni Houlihans round Dublin: one, like the traditional, in green dress, shamrocks in her hair, a little brian-boru harp under her oxter, chanting her share of song, for the rights and liberties common to all Irishmen; they who fight for me shall be rulers in the land; they shall be settled for ever; in good jobs they shall be, for ever, for ever; the other Cathleen coarsely dressed, hair a little tousled, caught roughly together by a pin, bare footed, sometimes with a whiff of whiskey off her breath; brave and brawny; at ease in the smell of sweat and the sound of bad language, vital, sweet and assuaged with immortality. Those who had any tinge of gentility in them, left the Citizen army for the refined Volunteers.[19]

What also irked nationalists was the contention that the cause of the workers was the cause of the nation, or as was expressed in the *Irish Worker* in September 1913, continuing the struggle of the 'Irish race ... which for eight hundred years of slavery and persecution has never once lost faith in the nobility of its mission'[20] (Connolly was a key thinker and writer in linking class and nation but did not choose the route of lazy polemic and layered his output with historical analysis). Earlier that month, the *Irish*

Worker had rounded on nationalist representatives for their passivity and accused them of being in cahoots with Dublin Castle authorities.[21] Larkin also accused Dublin Corporation of not doing enough and of using the idea of nationality for purely selfish reasons, part of a strategy of targeting the IPP as a party wedded to the interests of an elite. The stance of Sinn Féin was also interesting; Arthur Griffith in 1911 had described the ITGWU action as 'the English-made strike' and condemned syndicalism and the sympathetic strike as approximating to acts that were 'terrorist'.[22] Sinn Féin opinion, however, was not united in this regard; others were happy to depict the ITGWU as a nationalist union, but the republican monthly paper *Irish Freedom* was insistent that the labour question could not dominate: 'The interests of Ireland as a whole are greater than the interests of any class in Ireland, and so long as labour accepts the nation, Labour must subordinate its class interests to the interests of the nation.'[23] Others were more equivocal, including Patrick Pearse, a passionate educationalist, then beginning to contemplate nationalist rebellion but not yet completely divorced from the idea of gradualist nationalism: 'I do not know whether the methods of James Larkin are wise methods or unwise methods (unwise, I think in some respects) but this I know, that there is a hideous wrong to be righted'. Maud Gonne, an advanced nationalist and also devoted to social issues, condemned the employers and British rule but did not exactly give her full backing to Larkin: 'Larkin is a painful necessity, but a necessity and has done great good in many ways ... Larkin has a wonderful magnetic influence on the crowd, but I fear he is too vain and too jealous and too untruthful to make a really great leader.'[24] A none too modest Larkin had asked 'Is it any wonder a Larkin arose? Was there not a need for a Larkin?'[25]

Arnold Wright's *Disturbed Dublin: The Story of the Great Strike of 1913*, published in 1914 and commissioned by the Dublin Chamber of Commerce to give the perspective of the employers, pointed to the workers' low standard of living and energy which had reduced their value in the labour market, noting that because of this the strike's supporters should be 'chary of playing the role of critic to employers who have to utilise this damaged material'.[26]

Although the workers were defeated and those who were able or allowed to began to return to work in early 1914, the ICA was now part of a melting pot of organisations that was about to get bigger still. At the launch of the Irish Volunteers in November 1913, moderate nationalists and trade unionists were joined by cultural and language activists, GAA stalwarts, representatives of the AOH and the IRB, as well as a large body of university students. The meeting was chaired by UCD histo= rian Eoin MacNeill, who had written an article three weeks previously in *An Claidheamh Soluis*, the newspaper of the Gaelic League, calling for a nationalist force that would emulate the formation of the UVF in Janu- ary 1913.[27] The manifesto stated that the duties of the Volunteers 'will be defensive and protective and they will not contemplate either aggression or domination'.[28]

Various launches were held in other parts of the country and by the middle of 1914 police reports estimated membership had reached 150,000. At the time of the formation of the Volunteers, Europe was riven with con- flict and labour unrest; militarism on the part of civilians was evident in Germany, Britain and Poland and independent military action of smaller nations was evident in the Balkan wars of 1911 and 1912 and the emerging nation states of Serbia, Bulgaria and Greece, developments that did not go unrecorded in Ireland.[29] The ICA admitted women and spoke the lan- guage of equality but the Volunteers were not as enlightened; Cumann na mBan was launched in 1914 specifically as a female auxiliary force to the Volunteers, although its rhetoric and membership badge was militaristic.

A number of things were apparent from the early stages of the Vol- unteers' existence: while the electric atmosphere enthralled many, the sheer variety of nationalist opinions and organisations involved meant the potential for internal dissension was strong. A crucial question was whether or not the IPP would seek to control the Volunteers; its leader John Redmond's standing was high in Ireland but his position in West- minster was relatively weak, given the unionist and Tory opposition to the implementation of home rule. MacNeill sought to resist any Redmon- dite takeover but, fearing a split would ensue if there was no compromise, eventually accepted Redmond's nominees to the Volunteers' Provisional Committee.

While there was an uneasy tolerance for a period, growing distrust was inevitable and the outbreak of the Great War complicated things fur- ther. Redmond's call in September 1914 for the Volunteers to enlist in the British army as a moral imperative was met with accusations of treach- ery from MacNeill and his allies. But Redmond's standing was such that when the movement split that month, he took the vast majority of Vol- unteers, over 90 per cent, now styled the National Volunteers, with him.

Contemporary estimates of the number of Irish Volunteers who stayed with MacNeill were in the region of 9,000.

There were also particular local social and economic tensions that made for divided loyalties. Land agitation and poverty were dominant features of the west of Ireland, for example. Concern with the social conditions of the west had long been apparent with the formation of the Congested Districts Board (CDB) in 1891 (when it wound up in 1923, the area that had been under its jurisdiction had amounted to one-third of the total land mass of Ireland).[30] In Tuam in 1915, for example, much attention was devoted to local meetings of the UIL and the demand that 'graziers and grabbers stand aside ... so long as you are willing to associate with the grabbers they are justified in holding the land'. The contrast of tiny farms beside large pasture lands was noted; people were urged to reduce policing by giving the information necessary to capture the 'ruffians' who committed land crime.[31] The UIL made numerous calls on the CDB to divide bigger farms, and a meeting of the UIL in Waterford, organised 'to welcome persons who had undergone imprisonment for taking forcible possession of a farm', was suppressed.[32]

Urban poverty was also pronounced. Cooperative promoter Horace Plunkett highlighted stark statistics in 1917: there were 72,724 deaths in Ireland that year, a death rate of 16.8 per 1,000 of the population, compared to a figure for England and Wales of 14.4. There were 9,680 deaths from TB the same year, 2.23 for every 1000, compared to 1.62 in England and Wales.[33] On the eve of the First World War Dublin was a city socially and economically polarised, with 26,000 families living in tenements. The city produced many soldiers for the British army and by the end of the war, 25,644 Dubliners had served. This is unsurprising, given that a labourer could expect to earn between 16s and 18s for a forty-eight-hour week while the weekly separation allowance rate for the wife of a British army recruit was 12s 6d. The serving husband received one shilling a day, along with free board and lodging. If the couple had children the family was much better off, with separation rates rising to £1 a week for a wife and three children. Of Dublin men who enlisted in the British army, 19 per cent were killed between 1914 and 1918 and as the war progressed there were many domestic tensions and uproar over profiteering, food shortages, the requisition of hay crops and increased taxes and inflation.[34]

Undoubtedly, cost-of-living issues gnawed away at support for the war and a radical but small-circulation nationalist press also stoked anti-war feeling.[35] Milk supply in Dublin was referred to by concerned contemporaries as a 'public scandal' and 'scarce, dear and bad in a country better adapted to produce it than any other in Europe ... there are children actually dying for want of food in Dublin at present'. Nor was this just about those destitute: 'the man even at £150 a year who has a wife and 3 children ... and who has to have a house in a respectable neighbourhood and to wear respectable clothes, clean linen and good boots is performing something of a miracle if he does all this'.[36]

This is a reminder of the broader social context for Ireland during the war. For those with no jobs, or poorly paid jobs, British army service held certain monetary attractions unavailable at home. Undoubtedly many volunteers were motivated by loyalty to empire or Irish nationalism, having been encouraged to enlist by their political leaders either to strengthen the case for remaining within the British Empire or to be rewarded for their service through the implementation of home rule. Many Irish nationalists of that era did not feel their political affiliation was incompatible with service in the British army. Catholic nationalists from Belfast joined in significant numbers and fought alongside their unionist counterparts, and in April 1915, in response to the question of why they were joining the British army, three Irish brothers from southern Ireland declared: 'Because Mr. Redmond said that this was as much Ireland's fight as England's and we want to fight for Ireland.'[37] By that time, more than 50,000 men had enlisted from Ireland, north and south; by the end of the first year of the war, 80,000 had enlisted.

For others, family and community traditions of military service were relevant, as was peer example and pressure, and simple quest for adventure. Tom Barry, later famed as an IRA leader in the War of Independence, volunteered 'for no other reason than I wanted to see what war was like, to get a gun, to see new countries and to feel a grown man'.[38] Others were persuaded by the plight of 'little Catholic Belgium' and contemporary recruitment posters and propagandists made much of this, especially after the Central Council for the Organisation of Recruiting in Ireland produced posters specifically for an Irish audience. These asked Irishmen to

> Remember Belgium: Your place is on the Battlefield and no true Irishman should be sought or found elsewhere ... have you any women folk worth defending? Remember the women of Belgium ... the Irish are the most religious soldiers in the British army ... in the average

Irishman there is a blend of piety and militancy which makes him an effective soldier.[39]

But many 'true Irishmen' were confined to the agricultural fields; it was clear that farmers were reluctant to let their sons go, even though they were the class that had benefited most from the government's land legislation; the 1914 harvest had achieved the highest prices since the 1880s.[40] Levels of recruitment in Wexford, for example, were lowered by the involvement of nearly two-thirds of its occupied male population in agriculture; in contrast, the student population of Trinity College Dublin dropped dramatically from 1,074 in 1914 to 535 in 1918; 869 undergraduates gave up their studies to join the war effort.[41] But overall, the over-representation of working-class recruits in the ranks was noted unfavourably by the recruiters, who felt it diminished the chances of more from the farming and commercial classes joining.[42] In County Kildare, which provided 6,264 recruits, a local newspaper observed in February 1916 'the labouring classes have done remarkably well and the gentry have also done their bit. But there are 2 classes still that did not do their bit – the farmer's sons and the young commercial men.'[43] About 2,000 workers, mainly women, also found work in munitions factories in Dublin, Cork, Waterford and Galway.

Youth, fear, pride, excitement, courage and horror emanate from the many Irish war letters that were sent back to families and have survived. Nineteen-year-old Billy McFadzean, from a loyalist part of Belfast and serving in the 36th Ulster Division, left England for France in 1915 and wrote to his family: 'You people at home make me quite proud when you tell me I am the soldier boy of the McFadzeans. I hope to play the game and if I don't add much lustre to it, I certainly will not tarnish it.' He was subsequently killed by grenades that fell out of their boxes without their pins; he threw his body over them, killing himself to save his comrades, and was awarded a Victoria Cross.[44] Michael Lennon, who took part in the Gallipoli campaign in 1915, died less than two months after his arrival at the front. His last letter was sent in June:

> Went up to the firing line last Monday, stayed there about 10 hours and then was relieved by another regiment. The return journey was tremendously exciting, as we had to go down a passage which was almost perpendicular and was 70 or 80 feet from top to bottom ...

the shells flying above ... one of the chaps who left Cork with us was bowled out, but I am hoping for something better than that.[45]

Sligo lost 440 men to the war. Eight brothers enlisted from one Sligo family: four were killed in action, four made it home, one of whom later died of Trench Fever, while another lived the rest of his life in a local psychiatric hospital.[46] In the region of 6,000 women from Ireland volunteered for service in the British Red Cross and St John Ambulance, and 2,000 joined Voluntary Aid Detachments posted to front-line hospitals. Emily McManus, a nurse from Mayo, spent three years at the front and worked at a casualty clearing station at Noyons, recalling bedding 'foul with excrement and dried pus and blood and reeking with decomposition', the difficulty with sleep, and 'trying to forget and to keep from inhaling the stench of vomit and the agonised breath of the last man who died in my blanket'.[47]

Conor O'Brien, a Blackrock College student in Dublin (a prestigious private school), joined the 7th Leinsters 16th Irish Division in 1915 and kept a diary in his Sunday missal: 'Feb 3 1917. Left 4th Leinsters at Limerick for 6th at Struma, Macedonia. Within days of the Allies arriving in Struma, 7,000 came down with Malaria and there were many deaths ... weather very hot. Mosquitoes terrible.'[48] O'Brien survived and spent a total of thirty years in the British army.

There was a strong degree of political unanimity in embracing the war at first, with both the IPP and Ulster Unionists supporting it for different reasons. But there was a degree of ambiguity on the part of many, as can be traced for example, through the BMH statements. Nationalists, many ignorant of European affairs, could cheer on recruits with influential Catholic Church figures who threw their weight behind Redmond's call (though opinion was not unanimous within the Church); fear of German invasion was also paramount (German butcher shops in Dublin were attacked in the autumn of 1914).[49] The overwhelming support for the war that existed in nationalist Ireland at the outset dissipated, but the ties between that war and future Irish republicans were manifold. As pointed out by Deirdre McMahon:

Many of those who fought in the War of Independence and on the republican side in the civil war had close connections with the First World War. Jack Hunt, who won the DSO at Guinchy in 1916, later joined the IRA as did Emmet Dalton and Tom Barry. Emmet Dalton's younger brother Charles, later a close associate of Michael Collins, started his career in the IRA with a revolver his brother Emmet had brought back from France ... Erskine Childers, his cousin Robert Barton and their friend David Robinson, all from Anglo-Irish backgrounds, served in the British army during the Great War and took the republican side in the Civil War in 1922. Ernie O'Malley, author of two of the finest books about the 1916–23 period ... had a brother in the Dublin Fusiliers, was fascinated by armies and military manuals, and was planning to join up when the 1916 Rising impelled him to change course and join the IRA. These complex ties and allegiances, covering the First World War, the War of Independence and the Civil War, were repeated in hundreds of families.[50]

Irish survivors of First World War battles who became active in the IRA were matter of fact about this; Denis Dwyer, an IRA lieutenant in Cork from 1919–21, who fought in the Battle of the Somme, recalled in relation to guerrilla war in Cork: 'Were it not for my former battle experience it is very doubtful if I would have lived to tell the tale.'[51] John Riordan, a training officer with the IRA in Waterford, who fought with the British army in Mons and Ypres, noted that his IRA brigade commander 'decided that I should be attached to the Brigade staff probably because of my training with the British army'.[52]

In July 1914, when the Dublin battalion of the Irish Volunteers smuggled 900 German Mauser rifles into Howth in Dublin (the following week, more rifles were landed at Kilcoole in County Wicklow, and as a result of the Howth and Kilcoole escapades, a total of 1,500 rifles were landed with 45,000 rounds of ammunition), one of the victims of a shooting in Dublin later that day by British soldiers was Mary Duffy, a fifty-six-year-old widow with a son in the Royal Dublin Fusiliers. The other two who died the same day were Patrick Quinn, a coal porter and father of six, and James Brennan, a seventeen-year-old messenger boy. The funerals of the victims attracted massive crowds. The funeral procession was headed by Volunteers equipped with their new guns; it was a remarkable display of unity from nationalist Ireland and included Lorcan Sherlock, the Lord Mayor of Dublin, trade unionists, students, Christian Brothers and members of Cumann na mBan.

While all this gunrunning was partly just tactical and symbolic, it raised troubling questions about the precariousness of constitutional politics and the gulf between moderate nationalists and the more militant. As a result of the UVF and Irish Volunteers' initiatives there was now a significant presence of arms in Ireland. Although many of them were old – the Mauser was the first cartridge rifle adopted by the Prussian army in 1872 but by 1914 had been superseded by the 1898 Mauser Gewehr rifle – gunrunners were not too concerned about that; Darrell Figgis, one of the organisers of the Howth gunrunning, described the older guns as 'ideal for our purpose, cheap and undeniably effective'.[53] The First World War also 'presented a suitably violent model for political action and defined the moment when that action was likely to occur'.[54] Stephen Gwynn, a serving British army officer and Nationalist MP, made the point that the heroism of the Irish soldiers in the trenches was too abstract – and was demeaned as involving materialistic 'corner boys', 'slavelings' and 'wastrels' by the IRB's *Irish Freedom* – in contrast to those who ended up staging a rebellion in Dublin at Easter 1916 which 'offered to Irishmen a stage for themselves'.[55]

FOURTEEN

1916: AN IDEA 'ESSENTIALLY SPIRITUAL'?

Before that stage was ready, deception, secrecy and infiltration of the Volunteers by the IRB played important roles in the organisation of the Rising, as did extraordinary idealism, if not delusion. In 1967, F. X. Martin suggested the weakness of the Rising was ultimately its strength: 'It was imaginatively planned with artistic vision and with exceptional military incompetence. The revolt was staged consciously as a drama by its principal actors.'[1] The core strategists were 'a minority of the minority'.[2] IRB treasurer Thomas Clarke and secretary Seán MacDiarmada, active organiser for Sinn Féin and manager of *Irish Freedom*, fomented the plans for a rebellion, and they persuaded others, including Éamonn Ceannt, an Irish language enthusiast, employee of Dublin Corporation and devout Catholic, the increasingly militant educationalist and language activist Patrick Pearse, and eventually James Connolly, the socialist leader with a profound intellect, that the First World War gave them an opportunity, owing to England's obvious preoccupations elsewhere. In the summer of 1915 they established a military council of the IRB to secretly plan a rising.

They were not necessarily preparing for failure, but those who eventually became involved in the events of 1916 did not all think alike or share the same philosophies, which is why there was so much confusion in the lead-up to the Rising. Despite the postponement of the implementation of home rule due to the war (the Home Rule Act of 1914 followed the passing of the Home Rule Bill in 1912 but was parked under the Suspensory

Act to delay its promulgation into law), Eoin MacNeill, as chief of staff of the Irish Volunteers, though not a pacifist, did not believe a Volunteer uprising was feasible or justified, as it would lead to suppression of the organisation and abandonment of home rule. His logic, as enunciated in February 1916, was clear; the only justification for rebellion would be 'deep and widespread popular discontent', but 'no such condition exists in Ireland'. He also insisted that 'what we call our country is not a poetical abstraction ... it is our duty to get our country on side and not be content with the vanity of thinking ourselves to be right and other Irish people to be wrong'.[3]

Following a visit to MacNeill on 23 April 1916, Thomas MacDonagh, who himself had been informed relatively late in the day about the rebels' plans but whose involvement was vital as he was Dublin Brigade commandant of the Volunteers and co-opted in April 1916 to the IRB's secret military council, left a statement pointedly describing MacNeill as an 'honest and sincere patriot'. MacDonagh was a UCD colleague and something of a go-between connecting MacNeill and the conspirators; he was perhaps also feeling guilty because of his lies to MacNeill.[4] Patrick McCartan, another member of the IRB supreme council, acknowledged in June that MacNeill's actions had weakened the Rising but maintained 'I think he is to be pitied most of all because he is so misunderstood.'[5]

MacNeill also did not believe a Rising was justified unless there was an attempt to disarm the Volunteers, or significant help was forthcoming from outside Ireland. And just how likely was that? The judgement of F. S. L. Lyons was that Germans, while at war with Britain, were still likely to regard Ireland as 'a remote and improbable sideshow in which it would be folly to make a major investment of men and materials at a critical moment in the war'.[6] In the 1916 Proclamation, unveiled at the outset of the Rising, the reference to the support of 'gallant allies in Europe' was understandable in light of the promised guns from Germany, even if they were not to transpire. But at his trial after the Rising, Pearse also exposed that for the propaganda it was when emphasising 'Germany is no more to me than England is'. To him 'German domination was as odious as British'.[7] Roger Casement, one of the great humanitarians of his age owing to his work in the British diplomatic service to expose the barbaric treatment and exploitation of natives in the Congo and Amazon by European imperial powers, despite being knighted in 1911, devoted himself to Irish republican endeavour and attempted to recruit an Irish brigade from prisoners of war in Germany to fight against the British Empire. He was arrested after landing from a German submarine on the Irish coast, on his way to persuade those organising the 1916 Rising to hold off until more support could be arranged. His German brigade only amounted to a pathetic fifty-six men, a desultory return given that in November 1914, 2,486 Irish soldiers had been separated from British soldiers and transferred to Limburg. The volunteers never saw action against the British army, while Germany sent the SS *Aud* to bring 20,000 rifles (mostly captured from Russians) to Ireland for the Rising. It was scuttled.

MacNeill was obviously conscious that public opinion would not be in favour of an unprovoked rebellion, but most of the leaders of the Rising were not concerned with public opinion. *Irish War News*, issued the day after the Rising began, included the clearly propagandist statement from the newly declared President of the Irish Republic, Patrick Pearse: 'The population of Dublin are plainly with the Republic and the officers and men are everywhere.'[8] Robert Lynd made the point in 1917 that James Connolly, leader of the Irish Citizen Army, believed it was necessary to align the labour and republican movements because in looking at Irish history, 'he saw insurrection following insurrection apparently in vain, like wave following wave, but he still had faith in the hour when the tide would be full'.[9] In that sense, it was a certain mood of despair mixed with vague optimism within Irish republicanism and socialism that prompted the manoeuvres of Easter Monday. William O'Brien commented on the hostility that existed between the Irish Volunteers and the ICA before Connolly took charge of the latter in October 1914. O'Brien estimated the Citizen Army had only 339 members on its register by Easter Week, and 'some of these only joined a short time before'.[10]

As John Horne has argued, the First World War

> crystallised a deep pessimism in Connolly about the revolutionary possibilities of Labour ... Connolly rejected the war on the grounds of both class and nation, but this should not disguise how deeply his response was formed by it. Those who rejected the war (the Bolsheviks on grounds of class, the Irish revolutionaries of 1916 on the grounds of nation) incorporated much of the war (including its ideological and military violence) into their own projects ... the war itself, though Connolly would not have agreed, was one source of the violent mythologies that consecrated the new cultural and political orders it

produced. In this sense Connolly – and Ireland – were not peripheral and opposed to the Great Divide but stood at its heart.[11]

The original plan was to mobilise the volunteers on Easter Sunday and then inform them a rising was about to take place. The idea was that this would be a nationwide rebellion, not just confined to Dublin. On Holy Thursday, when they had got wind of the secret plans, IRB member Bulmer Hobson and MacNeill confronted Pearse in his capacity as director of military organisation for the Volunteers. Pearse convinced them military aid was imminent from Germany, as was suppression of the Volunteers by the government. MacNeill relented, but the rebels' plans subsequently collapsed. MacNeill discovered that the document purporting to provide evidence that the suppression of the Volunteers was imminent was a forgery. He countermanded the order for the Volunteers to mobilise – 'if he was astonished to find that a group of his colleagues ... could systematically deceive him, they were no less astounded to discover his power of decision in the hour of crisis'[12] – and the British authorities decided to wait until after the Easter holiday to round up the suspects. The chief secretary, Augustine Birrell, was in London for the holiday, as was army commander Major General L. B. Friend, satisfied that Casement's arrest would halt any planned rising.

The Crime Department Special Branch of the RIC had been keeping tabs on secret societies in Dublin in late 1915 and early 1916, detailing the moves of those they considered as holding 'very extreme political views'.[13] Notes from the Detective Department give details of the infiltration of the Volunteers by two British agents, 'Chalk' and 'Granite', and two days before the Rising Thomas MacDonagh was quoted in one report about the Volunteers mobilising on Easter Sunday: 'Boys, some of us may never come back.' There were also reports on 7 April of ammunition being moved around Dublin and 'rifles secreted at the residence of E. De Valera' in Donnybrook (de Valera was a battalion commandant during the Rising).[14] The month before the Rising, correspondence from the Detective Department, based on the infiltration reports, stated:

Granite adds that there is at present no fear of any Rising by the Volunteers – standing alone they are not prepared for any prolonged encounter with the forces of the Crown and the majority of them are practically untrained. In addition they are not sufficiently equipped for any such engagement and except that a favourable opportunity presented itself, they would not be of any much account in a general campaign against the law.

A week earlier 'Chalk' had written that 'the heads of the Irish Volunteers are against a Rising at present. McDonagh said it would be sheer madness to attempt such a thing if the help promised by Montieth [Robert Montieth, who had been sent by Tom Clarke to Germany to assist and monitor Casement] was not forthcoming'.[15] In March 1916 intelligence given to the British government suggested the number of Irish Volunteers was only 4,618 with 3,941 rifles and shotguns.[16]

On Easter Monday, 24 April, the rebels, numbering about 700 (they were joined by others during the week, bringing the numbers up to roughly 1,500) decided to mobilise. The sense of confusion and bewilderment created by MacNeill's decision to countermand the order given to the Volunteers to assemble on Easter Sunday was later recalled by many. Some felt in the loop; others outside. According to Christopher Brady, a printer on the staff of the *Workers' Republic* who printed the '2,500 copies' of the 1916 Proclamation, Markievicz arrived into the machine room with MacNeill's countermanding telegram announcing 'I will shoot Eoin MacNeill', to which he recalled James Connolly replying: 'You are not going to hurt a hair on McNeill's head. If anything happens to MacNeill I will hold you responsible.'[17] Paddy Browne, a member of the staff at Maynooth College, recalled, 'I had not the slightest notion that anything was going to happen, I did not know anything about dispatches going around the country,' whereas Min Ryan, who was at the centre of the fighting during the Rising, remembered 'a sort of seething undercurrent' of anticipation.[18] The account of James Cullen, an Irish Volunteer captain in Enniscorthy, was typical:

> On Tuesday and Wednesday rumours of all kind were circulating. Some said the Volunteers were sweeping the country, others that it was only the Citizen Army that had risen and that the Rising had been suppressed ... in the absence of any definite or authentic information it was very difficult to decide what to do ... commandant Gilligan, who had gone to Dublin on Good Friday, arrived back in Enniscorthy late on Wednesday night. He had cycled all the way from Dublin.

Gilligan persuaded them to stage their own rising, which was short-lived and resulted in him and others 'being put on a cattle boat in the North Wall and taken to Holyhead'.[19]

The Dublin rebels began their operations by seizing prominent city-centre buildings, including Boland's Mill, the South Dublin Union and Jacob's biscuit factory; Dublin Castle was not captured, but the first vic-tim of the Rising was Constable James O'Brien from Limerick who was guarding the castle and unarmed. He was shot by Seán Connolly, a mem-ber of the ICA who was killed an hour later by a British army sniper. The rebels took over the General Post Office (GPO) as headquarters, outside of which Pearse read the Proclamation. It had been printed in Liberty Hall the day before, and was a declaration from the provisional government of the Irish Republic to the people of Ireland: 'In the name of God and of the dead generations from which she receives her old tradition of nationhood, Ireland, through us, summons her children to her flag and strikes for her freedom.' The Proclamation was signed by Pearse, Seán MacDiarmada, Thomas MacDonagh, Joseph Mary Plunkett, Thomas Clarke, Éamonn Ceannt and James Connolly. Regarding the authorship of the Proclam-ation, Christopher Brady insisted: 'It certainly was not Connolly's as I was familiar with his scrawl.'[20] Whatever about the presence of his scrawl, his influence was certainly apparent in some of the references ('The Republic guarantees religious and civil liberty, equal rights and equal opportunities to all its citizens'), the commitment to universal suffrage and to 'cherishing all of the children of the nation equally'. But Pearse's influence, through his exaltations and war propaganda, was even more obvious ('supported by her exiled children in America and by gallant allies in Europe, but rely-ing first on her own strength, she strikes in full confidence of victory ... in this supreme hour the Irish nation must, by its valour and discipline, and by the readiness of its children to sacrifice themselves for the common good, prove itself worthy of the august destiny to which it is called').[21]

As the rebels had failed to capture Dublin Castle they opted for the adjacent City Hall instead, and members of the ICA positioned themselves in St Stephen's Green. A battalion of rebels occupied the Four Courts, and the rebels also seized Jameson's Distillery on Marrowbone Lane. The shortage of numbers meant the only significant outposts were at Westland Row Station and Mount Street Bridge. On Tuesday, government troops from Belfast and the Curragh, numbering some 3,000, arrived in the city (Crown forces would number about 16,000 by the end of the week) and retook City Hall and St Stephen's Green. On Wednesday, the empty Liberty Hall was shelled, British troops continued to land at Kingstown (Dún Laoghaire), while General Sir John Maxwell was dispatched from London to deal with the fallout, and a battle at Mount Street Bridge raged all day. Irish soldiers in the British army were also involved in fighting the rebels, including members of the Royal Fusiliers and Royal Irish Regiment; some were home on leave at the time the Rising began. Gerald O'Sullivan, an Irish member of the Royal Navy, wrote to his father a few weeks later that, on hearing of the Rising,

> I was worried and restless ... but I will not waste time in dogmatising on such madness ... it would seem as if the temple of glory built by our brave Irish regiments had been pulled down by their own kindred. In a paper that Maggie sent me I notice the name and address of Dot's brother as one of the rebels deported. I wonder what his own brother Jack will say when he hears the news at the Front. That half-demented, crazy, misguided fool ... Patriotism! My God! And he knows as much about Irish history as a Fiji cannibal.[22]

Despite the confusion about MacNeill's countermand, the efforts of 'bands of rebels' outside Dublin should not be dismissed, as they were enough to justify martial law being extended across the country. The BMH statements also reveal some of the immediate reactions to the surrender, such as the recollection that Major John MacBride advised the Jacob's factory battalion, 'if it ever happens again, take my advice and don't get inside four walls'.[23] This touched on but one of the military failures of the rising. Undoubtedly, the rebels could have made things more difficult for the British army if they had not centralised their forces, but they also failed to seal Dublin off from outside communication.

Looting, disruption of travel, food shortages and the destruction of buildings and commercial premises such as Clery's department store and the Imperial Hotel, added to the drama, tension and confusion that pervaded Dublin city during the week. The story of the rising, its participants, victims and opponents is now a much more textured one thanks to the variety of material that has been uncovered about the individual and collective experience. Who would have thought, for example, that buying a stamp in the GPO on Easter Monday could have had such consequences? An off-duty soldier was taken prisoner when doing precisely that: for the staff inside it was a working day, and some did their utmost to resist and communicate what was happening. A service message routed from Dublin via a telegraph relay station in Wales gave the first news of the Rising: 'Volunteers have taken possession of telegraph office ... and all lines stopped in consequence'; a little later there was another message: 'GPO Dublin taken possession of today at noon by Sinn Féiners',[24] under-lining the degree to which for some, Sinn Féin and the Volunteers were one and the same or interchangeable, even though Sinn Féin did not plan or orchestrate the rebellion.

The quick establishment of a communications link through Amiens Street Railway Telegraph Office by the Post Office's Engineering and Tele-graph staff was 'vital to the government' in establishing a line between Dublin and London. Rebels failed to capture the Crown Alley telephone exchange and there was praise for the 'plucky' telephonists under fire there. The secretary of the Irish Post Office, Arthur Hamilton Norway, who later penned a memoir about the week (for, it seemed, private circulation) was generous in his praise of them. He was also critical of the British govern-ment for taking its eye off the ball: 'everyone believed that the point was off the Irish pikes and the gunmen had forgotten how to shoot'.[25] One engineer employed by the PO since 1907 was Richard Mulcahy of the third battalion of the Dublin Brigade of the Volunteers, and future IRA chief of staff, who managed to cut the telephone and telegraph lines in north Dublin to Belfast and Britain.

Less dramatic was the determination of others to pursue business as usual: 'Michael Patchell, an assistant inspector of postmen, rescued the keys of some 1400 Dublin and suburban collection boxes from the ruins of the GPO and, by filing away the molten glass and brass that had stuck between the wards of the keys, enabled collections to resume within 36 hours.'[26]

In relation to the drama outside Dublin, there was upheaval in Wex-ford, where 600 volunteers seized Enniscorthy, and an attempted uprising in Galway, where the rank and file of the Irish Volunteers were made up, 'not of the "rabble" and the corner boys of the city, but of "plain men" of both the towns and the countryside, comprising small farmers and their sons, labourers, tradesmen, artisans, clerks and shop assistants'; according to British intelligence notes there were 530 suspected rebels in Galway.[27] One English visitor residing in the Railway Hotel in Galway during Easter Week found himself cut off and turned to writing bad poetry:

Instead of thirst, we'd plenty to drink
Of excellent Guinness coloured like ink
And while many a drink is left unsaid
We really had not very much to fear
From the rebels and that rebellion here[28]

Undoubtedly, there were worse ways to experience an Irish rebellion.

As the assault on the GPO continued, James Connolly was wounded on Thursday, and the following day General Maxwell arrived and declared that he would take 'the most vigorous' measures necessary to defeat the rebels. On Friday night the decision was taken to evacuate the GPO. Five of the seven signatories of the Proclamation – Pearse, Connolly, Plunkett, Clarke and MacDiarmada – retreated to a house on 16 Moore Street. At noon the following day Pearse decided on a ceasefire, his message carried to the British by Nurse Elizabeth O'Farrell. The rebels, however, were informed that the only acceptable conclusion to the Rising was unconditional surrender, after which Pearse surrendered, in his own words, 'in order to prevent further slaughter of the civil population and in the hope of saving the lives of our followers'. The trade unionist William O'Brien maintained that afterwards, when the insurgents were rounded up in Richmond Barracks, de Valera 'said he was glad that he had no responsibility for deciding anything and that he simply obeyed orders given to him'.[29]

Garrisons at Boland's Mill, Jacob's, the South Dublin Union and Marrowbone Lane surrendered the following day, after which they were marched to Richmond Barracks, enduring abuse from some Dubliners, which was hardly surprising. The figures for casualties reveal clearly that it was Dublin civilians who bore the brunt of the suffering during the week; 256 of them were killed, including 40 children, while 62 rebels and 132 members of government forces perished.[30] More than 200 buildings had been damaged and the cost of the destruction was later estimated at over £2.5 million. Military forces, too many of them drunk, caused more civilian deaths than the rebels; they were effectively given free rein in doing so. General William Lowe, general officer commanding the British troops, issued an order that if firing came from a house 'every man in such a house whether bearing arms or not, may be considered a rebel'.[31]

What did it mean to those involved? Is it possible to capture the 'authentic voice' of the rebel in 1916? Helena Molony found herself in the battle zone, 'carving, carving' the abundant food that seemed to exist for the fighters, who at least fought the British Empire on full stomachs. But their nominal commander-in-chief, Patrick Pearse, was shooting nothing except the breeze. According to Min Ryan, 'Pearse spent most of his time in the front part of the Post Office ... on one of the high stools, and people would come and talk to him'.[32] The role of women was commented on by contemporaries, although the extent to which they were basing their accounts on rumour rather than reality is debatable. A Kerry neighbour of Kathleen O'Connell, later Éamon de Valera's personal secretary, wrote to her six weeks after the Rising: 'Curiously enough, there appears to have been a large number of Irish girls involved in the rebellion. They fought with the men, many of them sniping away with rifles and doing serious damage by all accounts.'[33]

It is clear that not all participants were consumed by debates or thoughts about ideology or notions of the continuity of the republican struggle that they supposedly embodied; although many joined because they regarded the continued Anglicisation of Ireland as retrograde and akin to slavery, some were more focused on their pleasure and pride in looking 'swank' in their new Volunteer uniforms, and being able to hold weapons for the first time made them feel authentic and like 'the real thing'.[34] But other Volunteers were unflinching in their accounts of the casualties. Joe Good, for example, was attempting in the dark to find a teenage girl in a slum: 'He thought he put his fingers into her mouth as he thought he had felt her teeth, but when he struck a match, he found that it was through a hole in her skull he had put his fingers.'[35]

The battle of the Marrowbone Lane Distillery was recalled in great detail by Robert Holland from Inchicore, whose nineteenth birthday fell on the second day of the Rising. After the surrender, native Dubliners jeered the rebels, and 'the British troops saved us from manhandling ... I was very glad as I walked in the gate of Richmond barracks'. This is a statement which resonates with much hurt: 'Little did we think that the Dublin citizens would ever go so far as to cheer British regiments because they had as prisoners their own fellow citizens – Irishmen and Irishwomen – just as they were.'[36] As is equally clear from other recollections, rebels were not initially popular; some who survived recalled being attacked by the 'rabble' of poor exclaiming hostility and threatening them with violence. One Volunteer recalled 'a very fat dame in spotless white apron and voluminous shawl leapt in front of us and, beating her ample bosom with clenched fists, called on me to "put it through me now for me son who's out in France".[37] But there was also pride. In the words of Máire Nic Shiubhlaigh, who was in Jacob's factory:

> You never thought much of what the result of it all would be. You never assumed that victory was certain, but neither did you think of defeat. What might happen if we lost meant nothing; life or death, freedom or imprisonment, these things did not enter it at all. The great thing was that what you had hoped for at last had happened. An insurrection had taken place and you were actually participating in it.[38]

Parts of the country that were not mobilised in 1916 were nonetheless to be important in the aftermath of the Rising; in Limerick, for example, the Volunteers had neither the numbers nor the arms to rise and the older of them advised caution: 'the six members of the local leadership who wanted to commence hostilities on 25 April were younger and less cautious than their 10 colleagues who outvoted them'.[39] Initial accounts of the Rising to emerge in the Limerick press exaggerated the German link and the number of civilian casualties, but what was influential was the role of the local bishop, Thomas O'Doherty, whom both the British government and the RIC came to see as a danger owing to his public pronouncements. He praised the rebels for the 'purity and nobility of their motives' and their courage and decried Maxwell as a wanton, military dictator. O'Doherty had regarded Redmond's backing of the war effort as a betrayal and was a public subscriber to a fund for the Volunteers' dependants; he was, it seemed, in the Rising's aftermath, assuming the role of 'moral leader' of the nationalist opposition.[40]

But O'Doherty's peers did not share his certainty at the time of the Rising; the insurrection presented the Catholic Church with its own problems, including fears of loss of allegiance and discipline. Leslie Price stated that at the time of the Rising in 1916 Fr Michael O'Flanagan, later vice president of Sinn Féin, had remarked to her of the fighters in the General Post Office: 'let these people burn to death, they are murderers'; he later relented and agreed to travel across the city to assist with the injured. Price was disgusted that when she and O'Flanagan were on their way to the GPO and they passed a drunken tramp who had been shot: 'the priest did not stop for him', but did give absolution to another wounded man. 'You see the difference,' she wrote, 'here he knew a man who was respectable ... I said to Fr O'Flanagan, "Isn't it extraordinary you did not kneel beside the other man?"[41]

Class and respectability were not the only factors in determining the Catholic Church's attitude to the insurrection. The statement of Fr Thomas Duggan, secretary to Bishop Daniel Cohalan of Cork, is illuminating in this regard. Many in the Church, and indeed in the republican movement, saw no contradiction in supporting Irish republicans and simultaneously administering to wounded Irish soldiers in the British army:

> My generation in Maynooth embraced the ideals of Easter Week 1916 with a hundred percent fervour. That did not prevent us from becoming Chaplains in the British Army. In the First World War there were well over 100,000 Irish Catholics in the fighting ranks ... everyone admitted that these boys were spiritually intractable to anyone save to an Irish priest. Hence, when in 1917 Cardinal Logue issued a special appeal for Irish Chaplains I volunteered. And I went off to France with the blessing and encouragement of every friend I had in advanced Sinn Féin circles in Dublin.[42]

Fearghal McGarry has concluded that 'the complexities and uncertainties of this period of history, as illustrated by the conflicting views of those who experienced it, should defy the condescending certainty with which hindsight is deployed to endorse or condemn one side or the other'.[43]

But for propagandist reasons, some of the participants and their champions sought to narrowly frame their motives as essentially religious, or as Florence O'Donoghue was later to express it, 1916 'was the expression in action of an idea essentially spiritual'.[44] Aodh de Blácam, Sinn Féin propagandist during the War of Independence was also fond of this mode of interpretation; politics and constitutions were 'poor things' if there were no meaningful objectives underpinning them and no real idealists framing them: 'The strength of Ireland is the spirituality of her ideal.'[45]

FIFTEEN

THE PERFECT PATRIOTS

In the aftermath, however, it was the scale of the arrests and executions that were to have the most profound impact. Roughly 3,500 people were arrested and although many of them were quickly released, in the region of 2,000 were interned, with detainees deported to Welsh, English and Scottish prisons. The long drawn-out executions of the seven signatories of the Proclamation and nine others (including Roger Casement, executed in London for high treason) did much to change public opinion. One of those executed was Thomas Kent, executed for shooting an RIC man in Cork.

The executions began on 3 May and did not end until 12 May. John Redmond, as leader of the IPP, was well aware of the consequences the executions could have. After the first three men – Pearse, Clarke and MacDonagh – were executed in the stonebreaker's yard at Kilmainham jail, he warned the British prime minister, Herbert Asquith, 'If any more executions take place in Ireland, the position will become impossible for any constitutional party or leader.' The desperate and failed attempts by Wimborne, the viceroy, to prevent more executions, 'pointed up just how completely the civil government in Ireland had been superseded by the military'.[1] Redmond's colleague John Dillon, who was in Dublin during the Rising and characterised it as 'a clean fight, a brave fight, however misguided', was even more forceful in reacting to the executions: 'you are washing out our whole life-work in a sea of blood'.[2] But for Redmond's critics, his failing was that he was aware too late; a year before the Rising, a publication by the Irish Volunteers invoking the ghost of Robert Emmet, who led a failed republican rebellion in 1803, was authored by an Irish nationalist who had lived for many years in England, 'and I have tried the experiment of viewing Ireland from the House of Commons; and it is like looking through the wrong end of a telescope'. Such was the 'tragic failure of a foreign-spirited leader', John Redmond, in contrast to the 'perfect patriots' of 1798, 1803, 1848 and 1867.[3]

Drawing out the executions in this way was unwise and counterproductive; Robert Kee in 1972 referred to one woman who was heard to say that because of the way the executions were handled, some people began to feel they were 'watching a stream of blood coming from beneath a closed door'.[4] Cahir Davitt recalled in his BMH statement, with admirable honesty, the pendulum of emotions and confusion; the Rising

> appeared to me to be tragically insane. After a severe examination of conscience, I did not feel myself bound to participate and had no inclination to do so. At the same time I felt like a deserter and was miserably unhappy. During the course of the week, wonder at their insanity gave way to admiration for their courage and pride in the fight they made. Then came anxiety and apprehension as to their fate and eventually grief and futile indignation at the executions.[5]

But the response was not harsh enough for critics of republicans (and indeed the failures of Dublin Castle); Frederic Pim, a businessman, pamphleteer and chairman of the board of the Dublin, Wicklow and Wexford Railway Company, writing a month after the executions, cited the case of the Commune of Paris in 1871: 'If we compare Sir John Maxwell's methods with those of M. Thiers, we shall, I think, see reason to admire the clemency and moderation with which this outbreak, the most dangerous that has occurred in the UK since 1798, has been dealt with.'[6]

The aftermath also held out the prospect of destitution for those affected; Grace Gifford, a cartoonist and illustrator, for example, was penniless after the execution of her husband Joseph Plunkett and a year after the Rising, in one of the most bleak lines from any archive concerning the revolution, wrote: 'I think my having to go into the workhouse on the anniversary of my husband's sacrifice and my own will hardly fail to shock.'[7] The tragedy and pathos of the Plunketts – they married hours before his execution in the chapel of Kilmainham jail and were separated immediately after – may have made some contribution to increasing sympathy for the rebels, but clearly it did not put food on the table.

There was a prolonged quest by business interests for compensation in the aftermath of the Rising; Arnott's department store, for example, sought £47,000. A compensation commission chaired by the chairman of the Great Southern and Western Railway Company, who had close business associations with many of the claimants, awarded a total of £1 million. Underlining the class divides, Pádraig Yeates points out that 'the families of civilians killed in the fighting did not fare nearly so well as big business'. There were only 450 claims from them as opposed to more than 820 from property owners. Many of the families were put through a demeaning bureaucratic wrangle to prove they were destitute; a two-year-old whose leg was amputated after she was shot was eventually offered a paltry £100 (about £10,000 in today's terms).[8]

The prison experience was also to be a formative one for many and offered some of them time to enhance their studies; Sean T. O'Kelly wrote to James Ryan, medical officer to the GPO garrison, regarding his studies that he was 'glad to see you were turning your enforced idleness to such good account'.[9] Although there is plenty of evidence of hostility shown towards the departing rebels, Ryan maintained that he 'got a great send off – all the girls went down to wave us a fond goodbye and blew kisses after us. I quite enjoyed it,' though the boat to England was not so pleasant, 'amongst the cattle, the boxes of dead fish. Oh Lord ...'[10] A new status for the rebels developed which also added to their attraction to women; Ryan was informed 'you have all become great heroes now' and, regarding the conversion on the part of university students: 'you never saw such wholesale conversion. There are not half a dozen people in the college [UCD] who are not Sinn Féiners ... I for one want a souvenir of the Rising ... the very least of us would not be bothered with these that are left. An ordinary "beardless boy" has no attraction for us now.'[11] Martial law lasted until early November, and on 22 December most internees in Britain were released.

Women devoted an extraordinary effort to the relief of 1916 dependants after the Rising; Nancy Wyse Power suggested 'during the summer of 1916 there was little Cumann na mBan activity outside of the National Aid Association which was established within a few weeks of the suppression of the Rising'.[12] The amnesty campaign was also central to their contribution and they were critics of the conditions in Mountjoy and

Kilmainham jails and gave much publicity to this through pamphlets and articles and Easter week mementoes. Margaret Ward has argued that their efforts were essential to ensuring that by the time the first prisoners were released in 1916 they had 'to their great amazement, become heroes'.[13] Widows and mothers of the fallen in 1916 also became important, symbolically and politically.[14]

For individual Volunteers who had survived the Rising there were serious implications for their livelihood and future and it was particularly stark for those in government employment. Hugh O'Hehir, for example, an assistant clerk in the Irish Land Commission, was arrested after the Rising and spent a week in Frongoch; he was acquitted by the advisory committee set up to examine these cases but he was not permitted to return to work and he complained of 'animus against us on the part of the Land Commission authorities which may prejudice our cases'. According to a report of the Dublin Metropolitan Police (DMP) on Robert Rooney, another Land Commission employee, all the evidence they had against him were some 'SF newspapers'; the instruction was to 'reinstate'. In all, twelve members of staff of the Land Commission were arrested.[15]

Some Post Office staff who were suspects were being watched for quite some time afterwards. The Lord Lieutenant wrote to the secretary of the GPO at the end of 1918, noting that all of those listed had kept their undertakings, with the exception of Andrew Travers, a telegraph messenger:

> As regards Travers however, it appears that on the night of 11th November a crowd of persons paraded thru' village of Ballintra to celebrate the cessation of hostilities and during the passage of an orange band the police heard opposition cries from an archway – 'up the Irish Republic' – being made use of several times. On reaching the place where the shouting proceeded from the police found Travers in postal uniform, with 2 others, standing in the archway. Later on when an opposition party paraded the street, Travers was conspicuous in this party and was recognised with others singing The Soldier's Song [composed in 1912 and adopted by the Irish Volunteers as their marching tune, it had the status of a national anthem after 1916].[16]

Mothers wrote letters of desperation to the Chief Secretary's Office seeking clemency or leniency. Mary Byrne from Terenure in Dublin, for example, pleaded for her three sons:

As my three boys, Patrick, Frances and James have been arrested and deported to England I beg to appeal to your sense of justice and mercy as I am a widow and now penniless having nothing but the workhouse staring at me in the face unless these boys are released soon. I know that they did not understand what they were going out for on Easter Monday ... they were informed they were wanted to go for a march to Glencullen and I went to the trouble to get a lunch made up for them, along with a bottle of milk and expected them back to dinner about 6 O'Clock.

All three were GPO employees: a carpenter, inspector of telephones and compositor. The three – hardly boys – were in Knutsford prison and their own responses as recorded in their forms differed. The youngest, James (aged twenty-two), responded: 'I was not fully aware that I was going out on active service'; Francis (twenty-six) 'did not fire a shot. I was not fully aware of any active service' while the eldest, Patrick (thirty), was unrepentant: 'no claim for release whatsoever except as soldiers. I was on the defensive for 7 days. I was always prepared.'[17]

David de Loughery, a post office clerk in Kilkenny, it was noted in 1914, 'resides with his brother Peter who is an extreme Sinn Féiner', but David 'does not take any active part, outwardly at any rate, in politics and is regarded as a respectable young man'. But a further memorandum, two years later in July 1916, recorded that he was now

observed in the company of advanced Sinn Féiners and there is hardly any doubt that his sympathy is strongly with them. He has subscribed 10/– towards a fund which has been started by the editor of Kilkenny People for the dependants of the prisoners who were arrested in Kilkenny. I do not think this man ought to be retained in government service.[18]

Another memorandum from a detective sergeant in Dublin referred to W. Archer, a sorting clerk who did not turn up for work on Easter Monday: 'he is at present a patient in the Richmond hospital and has had the second largest toe of the right foot amputated'. He told the authorities he was shot 'out of the blue ... I was only rambling about the city, sight seeing'. It was noted that his family were 'bosom friends of notorious rebels ... it is rather strange that he should be sight seeing in Church Street going towards the Four Courts at such an early hour on this particular date given it was a lively centre of the disturbances.'[19]

The Rising's aftermath fuelled an array of publications and no shortage of kitsch propaganda as well as thunderous denunciations that 'the hooligan element of the population were left in possession of the city'.[20] A different tone, understandably, was struck in the publications of the Irish National Aid and Volunteers Dependants Fund, including their 1917 publication *Aftermath of Easter Week*, which exclaimed 'the nation's life has been purified and renewed, and, among other things the national literature has experienced a new impetus and inspiration'. It published poems that had been written for the benefit of the fund, inviting the public to respond, 'not so much for the sake of the poems themselves, as for the cause they are intended to help', which was probably just as well, given the verse on display. Fr Paddy Browne, for example, the Professor of Mathematics at St Patrick's College in Maynooth, was a close friend of Seán MacDiarmada, whom he had visited in Kilmainham jail on the two nights prior to his execution on 12 May 1916. Undoubtedly traumatised by this and other deaths, in the summer of 1916 Browne cycled alone to the West Kerry Gaeltacht, to reflect and find some solace, and obviously resolved to vindicate the sacrifices of the fallen republicans. In the process, he took a shine to himself as a poet; his tribute in verse to MacDiarmada included the lines

> Your pale and dead face with sure insistent calm
> Shall haunt my soul as long as thought endures
> Waking remembrance of your wasted frame
> Afire with that all-conquering soul of yours.[21]

Another publication, *The Sinn Féin Leaders of 1916*, which included lists of those injured, dead and deported, published by sympathisers, insisted 'the rebellion of 1916 abounded in romance of every kind' and also included a section called 'minor men': 'Take Patrick O'Flannagan, for example, of Hardwicke Street, who died in King Street, and left 3 children – himself only 24 years of age.' Rebellion souvenirs were also for sale on Grafton Street: 'Copies of *Irish War News*, only a few left. Five Guineas each.'[22] There were also abundant images published, including thirty-one quality photographs 'from the camera of T. W. Murphy, subeditor of *The Motor News*', which included the commentary that 'looting and

the destruction of business premises by fire was commenced by the mob'
and that property damage amounted to 'three million pounds sterling'.[23]
The Easons' publishing company also published a book of photographs
with, hardly surprisingly, as a member of the Dublin Protestant Business
community, an unsympathetic commentary; it referred to the Rising as
Dublin's 'black week' when 'the rebels and the hooligan element of the
population were left in possession of the city until the military authorities
brought up reinforcements'.[24]

The decisions that were made in the weeks following the Rising
ensured that in the long term, the Rising came to be seen as the starting point for all subsequent Irish history. It was claimed by many as the
founding act of a democratic Irish state, by others as a bloody conspiracy
of a minority ('the democrat and the theologian may question the means
they used')[25] that ushered in an era of unnecessary conflict, ultimately
achieving a twenty-six-county Free State in the early 1920s that could have
been gained peacefully. It was a momentous event that transformed the
focus of Irish nationalism, deepened political consciousness and created
its own mythology. Dublin writer James Stephens, who wrote an eyewitness account of the Rising, was insightful in suggesting at the time that
'Ireland was not with the revolution, but in a few months she will be, and
her heart which was withering will be warmed by the knowledge that men
have thought her worth dying for'.[26] The Rising also led to damning conclusions about the incompetence of British rule in Ireland, laid bare in the
report of the Royal Commission on the rebellion. Its compilers examined
twenty-nine witnesses and held nine meetings, five in London and four in
Dublin, and concluded that 'if the Irish system of government be regarded
as a whole it is anomalous in quiet times and almost unworkable in times
of crisis'. It highlighted that at the end of 1914 there were 8,000 Volunteers
drilling with 1,400 rifles: 'no opportunity should have been given for the
drilling'.[27] Countless warnings about a possible uprising had been ignored;
as early as September 1914 the RIC had warned that Irish republicans 'may
attempt some escapade before long' and ultimately, according to the commission's report, 'lawlessness was allowed to grow up unchecked' and law
was left 'in abeyance'. The chief secretary, Augustine Birrell, was deemed
to be 'primarily responsible', a responsibility he willingly accepted.[28] General Maxwell also expressed his views (though in private) on where the
blame lay: 'It is the government as a whole that are to blame, ever since
they winked at Ulster breaking the law they have been in difficulties.'[29]

Given Redmond's full-scale backing of a war that became increasingly unpopular in Ireland, the IPP was in grave trouble regardless of the Rising, but Redmond was also ruthlessly shafted in the summer of 1916 when Asquith sent David Lloyd George from the War Office to negotiate separately with unionists and the IPP, talks which lasted from May to July. Lloyd George, who in correspondence with his brother at this time complained of being immersed in 'the Irish bog', managed 'by a remarkable sleight of hand' and through deliberate ambiguity to persuade Redmond and Joseph Devlin that home rule would be granted during the war, and to get them to accept the exclusion of six, not four, Ulster counties from home rule 'on a temporary basis'. Asquith 'was bluffing', while Lloyd George was double-dealing, and deliberately vague about the duration of exclusion, and although the talks collapsed, the central issue around home rule was now partition; Fermanagh and Tyrone would be lost to nationalists as any proposed temporary arrangements were not likely to be reversed, and Lloyd George also had a tendency to discount southern unionists who were then furious with Redmond.[30]

Peter Hart suggests that the political upheavals of 1916–18 'mostly' grew out of the crises and circumstances left over from 1914 as generated by the war. Pearse's longed-for transformation in popular sentiment did not happen 'in the population at large but among the few thousand who actually made the revolution possible'.[31] What is indisputable is that it allowed the status of those involved to be elevated, gave the IRB more influence in the hierarchy of Sinn Féin, which benefited from an increased profile through the regular use of the description 'Sinn Féin rebellion' being applied to 1916, and ensured a steady flow of money from the US. The National Aid Association handled over £140,000 between 1916 and 1919. But this, of course, was not the full story regarding the legacy of the Rising. As Hart suggested, the Easter rebels and those who built on their efforts may have gained power and while 'they were quite right that the only way to get there was to use force ... they were very wrong in thinking that they could generate enough violence to overcome their political and military foes or that the people would back them all the way ... the Ireland of the 1916 Proclamation was far beyond the gunmen's reach.'[32]

SIXTEEN

1917–18: BONFIRES AND BALLOTS

How was the Irish Volunteer movement to rebuild itself in the wake of the Rising? General Maxwell had written to a colleague in September 1916: 'A strong effort is contemplated to bring the force into being again as a political factor. I hope we can stop it!'[1] They could not. The reception afforded to the release of the prisoners was a dramatic illustration of changed attitudes all over the country: in Kerry, for example, 'bonfires blazed' in Lispole and Dingle with 'huge crowds' to welcome home Thomas Ashe and other Kerry prisoners, 'accompanied by Austin Stack of Tralee'.[2] By February 1917 the reorganisation of the Volunteers had begun. Count Plunkett, the father of the executed Joseph Plunkett, won the North Roscommon by-election as an independent candidate supported by Sinn Féin; other by-election successes that year suggested the IPP was being beaten at its own game. In the summer of 1917 Sinn Féin also refused to participate in the Irish Convention – Lloyd George, now prime minister, suggested this as a way to negotiate a deal between unionists and nationalists in a series of meetings in TCD and the IPP was divided on its merits. At Sinn Féin's national convention in October, attended by 1,700 delegates, de Valera, who had been spared execution after the Rising (according to some accounts because of his American birth, according to others because his court martial had been delayed owing to uncertainty about whether he was a ringleader and in the meantime pressure was exerted on the British government to prevent any more executions)[3] and was now its sole surviving commandant, was elected president, replacing Arthur Griffith who became vice president. They pledged Sinn Féin to achieving a republic, with a promise that a referendum on the precise form of government would follow; a pragmatic temporary burying of the differences within the movement, but an attempted takeover of the IRB was less successful.

What did these developments mean for the constitutional nationalists and how did they cope with the post-Rising environment? The reports of the Crime Department Special Branch of the RIC give some idea, as they tracked and reported on the meetings of its constituency organisation, the United Irish League. It was quite clear that even in the run-up to the Rising the UIL was struggling, as a selection of the RIC reports indicate:

> Co Galway, 16 January 1916: a small meeting (120) without enthusiasm
> Meath, 19 March 1916: unimportant meeting of 84
> Frenchpark 19 March 1916: 200 attended, no enthusiasm[4]

Those who assembled after the Rising made clear their disapproval of what had occurred, but fewer meetings were permitted: just eleven were allowed in September 1917 including a very large one in Downpatrick with an estimated attendance of 2,000, at which 'speakers referred to the base ingratitude of the Sinn Féiners', while at Longford the local IPP MP 'spoke against Sinn Féin and said their capital was German gold'.[5]

In November 1917, J. P. Farrell MP was again vocal in Longford, where 300 were present and 'speakers pointed out the uselessness of the Sinn Féin policy and advised those present to stick to the green flag that got so many concessions for them during the past 40 years'. There was also a deliberate pitch for the youth, Farrell advising 'young men to keep away from Sinn Féin and its policy' and saying 'it was the Irish party saved them from conscription'.[6] A St Patrick's Day Meeting in 1918 heard from MPs and JPs: 'Speakers warned their hearers against being led away by young priests. 2 small Sinn Féin flags were torn down and burned.'[7] By the spring of 1919 in Ardara, Donegal, 540 were present and 'some free fighting between UIL party and Sinn Féiners took place which was quelled by the police'.[8] Meetings in the Ulster region could still attract big crowds: 2,200 were present in Carrickmacross, County Monaghan, in May 1919, when 'speakers criticised the SF policy and advocated the constitutional movement. Advised people to prepare for the next general election.'[9] But as the RIC recognised, especially in the west, Sinn Féin was also seen as a vehicle to advance demands for land distribution or 'as an agrarian movement for the forcible possession of lands ... This new phase of SF will bring many young men into the movement which had no attraction to them heretofore.'[10]

Tensions also abounded in relation to soldiers' wives, often referred to as the 'separation women'; there was much comment, public and private, on their behaviour and reports of their excessive drinking. One resident in Limerick suggested to the Secretary's Office of the Board of National Education: 'some of the wives of soldiers are living bad lives. Some soldiers' wives, though living well, get very excited against Sinn Féiners. I must say, in my experience, the Sinn Féiners are not those who provoke a quarrel.'[11] This was a reaction to a case in Limerick when one of the soldier's wives allegedly 'hissed and spat at an aged priest passing on the bicycle – evidently because he was wearing what are termed "republican" colours'. A witness, a teacher, responded to her, 'Well, I wonder what your convert husband thinks of you. Conduct like that would not go on, much less be tolerated, in the slums of London.' The wife allegedly replied, 'To hell with priests and to hell with religion.'[12]

John Flanagan, active in canvassing for Sinn Féin at the East Clare by-election in July 1917, which resulted in the election of de Valera, recounted strong anti-Sinn Féin sentiment in Ennis:

> The women were kept well plied with drink by a number of the publicans who were supporters of the Irish party and in their drunken condition they were a frenzied and ferocious crowd to deal with. On a couple of occasions the volunteers were obliged to use the ash plant in order to protect Sinn Féin supporters from being mauled by these infuriated females.

Ernest Blythe recalled that, after a Volunteer parade in Limerick,

> the rabble of the city, particularly the 'separation women', got into the mood to make trouble and a large crowd of them gathered near the station to attack the Volunteers as they moved to the train. There was a certain amount of stone throwing and blows were struck at Volunteers as they passed by.[13]

In contrast, republican women, some of whom had came together to resist their exclusion from Sinn Féin decision-making structures and four of whom were then co-opted on to the SF executive, heralded the 'splendid recognition of women's equality with men by the SF convention ... a triumphant vindication of the sound political wisdom of the Irish militants in placing suffrage first, especially during the trying period of the European war and perhaps the still more trying period since the rebellion.[14] On the back of the East Clare by-election the Volunteers resumed public drilling and organised a series of political meetings in August in defiance of a government ban.

The Volunteers' involvement in the funeral of Thomas Ashe in 1917 also provided the catalyst for a focused reorganisation. The president of the Supreme Council of the IRB, he died as a result of force-feeding while on hunger strike to achieve political status in Mountjoy jail. The careful choreographing of this funeral led in turn to the establishment of formal military structures for the Volunteers over the following six months and the formation of the Dublin Brigade, with Richard Mulcahy as commanding officer, from battalions that had previously lacked leadership and direction. The prominence of Michael Collins at the graveside of Ashe increased his profile and influence, and the General Headquarters (GHQ) Staff was born. Tom Garvin makes the point that Collins also had considerable organisational skills and administrative competence acquired 'in that flower of Victorian bureaucratic skills, the British post office ... [where] they kept files like civil servants'.[15] Mulcahy was central to the increased profile of the Volunteers. He had spent the spring and early summer of 1917 fundraising for the Gaelic League in Cork and Kerry; this was a cover for Volunteer reorganisation and he was one of the group which met to coordinate a Volunteer convention planned for October.

The conscription crisis of April 1918, when the British government introduced the Military Service Bill extending conscription, which had existed in Britain since January 1916, to Ireland, reinvigorated the Volunteers. Facing mounting pressure on the Western Front, the British government needed to boost the available manpower but, given the scale of opposition, abandoned the plan for conscription. When Lloyd George introduced the Bill to the Commons on 9 April 1918, he was warned that 'you will have another battle front in Ireland', with William O'Brien going as far as saying 'that is a declaration of war against Ireland'.[16] The Chief

Secretary's Office in Dublin received a letter from a contact in Kildare who referred to the idea of imposing conscription on Ireland as 'this mad step'.[17]

The impetus for nationalist public gatherings increased; in Kerry, for example, it was reported that

> the largest and most representative meeting ever held in Tralee and the most united in its determination to fulfil the object for which it was called, was the assembly on the square last night. The outstanding feature of the meeting was the attendance and cooperation of people who were hitherto diametrically opposed to each other in national principles, Sinn Féiners, Redmondites, pro-British etc.[18]

It also gave Sinn Féin a further boost in the aftermath of the death of John Redmond; at a convention in the Mansion House in April 1918 it was joined by the IPP and the Catholic Church. A pledge to resist included the wording 'denying the right of the British government to enforce compulsory military service in this country, we pledge ourselves solemnly to one another to resist conscription by the most effective means at our disposal'.[19]

Observing the national outcry, the *Irish Independent* predicted, 'If we judge rightly the determination of the people as evinced in their protests, the Rising of 1916 is but a trifling incident compared with what is to come, and it may take not one but many weeks to end it.'[20] Organised labour representatives meeting in the Mansion House on 20 April endorsed a call for a general strike three days later; the *Freeman's Journal* reported that it was a success: the response to it was 'most remarkable', with not just trade unionists downing tools but 'shops were shut, railway and postal services ceased and in Dublin all tram and vehicular traffic was stopped'.[21]

What was also significant was the way the crisis was used to hone the separatist claim; de Valera prepared a statement on behalf of the Mansion House conference for submission to Woodrow Wilson – *Ireland's Case Against Conscription* – insisting it was 'a battle for self-determination and for the fundamental principles of civil liberty' – which could according to Maurice Moynihan, be seen as 'a manifesto of Ireland's claim to separate and independent nationhood'.[22] Laurence O'Neill, Dublin's Lord Mayor, was deputed to deliver it to Washington; it included the assertion:

A century and a half ago, when the American colonies dared to assert the ancient principle that the subject should not be taxed without the consent of his representatives, England strove to crush them. Today, England threatens to crush the people of Ireland if they do not accept a tax, not in money, but in blood, against the protest of their representatives.[23]

The Mansion House Committee also issued a memorandum to local defence committees with a plan of action that included the stoppage of railway traffic, a general work stoppage and food rationing.[24] These were not idle threats; many contributors to the BMH commented on the extent to which the conscription threat re-energised the Volunteers and provided a new, more militant focus, born of a genuine anger or fear, or both: it 'roused the Irish people of all shades ... to a high pitch of enthusiasm to fight the conscription menace ... as a result of this threat the Volunteers were reorganised in most of the local parish areas.'[25]

Michael Curran, the secretary to the Catholic Archbishop of Dublin, William Walsh, suggested it made an older generation still reluctant to commit to Sinn Féin think again; such resistance also had a 'moral basis'. De Valera was also apt during this period to elevate the significance of religion: 'the higher the moral standard, the higher the life. True morality can only find a foundation in religion'; the Irish were the most spiritual people in the world and 'will show the world the might of moral beauty'.[26] There was also, according to Curran, a determination on the part of Archbishop Walsh to offer a corrective to Cardinal Michael Logue's mention of 'passive resistance', Walsh emphasising the necessity of 'giving definite instructions to those who were prepared to oppose conscription'. The crisis, maintained Curran, 'set Ireland ablaze'; he recorded in his diary 'great talk about tanks, poison gas and other frightening eventualities'. But what was also common according to a number of statements was that after the crisis had passed, those who had joined up 'became inactive again' or 'our numbers dwindled considerably'.[27]

Although some rogue priests upped the tempo in their sermons to talk of forceful resistance, most appeals by bishops and clergy focused on unity and discipline through passive resistance, one bishop warning against doing 'anything rash'.[28] Historian Leland Lyons, in his biography of John Dillon, suggested 'not even in his most strenuous labour for an Irish settlement had Lloyd George ever come near to producing such uniformity of view amongst so diverse a group of Irishmen as he did by this one action'.[29]

Dillon had replaced Redmond after the latter's unexpected death in March 1918. The *Northern Whig*, in reacting to Redmond's death, suggested the regret at his passing 'is not confined to one political party and it is no less sincere in Ulster than elsewhere. We differed immensely from Mr Redmond on public questions but we always found that no matter how strongly he advocated his own views he did so like a gentleman ... the empire loses a great practical imperialist'.[30] There was also recognition of the missions he had undertaken to Australia and America; the *Irish Independent* singled out the regret that would be felt 'by the Irish race the world over and also by the members of other races who sympathised with the claim of Ireland for self-government'.[31] W. B. Wells, in his biography of Redmond, suggested that through his actions 'he incurred all the odium of having accepted partition, without gaining any of the credit for his courageous attempt to effect a temporary settlement'.[32] Stephen Gwynn, meanwhile, emphasised that he was chairman rather than leader of the party, 'that is to say he was not to act except after consultation with the party as a whole, he was not to commit them upon policy'.[33] What was an exaggeration, however, was the *Freeman's Journal*'s contention that 'the reunion of the Irish parties under his leadership was so complete'; contrast this with the *Northern Whig*'s assertion that Redmond 'like every other nationalist leader, ended his career deserted by his own supporters ... death has relieved him of a humiliation as deep as any modern political leader has had to bear'.[34]

In relation to contesting the general election in December 1918, Kevin O'Higgins, soon to be Sinn Féin MP for Laois, was jubilant about an Irish manifestation of a wider impulse – 'at this hour when the world is ringing out with the cry of self-determination!'[35] – but Sinn Féin's path to victory was still not assured, indicated by defeat in by-elections in South Armagh (by Joseph Devlin), Waterford and East Tyrone. During the South Armagh by-election the IPP claimed it had 'enabled the farmers to purchase their own holdings, secured decent cottages for the labourers to live in and had brought education into the homes of the people'.[36] It was a message that worked for the time being and this, Sinn Féin's first foray into Ulster politics with Patrick McCartan as its candidate, exposed certain vulnerabilities. Uniformed Volunteers were active in canvassing, but there may also have been concern and embarrassment with the role

of Constance Markievicz, who was reported towards the end of the campaign as saying 'the liberty won by the Bolsheviks in Russia is the kind of
liberty the Irish people are determined to fight for.'[37]

The 'German Plot' arrests, involving the round-up of seventy-three
prominent Sinn Féin members in May 1918 on the pretext that a German
agent had been arrested off the coast of Clare and that there was a necessity to stamp out pro-German 'intrigues' in Ireland, backfired for Sinn
Féin's enemies. Regarding these arrests, a letter to the Chief Secretary's
Office insisted, 'You have got to prove your accusation or else your action
in arresting these men will be worse than useless ... if you merely imprison
these men, deport them to England and hush the whole thing up – the
course of action adopted with the arrested suspects after the 1916 rebellion – you will make things worse.'[38] Sinn Féin became an underground
proscribed movement, but Arthur Griffith was elected in the East Cavan
by-election and martial law was declared in areas of the south and west.
The arrests after the 'German Plot' provoked large crowds protesting; in St
Peter's College in Wexford, for example, 3,000 protestors gathered. In the
midst of all this, 'the establishment of GHQ defined a new era for the Irish
Volunteers. Within the space of six months, the Volunteers had evolved
from a loose organisation to one with clear structures and plans to instil
training and discipline throughout the country. Sinn Féin was also effective in soliciting donations; according to reports received by the Chief
Secretary's Office, 'it is estimated that £42,612.16 has been collected in
the provinces up to 30 June 1918'.[39] However the Volunteers' focus would
remain largely defensive until the end of the following year.

The expansion of the Volunteers also raised a fundamental question:
who would volunteer and why? There is 'no one size fits all' answer to
that question. Peter Hart suggested they were primarily unmarried men
from the middle classes and disproportionately urban-based, rather than
the 'mountainy men' of myth.[40] In her study of County Longford during
this period, Marie Coleman arrived at a similar social profile. Most of the
Volunteers she examined were born in the 1890s, were literate Catholics
and unmarried, and most from the rural townlands and villages of North
Longford.[41] Hart characterised them as 'plain, respectable, ordinary men',
while Joost Augusteijn saw them, socially, as falling in the middle ground
between 'the most well to do and ... the lowest social strata'.[42] What was
also notable was their youth: 'The revolutionary generation was made up
of mostly obscure people, whose most obvious common characteristic was

their youth'. Before 1919, the average age of a rank-and-file Volunteer was twenty-three and for officers twenty-five; after that, the average age rose by about one year.[43] Inter-generational conflict was apparent, with a desire on the part of the younger to challenge the dominance of authority figures, and in Mayo, the RIC suggested, 'sons are frightening their fathers as to what will happen if they don't vote Sinn Féin'.[44] Media representations of these Volunteers were jaundiced and simplistic – in Cork, for example, common descriptions included 'young men of no means', 'the loafers of the town', 'raw country bogcutters' and 'scum who didn't own a wheelbarrow of their own' and, invariably, 'corner boys', a common term of abuse at this time, creating a simplistic polarity between those with 'a stake in the country' and those without.[45]

In relation to Dublin, Laffan highlights that of those arrested in Dublin after the Rising, 55 per cent were labourers, shop assistants, salesmen and clerks and another 30 per cent tradesmen, while outside of Dublin, about 28 per cent were farmers and 23 per cent agricultural labourers.[46] Ernie O'Malley insisted that in his company of Volunteers 'there were no class distinctions. One judged a man by his previous training, efficiency and ability'.[47] An RIC assessment of SF candidates in the 1918 election suggested slices of middle-class and lower-middle-class Ireland: 'a few doctors, solicitors, farmers and shopkeepers, together with clerks, ex Post Office clerks, students, teachers, commercial travellers, a labourer and other persons of insignificance', but these kind of observations were impressionistic, prejudiced and not quantifiable.[48] The same problems are apparent in characterising the attitudes of farmers who, after all, had already experienced a social revolution in relation to the transfer of land and were keen to protect their status. But it was also in their interests to support a republicanism that might sideline a labour movement that scared them, and according to one Volunteer in Limerick, later 'the farmers fed the flying columns and subscribed thousands of pounds to the Dáil Éireann loan and Volunteer funds'.[49]

There is little doubt that many farmers had done well in the early stages of the war; Fitzpatrick pointed out, for example, that the agricultural wholesale price index rose by 60 per cent from 1914–16.[50] But compulsory tillage policies to feed the army had taken their toll by 1918 and created tensions as prices for potatoes, grain and other crops were poor and there was a scarcity of dairy products. In January 1918 the *Wexford People* newspaper was vocal about the ensuing consequences, and what was striking was how the memory of famine was invoked: 'food prices and the prices of other necessities have risen to an enormous pitch ... bread famine now stares us in the face ... of course the troops must be fed ... but the food which is the God given right of the people is being sent elsewhere before the eyes of the people'.[51]

Food shortages created militancy in Cork just before the conscription crisis in 1918 as separatists and militants formed the 'People's Food Committee', a product of Sinn Féin and organised labour which 'briefly threatened to use force to prevent the export of food supplies'.[52] For two years the Cork Poor Law Guardians had been requesting the Local Government Board to initiate price controls over bread and milk to no avail. In early 1917 the *Cork Examiner* referred to the 'acute distress' that existed and references to the possibility of famine were not uncommon there either: 'As the food situation worsened during the winter of 1917–18, Sinn Féin cries of "Never Again" resonated throughout the country.'[53] Potato supplies in Cork were also pitifully low in early 1917 and an Irish Food Control Committee established by the British government omitted Sinn Féin. One of the concerns was with preventing profiteering. In January 1918 there was further 'famine anxiety', an issue also addressed by the Catholic Church with resultant land agitation, as graziers, under pressure to provide tillage land, suffered from cattle drives and boycotts. The amount of livestock leaving Cork was a cause of great anger and with the formation of the People's Food Committee, exports dropped dramatically after direct action.

Cattle driving, pig seizures and rows with commercial leaders were common but it was also notable that 'recognising the growing upheaval and potential division of the independence movement between the landed and the landless, Republican leaders set out to put the genie back in the bottle',[54] discouraging land seizures and cattle driving. De Valera's instructions, as transcribed by a member of the SF Executive, were very revealing in this regard, and an apt summary of the determination of the SF leadership not to allow irksome social radicalism to complicate the purity of the struggle: 'Let us bide our time. Don't get us involved in side issues at present. You must get the whole country behind you if you are to win ... avoid challenges if you can.'[55] A good harvest for 1918 and the effectiveness of British food price and production controls also helped cool ardour, but perhaps SF's leadership had also set an important precedent; after all, the Labour Party did not contest the 1918 general election after pressure from Sinn Féin, in order not to complicate the 'national' question, a severe sacrifice.

In preparing for that election, pamphlets such as *How to Form Sinn Féin Clubs* and *Work for a Sinn Féin Branch* followed and Robert Brennan, appointed director of propaganda for the election, recalled in his memoir how the SF practice of sending party notes and news to provincial and local newspapers was another vital ingredient, starting from a base in the first week of thirty newspapers, which gradually increased.[56] By the beginning of 1918 SF was now, Griffith asserted, 'the dominant vital force in Irish national life ... it draws its strength not from party exigencies or incidental convulsions of current events, but from the re-awakened consciousness of the national mind.'[57]

The Representation of the People Act had expanded the electorate from 700,000 to 1.93 million, with women over the age of thirty with the requisite property qualifications allowed to vote for the first time. The run-up to the election provided an opportunity for a multitude of mass political meetings and such meetings could run simultaneously; six meetings were listed in the *Wexford People* as planned for Sunday 8 December 1918, for example. There is also evidence of generational tension within the Catholic Church, with younger curates more likely to back SF while their elders supported the IPP. Revd Mark Byrne in Wexford town supported SF and was adamant about the arrogance of the IPP: 'It seemed to be characteristic of Irish political leaders that once they held the reins of power for any considerable time they refused to lose their grip and refused to change their course, resented and ignored criticism until eventually it had to be wrenched from their hands by an indignant people.'[58] SF was characterised as 'manly and straightforward', with the IPP 'servile and slavish' and voters were urged to use 'the brains God gave them ... SF wants no unthinking mob to rush blindly to the polls.'[59]

The propaganda war was considerable: the election literature of Patrick Little, editor of various Sinn Féin newspapers and a member of the Sinn Féin executive 1917–22, who was elected as Sinn Féin MP for Dublin Rathmines, sneered at 'honest John Dillon' in cahoots with the British government. There was also a determination to root up old parliamentary contributions, such as Dillon's assertion in 1881 at Westminster that 'if you sent angels into parliament, unless they are controlled by a public body sitting in Dublin they would betray the people.'[60] IPP members were also characterised as both 'conscriptionists' and 'corruptionists', and 'parliamentarianism' became a term of abuse. This was also linked to economic arguments with particular leaflets and pamphlets aimed at business people and farmers: 'Ireland, thanks to parliamentarianism, has lost half her wealth in man-power and her expenses have been increased seventeen times.'[61] It was claimed that the Irish population of 4.39 million in 1918 paid £35 million a year in taxation, whereas in 1800, an Irish population of 8.5 million paid just £2 million a year in taxation. Indeed, SF trotted out all sorts of (supposedly) comparative statistics, figures and costings: 'Liberty has cost only $6 per capita per annum in Greece and Serbia, $7.50 in Bulgaria, $9 in Switzerland, $13 in Sweden, $14 in Portugal, $15 in Norway – while in Ireland, British militarism costs about $40 per capita, per annum.'[62] Sweden, Denmark, Holland, Serbia, Greece and Bulgaria were all elevated as ideal models; small countries with their own governments, armies and perceived freedom. Since the passing of the Act of Union between Ireland and Great Britain in 1801, according to another tract, 'the imperial government has abstracted from Ireland between £500,000,000 and £600,000,000 of over taxation.'[63]

There was also a specific appeal to women, and the pamphleteers scaled new heights:

> not without reason did the old time poets of Eirinn call the country they loved by a woman's name ... the women of Ireland have for seven centuries preserved to the Gael the ideal of independence ... when in the famine years the manhood of Ireland were scattered to the four corners of the earth it was the lonely, heartbroken women who crooned the old song of Irish independence to the children left fatherless ... the nation which all through its history was renowned for the nobility of its womankind and which stood out from all other nations in Europe for the honoured position women held in the Irish state can now be freed by the sex made reverent by the Gaelic tradition.[64]

This conveniently ignored the fact that emigration to the US from the second half of the nineteenth century was characterised by roughly equal sex ratios. But the argument now was that if women were to vote for the IPP, 'their sons and daughters fly from an impoverished Ireland into the Godless cities of the world ... but you can save Ireland by voting as MRS PEARSE will vote'. Then came the ultimate lie: 'In the future, the womenfolk of the Gael shall have high place in the councils of a freed Gaelic nation.'[65]

Weightier offerings were also apparent for both and Irish and British audiences to 'explain' Sinn Féin and the Irish race, which was 'pre-eminently intuitive, that is to say it feels its conclusions rather than thinks them'. P. S. O'Hegarty proudly trumpeted his offering, *Sinn Féin: An Illumination*, as 'the first book about Sinn Féin from the inside', depicting the movement as born out of the Gaelic League and representing 'a combination of forces'; the 'old Sinn Féin movement' Fenianism, and Arthur Griffith as the 'Hamlet of the piece ... There are many sections in it, separated on minor points but agreed on the main point, that Ireland must work out her own salvation.'[66] In relation to the Labour Party agreeing not to contest the election, Aodh de Blácam suggested it 'would not be wrong to say that a large majority of the Irish proletariat is now becoming socialistic in hope and policy', that the word socialist 'no longer terrifies ... Ireland had turned her back on bourgeois politics ... the policy movement of today, most of all, is committed to a social orientation if it is loyal to the ideals of Padraic Mac Piarais [Patrick Pearse] ... Sinn Féin leads inevitably to social Gaelicism'. He added that 'the actual programme that social Gaelicism will adopt is yet to be hammered out', but a native socialistic order would go, as it had historically 'as far as socialism did not part with the law of God'. Labour standing aside in the 1918 election was presented as 'the habitual indication of the self-sacrifice of the working-class.'[67]

But a more cautious tone was adopted by others:

> The labour movement has erroneously, I think, appealed to the workers of Ireland as a 'class'; the workers of Ireland cannot be regarded as a 'class' they are the nation: [SF] does not appeal merely to material considerations though such are incidentally involved ... the national movement must be broad ... the movement for national independence cannot possibly hurt the labour movement [another big lie]. SF is broad enough to admit every Labour man ... [The flag of SF] is the same that Connolly fought under ... economic freedom is contingent upon political independence.[68]

SF propaganda, of course, had no interest in the reality of the IPP identity, which was not monolithic or straightforward; it is clear from the work of Michael Wheatley, for example, that while the nationalism of its leader Redmond may have been deemed 'moderate', for the grassroots the kind of discourse common in the party was different, and was actually dominated by 'Catholicity, sense of victimhood, glorification of struggle, identification of enemies and antipathy to England'.[69] This is why many of its supporters could embrace SF; there was not a 'rigid dichotomy' between the two parties.[70] But it was also why SF strategists and propagandists went for the jugular of the parliamentarians in 1917 and 1918. As a contemporary one-act play put it, 'sparring at the English like young pups and then coming docile to the heel of your masters ... it's queer in the head you've grown from asking questions in parliament; your heart's not with your own people'.[71]

John Dillon, tougher, more aggressive and forthright than Redmond, conducted a frank exchange of correspondence with party stalwart T. P. O'Connor throughout the election campaign that reveals how despondent Dillon was about lack of party organisation and a sense that, in his own words, his followers were already beaten 'in their hearts'. He regarded those members of the party who backed away, having originally committed to stand, as demonstrating 'sheer cowardice', but he refused to fold up the party tent. As recorded by Leland Lyons, 'on the one side he placed the party with its proud tradition and long record of service to the people – the source of every major reform in Ireland since the New Departure [in 1879, to link the land question and nationalism] – on the other side stood Sinn Féin, politically inexperienced.'[72]

One of Dillon's major gripes was that the younger generation 'are ignorant of what our movement achieved for Ireland', but he also acknowledged 'our own blunders in not realising what was going on'. Dillon suggested there could be a positive side to the election loss, as 'the more the responsibility is fixed on the other side to deliver the goods and carry out the promises they have made, the better and more speedy will be their discomfiture and break up'.[73] It was a forlorn hope; Dillon had warned that SF's pursuit of a republic would lead to bloodshed and defeat, and characterised abstentionism as 'a policy of lunatics', but his pleas were ineffective.[74] (In relation to its quest for a republic, SF's manifesto stated it would use 'any and every means available to render impotent the power of England to hold Ireland in subjection', which was open to different interpretations.) Dillon himself lost his Mayo East seat to de Valera by a margin of two to one.

How had it all come crashing down for the IPP? Michael Wheatley's examination of nationalists and the Irish party between 1910 and 1916 offers many answers. There is little doubt, as with elsewhere, that the First

World War created a vacuum and such upheaval as to deprive the party of essential political leverage, and frayed its organisational abilities with a growing distance between grassroots and leadership. But Wheatley challenges the notion that the war just exposed weaknesses that were already evident by highlighting vigour and activity at local level: quite simply the party continued to be representative of nationalist opinion, or in Wheatley's clever phrase, 'more representative than rotten' in 1914.[75]

The results of the election were emphatic. SF won seventy-three seats, unionists twenty-six and the IPP just six: SF had, under the 'first-past-the-post' electoral system, won three-quarters of the Irish seats at Westminster with less than half of the votes cast. For those who supported SF the election result was one to be savoured and celebrated with panache. As with the conscription crisis, contemporary newspapers made much of invoking the sense of history, the *Derry Journal* reporting on New Year's Day 1919 that 'not probably since the days of the Land War was there such an immense concourse of people ... many houses were illuminated, Sinn Féin flags flew from several houses.'[76]

Fr Michael O'Flanagan, a compassionate but arrogant republican activist and priest in Roscommon who had been active in the Gaelic League and was elected joint vice president of the newly consolidated party, was put in charge of SF publicity during the general election and at its conclusion allegedly said, 'The people have voted Sinn Féin. What we have to do now is explain to people what Sinn Féin is.'[77] This was part of a wider dilemma about how to construct a new political framework or dispensation after the upheaval of the First World War and the impact that it had on the relationship between state and citizen and the attendant changes in ideology, alliances and allegiances. Terence MacSwiney's sister wrote to him in prison after giving him details of the election result and asserted, 'it isn't the men but the policy that's winning.'[78] The issue now was how exactly ideals would be realised to deliver on the idea that 'Belgium a nation again is music to Irish ears ... on the fate of Ireland rests the whole moral structure of the allied cause.'[79]

SEVENTEEN

WAR OF INDEPENDENCE (1): 1919–20: CATCHING THE WAVES

Shortly before his death in October 2007, Dan Keating, a native of Castlemaine in County Kerry, was the last living link to the Irish War of Independence. An apprentice barman in his youth, he was the eldest of seven children, and a nephew of uncles who had been active in the Land War. He became a product not just of that heritage but also of a more militant post-1916 Tralee, where he was educated by the Christian Brothers and where he worked and joined Fianna Éireann in 1918 and subsequently the IRA in 1920. His involvement was not born of intense study of history or revolution, but of contemporary practices: 'It was the thing to do at the time – there was a wave and you got caught up in that.'[1] One wave washed over in January 1919: on the day the first Dáil (the parliament convened by SF after its electoral victory) met in Dublin, two policemen, Patrick Mac-Donnell and James O'Connell, native Irishmen, were killed in an ambush at Soloheadbeg in County Tipperary, 'sounding a forbidding chorus to the Declaration of Independence proclaimed in the Dáil'. The rest of that year and much of the next two were mapped out by a catalogue of 'ambush and execution, of reprisal and assassination, fear, terror, curfew and martial law'.[2]

For all the high-profile killings and headline-grabbing moments,

all of these events were played out against the background of other small local wars ... war's character changed across counties, even within counties ... identifying sectarianism as a motive is one of the issues that still divides historians most. But it was only one of many motives, as local rivalries, old land disputes, were given freedom to express themselves in a country largely beyond police control since the winter of 1919–20.[3]

The war evolved from being one characterised by attacks on the RIC to being a war waged against British troops and 'it remains very unclear as to whether this was the kind of war that people had voted for at the general election of December 1918, indeed whether they had voted for any kind of war at all.'[4] Art O'Connor, director of agriculture in the first Dáil, was to acknowledge a few years later that initially, 'the struggle of the Volunteers was a struggle with the Irish people more than a struggle with the invader and indeed the real uphill fight which Sinn Féin has had is with the Irish people. The guerrilla war did not for a long time find favour with the bulk of the people'; with its escalation, he maintained, 'the people rallied to the Volunteers',[5] who were being increasingly often referred to as the Irish Republican Army (IRA) from 1919.

Measuring the veracity of O'Connor's assertion about the people's embrace of the IRA campaign is problematic. Soloheadbeg was not a confident unanimous declaration of war, but a local initiative and unauthorised. The Volunteers were not ready for war. Dan Breen, a key member of the IRA's South Tipperary Brigade, was worried that the Volunteers were serving merely as an appendage to SF, a reminder that the primary impulse at this stage was political rather than military; and it was his impatience, along with colleagues including Seán Treacy and Séamus Robinson, that saw them strike out on their own. They became famous as a result; £1,000 was offered for Breen's capture, for 'Without any knowledge of such tactics, Breen and Treacy had pioneered guerrilla warfare.'[6] Treacy was dead the following year, while Breen lived to old age, not dying until 1969, and lived to tell his tales, some of them tall.

The Volunteers of the Tipperary Third Brigade occupy a hallowed place in the history of the Irish revolution due to the Soloheadbeg attack, but it also begged the question as to the significance of location; why were some counties, including Tipperary, more active than others? Some of the answers may lie in the traditions of activism associated with certain counties. Tipperary, for example, had produced committed Young Ireland rebels in 1848, where there was an attempted rising in Ballingarry, and Munster labourers had also been active at the end of the nineteenth century in forming the Irish Land and Labour Association. There are also unusual statistics from individual counties; how much should we read into the fact that 45 per cent of Volunteers in Tipperary were fatherless, a much higher figure than in other parts of the country?[7] Was distance from Dublin also a factor? Tipperary volunteers in some ways seemed to be experiencing the same frustration regarding communication with Dublin as their Fenian predecessors had.

Media reaction to Soloheadbeg revealed much about the public perception of the RIC; both victims were described as being well liked: 'both deceased were popular and the double tragedy has caused a most painful sensation' was the verdict of the *Freeman's Journal*.[8] During the inquest, one of MacDonnell's sons inquired in an intervention whether 'the police had been given a dog's chance', but the coroner intervened, stating it was the function of the inquest to ascertain the cause of death only. Addressing the jury, however, he acknowledged 'the tragedy was the saddest case that had happened in Tipperary or any part of Ireland for many years'.[9] Concern was also expressed about the business consequences of martial law being proclaimed as it was after the ambush: 'Business people are very much concerned about the enforcement of military law in the area, as it is feared it is likely to lead to dislocation of their business.'[10]

There was also an opportunity for members of the church to comment on the ethics of what had happened. The Revd J. Slattery of Soloheadbeg maintained 'the most shocking feature of the sad affair was the thought that the perpetrators were actuated by what they considered a desire to further the cause of Ireland. But God could not bless a cause that thought to gain its end by criminal means'. The Revd William Keogh also had an interesting observation: 'Ireland's enemies would try to saddle this crime on the new popular movement striving for her independence but in that they were wrong. The leaders of that movement were far too logical and God-fearing to countenance such crimes.'[11] It is unlikely Dan Breen was God-fearing; one of the anecdotes about him concerns the end of his life when his friend Peadar O'Donnell visited him in hospital: a nurse told him that a bishop was waiting to see him. Breen's reply was "Ah, just tell him to fuck off."[12]

Protestant propagandists were adamant that Rome was behind SF: 'it is the priestly cloud which obstructs the light of freedom', with an estimated 4,000 priests in a population of 3.25 million Catholics, 3,000 churches and chapels representing a 'gigantic force which acts as a sucker on the whole country'.[13] But the War of Independence also presented the Catholic Church with new challenges, including the potential for undermining of allegiance and discipline. When Dr Fogarty, Bishop of Killaloe was interviewed a few decades later, the impression his interviewee got was that 'the Irish Bishops did not at any time discuss in council the question of the moral justification of the Easter Rising, or the Anglo-Irish conflict that followed'. Generally the attitude of individual bishops was a matter of age, with the older bishops more opposed to republicans. Dr Fogarty

> gave expression to the view that in any other country except Ireland the clash of Episcopal opinion might have meant a schism in the church there. Dr Fogarty maintained that in private conversation with Dr O'Dwyer, Bishop of Limerick, the latter mentioned that the rising in 1916 was morally justifiable ... Dr Fogarty declared that in the Anglo-Irish War the national interest would override such unpleasant happenings as the shooting of policemen.[14]

But Richard Mulcahy argued that the way to maintain support from both the Irish public and the international community was to 'move slowly and educate the people'.[15] This may also have been a reaction to the desire on the British side and from Irish constitutional nationalists to foment splits in the republican movement by encouraging anything that would separate what A. M. Sullivan, a lawyer and supporter of the IPP, termed 'the blackguards' from the moderates.[16] For these reasons, the IRA remained largely a defensive organisation until August 1919, when the Dáil attempted to impose its authority by assuming at least some responsibility for the army's actions. As Joe Lee saw it, 'The British, as if, not for the last time, in collusion with the extremists, drove the elected representatives more into the hands of the gunmen by suppressing the Dáil and Sinn Féin in late 1919.'[17]

In the meantime, the business of politics was ongoing and in some respects it was ill defined. In August 1919 for example, Constance Markievicz, the first woman elected to the British Parliament, suggested SF was 'not a solid, cast-iron thing like English parties. It is just a jumble of people of all classes, creeds and opinions, who are all ready to suffer and die for Ireland.'[18] This was patent nonsense; the War of Independence 'produced thugs as well as heroes',[19] and SF was not such a broad church as she declared. Not all those who wanted to die for Ireland wanted to redistribute for Ireland first: Tom Garvin makes the point that 'whenever social protest began seriously to threaten the interest of men of substance, republicanism ostentatiously dissociated itself from agitation'.[20] As Seán O'Faoláin was to characterise it, the Democratic Programme unveiled at the meeting of the first Dáil, which involved enunciating Sinn Féin's social ideals and promised to provide shelter for the weak, and abolish the 'odious' poor law system, 'was listened to and discussed for precisely twenty minutes and fifty seconds, and then buried forever. In any case, its terms were of a purely pious and general nature that committed nobody to anything in particular. The policy of Sinn Féin had always been since its foundation that simple formula: freedom first; other things after.'[21] De Valera had found a convenient way of expressing this impulse in March 1918: Sinn Féin aimed at the 'uplifting of the entire nation', encompassing all classes, 'which may be done and leave their relative levels and relative equilibriums undisturbed'.[22]

The Democratic Programme was, therefore, a product of compromise between the Labour Party and SF. One of its architects was Thomas Johnson, who in a sense, as leader of the Labour Party, was being rewarded for Labour's abstention from the 1918 election, but some of his initial draft was diluted or omitted, including the assertion, 'wherever the land, mineral deposits and other forms of the production of wealth are wrongly used or withheld from use to the detriment of the Republic, then the nation shall resume possession without compensation', in favour of 'it shall be our duty to promote the development of the Nation's resources ... in the interests and for the benefit of the Irish people'. Johnson's declaration of class war – 'the Republic will aim for the elimination of the class in society which lives upon the wealth produced by the workers of the nation but gives no useful service in return' – was completely censored. There was a consensus, however, about subordinating private property to the public good and that 'it shall ... be the first duty of the government of the Republic to make provision for the physical, mental and spiritual well-being of the children, to secure that no child shall suffer hunger or cold from lack of food, clothing or shelter'.[23]

What did this mean in practice? When, a few months after the unveiling of the Democratic Programme, the *Worker's Bulletin* in Limerick published an article entitled 'The New Era', it insisted on echoing the censored, more radical draft of the Democratic Programme, declaring that what workers wanted now was 'to release those things that constitute capital and real wealth from the base profiteers and financial gamblers who exploit them for their own aggrandisement' and replace it with 'a system of national ownership and democratic control'.[24] A strike, involving 14,000 workers in a city of 38,000 people, and the closure of shops, factories and warehouses, was declared by the Limerick United Trades and Labour Council to protest against the proclamation of the city by the British authorities as a special military area. It lasted ten days, and involved a strike committee (which became known as the 'Soviet') that regulated price and distribution of food, published its own newspaper and even printed its own currency. The *Irish Times* suggested in the midst of the strike that it was 'a very bold and candid experiment in Irish syndicalism', but that such 'Bolshevism' would not succeed, as nationally, 'the bulk of labour' was too cautious and 'in our farming classes the sense of property is as sacred and strong as in the French'.[25]

Initial support from Catholic clergy dissipated, but in any case, strong leadership of the workers was lacking, as was any socialist vision: 'surly' middle-class employers and employees were unlikely to give long-term allegiance to the cause; workers became disorientated and 'quickly found an accommodation within the new nationalist consensus'.

It was a revealing episode about the potential for the 'rabble' to successfully and defiantly act on their grievances; there was a tension between national and regional labour and republican priorities, fear of 'Russian anarchism' became widely articulated, senior Church figures became more thunderous, and there was, other than an acknowledgement of the workers' plight, a certain muteness on the part of Sinn Féin. The Irish Labour Party and Trade Union Congress feared that any escalation in support for Limerick 'would be entirely on their own heads and lack the enthusiastic national support of Sinn Féin'. Towards the end of the Soviet, Sinn Féin's Eoin MacNeill was getting increasingly concerned about reports in America that Sinn Féin was 'under the red flag' and told a Chicago newspaper: 'We Irish are neither Russian nor international ... the wind behind the Irish red flag is not strong.'[26] Establishing the Irish Republic, it became clear, was to be about a strong wind behind a green rather than a red flag.

The 'freedom first' impulse also had serious consequences for the police.[27] The RIC boycott was effective and the campaign to assassinate its members that followed was ultimately responsible for approximately 400 deaths during the War of Independence: 'The RIC's strength during times of relative peace – its closeness to the community among whom it lived – became a serious weakness. It was not difficult for determined IRA leaders to cultivate contacts with friendly, frightened or otherwise vulnerable policemen, to intimidate diligent policemen out of their jobs and encourage their less enthusiastic colleagues to remain.'[28] The RIC's methods became outdated and underfinanced.

Some of the statements contributed to the BMH by former members of the RIC are understandably defensive in tone, but the assumption that the force was overwhelmingly loyal to the Crown is not supported by those members who testified. Statements emphasise not only the moral probity and discipline of the force, but also the men's sense that by joining they were attaining a social respectability unachievable in many other jobs. Most insist that the relationship between the population and the police force was relatively good prior to the War of Independence. Understandably, many joined because it provided a secure income and pension, and even republicans could see the merit in this. J. J. McConnell, who joined in Dublin in 1907 and later became a sergeant and district inspector, stated defensively that even his Fenian father approved of him joining up and that by enlisting, he 'realised my childhood ambition. Indeed, it was the dream of all my boyhood pals to join the force that was greatly admired and respected throughout the country.'[29]

Eugene Bratton, a constable in Meath, maintained that 'in some cases the police actually assisted in the training of the volunteers for a short period, but not for long'. He also contended – and this is noted elsewhere – that the police resented the conscription threat of 1918. In a scenario that also seems to have been common, 'I wanted to resign from the force, but General Boylan of the IRA would not allow me ... I was more useful where I was.' John Duffy, an RIC member who carried out intelligence work for the IRA, advised Michael Collins, who became the IRA's director of intelligence, how to persuade young men to leave the force. 'Collins sent down a courier by return with instructions in his own handwriting that under no circumstances was I to leave the force and if I did so I would be looked upon as a coward. The word "coward" decided my determination to remain on.'[30]

In April 1919, the clerk of the Dáil, Diarmuid O'Hegarty, elaborated on what the social ostracising of the RIC needed to amount to:

... that they should be debarred from participation in games, sports, dances and all social functions conducted by the people, that inter-marriage with them should be discouraged, that in a word, the police should be treated as persons who having been adjudged guilty of treason to their country are regarded as unworthy to enjoy any of the privileges or comforts which arise from cordial relations with the public.[31]

As early as December 1919 the RIC's inspector general reported that his policemen were 'not strong enough to cope with it but for the assis-tance afforded by the military'; this could only add to their estrangement from their communities, and boycotting and ostracism were added pres-sures. The monthly RIC reports became a catalogue of woe that intensi-fied in 1920 but British counter-insurgency policy held that their place was still in the front line.[32] One member explained that this was despite the fact that they were ill-equipped to deal with guerrilla warfare: 'Excel-lent police officers, as many were, they were only suited from a *gendar-merie* point of view to deal with a few armed moonlighters. Dealing with formed bodies of IRA was completely out of the class of most of them.'[33]

The statistical summaries that were compiled between March 1920 and December 1921 document 2,690 offences against the RIC with short reports for 1,942 incidents. Between mid March and mid April 1920 alone as many as 129 empty stations were burned with over 700 experiencing that fate by the end of December.[34] Cork, Clare, Mayo and Longford were particularly dangerous counties for the RIC ('Queen's [Laois] was the only county in Ireland in which a policeman was not killed'). There were 860 casualties (576 wounded and 284 killed) in the almost 900 attacks and ambushes on the RIC recorded in these statistical summaries. Attacks on family members and intimidation was also rife and in 1920 'the intim-idation of those friendly to or conducting business with the police was comprehensive', though they occasionally fought back: 'The Mother of an RIC constable, Mary Boylan of County Cavan, showed remarkable cour-age in driving away an armed party of forty men with only her spade ... it does not appear that she was disturbed again.' Others were less fortunate: 'Mary Crean of Frenchpark Roscommon, was accused of supplying the police with information in the summer of 1920 and in reprisal had three pig rings fixed to her buttocks'; that same summer the McCarthy sisters of Portmagee had their hair shorn for being too friendly to the police and the sister of an RIC constable in Annagh suffered the same humiliation.[35]

The husband of a woman working as the servant at the RIC Barracks in Templemore in County Tipperary was told that, 'if your wife does not withdraw her services you shall undergo the extreme penalty'. But more would have nothing to do with them. In Cork, little progress could be made in investigating the robbery of bank officials: 'no reliable information can be obtained as the people will tell them nothing'.[36] And who was the money being robbed for? The RIC reported on house raids in Mayo in April 1920 by men 'demanding money in the name of the Irish Republic ... it is believed the money was for their own private use'.[37]

Those who conversed with the RIC were putting themselves at grave risk; a man in County Wicklow in April 1920 received this letter: 'We have good reason to believe that you are playing the spy and supplying the peelers with any information you can possibly get. Keep clear of the peelers or your days are numbered.' It was noted by the RIC that this man 'is friendly disposed towards the police and converses with them'.[38]

Resignations and a recruitment famine were inevitable. During the summer of 1920 over 1,300 left, half of them through resignation and 43 per cent through retirement, and by the autumn of 1920 membership of the force had fallen below 10,000, though this had recovered to 12,000 by the very end of 1920 as recruitment of Auxiliaries and Black and Tans bolstered their presence. But it is also clear that this reliance 'was disastrous for the image of the RIC as it further militarised the police role and increased their distance from the nationalist population', as was reflected in much contemporary newspaper comment, while the policy of reprisals 'terminally tarnished the reputation of the RIC as Ireland's civil police'. Former soldiers in the British army were also vulnerable; in April 1921 an ex-soldier in Clare, John Reilly 'was taken from his house by six armed and masked men and shot dead on a by-road. The party gained admission to the house on the pretence that they were police. He was shot in the presence of a priest who was taken there to administer the last rites. A notice was pinned on the dead man's coat as follows: "Spy. Executed by the IRA. Getting them at last – Beware".[39]

Propaganda was also an important part of SF's contribution to the war. Collins was later to make a revealing comment in a letter to George Gavan Duffy that 'real progress is much more to be estimated by what is thought abroad than by what is thought at home'.[40] SF's Department of Foreign Affairs report in June 1921 noted that special envoys have been sent to Germany, Russia, South America and South Africa, an accredited representative has been appointed in Germany; press bureaus have been established in Germany, Switzerland, Spain and Rome and the organisation of similar bureaus in South Africa, Australia, Chile and the Argentine is under way. In addition the organisation in the United States has been put on a new basis.[41]

Robert Brennan, active in SF propaganda after the 1916 Rising, also became an important character in the evolution of Irish diplomacy; along with producing the *Irish Bulletin* (see below), Brennan began to 'organise and professionalise what had from January 1919 been a diplomatic service without routine procedures.'[42]

They were needed, given the often painstaking if not desperate quest for international recognition of the Republic during this period. There was delusion on the part of individuals like Seán T. O'Kelly in Paris about the scale of what could be achieved, as well as divisions within the Irish delegations abroad, not to mention the schisms in Irish-American nationalism.[43] Laurence Ginnell was appointed director of propaganda in April 1919, but he was arrested after one month. The publicity department published fourteen information pamphlets and produced the film *Sinn Féin Review* (1919). What became more important when Desmond FitzGerald took over was the publicising of British outrages, then sent as a press release to various newspapers at home and abroad; this service, which began in June 1919, became known as the *Irish Bulletin* and its initial mailing list of thirty was said to have increased to 2,000 within two years. Effectively painting a grim picture of Britain's mission in Ireland, the department was satisfied with the number of newspapers that printed its 'Acts of Aggression'.

In a report to Diarmuid O'Hegarty, FitzGerald highlighted his meetings with various journalists:

On the whole I found them interested and sympathetic. They all assure me that they will do their best to represent Ireland fairly to the readers of their journals. Some of them have, to my knowledge, made a point of writing special articles on the present state of Ireland since my first visit to them. All of them expressed themselves very glad to receive our daily Bulletin and our pamphlets.

But he also acknowledged that this was not plain sailing; some of the correspondents' experiences during the war had 'made them very chary of anything in the nature of propaganda; I endeavoured to meet them through introductions of a non-propagandist nature'.[44]

Art O'Brien, who ran the propaganda office in London, was another key figure. After the establishment of Dáil Éireann he became chairman of the London Loan Committee and was representative of the Dáil in England, and focused on the spread of its propaganda as well as acting as a conduit hub for the Dáil and its representatives in Europe, and was on 'intimate terms with every visiting pressman ... he was a regular visitor to the offices of the *Freeman's Journal* where they usually congregated, at other times to be found in more discreet quarters, he contrived to keep himself in close and constant touch with the newspaper world of Europe and America'.[45] Later in 1921 he wrote an amusing letter about the extent to which he had to move around: 'Stopping on at the hotel is a very large expense. By the force of circumstances, I now have 2 flats, a house, a suite of rooms at an hotel and 3 offices; if fact, if we go on a little bit longer it looks as if I should want to start a special estate department to look after all these premises.'[46] But it was not all one-way traffic; FitzGerald also had to compete with well-established London-based news services that obtained their news directly from the British Home Office or Dublin Castle, which could be quicker and more efficient.

George Plunkett, Foreign Affairs Minister in January 1921, highlighted the importance of de Valera's 'rescue of the Irish voters in the United States from the control of American party leaders'.[47] But it was to become clear that Sinn Féin's contention during the election of 1918 – 'if you accept independence and reject any compromise, President Wilson is bound by his own words to see that you get it' – was a very simplistically optimistic reading of the American dimension.[48] De Valera's visit to the US from August 1919 to the end of 1920 was significant in this regard. Senator David Walsh, the son of Irish emigrants and the first Catholic to reach the Senate for Massachusetts, set the tone by referring to de Valera as 'the Lincoln of Ireland' who would 'take the shackles of tyranny from the limbs of the sons of Ireland'.[49] But the trip was often marred by fractiousness, underlined by the ferocious tone of a letter Arthur Griffith sent to Daniel Cohalan, the influential New York judge who believed that Americans needed to dominate the Irish organisations in the US, and his ally John Devoy, in June 1920, imploring them to stop the 'attacks being made at present by prominent citizens of America of Irish blood on the authority and credit of the president of the Irish republic'.[50]

Diarmuid O'Hegarty's influence was also vital due to his administrative talents; he was responsible for organising meetings of the underground republican government and coordinating the work of departments from his office in Dublin. A measure of his task, and indeed his success, was that it would be, as far as he could manage, 'functioning as any progressive government would be expected to function'.[51]

Dublin Castle, of course, had its own intelligence and 'Personality Files' assembled by the RIC's Crime Department Special Branch and the Dublin Metropolitan Police's (DMP) detective division from the very end of the nineteenth century. From 1899 to 1921 this amounted to 19,000 pages of secret documents on 500 republican suspects: 'Contrary to popular belief, neither was a particularly impressive organisation', and until the final year of Dublin Castle's rule, there was no 'secret service' in Ireland: 'Special Branch did not run undercover agents, rarely recruited informers and made little effort to penetrate the organisations of its enemies.'[52]

The largest proportion of documents relate not to household names but to public servants – such as teachers, clerks and postmen – with much comment on those teachers believed to be imparting 'disloyalty and sedition'. Such people, points out Fearghal McGarry, 'belonged to a class particularly drawn to republicanism; young men who were educated, status-conscious and ambitious but frustrated by the lack of social and political opportunities available to them in Ireland under the Union'.[53] There was a wealth of personal and political detail recorded and a variety of activism, not just republican, monitored, but it was not easy to secure convictions for political crimes owing to sympathetic justices and juries and reluctance of witnesses to come forward.

The recruitment of new soldiers to augment the under-pressure existing police and Crown forces complicated these challenges. The plight of the RIC was, of course, pivotal to the character of the war, and the need to reinforce its ranks and authority led to crucial decisions being made about military strategy in Ireland, including the recruitment of an Auxiliary division and the Black and Tans. It was civilians who would bear the brunt, as recalled by playwright Seán O'Casey, who referred to a raid on his tenement dwelling in Dublin. He distinguished between the Tommies (regular British army soldiers) and the Tans: 'Tans, thought Seán, for the Tommies would not shout so soullessly, nor smash the glass panels so suddenly; they would hammer on the door with a rifle butt and wait for it to be opened.'[54] The first Black and Tans arrived in March 1920, their nickname due to their mixture of police and army uniforms, and from early 1920 through to the truce of July 1921, nearly 14,000 new police recruits were added to the almost 10,000 members of the old RIC.[55] An account of them by David Leeson, published in 2011, and which drew on British records, made it clear they were recruited too quickly, without proper training or assessment of suitability and encouraged to treat republicans as they wished.[56]

The majority (52 per cent) were unskilled or semi-skilled workers, and skilled manual workers (36 per cent) made up most of the rest. The high rates of pay were a draw at £3 10s a week, with allowances. But it was not the case, as often contended, that they were frequently men with criminal records; rather they were a collection of British and Irish ex-servicemen (Leeson describes them as 'fairly ordinary men'), and those who had been hardened by First World War service had no monopoly on brutality; those with pre-war service in the army were also likely to act with impunity and indiscipline. Leeson does underline, however, the awful conditions they lived in, and that the IRA's ability to choose and vary ambush sites left them physically and psychologically vulnerable. Casualty rates, however, were not particularly high; Leeson points out that of the 1,153 who joined up in October 1921, 'the IRA killed only 21 of them'; another four died in accidents.[57]

One historian's examination of the registers of 2,300 Black and Tans reveals that one-third were recruited in London, over one-third in Liverpool and Glasgow and 14 per cent in Dublin. This was an overwhelmingly English force – 78.6 per cent of this sample – but 19 per cent of the sample were Irish-born; their average age was twenty-six and a half. One who resigned recalled, 'We were mercenary soldiers fighting for our pay, not patriots willing and anxious to die for our country ... our job was to earn our pay by suppressing armed rebellion, not die in some foolish ... forlorn hope.' The Black and Tans had a deserved reputation for brutality; they terrified the inhabitants of Balbriggan in Dublin with a 'sacking' of the town in September 1920 in revenge for the murder of an RIC district inspector and his brother by burning and destroying homes and businesses and beating two republicans to death, and as was well recognised at the time, the 'majority of those attacked were victims innocent of any documented complicity'.[58]

The Auxiliaries were ex-officers and in effect a paramilitary strike force; they were intended to be an elite cadre. Recruited in July 1920, they operated in counter-insurgency units independent of other RIC formations; former officers promoted following exceptional performance during the war, they too had their problems of unsuitability and lack of discipline.[59] The 'Burning of Cork' in December 1920, in retaliation for an IRA ambush, caused extensive damage to the city (costing an estimated £2 million with 2,000 jobs lost). One participant, Charles Schulze, an Auxiliary, wrote to his girlfriend and mother in its aftermath:

> You will have read all about Cork. Suffice to say I was there and very actively involved to boot until dawn on Sunday. I just escaped the ambush ... but later arrived as a reinforcement. We took sweet revenge ... Houses in the vicinity were set alight and from there various parties set out on their mission of destruction. Many who had witnessed scenes in France and Flanders say that nothing they had experienced was comparable with the punishment meted out in Cork.[60]

In terms of general intelligence, the IRA was not infallible; the broader British intelligence was actually better than it got credit for. What cannot be contested was the formidable achievement of Collins, a masterful organiser, in cultivating contacts throughout the government, but also turning some of the opposing players against their own side, and in organising the killing detectives and intelligence officers and their agents in order to protect his own intelligence network. Anne Dolan has made the point, however, as noted earlier, that 'the civilian experience is possibly the most overlooked aspect of the war. It gets lost in the eagerness to examine the combatants.' The experience of this war, she writes eloquently:

> was borne not just by those who fought but also by those who lived around it; by the men and women, who, in going about their daily lives, provided the necessary cover for guerrilla warfare, by those subjected to curfews, by those caught in the crossfire, by those who were made to dig trenches in country roads by the IRA and then made fill them in by the British forces that came upon them. It was borne by the girls with the shaven heads, the mark of fraternising with either enemy, by the women who brought whispers and messages and relief to any side. It was borne by those who feared the accusation of collusion, by

those who went the other way when the dying asked for help because they feared death coming to their own door.[61]

As Ernie O'Malley saw it,

police were inclined to get information but when people who talked loosely were located through the [IRA] intelligence system, or saw their friends suffer as a result of their looseness, things changed somewhat. For the enemy intelligence agents things were made so hot by the threatening and shooting of spies, and even more so by the clearing out of the local Royal Irish Constabulary garrison ... people found it did not pay as 'England was far and protection a name', so people eventually learned to shut their eyes and close their mouth.[62]

EIGHTEEN

THE CHIVALROUS SOLDIER AND THE CRUEL KILLER

High-profile events in late 1920, including the death of the Sinn Féin Lord Mayor of Cork Terence MacSwiney after a prolonged hunger strike; the execution of Kevin Barry, an eighteen-year-old IRA Volunteer and the first to be executed since 1916; Bloody Sunday, when twelve alleged British intelligence agents were shot and in retaliation a mixture of Crown forces killed fourteen civilians at a GAA match; and the Kilmichael ambush, when sixteen Auxiliaries were killed (and one who was captured later shot dead), underlined the intensity of the battle. So did the formation of IRA flying columns, while disputes between farmers and the ITGWU and the killing of informers by the IRA revealed strong social tensions.

MacSwiney's death made an international impact and provided much opportunity for propaganda. He died in Brixton prison on 25 October on the seventy-fourth day of his hunger strike, and one biographer dwelt on the enduring image of him 'pitted directly against the might of the British empire ... Terence MacSwiney's solitary protest would be seen, in the context of the Irish struggle, as personifying the triumph of the weak over the strong.'[1] His own words were also frequently quoted and provided succour for others, including those seeking independence in India (during their own struggle for freedom from the British Raj, some Indian nationalists would cite the Irish War of Independence as a source of inspiration): 'Not all the forces of all the empires of the earth can break the spirit of one true man ... it is not those who can inflict the most. But those who can endure most who will conquer.'[2] But at the time, there was also some discussion over the morality of his actions and the extent to which it could be reconciled with Catholicism. His wife Muriel, in some of her interviews, also underlined the extent to which the War of Independence all but destroyed family life for those involved at that level: '[Terence] really could not be with me at all. He could not be where they might find him at night. I hardly ever saw my husband at all, to tell the truth.'[3] They had one daughter, Máire, who was born when MacSwiney was in prison in June 1918; news of her birth made him feel, according to a prison letter 'grateful, proud, delighted, relieved happy beyond measure'.[4]

But it was back to the cause soon afterwards; he was adamant the following month that 'under no account is the registration of her birth to be done in English'; a few months later he was unfazed about deportation: 'this deportation will be nothing ... my form couldn't be better'.[5] Even allowing for propaganda and the censor's eye (he acknowledged in December 1918 that, because of the censors, 'I never try to say anything intimate in my letters'), there is a casualness here that suggests little room for the wider human and family picture. The focus towards the end of his life was not on the contemporary impact but the aftermath; he wrote to Cathal Brugha from Brixton in September 1920: 'If I die I know the fruit will exceed the cost a thousand fold.'[6] But there were also the more mundane practicalities which others had to sort out; that same month his sister Mary still had to deal with correspondence about Terence's bank account.[7]

The campaign to gain a reprieve to prevent the execution of Kevin Barry, a 'mere boy', gathered momentum after he was sentenced to death for an IRA attack which was one of the first to result in deaths (three) of British soldiers as opposed to RIC members. Accusations of torture while he was in custody were vigorously highlighted; Arthur Griffith declared he was a 'prisoner of war' while Erskine Childers, the former British civil servant turned ardent Irish republican, called it 'an unworthy act of vengeance, contrasting ill with the forbearance and humanity invariably shown by the Irish Volunteers towards the prisoners captured by them'. But the British, having achieved a first conviction under the Restoration of Order in Ireland Act (ROIA), which had suspended the normal courts system and provided for military courts with the power to enforce internment without trial and the death penalty, were not going to allow it to be diluted. General Nevil Macready, commander of the British troops in Ireland, was conscious of and sensitive about propaganda opportunities (complaining the following year that 'this propaganda business is the strongest weapon SF has') and the hostility of papers like the *Manchester Guardian* to the government's 'get tough' policy. It has been observed that the *Manchester Guardian's* story on Barry's execution was 'almost indistinguishable from those which appeared in the more moderate nationalist papers in Ireland' ('the boy met his death with cheerfulness and courage'), but other papers pointed out that the three soldiers killed were also 'mere youths'.[8]

As Macready saw it, in a letter to Henry Wilson, chief of the imperial general staff, 'I imagine there must be some game on to get a reprieve, and all I have to say is that if they do such a thing it will irritate the troops to a very great extent, because here is a clean-cut case of murder without any doubt, where three soldiers lost their lives and if the man is not hung, how on earth can we prevent troops making reprisals?' But that does not mean that the ROIA worked – clearly it did not – or that Basil Clarke, head of the government's propaganda agency at Dublin Castle, would be able to counteract the effectiveness and endurance of the propaganda built up around Barry, who was commemorated widely in song and verse, in contrast to the British soldiers killed that day, who remained 'faceless names and numbers'.[9]

Bloody Sunday was a stark reminder that there were two wars being fought in Ireland in 1920: the military one and the intelligence one. The murder of thirty people in a single day (along with those killed in the targeting of intelligence agents, and at the GAA match, two Auxiliaries and two Dublin IRA officers were also killed) was a microcosm of the War of Independence, in respect of the role of killing and espionage, heavy civilian casualties, the taking of significant risks, a fiercely fought propaganda battle, its contribution to the building and sustaining of myths about key individuals, and relevance to the debate about whether the war was to be long or short. The maintenance of law and order had long crumbled in Ireland and the conduct of the war from the British side was a disaster. Important sections of the British media, including the *Daily Mail*, reported what happened in Croke Park as a reprisal and an illustration that the Irish issue was not being 'contained'.[10]

Historians in recent years have been more sceptical about the scale of the damage inflicted by Michael Collins. Bloody Sunday undoubtedly contributed to the contention, to use the phrase of Arthur Griffith, that he was 'the man who won the war'. In truth Bloody Sunday was not 'a brilliant demonstration of pinpoint selective assassination'. Most historians now accept that not all that morning's targets were involved in intelligence work (one was a vet, some were court-martial officers). They were easy targets because they had never contemplated such attacks, as prior to this no spies had been killed in their residences.[11] Certainly, there is an onus on historians to cut through some of the more simplistic assertions; Michael Hopkinson points out that traditionally Collins has been depicted as the heroic leader of the IRA from the beginning of guerrilla warfare in January 1919, 'despite the fact that his role was that of an organiser rather than a fighter, and that he rarely journeyed outside Dublin. He advocated a cautious approach to any confrontation with British forces.'[12]

There is no doubt that to get results from his intelligence information his Squad – a group of gunmen, all IRB members and operational from July 1919 – was significant, as they eliminated the threat posed by the DMP, which had a detective division (G), through assassinations and then sought to destroy British intelligence agents. But while he was active in extending his intelligence system to the provinces, his organisation there

> was much less comprehensive ... Whatever influence the IRA headquarters had in the provinces was largely brought about by Collins's personal contacts and energy, but it should be remembered how critical local initiative was in guerrilla warfare, and how resented was his refusal to grant requests for arms and ammunition. He had a surer grasp of the limitations of his achievement than many of his biographers. His significance to a great extent lay in Dublin.[13]

The question of local initiative and the difficult relationship between IRA HQ and local IRA units also exercised Richard Mulcahy, who insisted on the importance of Dublin, asserting that 'no number nor any magnitude of victories in any distant provincial areas can have any value if Dublin is lost in a military sense', a priority that inevitably created tensions with the IRA outside of Dublin, especially in Cork.[14]

Researchers will find a variety of versions of Collins in various collections of papers, illustrating his need to let off steam, exaggerate, propagandise or express a sense of genuine uplift: in May 1920 he wrote to George Gavan Duffy suggesting 'things here are very thrilling ... I think in my opinion, Ireland is in for the greatest crucifixion she has ever yet been subjected to.'[15] Such declarations suggest a gross insensitivity to those who would be most affected by such crucifixion.

The mixture of various traits, attributes and failings associated with Collins can be extended; Charles Townshend contended as far back as 1979, for example, that 'the army of the Republic was a curious compound of the admirable and the unpleasant – the chivalrous soldier and the cruel killer, the selfless patriot and the swaggering jack – in office, the devout Catholic and the self-conscious martyr'. But he also concluded that their achievements 'could be used to establish a new framework for resistance against imperial power'.[16] More than twenty years later, Arthur Mitchell wrote about the variety of tactics the republicans employed and characterised them as 'intimidation, coercion, arson, murder and ultimately guerrilla warfare'.[17] But there were obvious weaknesses also; even though the DMP's G Division was virtually paralysed and despite the magnitude of the Bloody Sunday killings, the police under the leadership of Ormonde Winter were making some inroads in intelligence.[18]

In the short term, the backlash to Bloody Sunday left the IRA reeling; internment without trial, wide-scale arrests, including that of Arthur Griffith, and martial law (though it was telling that the martial law that was introduced was a diluted version of what the military chiefs wanted). The British intelligence effort was back on track. The IRA recovered too; how robust it was is open to debate, but it can be asserted that in the realm of 'secret service' the IRA was victorious; the republican spy network was not penetrated; the British did not succeed in effectively infiltrating the underground.

But politics was still relevant. It is no coincidence that at the time of Bloody Sunday, the militarists were also thinking in terms of length of conflict and possible channels of communication. The short-term backlash to Bloody Sunday was not as important as the fact that neither side could afford a repeat of events on that scale. The historian Michael Hopkinson uses a modern phrase, 'peace process', to describe what was emerging in 1920 and it is no coincidence that it developed more momentum in the aftermath of Bloody Sunday.[19]

The extent of British revenge attacks, or as one Cork IRA member described it, 'the viciousness and unbridled brutality of the enemy by taking revenge in reprisals both official and otherwise', was not just subject to the judgement of Irish republicans and those who 'gave us food and shelter'; it was also commented on critically and with clarity by the

British media, including, for example, the London weekly *New Statesman* towards the end of 1920. Senior British politicians and military figures, it maintained, 'know that murder, theft and arson are becoming commonplace in whatever part of Ireland the Black and Tans enter. They know that women and children have to hurry out of their beds at midnight to escape from houses deliberately set on fire by the agents of law and order', including those 'dragged from their beds, stripped naked and flogged'. It was also observed that British journalists 'have been threatened with murder for speaking the truth'. What all this amounted to was 'a state of government terrorism'.[20] Some members of the British forces, although they gave full vent to racism about 'dirty Irishwomen', 'thoroughly infuriated Irishmen', 'houses swarming with fleas', 'corner boys', 'fanatical rebels' and 'incidents that could only be Irish', also recognised 'our intelligence was not too intelligent and methods employed were sometimes unorthodox', that Irish republicanism was 'a national movement' and that 'the IRA were no fools in the conduct of guerrilla warfare'.[21]

The status of Britain's Empire, it seemed, would be better served by getting out of southern Ireland through the means of a political compromise, and crucially, the IRA was enough of a broad coalition to contemplate this. Hopkinson suggests, for example, that Collins was prepared to agree a truce in December 1920, and that this did not happen for another six months because of the stubbornness and lack of political bravery of the man they called the 'Welsh wizard', British prime minister Lloyd George, who allowed himself to be convinced by the hawks who had his ear. But the important point is that a beginning had been made prior to Bloody Sunday, and that willingness to work towards a truce was reinforced by the events of that day.

Vinnie Byrne was only aged nineteen on Bloody Sunday when he entered the room of a British officer and shot him; Byrne lived to the age of ninety-two. He had joined the Irish Volunteers at the age of fourteen and had fought in 1916, and in November 1919 joined Collins's Squad. For the duration of the Anglo-Irish war, Byrne took part in the stake-outs and killings of police detectives and military intelligence agents; his BMH witness statement recounts his participation in some fifteen such operations. On Bloody Sunday he commanded an IRA detail that killed two agents in their boarding house.[22] Anne Dolan has suggested that 'some hierarchy of horror had been grossly breached on Bloody Sunday morning ... nine of the men killed wore only their pyjamas'. While Collins could sanitise the executions ('my conscience is clear. There is no crime in detecting and destroying in war time, the spy and the informer. They have destroyed without trial. I have paid them back in their own coin'), some of the Squad were so young – just teenagers – when asked to join that they learned at a very young stage, after a short and brutal training, to be callous – one of the assassins ate his victim's breakfast on Bloody Sunday morning. But there were still reminders that they were just out of adolescence: Byrne recounted how he liked 'plugging' British soldiers 'but he still filled his pockets with liquorice like any child would when he took part in a raid on the B&I stores'.[23]

Bloody Sunday also cemented the GAA's relationship with Irish republicanism (a new stand at Croke Park, the Hogan Stand was named after the slain Tipperary captain in 1924), though that connection was not as intrinsic or all-embracing as sometimes believed. In the past it has been maintained that the GAA members contributed to the revolution in disproportionate numbers and this led to gloriously exaggerated assertions. Historian William Murphy has pointed to a quote from the *Irish Independent* in 1923:

> In 1916 when Pearse and his companions unfurled the flag of liberty, the men of the hurling and football fields rolled in from far and near, and it is no exaggeration to say that they formed the backbone of that company ... when the Anglo-Irish War developed, go where you would up and down the country, it was difficult to point to even one man, other than a hurler or footballer, who took any prominent part in the fight.[24]

Such notions endured, but while the formation of the Irish Volunteers witnessed the GAA in many respects facilitating and promoting the new venture, both groups also had to compete for the time and commitment of members and involvement with either group was not necessarily 'synonymous with radical separatism'. Collectively, these nuances point to 'the importance of treating with scepticism the notion that the GAA was politically and nationally minded above all else'. But during the summer of 1918 the GAA did defy bans on public meetings by going ahead with its matches and police did not have the resources to deal with defiance on such a scale. Many GAA clubs were named after dead republicans and clubs organised games in aid of prisoners, including the match that was being played on Bloody Sunday which raised £160, 'despite the mayhem and confusion'. The playing calendar was inevitably heavily disrupted by the intensity of the war, but broadly, 'it seems that revolutionary activists and their opponents had more impact upon the GAA than the association or its members had upon the revolution'.[25] A recent study of the GAA in Kerry, a pioneering county for the association, highlights the gulf between popular nationalism and the ambiguity that remained at official GAA level regarding endorsing the separatist agenda.[26]

Much energy has been expended trying to get to the bottom of the Kilmichael ambush in Cork on 28 November 1920, when an IRA flying column under Tom Barry killed seventeen members of the Auxiliaries. Given the scale of the body count it assumed folkloric status. Barry maintained that no prisoners were taken because the Auxiliaries faked a surrender and then opened fire again, killing three of the ambushers. It was a version accepted for decades but disputed in *The IRA and Its Enemies* (1998) by Peter Hart, who rubbished the idea of the false surrender; they were, he maintained, killed in cold blood. None of the arguments about the ambush have been proved conclusively and the contradictory evidence over what happened does not merit emphatic conclusions, but given the scale of the Bloody Sunday killings a week before, the Kilmichael ambush inevitably provoked a severe backlash. Shortly after it, martial law was declared for much of Munster, wide-scale internment was resorted to and official reprisals were authorised. But this was not to deter Barry and his colleagues – six months later, he could boast of commanding the largest IRA flying column in the country, with over a hundred members. They made mistakes and took risks, a consequence of Barry's insistence that they could not be a 'paper army' and had to act spontaneously and in response to local circumstances, which resulted in both spectacular successes and obvious failings as well as ruthlessness, but underlying all of that within the IRA was also distrust and resentment. Isolated triumphs 'could not hide the fact that pressure was increasing on the column, and Barry became increasingly critical of inactive regions. He was later to say that all Kerry did during the war was to shoot one decent police inspector at Listowel races and a colleague of his. Barry was strongly critical also of the lack of assistance from GHQ.'[27]

Despite the IRA's often effective use of guerrilla warfare tactics, there was often a pitiful shortage of weapons, as well as communications problems between IRA headquarters and the regional brigades. The BMH statements invite reflection on the extent to which the independence struggle was under effective central control. Patrick Cannon, a Volunteer in west Mayo, testified that 'we had no information about the enemy and just anticipated that some such would pass that way some time during the day ... we had no arms at the time'. In east Mayo, Patrick Cassidy recounted, he and his colleagues were ill equipped: 'we got no rifles of any sort. We had one old Martini rifle and a large sporting type rifle for which we had no ammunition ... we did not appreciate then the importance of intelligence and did not give this subject the value it deserved.' These are among the many statements that, far from being triumphalist or boastful, were frank about the shortcomings of the IRA's campaign. But it is clear that other Volunteers were relatively well armed and had access to more information.[28]

A particularly interesting statement was contributed by James O'Donovan, a university student of chemistry and director of chemicals on the IRA's GHQ staff, who detailed the tests and research he carried out in UCD using gelignite, nitro-cresylic acids and poison gas. He refers to the importance of an awareness of 'bacteriological warfare', not a phrase one normally associates with the War of Independence, and suggests that the IRA at one stage considered the possibilities of infecting British military horses with 'glanders or some similar infectious disease' and of spreading botulism. O'Donovan wrote with great passion and pride about his work, relishing the memory of

> getting a beautiful grenade turned out in a week – a vast improvement on anything that had been done in the way of moulding the wall with its sectional grooves. I always maintained that our final grenade was really superior to the Mills ... The whole problem with me, if I was going to produce explosives more or less on an army scale, was that they had to be made so simple that men with practically no knowledge could make them in a farmhouse kitchen and places like that. Yet, they had to be fairly foolproof, because we could not have people all over the country having their heads blown off. We had some accidents, but not many.[29]

But the IRA was to face what became a recurrent problem: if it was fighting a war in the name of 'the Irish people', how did it deal with Irish people who stood in its way or were alleged to have undermined its efforts? In September 1921 Bishop Michael Fogarty wrote to Arthur Griffith enclosing money for a prisoners' fund, but was 'very uneasy about the shape things are taking ... A war of devastation without the good will of the people behind it would be a ruinous disaster and it looks, at least in the papers, as if things are drifting that way.'[30] The IRA had few qualms about killing informers and alleged informers; the difficulty for the historian is establishing how many were in fact informers, perhaps an impossible task. The cloak of the conflict could also be used to cover the ostracising of those who were simply an inconvenience, like one man arrested for questioning by the IRA in Cork: 'he is a man of rowdy nature, dishonest and a nuisance in the locality.'[31]

In April 1921 Kitty Carroll, a forty-one-year-old Monaghan woman, was shot dead by the IRA after she had informed police about illicit distilling. Brian Hanley points out that Carroll was a Protestant and 'there have been recurring allegations that the IRA was more likely to kill "spies" if they were ex-soldiers, Protestants or marginal figures ... rather than "respectable" members of the nationalist community.'[32]

Anne Dolan's arresting opening to an account of Carroll's death underlines the brutality but also the myths, five months after IRA HQ had prohibited the killing of female spies:

> There were five bullets in Kitty Carroll's body when it was found in April 1921. Her hands were tied behind her back: 'Spies and Informers beware, Convicted IRA' was written on the calling card pinned to her breast. Either the bullet to the head or heart had certainly killed her. The other three, one through her cheek, were just fired for good measure. [33]

Carroll had been fined by a republican court for distilling *poitín* but had persisted; she was a spinster living in complete poverty with her parents and 'deranged' brother in Monaghan and was, according to a local IRA man, 'by any standards a half-wit' who may have had amorous intent towards an IRA man. Was this really about spying? Or personal grievance? Or getting rid of nuisances? Likely the latter, and this was not uncommon, leading to a fundamental question: 'How do you reconcile the details of the deaths of 1919–23 with the need for a myth of independence?' There were many cases like this, revealing a 'new, intimate, local kind of killing'; the battering, mutilations and excessive bullet count were meant to terrify and shame and deter. Unlike other confrontations, many of the killings were face-to-face, sometimes involving people who knew each other. Tom Barry referred to it as 'going down into the mire to find your freedom', a euphemism at odds with the brutal reality and psychological consequences of such killings and the callousness of young, often inexperienced killers.[34]

There is relatively little documented sexual violence during the conflict; the *Irish Bulletin* did occasionally refer to rape, though there was a perceived conflict between the need to protect female modesty and the urge to publicise brutality.[35] In April 1921 the *Bulletin* devoted a special edition to 'outrages on Irish women', which explicitly used the word 'rape' and, though breaking taboo with its frank statements from victims, suggested there were other victims who were not prepared to see their names and addresses published. At this stage the *Irish Bulletin* writers seemed to think the need to record the brutality outweighed the need to protect the women's modesty.[36] Republicans and British soldiers cut off girls' hair, and women in their nightwear did face uniformed and armed men. There was a tendency for republicans to suggest that 'no girls, except the unfortunates' would meet British soldiers, but the British in turn distributed leaflets that suggested republican men were 'safely hidden in the bedrooms of their female admirers in Dublin ... Many of our once pure Irish girls have lost their virtue in the abnormal lives they are leading.'[37]

There are very few references to rape in the BMH statements, though Seámus Fitzgerald, a Cork IRA Volunteer, referred to incidents of rape and attempted rape in his locality: 'I regret to say I had two such cases. One, an already middle-aged pregnant woman was raped in Blackpool by the Black and Tans, and in the same locality another middle-aged woman successfully resisted a similar attempt.'[38] Frank Henderson of the Dublin IRA referred to a fellow Volunteer arrested on a charge of rape who was brought before a republican court, though he provided little detail: 'The Court took a certain view in regard to the case, but it was thought it would be well to obtain expert advice on the moral side of the question and it was agreed to defer announcing a decision pending consultation with a clerical authority.'[39]

Women active on the republican side experienced mixed fortunes. No doubt some had been energised by the promise of equality in the 1916 Proclamation, but what did that actually mean in practice during the war? At Cumann na mBan's conference in 1918 the importance of militarisation was emphasised; one historian has suggested that 'Cumann na mBan was an organisation almost entirely practical in nature. It did not explore new venues of political theory, being content to stay within the framework of the new nationalism by following the new ethos of the Volunteers, and also by embracing the Irish-Ireland ideas espoused by Sinn Féin.'[40] But because of gender it was more complicated than this; the women were seen as troublemakers in a category of their own. Some of the proclamations after the Rising specifically aimed at them could also empower them in their attitude and their militancy, and they felt that they, through their participation in 1916, had earned the claims to equality.

Nancy Wyse Power was a central figure in the reorganisation of CnB after the Rising, following her appointment as one of two honorary secretaries (Markievicz was president of the National Executive); reorganisation and restructuring meant that by 1920 there were in the region of 500 branches in the country. Women also played an important intelligence role, and were involved in prisoners' rights and welfare, propaganda and relief work, which would suggest that the assertion that 'instead of passing resolutions, mothers and sisters served the cause by bringing out tea, griddle-bread, butter and bandages to the ambushers' is overly dismissive and not supported by the array of testimony now available; one CnB member remembered 'getting up on one policeman's back and getting my two hands round his throat.'[41] Women also found themselves working as justices in the Sinn Féin courts, but their liberation should not be exaggerated. An activist from Enniscorthy highlighted the limitations: 'I had a first aid certificate, but it's the rifle I would have preferred.'[42]

Some were also apt, from an early stage, to invoke the supposed spiritualism and religiosity of republicanism. Mary MacSwiney, a sister of Terence, for example, continually articulated the morality of republicanism and Markievicz used her conversion to Catholicism in 1917 to hone her equation of her cause with religion; though she was 'notoriously ignorant of the finer points of catholic theology, she nonetheless embraced her new faith wholeheartedly, claiming to have experienced an epiphany while holed up in the College of Surgeons' during the 1916 Rising.[43] CnB stalwarts encouraged MacSwiney to

> always put the real views here before the Americans and showing that we do <u>not</u> want peace 'at any price' ... far from being oppressed or intimidated by martial law our girls in the areas where it prevails are

magnificent – defiant in the face of all threats ... the splendid example
you gave in your sorrow helped them to bear theirs with fortitude too.[44]

When in the US, MacSwiney insisted that 'besides in first aid CnB is
useful in scores of other ways. In districts where there are flying columns
of our men, their washing, cooking etc is done by our girls and they are
provided with shirts, socks and often boots. Despatch carrying is another
activity and we shine here too'. She also referred to 'our roll of honour' of
thirty in jail.[45]

For those who were organising for CnB, there were obvious societal
prejudices to overcome based on the perceived inappropriateness of the
marrying of women and militarism. Bridget O'Mullane recalled:

> I had a good deal of prejudice to overcome on the part of parents who
> did not mind their boys taking part in a military movement but who
> had never heard of, or were reluctant to accept, the idea of a body of
> gun-women. It was, of course, a rather startling innovation and, in that
> way, Cumann na mBan can claim to have been pioneers in establishing
> what was undoubtedly a women's auxiliary of an army. I fully under-
> stood this attitude and eventually, in most cases, succeeded in over-
> coming this prejudice.[46]

The question for the organisation as the war progressed was the extent
to which its members would be full combatants; they managed to organise their own training camps and drills and some acted as snipers; they also
acted as intelligence agents, establishing contacts with informers in Dublin Castle and undertaking courier work.[47] Calls for boycotts were another
part of its strategy. Some CnB activists suffered house raids and serious
physical assaults; Sineád McCoole records the case of Agnes Daly, sister
of Kathleen Clarke, who in October 1920 was pulled from her house, had
her hair cut off and was slashed with a razor, only to be saved by the first-
aid training of another sister.[48] Roughly fifty women were interned during
the conflict, a relatively low number, suggesting that the mores of the time
contributed to a reluctance to imprison too many women; a number of
them went on hunger strike in Mountjoy in late 1921, when, after an escape
by four of their members, restrictions were placed on their association and
they were placed under guard by Auxiliaries.[49]

Markievicz was also an intriguing character and her increasing militancy 'must have horrified Constance's mother Lady Gore Booth of Sligo who didn't want a rebel heroine for a daughter'. But Constance began to 'forge her own image. She had herself photographed – smocked and smoking – in her studio, a dishevelled Bohemian chaos.' Other images from these years, including those of her in bicycling gear, declared 'in black and white that whatever Constance ... might choose to do with her future, it would be both whole-hearted and unpredictable.'[50] She also had a tendency to describe revolutionary events as 'wonderful', writing to her sister: 'Isn't it wonderful to think of these boys in Mountjoy? Some are just rough country lads all going in smiling and confident and facing up to things like this,' or on another occasion: 'Life is so wonderful. One just wanders around and enjoys it.'[51]

Julia O'Faoláin, the daughter of Seán, herself later a renowned novelist, saw the revolutionary period as central to her parent's courtship and indeed their life after it; they had 'entwined their feelings for each other with those they cherished for the national cause', which did not necessarily make for a straightforward relationship or for equality. Eileen told her daughter stories about how she and other members of CnB during the War of Independence would cut up an ox for the retreating men: 'these were definitely menial jobs that were given to the women ... there was no question she would have a gun. No.'[52] In the local elections in Dublin in 1920 The *Cuala News* encouraged voters to vote for women: 'On such questions as education, housing, public health the woman's opinion is of particular importance. Women are by nature orderly; undoubtedly the cleansing department of any city would benefit by the inclusion of some women ... women have too intimate a knowledge of the purchasing value of money to acquiesce in the squandering of public funds.'[53]

NINETEEN

GOVERNING, SOCIAL REALITIES AND JUSTICE

The 1920 local elections highlighted that there was a parallel political War of Independence in train. SF used the elections (held in urban areas in January and rural areas five months after) to cement its authority, but not without pain. It gained control of twenty-five out of thirty-three county councils and 172 of 206 rural district councils but it did not have the field to itself and suffered in some urban areas. It won, for example, only forty-two out of eighty seats on Dublin Corporation; only ten of twenty-four in Galway; and in Cork, thirty of fifty-six. Nonetheless, the RIC in Longford concluded that 'the local councils in this county are now in the hands of the rabble'.[1]

But the 'rabble' also impressed some; in mid 1920 the British government's Irish Affairs Committee was informed that some southern unionists were impressed by SF's attempt to administer local government, even if compliance was sometimes induced through fear. It was noted in Limerick that 'everybody is going over to Sinn Féin, not because they believe in it but because it is the only authority in the country and they realise that if their lives and property are to be secured they must act with Sinn Féin'.[2]

When William T. Cosgrave gave his statement to the BMH in 1949, he sought to focus on the significance of the 'loss of civil control' by the British government in Ireland during this period. As Minister for Local Government in the underground Dáil Éireann, he managed to achieve much with a staff of just sixty-five, one-quarter the number in the official

Local Government Board for Ireland. He recounted how on one occasion 'the chairman of an important County Council walked freely through the city of Dublin with £50,000 on his person'. But he also pointed out that some local public representatives paid with their lives – 'two lord mayors of Cork were done to death, one outside his own home; one mayor of Limerick, two members of the Limerick Corporation and the chairman of the Limerick County Council'.[3]

There was also an obvious tension between the politicians and the IRA soldiers; Tom Barry had contempt for 'the way headquarters was carrying on ... big carpeted suites of rooms in the Gresham Hotel and bottles of whiskey and brandy all round'. Dan Breen was also dismissive of those who 'preferred the drawing room as a battleground; the political resolution rather than the gun as their offensive weapon ... we had heard the gospel of freedom preached; we believed in it, we wanted to be free, and were prepared to give our lives as proof of the faith that was in us. But those who preached the gospel were not prepared to practice it.'[4]

But people working in a variety of government departments and as civil servants were also enduring grave risks; for those working for the Irish language department,

> two of our eight organisers are in prison; the organiser for Mayo was seized and imprisoned for 3 months: this organiser had a narrow escape with his life by the army of occupation. On the occasion of his arrest they compelled him to come on his knees and repeat fulsome praise of King George; they pressed firearms against his head and lips and murderously assaulted him. They stuffed his mouth and throat with bog almost to the point of suffocation and finally threw him into a lake where they left him until he was all but drowned.[5]

The political War of Independence posed serious communications problems, frequently commented on by all departments; a system needed to be devised for 'weekly messengers from various towns throughout the country ... these towns to be collecting and distributing centres for definite areas'. In October 1920, Kevin O'Higgins, Cosgrave's assistant, made the point that the Department of Local Government 'for efficient functioning requires free and frequent communication with every public body in the country. An estimate of the number of letters issuing would be from three hundred to five hundred each week.'[6] Given the scale of the correspondence that has survived, this was clearly a challenge that was met successfully, though not without interruptions and raids, including a raid on the office of Austin Stack, the Minister for Home Affairs, in May 1921 during which 'all papers, files and office furniture were seized. The office stamp and the name stamp used by Mr Stack were also seized.'[7]

Diarmuid O'Hegarty was vital as secretary to the Dáil cabinet from 1919–21 and played a key role in its success by organising secret meetings of the parliament and coordinating the work of various departments from his offices on the corner of O'Connell St and Abbey St, and later in Middle Abbey St, and handled all correspondence of the cabinet. Demonstrating the blurring of the lines between political and military and civil, he was also a senior member of the IRB and director of communications for the IRA, and after that the IRA's director of organisation. CnB was also credited with having 'efficient lines of communication through Leinster and the South.'[8]

In August 1920 it was decided that 'Ministers who devote their whole time to ministerial duties shall henceforth receive £500 per annum ... directors of departments shall receive £400 per annum.'[9] Clearly, it was a war that needed to be financed and money was very frequently on the agenda of the first Dáil. It helped that one of the members of the first Dáil was millionaire businessman James O'Mara, who organised the government's first bond-cert drive in the US between 1919 and 1921, when over $5.1 million was raised, but it was also a grubby business, and O'Mara resigned his post over concern about the management of the funds; not all of the money was sent back to Ireland and there were to be several lawsuits over disputed ownership. Over 300,000 people bought certificates, most buying amounts of $25 or less. O'Mara had to devise elaborate schemes to launder the money: 'An early dispatch of $200,000 was sent through 3 different bank accounts to remove all traces of its origins and eventually drawn down by a New York Priest who gave it to the Bishop of Killaloe, Michael Fogarty, then also a Dáil trustee.'[10]

Domestic fundraising was also required; the first Dáil Loan raised £371,000, which was extraordinary given that the IPP considered it a great achievement to raise £10,000 a year.[11] Joseph Connolly, the Irish Consul in New York, was wary of numerous inquiries made by Americans regarding investment in Ireland, warning of the need to prevent Wall Street exploitation due to the 'dangers of American finance ... the fact is that quite a number of these people imagine that the whole Irish race is pauperised and that we can do nothing for ourselves without Wall Street money.'[12] Of the money raised in Ireland, most came from Munster; Dáil Éireann records suggested a total figure of £500,000 secured by September 1920.[13]

This, however, was not deemed enough and thoughts turned to the possibilities of raising money through income tax, though putting this into practice was not straightforward; it was recorded, for example, in March 1921 that 'it would be quite impractical to collect income tax in present circumstances. It would be practicable to instruct Income Tax Payers not to pay but to hold the money for the Republican government.'[14] Given that local authorities in pledging allegiance to Dáil Éireann lost in the region of 15 per cent of their revenue from the British government, the solution to this dilemma was deemed to lie in cuts to spending. The Irish republican government loan in Argentina was little to celebrate; by early 1922, $19,155 had been raised from twenty people, but 'the necessary expenditure incurred directly on account of the loan, fully checked and duly audited amounts to $11,280'.[15] Foreign consuls were recorded as being paid a salary of £500 per year in May 1922 (about £50,000 in today's terms).[16]

The withdrawal of British government grants, amounting to over £1.5 million per annum, complicated matters, as did rising agricultural prices and demands for wage increases. These years were dominated by repercussions of lack of finance, disputes over rates, trade union militancy and concern over the Dáil's proposals for reform of the poor law system and the administration of health care. The struggles of ordinary employees of local government authorities generated much correspondence and anger. Thomas Meaney of the ITGWU complained to the Department of Labour that the ceasing of grants paid to Limerick County Council in September 1921 had led to it refusing to employ two-thirds of casual labourers as road workers, which had led to

> dismissing unfortunate workmen, many of whom have large families to support, and keeping useless officials in luxury, thus creating discontent amongst the workers and furnishing propaganda for reactionaries ... the peace outlook is bright so for God's sake do not let us follow the example of Russia [and] let penury be the first fruits of the victory that seems to be at hand.

More scathingly, he maintained,

> the new co. council you have said is exclusively composed of the real
> representatives of the people and is determined to give the Irish worker
> a good means of living and thus make him content and happy in his
> native land. But the 'real representatives' have proved their 'determina-
> tion' in this respect by dismissing unfortunate working men.[17]

Minister for Labour Constance Markievicz drew attention to trade
union disputes and the bleak prospects for labourers in a letter to Limerick County Council and she admonished them for not supporting a
motion that the council employ only trade union labour:

> Far from being a coercive measure, it is a measure for the protection of
> the worker against the constant encroachment on their liberties by the
> employing classes. It has been accepted and approved by all lovers of
> liberty in all countries and it surprised me that such a well known and
> approved principle was not even allowed a fair discussion in a demo-
> cratic council composed of lovers of liberty.[18]

But was such devotion to the labour cause widely shared and was it
meaningful in the first place or was it just a sop to SF's allies? The Labour
Party promised advances in housing, education and health of the working
classes and all its candidates in the 1920 local elections were trade unionists, but it was also prone to divisions due to SF's insistence that cross-class
alliances rather than class confrontation should be prioritised: 'this argument was accepted by some within the labour movement and rejected
by others'. In June 1920, despite an impressive tally of 329 seats in the
municipal and urban elections, and acknowledging that its support was
likely to be higher in urban areas, it is still noteworthy that Labour only
contested a handful of seats in the rural elections and 'in fact, Labour's
role in the 1920 local elections is hardly remembered at all'.[19] While SF
eschewed socialist ideas, instead preferring to focus on securing 'efficiency
and purity of administration', the issue of class permeated the Labour
Party's programme and it focused in particular on housing, the low wages
of some council workers who were receiving just 16s 9d for a seventy-two-
hour week, and the need to 'recover for the national possession' Ireland's
natural resources.

Labour trouble during the War of Independence was being reported on for the British authorities by the Crime Department Special Branch, an indication that many of those involved were regarded as subversive. In the spring of 1920 it was reported that, in Kerry,

> 70 farm labourers have been going about Listowel District calling on each farmer to give an acre of land to a labourer. The farmers refused the demand with the exception of a few. The labourers struck work in the hope of embarrassing the farmer during spring season and thereby compelling him to yield. There is no question of wages and the labourers are beginning to tire of the strike and an early settlement is expected.[20]

In August 1920 there was a strike at the Hills Woollen Mills in Lucan, Dublin, in pursuit of a pay rise of 10s per week, but the owners could not comply as 'trade is distressed and no orders are coming in. Even if the strikers resumed work there are only enough orders to keep them working for about 2 weeks.' Others reported as striking included bakers in Drogheda and bread-van drivers, and the workers secured increases, while 'at Charleville, Buttevant and Churchtown small strikes took place between farm labourers and their employers. The labourers made a demand of 15/– per week increase in wages. The employers offered 10/– per week, which was accepted. The dispute was settled in about 3 days.'[21] At the end of 1920, the Irish Ministry of Labour was boasting that, 'of the 60 labour disputes that have passed through the Labour Department, 45 have been dealt with. In 6 cases intervention was not accepted. 39 disputes have been settled in a satisfactory manner.'[22]

SF leaders were always alive to the danger of trade union militancy; in February 1921, Michael Collins corresponded with Art O'Brien in London about trouble on the railways, especially after the death of railway workers in Mallow, County Cork. According to O'Brien, 'unfortunately the leaders of the Irish railwaymen are what might be described as "old timers" and are without vigour and national spirit'; as far as he was concerned, this was just a union turf war between the NUR and the Union of Locomotive Drivers and Firemen (both English unions with Irish members), who 'are always at loggerheads ... it would be a good thing if we had no members of English unions in Ireland'.[23]

But it was also clear that month that the Department of Home Affairs was prepared to 'instruct police [the Irish Republican Police

Force, formed in 1920] to proceed with aid to Volunteers to eject strikers' from their place of work if it deemed it necessary'.[24] De Valera responded piously to a complaint from the Irish Farmers Union in April 1921 about disputes it was having with the ITGWU with the assertion that 'he feels confident that the common patriotism of all sections will prove superior to all special class interests and that a basis of accommodation will be found accordingly'.[25] A few months later he addressed the ICTU at the Mansion House: 'We know what your support and what your refusal to put forward even your own special interests has meant to the cause of Ireland in the past two years, and I feel perfectly certain that if the fight is to continue we will have the same support from Labour as we have had in the past.'[26] In October of that year *The Voice of Labour*, the official organ of the ITGWU, posed a simple question – 'Who will own Ireland when Ireland is free?' – and singled out shopkeepers for opprobrium.[27] A few months later in January 1922, the same newspaper was urging those in the labour movement to 'build your political machine now ... the other parties are building for themselves. Let Labour build for itself.'[28]

Contemporary newspapers also underlined the difficulties of urban poverty and the 'hungry children of Dublin'; in September 1921 it was reported that the Irish White Cross was spending £50,000 per month on relief, and that charitable endeavours such as Mrs Meade's penny dinners in Sandwith Street were vital.[29] Two months later, the White Cross issued a public appeal suggesting 'about 100,000 men, women and children are in actual want or homeless as a result of the destruction of houses and property ... about 1,000 buildings – farmhouses, shops – have been utterly destroyed ... 40 cooperative creameries utterly destroyed ... at least 6,000 men imprisoned or interned – most of these were the sole, or the main, support of their families.'[30]

The Child Welfare Section of the Women's National Health Association organised babies clubs that had a membership of 1,269 mothers and it stressed that intervention was effective; there had only been one infant death in a recent outbreak of diarrhoea.[31] In County Wexford it was suggested there were, however, 'thousands of unvaccinated children. This state of affairs might be a serious menace in the event of an outbreak of smallpox.'[32] The War of Independence had also been preceded in 1918 by the outbreak of the international influenza epidemic; 20,057 people were reported as having died in Ireland as a result of it from 1918–19: 'in addition, an increase in deaths caused by related illnesses, most notably pneumonia (from which over 3,300 died above what would usually have been expected) can be attributed to the epidemic'.[33] There were undoubtedly other deaths that were not certified. The first wave hit Ireland in early summer 1918 with a more virulent wave from October to December and a third wave from February to April 1919. Schools, retailers and businesses were all affected, as were, disproportionately, those involved in dealing with the public. Given the number of prisoners with influenza, Sinn Féin complained of prisoner mistreatment and neglect; Fionán Lynch, one of the Sinn Féin activists jailed in Belfast, 'attributed the prisoners' preferential medical treatment to Sinn Féin's highly efficient propaganda, as the British authorities wanted to avoid the negative publicity that would follow prisoner deaths. Ironically, with not a single fatality among the prisoners, Belfast jail seemed to be the safest place in the city during the epidemic'.[34]

Dublin County Council also recorded 'how difficult it was for the first city in Ireland to deal with the TB scourge in view of the action of the British government'.[35] Children described as 'delicate' were afflicted with rickets, TB and 'undeveloped frames'.[36] A report on the outbreak of dysentery in the Limerick District Asylum in September 1921 revealed that 'altogether there were over 100 cases with 14 deaths. Dysentery is not uncommon in asylums.'[37]

The *Freeman's Journal* posed the simple and stark question in September 1921: 'why is food so dear?' highlighting the campaign against profiteering by Dublin Corporation; in relation to bread, 'the loaf in Dublin costs 3½d more than the loaf in London'. While, as a trader, Ireland was a creditor nation, it was tied to the British fiscal system and adversely affected by exchange rates, and Britain milled twenty times the proportion of flour Ireland milled.[38] Anti-profiteering decrees featured on the business agenda of the SF government in November 1921,[39] but by the spring of 1922 it was acknowledged that the orders during the War of Independence prohibiting a variety of British goods had been 'part of a policy too rigid and arbitrary to be really sound economically ... almost all Irish industries are at present feeling very keenly the pressure of foreign competition. In many cases the pressure comes principally from countries with depreciated exchanges.'[40]

The amalgamation schemes affecting welfare institutions also generated heated correspondence; the Ballyvaughan Union Board of Guardians was scathing about the scheme of amalgamation put forward by Clare County Council, for example, describing it as 'the most cumbersome and

uneconomic scheme prepared for the reform of the Irish poor law system'.[41] (Under that system, after the Poor Law of 1838, the country had
been divided into 130 unions, each with a workhouse at its centre; the
1919 Democratic Programme committed republicans to abolishing the
system as it was 'odious' and 'degrading'.) But there was a logic to the
amalgamation schemes; a memorandum regarding Roscommon, for
example, made the point that 'the 500 inmates belonging to County
Roscommon are scattered over 7 workhouses built to accommodate over
5,000 people, each workhouse being supervised by a comparatively large
staff of officials'.[42]

The Dáil appointed fourteen local government inspectors and
reports of visits to neglected and isolated workhouses and hospitals are
a reminder of the scale of the task faced and the attitudes that prevailed.
In November 1921 these were the impressions recorded of Belmullet: 'For
absolute neglect and waste this is the worst case I have yet come across. It
is 40 miles from any railway station and in consequence has been immune
from inspection. It is the last word in the rotten poor law system. With
the exception of the qualities [of] the nuns the whole place is a wreck.' The
inspector could not get written data for the number of fever cases in the
previous two years and there was a register of notification for infectious
diseases which had not been written up.[43]

In Sligo, an irate inspector

> found the imbecile and idiot inmates belonging to Tobercurry (about
> 16 females) huddled together in a small ward where they have been
> confined and congested since they were removed over a fortnight ago.
> They have not been allowed in the open since. This is a scandal in view
> of the fact that there is abundant room in the institution.[44]

In the Limerick Union there were 481 beds of which 323 were occupied, including

> 80 imbeciles and 60 fever cases ... no effort seems to have been made
> to get rid of cases which are either unsuitable or have completed con-
> valescence. It indeed seems that once a patient is admitted the length
> of time is not strictly limited to the necessity of treatment ... there are
> 19 unmarried mothers acting as attendants (unpaid). In one sense this
> may be economic but it is obviously subject to abuses. There is also no

sufficient effort made to get inmates who can afford it, to pay anything for their maintenance.[45]

What sort of attitudes were these situations generating and how did they stand in contrast with the social aspirations of the revolution? The concentration in Sinn Féin's political manifesto on efficient and honest administration was significant, particularly its call for appointments to be made on merit and open competitive exams for all clerical posts. It also called for improvements in the health services and the provision of housing. SF have generally been credited for their ability to supplant the British administration in their management of local government during this difficult period, but whatever political radicalism propelled them was not matched by a similar concern with the most vulnerable in Irish society. The loss of British grants ensured that cost-cutting was moved to the top of the agenda of local government. This worked to their advantage in certain areas. Tom Garvin notes that the replacement of contract by direct labour had the dual advantage of 'cutting out traditional businessmen, unionist and/or Protestant in many areas and creating a considerable source of petty patronage to the advantage of new local councillors'.[46]

But in relation to saving money, it was in the area of welfare that SF often sought to economise. The principal victims were the weakest.[47] The commitments in the Democratic Programme, including to look after the aged, infirm and vulnerable, became somewhat hollow promises, forgotten in the midst of a primarily political and military revolution which was being managed in the main by men with Victorian mindsets. Cosgrave demonstrated this vividly in May 1921. In a letter to Austin Stack, Minister for Home Affairs, he maintained:

> People reared in workhouses, as you are aware, are no great acquisition
> to the community and they have no ideas whatever of civic responsibilities. As a rule their highest aim is to live at the expense of the
> ratepayers. Consequently it would be a decided gain if they all took
> it into their heads to emigrate. When they go abroad they are thrown
> on their own responsibilities and have to work whether they like it or
> not.[48]

Cosgrave's views were not only an early indication that Irish leaders would prefer to export rather than solve Irish problems, but indicative also of the extent to which issues of welfare at both local and national level were to be dominated cruelly by the issue of class. The inmates were not without their champions – a correspondent who signed himself 'Humanitarian' referred pointedly to the condition of 'friendless and helpless poor' in workhouses: 'the plea of economy does not hold as it is well known that of every £1 spent on poor law, 15s goes towards administration and 5s for the maintenance of the poor. Beyond doubt, a dumping ground has been selected for what may appear to those who lack human sympathy as the "scrap heap of humanity".'[49] Despite her reputation for radicalism, Constance Markievicz, now Minister for Labour, had also expressed reservations in private about the rights of labour when she was in prison after the 1916 Rising: 'The trade unions' appeal always seems to me to be so very sordid and very selfish. Till something suddenly makes them realise the value of self-sacrifice they will never be much use to humanity. They are only scrambling for champagne and frock coats in the end.'[50]

Idealism clashed with pragmatism at various stages, notably in a dispute over the Richmond Lunatic Asylum in Dublin in 1921, which had 3,252 patients. Dublin Corporation asked the board of guardians overseeing it to boycott the Local Government Board which had funded it and seek private funding, but the guardians refused and submitted the asylum's books to the Board, and duly received funding, saving patients from discharge, as well as the jobs of 160 people employed there. The resident medical superintendent insisted that Dublin councillors 'could not carry on high-falutin' language and indulge in heroics at the expense of the most unfortunate people'.[51]

Another relevant issue was the extent to which there would be any clear water between the politicians and the soldiers. In October 1921 James Gilligan, the chairman of Sligo County Council, wrote to Cosgrave. Gilligan was an IRA member but he was troubled by 'the important question as whether the civil or military side of our government is the supreme authority'; he wanted to know if the IRA, which was making numerous orders, was 'entitled or empowered to dictate to County Councils … councillors should be allowed freedom of speech and action and should not be dictated to or interfered with by the IRA … I have been told that because I made this protest against what I considered was the dictation of the IRA I will be dealt with in another quarter, but be this as it may.'[52]

One of his chief concerns, continually expressed, was regarding the collection of rates, and consternation at rate collectors being appointed by the IRA and the lack of collecting being carried out in a variety of districts. Cosgrave's response to this problem in Listowel (where rate collection was described in June 1921 as 'gone from bad to worse') was that 'defaulting tenants should be summoned to the local republican courts'.[53] In Belmullet, a rate collector 'has £137 which he will not hand over'.[54] The Dublin County Ratepayers Association, inaugurated in May 1921, accused Dublin County Council of referring 'contemptuously' to the association when it complained about a doubling in rates.[55]

In Mayo, in the Castlebar and Westport districts, the IRA

> have taken upon themselves to impose a tax of 1d per bottle of stout ... the publicans are expected to hand over part of the receipts from the tax to the IRA ... So far as this is intended to prevent drunkenness it is an admirable thing in itself, but the fact that the shopkeepers are being vested with powers to increase already inflated prices ... is nothing short of an incentive to the profiteering evil which has already been carried too far ... Eventually it is going to put the thinking man in a very pessimistic attitude as regards future administration under a home government.'[56]

Another symptom of the loss of civil control by Britain was the operation of the republican courts, which worked effectively in some areas, though the judges were sometimes unconventional. Conor Maguire, later Chief Justice of the Irish Free State, submitted a statement to the BMH concerning his work in connection with the courts in 1920–21 in Mayo, where land agitation led to the courts considering claims between owners and landless men, thereby assuming a jurisdiction for which there was no counterpart in the British system. He described one incident that occurred

> at the close of one sitting of Kevin O'Shiel's court in an out-of-the-way deserted mansion on the edge of a bog. Michael Maguire, who was chief of the IRA police, presided at a court-martial on a prisoner who had been held for some days. He was a young man who looked to be frightened out of his wits. The charge against him was that he had pretended to be an IRA policemen and in that capacity had ordered all the public houses in Multyfarnham to close one evening about 3 hours before closing time. He pleaded guilty and received a sharp lecture from Michael Maguire who fined him £1 and let him go. I well

remember the look of relief on the prisoner's face as he left. We then
had an unexpected treat in the form of a recital of Gilbert and Sullivan
songs by Michael Maguire who had a very fine tenor voice.[57]

Mayo was both the first county to organise a system of tribunals to
deal with civil disputes and the first to set up parish and district courts
early in 1919, which amounted to 'a relentless campaign to procure ad hoc
solutions by force to grievances about land'. Maguire, at that stage a young
solicitor from Claremorris, initiated the holding of a court as Ballinrobe
about a disputed farm.[58] It was clear that this was also about SF wanting to 'put a brake' on agrarian agitation, but it was ultimately the agitation of the people themselves that forced politicians to do something
about it. A grisly double murder south of Castlebar was the catalyst when
Michael O'Toole, manager of the estate of James Fitzgerald Kenny (who
had refused to sell his estate to locals who instituted a boycott) because
he had a large family and could not afford to obey the boycott, helped a
neighbour plant oats and was tied to a tree and savagely beaten to death;
Kenny's coach driver was also attacked and later died from his injuries.[59]

Many of the court decisions dealt with minor offences: a donkey's harness was stolen in County Limerick and the person convicted 'had to walk
over the mountains in his bare feet with the harness on his shoulder as a punishment, 5 miles'. In another case a man owned a pig that ate the neighbour's
cabbage 'and the punishment was that the man had to grow on his own land
as many rows of cabbages as the pig had eaten'.[60] But there was clearly something much bigger going on here if even the unionist *Irish Times* was moved
to remark that 'the whole countryside now brings their rights and wrongs
to the courts of Sinn Féin'.[61] Not all obeyed; in Donegal one man decided to
bring his case to the official County Court at Letterkenny, and as one IRA
veteran recalled: 'We called on him with the intention of kidnapping him
as to prevent him appearing.' The IRA arrived at his house and found him
'looking so frail and ill that we thought he might die on our hands. We made
him swear on his knees that he would not attend the court. Despite this he
appeared, making us determined to be less soft-hearted in the future.'[62]

The operation of the courts involved an audacious but high-risk defiance of British authority in Ireland; the 1919 decree setting up national
arbitration courts had been passed by the Dáil but it became clear that
a more elaborate system was necessary to administer justice effectively.
By the summer of 1920 they began to build this system, and sought 'to

build regulated structures on foundations laid by the people themselves'.[63] Volunteers had already formed spontaneous local court systems that had little to do with the government and it was on these foundations that the arbitration courts were established at district and parish levels by May 1920. The scheme of courts had envisaged a supreme court, a district court corresponding to the county courts under the existing system and petty courts corresponding to the extant petty session courts.

Parish courts dealt with minor crimes (they could only hear claims of less than £10) and were composed of three people elected by the parish, while district courts were composed of five members elected by parish justices. Circuit courts for each of the four provinces were also proposed.[64] Lack of prisons and enemy interruption were problematic, as was the difficulty finding suitable high court members, and as was recognised in June 1920, 'I see at least one great obstacle in the way, namely, the want of machinery and power to enforce the decrees of the courts, especially where the defendants fail or refuse to attend or to obey the decision, or attend and refuse to carry out the court's orders.'[65] The courts were also forced to work underground, in farmhouses, barns and schools, and in relation to criminal courts, 'we would be without the mode of punishment usual in most countries – imprisonment'.[66] By August, some of these problems had been overcome; suitable men had been found to sit on the high court, and two circuit court judges, Diarmuid Crowley and Cahir Davitt, son of the legendary land and tenant rights campaigner Michael. Davitt was the 'kingpin of the fledgling judicial system throughout Munster ... and gave it an authority and status that could not have been achieved without some hierarchical framework'.[67] He was also more circumspect than Crowley, who was arrested and subsequently imprisoned for holding his court in public and refusing to abandon procedures when asked.

By August 1921, the Minister for Home Affairs, Austin Stack, had to admit that 'the courts for a time fell into abeyance in many places' but suggested a reorganisation of the system so that 'no effort on the part of the British forces will be able to dislodge them'.[68] He also referred to the 'vital' importance of keeping the courts going 'at all costs'. Part of the solution was deemed to lie with the creation of a police force to be 'the executive arm of the courts', as well as regular fixed sittings and the compilation of monthly reports and an insistence on the boycott of 'enemy courts'. Monthly reports, however, were often late and incomplete, and thus 'of very little use'.[69]

But there were successful aspects also; the report of the Ministry for Home Affairs for April 1922 recorded that since the August 1921 report, 'the causes retarding the work at the courts have disappeared ... the courts are now functioning throughout the country generally',[70] though the volume of letters to the Ministry requesting circuit court hearings to hear district court appeals would suggest that they did not sit as regularly as was needed.[71] Again, there was considerable success in addressing the backlog in early 1922. Overcoming the problems and, indeed, surviving and gaining wide acceptance was a significant achievement. The historian of the courts has gone as far as to suggest that 'nowhere was Sinn Féin more successful than in the creation of an alternative administration of justice'.[72]

TWENTY

LAND FOR THE PEOPLE?

One of the issues on which the courts frequently had to deliberate was land. The land agitation was born of the continued issue of congestion in western areas, where it was estimated that one-third of farmers were occupying holdings too small to make a reasonable living and they required additional land. Restrictions on emigration also meant there was a surplus of labourers and the acquisition of grazing land was attractive at a time of rising agricultural prices. Nor was the RIC in much of a position to devote itself to counteracting this agitation, for obvious reasons, while land purchase activities of the Congested Districts Board (CDB) had ceased: 'the majority of the agitators were small farmers, congested tenants and landless labourers'.[1]

SF was opposed to forced redistribution, seeing it as a threat to a cross-class support base; internal social conflicts were hardly deemed to be compatible with the war against Britain, and, most importantly, SF feared that the agitation would undermine its attempt to establish an alternative state in Ireland which is why it opted for the land courts. Much of the Land War had ended with the Wyndham Act of 1903, which had established financial parameters for sale agreements between landlord and tenant that were guaranteed approval by the Land Commission, and ensured that mortgage payments were lower than existing rents. Between the Wyndham Act and a further Land Act in 1909 almost 124,000 farmers were advanced money through the Land Commission, receiving £77 million to buy 7.3 million acres, with another £7.5 million paid to the Congested Districts Board to purchase 47,000 holdings on 729 large estates. But great resentment at inequalities remained; of the 570,000 holdings in Ireland in 1917, 227,000 were less than ten acres. The disputes during the revolutionary era 'were increasingly defined by anti-colonial nationalism as a damaging social concern that detracted from the more important political issue of the state', and in reality this involved abandoning arbitration in favour of the coercive system of Dáil courts.[2]

But it had been established as a SF principle that some form of land redistribution was necessary; a series of land conferences sought to hone strategy in this regard. In May 1920 'the republican leadership accepted in principle that grazing land should be redistributed, but that eviction proceedings should only be instigated with Stack's permission. These principles were later adopted by the Land Settlement Commission, which was approved by the ministry on 26 June 1920.'[3] Those overseeing the Land Settlement Commission (LSC) maintained that between 1 May 1920 and 31 December 1920, 50,000 acres had been redistributed.[4] Financial assistance for housing, however, was not forthcoming; when a request from Nenagh Urban District Council was received for the 'promotion of housing schemes for the working classes' the reply was that, while Dáil Éireann was 'alive to the urgency of the housing problem and they hope that at a later stage it may be found possible to make provision for affording financial assistance', it could not, 'in view of the large amount of money which would be required ... undertake to provide funds'.[5]

The LSC faced a formidable task and its archive is an unrelenting record of the passions and divisions disputes about land gave rise to. Signs such as 'The man that buys hay here signs his own death warrant' and 'Hell with the land sharks' were very common.[6] RIC reports from 1920 made it abundantly clear that shadowy characters such as 'Rory of the Hill' in Waterford were making menacing threats: 'If the land in your possession is not divided amongst the people you are doomed.' In Galway, a notice was found warning that no grazing stock were to be put on the farms at Rusheen: 'The young men of the district want the land stripped and they want no outsiders in any of the farms.'[7] Little was left to the imagination, a County Clare farmer being told: 'Clear out of here. Your grave is made. Fall into line at once with the rest of Clare. If not you will suffer the same fate as Shaw-Taylor. Head separated from the body.'[8]

In August 1921, shots were fired close to a house in Raheen in Offaly;

the solicitor to the occupant noted 'my client is a Protestant and was not in any way sympathetic with us, but in common with many others of his creed and views, recognised the fairness of the arbitration courts'. He insisted the 'flouting' of the court decrees had to cease: 'If the High Land Commissioner does not soon deliver his judgements we will all be shot.'[9]

Jim Gralton, who returned to Ireland in June 1921, having joined the American Communist Party after disillusionment with the conservatism of the Fenians, raised funds for the IRA, and began training Volunteers in Leitrim, placing a strong emphasis on social issues. Land on the family's farm was used for the construction of a Pearse–Connolly Memorial Hall, built with local voluntary labour and used to provide educational classes for young school-leavers and for social events. The committee established to run the hall consisted of republicans, farmers and trade unionists, and the hall was also used for SF courts, where a local land committee settled land disputes.[10]

Gralton's efforts created suspicion and tension, and his experiences were particularly instructive about the local forces and dynamics at play during the War of Independence and civil war era and their legacy. The south Leitrim area that he hailed from (Gowel) witnessed considerable social unrest during the revolutionary period. The national movement was fragmented owing to the demand for land redistribution and the fear that it would distract from the 'national' question, which meant Gralton laid bare in the early 1920s (and again a decade later) 'the nerve centres of power in the local community and for this he came up against an array of opposition ... which attempted to turn him into an exile even in his own locality'.[11] Luke Gibbons makes the point that the social and material questions around which republicans had organised, including trade union militancy, land seizures and the outbreak of Soviets, became embarrassing and complicating for the national leadership.[12] Austin's Stack's pamphlet *Constructive Work of Dáil Éireann* warned of the dangers of agrarian agitation subverting patriotic opinion and pointed to the importance of the republican courts in undermining such revolutionary sentiment. But the truth was that these issues had not been resolved and that was why Gralton became a compromising factor and a threat.[13]

All this underlined the crucial point about the variety of motivations, expectations and opportunities the revolution served to generate and whether or not it was a revolution at all: a revolution that needs, as seen earlier in the words of Peter Hart, to be 'reconceptualised and to have all the myriad assumptions underlying its standard narratives interrogated'.[14]

As Fergus Campbell has underlined, a rebel's conception of freedom in the west of Ireland was economic as well as political, 'and the two struggles against the British state and the landlord class were viewed as one and the same'.[15] In the words of Tom Garvin, 'status resentment' loomed large and was an important motivating factor.[16] For proponents of 'the nation' there was no toleration for land agitation even though the process of redistribution was by no means finished.

In August 1921, the propagandist *Irish Bulletin* referred to 'The Land agitation: a grave danger' and looked back to spring 1920, when there was 'an agitation, more or less chronic' for breaking up ranches for the landless. What this involved was 'revival of ancient and unwarrantable claims, gross intimidation, cattle-driving, fence-levelling and an "ugly rush" for land. The mind of the people was being diverted from the struggle for freedom into a class war and there was even a possibility that the IRA, itself largely composed of farmers' sons, might be affected'. This fear, it continued 'proved wholly groundless' as 'agrarian lawlessness was steadily suppressed, cattle-driving and boundary-breaking punished and ruffianly elements brought to book'. This was a way of heralding and exaggerating the success of the arbitration courts so that it could be maintained that 'the double revolution in civilian and criminal justice was complete'.[17]

Kevin O'Shiel characterised the spring of 1920 as 'the last Land War', spreading into sixteen counties and involving more 'agrarian outrages' in Ireland than any other year since 1882.[18] Art O'Connor reported to the Dáil in May 1920 regarding his mission to Connacht that 'many unjust acts undoubtedly have been done in the name of Sinn Féin but the situation is rapidly changing: "Out of evil cometh good!" Recent happenings have proved that the majority of the people readily turned to the organised republican opinion to save society from a complete collapse.'[19] In his view,

> a fever of land hunger breaks out at the 1st May each year, this year it was more violent than heretofore, probably due to uncertainty of our point of view ... now that 1st May has passed the fever has very much subsided ... owing to the establishment of arbitration courts and the knowledge that we will not back up or tolerate the attempted robberies which were in progress or in contemplation.

But he also believed that a 'regular and well considered land policy' was necessary:

Fortunately for us the feelings against the CDB and impatience for its delaying tactics are very strong and general in Connacht and this coupled with the disposition which even large landowners have recently developed towards us, such as faith in our fair play and power over our own followers will make them very ready to come forward to assist in drafting a proper workable scheme with special reference to its financial requirements.[20]

The following summer, however, it was admitted privately that the LSC was functioning under 'grave difficulty'.[21] At the same time, a disgruntled son wrote from a farm in Clare:

I am a poor struggling boy living with my father, mother and brother on a few poor acres of craggy land. My father's house is on the bounds of this farm, so near so that from his fireside I could pitch a penny through the window into the farm ... I myself hold 3 acres of this farm surrounded by outside invaders. Surely it is time this sort of thing should be looked after and the needs of the poor people adhered to. This farm has caused more trouble than any other farm in Clare and yet it is not settled. It was cleared about 10 years ago and was made a commonage for a few years until the fight for freedom of our country started.[22]

There were success stories nonetheless, including the decision of Colonel Spaight in Ardataggle in Clare, who 'generously divided some 170 acres ... amongst his workmen and small holders. The action has caused the greatest satisfaction in the district'.[23] In tandem, there were also those who, in 1922, were claiming agreements made in 1920 were made 'under duress' and would not now abide by them.[24]

After the courts were established to implement land redistribution in an orderly and non-violent way and new tribunals convened to ensure landowners were paid for the land, Robert Lynd suggested landowners preferred to sell to the SF courts rather than the CDB 'because it paid in cash'. But this was never going to be seamless; force was also necessary to control the agitation and republicans policed dissent. O'Shiel in his memoirs of this period emphasised the legitimacy of the land courts and lack of police informants ('the public had faith in their impartiality and were solidly behind them') and that the landowners supported them ('terrified landowners who came looking to the Dáil for protection'), though Fergus Campbell has made the point that this leaves much out, particularly the effectiveness of intimidation and duress and the extent to which the courts behaved justly towards all.[25]

Land disputes also bred a suspicion of the 'outsider'. In the summer of 1921, Richard Mulcahy received news from the IRA in east Limerick that a ranch had been split up by the Land Commission and that 'ex soldiers from a distance have been given land and are now settling there'. Mulcahy's question to the Minister for Defence was 'What attitude is to be adopted?' Six days later the IRA issued a 'warning to settlers'.[26] In September the issue was still festering; apparently 'three of the lesser officers of the IRA, evidently goaded by some taunts from Cumann na mBan, took action on their own account in the matter and went and cleared out the chap in residence and burnt some of the boundaries'. Following this they were waiting for 'official action from our own government ... nothing however has been done'.[27] An interesting twist was that one of the soldiers, who was Australian and not British and had helped the IRA, asked for special consideration and it was agreed he 'would be considered as a small holder'.[28]

Some areas that simmered eventually boiled over, as was the case in Laois, which had 'a reputation for freedom from crime and lawlessness such has not, perhaps, been equalled by any county in the south of Ireland. It is now threatened with such a deliberately well organised and determined land agitation', though one observer insisted that 'it is without foundation to allege it is because they are Protestants they were so treated. In similar circumstances Catholics might have been treated worse.'[29] In September 1921 Collins wrote to Cosgrave suggesting

> the number of defaulting annuitants [those who had to pay a fixed yearly sum in return for the money advanced by the Land Commission for land purchase] or at least annuitants who are holding up their payments is very greatly increasing. I was trying to get some definite particulars but this is a very difficult matter. The effort is of course spasmodic but I think in case of resumption of hostilities there will be a very large backing for suspending payment altogether.[30]

Despite the fact that the LSC courts had dealt with claims for ownership and transfer of land, the poor were still the land's most hapless victims. By 1922, an average of about 65 per cent of all agricultural holdings

in each Irish county came under the definition 'uneconomic' as defined
by the Land Commission, meaning they had a valuation of below £10 or
roughly twenty acres of 'reasonable' land.[31] In Kerry, the Ardfert village
tenants' petition to the government was representative of a wide-scale pre-
dicament, particularly after arbitration had been refused:

> Our group comprises tradesmen, small shopkeepers, business hands
> etc., all married and with families. The provision of milk for our
> children is one of our great difficulties. It is impossible to get grazing
> for a pony and a pony is a necessity with most of us. We seek only a
> few acres each, enough to keep a cow and graze a pony, or if it would
> smooth matters we would accept less – say, what would keep a cow.
> Thus among nine of us we would only ask what would scarcely make
> an economic holding for one person. We live right on the edge of this
> land, and have had to look at the bullocks of the Grazier for years
> while our children pined for milk. There are among our families 19
> children either babies or little beyond the baby stage. The widow and
> female orphans of one of our former members who was murdered by
> the Black and Tans live in a small shop. They haven't a perch of land.[32]

TWENTY-ONE

WAR OF INDEPENDENCE (2): 1921–2: THE JUGGERNAUT OF POLITICS

How did republicans assess their progress by the end of 1920? Kevin O'Higgins had certainly moved far, mentally as well as politically, during that year in relation to how he viewed what he and his colleagues had been living through; writing to his fiancée Brigid Cole in May 1920, about a 'queer complex kind of old world ... with the juggernaut of politics butting into every phase of our existence. It's different for us, we have the fun of the fight, but its bad to think of the old wheel catching little people who didn't go looking for trouble.'[1] The following month he referred to 'the man on the hedge', but that 'there oughtn't to be any man on the hedge at present', while in relation to Bloody Sunday, he acknowledged its impact on those 'who are in close touch with the crude horrors that occur'.[2] But how long was the war likely to last and did the mood alter? O'Higgins wrote again in March 1921: 'I have very definitely the conviction of a crisis safely passed, there is a corner turned and we're on the straight run for home – a long run, perhaps.'[3]

O'Higgins moved between different assessments, and his concern for individual suffering and that of his own family was especially apparent after the imprisonment of his father: 'Justice is vindicated on earth by the patient and dignified sufferings of people like them rather than the mean-spirited effusions of the Bishop of Cork [Daniel Cohalan, who issued a decree excommunicating Catholic IRA members involved in ambushes] and many of his colleagues.' But he was also moved to zealous and righteous conviction about the purity of the battle: 'Whether we win, lose or draw eventually, the moral value of the struggle is unquestionable. Probably not since the persecutions of the early Christians has human nature risen to finer heights in endurance for an ideal than in Ireland today.'[4] (Ironically, it was that very mindset which O'Higgins was to denounce a year later.) But he also recognised the complete absorption of the revolutionaries in their task and the consequences for their behaviour and temperaments: 'What monomaniacs we'll all be if we don't pull things off soon. Five years' concentration – is it any wonder that some of us have no small talk?'[5] In truth, however, O'Higgins had little faith in the capacity of the people on whose behalf he was supposedly fighting and on whose support he depended to withstand the enemy; the British, he suggested 'may well be relied on to try every trick in their dirty bag to stampede a not very wise or educated people'.[6]

For those people, patience was under strain. It was observed by the Ministry for Home Affairs in May 1921, for example, that 'the number of prisoners taken by the enemy in private residences principally have continued to increase'. A few months later, Minister for Labour Constance Markievicz suggested 'the people's nerves are wrecked as a consequence of the war that has been waged against them up to their very hearth stones ... many of the people are armed. Some of these are not members of the IRA and therefore not subject to any discipline ... in some parts of the country men belonging to the IRA have taken the law into their own hands.' In relation to labour and workers' discontent, she sounded an ominous warning: 'If a violent popular leader should emerge from among the disaffected workers it would be impossible to predict how far the trouble would develop.'[7] The solution, she insisted, lay in the cooperative sale and distribution of agricultural products.

Later that summer a disaffected fruit grower in Roscommon underlined the need for farmers to have guns in order to prevent a 'fruit famine ... This is very urgent as all fruit is ripening. I did not get one strawberry though I had over 500 plants.'[8] The Presentation nuns in Fethard, Co. Tipperary went as far as to ask the British army to send in a sniper to control vermin as the locals were not permitted to carry guns; the Reverend Mother asked if the local military barracks commander could 'kindly send down one of your men to shoot some jackdaws and crows which are ruining our potatoes, peas and other vegetables in our garden'.[9] It is not known if there was a response.

Internment also had devastating consequences for many; a road sur-
faceman in Limerick who had been interned in Ballykinlar for thirteen
months wrote to the chairman of the County Council in December 1921:

> Previous to my internment I was the object of constant attack by the
> Black and Tans, my house being frequently visited by them and on
> one occasion all my furniture was completely destroyed, doors and
> windows of my house broken and I had to flee for my life. During
> my internment of course the half acre plot attached to my cottage was
> untilled and this used to be a nice source of income to me. This loss,
> together with that of my wages for the time, has left me in a bad way
> for a little money.[10]

Inmates in prisons and internment camps were enduring difficult
conditions, and the use of the hunger strike in pursuit of political status
was vividly recorded in some cases. Seán Moylan, a member of an active
service unit of the Cork IRA, described his experiences:

> I shall always hate jails and sympathise with prisoners. The food was
> uneatable; the bullying tones of the warders unbearable; the harsh
> routine of prison life a constant insult. I went on hunger strike. Then
> began the struggle for freedom. Day after day I found my mind pre-
> occupied with the devising of menus. Elaborate and often incongru-
> ous combinations of food – flesh, fruit, vegetables – passed on the
> assembly belt of imagination before my eyes, leaving the craving that
> encompassed me more insistent as the days went by ... Wearisome,
> interminable, the days of the hunger strike dragged out at slow length.
> Threatened, abused, ridiculed at first, later I was wooed and tempted
> with specially prepared delicacies. I refused to break.[11]

An inmate at the prison camp in Rath described prisoners being 'up
to our ankles in mud as our tent is leaking badly'. The verdict of Michael
Staines, director of the Belfast boycott, who spent time in prison, as did his
father, was that Rath was 'absolutely unfit for human habitation'. Conditions in Ballykinlar were also horrendous; in 1921 there were 1,800 inmates
housed in filthy huts that were frequently flooded. There was a scarcity
of drinking water, inedible rations and a refusal to release ill prisoners,
while another prisoner wrote to Desmond FitzGerald in April 1921: 'We

are packed into a small cell, about 12 × 14 feet ... no sanitary arrangements, no exercise, no wash, half the food which is sent is kept from us.'[12]

William Murphy highlights that by June 1921, 6,129 men and women were imprisoned as a result of the unrest, and that imprisonment 'was one of the most common experiences shared by activists and suspected activists during this period'. Prison generated agitation inside and outside the prisons and thus could also be transformed into

> a pulpit, a soapbox, a stage and, providing one survived, time served as a political prisoner became an important qualification for public life in Ireland, as in many European countries ... More than that, imprisonment provided Irish activists with another opportunity to rebel, turning the sites that were supposed to 'quell political dissent' into places where resistance, even revolution was nurtured and enacted.[13]

For IRA combatants, there was still an obvious shortage of arms; in November 1921 the number of rifles reported to GHQ was just 3,300; over a quarter of these belonged to Liam Lynch's First Southern Division.[14] The notion that the IRA was facing defeat by the middle of 1921 is debatable; the scale of the body count in 1921 did not suggest an IRA that was about to collapse (T. Ryle Dwyer gives a count of 317 security force deaths in the first six months of 1921)[15] and Macready referred to the psychological exhaustion of his own army and his desire to see the war come to an end by autumn. In June, chief secretary Hamar Greenwood referred to an increase in IRA activity but it was also the case that, given some of the British successes in the spring of 1921, a further push could have left the broad IRA vulnerable, whatever about the more robust units. Regardless, however, of the military upper hand, it was simply far too late to repair the political damage that had been done by the British failures in Ireland.[16] In early 1921 it was estimated the Irish military campaign was costing the British government £20 million annually, but the Irish question could not be viewed in isolation: 'Throughout 1919, 1920 and 1921 the gloomy quartet of Ireland, Egypt, Mesopotamia and India appeared with monotonous regularity on the cabinet agenda. The fear of a domino effect in each theatre of imperial unrest gripped British ministers as they thrashed around for a solution.'[17]

The reappearance of de Valera after his American sojourn was also significant; Desmond FitzGerald, in his capacity as director of propaganda, told the Sinn Féin ministry on 18 January 1921 that 'while the truce talk had associated with it suggestions that Ireland was prepared to surrender, which were damaging to us ... this has been overcome to a large extent by the return of the president'.[18] But crucially, what had been established was that moves towards peace and negotiations could take place in parallel with the armed campaign. De Valera reputedly criticised the IRA's guerrilla warfare campaign to a flabbergasted Richard Mulcahy, with the warning: 'You are going too fast. This odd shooting of a policeman here and there is having a very bad effect, from the propaganda point of view, on us in America. What we want is one good battle about once a month with about 500 men on each side.'[19] Immediately after he returned from the US de Valera was trying to get Collins to go there, so that 'we will not have here, so to speak, "all our eggs in one basket" and that whatever coup the English may attempt, the line of succession is safe, and the future provided for'.[20] Collins was having none of it, not just resenting potential isolation from the domestic situation, but also concerned about passage to the US being far too risky.

The names and numbers of victims were recorded by those compiling police reports for Britain's Irish Office, and as the war intensified and became more brutal, the increasing numbers of atrocities were noted often in a detached, administrative way, but not without detail and the occasional hint of anger and emotion. They also suggest other scores that were being settled under cover of the war. For Kerry, this report was compiled on a murder similar to that of John Reilly in Clare (above, p. 193):

> Between 1pm 12th and 10am 14th, James Kane, RIC pensioner, inspector fisheries Listowel district, murdered by members IRA. Police found body lying on roadside, Bunegaragh with handkerchief tied round eyes. A card tied to body which bore 'Convicted Spy. Let Others Beware. IRA.' Head and body riddled with revolver bullets which goes to show that man was murdered by IRA in most brutal and cold blooded manner. Deceased had 25 prosecutions for poaching at the next petty sessions which police believe was motive [for] which the IRA murdered him.[21]

Not all were left with placards:

> 10am, 14th, Police at Kinsale informed that dead body Michael Driscoll labourer was lying in field at Waterland-party. Police went

to scene found Driscoll's nude body lying on left side under hedge in field next public road. Driscoll not identified with politics, police have found nothing to indicate that he was executed as a spy.[22]

There were also particular punishments reserved for women deemed to have violated certain codes. In King's County [Offaly] in September 1921 'Jennie Green and Margaret Byrne were chained to telegraph poles in Harbour Street by 8 men. Over each girls head was a paper with printed word: "Immorality" on it. The girls were taken to a shed and their hair cut off.'[23] One wonders if the irony of it all ever dawned on the eight men. Those in a hurry could also make haste for the sake of the Republic, as a report of a JP's loss in Nenagh illustrated: 'his bicycle stolen in the name of IRA'.[24]

But there were also tensions within republicanism, reflected, for example, in the rows between Cathal Brugha, Minister for Defence, and IRA chief of staff Richard Mulcahy over control of headquarters and discipline. Brugha was strict in this regard and disapproved of independent actions by Volunteers without Dáil approval, and was not keen on the shooting of either police or intelligence officers. In his life of Collins, published in 1926, Piaras Béaslaí, who had been a good friend of Collins, considered Brugha 'hopelessly out of touch' with the reality of the grassroots IRA campaign.[25] This lack of control coupled with individual initiative and the continuing allegiance some had to the IRB made Brugha's job difficult; he simply did not believe membership of the IRB and IRA were compatible. It was Brugha who had originally proposed in 1919 that Volunteers and TDs should take an oath of allegiance to the Irish Republic and its government, Dáil Éireann; but while many did so, the proposal was never formally approved by the IRA:

> One notable occasion when he asserted his authority was before 'Bloody Sunday' when he removed several names from Collins's assassination list, claiming there was insufficient information against them ... Given Collins's positions as IRA adjutant general and director of intelligence, his activities extended into many areas that Brugha considered his domain ... With ample scope for conflicts of authority, an ill-concealed antagonism simmered on between them throughout the War of Independence and beyond.[26]

The second phase of the War of Independence involved not only more death, destruction and confusion but also a hardened public stance on both sides, with parallel strands of contacts, holding out the possibility of a truce or some form of dialogue. Martial law was extended to Clare and Waterford and by February 1921 Frank Crozier, the commander of the Auxiliaries in Ireland, had resigned; he had taken over the Auxiliary division of the RIC in August 1920, but did not have the power to enforce the discipline he wished. Even when Crozier dismissed men following rampant revenge attacks and indiscipline in February 1921, Henry Tudor, the chief of police, refused to support him and what was significant in this regard was that Crozier did not blame Tudor, or indeed Nevil Macready, the military commander, but those whom he termed 'a small, silent, powerful, unscrupulous, and vicious gang of men'.[27] The bottom line was that, like Tudor, he failed to win the disciplinary battle, though perhaps due to his friends in high places, he was more protected.

Macready was faring no better; he put much effort into improving the logistics and efficiency and indeed modernisation of the military effort in Ireland, but he did not seek to control or curb the excesses of the RIC or Auxiliaries, believing only a vicious rout, which would have had enormous and presumably unacceptable political consequences, would quell Irish disturbances, and he recognised that dialogue with republicans would have to substitute.[28] Over the course of two days, between 14 and 15 May, the IRA killed fifteen policemen.

All SF candidates were returned unopposed in the May 1921 election, but the burning of the Customs House that month was a disaster; it has been described as 'the most ambitious IRA operation in Dublin since the Rising' and may have been designed by de Valera, ironically, to be 'a demonstration of strength in the capital to underpin victory at the polls. Such a protest in arms would carry far more weight in the period before peace negotiations than a multitude of minor actions', and all five city battalions were mobilised for the attack.[29] It was a military fiasco and resulted in the capture of nearly one hundred members of the IRA's Dublin Brigade and the deaths of several others. It also had no military significance, and was described by Henry Robinson, vice president of the Local Government Board, as 'probably the stupidest thing Sinn Féin ever did'.[30] Five civilians were also killed; when the staff there resisted the IRA's occupation a caretaker and temporary clerk were shot dead. The action also resulted in another massive bill of £35,000 for the Dublin ratepayers. Oscar Traynor,

OC Dublin Brigade, commanded the attack and some of the responsibility for the disaster was attributed to him.

In relation to political dialogue, in May 1921, James Craig, who had replaced Carson as leader of the Ulster Unionists, and de Valera met in Dublin. This was a tense affair, and while it might have been regarded as courageous it was also largely pointless; it was arranged by Alfred Cope, Lloyd George's go-between linking London and Dublin Castle. Both men were led to believe the other had requested the meeting. Craig, in any case, could be confident at that stage, with his status as premier of a nascent northern state. The following month, in opening the Northern Ireland parliament, King George V made a conciliatory address while by July General Jan Smuts, prime minister of the South African Union, in the UK on imperial business, was in Dublin to explore the peace options.

Two questions were now paramount: could there be a political response to a military impasse, and was complete military victory impossible for both sides? There was concern about regional disparities in the IRA's strength; it was often badly equipped and poorly trained, deficiencies sometimes complicated by the recklessness of youth: for all the casualness of some of their actions and utterances and justifications, killings also took their toll in the form of drinking, mental breakdown and induration to the consequences of killing in cold blood (the fallout from which the new state later had to deal with).

As Dolan notes, 'it was also a war of veterans; the Great War's veterans were combatants on every side', as well as a guerrilla war which of course unnerved soldiers used to more open combat, and 'for the IRA it was not necessarily about winning, but about carrying on'.[31] For the British soldiers, 'living under the threat of violence, as much if not more than the violence itself, had undermined the very essence of their army and service. One of the Essex Regiment in Cork put it plainly: "I did not like myself in Ireland. I don't think anybody else did either."'[32] Dolan makes the point that Britain

was conscious of pressure from its American allies, never mind the cost of keeping some 50,000 troops in Ireland when they were needed elsewhere. Once the question of the Northern Parliament had been settled, there was every reason to try and end the troubles in Ireland ... the nature of war suggests a local, intimate kind of violence. It cost approximately 2,000 lives, which, in comparison to other conflicts after 1918 was remarkably low. Yet in a small townland where every face was known just one death could seem like everything of war.[33]

Michael Collins suggested in June 1921 in relation to 'peace talk' that 'it would be a great pity if well-meaning people queered the position by too much of this', but was also conveniently disingenuous in asserting: 'I don't know whether there have been cases under stress of actual field conditions where spies have been executed without being given a chance to defend themselves, but such would be a very exceptional case. A remarkable thing indeed it is that most of them have confessed.'[34]

TWENTY-TWO

TRUCE AND TREATY

There is no unanimity concerning the strength of the IRA prior to the truce of July 1921. Richard English suggests it was 'far from clear' that the IRA was on the verge of defeat in 1921; as Ernie O'Malley saw it, it was the British campaign of terror 'that was defeating itself'.[1] Just what was the body count as a result of the war at that stage? One of the most significant projects undertaken in recent years, by Eunan O'Halpin and Daithí Ó Corráin, has produced much more concrete detail regarding deaths during the War of Independence. With a starting date of January 1917 and a finish date of December 1921, *The Dead of the Irish Revolution* has recorded 2,141 fatalities, and what is particularly striking is the regional variation; at one end of the scale, Cork returned 495 dead but at the other, County Wicklow just 7.[2]

In comparative terms, the killings of the War of Independence were minute in scale – 'in the frame of global conflict it hardly registers' – and barely qualifies as a war in the numbers game, dwarfed by the scale not just of the titanic world war but conflicts such as the Turkish War of Independence or the Russo-Polish conflict.[3] David Leeson suggests 'the British and Irish let each other off lightly',[4] but as Charles Townshend has pointed out, this was not just a question of statistics: 'ideas and attitudes are as relevant as legal definitions and statistical indices ... We need to try to recover something of the texture of that warlike experience ... the domestic context is obviously crucial to understanding the war.'[5]

The agreement of the truce in July 1921, the subsequent correspondence between de Valera and Lloyd George, the decision to send a delegation to London and the signing of the Treaty in December involved an extraordinary six months characterised by hope, impatience, apprehension and vagueness concerning objectives. For the IRA, the truce led to a certain liberation, later seen in a misty-eyed way by Frank O'Connor; he wrote of the summer of 1921 as one when Volunteers and post-truce recruits attended dances and concerts, commandeered cars and were 'tearing up and down little country roads with girls, all the bright hot days of summer'.[6]

After the parties, in a letter to de Valera, Michael Collins described the situation in Cork in mid July: 'fine spirit, fine confidence and although there was a little more relaxation than I should have liked, everybody is working *fairly* hard again'.[7] But there was odium for the post-truce recruits who were referred to by some as 'Johnny come latelies', 'Trucileers' and 'Sunshine Soldiers'.[8] Unsurprisingly, the British military were less satisfied; the divisional inspector commanding the Auxiliary division in Dunmanway reported in October 1921 that drilling, enrolling and insults had continued long after the truce: 'In this district the truce between the British government and the so called Irish Republic is maintained in one respect only, and that is, except on one occasion, there has been no actual shooting. In all other respects the truce has been broken by members of the IRA.'[9] But that was hardly a bad result either, given the intensity of the conflict a few months previously.

Jan Smuts tried to persuade de Valera to accept dominion status and when de Valera responded that such a question was for the people to decide, Smuts tellingly responded: 'The British people will never give you this choice. You are next door to them.'[10] He wrote to de Valera from the Savoy Hotel in London, telling him he had to leave the Ulster question alone for the time being; unionists could not be coerced and 'the force of community of interests will over a period of years prove so great and compelling that Ulster will herself decide to join the Irish state ... To you, as you say, the Republic is the true expression of national self-determination. But it is not the only expression.'[11] That was a fair point; de Valera had acknowledged as much at the Sinn Féin convention in 1917.

At no stage was the recognition of an Irish Republic by the British government a serious possibility, but what became crucial was the importance of symbols. The likelihood of failure was also ever present. Lloyd

George offered dominion status, Ireland within the Empire and an oath of allegiance to the Crown; de Valera replied by insisting on the Irish people's indefeasible right to decide their own destiny, while privately developing the idea of a treaty of free association within the British Commonwealth (an 'external association'). Lloyd George offered a tripartite conference and dropped his insistence on an arms surrender, and when de Valera travelled to London for talks with Lloyd George he was offered dominion home rule for the twenty-six counties of southern Ireland which was rejected with an insistence on recognition of an Irish Republic. When the second Dáil met in August, de Valera may have been afforded the title President of the Irish Republic, but it is undoubtedly significant that he also used this forum to declare 'we are not doctrinaire republicans', suggesting there was wriggle room.[12] When in London, he wrote to Collins: 'things may burst up here suddenly, so all should be prepared. I intend adhering to our original plan as closely as possible, but the changes in the situation have to be met as they arise.'[13]

Megaphone diplomacy and accusations of bad faith continued between the two sides over the course of the summer until it was agreed that 'conference not correspondence' (without preconditions) would be the most practical and hopeful way to an understanding. At the end of September a conference was arranged in London 'with a view to ascertaining how the association of nations known as the British Empire may best be reconciled with Irish national aspirations', and the Treaty negotiations lasted from 11 October to 6 December. De Valera's bombshell at the outset, however, was that he was not going to London. He offered various explanations: that he needed to avoid compromising the Republic; to be in a position, uncontaminated by negotiations, to reopen dialogue in case of a breakdown in the conference, to rally the people in the event of resistance, or to act as a kind of 'final court of appeal to avert whatever Britain might attempt to pull over'. Above all, he remained 'anxious to convey the impression that his decision not to go to London was not his alone but was somehow a collective one'.[14]

Nonetheless, the accusation that he had made a scapegoat of Collins, who was a member of the Irish delegation, persisted, facilitated by a much more sympathetic approach to Collins than de Valera from historians. But as Collins's most recent biographer, Peter Hart, has pointed out, of all the Dáil ministers, it was de Valera that Collins was closest to until the Treaty split. He did not want to travel to the negotiations without de Valera, but the notion of Collins as the simple soldier, unused to or unable to grasp the art of negotiations is not credible; he sat on the executive of his party, was Minister for Finance and a skilled administrator, and was not going to baulk at the prospect of being centre stage in the search for a solution.[15]

Curiously, in all his post hoc justifications, de Valera hardly mentioned one reason for staying at home which emerges from contemporary documents: the high tensions between Cathal Brugha as Minister for Defence and Richard Mulcahy as chief of staff of the IRA. Brugha had sent Mulcahy a letter on 13 September 1921 firing him, one of two occasions on which he did this, and it was quite clear the truce 'was devastating' to relations between the two men.[16]

De Valera justified his selection of the negotiating team (or plenipotentiaries, to give them their official title) on the basis that the team he chose, especially Collins and Griffith, representing the IRB and 'moderates' respectively, 'would form a well balanced team'. He also suggested, 'There seemed to be no good reason why I should be on the delegation.'[17] This was disingenuous. There were very obvious reasons, including his experience, stature, and the fact that members of his own party wanted him there. He also made a reference to his 'external association' proposals (by which Ireland would be an independent country within the Commonwealth, associating with it for defence purposes, and recognising the Crown as 'external' head), observing that he knew such proposals would probably be 'unacceptable to those whose political upbringing had been based on separatism'.[18]

The plenipotentiaries were furnished with credentials, which, it appeared, gave them the right to 'negotiate and conclude on behalf of Ireland, with the representatives of His Britannic Majesty, George V, a Treaty or Treaties of Settlement, Association and Accommodation between Ireland and the community of nations known as the British Commonwealth'. They were also told to remain in contact with the cabinet, issuing details of the talks, and to supply the cabinet with a copy of any draft treaty before signing the final version. This was confusing: did the delegation actually have full plenipotentiary rights? Was their whole mission framed in a paradox? Or was this sleight of hand? After all, the Dáil had agreed that the delegates would be plenipotentiaries and 'be given a free hand in [the] negotiations and duly to report to the Dáil', but the cabinet in effect privately limited their power and directed that it should have the final word on any agreement.[19]

In private correspondence Collins voiced his suspicions that he and Griffith had been 'set up' by de Valera to negotiate a compromise that Valera himself did not wish to make. Robert Barton had a different perspective:

> My memory of it is that I pressed de Valera to return with us to London on the score that it would be impossible for us to get the maximum terms without his being present and that it was unfair to expect us to get best terms without his assistance. He was however unwilling to move from the decision which he had made earlier that he would stay here as being the last defence. If negotiations should break down when he was with us that was the end but if they broke down without him there would always be a last recourse to him. It was good tactics. I remember him particularly referring to the fact that he represented a reserve in the battle, which could be thrown in when all else was lost. I entirely agreed with the original decision but thought it should have been reversed by the time we reached the final stage.[20]

The *Freeman's Journal* did not dwell much on de Valera's absence, but sent its prayers with the delegation who will have 'crowned their work for Ireland if they safely gather the harvest that is already ripe'.[21] But what exactly was ripe? A few days later de Valera was quoted in the same newspaper as warning the public against too much optimism, discouraging 'foolish hopes'.[22] Frank Pakenham was later to make the point – which deserves consideration – that de Valera staying at home was 'generally accepted in Ireland and the question did not become a serious issue until the articles of agreement had been signed and the political division had occurred'.[23]

The negotiation of the Treaty was fascinating because of the political strategies employed by both sides, the human dilemmas it created, the split it caused and the subsequent manner in which all these issues were framed. The British were particularly preoccupied with Empire, Crown and defence, but there was still an ambiguity as to what dominion status meant.[24] The Irish delegation was 'badly briefed; in particular the negotiations were already under way before de Valera revealed to Griffith what his policy on the Ulster question should be (and even then he had not shown it to his colleagues in Dublin)'.[25] Thomas Jones, secretary to the British delegation, recorded in his diary that Lloyd George feared that, if Irish allegiance to the Crown and membership of the Empire were not made non-negotiable, 'the discussion might become entangled in the Ulster problem' and he did not feel he had a strong case in this regard: 'Men will die for throne and Empire. I do not know who will die for Tyrone and Fermanagh.'[26]

The Irish delegation had to contend not only with internal divisions – it was revealing, for example, that Erskine Childers was reporting back independently to de Valera and was distrusted by the British side to the extent that they sought to set up separate meetings that would exclude him – while Robert Barton, chosen as the economic expert, was considered by the British government to be the head of the de Valera–Childers faction and it 'sought to exclude him from the talks at every opportunity. Their antipathy came to be shared by Griffith, and it was not long before the Irish delegation split along this fault line.' Barton was there to push the 'external association' idea but Griffith criticised Barton and Gavan Duffy for 'being too emphatic and creating the wrong atmosphere' in talks concerning trade and neutrality.

Of Griffith's performance, Barton wrote that 'he fell for the baited trap' and it was Barton who struggled most when it came to signing the Treaty[27] – but a gulf between the representatives in London and what was left of the cabinet in Dublin was also apparent. The Irish did not want to collapse the talks over the question of the Crown, and the British 'were equally concerned to avoid a break over "Ulster" where – as Lloyd George remarked to his colleagues – they had a very weak case'.[28] The British side, which included political heavyweights, would also have been cognisant of the 'domino' effect 'in Britain and throughout Europe' of continued Irish sedition and wanted to settle it once and for all.[29]

In 1935, writer and politician Frank Pakenham produced a quality account of the Treaty negotiations, *Peace by Ordeal*, which has retained its status. He had the advantage of being able to talk to key participants on both sides and managed, with verve, to produce a balanced assessment, at a time when the issues were still raw and emotive. He included vivid portraits of the participants, underlined the consequences of the tensions and distance between the Irish negotiators in London and their colleagues who remained in Dublin, and the extent to which the Irish delegation was outmanoeuvred by the British in relation to a boundary commission clause in the Treaty which they were led to believe would result in an alteration to the border making the state of Northern Ireland unviable.[30]

They had been sold a pup on that issue and if there was one clear winner during all this, it was Northern Ireland prime minister James Craig, who was assured of his position and capable of securing exactly what he wanted. As he said to Lady Craig, 'If I can bring off "not an inch", I will be very pleased.' He had every reason to be pleased; one of the most notable features of this period was the 'resounding success' of Craig's attempts to differentiate the six counties as much as possible from the rest of Ireland (see chapter 26).[31]

But overall, the Irish delegates negotiated a measure of independence that some more than others believed was substantial. The issues that had come up for discussion during the negotiations included dominion status, recognition of the right of Northern Ireland to self-government, British military presence in Ireland and the oath of allegiance to the British Crown. De Valera, staying at home and yet wanting to fully participate, was eventually to frustrate members of the Irish delegation, as they pointed out in no uncertain terms to him on 26 October 1921, in a letter in which they berated him for tying their hands in discussion and raised doubts about the powers they had:

> It is obvious that we could not continue any longer in the Conference and should return to Dublin immediately *if the powers were withdrawn.* [Griffith's emphasis]
>
> We strongly resent, in the position in which we are placed, the interference with our powers. The responsibility, if this interference breaks the very slight possibility there is of settlement, will not and must not rest on the plenipotentiaries.
>
> As to your coming to London, we think, if you can come without being known, it is important you should do so immediately. But if you cannot come privately do not come publicly unless we send you a message that in our opinion it is essential.[32]

Griffith and Collins kept de Valera and the cabinet in Dublin in the dark about their secret dealings with Lloyd George and Tom Jones, who referred in his diaries to the 'private discussions and bargaining' that went on.[33] Barton recalled in his BMH statement that

> possibly Lloyd George felt that he could make more progress with Griffith and Collins than he had made with a full delegation ... It was

not until later that Gavan Duffy, Childers and I realised that Griffith and Collins were prepared to settle for less than we thought it possible to obtain. We had trusted them fully. We had complete confidence in them up to that time. Griffith fought magnificent actions during the full conference. We had no reason to suppose at the time that he would agree in private to anything which he had not been agreeing to with five of us present ... It was decided that one of us must go to Dublin to acquaint the Cabinet and de Valera that we were not at all sure that the reports given us of what transpired at private conferences were comprehensive.[34]

By the middle of November a few things were clear: dominion status within the Empire was on offer, with British bases in Ireland to guarantee security and defence, a provision to allow unionists one year to opt out of the new Irish state (which would make them subject to the 1920 Government of Ireland Act that had created the new state of Northern Ireland), and a boundary commission to examine the future of Irish partition.

The Irish responded with the idea of external association, which was firmly rejected. The sop given by the government, after a forceful intervention by Childers, was that the Irish could use 'any phrase they liked which would ensure that the position of the Crown in Ireland should be no more in practice than it was in Canada or any other Dominion' and, according to Griffith, a promise to try to modify the oath of allegiance 'if that would help us'.[35] Jones recorded the degree to which events were taking their toll on Griffith: 'He was labouring under a deep sense of the crisis ... one was bound to feel that to break with him would be infinitely tragic.'[36] But there was more drama, as also recorded by Jones: Lloyd George would countenance no more cross-Channel hopping: 'The Irish had to sign and disregard whatever their Sinn Féin mandate said, or, if they believed the prime minister, face the accumulated might of the British forces ... Griffith undertook, whatever the reply, to sign the Treaty himself ... but this was not enough for the prime minister who wanted the same assurances from Collins and Barton.' Lloyd George held up two letters addressed to James Craig, one indicating agreement had been reached, the other indicating breakdown, and repeated a threat of war within three days if the answer was no.[37]

And so, after signing, the Irish cabinet split and the debate began; was this a stepping stone to further freedom or a betrayal of republican ideals?

Perhaps it was both, but what was focused on during the debates was the oath of allegiance and the right of the delegates to sign. As Collins saw it, the following clarification was necessary: 'Ireland is fully free to accept or reject [the Treaty]. Many a parliament of a country has refused to accept decisions of plenipotentiaries even if these decisions might be considered legally and morally more binding than the present decisions. I can only make plain again that the document is agreed to by the signatories and recommended to the Dáil for acceptance.' Griffith backed him up: 'The British ministers did not sign the Treaty to bind their nation. They had to go to their parliament and we to ours for ratification.'[38]

There was little said about Ulster: 'Either they felt that partition was already an established fact and that nothing could be done, or they assumed that the boundary commission clause would take care of the question. Some people were later embarrassed by this omission and tried to rewrite the record.'[39] Griffith and Barton may have claimed that 'they had only signed under conditions of extreme duress' but this did not assuage their opponents in cabinet, who felt that 'their trust had been misplaced'.[40] On 14 December, at the outset of the Dáil debates, the *Freeman's Journal* seemed to have a misplaced confidence that 'the utmost good feeling exists, and nothing but a most exemplary discussion wholly worthy of the great movement that has accomplished the freedom of Ireland is anticipated'.[41] Significantly, when it became apparent a week later that the newspaper's prediction that 'the men who have been staunch comrades throughout the days of the terror are not likely to descend to the indignity of abuse' was increasingly under strain, it adopted a more strident and partisan stance, referring to opponents of the Treaty as 'persons calling themselves the representatives of the Irish people ... The peace has been won but there are those who would destroy it.'[42]

Barton's contribution to the debate on 19 December was striking: 'I do not seek to shield myself from the charge of having broken my oath of allegiance to the Republic – my signature is proof of that fact.' He then referred to Lloyd George's threat of immediate war in the event that there was no signing: 'For myself, I preferred war. I told my colleagues so, but for the nation, without consultation, I dared not accept that responsibility ... I signed.'[43] The following week, the *Freeman's Journal* made reference to the Christmas break: 'Some advantage might be derived from the adjournment if the opponents of the Treaty had any longer any respect for Irish democracy,' while immediately after Christmas, the newspaper referred to

Christmas Day sermons delivered by priests in favour of acceptance and claimed that 'public opinion in every province favours ratification.'[44]

County Councils, agricultural, labour and trade bodies were also coming on board, but the *Freeman's Journal* was deemed to have gone too far by 5 January when it claimed of de Valera 'he is ready to sacrifice the country ... he has not the instinct of the Irishman in his blood ... it is the curse of Ireland at the moment that its unity should be broken by such a man acting under the advice of an Englishman who has achieved his fame in the British Intelligence service' – a reference to Erskine Childers.[45] Both sides of the debate criticised the newspaper. At the conclusion of the debates, the Dáil voted narrowly in favour of accepting the Treaty by 64 votes to 57; de Valera went into opposition and was replaced by Griffith and Collins became chairman of a new provisional government.

Michael Laffan has suggested the Dáil and cabinet were not representative in some ways: 'Perhaps the most serious disadvantage was that the priorities of the Dáil and its cabinet differed from and were even opposed to those held by the great majority of Irish nationalists.' And what did that majority want? 'An end to fighting, accompanied by Irish independence, the reunification of the country and, finally, and least important, the achievement of a republic.'[46] Michael Hopkinson has echoed some of these observations: 'The Treaty's fate was to be decided not by popular will but by organisations – military and political – which did not have a close, clearly defined relationship with the huge majority of the Irish population.'[47]

Nonetheless, there were those more than prepared to insist on what those people should endure to keep the purity of the Republic. According to Liam Mellows: 'We would rather have this country poor and indigent, we would rather have the people of Ireland eking out a poor existence on the soil, as long as they possessed their souls, their minds and their honour.' Was this completely at odds with the reality of public sentiment, or could that be in any way measured? Mellows knew such piety lacked practicality, which is why he also produced a document more in the way of strategy: 'How to capture Irish labour – the use to be made of unemployment, starvation, the postal strike and the desire for land.'[48] Eoin MacNeill, who occupied the speaker's chair during the Treaty debates, insisted that 'deputies who are against the will of their constituents should be called upon to resign ... publicly, insistently, repeatedly'; or as the *Freeman's Journal* put it, after describing the Treaty as 'peace with honour': 'Let the war party go to their constituents, consult their constituents, obey their constituents.'[49] An article by a pro-Treaty TD ridiculed Robert Barton: 'First he signed the Treaty, then he voted for its acceptance by Dáil Éireann and since, he has been doing everything he can to smash the Treaty.' Michael Collins felt such a highlighting of inconsistencies 'may be useful'.[50]

What was of significant benefit, however, was the release of Irish political prisoners; it was reported a few days after the Treaty had been signed that 5,000 Irish internees would be released by order of a Royal Proclamation.[51] At the end of January 1922, the British cabinet agreed on these releases and Winston Churchill, as Secretary of State for the Colonies, requested in February 1922 the 'immediate release of prisoners held in custody for offences committed in England and Wales prior to the truce who were, in the judgement of the Home Secretary, actuated by motives connected with the political movement in Ireland'. A memorandum from the Home Office the following month asserted 'it is quite clear that it is a question of an amnesty for all or none', and there was no scope for selectivity in the matter.[52]

And what of the reaction to the Treaty on the part of the IRA? In December 1921 its journal *An tOglách* maintained that 'Volunteers will receive the news without any undue excitement ... The army is the servant of the nation and will obey the national will expressed by the chosen representatives of the people.'[53] In the following weeks it became more direct: 'Our army can never become a menace to the Irish people. Whatever political differences may divide the country will not be allowed to affect the discipline and organisation of the army.' Two weeks later it asserted that 'the Volunteer spirit is the antithesis of the spirit of militarism. It is the spirit of the good citizen soldier.'[54]

This was an interesting piece of pro-Treaty spin and a revision of how the Volunteers had evolved and stated their case in the past. Peter Hart has highlighted the extent to which the Volunteers had remained aloof from politics: 'They did not frame their struggle in terms of democracy but they never denied its validity except in so far as it constrained their own actions.'[55] That caveat, of course, was the issue in 1922 which *An tOglách* was alluding to: how many Volunteers would deny democracy's validity because it constrained their actions? Could Treaty supporters, even if a minority within the IRA (an estimated 70 per cent of IRA brigades were opposed to the Treaty, but nine out of its thirteen GHQ staff were in favour),[56] still claim, as *An tOglách* frequently had done in relation to the Volunteers in 1918, that they were 'the agents of national will?' But that did not mean a coup d'état was ever seriously contemplated, according to Hart; even at this difficult stage in 1922 'the guerrillas wanted to fight for Ireland, perhaps even die for Ireland, but they did not want to run Ireland.'[57]

Regarding the numerical strength of the IRA at this stage, in December 1921 its new director of organisation Éamon Price estimated membership at between 72,000 and 82,000 men, but he had written to Eoin O'Duffy, deputy chief of staff to Michael Collins at IRA GHQ, two weeks before the Treaty: 'to a certain extent the figures may not be quite accurate, as since the Truce a certain amount of recruiting has taken place. You could safely add another 10,000 to the figures I give.'[58]

TWENTY-THREE

THE DRIFT TO
CIVIL WAR

Souls, minds and honour were deemed by some anti-Treaty republicans to be their preserves, but to characterise those involved as either 'die-hards' or 'moderates' does not suffice; David Fitzpatrick, for example, in his biography of Harry Boland, who had acted as private secretary to de Valera in America but was also close to Collins, suggested that he 'was at once a dictator, an elitist, a populist and a democrat'.[1] He also believed reconciliation between the two sides was possible, as did others; Michael Hayes's papers record his and Eoin O'Duffy's report of a meeting informally arranged between five pro-Treaty and five anti-Treaty TDs, held in the house of Seán T. O'Kelly, to discuss possible action to try and prevent a split in the Dáil in January 1922.[2]

What had changed profoundly was the degree to which it was now apparent that Ireland needed to be dealt with by the Irish, but British influence and demands were not yet irrelevant and the threat of renewed conflict remained. As was reflected in reports from the British army camp in the Curragh at the end of December 1921, there was much uncertainty: was it possible that the IRA would 're-activate' and 'will the enemy try to take advantage of our scattered forces? ... It is safer to assume that, should hostilities be renewed the Crown Forces will, at first, be up against a very much more active and stronger enemy than prior to July 11th.'[3] Further communications from the Curragh and Dublin in April 1922 suggested raids for arms were 'not unlikely' and 'there is a probability that officers and other ranks may be attacked or otherwise molested whenever a favourable opportunity occurs'. A few days later it was maintained that, owing to the split in the Irish republican movement, there needed to be plans for 'evacuation at short notice' and a readiness to destroy all stores and 'despatch all married families to England', as well as a need to avoid the 'unnecessary clashing' of Free State Troops and British troops ('troops will march to attention, no compliments will be paid').

A report in February 1922 signed by the major general commanding the Dublin district, referred to an interview with an 'official' of the provisional government who maintained that 'the biggest blow struck at the provisional government's prestige had been the suspension of the evacuation of imperial troops'. The chief concern in the Curragh by April was that 'the administrative work in connection with the evacuation of the Curragh is very heavy and the time available to complete the evacuation is very limited'.[4]

It became difficult to contain the divisions in Sinn Féin, and the debates became much more personalised; there was growing pressure from the farming community, the labour movement, business interests and the Church to accept compromise and move on and others just wanted to prioritise bread-and-butter issues. When the writer Liam O'Flaherty returned from his travels abroad a convinced communist in late 1921, he began organising the Dublin unemployed, some of them ex-servicemen like himself. His group seized and held the Rotunda in Dublin for a short time in January 1922 after he had founded, with Roddy Connolly, son of James Connolly, the first Communist Party of Ireland (CPI) in November 1921. The CPI rejected the Treaty and urged civil war in resistance, aligning themselves with the republicans. O'Flaherty and Connolly co-edited the party's newspaper, *The Worker's Republic*, in which, in February 1922, James Larkin was dismissive of Arthur Griffith, as he 'was not and never could be one of us. He does not know the real Ireland, for men such as he can never know the Ireland that our men and women gave up their lives for.'[5]

The provisional government formed on 14 January saw Arthur Griffith returned to the leadership of SF while continuing to lead a parallel SF government, while the symbolism of the surrender of Dublin Castle by Britain was profound. February and March were horrendous months in Belfast with over a hundred killed during sectarian violence, while in March the anti-Treaty IRA repudiated the authority of the Dáil and formed a separate command structure. CnB also rejected the Treaty. On 14 April, republican forces took possession of the Four Courts and Liam Lynch was appointed chief of staff of the anti-Treaty IRA; for him the Treaty was unacceptable as 'We have declared for an Irish Republic and will not live under any other law.'[6] At a meeting of the supreme council of the IRB a few days after the Treaty he was in a minority of one against its signature and insisted that an army convention should be called to discuss it. He was raising the prospect of an IRA that no longer accepted the authority of the Dáil.

But Lynch also did much to avert civil war (and was regarded as too moderate by the likes of Rory O'Connor), suggesting one way to achieve unity could be through the enacting of a republic. The attitude of some of the republicans to the notion of popular support for the Treaty was interesting; Lynch suggested the people 'were merely sheep to be driven anywhere at will'.[7] Contrast that with those who saw a bigger picture; Paddy Lalor, an IRA member from Meath, insisted that 'Irish history ended on the day the Four Courts were shelled [in June 1922]. I wanted no part in the Civil War ... I had been soldiering for four years and was anxious to get back to the family tailoring business since a green flag wasn't going to fry food in the pan.'[8] Playwright Seán O'Casey undoubtedly concurred, recording at a later stage his response to the 1922 Irish dilemmas: 'a civil war should be waged only for a deep and a great cause ... We should be careful of personal idealism; good as it may be and well meaning, its flame in a few hearts may not give new life and new hope to the many, but dwindle into ghastly and futile funeral pyres.'[9]

Michael Collins got irate in correspondence with Seán T. O'Kelly, who referred to 'my new found political opponents, so many of whom like yourself have been such good friends of mine'. Collins wrote that he had been informed O'Kelly had been overheard saying 'that Collins is a drunkard and spent the time during the Truce boozing with [Alfred] Cope [a civil servant in Dublin castle] ... [and] that Birkenhead [Lord Chancellor and member of the British negotiating team] told [John] Chartres [the lawyer on the Irish side who drafted various constitutional proposals] that he was willing to accept Document no. 2'. A macho Collins, regarding the Cope allegation, thundered, 'I should like to meet the man who says it or repeats it.' Of more substance was Document no. 2, which was de Valera's alternative to the Treaty, arguing for a constitution in which all authority was derived from the people and an oath to obey this constitution, not an oath to the Crown, and 'external association', which would involve recognition of the Crown 'only as head' of the association of Commonwealth countries. O'Kelly insisted Collins had told him in confidence England would concede on this, but was now showing 'complete indifference even distaste' for it. Collins was forceful in reply: 'I certainly would not ask any man to risk his own life or take the life of a brother Irish man for the difference which was described by Mr de Valera himself as "only a shadow".'[10] (The way the *Freeman's Journal* had described this was 'War for a grammarian's formula.')[11]

With a general election approaching, something insisted on by the British but also necessary for domestic reasons and to create some clarity about public opinion, and the provisional government tortuously attempting to frame a new constitution that might satisfy both republicans and the British government, de Valera and Collins agreed an electoral pact in May 1922 proposing a national coalition panel, which was by no means guaranteed to hold. The idea was that pro- and anti-Treaty Sinn Féin would run a joint panel of candidates to maintain their existing strength in the Dáil, with third parties running against these panel candidates. The process was widely regarded as undemocratic and came under increasing strain.

But it was the occupation of the Four Courts by republicans led by Rory O'Connor in April that had ensured civil war was likely. Collins and his colleagues were under considerable pressure to react to this defiance, and the increasing impatience of the British government was reflected in the tone of letters from Winston Churchill to Michael Collins: 'I write to you as man to man ... It is obvious that in the long run the government, however patient, must assert itself or perish and be replaced by some other form of control.'[12] The assassination of Sir Henry Wilson in London (which Kevin O'Higgins succinctly and mournfully described to his wife as 'another barrel of oil to the conflagration'[13]), witnessed Britain formulating plans for military reprisals in Dublin. Wilson had served as a Unionist MP for Down and before that at the War Office and was now chief security adviser to the Northern Irish government; he was killed on his doorstep in London by two members of the IRA, both of whom, ironically, had served in the British army during the First World War. This certainly played a role in the decision to attack the occupants of the Four Courts on 28 June, marking the beginning of the civil war. By this stage Rory O'Connor had split openly with Liam Lynch by refusing to

countenance compromise army unity proposals, and had led his supporters in a walkout from an IRA convention on 18 June and barred Lynch and
his supporters from the Four Courts.

Nonetheless, peace negotiations in the spring of 1922, which Harry
Boland was also involved in, should not be dismissed; indeed, Boland
seemed to be more firm in his conviction than Collins that 'fraternal
solidarity could surmount all divisions, and spent the first half of 1922
seeking a reconciliation between Collins and de Valera. Ever optimistic
and cheerful, he imagined that goodwill and belief in the cause of freedom
could prevail against sectional and personal animosities.' He was central
to the negotiation of the abortive 'pact' before the election of June 1922.[14]
A Dáil 'peace committee' initiated by the IRB actually met eleven times
but could not reach agreement.

Frank Aiken was also feeling the heat; as early as October 1921
Mulcahy had sounded him and others out as to whether or not they were
prepared to accept a compromise that involved less than a republic. Aiken
was disgusted at the suggestion; when it came, he clearly did not like the
Treaty, but he was also worried about fracturing the IRA's 4th Northern Division, which he had commanded since March 1921. He sought to
prevent a split in the IRA in the south while also cooperating with potential pro-Treaty opponents to reinforce the IRA in the north to go on the
offensive against the northern government. But while Aiken was disgusted
with Collins, he also attacked Rory O'Connor for his inflexibility. By the
summer of 1922 he had swung around again, accusing those who defended
the new constitution, Article 17 of which incorporated an oath of fidelity
to the British king, and which was published on the day of the general
election, as being 'dishonourable Irishmen' who would become 'as British
as the British themselves'.[15]

The decision to attack the Four Courts after the occupants had
ignored an ultimatum to leave was followed by the provisional government's issuing of a call to arms. By the end of the war there were more than
50,000 troops in this new National Army (also referred to as the Free State
Army) and it was, according to James Hogan, its director of intelligence,
'honeycombed with factions', but it was also fighting a civil war the republicans had neither the resources nor the popular support to win.[16]

The tone and threat from London, in relation to elections and the
possibility of a coalition government of pro- and anti-Treaty politicians,
and now in relation to the Four Courts occupation, would have been

major considerations for the provisional government in deciding to move against the Four Courts garrison, a reminder that the description of the civil war as the 'madness within' does not do justice to the balance of forces at work and the role of Britain in creating the conditions for conflict.[17] But domestic personalities and mentalities were also factors; Collins was desperate to avert civil war, but when he realised he could not achieve compromise with the republicans he decided there was no alternative to a military showdown, and one of his characteristics was his decisiveness in following through once he had resolved to take a particular course. The last thing the National Army and provisional government needed in 1922 was a half-hearted or less than successful defeat of the republicans in the Four Courts as this would have been a disastrous start to a civil war the National Army needed to win quickly and emphatically. The provisional government accepted the British offer of military equipment to boost its civil war effort. Facing a bombardment that could not be resisted, the Four Courts occupants surrendered two days later.

The general election the same month was watched with intense interest. Pro-Treaty Sinn Féin won fifty-eight seats, anti-Treaty Sinn Féin thirty-six, the Labour Party seventeen, Independents and Unionists ten and farmer's representatives seven. A breakdown of the votes is even more revealing; of the 620,000 votes cast, pro-Treaty Sinn Féin won 239,000, anti-Treaty Sinn Féin 132,161 and the combination of the rest, 247,082.[18] Overall, the election result did not suggest an electorate obsessed with symbols, oaths or constitutional formulae, all of which had been vigorously debated by SF after the signing of the Treaty.

Different perspectives have emerged on these crucial months. Tom Garvin's denunciation of the anti-democratic tendencies of the anti-Treatyites lies in contrast to a more nuanced reading, which would suggest that the British threat of 'immediate and terrible war' made the election of 1922 less than a 'fully free choice'.[19] What was painfully apparent was the disintegration of the Sinn Féin movement, a crisis that has often been analysed in terms of a preoccupation with some of the principal political personalities of the period, although there has been too great a tendency to write this story from the 'winners' perspective (the supposed 'democrats' in opposition to the anti-democrat diehards), which raises interesting questions as to what democracy actually meant in 1922.[20]

Bill Kissane's survey of the politics of the civil war highlights that there was a democratic culture in pre-independence Ireland, so 'the vista of a heroic elite forcing democratic values down the throat of a recalcitrant society should not be taken at face value'. Some of the subsequent approach to the distribution of power by those on the winning side, after all, 'showed how far Ireland's new governing elite had moved from any concept of participatory democracy, and were firmly tied to a Victorian conception, which favoured the symbolic and executive elements of the state over the representative and the legislative'.[21]

The alternative argument is that sovereignty was necessary for an electorate to express itself freely and that a treaty signed under threat of war did not provide those conditions. The class arguments put forward – that anti-Treaty feeling was stronger in poorer areas more affected by emigration, for example – does not withstand the scrutiny of Peter Hart, Michael Farry and Marie Coleman; Farry, for example, found that in Sligo, the 'men of no property' were actually more likely to be found in the ranks of Free State than with the republicans.[22]

The Treaty divide was also brought briefly abroad. Seán Mac Caoilte was part of a pro-Treaty delegation who made a trip to the US and his letters to his wife in May 1922 highlight how he agreed with her 'that there is little use arguing our differences all over the USA' ('I sincerely hope I shall never again be entrusted with a diplomatic mission'). Writing from Indianapolis, he noted 'the sentiment here is just the same as elsewhere. There is no keen desire to throw away the chance Ireland has of recuperating under the terms of the Treaty, though of course no one is particularly enamoured of the whole thing.'[23] But things got better in Pennsylvania: 'Beasley and Jim are gone down to the smoke room to buy some cigars. I hope shortly to join them. I am beginning to enjoy this tour ... by the way, our youthful appearance seems to have caught the American imagination. They find it difficult to believe that I am 36 and the father of four children.'[24] There were certainly advantages to being out of Ireland at that stage; tragically, however, Mac Caoilte was dead less than a year later, a victim not of civil war, but pneumonia.

And what of the Labour interest at this juncture? In August 1921, Labour Party leader Tom Johnson had insisted that 'the employers by their thick headedness and inactivity have declared war ... It means that we may have to face a definite social revolution.'[25] But worries of a split remained; a proposal that it should abstain from the 1922 general election was 'defeated by a surprisingly narrow margin: 115 votes to 82. Such lack of enthusiasm boded ill for Labour's prospects.' However, the delay in holding the election and the desire, as expressed in the pact, that the Treaty should not be centre stage and the use of proportional representation all helped Labour; four of its candidates withdrew but eighteen stood for election and seventeen were elected, a performance that was 'astonishing'. The party won 21.4 per cent of the first preference vote 'an achievement it never matched in any of the following 28 general elections'. (Even with the collapse of the once mighty Fianna Fáil in 2011 it only managed a 19.5 per cent share.)

But Michael Laffan has suggested that in some respects 'this outcome was deceptive or even misleading'; Labour benefited from republican divisions and a desire to punish those responsible; it was benefiting in that sense from 'borrowed' votes and its vote dropped in the general election of 1923, when it returned only fourteen candidates.

References to the needs of an estimated 130,000 unemployed were common, but just what could be done for them in this environment, and just what was the function of the Treaty-supporting Labour Party to be in this Dáil, given the role that Johnson had played in providing material for the Democratic Programme of 1919? Certainly it sought to put such notions centre stage, mentioning the need for 'fundamental rights' in socio-economic terms but it had no input into the drafting of the 1922 constitution. It pushed for protectionism and economic self-sufficiency but it was affected by internal disunion.[26] This was exacerbated by the return to Ireland of Jim Larkin, who, from abroad, had denounced the Treaty and opposed the Free State. Tensions remained with the ITGWU about the notion of giving 'sanction to the Free State' and the desire to resist any attempt by communists to infiltrate the ICA. A sizeable proportion of the ICA was opposed to the Treaty, but, given its size and Dublin centricity (where it had, the IRA reckoned, about 200 members), it could exercise little influence.[27]

Were these the crucial months when radicalism was deliberately and swiftly snuffed out with serious long-term consequences for the left? The degree of social discontent has not received the attention it deserves and conflict between farmers and farm labourers was widespread in 1922. The index of agricultural prices (with a base figure of 100 in 1911) reflected the collapse in the economic boom, with prices falling from 288 in 1920 to 160 in 1922.[28] A letter to the Department of Home Affairs from the court organiser in Corofin in Clare, on behalf of the district justices, pleaded for a justice or resident magistrate for Clare:

much cattle driving is taking place and when arrests are made in connection with same and prisoners brought before parish justices they are invariably set free. Can anything be done in this respect; it certainly is not a wise policy to take this class of prisoner – the cattle driver – before the justices of his own parish, or of a neighbouring parish.[29]

Industrial relations were also dire; at the beginning of the year the *Irish Independent* had warned in an editorial, reacting to the strikes in the docks, railway and canals, that 'every strike now is an obstacle in the path of progress and if the strikers proceed to pull down the temple of industry, they will like Samson, bury themselves in the ruins'.[30] Trade unionists were much more numerous – 303,000 spread across forty-one unions, in contrast to 110,000 in 1914 – but the difficult economics of the period undoubtedly reduced their bargaining power; the main demand was that wages would not be reduced. What was instructive during this period, however, was the government's determination to crack down on labour unrest on national security grounds. There was no shortage of strikes to react to: 1,600 railway engineers in Dublin were on strike in the autumn of 1921 and by early 1922 there was serious industrial unrest across the railway sector and after a British-imposed reduction in the bonuses of post office clerks and postmen in autumn 1921, serious disgruntlement in that sector.

Postmaster J. J. Walsh won a bitterly fought dispute with his employees (from September 1922) by dismissing strikers and replacing them with new recruits; Walsh had also claimed, erroneously, the strike threat had little to do with wages and was designed to undermine the government.[31] What was also significant here was the issue of the right to strike; a government proclamation claimed the strike was illegal: 'The Government does not recognise the right of civil servants to strike ... the post office service is a vital state service. The government is prepared to use, if necessary, all the forces at its disposal to ensure that no official who continues his service to the state is subjected to interference or intimidation'. The military was authorised to use force if warnings and arrests were not heeded; Kevin O'Higgins's contribution to a Dáil debate made it clear that this strike was being treated as a war issue: 'Members must understand if this state is to be founded, if it is to live and flourish, it must be able to depend on loyal and constant service from its officials.'[32]

Lack of protectionism meant Ireland could be used as a dumping ground for produce not sold elsewhere and emigration was negligible; the desire to force down wages to cut costs created a backlash. Dáil questions referred to 'the extent of privation being endured by large numbers of the working class population'.[33] The withdrawal of British troops had also caused economic dislocation; their presence had generated much employment, most obviously around the Curragh in Kildare. In addressing the Dáil on 10 January 1922, Johnson, leading a delegation of the Labour Party and the ICTU, was able to paint a vivid portrait of poverty:

> There are at this time probably one hundred and thirty thousand men and women walking the streets, unemployed ... . We are in the situation to-day that a very large proportion of the population is at its wits' end to know how things are going to move. Thousands of children are hungry and naked, huddled together like swine in their so-called houses ... The patience of the workers, of the people, of the poor unemployed, and the wives of the unemployed, is becoming exhausted.[34]

In response to these various concerns, however, a new version of the mantra 'Labour must wait' was formulated; solving the problems had to be postponed until peace had been restored, as was enunciated by Ernest Blythe, the Minister for Local Government:

> It is all very well to suggest a number of small things that might be done to remedy unemployment. But these things would be like trying to keep out the sea with a broom ... they will only delay the trend of things economically ... The only way that is worth talking about of assisting trade and industry at the present time is to produce stabilised conditions in the country.

Kevin O'Higgins gave another version of this argument a few months later:

> One does not usually build in the path of a forest fire, one gets after the fire and faces the building afterwards. We have been asked about unemployment; surely it is wheels within wheels ... the thing that most makes for unemployment is the fact that there is no credit, no security and no system of justice ... Until you re-establish normal conditions, unemployment will go on increasing and no man and no government could stop it.[35]

The same month, a member of the Farmer's Party suggested 'there were not enough lamp posts in Ireland to hang agitators from Liberty Hall', the headquarters of the ITGWU.[36]

In an atmosphere of civil war, claims that simplified the recent past and its class tensions and ugliness were likely; O'Higgins, for example, had maintained during the 1922 election that there was a need to dispense with notions of radicalism, to 'trust in evolution rather than revolution'.[37] Alfred O'Rahilly insisted that when the Treaty negotiations began it was clear that the idea of 'an immediately attainable republic was dead. Compromise was inevitable ... it was forced on us, of course it was', but

> the admission of force merely strengthens the case for acceptance; it enables such decision to be based on the highest ground of all – preservation of our national existence ... the delegates might have secured better terms? Perhaps. There are always onlookers, hurlers on the ditch who think they could play better than the selected team. But the might have been is not a practical proposition.[38]

The writer George Russell characterised the dilemma as the 'agony of conscience'.[39]

The outline of the pro-Treaty arguments and case in the civil war are also clear from the pamphlets, leaflets and handbills in the papers of Desmond FitzGerald, under titles such as 'The cost', 'A painful necessity', 'Civic virtues', 'Ireland's opportunity' and 'His neighbours pay'. They were also fond of invoking the example of Abraham Lincoln's calls for national reconciliation in the context of the US civil war and, indeed, William Jennings Bryan, the supporter of popular democracy who had been a candidate for the American presidency in 1908, regarding the right of people to control their government and use that government to protect their rights and promote their welfare.[40] O'Higgins was also determined to personalise the debate, accusing Erskine Childers of 'mental disorder', Mellows of 'lofty transcendentalism', with de Valera the leader of a 'motley coalition ... only held together on a destructive programme ... rabid republicans' and 'rabid document-twoites' with contempt for 'plain people'.[41]

And what of the people's expectations? Tom Garvin has commented that 'an insecure and inexperienced elite found itself presiding over a population that wanted unheroic things'.[42] It was also an elite that was executively aggressive and frustrated and undoubtedly psychologically scarred by the frequency of death, funerals and violence during this period.[43] In 1980, J. M. Curran painted this memorable portrait of the situation on the eve of civil war:

'The Free State leaders faced a host of problems. They had to take over the Executive from the British, maintain public order during the transitional period, and draft a constitution. They also had to prepare for an election on the Treaty and coordinate the work of Dáil departments with those taken over from the British.' O'Higgins later described the provisional government as 'simply eight young men in the City Hall standing amidst the ruins of one administration, with the foundations of another not yet laid, and with wild men screaming through the keyhole'.[44]

TWENTY-FOUR

CIVIL WAR

Who were the wild men, what did they want, and were they responsible for starting the civil war? Contemporary polemics were adamant that blame needed to be attached: 'Who has caused this war which is tearing the heart out of Ireland? One side or the other must be responsible. Which is it?'[1] This deliberate polarisation did much to simplify the dilemmas of 1922. There was a tendency for contemporaries of the 'diehards' to immortalise them in print; in Ernie O'Malley's *The Singing Flame*, for example, he characterises compromise as involving the loss of soul, and Liam Mellows is lionised as 'a clear flame, steadfast, burning of its own strength'.[2] Mellows was apt in the aftermath of the Treaty to speak of 'the people's will' that 'cannot be broken ... It is not a question of negotiations or concessions, it is a question of our rights.'[3]

There was much comment on 'wild' women too. On 24 April 1922, Mary MacSwiney wrote to Richard Mulcahy: 'No matter what good things are in the Treaty, are they worth this unhappiness Dick? Do you not realise, we hold the Republic as a living faith, a spiritual reality stronger than any material benefits you can offer – cannot give it up. It is not we who have changed. It is you.'[4] This was no impetuous, rash conclusion; after all, MacSwiney had spoken against the Treaty for longer than anyone else in the Dáil, for two hours and forty minutes on 21 December 1921. She treated the Dáil majority in favour with contempt and went on hunger strike twice when imprisoned.

Regarding de Valera's position early in 1922, Owen Dudley Edwards has asserted that, given the depth of republican militarism, 'the civil war would have happened if he had supported the Treaty'.[5] This is indeed likely, given the difficulties that de Valera already had in dealing with the militants and his honest admissions about his own lack of extremism. It is a reminder of the danger of isolating de Valera as the embodiment of intransigence in the immediate aftermath of the Treaty. During the civil war, he sought to explain why he could not share MacSwiney's uncompromising republicanism:

> Reason rather than faith has been my master ... I have felt for some time that this doctrine of mine ill fitted me to be leader of the republican party ... Nature never fashioned me to be a partisan leader in any case and I am sorry that I did not insist on Cathal's [Brugha] assuming the leadership when the party was being formed. For the sake of the cause I allowed myself to be put into a position which it is impossible for one of my outlook and personal bias to fill with effect for the party ... Every instinct of mine would indicate that I was meant to be a dyed-in-the-wool Tory, or even a Bishop, rather than the leader of a revolution.[6]

Other republicans dug deep to seek solace in their faith and apostolic succession; Fr Albert's diary of his time in the Four Courts (he was a Capuchin friar and long-time republican sympathiser) recorded that 'the boys all knelt down and recited a decade of the rosary in Irish, placing themselves and their cause under the protection of the Blessed Virgin and all patriot martyrs of the Irish republic'.[7]

It is easy to lose sight of the sincerity and devoutness that underpinned civil war decisions and the air of doom. After the execution of Erskine Childers in 1922, the *Irish Times* sketch writer 'Nichevo' (Robert Smyllie, a future editor of the newspaper) recalled the impact of the loss of the Treaty vote:

> That last night at Earlsfort Terrace ten months ago will never be forgotten by those who witnessed the scenes following the passing of the Anglo-Irish Treaty. Arthur Griffith, flushed to brows, was nearly bursting with suppressed excitement. Michael Collins was dashing his nervous hand through his shock of jet-black hair while on the other

side of the room Harry Boland was crying like a child and Cathal Brugha was biting his lip in bitter disappointment. A few seats away from Brugha, Erskine Childers was sitting. His face was drawn and haggard. Bloodless lips were parched and twitched in painful grief. But this strange man never moved in his place. Like Arthur Griffith, he knew how to master his emotions. And now they are dead. Griffith died of worry. Collins and Brugha fell in the heat of the fight, Boland was killed in a scuffle at Skerries and Childers faced the firing party yesterday at dawn.[8]

Propaganda, censorship and personalisation were also factors during the civil war, as were heroic last stands; after the shelling of the Four Courts, Cathal Brugha reported for duty to the Hammam Hotel in Upper O'Connell St, which, along with the Gresham and Granville hotels, had been taken over by anti-Treatyites. The hotels came under heavy fire and after a week, most occupants surrendered, but Brugha insisted on fighting on. With the Granville ablaze, he ran onto the street that now bears his name, firing a pistol, and was shot in the thigh and seriously wounded, dying later in the Mater hospital. Kathleen O'Connell recorded in her diary: 'Poor Cathal died at 7.45 this morning. Our Minister for Defence! Strange irony of fate. The first life given in defence of the Republic.'[9]

There had also been something of a battle of the sexes going on in the Hamman Hotel; there were five members of CnB present and one of them, Kathy Barry, sister of the executed Kevin, recalled that

> the men didn't allow us to stay. We just stayed ... Dev kind of carried me across the room and then he turned round to see if there were any more neurotic girls ... it wasn't fair to drive us to mutiny in order to be let stay ... I had to dodge Cathal [Brugha] all the time. He approved of me making tea and Bovril but not of me filling sandbags in my leisure moments, but others were sports and let me do heaps of things ... I loved those 3 days at the end because I felt I was nearly as useful as a man and you don't know how helpless a feeling it is to be a woman when you feel you ought to be a man.[10]

There was also ill behaviour and problems of discipline. The establishment of a War Council and the appointment of Collins as commander-in-chief of the National Army signalled the growing gravity. Collins's devotion to constitutionalism in 1922 has been exaggerated; he was commander-in-chief at the same time as he was president of the IRB and John Regan declares it cannot be claimed with certainty that 'the Treatyite regime was independent of the IRB executive'. It is, however 'impossible to say' how much power the IRB had. In August 1922, by vetoing demands to have parliament assembled, Collins also transferred executive powers to the military command. The lack of legal relationship between the Treaty-ite government and the army during the civil war was another anomaly.[11]

In July 1922, when the raising of up to 35,000 men for the new army was formally approved, Mulcahy insisted that new army recruits and a volunteer reserve were needed to 'flabbergast those who would like to protract things indefinitely in the country with the intention that the government would never function'.[12] The language of Collins had also become more resolute; he suggested to Griffith the same month that republican opposition was 'largely brigandage and when not this, it is opposition to the people's will'; what the new army recruits would be fighting for was 'the revival of the nation'.[13] De Valera refuted such a description; a memorandum of his from June 1922 insisted the men fighting to defend the Republic were not 'bandits' or 'brigands' but 'soldiers'.[14]

But the National Army men were also fighting for money; pay was set for recruits at 3s 6d per day with a family allowance of 4s per day for a wife and 6s 6d for up to two children, which were at that time generous allowances. According to Joseph Brennan, the comptroller and auditor general of the Department of Finance in June 1922, overall national expenditure on public services for 1922–3 would be in the region of £26.5 million, of which £10 million would go on the army, civic guard and reconstruction schemes; of this, £7.2 million was for the army alone.[15] And this was before the civil war which it is estimated cost the army 500 men killed, up to 5,000 wounded, damage to property of £30 million and army costs of £17 million with, at the end of it all, a bloated army of in the region of 55,000 who were all uniformed up with nowhere to go once the war ended.[16] George Russell had a suggestion in that regard, in a letter to Michael Hayes: 'Perhaps we might have a dual purpose army, working at works of national importance in time of peace and quitting those for fighting when there is a state of war.'[17] A memorandum in April 1922 recorded that Cosgrave, Collins and Kevin O'Higgins 'have not drawn any salary since 5th January last'.[18] Ever punctilious, the accountants also recorded that 'a bicycle, the property of the Department of Trade, was taken by the messenger of that department on his leaving to join the forces in possession of the Four Courts'.[19]

With the move to oust the republicans from the Four Courts another momentous happening was in train: the destruction of the Public Records Office, housed within the Four Courts complex, responsibility for which had been handed over to the provisional government just a few weeks previously on 1 April. At the outset of the civil war, history was thus not just being made, centuries of it was literally floating in the air above the Four Courts or smouldering within it. When the Deputy Keeper of Public Records came to compile his report for the year 1922–3 he noted, 'to a great extent the loss is irreparable, but in certain respects much may be done to mitigate it'. But he made the point that

> the losses suffered in the past through fire, neglect, unsuitable places of deposit or otherwise, serious as they were, cannot in any way compare with those suffered in the Public Record Office in June 1922, whether we consider the volume, the diversity of nature, or the importance to the public and private persons of the documents destroyed by the calamitous fire in the Four Courts.[20]

There was, in retrospect, a bitter irony to the words of Rory O'Connor, as reported in the *Irish Independent*: 'The business of the courts, he said, would not be allowed to go on but every care would be taken to preserve all documents etc.'[21] According to Ernie O'Malley, it had been agreed that the Four Courts would be blown up or set ablaze rather than handed over to Free State troops. Éamon O'Neill, assistant keeper of the PRO at the time of the bombardment, insisted a year later that 'on the occupation of the Four Courts I sent immediately a reasoned and detailed statement to Rory O'Connor of the great historical value of the records that were endangered'.[22] It is likely the archive would have suffered even without the mines, given the determination to rout the occupants, but perhaps not to the extent it did.

The notes of Michael Collins at this stage, after the fall of the Four Courts, were interesting: 'The surrender of Rory O'Connor and Mellows important. We do not want to mitigate their weakness by resolute action beyond what is required.'[23] He was conscious, it seemed, of the dangers of humiliating them, but what was the measure of what was required? To what extent, in the words of George Gavan Duffy, would it be the case that for the provisional government, it was 'obstinacy that they mistake for strength?'[24] Because of the extent of Collins's own inner conflict about this there was a suggestion that, had he lived, 'there would have been no firing squads because the power of his humanity would have found the solution which those who followed him sought desperately in vain'.[25] This is far fetched, however, and part of the stained-glass approach to the Collins legacy; both he and his colleagues became quickly convinced that 'what is required' was ruthlessness.

The incoherent and haphazard occupation of buildings in the city by the Dublin No. 1 Brigade of the IRA was inevitably doomed to failure. Liaison with the Four Courts was often dependent on Máire Comerford and her bicycle as, in carrying dispatches, she strove to confirm CnB's status as indispensable republican auxiliaries. Her subsequent involvement in an unsuccessful attempt to kidnap W. T. Cosgrave in January 1923 led to her arrest and imprisonment in Mountjoy jail, where her protests resulted in three months' hard labour and in response to which she went on hunger strike. During her imprisonment she was also shot in the leg by a Free State soldier because she had been waving to fellow prisoners, a measure of the brutality but also the fury directed at 'the furies'.[26]

Retarded communications, as the IRA was hounded from one building to another, were to be the hallmark of the conflict in the city. Seán T. O'Kelly's arrival at the Hamman Hotel, armed only with an umbrella, was indicative of an army ill prepared and ill equipped. O'Kelly, by no means a diehard, had attempted to mediate between bishops and fellow republicans and shortly before the outbreak of the civil war he told Bishop Edward Mulhern of Dromore that he believed republicans should act as a constitutional opposition.[27] But after the outbreak of civil war he was arrested and detained at Kilmainham jail and Gormanston internment camp until the end of 1923. That those involved had so recently been united as combatants with their now sworn enemies not only fuelled a lust for retribution, but also meant the IRA had literally nowhere to hide, as Collins's (ruthless) Criminal Investigation Department, based in Oriel House, discovered to its satisfaction. The viciousness and personalisation of the divide was striking; the pro-state publication *An Saorstát* [The Free State], regarding the Treaty and the IRA's incursions into Northern Ireland, declared in April 1922, 'Mr de Valera will wade to his dictatorship, if necessary, through the blood of Belfast babies. The cost is nothing when one has to save face.'[28]

But just how much in control was de Valera at that stage to justify such viciousness? In 1958, the UCD historian Desmond Williams wrote to Michael Hayes regarding the civil war: 'the most obscure thing of all is Dev's actual attitude towards O'Connor and Mellows between January 7 and June 1928. All the Fianna Fáil apologists shroud this in mystery.'[29] What de Valera did suggest in 1922, however, was that the IRA had made a decision to 'act temporarily as a de facto military government'.[30]

The six weeks that followed the Four Courts and O'Connell Street bombardment in Dublin saw the speedy capture of republican strongholds in Cork, Limerick, Waterford and Tipperary; National Army forces numbered in the region of 38,000 at that stage and the IRA not more than 6,000 and was not as well equipped. Seaborne landings also worked against them; on 7 August, Emmet Dalton sailed with 500 men from Dublin to Passage West, Cork. Encountering little opposition, the National Army had control of Cork city by 11 August.

Ten days later Arthur Griffith died, and he died an angry man:

> He shared none of Collins's forbearance towards his old comrades, and demanded constantly that the pro-Treaty authorities should act firmly against those whom he regarded as anti-democratic militarists. Ministers would be 'poltroons' if, having stood up to British tyranny, they now submitted to 'a tyranny just as mean and less supportable'. In turn republicans regarded him as a warmonger, and even his supporters were embarrassed by his intemperance.[31]

He was undoubtedly mentally and physically exhausted, travelling to London to defend decisions like the postponement of unveiling the constitution and the pact election proposal to a sceptical British government, decisions which in any case he had little time for. He was also an assiduous attendee of provisional government meetings; his health broke down and he died of a cerebral haemorrhage. Although he was aged only fifty-one 'he seemed already a father figure to the younger men around him, a relic of an earlier age. He died despondent, believing that many of his achievements were being undone and that his old suspicion of bloodshed had been vindicated at last.'[32]

George Gavan Duffy was also in considerable turmoil at this time: like many of his contemporaries in 1922, Duffy, the Minister for External Affairs in the provisional government, was struggling to reconcile his aspirations for Irish independence with the reality of what the Anglo-Irish Treaty had made possible. As a member of the Irish negotiating team, Duffy had been a reluctant signatory of the Treaty, but he saw little to be gained in rejecting it; as he pointed out in a subsequent Dáil debate: 'My heart is with those who are against the Treaty, but my reason is against them, because I can see no rational alternative.'[33] Nonetheless, he resigned from his ministry in the summer of 1922: he felt the new state was not doing enough to assert the limited independence he believed was conferred on it by the terms of the Treaty; he maintained parts of the 1922 constitution conceded more to Britain than was necessary; objected to the speedy disbandment of the Dáil courts established during the War of Independence; and was uncomfortable with the way the government was dealing with the civil war.

In March 1922 he had written to Collins concerning the draft constitution suggesting the draft not be showed to the British side 'as if it is as good as the Treaty allows it to be it will knock the bottom out of the opposition and ... should give a priceless opportunity of uniting the country'. But he also knew Britain would make 'desperate efforts' to get the oath of allegiance included in the constitution; at one stage he suggested using the words 'the British agent' whenever the phrase 'representative of the King' was proposed.[34] He resigned in July, insisting he was loyal to the government regarding the civil war but disagreed with them on most other things, though subsequently he criticised the execution of republicans.[35]

Despite these dilemmas, while he was briefly a minister in 1922 he articulated what he felt were the opportunities for a new small state at that time. In a letter to a priest, he refused to comment on the defects of the Treaty but instead chose to 'rejoice' in his belief that 'Ireland emerges at last from her dungeon into the sunlight'. The new state, he asserted 'will bring into a tired world a freshness of vision, coupled with a directness and a tenacity of purpose that will gradually make her an active factor in the redemption of Europe'. He concluded defiantly that the new state would 'rapidly prove itself justly entitled to be called the first of the small nations'.[36] These rhetorical flourishes were born of hope and aspiration rather than acceptance of reality, but they encapsulate the genuine idealism of that revolutionary generation. At the same time, Duffy's more sober admissions captured the reality of the limitations that curtailed the state's room for manoeuvre.

But the ultimate drama was to come – 'the great public tragedy – indeed the only *public* tragedy – of the civil war',[37] with the shooting dead of Michael Collins. On 18 August Emmet Dalton informed Collins of possible moves towards peace he had heard through intermediaries. This prompted Collins to visit Cork to arrange meetings with the anti-Treaty-ites, but on 22 August 1922 he was shot dead during an inspection tour of the south-western command. Contemporary reports suggested the ambushers could have numbered 200, which was a wild exaggeration.[38] More importantly, the government publicity bureau moved to quickly secure the halo around Collins: 'The genius and courage of Michael Collins lent an inspiration to the race ... in every phase of the awakened activity of the nation, constructive, administrative, executive, military, the personality of Michael Collins was vivid and impelling.' Tributes from the British side were also fulsome; Lord Birkenhead described him as 'a very remarkable personality; daring, resourceful, volatile and merry', while Lloyd George contented himself with the observation that 'his engaging personality won friendships even amongst those who first met him as a foe'.[39]

Playwright George Bernard Shaw, as usual, was much more interesting and original, if also insensitive with his timing, writing to Collins's sister Hannie a few days later:

> Don't let them make you miserable about it. How could a born soldier die better than at the victorious end of a good fight, falling to the shot of another Irishman ... I met Michael for the first and last time and am very glad I did. I rejoice in his memory and will not be so disloyal to it as to snivel over his valiant death. So tear up your mourning and hang up your brightest colours in his honour and let us all praise God that he did not die in a snuffy bed of a trumpery cough, weakened by age and saddened by disappointment that would have attended his life had he lived.[40]

When his body was returned to Dublin, thousands filed past it in City Hall with an estimated 300,000 lining the streets of the capital as the body passed to Glasnevin Cemetery.[41] There was a specific local sorrowful patriotism at work in his native Cork and it was reported, erroneously, that his last words were 'forgive them'.[42] He was also described as 'a kindly, generous and brave Corkman who typified in his personality all that was best and noblest in the Irish character'.[43]

The unionist response was a curt iteration of the maxim that those who live by the sword die by it: 'The latest victim of this blood lust is Mr Michael Collins who played such a prominent part in the murder campaign ... The cruel measures he meted out to police and soldiers have in turn been meted out to him by the men with who he formerly worked.' There was, however, some muted praise in relation to his signing of the Treaty: 'Whatever Collins' failings were, and there were many, he was a fearless man and this very quality has been his undoing.'[44]

The rhetorical flights were by no means confined to Ireland; the *Boston Daily Globe*, for example, published elaborate articles: 'Collins, chivalric figure of Irish revolution: won friend and foe'; subtitles included 'Heroic figure of revolution', 'Irish to the core' and 'Picturesque figure'. Journalist Charles Merrill had a field day, describing him as having his 'strong right hand flash the winning sword of justice', the 'best type of young Irishman' and 'a handsome youngster'.[45] The myth of the one man who forged a nation's destiny was in production at a very early stage but Lionel Curtis in the Colonial Office in London took a more pragmatic view, writing to Cosgrave on 24 August that Collins and Griffith had 'both made great places for themselves but none of us here doubts that Ireland knows how to fill those places'.[46]

To his credit, Richard Mulcahy, who succeeded Collins as commander-in-chief, warned in Collins's funeral oration against reprisals, and he was still intent on exploring possibilities for conciliation, meeting de Valera secretly on 5 September without the knowledge of his cabinet colleagues, who, when made aware, saw it as a breach of collective responsibility. Kevin O'Higgins was scathing but, in any case, he regarded Mulcahy holding the posts of both Minister for Defence and commander-in-chief as a dangerous complication in relation to the government's control over the army.

TWENTY-FIVE

STONE HEARTS

There was a limit to Mulcahy's quest for compromise nonetheless; he supported the Public Safety Act of 28 September that established military courts empowered to impose the death penalty. John Regan has suggested that as Minister for Defence, both during the civil war and after, Mulcahy 'resigned himself to the realities of the army he inherited from Collins and ignored its excesses' in the interests of balancing 'the internal stability of the army against the application of rigorous discipline'.[1] The death of Collins also brought William Cosgrave to a new prominence, when he was elected president of the Dáil and chairman of the provisional government. In September or October, during the passage of the Free State constitution through the Dáil, 'Under threat of assassination, he wrote a note forgiving whoever might kill him.'[2] On 6 December 1922, on the formal establishment of the Irish Free State, Cosgrave became president of the executive council. In the Dáil, amidst tight security and without anyone in the public gallery, Cosgrave took the oath of allegiance to the king and made a sombre speech: 'On this notable day when our country has definitely emerged from the bondage under which she has lived through a week of centuries, I cannot deny that I feel intensely proud to be the first man called to preside over the first government which takes over the control of the destiny of our people.'[3]

But it was not an event that lent itself to celebration. Little changed with the formal creation of the state; the actual powers of administration and control over internal security had already been transferred to the provisional government in March 1922, and the day after the formal birth of the state the reality of Irish partition was again underlined when the Belfast parliament formally opted out of coming in under the Dublin parliament, as was its right. As Cosgrave acknowledged, it came at a time of trauma. In the midst of a civil war that had become vicious, the formal establishment of the state was sandwiched between horrendous events.

The execution of anti-Treaty republicans by the Free State authorities had begun on 17 November, and the day after the inauguration of the new state, pro-Treaty Cork TD Seán Hales was shot dead. In retaliation, the government authorised the illegal execution of four prominent republicans, including Rory O'Connor. Liam Lynch warned the speaker of the Dáil, Michael Hayes, that the IRA was giving to each TD 'due notice that unless your army recognises the rules of warfare in the future we shall adopt very drastic measures to protect our forces'.[4] The following week George Gavan Duffy wrote to Hayes about his increasing isolation in the Dáil due to his opposition to the execution of Erskine Childers and the 'vilification' he was subjected to as a result.[5]

Duffy also corresponded with P. J. Hooper, the editor of the *Freeman's Journal*, who had spent a month in Mountjoy jail for publishing a story of army brutality during the War of Independence but who was now editing a paper that was virulently dismissive of the anti-Treatyites. Duffy complained about the venomous attacks on Childers, to which Hooper replied that Childers was the most dangerous enemy to the peace 'because of his extremism' and owing to 'his great influence with Mr de Valera'.[6] This was a commoner misnomer; the reality was that both Childers and de Valera were quite marginalised in the republican movement at this stage. Kathleen O'Connell's diary records that de Valera and his companions were 'stunned' by the executions on 8 December.[7] But there was also intimidation of newspaper proprietors and editors by republicans in the areas where they exercised control, and the *Freeman's Journal* was one victim.[8]

Kevin O'Higgins defended the executions:

There are no real rules of war. They may be written in a book; they may get lip service from philanthropists. When war breaks out they are more honoured in the breach than in the observance. I have spoken to men who were [sic] through the late European war, and I could not come here to this Dáil and talk with any seriousness of the rules of war or the laws of war after what I heard from these men. So let us not proceed just on those lines ... the safety and preservation of the people is the highest law.

Cosgrave added that the jackboot would now take precedence over all else: 'I know fully well there is a diabolical conspiracy afoot ... there is only one way to meet it and that is to crush it.'[9]

In his response, the leader of the Labour Party, Thomas Johnson, said in the Dáil: 'There was no pretence at legality. I am almost forced to say that I believe you have killed the new state at its birth.' Hearts had turned to stone; two days after those executions, the house of another pro-Treaty TD, Seán McGarry, was set on fire and his seven-year-old son Emmet died as a result.

De Valera's continued correspondence with Mary MacSwiney reflected a certain weariness with the Republic as a living faith/spiritual entity argument, which he effectively negated with a telling rebuke to MacSwiney, one which underlined the dilemma of republicans during the civil war and the inevitability of their defeat: that there was a 'difference between desiring a thing and having a feasible programme for securing it'.[10]

Cosgrave and his colleagues remained wedded to a ruthless military and political strategy that ensured, by May 1923, a decisive win over the republicans and the end of the civil war. In February 1923, Cosgrave's analysis was that 'the executions have had a remarkable effect. It is a sad thing to say, but it is nevertheless the case'. He could also be chilling in his resolve: 'I am not going to hesitate and if the country is to live and if we have to exterminate 10,000 republicans, the 3 millions of our people are bigger than the ten thousand.'[11] Perhaps this realism was also beginning to affect the men of faith, Dan Breen telling his fellow republicans: 'In order to win this war you'll need to kill 3 out of every 5 people in the country and it isn't worth it.'[12] There is, nonetheless, evidence that the National Army was instructed to treat republican prisoners being prepared for execution 'with the utmost humanity'.[13]

The opposition of many in CnB (whose convention rejected the Treaty by 419 votes to 63) was also significant; more republican women were opposed to the Treaty than republican men and this resulted in much bitterness and blame. P. S. O'Hegarty, the civil servant and pro-Treaty historian, devoted a chapter in *The Victory of Sinn Féin* (1924) to the role of women in the civil war under the title 'The Furies – Hell hath no fury like a woman ...' and he elaborated:

> Left to himself, man is comparatively harmless. He will always exchange smokes and drinks and jokes with his enemy and he will always pity the 'poor devil' and wish that the whole business was over. The thought of his parents, or of his wife or his children, is always with him to make him consider a friendly arrangement rather than a duel, to make him think of life rather than of death ... It is woman adrift with her white feathers ... with her implacability, her bitterness, her hysteria, that makes a devil of him.[14]

This was just one example of the concerted determination to marginalise women in the new Free State and to belittle their War of Independence and civil war contributions, not to mention discarding the promises of equality in 1916. In the midst of civil war, Cosgrave was adamant in his correspondence with Archbishop Edward Byrne of Dublin that women were an especially malign influence, referring to 'the prominent and destructive part played by women in the present deplorable revolt ... a law unto themselves'.[15]

There was also a tendency to characterise women's opposition to the Treaty as personal and emotional and out of place in what purported to be a 'rational' discussion of Ireland's future; Batt O'Connor, a close ally of Collins and defender of the Treaty, wrote privately:

> There is not much real division noticeable at all among the people, but the women are 'holy terrors'. They are mudslinging and name calling and spitting and froughting [sic] to the mouth like angry cats, and always casting up about their relatives that died for Ireland. I think the Irish people will not be in a hurry again to elect women to represent them.[16]

Some even went as far as to suggest that women adopted extreme positions as they did not have to fear for their lives during the War of Independence. At the height of the civil war, Kevin O'Higgins simply referred to them as 'certain neurotic women'; he even referred dismissively (and ironically, given the way contemporary and future male Irish republicans used it) to the 'women's weapon of the hunger strike'.[17]

Another notable development during the civil war was the strong intervention of the Catholic hierarchy. Archbishop Byrne had been quick to state his support for the provisional government and had urged de Valera to avoid fermenting a split. He also attempted, with Laurence O'Neill, lord mayor of Dublin, to broker a peace by calling a conference of opposing leaders, which was a respected though doomed effort. Significantly, he tried to persuade Cosgrave, with whom he corresponded regularly, not to execute republican prisoners; he regarded the summary executions as 'not only unwise but entirely unjustifiable from a moral point of view'.[18] Writing to the rector of the Irish College in Rome, John Hagan, Bishop Fogarty of Killaloe criticised anti-Treaty propaganda, suggesting that voters should 'pay no attention to all the talk about surrendering their birthright. They know their own minds.'

The bishops were clearly intent on taking ownership of the issue of Treaty acceptance and filling any vacuum that existed at that time as well as being hostile to the arrival of a papal envoy, Monsignor Salvatore Luzio, in 1923, hostility shared by the new government. Republicans were firmly in the firing line with their emphasis on the 'moral superiority' of their opposition, or, as one historian described it, 'republican spiritual rhetoric'.[19] Their constant use of the word 'faith' was striking, along with the preponderance of utterances and declarations that referred to soul and righteousness, what Michael Tierney, UCD academic and firm supporter of the Treaty, lampooned as 'Hiberniorism'. This prompted an increasingly aggressive reaction from the Catholic bishops and in their pastoral of October 1922 they lamented 'how decent Irish boys could degenerate so tragically'; the pastoral had its critics, including Fr Paddy Browne, who saw it as 'an abuse of their spiritual power', as was, he maintained, withholding absolution to prisoners in jail.

As influential rector of the Irish College in Rome, John Hagan did his utmost to keep the Vatican out of all this and had to juggle his opposition to the Treaty and to pro-Treaty bishops and their pronouncements with the need to correspond with them on regular Church business (they certainly could not afford to ignore him given his influence).[20] Hagan reported in March 1923 that Luzio would be sent to Ireland 'for the purpose of bringing the warring leaders together and making peace', which Bishop O'Doherty thought was 'ludicrous'.[21] Cardinal Logue's position was also significant; although disappointed by partition, he was firmly in favour of the Treaty. He suggested that the opponents of the Treaty did nothing but 'talk and wrangle for days about their shadowy republic and their obligations to it' while the Treaty granted everything that was necessary for the progress and welfare of the country.[22] He wanted his fellow bishops to be more vociferous in their praise of the agreement, and during the civil war he was keen that the Vatican intervene and condemn the state of unrest.

Luzio's mission was also a product of a visit to Rome in December 1922 by two Irish republicans, Arthur Clery and Conn Murphy, who came to formally complain that the Irish bishops had exceeded their authority in excommunicating opponents of the Treaty.[23] There were reasons beyond the civil war for Luzio's cool reception from some when he arrived in Ireland. While republicans were pleased to claim that the Pope had sent Luzio as a mediator, and thus conferred equal legitimacy on them in the civil war dispute, the government pointed to its mandate and its need to do whatever was necessary to protect the state from a minority of armed rebels. The bishops also feared, it seemed, that the visit might presage the appointment of a permanent nuncio, not necessarily to promote Irish affairs but to use Ireland as a base to strengthen Vatican diplomatic relations with the British Empire. Luzio was there, believed some, 'to ascertain if there would be much objection to a delegation of a permanent nature'; he was in Ireland for three weeks before there was any effort to contact members of government and, 'more insulting yet, he had spent a great deal of this time meeting with prominent republican leaders many of whom were wanted criminals who had been denied the sacraments and excommunicated'. Cosgrave in turn, wanted the Vatican to know that Luzio's actions 'are in the highest degree embarrassing to the government'.[24] Meanwhile, Desmond FitzGerald sent a representative to the Vatican to successfully demand Luzio's recall. Amusingly, Luzio complained that the Irish bishops regarded themselves as 'twenty-six popes'.[25]

The bishops were also unusually mute in relation to the executions and hunger strikes, and Byrne's private complaints to Cosgrave were responded to with polite defiance; O'Doherty depicted those behind the hunger strikes as 'the crowd that have tried to blacken the bishops in Ireland and all over the world'.[26] Ever since 1916, the support of the Church had been vital to SF, but as the history of radical nationalism had demonstrated, there were limits to its influence, not just with the flock but also its own clergy. What was striking about Byrne's correspondence with Mary MacSwiney, however, was the emphatic closing down of political debate:

'With regard to your political beliefs, hopes and aspirations I have nothing to say. I too, have ideals, many of them impossible of realisation.'[27]

The Church may also, suggests Patrick Murray, have underestimated the ferociousness of republican opposition; a woman from Kenmare, for example, told the Bishop of Kerry that she would no longer be attending Mass or contributing to the Church because on successive Sundays 'republicans have to sit there and listen to insulting remarks cast at our men and boys whose only crime is being true to their oath of allegiance to the Republic'. Murray also underlines that these were the kind of interventions by women which confirmed the view of some bishops that republican women were unreasonable and extreme: Bishop Doorly wondered, 'Who respects them or would marry one of them?'[28]

Significantly however, republicans were not without their clerical supporters at home and abroad, which meant complete alienation was never a possibility and Murray suggests that without that support, a more pronounced form of anti-clericalism could have been part of the civil war legacy, a reminder that throughout the revolution there were responses to political and military controversies that were complex and variegated. One republican prisoner publicly criticised the bishops for their 'partisan excess' and a pastoral which 'presses into theological use the catchcries and terms of abuse of the Free State party ... I see here in prison the injury done to the souls of splendid men by the reckless attitude of the hierarchy.'[29]

Archbishop Byrne also exerted pressure when it came to the issue of the hunger strikes of republican prisoners. Mary MacSwiney was notable in this regard after her arrest, and her plight in November 1922 was attracting much attention and sympathy. Women even protested in the grounds of Dr Byrne's residence.[30] Many who wrote to Cosgrave invoked the ghost of her late brother: 'I pleaded with English people to use their influence to try and save the life of the late Lord Mayor of Cork when he was hunger striking in England. So I venture to plead with you to save the life of Miss Mary MacSwiney now hunger striking in Dublin among her own people.'[31] Not allowing her sister to visit her was another controversial decision; MacSwiney twice managed to embarrass the government into releasing her, after a twenty-four-day hunger strike in late 1922 and again in April 1923. Edward Byrne had suggested the request of her sister 'does not seem to be unreasonable and to be on the side of humanity'.[32] Cosgrave demurred but Byrne also had his own strictures; MacSwiney was refused Holy Communion and when she complained, Byrne informed her that she was breaking a divine law by hunger striking and 'all who participate in such crimes are guilty of the gravest sins and may not be absolved nor admitted to Holy Communion'.[33] But one factor Cosgrave and his government had to consider was which was the lesser of two evils; one of his supporters wrote to Cosgrave: 'If she dies she will live forever.'[34] MacSwiney positively embraced her martyrdom to an almost messianic degree, announcing to her supporters in America in November 1922, 'Whether I am released or whether like my brother my sacrifice is to be consummated, I am happy to suffer for Ireland.'[35]

Many other republicans went on hunger strike, surviving on a 'diet' of Turkish cigarettes ('helped to dull the eternal craving for food'), lemon sweets and chewing gum: 'surely such suffering cannot go unrewarded either here or hereafter', Phyllis Ryan wrote to her brother James as she enclosed the hunger strike 'provisions'.[36] After the civil war had ended, suffering republican prisoners in Mountjoy prison, via Sinn Féin, complained to the Catholic bishops that 'a plague of flies from rotting rubbish heaps under the windows of the two wings has come as added torment to the bed-ridden men'.[37] For the young Todd Andrews, the greatest challenge of internment was boredom.[38] Writer Francis Stuart, interned for eighteen months in various prison camps, later romanticised the incarceration; he had decided, he declared, to step outside of history: 'One can open one's arms to life more widely in a cell than anywhere else perhaps ... Those days were not unhappy.'[39] Contrast that with the recollections of Michael O'Donoghue:

> Weeks passed and no word of release. I became infested with vermin – lice and fleas, but especially lice. A large abscess formed inside my cheek, the result of infection from my diseased gums. A doctor came and advised me to submit to medical and dental treatment from the Free State Army medicals. I refused, demanding release. The abscess burst.[40]

A measure of the ruthless resolve and the sheer power of the National Army Council was evident in its order of February 1923: 'In every case of outrage in any battalion area, three men will be executed ... no clemency will be shown in any case.'[41] The previous month, another thirty-two had been executed and by the end of the civil war the Free State had authorised the execution of seventy-seven; this was fifty-three more than the British had executed during the War of Independence. It has also been estimated that 11,480 republicans were jailed under public safety laws. One of the arguments used by Mulcahy was that permitting official executions would prevent National Army troops from carrying out unofficial killings.[42] But these unofficial killings occurred anyway, including three teenage Fianna Éireann members from Drumcondra who were arrested for putting up anti-Treaty posters and then killed. So too was Noel Lemass, brother of Seán, who was an intelligence officer on the anti-Treaty side and had spent periods incarcerated and on the run. An added tragedy was that Lemass was killed after the end of the civil war; his badly mutilated body (some of his fingers had been removed and he was shot three times in the head) was found in the Dublin mountains in October 1923. The grotesqueness of his death caused outrage, and no one was convicted of the crime; it was widely believed the CID was responsible. Seán Lemass did not mention it in public in the course of his subsequent career.

At the end of the war, Dorothy Macardle wrote of 'dark, fearful and secret happenings', cold-blooded revenge killings and psychological torture. In her *Tragedies of Kerry* (1924) she also focused on the Ballyseedy massacre, when nine republican prisoners were tied to a land mine which was detonated, in revenge for the killing of Free State soldiers at Knocknagoshel in Kerry:

> One of the soldiers handed each of them a cigarette: 'the last smoke you'll ever have', he said ... the soldiers had strong ropes and electric cords. Each prisoner's hands were tied behind him, then his arms were tied above the elbow to those of the men on either side of him. Their feet were bound together above the ankles and their legs were bound together above the knees. Then a strong rope was passed round the nine and the soldiers moved away. The prisoners had their backs to the log and the mine which was beside it; they could see the movement of the soldiers and knew what would happen next. They gripped one another's hands, those who could and prayed for God's mercy upon their souls. The shock came, blinding, deafening, overwhelming ... for days afterwards the birds were eating the flesh off the trees at Ballyseedy Cross.[43]

Remarkably, there was a survivor, Stephen Fuller, who was blown into an adjoining field, went on the run and was treated by a doctor who 'found him in a dug out on a mountain'; he was, after it, 'a complete and permanent invalid'. In the 1930s he was awarded a wound pension of £150 a year; most of those who testified on his behalf were remarkably understated ('I understand his health has been greatly impaired as a result of his activities ... [He] is now suffering from shock received from a mine explosion at Ballyseedy'), though one was moved to declare that he was 'blown up in the Ballyseedy massacre providentially escaping alive'. As well as TB, 'an X-ray also reveals the presence of several fine bodies embedded in the musculature of his back'. Fuller, however, went on to outlive many of his contemporaries, dying at the age of eighty-four.[44]

The survivor of the Knocknagoshel tragedy was not so lucky. Annie O'Brien in Dublin received a telegram on 13 March: 'Regret to inform you that Vol. Joseph O'Brien No. 1596 lies badly wounded at the infirmary, Tralee. Should you desire to visit him a free voucher will be issued.' Her husband was the only National Army soldier who survived the triggering of the mine that killed five of his colleagues; both his legs had to be amputated below the knee and he had severe impairment of vision in both eyes. A year after the end of the civil war the recommendation of the Army Pensions Board was that he receive a wound pension of £2 2s weekly 'and artificial limbs' but thereafter, his wife had to go to great lengths to find suitable accommodation, as he was 'living in a top room' but 'he is unable to get up the stairs'. The Department of Defence curtly replied that 'the question of suitable housing accommodation is not one that can be dealt with by this department'. His wife also had to plead for a wheelchair – 'It is the only means I would have of getting him out for air each day' – which took six months to be provided, his brother stating: 'It is a shame for him to be treated in such a way.'[45]

Thomas Roche, a National Army soldier wounded during the Four Courts explosion, 'after the very heavy strain of all the fighting', was admitted to Clonmel mental hospital in December 1922, where he stayed for five months before he was discharged from the army as medically unfit, and was destitute by the end of the civil war. 'I certainly lost good opportunities in my young life' was how he succinctly and mournfully summed up his civil war experience.[46]

Lennox Robinson, in editing Lady Gregory's journals for publication, observed that during the period of the civil war the journals 'are filled with accounts of grabbing of land, driving of cattle and general confusion. These doings are merely of local interest and I do not record them.'[47]

This was an interesting insight into why many of those themes have been unjustly neglected; after all, they were precisely the sort of happenings that prompted Kevin O'Higgins to assert in the Dáil in March 1923, 'We were the most conservative minded revolutionaries that ever put through a successful revolution.'[48] The remark was made during an ill-tempered Dáil debate about the seizure of cattle by the Free State Army after the cattle had been stolen and were being grazed on illegally captured land. The *Irish Independent* characterised the government's response the day after this Dáil debate as 'Checking Anarchy'. For O'Higgins, the cause was 'greed; the desire to get rich quick on the part of people who think they have a vested interest in disorder; to get rich quick regardless of law human or divine; to get something for nothing; to get the fruits of work without work.'[49] As Peadar O'Donnell saw it, however, this was about a new social polarity and a perpetuation of the 'rabble' theme – 'city minded' Sinn Féiners, suspicious of the 'wild men on the land', with republicans as the champions of the dispossessed and the small farmers.[50]

Such activities had continued because the promise that things would change had begun to wear thin. The previous year, a soldier in the western division wrote to Patrick Hogan, the Minister for Agriculture, 'the number of disputes about land in this divisional area are increasing daily. Very many volunteers and volunteers' friends are concerned in the disputes. They don't recognise that all that can possibly be done for them will be done in due course.'[51]

The anti-Treaty IRA in some districts encouraged boycotting of Protestants and intimidation was widespread.[52] In a few days in April 1922, thirteen Protestant civilians were murdered in and around Dunmanway in west Cork; the killings were condemned by both sides of the Treaty debate and the IRA. The commander of the British navy in Cork harbour stated, 'In view of what looks like the beginnings of a pogrom against the Protestants in the South, it may be necessary to send ships to evacuate Protestant Loyalists from Southern sea ports.' Peter Hart suggested the motive was sectarian and 'ethnic cleansing' in operation: 'The accuracy of his thesis dominates debate to this day, particularly in the face of counterarguments that the victims may have been informers.'[53] It has also been asserted 'these killings were exceptional'.[54]

In 1911 southern Protestants numbered 311,000, 10 per cent of the population, but they were spread unevenly, with 21 per cent in Dublin and only 4 per cent in the west of the country. By 1926 their proportion had declined to 7 per cent of the total population, yet Protestants still accounted for '40 per cent of the lawyers, over 20 per cent of the doctors, and well over 50 per cent of the bankers. More than a quarter of large farms were still in Protestant hands in 1926. Of the managerial classes, nearly one-fifth were Protestants.'[55] While the decline of the 'big houses' of the Anglo-Irish aristocracy had been an obvious symbol of their demise, this was also 'overwhelmed by the fiction; it needs careful treatment'. There are, for example two contrasting assertions and perspectives in Lennox Robinson's play *The Big House* (1926) after the house, Ballydonal, becomes a charred and smoking ruin: 'I'm just damn glad its all over and there's no reason to make an effort anymore,' alongside 'I believe in Ballydonal, it's my life, it's my faith, it's my country.'[56]

But how many Protestants were actually compelled to leave? While between 1911 and 1926, the decline was 33 per cent (in contrast to only 2 per cent for Catholics), there are obvious caveats to be factored in to these figures, including departure of military families, police, civil servants and the effects of the First World War. Nonetheless, there is still 'the inevitable conclusion that a significant proportion of the overall decline was due to involuntary migration, recently assessed at about 39,000 from the south ... This exodus constitutes about 37 per cent of the Protestant population decline between 1911 and 1926.'[57] The decline, however, did not begin with the War of Independence; it had begun with the Land War of the nineteenth century and especially the Wyndham Land Act of 1903 and entered its last days when the First World War began. As Elizabeth Bowen recorded, 'Not a family had not put out, like Bowen's Court, its genera-tions of military brothers – tablets in Protestant churches recorded deaths in remote battles; swords hung in halls.'[58]

Terence Dooley has estimated that between February 1920 and April 1923, 275 big houses were burned, which was only about 4 per cent of such houses in Ireland; they were particularly targeted in Munster.[59] Many other Protestant businesses and homes were targeted (Peter Hart suggests at least 400 Protestant homes and businesses were burned dur-ing the revolution) and they were victims also of agrarian outrages as they were overrepresented on the larger farms and there had been a slowdown in the transfer of land during the First World War.[60] Andy Bielenberg has reached a fair and balanced conclusion: while acknowledging the shades of grey, he concludes the likelihood is that 'fewer than 16,000 people (representing under 15 per cent of the drop in the Protestant population) could plausibly have been driven out by violence, intimidation and terror during the nationalist revolution'.

That, of course, amounted to trauma on a serious scale, but,

> Ultimately, the majority of Protestants remained in Ireland and, if we exclude the language question, the political question was reasonably sensitive to their position. At the outset, at least, they were over rep-resented in both the Senate and the Dáil; they retained ownership of a disproportionate share of land in the state and retained a dominant position in industry, finance and the professions. While it is impor-tant to acknowledge the impact of revolutionary violence and terror on minority emigration, it is also important to recognise a wider spectrum of forces at work in this period, which was collectively far more significant in explaining the exodus.[61]

It hardly amounted to ethnic cleansing, but some republicans, in the way they framed this issue, were deliberately vague or disingenuous, Tom Barry asserting, for example, that 'we never killed a man because of his religion ... but we had to face up to facts'. Charles Townshend asserts in response that 'the most salient fact was that nearly all Protestants were unionists'.[62]

Undoubtedly there was a new emphasis in civil-war and post-civil-war Ireland on recognising hierarchies and people knowing their place; this was also evident in the army, where, in July 1923, Mulcahy issued an order to officers demanding that there be no longer a sense of fraternal and equal brothers in arms. There was to be no repeat of 'discourtesy or smartness' or correspondence using the term 'a chara' [friend]; correspon-dence to the Minister for Defence and Army Council should now end with 'I have the honour, sir, to be your obedient servant'.[63] This was true in other walks of life also; the power vacuum was being rapidly filled, and the rabble would know, and be required to acknowledge, its place.

Even after the end of the civil war, the 'rabble' theme continued to be aired, this time in the context of the electoral battles between Sinn Féin and Cumann na nGaedheal (CnG), the new name for pro-Treaty Sinn Féin from 1923, which in turn evolved into Fine Gael. In August 1923, Cosgrave and O'Higgins addressed an election meeting in Drogheda where a brass band and an estimated 2,000 listeners were confronted by in the region of a hundred women with banners demanding the release of prisoners, who, according to the *Irish Times*, began 'howling in chorus'. The local monsignor spoke to endorse CnG and urged that 'madmen should not be allowed to deprive them of the freedom they had won'. Cosgrave went further, comparing the government's experience in the previous eighteen months to 'that which Abraham Lincoln had in America'. Announcing de Valera's arrest (he was imprisoned from August 1923 to July 1924), he suggested 'many a grave is in the graveyards of the country tonight because of the formulas, the metaphysics and nonsense he put before the needs of the nation'. O'Higgins was left with the last words: 'Here they had the decent, silent masses of the people, anxious to restore the nation's credit and, on the other side, they had the noisy, ignorant rabble, that could only shout and destroy instead of building up.'[64] In that election, SF actually did very well and 'performed much better than most observers had expected'; it won 27.4 per cent of the vote with forty-four TDs returned.[65]

But, as abstentionist TDs, they were all dressed up with nowhere to go; it was still a coalition of different interests and de Valera was well aware of its limitations. He was conscious of the extent to which the civil war had narrowed his options and left him bereft of control, and the need to try to regain the semblance of unity that had existed in 1917. In May 1923 he had sent a letter to the organising committee of SF concerning its resolution that a political organisation – the Irish Republican Political Organisation – be formed. De Valera objected to this on the grounds that 'purely republican needs' were already catered for by the IRA:

> We wish to organise not merely Republican opinion strictly so-called, but what might be called 'Nationalist' or 'Independence' opinion in general. If we do not do it, the other side will and the loss will be immense ... to attempt to found a further Republican organisation would be a wasteful duplication that would serve no purpose whatever ... the position is in many respects similar to that we had to face in the middle of 1917. If we act as wisely and as energetically as we acted then, we shall win the people over once more.[66]

The civil war had ended without negotiations or a truce; IRA chief of staff Liam Lynch was killed in action on 10 April 1923, which quenched whatever fire was left in the republican fight, and was succeeded by Frank Aiken. In his letter to his republican comrades requesting them to dump arms in May 1923, as had been commanded by Aiken, de Valera reserved his most damning criticism for the Church, with scathing references to 'the moral leaders especially, whose influence in [a] crisis like this would be beyond price, have allowed themselves to be so entangled in the conflict that they are now useless. They have displayed a spirit of hate and vindictiveness more narrow and bigoted even than that of the professional politicians.'[67]

He established his new party, Fianna Fáil, in 1926, not just to mark the change of policy on abstention, but also because, as pointed out by Pauric Travers, this 'gave de Valera unfettered control, which he had not enjoyed with Sinn Féin'. Within six years it was in power, where it remained for most of the next seven decades, and in relation to his republican past, de Valera was just one of many of that generation who made the successful transition from poacher to gamekeeper. In 1940, in the run up to the twenty-fourth anniversary of the Easter Rising, he made it clear that he and his government would not tolerate armed republicanism, and that law and order had to be upheld: 'Without such discipline we must inevitably degenerate into a rabble.'[68]

TWENTY-SIX

ULSTER'S WOUNDED
SELF-LOVE

The main political challenge for Ulster Unionists during the First
World War was to gain acceptance of permanent six-county exclusion from any Anglo-Irish home rule solution. The 'Ulsterisation' of this
issue was a device to prevent the imposition of home rule for the whole
of Ireland and partition was a tactic rather than a solution; in July 1914 at
the Buckingham Peace Conference, Edward Carson had proposed that
Ulster be separated from Ireland in its entirety and suggested if this was
done generously it probably would in time rejoin. One of his biographers
has suggested this idea was 'far-sighted. Carson foresaw, as eventually happened, that a smaller Protestant-dominated block in the north-east, if
split off, would have less and less in common with the rest of Ireland and
would eventually become an alien redoubt.'[1]

Carson and James Craig served in coalition government during the
war, which helped their standing and maintained their influence, but in
the post-war period they began to drift from each other. Craig remained
an office holder after the war, while Carson returned to legal practice,
and Craig was well positioned to influence draft measures based on a six-
county partition scheme, giving continuity to unionist demands; as was
the case in 1916, Craig in 1920 insisted that the six-county formula was
imperative. Craig's ministerial boss, Walter Long, was in charge of the
cabinet committee responsible for devising the Government of Ireland
Bill. Crucially, Craig was able to persuade the Ulster Unionist Council to

accept the bill, which passed in December 1920, as well as insisting on the creation of a new police reserve drawn mostly from a reactivated Ulster Volunteer Force to hem in the new political entity.

The bill created two parliaments, one in Belfast and one in Dublin. Sinn Féin, inevitably, rejected it; Craig, however, now had what he needed: a constitutional framework for the creation of the state of Northern Ireland. Acceptance of the bill was described by Craig as 'the supreme sacrifice', words that must have seemed horribly hollow to southern unionists. With the bill, according to a contemporary, 'the Irish question has ceased to be a dividing line in British politics ... There is perhaps no better testimony to its intrinsic merits than that it fails to satisfy either the political necessities of English political partisans or of Irish extremists of all sorts.'[2]

For all the Ulster Unionist defiance and militancy on display in rejecting Irish republicanism during this period, some politicians were also keen, behind the scenes, to insist on the demarcation between politics and paramilitarism. During the War of Independence, Fred Crawford, who had formed the Ulster Brotherhood, an armed undercover body nicknamed 'Crawford's Tigers', also discussed plans to infiltrate the IRA in Dublin but Craig was quick to point out to him in the summer of 1919: 'When peace is signed it will be up to you to consult Dawson Bates [secretary of the Ulster Unionist Council] and take whatever action the two of you deem judicious but under no circumstances should either Sir Edward Carson or myself be implicated – we should know nothing whatever about it.'[3] Perhaps during the War of Independence unionists were also worried that the performance of the IRA exposed the limitations in loyalist paramilitarism; in June 1920, Crawford suggested to Craig that what was going on militarily in Dublin 'proves my contention that we have "boys" here instead of soldiers.'[4]

There was serious rioting in April 1920 in Derry, the emergence of Protestant vigilante groups and the decree of a trade boycott of Belfast by the first Dáil. In the summer of 1920, according to Sinn Féin, up to 10,000 Catholics were intimidated out of their workplaces (David Fitzpatrick suggests that in July 1920, 5,500 Catholics and 1,900 Protestants suspected of nationalism or socialism were expelled from Belfast shipyards.)[5] The British labour movement was either unwilling or unable to challenge this.[6]

In November that year, enrolment in the Ulster Special Constabulary began, the biggest and most notorious division of which became the B Specials, who were given official status in 1920 despite a recognition that many of them were 'the younger and wilder'. Thus, the formation of the state 'had been anticipated by the formation of one of the most critical apparatuses – an independent paramilitary force whose populist flavour of Protestant self-assertiveness was not to be diminished by its new status. The official endorsement of this spirit was to shape both state formation and Catholic attitudes to it.'[7] The B Specials had a membership of 16,000 and were regarded by nationalists, with much justification, as the UVF 'in state uniforms', or, as Fitzpatrick put it, 'the new force embodied Britain's belated blessing of bigotry'.[8] Its champions preferred to refer to it in the summer of 1920, in the words of Fred Crawford's diary entry, as having 'a splendid spirit of discipline'.[9] (The B Specials were named as such because they were part-time, unlike the A Specials, and had a reputation for aggressive targeting of Catholics.) Those sympathetic to the unionist case described republican activists in Derry in the summer of 1920 as little more than 'armed ruffians'.[10] In private, Craig was prepared to admit the following year that 'above all' a good general officer was needed to command troops in Northern Ireland as 'I know we have not been well served on certain occasions in the past.'[11]

Crawford's diary of the disturbances in Belfast in the summer of 1920 was a partisan journal that underlined the polarisation. A twenty-year-old Protestant who said he was going to 'bate' the police was told by Crawford 'he was no Protestant or Orangeman but a mean low Sinn Féiner and he would not interfere with the soldier doing his duty ... When the youngster saw he was likely to be taken for a Sinn Féiner and realising that this would mean a good hammering once it was believed, he disappeared about as quickly as it was possible to do so.'[12] Crawford was involved in inspecting the UVF and 'giving the lads a bit of advice', especially 'after a police inspector was shot in cold blood coming from Church last Sunday in Lisburn', but what troubled him was the class divide: 'On the way home I saw big fires in Sandy Row. It is so senseless this destruction of property but we can't get the responsible better class working men to interfere, with the result that they will have to pay for all this destruction of property.'[13] The following month he recorded that 'nearly every day people are coming up to me for rifles and ammunition. I have none of the former to hand out but I am glad to say I have plenty of rifle ammunition but very little revolvers.'[14]

Crawford also saw himself as a likely target: 'they would willingly point me out to some of the RCs [Roman Catholics] from Lisburn and

who are very much enraged for having been burnt out of their homes';
he also told 'the boys' to hide their rifles from the police. He was critical
of the lack of condemnation from the Vatican of republican violence but
acknowledged that 'some of the older priests to give them their due have
spoken out', but there were so few they were 'crying in the wilderness'.[15]
Crawford made numerous references to 'the apathy of the old leaders. I
have been doing all I could to get them together since March when Sir
Edward Carson asked us to mobilise them again but a great number of
our men are fed up with fighting and want a rest and to enjoy the result of
high wages and better times, consequently there has been a tendency with
the men over 30 to stay out of it.'[16] Meanwhile, Craig in October 1920, as
recorded by his wife, 'goes down to Harland and Wolffs [shipyard] in the
dinner hour and unfurls a big Union Jack for them and makes a splendid
speech. He tells them that he approves of their action in not allowing the
disloyal element in their midst.'[17] A Firearms Act of 1921 passed by the
Northern Ireland government stipulated that 'all persons found in the
possession of firearms are liable on conviction to be sentenced to penal
servitude and to receive in addition certain strokes of the instruments
known as the Birch or the Cat'.

What were republicans to do about the reality of the northern state?
Delusion certainly endured. Poet and founder member of the Irish Volunteers, Joseph Campbell, a Sinn Féin activist and county councillor based
in Wicklow, wrote to Arthur Griffith in November 1921 as a 'pragmatist
in politics'. What he proposed, in order to 'save Great Britain's face, salve
Ulster's wounded self-love and satisfy the historic sense of the majority of
the Irish people', was a Union of the Free States of Ireland: 'I would take
the northern six county state as a basis, boldly acknowledging its independent status, without reservation or guarantee. I would divide Ireland into
five such free states of six counties.' He made the observation that Tyrone
and Fermanagh, 'although republican in politics are essentially northern
in character. Take them away from Derry, Antrim, Down and Armagh
and you are penning the Protestant population into what I may call a
"compound of peculiar folk"'. For Northern Ireland's agreement to such a
'National Confederation', a trade boycott and resistance by nationalists to
its laws would 'see its submission'.[18]

But the success of the trade boycott of Belfast goods is open to question; in January 1921 a report compiled for the SF cabinet suggested
there were more than eighty local 'boycott committees' in the south and

west, organised through municipal bodies, but it was acknowledged that
'very little at present can be done at the port as the goods arrive without
any trace of their Belfast origin'.[19] By the end of 1921, a frustrated Joseph
MacDiarmada informed the cabinet that the Dublin United Tramway
Company was a 'flagrant offender' of the boycott; it not only facilitated
the movement of Belfast goods, but was advertising boycotted firms on
its tickets and windows; a fine of £300 imposed was 'absolutely ignored'.[20]

FitzGerald and Childers's propaganda department produced a
pamphlet early in 1920 entitled 'The Ulster Difficulty' and in May proposed the 'constitution of a propaganda paper' for 'North East Ulster'.
There was a vote of £1,000 for the purposes of 'propaganda against partition' in April 1921, while by December 1921, those involved in coordinating the Belfast Boycott heard that 'further economic help was needed to
"Irishise" Belfast'.[21] But these were secondary issues; by the end of 1921,
more than a hundred people had been killed in Belfast alone. David Fitzpatrick suggests that 'as in the campaign for civil rights in 1967–70, Northern Protestant belligerence helped unify southern Catholics in righteous
indignation, so providing a welcome distraction from the moral quan-
daries of the Anglo-Irish struggle'.[22]

It was not just the poets who were in the wishful thinking club.
Michael Collins wrote to Griffith that same year about the elections in
Northern Ireland, noting that de Valera had met Dr Joseph MacRory, the
Catholic bishop of Down and Connor, 'and his Lordship is very good and
very strong on the whole thing. He thinks it quite possible that all parties
– I mean nationalist parties – will stand down in favour of Sinn Féin. If
this result is brought about we can go on a straightforward fight, then we
can at the outset give partition what ought to be an almost fatal blow.'[23]
But the result of the election would prove that no such blow was even
remotely possible.

A measure of the dilemma facing nationalist local authorities in the
north was reflected in a letter sent by nationalist chairman of the Kilkeel Board of Guardians in Newry, Co. Down, which had ten Sinn Féin
members and three unionist, to William T. Cosgrave, SF's Minister for
Local Government. The difficulty was that its parent body, Down County
Council, was unionist and in control of the rate:

> We have placed a motion on the books after the election pledging
> allegiance to Dáil Éireann but I considered it better in view of

information stated above [unionist domination of the county council] not to totally break for the moment with the English Local Government Board. We would not have been able to obtain the grants and we would not have been able to levy a rate to meet the care of the poor ... if we decided to send minutes to your department to break off with England altogether, could you suggest any means of meeting the claims of the poor in the infirmary? And again, I would like to get a clear idea of the manner in which your department intend to deal with the poor law institutions in the future. If we resist England, can we secure the grant and rate by any other method?'

Cosgrave sent him a holding letter asking him not to take 'any action' for the time being.[24]

This mixture of the political and social realities and immediacies was common throughout this period at local authority level. The minute book of the Council of the County Borough of Londonderry was filled with this mixture during the second decade of the twentieth century; insurance, rates, rents and sewers fight for space along with resolutions about political harassment and upheaval. A pressing issue throughout was 'the question of finding another source of supply to prevent the possibility of a water famine', while the conduct of the 'RIC force brought specially into the city for the purposes of the peace during the past week' merited a 'sworn inquiry into all the circumstances in connection with the recent unfortunate occurrences'.[25] Meanwhile, the rural district council minutes record a bemoaning about an abundance of 'petty complaints received from Labourers about trivial matters' as well as typhus, drainage issues, cottage repairs and malicious injury claims.[26] Nationalists won control of Londonderry City Council between 1920 and 1923; there was a lot of tension in the city from the spring of 1920 onwards with reprisals, cold-blooded executions and property destruction. Nationalists, too, experienced their own divisions at municipal level and the dreams of the mayor, Hugh O'Doherty, of improving the status of nationalists and the city itself remained unattainable in such an atmosphere.[27] In the midst of the War of Independence, in Magherafelt, another troubled part of the county, '2 labourers were taken from their beds in their employer's house by armed men and blindfolded, taken to an adjoining field and tarred.'[28]

Craig succeeded Carson as Ulster Unionist leader in February 1921. Carson, it seemed, had done more than enough to secure his legacy; he had

not only mobilised Ulster Protestants, but also organised a 'largely successful rebellion' and was a central player in British politics, twice in cabinet,
before becoming a law lord: 'It is this duality that made Carson's position exceptional in Anglo-Irish relations and contributed to the immense
authority he periodically enjoyed. Indeed, in Ulster before the Great War,
after which the Irish question in British politics was marginalised, his sway
assumed near-charismatic proportions.'[29] According to Andrew Gailey, an
'intricate blend of cultural anxiety, political opportunity and force of personality' was of utmost importance up to 1914. Carson had also been keen
to espouse the values of the 'honest Ulsterman', and was 'acutely sensitive'
to the power of symbolism: 'It was his idea to light a chain of bonfires over
Ulster, re-enacting the traditional warning of Catholic invasion since the
Spanish Armada.'[30]

As with de Valera in the south, much was made of the notion of Carson as 'the chief', and he received adulation and deference; in May 1921
Crawford wrote to him as

> My dear old chief ... I know how essential it is for your physical welfare
> that you should leave the active arena of politics ... there is only one
> man that I have implicitly trusted and whose advice I have always
> taken without question during the three or four years of extreme
> political stress Ulster passed through prior to the War, that man is
> yourself.[31]

Significantly, though, it could be argued that Carson was in the long
run undermined by the emergence in Ulster of 'militant self-reliance'. His
habit of 'speaking of Ulster as if it were Ireland disturbed Northern Paro-
chialism'. Craig, it seemed, transformed it into the narrow state Carson
had warned of, but neither did Carson seek to shape it himself.[32] In January 1921 an Ulster Unionist Council deputation met Carson – 'our great
leader' – in London; they were on a mission to persuade him to stay on,
as 'we cannot do without him yet'. Tellingly, however, many did not want
or could not go to London owing to age and infirmity.[33] Carson felt likewise, telling the deputation that 'he felt that he had insufficient reserve of
strength at his age' to bring into existence a new parliament'.[34] The Duchess of Abercorn was not pleased about the sense of the UUC as an old
boys' club, severely rapping Dawson Bates on the knuckles:

I have received the notice summoning me to the annual council of the UUC ... I notice in second paragraph that delegates to the standing committee are to be elected and we are asked to send in the name of any 'gentlemen' who we may wish to nominate. I am sorry to see that it is not worded 'member' or 'delegate' as it entirely knocks out any woman's name being sent in.[35]

Whatever about the Government of Ireland Act, Ulster politicians and paramilitaries still distrusted the British government, as did many in the labour movement. It is interesting, for example, that Robert McElborough, a trade unionist in Belfast who kept a diary of his activities as he worked on the tramways and then in the expanding gas industry and who experienced, like his colleagues, harsh management and dangerous working conditions that ensured his deep trade union commitment, struggled somewhat when it came to unionism and nationalism. In attempting to be neutral, but clearly preferring maintenance of the union, what also emerges is his pride in his Ulster Scots roots and his belief that Belfast workers would be best served by locally based trade unions, and he was annoyed at what he regarded as the tawdry response of English unions to 'Ulster' labour concerns. There was a sense of 'Loyalism' in Protestant working-class areas of Belfast that was proudly independent.[36]

The general election in Northern Ireland in May 1921 saw Ulster Unionists win forty out of fifty-two seats; the IPP and SF (abstentionists) won six seats each. It was a 'triumph of discipline for the Orange Institution'; the Orange Order had told those in County Down 'it was their duty. They must vote and work for them, whether they liked them personally or not',[37] and Craig became the first prime minister of Northern Ireland. Some County Down unionists celebrated electoral success at Terrace Hill in Belfast by preparing a bonfire; after a mock trial at which de Valera was indicted and found guilty of treason he was 'condemned to death by burning. The Republican leader's effigy was then saturated with oil and placed on the burning wood. Finally, the "Dead March" was played.'[38] (It was hardly surprising, given these kind of developments, that senior Sinn Féin figures were minded to refer to Ulster Unionist grassroots activists as 'the Orange Mob'.)[39]

In contrast, King George V used the occasion of the opening of this new parliament the following June to make an impassioned and personal appeal for peace. The priority for Craig was to institutionalise northern home rule as soon as possible to make it 'impregnable' before the Treaty; the solution also absolved Britain 'of direct responsibility for the application of that power'.[40]

For Craig, the task of establishing a viable state was complicated by the multitude of political posturings in 1921–2. In the context of the Treaty negotiations, a memorandum of a meeting at Churchill's house on 30 October 1921 recorded Lloyd George maintaining that 'he could carry a six county parliament subordinate to a national parliament. Alternatively he said he would try to carry a plan for a new boundary or a vote on the conclusion or exclusion of the whole of Ulster as a unit but he was not hopeful of doing so.'[41] Carson wrote to Craig in November 1921 about saving Ulster from this 'threatening disaster'.[42] Craig wrote to Lloyd George in mid December reminding him that he had promised on 25 November that 'the rights of Ulster will be in no way sacrificed or compromised', objecting to the proposed boundary commission as a breach of the Government of Ireland Act 1920: 'At our meeting on December 9 you complained that it was only intended to make a slight readjustment of our boundary line, so as to bring in to Northern Ireland loyalists who are now just outside our area and to transfer correspondingly an equivalent number of those having Sinn Féin sympathies to the area of the Irish Free State,' but members of government had 'given encouragement to those endeavouring to read into it a different interpretation'.

Craig objected to automatic inclusion in the proposed IFS even if it came with the right of unionists to then opt out.[43] He also refused to be bribed by Lloyd George in relation to the supposed economic unviability of Northern Ireland. A secret Ulster draft clause, circulated during the negotiations, held that certain nationalist constituencies could elect to be directly represented in the southern parliament but this and other draft clauses came to nothing. Griffith had written to de Valera detailing meetings between himself Collins, Lloyd George and Birkenhead: 'The gist of it was if we would accept the Crown, they would send for Craig, ie. Force Ulster in as I understand.'[44]

Eventually, agreement was reached on the establishment of a boundary commission to determine the future border. Interestingly, in the same month the Treaty was signed, there was questioning by some republicans of the wisdom of attempting to economically penalise Northern Ireland. A memorandum from Diarmaid Fawsitt of SF's Economic Relations committee, noted that

Belfast commercial men are prone to believe that the SF leaders desire to abolish her industries and to cripple her prosperity. They fear above all things, fiscal legislation. They need to be assured that no tax whatever will be imposed on any raw materials used in her manufactures and that no attempt will be made to levy taxes on exports.

It was necessary, he concluded to 'display friendliness towards Ulster'.[45]

Significantly, Carson made a speech in the House of Lords denouncing the Treaty; even though he had resigned from the leadership of Ulster unionism that did not mean he was incapable of creating difficulties for Craig and this speech 'greatly embarrassed' and angered Craig. As historian R. B. McDowell saw it, this last important speech 'was fundamentally that of an Irish unionist, a member of a deserted garrison, a Conservative facing defeat and seeing the close of a great tradition'.[46]

Following the ratification of the Treaty, however, it was still the violence which made the headlines, despite the series of meetings between Craig and Collins, with continued persecution of Catholics, and heavy IRA activity in border areas, the details of which Craig emphasised continually to Churchill. Collins was engaged in the same practice in relation to violence against nationalists in Northern Ireland.

In July 1921, in the run-up to the truce, on account of the peace overtures, de Valera had been advised by Collins to 'avoid any form of language which will reflect on or belittle the position of Ulster'.[47] There was something of an irony here, given the continuing operation of the IRA in Northern Ireland from 1920–22, before it collapsed in the autumn of that year, an issue that was not explored in any depth by historians until very recently.[48] In January 1922, Collins established the Northern Military 'Ulster Council' under Frank Aiken; when Monaghan GAA footballers were arrested in Dromore later that month, over forty unionists in Tyrone and Fermanagh were kidnapped in response by the IRA. In 1922 there was tragic drama in Clones when a party of A Specials fought a gun battle with the IRA that led to five deaths:

At the time its impact was enormous, leading to the suspension of British troop withdrawals from the South and nearly forty deaths in Belfast during the following three days. Today, however, the incident, like so many others in the North during the revolutionary period, is almost completely forgotten ... if such an event had occurred in Cork or Kerry would it have been so easily ignored?[49]

A lack of reference in Irish republican tradition to the Northern IRA was a reminder that historical amnesia could work internally also, this one a product of the complete defeat of the Northern IRA, and its failure to make any inroads into partition, and that in turn produced what Paul Bew called 'partitionist history'. Robert Lynch also made the point that, with over 500 deaths in such a small area, 'the violence and political upheaval that occurred in the North between 1920 and 1922 was on a scale virtually unmatched in the rest of Ireland during the revolutionary period'.[50]

In May 1922 the regular police were reconstituted as the Royal Ulster Constabulary (RUC), after control over police had passed to the North in November 1921. At that stage, in November, Craig was not able to 'absolutely vouch for' the number of constabularies in Northern Ireland; he estimated the number of RIC at 2,324 with a deficit of 387, along with 3,472 A Special officers and 15,780 B Specials. The strength of the RIC and Special Constabulary 'is about 5,800 or 2,800 in excess of our peace time requirements and my suggestion is that the Imperial government should pay for this surplus force until it reaches the normal peace establishment of 3,000'.[51] By January 1922 he was complaining to Hamar Greenwood of a 'good deal of delay' regarding the allocation of special funds for payment to the Special Constabulary; as a memorandum of Britain's Provisional Government of Ireland Committee put it, 'the expense of a police force of a quasi-military nature is one which cannot be regarded as chargeable upon the revenue for ordinary civil purposes in Ulster; the cost is incurred in connection with the protection of a part of the empire with particular circumstances'.[52]

A conference between Craig and the Chancellor of Exchequer Robert Horne the following month heard there was no longer any doubt the Special Constabulary had

> justified their existence ... he was aware that when the Constabulary were first formed grave doubts had been entertained whether the new force would not merely serve to provoke further partisan feeling in Northern Ireland. He was glad to say that the critics of the force were now satisfied that they were doing work which no other body and

certainly not a military force would be capable of performing. He was certain there was no cheaper way of maintaining the peace in Ulster [and] felt that he could not take responsibility for what might happen in Northern Ireland during the next 6 months if the special constabulary were not maintained.[53]

The Chancellor was less enthusiastic, of course; he was 'certainly not prepared to admit that this obligation would hold good for several years to come'. While there would be a contribution for the first six months of the financial year 1922–3, 'NI must understand that this contribution was final', to which Craig agreed.[54] This was not to be the case however; in October 1923 Neville Chamberlain, who now occupied the office of Chancellor, pointed out that in 1922–3 a grant of £2.85 million had been given and a further £1.5 million committed for 1923–4. Chamberlain found it 'very disconcerting' that a further contribution was being sought and that it was 'out of the question' that the further £1.5 million sought would be granted; he offered £1 million: 'I hope very much however that this really will be the end and that you will not have to ask a harassed chancellor for any further aid not hitherto contemplated in this or any other direction.'[55] He certainly would not be the last Chancellor to be harassed by the financing of Northern Ireland.

TWENTY-SEVEN

THE TYRANNY OF
THE 'SPECIAL'

In October 1921, the commandant of the 2nd Northern Division of the IRA wrote to Richard Mulcahy in despair: 'Orange outrages against our people have become so serious that some steps must be taken for their defence ... there is nobody else to do this.'[1] A meeting between Craig and Collins in London in January 1922 (Craig was initially much more impressed with Collins than with de Valera) led to an agreement to end the trade boycott, but little else. Further killings (an estimated forty-four killed in February and sixty-one killed in March) were accompanied by the widespread torching of Catholic houses; an attempted pact between Collins and Craig concerning IRA activity in Northern Ireland and the release of political prisoners failed.

The killings continued and were receiving much publicity in the south; the *Freeman's Journal*, for example, carried a photograph of five murdered Catholics at Kinnard Terrace on the Antrim Road, with the observation 'this is one of the most poignant pictures which it has ever fallen to the lot of a newspaper to publish'.[2] Some 500 republicans interned on the prison ship *Argenta*, a converted cargo vessel in Belfast Lough, endured horrendous conditions, including Cahir Healy, a leading member of the SF movement in Ulster from 1918, who supported 'non-recognition' of the northern state in education and local government from January 1922 but also made the fair observation that Sinn Féin leaders did not adequately understand the 'northern situation or the northern mind'.

In April 1922 Collins appointed Healy to serve on the provisional government's north-eastern advisory committee, set up to formulate a northern policy following the breakdown of the 'Craig–Collins pact' of 31 March, but he was interned in May 1922 on the *Argenta*. He was twice elected to the Westminster Parliament – in 1922 and 1923 – as a Sinn Féin MP for Fermanagh and Tyrone.

From the *Argenta* in the summer of 1922 he insisted that he and fellow republicans had not been 'active against law and order, but only offering constitutional opposition to the question of the Craig administration'. Significantly, he complained that since internment they had received 'no light or leading' from Sinn Féin: 'Are we to look to Dublin now from the 6 counties?'[3] A despairing Healy took to writing poetry about his plight:

> Like lions in a cage we pace
> The short deck to and fro
> While tossing free through Antrim's glens
> The singing waters go

He found insomnia a 'torture', despaired at his lack of privacy and the refusal to release him even when he was elected an MP, and had to beg for small mercies, including for a filling in his teeth; it was required first to establish the political sympathies of any proposed dentist.[4]

The British government continued to sit on its hands. In February 1922, Collins replied to a Northern Catholic who had furnished him details of persecution: 'When I was in London I read every line of it to Mr Churchill, and in this regard it was of considerable use to me. When I have to meet the British people and talk to them about atrocities one incident recounted is worth all the general statements that can be made. The definite cases you stated in your letter are exactly what we want. It is no use talking vaguely of the tyranny of the "Special" unless we can support our statements with details of actual happenings.'[5]

The following month, Collins received confidential information from Department of Foreign Affairs sources in London alleging there was a civil war being planned in Ulster designed to dupe English public opinion, enabling more British troops to be stationed in the North who would later find it necessary to cross the border. They were not the kind of reports which, given the tension and air of violence, were easy to discount. Patrick Riddell in *Fire Over Ulster* (1970) summed up his take on what was going on: 'The Protestant mobs in certain notoriously backward districts, provoked to fury, behaved dreadfully. Every city has its guttersnipes.'[6] A bomb was thrown among a group of schoolchildren at Weaver Street in Belfast in February 1922, killing six: Collins wrote furiously to Churchill, denouncing 'the campaign of slander', as the *Daily Mail* had reported that the bomb 'fell' among children at play.[7]

There was a palpable frustration about the propaganda battle: Collins wrote to Desmond FitzGerald, in charge of publicity, telling him, 'Your task is to show that the Belfast parliament is no parliament, that it is not able to protect the lives of people there.'[8] Churchill preferred Britain to wash its hands of the violence by suggesting to Collins in March 1922, 'the state of affairs is lamentable. There is an underworld there with deadly feuds of its own.'[9] The provisional government in Dublin also kept a series of signed statements from victims of Loyalist attacks. While their propaganda value was undoubted, what strikes the reader is the extent of the human isolation and personal tragedy that was coming to characterise Northern Ireland. The following was from a Catholic woman in Argyle Street whose house had been looted and set alight:

> As we were huddled together to save ourselves from the stones which were coming through the windows, we heard the front door being attacked, and then burst open. A leader of the mob who was well dressed compared with the others, came to us and told us to get out, giving us a minute to do so. He called us Sinn Féin B—s and said to do as we were told or we would all be blown up. He then joined the mob outside. This occurred about 5am. There was only another Catholic woman in the street besides ourselves, the rest having been previously cleared.[10]

The introduction of the Special Powers Act and internment without trial and the setting of over forty major fires in Belfast by the IRA underlined the extent to which the new state of Northern Ireland was baptised in blood and mayhem, while the killing of the Unionist MP for West Belfast, William Twaddell, shot on his way to his outfitter's shop by a gang of five, saw republican organisations declared illegal. Meanwhile, the civil war in the south diverted the northern command of the IRA, creating some respite for the state of Northern Ireland to gain some control over law and order. Collins sent a telegram to Churchill in March 1922:

Total death roll from eleventh February now amounts to 48 and 198 wounded while total casualties since Orange Pogrom beginning July 1920 number 257. Vast majority victims were Catholics ... our people also complain that civilian authorities when requisitioning military always direct them into Catholic localities instead of the border areas or strongholds from where Orange gunmen have been firing on Catholic areas ... Belfast parliament apparently powerless.[11]

The secretary of Northern Ireland's cabinet, Wilfrid Spender, wrote to the Department of Home Affairs, with the instruction that 'a careful and exhaustive reply' be prepared to 'these one sided statements passed through Mr Churchill'. Two days later the RIC Commissioner's Office in Belfast suggested that the total number killed from 1 July 1920 to 8 March 1922 was 123 Catholics and 112 Protestants, and the allegations by Collins were dismissed as groundless 'so far as can be ascertained'. Spender's reply, to be passed on to Churchill, was that 'it is very difficult to allocate the responsibility for commencing hostilities on any particular date to either party as the tension is extremely high on both sides.[12] In the summer of 1922 the British government agreed with Stephen Tallents, the Imperial Secretary for Northern Ireland, that a commission 'should be sent over to Northern Ireland to investigate the whole expense of the Special constabulary on the spot and to effect economies ... one of whom should be acquainted with military matters and be a good economist'.[13]

Tallents himself stayed in Belfast from 21 June to 1 July and prepared a memorandum for cabinet, so there was no question but that it had access to information on the extent of the killings; the reported casualties from 6 December 1921 to 31 May 1922 in Belfast were 73 Protestant civilians killed and 147 Catholics:

A large proportion of the deaths and woundings to which it relates were caused accidentally during street fighting; the Catholic casualties include an appreciable number of casualties inflicted by Catholics upon Catholics ... in brief, among a population that numbered just over 1¼ million at the census of 1911, there have been 283 deaths by violence and 427 cases of wounding reported during the five months ending May 31st last.[14]

There were other causes, Tallents believed, apart from 'the historic cleavage of race, temperament and religion', including fear of the boundary commission, violence fuelled by 'close cooperation with sympathetic organisations in the south' and 'terrible unemployment in Belfast'. He had some other interesting parallels and observations to make and also spoke with Bishop MacRory ('did not find him unreasonable'):

> The social cleavage between the Protestants and Catholics in Belfast is almost absolute – greater, I should say, than the division between Pole and Jew in Warsaw ... the Protestant community of the North feel that it is an outpost of civilisation set precariously on the frontiers of Bolshevism. It believes that the British government has betrayed it and at best that its cause is misunderstood in England.

He ruled out the idea of an independent judicial inquiry into events in Belfast: 'I am sure it would lead to a revival of propaganda about matters that are best forgotten.' He also suggested what was necessary was 'the kindly removal of the present Minister for Home Affairs to a less responsible ministry'.[15] Dawson Bates, the minister in question, was to hold that post for another twenty-one years.

Craig remained arrogantly upbeat in the midst of the turning of blind eyes to atrocities, boasting to Bates in June 1922 that he was making headway in London: 'we're gradually gaining the upper hand'; but he found it 'very necessary to act as a "corrective" when British ministers have been closeted for hours with the Collins crowd. They get clean off the rails and require nursing like children.'[16] In the previous week, 436 Catholic families had been driven from their homes in Belfast.

Craig's 'great success, apart from the stifling of the Northern civil war in June 1922, was to hold the line of the six counties until Cosgrave's government acknowledged the *fait accompli*'.[17] It was suggested in the mid 1990s that historical work prior to this had exaggerated the degree of support for the unionist security apparatus, but it was also the case that unionist attitudes were seriously affected by violence against southern Protestants in 1922 and their marginalisation thereafter. Richard English warned in 1995 of the lack of nuance that could pervade literature in this regard: 'When we are presented with an island overwhelmingly populated by "bigots" then the term loses any academic or analytical acuity.'[18] Historians have also asserted that there is 'no evidence to suggest that Belfast

Catholic non-recognition of the regime was automatic' and that the persecution of Catholics was 'not the inevitable consequence of partition but the result of a particular form of administration'.[19] There was also a multitude of criticisms of Craig's populism from senior unionist cabinet ministers and officials, while a private British report found that 'ministers are too close to their followers', and the British government was annoyed at the blocking of reform of the B Specials, while reports of their atrocities were suppressed.[20]

Craig's government from the outset was beset with other financial and social woes; in relation to unemployment, 'some of the hardest cases are those of young men whose service during the [1914–18] war prevented them from establishing themselves as skilled tradesmen'.[21] When in London in December 1921, Craig secured, according to Spender, 'a sum of something over £500,000 being transferred to government of NI this financial year ... £530,000 has been earmarked by the prime minister for the purpose of giving temporary assistance to the Minister for Labour in regard to the unemployment deficit', which was necessary 'to prevent the unemployment deficit from being unduly embarrassed owing to the fact that unemployment in one of Ulster's staple industries e.g. Linen is greater in the general average of the industries of Great Britain.'[22] Craig stated at a cabinet meeting in March 1922 that the £530,000 'was really a windfall' but a year later this had become, in the words of Labour Minister John Andrews, a 'distressing controversy ... like yourself I was shocked today to know that there is a grave doubt as to whether the £530,000 is available'. Andrews wanted the money to be given rather than loaned, as when Northern Ireland took over the Ministry of Labour there was a deficit in the unemployment fund of £200,000 with an additional deficit of £330,000 likely to be incurred by April 1923.[23]

A memorandum in 1923 recorded that shipbuilding was 'a notoriously unstable industry' and the linen industry

> being in the nature of a quasi-luxury, has suffered ... Whatever may
> be the causes of unemployment I can find no adequate reason in past
> experience for assuming that a revival in the staple industry in the
> province would bring such an amelioration in its economic condition
> as to justify the assumption that unemployment in Northern Ireland
> would eventually equate with that in Great Britain ... in the normal
> period of about 18 months prior to the War and in the abnormal

post-war period the rate of unemployment in Northern Ireland was consistently in excess of that of Great Britain by as much as 50 per cent and even during the war period of quite exceptional employment, Northern Ireland had more unemployed than the UK generally by an average of nearly 100 per cent.[24]

The Catholic Church sought to step into the breach for nationalists and remained oblivious to Protestant fears in relation to its role in politics; it became an indispensable voice of the nationalist people while nationalist politicians licked their wounds (their recognised leader, Joe Devlin, won a parliamentary seat in the Northern Ireland parliament for West Belfast in 1921 but did not take it up until 1925).[25] Cardinal Logue was also preoccupied with the worsening situation, particularly internment and violence against Catholics: he was himself frequently harassed by the B Specials. In 1923 he and the northern bishops issued a statement condemning the systematic abuse of the Catholic community under the laws of the northern parliament. What concerned them most, however, in relation to northern Catholicism, was 'a Catholic education for a Catholic people'.[26]

Logue may have seen republicans as hopelessly and naively idealistic but that did not mean he was not, at times, a fierce critic of British misgovernment, though it is perhaps going too far to suggest that his 'uncompromising and unflinching support for the Treaty contributed to the survival of the Irish Free State'.[27] Meanwhile, Bishop MacRory faced the dilemma in 1920 of urging northern nationalists not to give the state any formal recognition, on the one hand, while on the other attempting to handle the growing sectarian tension and violence in the north, particularly in Belfast:

> For some, the justification for this lay in the fact that northern nationalists, with their policy of boycott and abstention, had only themselves to blame. MacRory dismissed this as an excuse and in the troubled circumstances of 1922 he urged the authorities in London as well as the provisional government in Dublin to take decisive action. Within Belfast he took on the role of chairman of the Catholic Protection Committee, which attempted to provide practical assistance to those driven from their jobs or homes.[28]

And what of the voice of Labour? Harry Midgley, the future chairman of the Northern Ireland Labour Party, had packed a lot into his life by the time of the creation of the state of Northern Ireland: he had been attracted early to socialism and supported James Connolly, emigrated to the US, enlisted in the British army, and on his return to Belfast, wounded and gassed, he worked as a shipyard joiner with Harland and Wolff until his appointment as organising secretary of the Irish Linenlappers' and Warehouse Workers' Union. An over-the-top but for many effective and dramatic orator, he promoted the cause of unemployed ex-servicemen, as well as heralding the workers' uprisings in Russia and Germany. Like the Belfast labour majority, he supported all-Ireland home rule and opposed partition as fatal to the Irish labour movement, as it would facilitate the evolution of two reactionary capitalist states.

With the expulsion of Catholic workers from the shipyards, he was subjected to vicious abuse and performed poorly as an Independent Labour candidate in Belfast East in the May 1921 elections for the Northern Ireland parliament, but contributed to improved labour performances in both the December 1923 and October 1924 UK general elections. Midgley's election literature from 1923 gives an idea of how and to whom his message was pitched; not only was he challenging 'the whole conception of economic relationships underlying our present economic system' but also 'as one who served on the battlefields of France and Flanders I have realised from bitter experience how dearly the workers have to pay in blood and money for the harvest of secret diplomacy carried on by Conservative and Labour governments'. He demanded a national minimum wage, a universal eight-hour day and reduction of the age limit of OAPs to sixty; only by forgetting 'partisan cries' and 'remembering only that their poverty and distress spring from a common source and demand a common remedy [can] the workers of West Belfast ... unitedly return one of their own class'.[29]

The poverty, however, was to get worse; the following year the Unemployed Worker's Association (UWA) wrote to Craig, insisting outdoor relief – schemes that employed married men at tasks such as repairing roads for a minimal wage – was necessary for unemployed people 'on the same terms as in Britain, in view of the exceptional distress at present'.[30] In contrast, a businessman opposed to socialism wrote to Craig: 'While I agree that there is a great deal of poverty and suffering in our city, at the same time I have come to the conclusion that a good deal of this demonstrably is for propaganda purposes.' Regarding the leaders of the socialist Labour Party in Belfast, he was scornful: 'I am sure you will agree that these socialist fellows can do no more for our people than we have been doing.'[31] The UWA was informed by the cabinet secretary that Craig, 'acting under his medical adviser's instructions is away from home' and would not be dealing with any business until 'his return from a sea trip to the Mediterranean'.[32] Like their southern equivalents, the northern 'rabble' were in for a long wait.

So too, were those who believed that the boundary commission would deliver them to southern Ireland, or make Northern Ireland unviable. Why had the Irish delegates been duped into believing that the commission would solve, from their perspective, the partition dilemma? Dublin's approach to the issue was problematic and naïve throughout, but Lloyd George's duplicity was also a major factor; it is ironic indeed that it was James Craig who, when he met de Valera in 1921, warned him never to meet Lloyd George alone as he would give any account of the interview that suited him.[33] Carson also claimed (in 1924) that he had received a letter from Lloyd George in 1920 assuring him of 'permanent' exclusion of the six counties from any settlement with nationalist Ireland.

Was partition really avoidable, given the strength of unionist resistance and influential support from London and lack of a realistic approach on the part of Dublin? Did nationalists ever really confront 'the Ulster question' and what was their strategy? What all this amounted to was a combination of 'hope, fear, pressure and illusion'.[34] The section of Article 12 of the Treaty that dealt with the boundary commission was ambiguous: in the (inevitable) event of Northern Ireland opting out of the Treaty settlement,

> a commission of three persons, one to be appointed by the government of the Irish Free State, one to be appointed by the Government of Northern Ireland and one who shall be Chairman to be appointed by the British Government, shall determine, in accordance with the wishes of the inhabitants, so far as may be compatible with economic and geographic conditions, the boundaries between Northern Ireland and the rest of Ireland.

This raised obvious, troubling questions, including how 'the wishes of the inhabitants' were to be defined and measured, and how much influence

Britain would have on the conclusions of such a commission. Paul Murray makes the point that it is obvious the ambiguities were very deliberate; if it had not been ambiguous it would not have made it to the final text.[35] As early as 16 December 1921, Lloyd George insisted in the House of Commons that the phrase 'economic and geographic conditions' would not allow for large-scale transfer. The hope for somewhat deluded nationalists was that the commission would 'deliver' Tyrone, Fermanagh and large parts of South Armagh, South Down, Newry and Derry city; that a new mutilated North would not be a viable entity. What was notable after the Treaty was signed was the degree of acceptance of the proposed commission as a game changer by both pro- and anti-Treaty sides, evidenced by the relative silence on the issue of the border during the Treaty debates. The Irish delegation's legal adviser, John O'Byrne, viewed the text as ambiguous but nonetheless as Attorney General in 1925 he still argued that the commissioners were empowered to transfer large swathes of territory.[36]

Ernest Blythe believed that persuasion rather than coercion, either politically or economically, would be more effective, but he still believed coercion was justified – a contradictory stance.[37] But he saw the error of this at a later stage in 1922; shortly before the death of Collins the provisional government set up a five-man committee, including Blythe, to formulate a more realistic northern policy. An Ulster protestant, Blythe had greater claim to an understanding of the Ulster political mindset and was implicitly critical of Collins's policy of secret violence and confrontation, which he considered 'useless' in terms of protecting Catholics.[38]

But the over-optimism in relation to boundary changes was not, it seemed, subjected to the same critical and realistic scrutiny, at least in public. Another difficulty was the potential for great instability in the new Irish Free State if unionists were forced into it against their will, but there was no appetite for dealing with this issue publicly, while the British line was simple: any possible changes would be about minor adjustment rather than about any pretence towards self-determination.[39] In terms of achieving support within unionism, Craig was on more solid ground in not caring a jot for the notion of self-determination or minority rights, despite the stated aspirations he had towards presiding over a tolerant Northern Ireland, aspirations that were quickly allowed go up in smoke; crucially, unionists were in possession of the territory. After the commission's deliberations, a leak in 1925 revealed that the border would be virtually unchanged, and it was decided to bury the commission's report. It was not just northern nationalists or socialists who felt abandoned. David Fitzpatrick points to 'Loyalists on the wrong side of the border' – those in Cavan, Monaghan and Donegal; in these three Ulster counties, Protestants accounted for over one-fifth of the population in 1911 that ultimately came under the Free State. For them, the pragmatic partitionism of Craig and Carson 'constituted both a callous betrayal and a repudiation of the very essence of unionism', leaving them with a hardly attractive set of options: 'coexistence with nationalists, emigration or "diehard" resistance'.[40]

By the time of the boundary commission leak, Cahir Healy complained that northern nationalists had been 'sold into political servitude for all time'.[41] But northern nationalists had reason to be suspicious of southern political intentions well before the boundary commission debacle. In October 1922, a deputation from Northern Ireland to the provisional government, including priests, solicitors and local councillors, arrived in Dublin looking for funds to counteract unionist propaganda. They got short shrift from Kevin O'Higgins: 'We have no other policy for the North East than we have for any other part of Ireland and that is the Treaty policy.' He suggested that what northern nationalists needed was not just funds but 'a great deal of strenuous voluntary work – just the same sort of strenuous work that brought the national position to the stage it has reached'.[42] The washing of southern hands could hardly have been more apparent; O'Higgins claimed the real problem was the lack of cohesion on the part of nationalists. An interned teacher in Belfast in January 1923 wrote to the Free State's Minister for Education, Eoin MacNeill: 'The bitter part is the reflection that when I do get out I shall probably be forgotten.'[43]

He was right.

PART III

LEGACY AND COMMEMORATION

TWENTY-EIGHT

'IN DANGER OF FINDING MYSELF WITH NOTHING AT ALL'

Tom Barry, best known for leading the IRA flying column in west Cork during the War of Independence, survived both that conflict and the civil war, during which he fought on the republican side and was instrumental in efforts to end that war. He remained on the run until 1924, and from 1927 until his retirement in 1965 was general superintendent with the Cork Harbour Commissioners. Described as 'often prickly and autocratic' but also generous and charismatic, Barry was quick to take on lawyers and bank managers over matters relating to his IRA column's activities.[1] He also had to take on the Military Service Pensions Board over another perceived slight – its decision that his activities during the revolutionary period did not merit the award of the most senior rank and grade for the purposes of payment of a pension; these pensions were awarded on a sliding scale, from A to E, according to both rank held and time served as a combatant during the War of Independence.

In January 1940, he received his military service pension award of Rank B, which he emphatically rejected as unjust and humiliating.[2] Senior politicians, including Fianna Fáil ministers Éamon de Valera and P. J. Ruttledge, had already written statements of evidence on his behalf but, later that year, Barry personally gave further evidence to the pension assessors and in August 1940 he was granted the rank of Grade A for pension purposes on the basis of which an annual pension of £149 7s was payable (about £8,500 in today's terms).[3] His perseverance, righteousness, attention to detail, friends in powerful positions and adamant testimonials on his behalf had paid off. The saga surrounding Barry's application for a pension and his vehement rejection of the Pensions Board's initial decision is a reminder of the longevity of battles over the legacy of the War of Independence in the state that was created at its end. Undoubtedly, as with Barry, status was a preoccupation for many applicants, but the monetary award was often of more immediate consequence.

In the process of building and sustaining the pensions process, including the key legislation, the Army Pensions Acts from 1923 to 1953 and the Military Service Pensions Acts from 1924–49, there were numerous difficulties in relation to defining service (around which there was much ambiguity), eligibility and the application and assessment procedures. The fact that part of the War of Independence was a guerrilla conflict exacerbated these difficulties; proving membership of an underground movement was fraught, and what constituted sufficient sacrifice was open to a variety of interpretations. Wound pensions differed from military service pensions and there was a hierarchy of victims, with the immediate families of the 1916 signatories of the Proclamation, for example, specially catered for with annual allowances. Crucially, the anti-Treaty IRA was initially excluded and there were allegations of political bias in the award of pensions; in 1929 a member of Fianna Fáil accused the government of using the pensions 'for the purposes of political graft'. But when it came to power, Fianna Fáil was more than willing to extend the benefits of pensions to anti-Treaty republicans, which meant its supporters. There were also administrative changes that replaced the Board of Assessors with referees assisted by an advisory committee composed of former volunteers and civil servants. It was estimated in the 1930s that the pensions would lead to an annual bill of £400,000 (about £25 million in today's terms).

Not everyone was happy about this expenditure; P. S. O'Hegarty was later to describe the clamour for monetary reward as telling 'a sorry tale of patriotic degeneration and lack of public spirit'.[4] But this assertion needs to be balanced with the fact that there was extensive hardship experienced by revolutionary veterans and their dependants ('this was referred to in every Oireachtas debate on [Military Service Pensions] legislation'[5]). This is one of the reasons why the archive reveals so much about the revolution's afterlife, and the files in the archive cover the full life trajectory of those awarded pensions, each file closing with the issue of a death certificate and a cancelled pension warrant.

The Military Service Pensions Board, its members and the assessors, referees, civil servants and government officials involved in administering the pension process were thus both keepers of a precious national record and arbiters in disputes about survival and status. Some of the recipients led lives of financial ease, became holders of high public office and had elevated status as a consequence of their activities. Many, however, paid a high price for their involvement, enduring humiliation, disability, poverty, obscurity and even death. Many women and children were left without any means of support other than the prospect of a dependant's pension. The Board of Assessors overseeing the Military Service Pensions Act of 1924 approved the payment of pensions to 3,855 applicants; however, about 9,900 other applicants were stated to have *prima facie* cases but were deemed persons to whom the Act did not apply. The Military Service Pensions Act of 1934 amended and extended the Act of 1924 and included members of Cumann na mBan within the definition of those who constituted the 'forces'. It also allowed for pension applications from people who had pre-truce (July 1921) service, but took no further part and those who participated in the civil war on the anti-Treaty side. There are approximately 121,000 files in the 1934 series, but up to July 1957, only 10,832 awards were made. Even allowing for dubious or even dishonest claims, such a gulf between the numbers of applications and awards meant it was inevitable that there was a very large constituency of people who would have been, at the very least, disappointed at the decisions of the assessors. As noted earlier, a government memorandum in 1957 revealed that 82,000 people applied for pensions under the 1924 and 1934 Acts; of these, 15,700 were successful and 66,300 were rejected.

Those affected by the events of Easter Week 1916 and who were in drastic financial circumstances as a result of the Rising feature prominently in the correspondence generated by the pension and compensation process from the 1920s, and it is clear that civil war politics intruded in some of the decisions that were made. In May 1925, for example, Mary Malone from Drumcondra in Dublin wrote to the Minister for Defence on behalf of her sister Annie Malone, who was 'badly wounded with a bullet that lodged in her hip' on Easter Monday 1916 outside the College of Surgeons in St Stephen's Green. The bullet was extracted over a week later at Mercer's Hospital:

> Previous to her injuries she was training as a draperess, which occupation she is unable to follow owing to the injury to her hip, as she

is absolutely unable to stand all day, as is required in drapery establishments as the injured hip to the present day gives her great pain,
especially during the winter months ... After my sister was wounded a
claim was lodged on her behalf, but owing to the fact that our brother
Michael was 'killed in action' in Easter Week, her claim was dismissed
because we were 'rebels'. If our brother Michael had not taken part in
the Rising, my sister would have got compensation for the injury to
her hip. I feel sure that my sister's case has only to be brought to your
notice, when you will have it satisfactorily dealt with. As our mother
died on the 4th ult. my sister must now look out for herself. Were it
not for the injury to her hip she would be independent, earning her
living as a draperess.[6]

Three weeks later a confidential letter to the Department of Defence
from the Office of the Director of Intelligence reported that 'this lady
appears to be a sister-in-law of Dan Breen's. In that case, the whole family
is tainted with irregularism.'[7] Breen had been a key figure in the establishment of the IRA's South Tipperary Brigade, and his fame had been
established by the Soloheadbeg ambush on 21 January 1919 at the outset
of the War of Independence. He had married Bríd Malone, another sister
of the letter writer, and had often stayed with the Malone family while
on the run. Breen had reluctantly opposed the Treaty and was involved
in efforts to achieve reconciliation between the opposing sides. He had
led a republican column during the civil war, but was keen to find some
basis for a truce. Imprisoned in April 1923, he participated briefly in the
republican hunger strike that autumn but was subsequently released after
signing a pledge to desist from offensive actions against the Free State.
In August 1923 he was elected a TD for Tipperary. He subsequently left
the IRA. He had, according to Michael Hopkinson, 'major financial and
employment difficulties for the first decade after the war',[8] despite the
success of his ghostwritten autobiography *My Fight for Irish Freedom*
(1924).

One of the interesting aspects of the report from the director of intelligence, Colonel M. Costello, was the assertion that the Malone family
'are supporters of the Irregulars in a similar sense to Dan Breen, probably
for outward appearances and contrary to their better judgement'. It was
noted that her brother Brian Malone sympathised with republicans during the civil war 'but was not known to have taken any active part himself.

I believe the only case that could be made against the family is an effort to keep up the "family traditions" exemplified in "My Fight for Irish Freedom". It was also noted that two grants of £100 each (about £9,000 in today's terms) had been paid by the National Aid Society in respect of the death of Michael Malone after he was killed during the 1916 Rising.[9] The compensation claim was rejected.

Others in difficult circumstances in the aftermath of the Rising included Lily Connolly, the wife of James Connolly, a woman long used to penury. Writing on her behalf in February 1924, William O'Brien of the ITGWU contacted Minister for Defence Richard Mulcahy, pointing out that she was still waiting to hear about her application for a pension: 'She has found it rather difficult to make ends meet during recent years and at the moment is rather embarrassed for the want of some ready money. She has one daughter who is a medical student in her last year and it is hoped she will be qualified in the next six or eight months.'[10]

In the aftermath of the Rising, the National Aid Association had given Lily £1,500 at the time of James's execution, and she received £75 from the White Cross. Two days after the letter was written on her behalf, the secretary of the Department of Defence wrote an irate note to an army finance officer, complaining of the 'utterly inexcusable' delay in getting the matter sorted:

> It should not take one day to get evidence that James Connolly was executed in 1916. It should not take one other day to verify that the applicant is his widow ... those dealing with the matter of such pensions might have some appreciation that if a woman loses her husband and has a family that she has been through very difficult circumstances and is actually in very difficult circumstances at the present time – whatever bit of luck even may come her way.[11]

Nonetheless, she was interviewed the following week by an army sergeant who suggested 'she appears to be in comfortable circumstances as she has one unmarried daughter practising medicine and a daughter a boarder at the Loreto convent in North Great Georges Street'. By 1927, due to increases in allowances payable, she was entitled to a pension of £180 per annum, and her daughter was entitled to £40 per annum until she reached the age of eighteen. By the time Lily died in 1938, her pension was worth £500 per year (almost £30,000 in today's terms).[12]

Seventeen years later Kathleen Clarke, the widow of 1916 Proclamation signatory Tom Clarke and a former Fianna Fáil senator who served as Lord Mayor of Dublin from 1940–41, wrote to the Pensions Board on behalf of the destitute Nora Connolly O'Brien, James's daughter, pointing out that Nora's husband 'is idle through no fault of his own and they have nothing. It is an awful position for James Connolly's daughter.'[13] There was relatively good news for Connolly O'Brien in October 1941 when she was awarded an E grade pension of £29 7s 6d per year (just under £1,500 in today's terms).[14]

A number of sisters of the men of 1916 had been wholly financially dependent on their brothers. Some of their files bristle with rage, wounded pride, pathos and occasional triumphalist vindication. Another interesting case was that of Grace Plunkett, the widow of Joseph, executed in 1916, was in receipt of a widow's allowance of £90, later increased to £500 (free of tax), but was unsuccessful in her claim for a military service pension. She was never a member of CnB, but was 'in active connection with the national movement', attending political meetings, producing political cartoons and collecting funds for republican causes and was imprisoned for six months during the civil war. Owing to her relationship with Joseph 'she was disinherited in 1916 from her father's will and was ejected from her home', but the assessment of the advisory committee was: 'This lady does not appear to have any service which could be regarded as qualifying service ... she had no Cumann na mBan activities prior to the Truce. She stated that the mere sight of a gun would cause her to faint.'[15]

Plunkett believed others were faring better: 'That which I receive is less by £20 than that given to the children of Arthur Griffith and (I believe) less by some hundreds than that given to his widow [Maud] ... the reason why he is put in a lower position to Arthur Griffith has never been explained and is an insult to the seven signatories.' This was ironic, given the travails of Maud Griffith, and in the words of Anne Dolan, 'the struggles with her husband's colleagues that turned much of her sorrow to rage'. By October 1922 the £100 Maud received from Dáil Éireann funds to meet the expenses of his death was gone and she was 'forced to beg' until a Griffith settlement bill 'limped into the Dáil' in February 1923, ensuring she would receive £500 annually (about £21,000 in today's terms) for life when William T. Cosgrave, the head of government was earning £2,500 a year (about £107,000 in today's terms) and 'the government added insult to her injury by taxing every penny she received'. Maud vented her fury:

'only for his life work Mr Blythe [the Minister for Finance] would have nothing to do with Finance ... no honour or even a thought to a desolate woman has ever occurred to one of my husband's associates.'[16]

In 1953 Elizabeth and Brigid Colbert, the sisters of Con Colbert, who was executed in 1916, sought compensation and Elizabeth made a 'bitter complaint' as 'she was visited by a lady investigation officer from the SW [Social Welfare] department and she regarded the whole thing as a terrible inquisition'.[17] The sisters were entitled to £125 per annum. Brigid, a nurse who could not get full-time work, had ended up as housekeeper to a group of priests in Bristol, and a nun from the Convent of Mercy hostel where she was staying wrote to the Minister for Defence without her knowledge: 'I feel she should be able to settle down in Ireland in her old age and not be looking for Public Assistance in a cold place like Bristol ... Anyone who had any connection with Easter week should get a wee bit of consideration.'[18] As Brigid put it, a pension 'would enable me to spend that latter part of my life in Ireland'.[19]

They certainly were not the only victims of excessive bureaucracy and interrogation; the pensions administration required constant form filling and declaration forms with notification of any change in circumstances ('I further declare that I have not remarried since the grant of my pension'). In 1967, Margaret Pearse, sister of the executed Patrick, who had been a senator since 1938, wrote furiously to the Minister for Defence on Seanad notepaper, returning one such form: 'Enclosed notice is a piece of impertinence and shows a great lack of Irish history. I have been seriously ill since March and surely at the age of 89 I am not considering marriage. I am deeply insulted at the enclosure. It shows complete ignorance of the writer regarding my brothers Padhraic [Patrick] and Willie Pearse and their part in securing Irish freedom.'[20] Margaret died the following year.

For other relatives of executed 1916 leaders, financial support from the state was vital in allowing them to qualify as professionals, even decades after the Rising; it helped that their names carried considerable political clout and that they had relatives and friends who lobbied politicians on their behalf, ensuring some did not experience the impoverishment that threatened others. In June 1930, the sister of Muriel MacDonagh, wife of Thomas MacDonagh, another signatory of the Proclamation who was executed after the 1916 Rising, wrote to Dr T. Hennessy TD to point out that both their children, Barbara and Donagh, were supported and educated by an allowance of £80 per annum each and payment of school fees under one of the Pensions Acts, but as Donagh was approaching the age of eighteen, both allowances would soon cease.

As his maternal aunt, she pleaded for the pension and allowances for education to be continued for his third-level studies:

> His father, who was a lecturer in the National University, refused, to my knowledge, at least 2 professorships in Universities abroad in order to remain in Ireland and play his part in the 1916 Rising, thereby leaving his family to the care of the nation. Thomas MacDonagh would certainly have given his son a university course. His mother was drowned in 1917 and her two children have since been in the care of friends, as none of their relatives are in a position to keep them. Had she lived, she would have been in receipt of the pension awarded to the widows of the 1916 leaders and this present application might not have been necessary.

She also pointed out that there was a sum of just under £3,000 invested for the children but that 'Donagh's share, if realised now, would produce only about £1,200. This sum would be sufficient to maintain him till qualified but would leave him with nothing to carry him over the first few years until he could be self-supporting.'[21]

In October 1936, Donagh himself, then living in Sandymount in Dublin, contacted the Department of Defence with the information that, with the payments made to him to date, he had completed both his BA and BL degrees:

> As you probably know the first few years at the Bar are at once hazardous and unremunerative; of those who have been called in the last few years I know only one or two who have made more than £20 or £30. I hope you will find it possible to extend my allowance for some period as otherwise I can see no possibility of practising – as it is we are living on capital. Further grants would need to be much less than in the past as now there are no educational or examination fees to be taken into consideration. I hope you will be able to do something; I am very grateful for your help in the past, without which I could never have qualified and I hope you will be able to help me further until I am able to actually earn money.[22]

At that stage his pension was £80 a year, which, along with National Aid money, was, as he had earlier that year noted in a letter to Éamon de Valera, 'the whole of my income ... This leaves very little, if any, margin, so that I am always in danger of finding myself with nothing at all.'[23] He was looking for an increase. Early the following year, in 1937, a priest acquaintance of his appealed to the Minister for Finance Seán MacEntee to reimburse MacDonagh for expenditure in connection with his final examinations: 'The purpose of the annual grants was to equip the two MacDonaghs for the battle of life and I put it to you that it is not fair on Donagh to saddle him as he starts in life with a debt of £116.18.0 ... surely if we wish an end we must also wish the means to that end.' MacDonagh was granted the extra funds through means of 'extra statutory grants'.[24]

As mentioned in the letter written by his aunt, Donagh had a difficult childhood; he was only three years old when his father was executed and his mother Muriel Gifford drowned in 1917 while the hunchbacked MacDonagh was in hospital with TB. A talented writer, he was noted for his erudition in UCD and had spent a part of his second undergraduate year at the Sorbonne in Paris. He was an exceptional student and in 1934 his talent for poetry was revealed in a published collection. By the time he wrote the letters referred to above he was married and soon had two children to support and was later to describe himself as a 'briefless barrister'. He lost his wife after she drowned in the bath during an epileptic fit and he subsequently married her sister. But his professional life improved, as he was appointed a district justice in Wexford which provided him with a steady income until his death in 1968.[25] His was a life marked by both the privilege and the burden of his father's legacy, but it is clear that the pensions he received were essential to his education and professional status; quite simply, as he recognised, he could not have succeeded without them.

TWENTY-NINE

'FOR THE LIFE OF
MY HEROIC SON'

Elizabeth Traynor, the widow of Thomas Traynor, executed in Mountjoy prison in 1921, wrote to the Department of Defence in 1951 pointing out that she had a pension of 17s 6d per week (less than £40 in today's terms):

> I have applied several times for an increase and have always been refused. I know a woman, Mrs Doyle, whose husband was killed in action at the Custom house. She informed me that she got a substantial rise in the pension ... I am nearing 70 years of age. I have the same pension that I got 30 years ago when my husband was executed. He was not only a hero but a father ... 9 of [10] children are married and find it hard enough to keep themselves without keeping me.

The response was simple: the Army Pensions (Increase) Act of 1949 'makes no provision for the grant of an increased allowance in cases such as yours'.[1] Peadar Cowan, her local TD, also made representations on her behalf pointing out to Seán MacEoin, the Minister for Defence, that for a widow with ten children to be paid such a paltry sum was 'disgraceful and I see no reason why she should not be treated in the same way as widows of other persons executed or shot out of hand. The recent grant of a pension to the widow of the late Terence MacSwiney is [a case] in point.'[2]

In September, Cowan wrote again to MacEoin, pointing out that her pension had now been increased to £1 6s 3d per week: this was still totally inadequate: 'I may say that Mrs Traynor pays 18/10 rent which leaves her with the sum of 7/5d after her rent is paid.' Her contention was that under the terms of new legislation dealing with Volunteers killed on duty she should have been awarded £250 a year.[3] (The correct figure according to the new Act was actually £135 per year.) One of the arguments made by Traynor was that, as her husband had fought in 1916, she should have been treated the same as the widows of 1916 leaders, even though Traynor was not executed until 1921. This was an interesting exposure of the anomalies in the process; the Minister for Defence had wondered in 1951 'as to why the rates vary so much, particularly in the case of Mrs Keane [the widow of Thomas Keane, executed by firing squad in June 1921] and Mrs Traynor, both of whose husbands were executed about the same time'.[4]

A memorandum generated as a result of this case underlined in clear terms the disparity; it dealt with allowances being paid under the Army Pensions Acts to relatives of men executed from 1916 onwards. Three widows of 1916 Proclamation signatories were being paid £500 per year, seven sisters of signatories were being paid £100 per year and two widows of men executed during the War of Independence were being paid £135 per year while Elizabeth Traynor was being paid just 17s 6d per week. Two widows of republicans executed during the civil war were being paid £67 10s per year, while the mother of a man executed during the civil war was being paid just 15s per week.[5] Two years later Limerick TD Donnchadh O'Briain wrote to Minister Oscar Traynor (no relation to Thomas): 'You agree with me that the relatives of Easter week men are in a class apart.'[6]

Brigid Treacy, the mother of Seán Treacy, killed in 1920, was a claimant under the Army Pensions Act 1923 and also crossed swords with the Pensions Board. She was living on a small holding of fourteen acres in Tipperary and was offered a gratuity of £100 which she refused :'£100 for the life of <u>Sean Treacy</u>?' she wrote:

> A few lines to let you know of the humiliation I have experienced this morning at receiving the enclosed paper offering me the paltry sum of £100, for the loss of my noble son <u>my only child</u> and <u>only help</u> in this <u>wicked world</u> ... had I to beg from door to door for the remainder of my life <u>I could not nor would not</u> accept the meagre sum of £100, for the life of my heroic son. The Army Pensions Board must have a goodly

mixture of the old hated class in it or I would not be so humiliated by
them or E. Blythe ... Other men will do justice to my son's worth and
character and protect me from the insults I am receiving.

The gratuity on offer was subsequently increased to £150, the maximum
allowable, owing to 'special circumstances'. She was also incensed as she
was 'lately informed' (completely inaccurately) that 'Dan Breen, my son's
subordinate received for himself and his mother £780 and £800 yearly'.
She also refused the £150 but later accepted a pension of £1 per week. She
was described in administrative correspondence as 'an old feeble woman
and Seán Treacy was her only son'.[7]

Nor was the mother of Liam Mellows, executed in 1922, satisfied with
her treatment. In January 1940, she wrote to the Minister for Defence
expressing her confusion about the pensions process and the relevant government departments: 'Now, 17 years after my son Liam's death, my only
means of support are my surviving son, and the old age pension.' Again,
the belief others were doing better prevailed: 'In other cases I know people [for whom] better circumstances have been provided.'[8] She had been
awarded a gratuity of £112; from 1942 to 1948 her sole income was the old
age pension of 10s a week, rendering her eligible for an allowance of just
under £14 per year during that period, but because the old age pension was
increased in 1948, her allowance was reduced to just 15s per year because
for the special dependant's allowance there was a £40 annual income
ceiling.

Individual material circumstances did change and, for some veterans,
prompted a rethink about an application. In March 1944 historian and
political scientist James Hogan applied for a pension. Hogan had joined
the 3rd Battalion of the Dublin Brigade of the Irish Volunteers in 1915;
his promising academic career had been interrupted at UCD by the outbreak of the War of Independence and he was a member of the East Clare
flying column. He took a leading part in military engagements in Clare,
Galway and East Limerick. He was successful in his application for the
Chair of History in University College Cork in 1920, but did not take
up the post until 1924; he subsequently became a very active member of
the Irish Manuscripts Commission, and he remained active in Fine Gael
politics. He married in 1935 and had six children. In his letter to the Pensions Board, Hogan noted that he had not applied for a military pension
in 1924:

I was at that time unmarried, and holding a professorship ... my circumstances were such that I did not think it necessary to look for any compensation for my services such as they were. But my position is very different now. I have been married for several years and have heavy domestic responsibilities. Moreover, my health has deteriorated in such a way as to impose upon me the duty of providing for the future of my family, and this disimprovement in my health I believe would not have arisen were it not for my participation in the national struggle. This then is why I have altered my old attitude and beg to submit to you my claim for a military service pension.[9]

The following month, the secretary of the Department of Defence noted that the Minister for Defence, Oscar Traynor, 'does not consider as satisfactory the reasons put forward' by Hogan, but significantly, indicating that senior politicians could and did intervene to reverse refusals, Traynor wrote in May that 'in view of certain information conveyed to me verbally, I have now decided that Professor Hogan's application may be accepted'.[10] From September 1945, Hogan was awarded an annual pension of £120[11]; by the time of his death in 1963 it was worth £227 a year, though as was always the case, his widow was informed that she could not claim it after his death.

Hogan's case was unusual in the length of time it took him to apply, but also because of the speed with which his case was processed. Some applicants had to endure years of waiting, frustration and tortuous correspondence, often with no positive outcome from their perspective. The tone of many of their letters conveys an anger with seemingly endless bureaucratic delay and, as many saw it, inertia. What was an added insult to many was their genuine feeling that their services and sacrifices were not officially recognised, sometimes because of the difficulty of verifying the exact level of service or number of military engagements. Poverty formed the backdrop to many of the cases being considered, which gave an added urgency to appeals.

In November 1937 Mrs Annie Maher from Friar Street in Cashel, County Tipperary, made an appeal 'on behalf of my daughter', noting that

my son always voted for the government and my son William did 3 weeks hunger strike in Hare Park camp and he has always given his services to the cause since 1916. He has not received any pension so far and is now out of work for the past 10 months and living on me, a widow on the side of the street, but so far as I can see, it is the parties that are up against the government [that] are getting all. My daughter who has worked for the cause since 1916 is employed in the Labour Exchange Cashel on a wage of 10/– per week to keep herself and her brother. It was Mr [Seán] Lemass that gave her this job as she was in communication with him for some time ... is not that a miserable wage for a girl to work for. Surely the people that suffered should get more consideration. My daughter also is in for a pension but was not called yet and is waiting nearly three years ... if things don't improve I must send my son and daughter to England to seek for a better living.[12]

The file containing William Maher's application includes correspondence that ran for over twenty years. He gave sworn evidence before an interviewing officer in January 1942 in which he detailed his IRA service blocking roads and carrying dispatches as well as transporting IRA men and taking part in one military engagement before the truce. He also had extensive civil war service and was interned for eighteen months and released from Hare Park, where he partook in a hunger strike for nineteen days, in March 1924. A note attached to the end of the transcript of his sworn evidence for the advisory committee read: 'Good Civil War service. His one scrap before the Truce may pull him through.'[13]

But it did not pull him through. In April 1942 he was informed that he was 'not a person to whom the Act applies' and was therefore not eligible for a pension.[14] Under the terms of the Military Service Pensions (Amendment) Act 1949, a referee could reconsider applications. The next batch of correspondence concerning Maher commenced in October 1956, when William's brother John, who was town clerk of Cashel, wrote to explain that a letter had arrived requesting William to appear at the Courthouse in Cashel to deal with a review of his case. John explained that his brother had in fact died in November 1955 and the letter regarding his review had been sent to the wrong person. He pointed out that two IRA colleagues of his brother were available 'to vouch for my late brother's service'.[15] He was informed in November 1956 that his brother's application was still under consideration. In September the following year those reviewing the case noted 'applicant claims an exchange of fire which lasted 20 minutes with British military. This incident has not been verified by witnesses. The Act doesn't apply.'[16]

Verification of that alleged twenty minutes of gunshot was the difference between the award of a pension and refusal. In June 1958 John Maher
was again 'reluctantly compelled' to write to the Office of the Referee. Not
unreasonably, he suggested 'surely after such a long time and especially in
view of the fact that my brother is dead since November 1955, close on 2½
years ago, a decision as to whether he was or was not entitled to a service
certificate and allowance should long since have been arrived at'. The following month he was informed that reconsideration had resulted in the
same conclusion and decision as before: that William was not a person to
whom the Act applied.[17]

An emotionally charged John Maher wrote a subsequent letter to
the secretary of the Department of Defence, maintaining he could not
understand the decision, given his brother's obvious sacrifices during the
revolutionary period: 'Incidentally, I may remark that I am not in receipt
of a certificate of allowance and though qualified for such, I have declined
for same.' John had been in Maidstone prison in England:

> Within the past week spring cleaning and painting was being carried
> out by my sister in the house where she and my brother resided, and
> in an old box put safely away was found some papers on which were
> written details of his activities since he joined the IRA in 1917 ... they
> show sufficient evidence to prove that he was certainly a person to
> whom the provisions of the Act of 1934 apply.[18]

The reply he received informed him that the minister had no function in the matter; that the referees' decision was 'final, conclusive and
binding' and that there was no action that could be taken to further
review the case.[19]

The archive of the Military Service Pensions files is littered with such
disappointments and desperate pleas against what must have seemed like
a cold, harsh bureaucracy. It was not just the Department of Defence that
had a role in the pensions process; for obvious reasons relating to expenditure controls, the Department of Finance was also involved and could
be calculating in seeking to minimise spending on the pensions. Such
an approach was evident in its reaction to a successful appeal by Denis
Doran, who appealed against the abatement of pension payable to him
due to his receipt of public monies prior to the granting of his pension
award but during the period from which the pension ran (under the terms

of a public service abatement, pensions for those in receipt of other remuneration from the state were reduced on a pro-rata basis). Doran, from Enniscorthy in County Wexford, who had been a member of the Irish Volunteers, was active in 1916 and interned in Frongoch, and had been a district court clerk from October 1934 to May 1938, when he ceased to be employed. His pension had been abated for that period. But the pension was not awarded to him until he was fifteen months out of employment, at a time when he was not in receipt of any remuneration. He had been awarded an E grade pension of £11 17s 11d annually.

L. M. FitzGerald, a civil servant at the Department of Finance, recommended settling Doran's claim, but not seeing it as a precedent; he suggested that Doran be repaid the pension amount previously abated but that in general, the policy of pension abatements should continue with repayments occurring only where the pensioner challenged the practice in their own case and to ensure that when repayment took place, it did so before legal action commenced.[20] In January 1942 Doran had approached Richard Corish, the Mayor of Wexford, informing him he was not in the employment of the government at the time the pension was granted. His solicitor had to point out that he had sent four letters from December 1939 to December 1940, to no avail as elaborated by Doran:

> You will therefore see that another 12 months have now passed and still no word ... surely it doesn't take 2 years to decide a simple legal matter? My whole argument is: the Pension was not awarded to me until I was 15 months out of the government's employment and consequently, I was not in receipt of salary or remuneration during the continuance of such pension. There could be no continuance until there was a beginning and I was not in their employment at the beginning of the pension.[21]

The reason for the department's stalling was an obvious desire to prevent the payment of money legitimately due to pensioners. The Attorney General agreed with Doran's interpretation; he had 'no doubt' that a court would agree likewise, and the Department of Defence knew that

> there are a considerable number of cases which would be affected by whatever decision may eventually be reached in the present case ... these are the cases of persons who on the commencing date of the

pension (1st October 1924 or 1st October 1934, as the case may be) were in receipt of remuneration payable out of public moneys, but who were not granted Military Service Pensions for some time after that date. Their pensions were abated with effect from the commencement date of pension. In view of the advice received in the present case it would appear that abatement of pension should not have been effected during the period from the commencing date of pension to the date when pension was actually granted, in each case.[22]

It was estimated that the number of cases of this nature was a substantial 2,001. The Army Finance Officer, J. O'Connell, was informed by L. M. FitzGerald:

> We have come to the conclusion that in that type of case ... you should continue your present practice of abating from the date from which the pension notionally begins to run, but should, if challenged by or on behalf of the pensioner, repay abatement ... if a pensioner challenges you, however, you should repay to him the sum, if any, by which the amount of the abatement on the basis of the annual rate exceeds the amount of the abatement on the basis of the annual amount. You should, of course, in all cases, make the repayment before matters have been carried so far as to involve you in the payment of legal costs.[23]

This was a cynical move that sought to make savings from the hoped-for ignorance of those affected, and the probability that many of them would not have the means to pursue legal action.

In October 1942 a clearly distraught, but dignified, Doran – and this was characteristic of many of these letter writers who struggled not to become too emotional in the face of bureaucracy's stone wall – wrote to the secretary of the Department of Defence: 'I am a married man with a wife and 3 children to keep and being unemployed, I am at a big loss in not receiving the pay order punctually.'

Understandably, the Department of Finance was continuously vigilant about policing the cases of those whose pensions had been abated or suspended, as arose in relation to Patrick Wade from Balla, County Mayo. In 1943 he was indebted to the Department of Agriculture for £59 under levies incurred under the Slaughter of Cattle and Sheep Acts; the amount due was to be recovered from the Military Service Pension payable to him and the payment of his pension was suspended. In October 1946 he wrote a plaintive letter to the Department of Finance:

> My pension has been stopped for years for cattle levy due ... I have 11 children and my wife dead. I lost £620 in the fight for Irish freedom in Cork and Mayo. My shop was closed for a few years owing to this levy ... I am now starting the world over again with a big expense over my head and my 11 children and can't get a job for them.[24]

Forfeiture of a pension could also occur if a recipient was convicted of a criminal offence. In 1940 John Guiney, a small farmer in Meath who was in receipt of an annual pension of £50, was convicted under the Offences Against the State Act arising out of a milk strike in Dublin; he was bound over to keep the peace for twelve months. In this instance, however 'the special criminal court considered ... that the loss of pension consequent on the conviction constituted an unduly severe punishment for the offence' and the pension payments were resumed.[25]

Financial penury was certainly a factor in prompting applications, but intertwined with that were issues of pride and status and the difficulty of verifying the historical record, and what constituted active service, particularly twenty years after the events. In this regard, the judgements handed down by the pension bureaucrats were short, sharp and potentially devastating. In October 1941 Katie Walsh from Clonmel, County Tipperary, wrote to the Office of the Referee to appeal the refusal to award her a pension; she had been a member of the Touraneena branch of Cumann na mBan: 'I claim that my services which entailed hardship, privation and danger from the time of my enrolment to the end of hostilities entitle me to a just consideration from the government of this country.'[26] She had requested an opportunity to testify in person, which she did in July 1941. On the basis of this, the advisory committee was informed by the interviewing officer:

> Applicant had fair activities. She seemed to be very vague about periods. Her principal activities would appear to have been catering for the men who came to her cottage, none of whom stopped overnight, owing to lack of accommodation. She may probably have done more work than she can recall and her case may be worth consideration. Hold for officers.

Three months later the verdict from the advisory committee was succinct and negative. 'No Change. On appeal, applicant gave evidence. There does not appear to be anything outstanding in her service.'[27]

Others who were disappointed with the decision reached about their rank expressed their dismay but did not pursue an appeal, being well aware how long the process could take. As John Scollan from Dublin, on whose behalf leading politicians Seán T. O'Kelly of Fianna Fáil and Richard Mulcahy of Fine Gael testified, put it in May 1938: 'The question of rank is certainly disappointing. As I am now 62 years of age it would only delay matters considerably if I were to appeal. This I am not going to do.' Scollan had been director of organisation, intelligence and munitions for the Hibernian Rifles, a nationalist militia group arising out of the AOH, about thirty of whom fought in the GPO in 1916, and a member of the Executive Council of Sinn Féin, and had, at various stages, been a prisoner in Frongoch, Wormwood Scrubs and Reading jails. Although he had made his sworn statement in October 1935, he had still heard nothing by November 1936. In May 1938 he was informed his pension would be £20 per annum.[28]

Many of the pension files also reveal the long-term effects of the loss of a significant earner within the family and the levels of dependency within families. In January 1933 Mrs Margaret Murphy, an invalided sixty-eight-year-old widow with an unmarried daughter, sought a pension: her only son, John Murphy, had been executed in Beggars Bush Barracks in November 1922 at the age of nineteen: 'He was a promising boy and a great help to me in keeping my home and if by the will of God he had been spared to me he would now be able to replace his father in keeping a home for myself and my only daughter.'[29] The secretary of the Army Pensions Board subsequently received a report of an investigation of her claim, which involved a personal visit: she was 'confined to her bed and barely able to move'. At the time of her son's execution, her husband had been a labourer for Guinness; her eldest daughter was married and living elsewhere; her twenty-two-year-old daughter was earning 15s a week in a draper's. According to the report, John

> appears to have been a very intelligent lad because at the age of 16½ years he secured a clerkship in the railway ... he was stationed in Tullow ... and had, his mother thinks, about £2.10s a week. He used to send her on an average of 25 shillings a week ... about a month before his death he told his mother and sister that he had secured a job in

Suffolk Street, but they have never been able definitely to say what it was ... the probability is that he was wholly engaged in IRA work.

The situation in 1933, two years after the death of her husband, was bleak. She had an allowance of 16s a week from her late husband's employer, Guinness; she was keeping the two children of her middle daughter aged seven and 10; the children's father gave her 10s a week for their upkeep: 'Their mother it was who opened and first read the official notification of her brother's execution, and she never recovered from the shock.' The matriarch was paying 5s a week in rent and her younger daughter 'is obliged to devote her services to the household duties'. It was decided that this applicant was 'obviously in necessitous circumstances' and that there had been a 'partial dependence' on the executed son in terms of the income of the house.[30]

Understandably, at a time of high unemployment, economic stagnation, and very limited prospects for the next generation, this dependency issue permeates the Military Service Pension files. In 1946, the thirty-four-year-old daughter of an army pension recipient who had recently died asked the Department of Defence if her father's last cheque could be made payable to her

> as I am absolutely dependent for my support on my father's pension ...
> I should also like to point out that I am an invalid for over twelve years
> and I am not in receipt of any monies from any source whatsoever. I
> am unable to work, I get no relief or insurance benefits, and I have
> nothing left out of my death policy as any money received went to pay
> doctors for my father's illness and funeral expenses. My brother in law
> has asked me to live with him for the future.[31]

The sum was paid to her as requested; it amounted to 13s 9d. For those seeking to survive or eke out a bare subsistence in the 1930s and 1940s, every penny generated by War of Independence service was precious.

Others resented the idea that they were charitable cases. James Butler, a 1916 combatant at the age of seventeen (his youth ensured his early release after the Rising) and later injured during the War of Independence, was awarded an E grade pension in 1935 but successfully appealed the number of years accredited service. In September 1935, after numerous attempts to put together all the pieces of his military services jigsaw (not helped by some of the difficulties in his referee's accounts, underlined by such assertions as 'without being definitely able to say so, I believe he was on a raid' or 'I remember him to have been wounded; to what extent and how badly I cannot remember'),[32] he wrote to the Board: 'I cannot understand how the referee came to his decision in only allowing me £22–1-1 per annum.' Two years later he complained of the delay in progressing his appeal which was 'causing a great and unnecessary hardship ... this is not charity, I am justly entitled'.[33]

As he was also making a wound claim (only partially successfully as the Board disputed the cause of his paralysis) he had to be subjected to a medical examination and was reminded by the Pensions Board: 'You will be submitted to a very thorough medical exam. Many claimants have heretofore presented themselves in a dirty condition. Cleanliness of body and clothing make things much [more] pleasant for all concerned. You are requested therefore to have a bath before reporting to this office.'[34] By 1950, Butler was on the verge of death due to paralysis but had to endure a final humiliation when payment in December 1949 was withheld 'as it was not witnessed by a qualified person'. His neighbour wrote to the Board: 'The paralysis has now reached his fingers and he finds it increasingly difficult to even make the "mark" which I witness.'[35] He died ten months later.

Whatever about the difficulties of some of the male veterans, some of the women had to fight battles just for it to be accepted that they had served as soldiers. Margaret Skinnider, who fought in 1916, claimed under the 1923 Pensions Act 'in respect of wounds received in the course of duty, as a member of the Irish Citizen Army' on 27 April 1916. Nora Connolly O'Brien later wrote on her behalf:

> She was wounded early on Thursday morning while engaged in the task of trying to cut British lines in Harcourt Street. During that engagement she was in command of a squad of 5 men. The wounding consisted of a bullet wound near the spine and a bullet wound in the upper right arm which had ploughed through the flesh upwards and expanding had blown away the flesh connecting the arm and shoulder ... I know that for a very long time she had no use of her right arm and that even now she suffers disability as a result of her wound.

These wounds hardly mattered, it seemed, for those adjudicating on the pension applications in the 1920s, it having long since been determined by the Board that the Act of 1923, while mentioning allowances or gratuities to 'widows, children and dependants' presumably contemplates that the deceased members should be of the male sex. It would be illogical therefore, to include female sex under the term 'wounded members' ... Section 3, which applies to this case, uses the words 'any person' as referable only to the male sex ... The definition of 'wound' in Section 16 only contemplates the masculine gender.[36]

The Treasury solicitor concurred: 'I am satisfied that the Army Pensions Act is only applicable to soldiers as generally understood in the masculine sense.'[37] Skinnider was thus informed curtly that her claim 'is not admissible'; she appealed and had to wait for another thirteen years before she was awarded a wound pension.

Bridget O'Mullane, a member of the executive of CnB, was awarded a pension for service between April 1917 and September 1923. She had initially established CnB branches in Sligo, spent two months in solitary confinement for seditious speeches in 1919, then began organising branches in Wexford, Kildare and Meath, 'cycling about 40 miles a day in all weathers ... and sometimes failed to get up a bye way in time to escape'. She became director of propaganda for the organisation during the civil war and was then imprisoned in Dublin, where she embarked on a hunger strike. One of her male contemporaries recalled that 'wanted men always found a welcome' at her home in Dublin during the civil war.[38] That was the male view, or how the men remembered her; for some of the women she worked with, however, it was different: 'The growth and efficiency of our organisation throughout the country was due almost entirely to her untiring zeal, energy and ability as organiser.'[39] When asked about the districts in which she was active, O'Mullane made the point emphatically on her form: 'Prisons!!!' During her evidence, O'Mullane observed that she 'had to set about looking for work, worn out in mind and body after 6 years constant active service. In earlier years I gave up a thriving business left me by my mother to go out organising for CnB.' O'Mullane was unhappy with the rank that she was accorded for pensions purposes (D instead of the desired C), but, like others 'unfortunately for myself, I require the cash and so cannot afford to appeal ... financial necessity accordingly leaves me with no option but to accept.'[40]

THIRTY

HOMES FIT FOR HEROES?

In relation to status, compensation and living conditions, there was also much disappointment for many Irish men who had served in the British army during the First World War. For those from southern Ireland who enlisted and were fortunate enough to return, there were to be few homes fit for heroes; indeed, quite the opposite. A committee established in the Irish Free State to examine the claims of British ex-servicemen, chaired by lawyer Cecil Lavery, created substantial files, bursting with a sometimes eloquently expressed desperation and indignation. Land, cottages and allotments had not materialised in the way promised; a statement of some of the war veterans from Wicklow simply asserted that 'nothing whatever has been done in this area ... although some of us are living in houses not fit for human habitation'. The other complaint was that ex-servicemen, 'who chiefly belong to the Labouring class, have to pay very high rents'. An interesting indication of the hierarchy that then existed in Ireland was the assertion that one of the difficulties was in finding land that would be suitable for the building of houses 'because nearly every field near the town belongs to a shopkeeper'.[1]

J. R. Dagg, who had acted as a recruiter for the British army during the war, recalled Lloyd George's famous promise that those who returned would get homes fit for heroes; three of Dagg's own sons had volunteered, and, as he recalled, 'we induced those people to go out and fight for what we thought was their country. On the public platforms we held out that inducement.'[2] The British Parliament had passed an ambitious Housing Act in 1919 to help finance the construction of half a million houses for British ex-servicemen, though only 213,000 had materialised by the early 1920s; in Ireland, the Irish (Provision for Sailors and Soldiers) Land Act of 1919 was designed to enable the Local Government Board, which frequently clashed with the Board of Public Works about housing, to provide cottages and plots. Up to 20,000 applications were received under this Act, but by the spring of 1921, only 134 ex-servicemen had been given farm holdings and only seventeen dwellings had been completed, with a reported 926 cottages in construction.[3]

A major urban housing scheme for ex-servicemen was undertaken in Killester in Dublin, which employed 900 former soldiers and sailors, but, inevitably, progress in all these schemes was complicated by the War of Independence; the Sinn Féin cabinet was told in early 1921 it was republican policy to 'temporarily suspend these schemes as there is a grave danger of serious trouble in rural areas over this matter'.[4] Hundreds of ex-servicemen were dismissed from the Killester project in April 1922, though by the end of that year, nearly 250 houses were ready at that site.

An Irish Sailors and Soldiers Land Trust was established in early 1924 after legislation was passed in London, Belfast and Dublin, based on an agreement that over 2,500 houses were needed for the south and just over 1,000 for Northern Ireland. The Trust had an initial allocation of £1.5 million which was inevitably cut, with just under £800,000 being allocated to the Free State by 1926. The problem was that more than 18,000 requests for housing were received and the Trust believed that at least 10,000 houses were needed to meet even modest demands; by 1928 just under 2,000 houses had been built under the auspices of the Trust.

The Committee on Claims of British Ex-servicemen (CCBE) heard tales of destitution and woe and neglected graves from all parts of the country; the Cobh Branch of the British Legion asserted that 'no part of the Free State contributed more, in terms of its population, to the service of Great Britain during the European War', but only sixteen houses had been built by the Trust, and 'hundreds of our people, married, are living in squalor or tenements ... We can give as an example one man, who suffers from 100 per cent disability, has a family of 6 children and lives in a single room.'[5] The Kinsale Branch of the Legion suggested 'about 1600 men left this town and district to serve in the British navy and army during the Great War. Not one cottage has been erected in the urban district of Kinsale up to the present.'[6] In Waterford, it was claimed 'Waterford City sent 2,000 men to the Great War and as a recompense for the services which they rendered the Land Trust could only see their way to allot 30 houses which are not yet completed.'[7] In Cavan, it was claimed there were 1,275 ex-servicemen in the county and that only four houses had been built. Moreover, 'these houses are built approximately 5 miles from the nearest town in what is practically a swamp ... it is really a bog'.[8]

Another regular complaint was from clerks who were dismissed at the time of the emergence of the new Free State and replaced by men who had served in the National Army, and orphans of ex-servicemen who were 'at present in various schools and institutions'. The Free State was not necessarily the villain in this regard; one high-profile case was that of the rents paid by the ex-servicemen tenants in Killester in Dublin. In relation to this, William T. Cosgrave had intervened, and the British Legion in Dublin was fulsome in its praise for him, expressing the sincere appreciation of the Killester tenants 'at the spontaneous and manly action' of Cosgrave 'in preventing the wholesale evictions threatened by the Sailors and Soldiers Land Trust a couple of years ago'.[9] In 1926, Dublin Corporation had 'pressurised' the Trust to get 547 ex-servicemen housed, but the British Legion also estimated that at least 8,000 houses were needed 'to meet even the most modest demands of the British ex-servicemen'.[10] In relation to the war dead, evidence given to the CCBE suggested there were 1,974 registered graves in the Free State at the end of 1926, 'scattered in 323 cemeteries' and they were in a 'most unsatisfactory condition'.[11] The Commonwealth Graves Commission register of war graves for the period 1914–21 recorded 3,829 graves in Ireland, north and south, and the remains of British military personnel who died in Ireland from 1916–21 were also eventually deemed to deserve war grave status; their remains lay in twelve burial grounds in the area that became the Free State.[12]

Disappointment about housing and dire living conditions was only one part of the First World War legacy; there were also the physical ailments born of trench warfare: bronchitis, heart trouble, neurasthenia and allegations of 'callous, cruel treatment inflicted upon an old pensioner by agents of the British Ministry of Pensions at Dublin'.[13] Some of the cases were truly tragic; the Cork British Legion in its evidence drew attention to the plight of a war veteran who had been nerve shocked in the Dardanelles: 'He is in the Cork Mental Hospital and his wife and children are in receipt of no allowance. Walker himself is being treated as a pauper lunatic in the Cork Mental Hospital. We say that his lunacy is due to his service, but the Minister says otherwise.'[14]

Significantly, at its inaugural meeting, the CCBE decided not to hold public sittings as it judged that such hearings 'would be undesirable as in our opinion, public criticism might be calculated to prejudice rather than assist the case of the men concerned'.[15] This was criticised by William Archer Redmond, one of seven nationalist MPs to serve in the British army during the war, and the only son of John Redmond. In September 1926, along with another former Nationalist MP Thomas O'Donnell, he was involved in the formation of the Irish National League Party, essentially a reincarnation of the IPP, which sought to provide a constitutional pro-Treaty opposition to Cumann na nGaedheal.

It contested the June 1927 general election urging a reduction in taxes and increased welfare spending for the elderly and British ex-servicemen, winning eight seats, but this was reduced to two seats in the September 1927 election. Redmond was particularly vocal on the ex-servicemen issue; as a member of the Irish council of the British Legion, and the Irish Free State representative on the Legion's council in London, he articulated their cause and welfare as one of his main political priorities and wanted the hearings of the CCBE to be in public: 'Let the general body of ex-servicemen see what was going on.'[16] The question of public attitudes was significant both in relation to how the ex-servicemen were treated when they came home and subsequently during the revolutionary years; another frequent complaint in the statements of claim heard by the committee was from individuals who had property damaged owing to the hostile activities of the IRA. In December 1927 one victim referred to his land being rendered useless by the IRA: 'This discrimination was carried out by means of threatening letters circulated and in all cases signed by order IRA.'[17]

One soldier from Kerry, who had served nine years in the British army, was at home on leave in Listowel in 1918 when 'the IRA came to me and informed me if I rejoined the army it would mean instant death, so through fear I never did. I never got a penny gratuity or anything else.'[18] One Cork soldier who served in France took up his old postman's job after demobilisation and 'on proceeding to perform the route I was threatened and told that ex-British soldiers were a thing of the past ... I knew it would be certain death if I attempted to carry on.' He also claimed that after the establishment of the new state in 1922 it was clear that any job vacancies would only be given to 'ex National Army men'. This was a common complaint also from clerks who claimed they were dismissed in favour of ex-IRA men; as one saw it, he was removed from his job in order to 'make way for the IRA men'.[19]

A soldier from Mullingar 'found on my return to civil life that the reception given to ex-British servicemen in the particular locality where I resided was one which I least expected would be given any man who fought for his country. Contempt to say the least of it was what I received.' After he joined the RIC and was home on leave from that position, the IRA surrounded his house 'took me out and under the threat of being shot compelled me to give up my only means of living'. He added for good measure 'the direct cause of losing my livelihood was brought about by members of the present government then acting as officers of the IRA'.[20] In all, the committee held eighteen meetings; it estimated the number of British ex-servicemen ordinarily resident in the state at about 150,000, but 'nothing was brought to our notice to suggest that such ex-servicemen form a class with grievances or disabilities common to them as a class'.[21] While this conclusion might appear a haughty dismissal of the grievances outlined to the committee, underpinning it was a well-founded belief that the ex-servicemen in Ireland did not fare any worse than ex-servicemen in Britain; indeed, in relation to housing, state support and employment 'they were treated somewhat better' than their British counterparts.[22]

There were many others affected by the question of recompense as a result of violence in Ireland during the revolutionary period; conflict caused up to 20,000 people to flee to Britain, where they were given refugee status, while others moved either north or south in Ireland. In the words of historian Niamh Brennan, the issue of compensation became 'a political minefield'.[23] As late as 1943 a former British soldier, sent to Ireland in 1904, appealed to the British prime minister Winston Churchill about his plight. During the War of Independence he had been threatened by the IRA and was advised by police to move to a hotel in Galway; he complained 'I have never received a penny' regarding the hotel expenses, and 'all my life savings have gone'.[24] He was told it was too late to seek recompense, the most recent Irish Grants Committee having sat between 1926 and 1930. There had been a number of committees prior to this; the Irish Distress Committee was established in 1922 with a budget of £10,000, and dealt with 3,349 applicants in its first six months. It was originally 'intended to give immediate financial assistance to Irish loyalists who had been driven out of the country', but by 1923 its functions extended to compensation and it was reconstituted as the Irish Grants Committee. 'Almost equal' numbers of Catholics and Protestants applied and its second report in January 1924 noted that 7,500 applicants had been dealt with, of which 4,330 were approved for grants amounting to £13,501 and loans amounting to just over £10,000.[25] The British government had hoped to obtain a refund of this money in accordance with the terms of the Anglo-Irish Treaty, and while nearly £12,000 was paid over, the Irish government was reluctant to commit more, pointing out that it had spent nearly £18,000 dealing with the needs of nationalist refugees from Northern Ireland. The British government in turn paid over this money and then looked for reimbursement from the government of Northern Ireland: 'Not to be outdone, [James] Craig, in his turn, joined this bewildering merry-go-round and demanded from the Imperial Treasury a refund for money spent on southern loyalist victims who had fled North.'[26]

Another committee dealt with the claims of disbanded members of the RIC for increased expenses through being obliged to leave Ireland; a memorandum from 1927 recorded that a total of 1,263 replacement grants were paid, amounting to £98,845, along with 727 other grants amounting to £20,389.[27] Grants 'on account of danger were confined to exceptional cases, where it appeared that a disbanded man might be in danger even after leaving Ireland'. Five grants were made under these terms. A grant of £1,500 was made to one man, head constable Eugene Igoe, 'who had good reason to fear that he would have to seek refuge in distant parts of the globe, and even then be ready to move once more if his identity was discovered. As a matter of fact I believe he has been in England or Ireland ever since disbandment.'[28] An RIC tribunal appointed by the chief secretary in April 1922 reported early in 1924 that, since its establishment, it had arranged 228 sittings and dealt with 'upwards of 4,000 applications for increased grants and about 5,400 applications for commutation, besides dealing, as required by the terms of disbandment, with the accounts of disturbance allowance granted to some 7,000 men'. It was noted that those presiding over this process had 'interpreted the terms of disbandment as generously as possible and for various reasons a large proportion even of those who have not moved have been allowed to retain the whole or part of their disturbance allowance'.[29]

In 1926, a new Irish Grants Committee was established, the same year the British Treasury estimated the Irish Free State owed nearly £27,000 in grants committee payments; this sum was waived after the Irish government agreed to increase the sum it owed to the British government for damage to non-transferred British government property during the civil war. An Irish Claims Compensation Association was also formed; it estimated the total number of claims to be lodged 'will not exceed 2,000'. There was also a Southern Irish Loyalists Relief Association which warned the new Irish Grants Committee not to correspond with residents in the Irish Free State in official envelopes: 'anyone who is familiar with rural Ireland today knows only too well that the local post office is frequently the source through which information as to the contents of letters leaks out. A letter in an official envelope – OHMS [On His Majesty's Service] positively invites inquiry.'[30]

This second Irish Grants Committee produced a memorandum in October 1928 indicating it had submitted 1,300 recommendations for a total sum of £1,050,873; the overwhelming majority were from £1 to £1,000 and five had been over £12,000. At the end of the previous year, Winston Churchill, the Chancellor of the Exchequer, interviewed Sir Alexander Wood Renton, a senior legal official, about these claims. Churchill

> referred to the question of the £400,000 limit which he said had been fixed by a decision of the cabinet as the maximum sum that the government was prepared to pay on foot of the recommendations of the Irish Grants Committee and expressed some surprise that he had not been communicated with when it became apparent that this maximum would be exceeded.

He suggested a maximum of £625,000 but Wood Renton insisted this was not enough and that the compensation his committee had recommended 'did not err on the too generous side'. Churchill 'spoke in appreciative terms of the work of the committee apart from its financial aspects'.[31] From 1926–30 this committee processed 4,032 cases of which 2,237 were compensated.[32]

THIRTY-ONE

SCRAMBLING FOR THE BONES OF THE PATRIOT DEAD

Official and unofficial commemoration of the Irish revolution was also a thorny issue from the foundation of the Irish Free State. The Office of the Director of Army Intelligence reported in November 1924 that a national soldiers' commemoration in Cork of the death of Terence MacSwiney had been disrupted; anti-Treatyites arrived and 'an officer who was carrying a wreath to lay on the grave was confronted by Miss Annie MacSwiney [Terence's sister] who smashed the wreath with her umbrella and threw the pieces over the cemetery wall.'[1]

How to commemorate the 1916 Easter Rising in the aftermath of the establishment of the Free State was also problematic and a question that confronted both government and opposition. It frequently led to political disagreement, cantankerous debate and uncertainty. For many, rather than being a question of solemn remembrance, it provided an opportunity to create political capital out of the contested republican legacy and to emphasise the divisions that existed within the Irish body politic.

Unsurprisingly, there was a variety of views as to what should and should not be done and who should and should not be involved. More surprisingly, given the tendency to believe that its commemoration only became difficult after the supposedly glorious, triumphant and retrospectively embarrassing fiftieth anniversary celebrations in 1966, it seems that well in advance of 1966, there was a growing resentment about commemoration of the Rising, which evolved into a general indifference.

The issue was often complicated by confusion as to whether commemoration was a religious or political event, and the extent to which it could be 'a credible focus of reconciliation'.[2] There were also disagreements as to whether commemorative events and gestures should be focused on the capital city of Dublin or should be nationwide, the degree to which the government of the day or the former participants should spearhead such events, and whose rhetoric should be invoked.

The words of Anne Dolan, in her book *Commemorating the Irish Civil War* (2003) are partly applicable to the issue of 1916: 'There were years when it was useful, when it was embarrassing, when it suited best to say nothing at all. There were fashionable and fickle years, controversial and inconsequential years. But there were always some who never noticed or cared about the difference.'[3] But to what extent would the words of Edna Longley, also quoted by Dolan, be true in relation to 1916? – 'Commemorations are as selective as sympathies. They honour our dead, not your dead.' How different was it for the 1916 commemorations than for the civil war ceremonies? Dolan has suggested that with regard to commemorating 1916, 'there was never the same sense of regret; never the sense that death and ceremony were so plainly intended to divide. At civil war graves it was a solemn return, a return to the death of 1916's type of hope.'[4]

There is a degree of truth in that assessment, but it underestimates the extent to which remembrance of 1916 encouraged political confrontation. Particularly in the 1930s and 1940s, the legacy of 1916 *was* divisive, a divisiveness which seems to have turned to tedium by the 1950s and 1960s. David Fitzpatrick suggests that both Cumann na nGaedheal [CnG] and Fianna Fáil were 'hesitant in exploiting the emotional capital' accumulated as a result of the national struggle, because such actions would be tainted by politics and potentially counterproductive.[5] Nonetheless, this is only partly the case, and there has been a tendency to overlook some of the more interesting rows that commemorating the Rising caused.

The difficulties were obvious during the 1920s; a Sinn Féin movement so united on the surface in the aftermath of the Rising had been irrevocably split, and the country was red raw in the aftermath of the civil war. Many who had fought side by side in 1916 were now fierce opponents. Fitzpatrick records the suggestion in 1923 by Clement Shorter, widower of the poet and sculptor Dora, that William T. Cosgrave, President of the Executive Council of the Irish Free State, and leader of the CnG government, accept £1,000 from his wife's estate in order for her sculpture commemorating the executed 1916 rebels to be fashioned in marble, set on a pedestal of Irish limestone and erected in Glasnevin cemetery in Dublin with an image of Patrick Pearse as its centrepiece.[6]

Cosgrave doubted Patrick's mother Margaret would want anything to do with a proposal that had his government's blessing. He wondered would the sculpture be better placed outside Leinster House, the location of Dáil Éireann, and was worried about the neglect of those killed other than by execution in 1916. He also feared the proposal would 'look as if we wanted to have one last slap at the British'. Eventually, the proposal was reluctantly agreed to, but for the next four years there were disagreements about where it would be located, recriminations about the danger of it overshadowing the grave of Arthur Griffith, and disputes as to exactly whose names should be included. By 1927, when matters were settled, it was nonetheless decided that it would be politically wise to have no formal unveiling to avoid squabbling over the inheritance of 1916.[7]

Publicly, things had not been much easier for CnG. In 1924, the year in which CnG hosted the first formal military ceremony to commemorate the Rising, invitations were issued to relatives of the executed 1916 leaders, but only one, Mrs Mallin (widow of Michael Mallin), attended. It is no surprise Mrs Mallin was on her own, given the political affiliations of the other relatives, who were avowedly anti-Treaty and hostile to the ruling government. In 1925, the government did not issue invitations to the ceremony at Arbour Hill, where the executed 1916 leaders were buried, to those TDs deemed 'Irregular'.[8] Rival republicans marched to Glasnevin cemetery for an alternative commemoration, as they did the following year for the tenth anniversary.[9] CnG opted to keep the ceremonies low key, with a requiem Mass, a slow march with band, wreath laying and a graveside rosary (later replaced by 'The Soldier's Song'), the firing of a volley, and the performance of the Last Post.

The question for the 1930s was how the new Fianna Fáil government would handle this issue. In 1932 there was an unprecedented ceremony, which the *Irish Press* insisted was 'not for one party but for the people'.[10] Fianna Fáil also sought to gain political capital out of the death of Pearse's mother in 1932, despite the contention of the *Irish Press* in April 1932 that 'whenever she appeared men felt the near presence of the inviolate tradition of nationhood. Party divisions dropped away'.[11] This was an exaggeration; Margaret had been elected to the Dáil in 1921 and opposed the Treaty but was defeated in the 1922 election and was later on the executive of Fianna Fáil. While she was prominent in Ireland and America, making speeches about her martyred sons, some republicans also felt that such promotion overshadowed the sacrifices of their dead loved ones.

In May 1933 Richard Mulcahy, former CnG minister, asked Frank Aiken, Fianna Fáil's Minister for Defence, if invitations to the state's 1916 commemoration were withheld 'from a number of persons who in previous years received such invitations'. Aiken's response indicated that Fianna Fáil was now going to attempt to take control of the legacy and strike off the list the perceived bogus pretenders:

> There was no good reason why some of those on the original list should have been included. 241 persons who were invited in former years were not included in this year's list; it is not known how many of them took part in the 1916 Rising. Neither is it known how many persons who took part in the 1916 Rising were excluded from the list in previous years.[12]

Fianna Fáil also made a point of allowing the public to gain access to the graves at Arbour Hill, which CnG had prohibited, and also initiated a further commemoration ceremony, which coincided with the actual date of the first executions of the leaders of the Rising.

As the 1930s progressed, and with the IRA declared an illegal organisation in 1936, the year of the twentieth anniversary of the Rising, it was even more important for Fianna Fáil to claim sole right to the 1916 inheritance. A year after Fianna Fáil's ascent to power, the first moves were initiated to get a 1916 memorial erected in the General Post Office, and it was with the commencement of this project that deep political divisions over the commemoration of the Rising came into the open. It was first mentioned publicly in the *Irish Press* in 1933,[13] and a year later the idea of installing sculptor Oliver Sheppard's work 'The Death of Cúchulainn' was mooted.

The provision of £1,000 for the project was approved in the Dáil in August 1934, and the Minister for Finance indicated that the memorial 'was intended to be merely a feature of the building and not in any sense a national monument to commemorate 1916 in general and he indicated that the object of the memorial was to mark the special historical relationship of the GPO building to the events of 1916'.[14] A subcommittee of the government (the Easter Week Memorial Committee) was appointed to consider and propose an inscription. A year later, it was decided a section of the Proclamation would be suitable.[15]

A row broke out soon afterwards about who should be at the unveiling ceremony. At a conference which included civil servants, ministers and Gardaí 'it was felt that a distinction could not be drawn between TDs ... with 1916 service and those without'; but for ex-TDs, only those with 1916 service would be invited.[16]

A remarkable number of groups then lined up to announce they would have nothing to do with this ceremony, as reported by the *Irish Press*: Clann na nGaedheal (the pre-truce IRA), the 1916 Club, the Irish Republican Soldiers Federation and the Old Republican Rights Association, and eventually, and perhaps most significantly, Fine Gael (the new name for CnG after 1933), who issued a statement hoping 'All republicans will realise the necessity for the unity which will enable all organisations believing in the Proclamation of 1916 to take a fitting part in honouring the dead of the Nation without entering the sphere of internal differences of republican thought.'[17]

In the Dáil, Richard Mulcahy, chief Fine Gael critic of Fianna Fáil's attempt to monopolise the 1916 legacy, queried the composition of the Easter Week Memorial Committee and Fianna Fáil's partisan approach to the matter. An internal government memorandum acknowledged there was disquiet, noting, 'The suggestion has been made that the personnel of the Firing party has been taken exclusively from men who took part on one side in the civil war. This has also been indicated as a possible source of bitterness which should be, if possible, absent from a function of this nature.'[18]

The growing unease about the ceremony led to stormy debates in the Dáil, as well as the resignations of the Clann na nGaedheal representatives from the Memorial Committee because they could not consistently identify themselves 'with any of the various ceremonies being held by different republican bodies'. Also in the Dáil, Fine Gael made much of the fact that Fianna Fáil was proposing to hold a flag day on Easter Sunday, accusing the government of using the army 'for the purpose of making a Fianna Fáil holiday to add to their Flag Day collection.'[19]

Fianna Fáil also faced criticism from the other side – 'true Irish Republicans' – whom, Maud Gonne MacBride (republican activist and former wife of Major John MacBride, executed for his role in 1916) hoped, 'would not go near the GPO'.[20]

Clearly, the activities of the Memorial Committee were seen as politically controversial, and it was even wondered if civil servants should have to be specially authorised to associate themselves with it, although ministers insisted such involvement was acceptable. On 17 April 1935 William T. Cosgrave turned up the political heat and replaced Richard Mulcahy as the opposition's chief critic of the plans by releasing a powerful statement. He was not attending the unveiling, he insisted, because 'the time is not yet ripe for an adequate commemoration of 1916 which would be accompanied by that generous national enthusiasm indispensable to success'.

He went on, in his cleverly crafted contribution, to assert:

> The anniversary of Easter week is an occasion which might be suitably employed by every party in sober reflection. Bitterness, suspicion, envy, we have in abundance – as well as parties. It was for a noble purpose that men fought in Easter week 1916, not for divisions in the homes of the people, in their associations, or in the national ranks. It is not possible to hide these national humiliations today or to cover them with a veil lifted from the bronze statue of Cúchulainn.[21]

The *United Ireland* newspaper, a publication that supported Fine Gael, echoed his comments a few days later. Insisting Fianna Fáil TDs had nothing on their minds except a desire to make political capital for themselves and their party, it editorialised: 'It is always unseemly, if not indecent, for political parties to engage in a figurative scramble for the bones of the patriot dead.' Furthermore, this article maintained that the Cúchulainn statue had not even been specially made for this occasion but had been made twenty-five years previously, and 'lay ready to hand'. The ceremony in 1935 was also notable for the arrival at the GPO of a rival republican procession, en route to Glasnevin.

From the late 1930s there were also frequent demands from Old IRA associations to have 24 April, the date of the commencement of the Rising, declared a public holiday; it was considered by the government, but it was decided to adhere to commemorating it at Easter, whenever that fell. Éamon de Valera also presented the National Museum with an ornamental role of honour, listing, in Fitzpatrick's words 'thousands of supposed participants in the Rising'. It was a low-key affair with no speeches. More contentious, suggests Brian Walker, were the disturbances in the 1930s, when members of the Communist Party, 'all 28 of them', would fall in 'uninvited behind the IRA ranks and display conspicuous red rosettes in their buttonholes.'[22]

In 1940, it was suggested that there might be something unseemly about neutral Ireland having an elaborate military celebration for the twenty-fifth anniversary of the Rising while the Second World War was being fought elsewhere, a memorandum in February 1940 questioning, 'whether there should be any form of commemoration' and, if there was, 'whether it should be of a purely religious character or of a military character or whether it should be both'.[23]

Notwithstanding this sober reflection, some of the plans that emerged from the Department of Defence were exceptionally elaborate, including the idea of a pageant of history in the Phoenix Park, on an 'ambitious scale with searchlight effects', a 'mass victory parade past the GPO', a state ceilidh (a communal Irish dance) 'to be organised on the most extensive possible scale', athletic functions, and a ceremony involving the carrying of torches of freedom from the four provinces 'based on the Olympic games ceremonial'. The department also wanted the cooperation of all theatres and picture houses 'in staging distinctively national programmes', including, ironically, Seán O'Casey's *The Plough and the Stars*, a play that had sparked controversy in the 1920s due to its depiction of aspects of Dublin tenement life during Easter week 1916 and its thinly veiled assault on the militarism of the era.[24]

De Valera as Taoiseach was quite adamant in his negative response to these ambitious plans. Clearly, the officials in the Department of Defence had got carried away, and the words 'no question' were scribbled in the Department of the Taoiseach's response to the memorandum mentioned above; or as de Valera put it more officiously: 'In present circumstances the holding of a commemoration on elaborate lines would not be appropriate.' In October 1940, he suggested the commemoration 'should be of a purely military nature and that it might be a single event ... confined to one day only'. In December, in a memorandum from the Department of Defence headed 'Victory parade past the GPO', the Department of the Taoiseach bracketed the word 'Victory',[25] and in January 1941 it was dropped altogether; now, it seemed, it would just be a parade. But despite this apparent preference for a scaling down of commemoration plans, on 14 April 1941 de Valera was reported in the *Irish Independent* as having reviewed 25,000 men in the 'largest and most spectacular military parade the city has seen'. Special 1916 service medals had been minted; de Valera received the first one.[26] Interestingly, the Fianna Fáil-supporting *Irish Press* had warned against the practice of such commemoration, which had a tendency to 'fashion the Rising into a story heavy with sentiment and forget what it achieved'.[27]

De Valera was conscious of the sensitivities of the government appearing to overdo the republican celebrations, not just because of the Second World War, but also because of the ongoing IRA bombing campaign in Britain. In March 1940 he had made a radio broadcast with these issues as a backdrop and, significantly, spoke of Pearse's ideals, insisting that they could be realised only if the people of Ireland worked for them under the guidance of government:

> It is not the moral right of any individual or group of individuals to choose a means that is contrary to the public good or justice. The claim to choose such means can never be substantiated by an appeal to the facts or the conditions of Easter Week 1916 – nor to the sentiments of the leaders. We can conceive of these men as wishing only the true good of their country and it cannot possibly make for the good of the nation to refuse due obedience to the freely elected Irish government which now controls the major position of our land.[28]

There were complaints from the Dublin Brigade of the Old IRA in the mid and late 1940s that the commemoration momentum was on the wane; in a letter to the Minister for Posts and Telegraphs they informed him that 'the national flag is not flown from any of the post offices in the South County Dublin area on Easter Sunday'. The following year, the Old IRA Men's Association wanted all buildings under government control to have the flag flying on Easter Sunday and the week following, to which the government's response was that the flags would only be flown on the Sunday and Monday.[29]

There were two reasons for a military parade in Dublin at Easter 1949; to celebrate the Declaration of the Republic, the state's formal exit from the Commonwealth, and also to commemorate the Rising. Now that there was a coalition government in power, it was interesting that 1916 still seemed to cause suspicion in the party ranks, and that it was difficult to find unanimity. Seán MacBride, for example, the leader of Clann na Poblachta, one party of the coalition, and who had served as IRA chief of staff in the late 1930s, was present at the annual IRA commemoration of

1916 at Glasnevin cemetery, while Fianna Fáil boycotted the ceremonies at the GPO and went instead to Arbour Hill.[30]

Fianna Fáil certainly did not seem to have much enthusiasm for the idea of celebrating the new Republic. Taoiseach John A. Costello, in a magnanimous gesture, invited de Valera as leader of the opposition to join him in a broadcast to mark the occasion, an invitation de Valera rejected on the following grounds:

> We in Fianna Fáil are glad that henceforth there will be agreement amongst all parties in Dáil Éireann that the state shall be described as a Republic. We cannot convince ourselves however that the Act merits that its coming into operation should be marked by national celebrations. Indeed, when the constitution came into operation in 1937, we decided that celebrations such as those now proposed ought to be reserved until the national task which we have set ourselves is accomplished. We still believe that public demonstrations and rejoicings are out of place and are likely to be misunderstood as long as that task remains uncompleted and our country partitioned.[31]

There was a glaring hypocrisy in these sour lines, as, to use de Valera's logic, Fianna Fáil should never have commemorated the Rising either.

The *Irish Press* went so far as to maintain that the coalition government was doing a huge disservice to nationalists in the north, who 'have now seen the 1916 Rising linked with a Bill which changes nothing in their regard'.[32] Since the 1920s, northern republicans had attempted to commemorate the Rising in such places as Milltown cemetery in Belfast and Derry City cemetery, but they were banned by the government and remained prohibited until 1948. In 1950, the commemoration at Milltown cemetery incorporated services held by the National Graves Association, the Irish Labour Party and the Old IRA, and during the 1960s, marches continued to be held relatively unhindered, though there was some confrontation with police over the flying of the tricolour.[33]

By the 1960s, there were numerous complaints from members of Old IRA brigades regarding the lack of centralisation evident in the commemoration of 1916 and the over-proliferation of parades. In June 1962, this prompted Frank Casey and Peter Nolan, of the Federation of IRA 1916–21, to write a letter to Taoiseach Seán Lemass:

The Easter week commemoration parades held in Dublin this year occasioned a great deal of adverse comment among the Old IRA and there is no doubt that every year these parades are becoming less impressive and have ceased to command the respect to which they are entitled from the public. The position is that an official state ceremony is held on Easter Sunday centring on the GPO. Another state ceremony is held at Arbour Hill early in May. The old Dublin Brigade also hold a parade on 24 April, with a ceremony at the GPO and the different battalions are accustomed to hold separate commemoration parades in the different battalion areas, usually in association with a memorial Mass. This multiplication of parades has not been for the best. The citizens of Dublin have become so used to seeing handfuls of old men marching behind the national flag that they no longer turn their heads to look at them, while the drivers of buses and cars hoot them out of the way and break their ranks with indifference, if not contempt.[34]

THIRTY-TWO

'HE KNEW AS MUCH ABOUT COMMANDING AS MY DOG'

Undoubtedly, by the early 1960s some were turning their attention to the commemoration of the fiftieth anniversary of the Rising in 1966, but it is also the case that in light of these preparations, the government was conscious of two things – the general indifference of many people and the danger of reopening old wounds. With regard to the first, as the *Irish Times Annual Review* put it in 1965, during the general election of that year, 'partition, the Republic, the language and all the old constitutional questions were completely replaced by the social and economic questions of the new era ... It saw the resignation of many veteran leaders and the take over of a new generation.' The *Irish Times* went even further a month later in January 1966: 'Our young people want to forget. Boys in Dublin gravitate to coffee-skinned girls ... The past is not only being forgotten by the young, it is being buried with great relish and even with disdain.'[1]

Taoiseach Seán Lemass was also undoubtedly frustrated by the correspondence he had to deal with in 1965 as another issue raised its head – the question of who should figure most prominently in the 1966 commemorative events. Kathleen Clarke, widow of veteran Fenian Tom Clarke who had been executed after the Rising, signed her correspondence as the 'only widow alive of the signatories of the 1916 Proclamation', indicating her proprietorial view of 1916. She insisted in a letter to Lemass 'I know more about the events both before and after the Rising than anyone now alive', and demanded she be given a central role in the plans to commemorate the fiftieth anniversary.

She further insisted that Tom Clarke had been president of the Republic in 1916: 'Seán MacDermot [MacDiarmada] was always complaining to Tom that Pearse wanted everything. He was not satisfied with getting honours he may have earned but wanted to grab what was due to others.' Pearse, she alleged, during Easter 1916, had 'sat all the week writing in the GPO', and was 'beneath contempt', as he had taken advantage of the confusion in the GPO to sign himself 'President' on the documents of the week. She continued:

> Surely Pearse should have been satisfied with the honour of Commander-in Chief when he knew as much about commanding as my dog ... I have remained silent in public for fifty years but the circumstances which first forced me to remain silent no longer exist and the matter is now one of history. I had not intended raising the issue in public but I shall be forced to come out very strongly in public if the powers that be attempt to declare Pearse as President.[2]

Lemass had to look to one of his ministers, Jack Lynch, for advice on how to bat away Clarke; her own son did not agree with her and accepted the official version of Pearse as president, but she lined up formidable supporters for her view, including Muriel MacSwiney, Terence's widow, while Lemass's secretary insisted 'there is no proof that they all actually signed' the 1916 Proclamation: 'one of them certainly did not'. There were even disputes over who painted the words Irish Republic on the flag flown over the GPO.[3] Lemass had other, more personal reasons for being uneasy about contentious or triumphalist commemorations. He deliberately downplayed his own role in 1916; his brother Noel had been savagely killed during the civil war and his body dumped in the Dublin mountains and Seán himself had accidentally shot his baby brother dead at home in January 1916, perhaps when experimenting with an Irish Volunteer's rifle.[4]

The tone of the correspondence emanating from the Department of the Taoiseach suggests that Lemass was not keen on vigorous debate on the Rising or Pearse in the 1960s, particularly in the context of his determination to promote 'the building of Anglo-Irish good will'.[5] When pondering the suitability of Pearse's poem 'Invocation' as an inscription on the memorial wall in the Garden of Remembrance, he was 'disturbed by

the fierce and vengeful tone of the poem, which was entirely appropriate
to the circumstances of 1916, but will be less so to those years after 1966'.
This was not the observation of someone who was keen to get involved
in a scramble for the bones of the patriot dead. Other evidence suggests
there were others involved behind the scenes in coordinating 1916 commemorations in 1966 who did not see it as an inevitable opportunity for
grandstanding; the secretary of the government in 1965 declared he would
be 'rather nervous about recommending too elaborate a programme just
in case it might turn out to be a flop'.[6] Meanwhile, Dom Bernard O'Dea
of Glenstal Abbey, home to a prestigious private boys' boarding school,
suggested that it might be a 'worthy' motive of the jubilee to interest Irish
youth in the 'heroism' of 1916 but that 'the thinking youth are contemp-
tuous of the inconsistent, they will not submit to an emotional unreality
fostered by people they no longer believe in'. The *Irish Times* suggested the
best result of the commemoration 'would be an increased interest in the
educational field'.[7]

In October 1965 the Secretary of the Department of External Affairs,
Hugh McCann, reported on a discussion he had with the British ambassador to Ireland, who was worried about his presence in Dublin during the
fiftieth anniversary commemorations:

> The Ambassador asked about the character of the commemoration,
> and, in particular, whether it would be oriented towards the future or
> a re-enactment of the past. I referred to the Taoiseach's recent speech
> on the subject and told the Ambassador that I felt sure he could take
> it that the commemoration would be a forward-looking occasion
> without any attempt to re-open old wounds.[8]

Much has been made of the downplaying of the iconography of 1916 after
the fiftieth anniversary, but there is evidence to suggest that prior to 1966,
it was already becoming a sensitive and somewhat delicate subject.

In December 1965 G. A. Lovett, the first secretary at the British
embassy in Dublin, wrote to the Commonwealth Relations Office, noting

> the possibility that these celebrations might embarrass us has not
> escaped the notice of the American Embassy. The American Counsel-
> lor called on me the other day to say that he wished to avoid the danger
> of any action by his government causing needless embarrassment to us.

This was a friendly gesture ... it is known that the Taoiseach is anxious that this should not degenerate into just another occasion for reliving the past and rekindling old controversies. We have it on good authority that he has already made it clear that he sees this as a domestic Irish event and not an occasion for international rejoicing [a joker in the British embassy had suggested there should be extensive British military involvement in the commemoration, involving 400 regiments and a fly-by of the RAF].[9]

Hugh McCann had told the British embassy that the Taoiseach's intention was to avoid the occasion being 'backward looking' and it was agreed the British ambassador should attend 'the 2 or 3 functions' he was likely to be invited to, while the Commonwealth Office 'would see considerable political advantage in demonstrating the close and most friendly relations developing with the Irish Republic by presenting the flag to them' – a reference to the flag that had flown over the GPO in 1916.[10] The flag was to be given as an 'outright gift' but there were concerns that, regarding other relics wanted by the National Museum, they had not 'even acknowledged our offer ... all this had created a deplorable impression at the Imperial War Museum. We should be glad if an opportunity could be taken to inform the Irish authorities in suitable terms of the resentment felt at the behaviour of the National Museum of Ireland.' But the British embassy was still content that 'the Irish authorities seem to have taken our hint about avoiding unnecessary embarrassment to the British ambassador'.[11] Noble Frankland, the director of the Imperial War Museum, acknowledged that 'in many ways the Irish have a better claim to the flag than we have' but the CRO was anxious 'to get the maximum credit for this gesture'.[12]

The British ambassador, Geoffrey Tory, however, did not want 'to be physically involved' in the handover of the flag as he had taken part in the ceremony around the return of the body of Roger Casement the previous year. (After his execution in 1916 Casement was buried in Pentonville jail, and his remains were returned to Ireland only in February 1965.) After an elaborate state funeral Casement was reburied in Glasnevin cemetery and 'the photograph of myself, bareheaded, marching behind the gun carriage ... caused considerable heart burning amongst the British ex-servicemen here in Ireland but also in the bosoms of a number of Conservative backbenchers'. As a result, in relation to the return of the flag, there was a desire 'not to get involved with any sort of press conference or TV coverage'.[13]

It was not a smooth unfurling, however; the arrangement was to give the flag to the Irish ambassador in London but there was a panicked mix-up over which was the correct flag, as there were two – a tricolour and a green one; if the Imperial War Museum agreed that the green flag was the one which flew over the GPO, this 'would have put them in the wrong for the last 50 years! ... Thank goodness we arranged it in London and not in Dublin.'[14] The confusion was cleared up; it appeared the British museum had been displaying a tricolour that originated in Limerick; the one from the GPO was the green one which had the words 'Irish Republic' on it. One of the more bizarre requests that year was contained in a letter from the 1916 Commemoration Committee in London, of which the Irish ambassador was honorary president, to the Treasurer to the Queen 'for the use of the Queen's box at their charity concert' in the Royal Albert Hall. The treasurer responded 'although the application seems somewhat Gilbertian [comic and improbable] I can see no particular reason for refusing it'; Sir Saville Garner in the CRO agreed 'that the application is Gilbertian – or perhaps merely "Irish!" But I find the idea rather appealing' and the request was granted.[15]

There were also calls from academics and politicians for the rejection of a one-dimensional celebration in 1966. The Jesuit-published periodical *Studies* editorialised that, in relation to Eoin MacNeill, who attempted to prevent the Rising, 'history has attached to him that most damning label – it tells us that he meant well'; his memorandum on what would justify rebellion, it was asserted 'is a profound and inspiring profession of Ireland's nationhood. It is the sober, realistic and comprehensive declaration of Irish independence.'[16] David Thornley suggested in relation to Patrick Pearse that it had been 'not merely difficult but almost blasphemous to discern a human being of flesh and blood' but that 'in his own time he was an unrepresentative figure', while Garret FitzGerald argued the rebels were 'limited and naïve' and 'they did not regard themselves – nor were they in fact – great thinkers'.[17] But as he revealed much later in his autobiography, FitzGerald also had to seek an apology from *The Economist* magazine, after his article on the fiftieth anniversary appeared under the heading 'This week, 50 years ago, a group of hotheads seized the GPO in Dublin', accompanied by a photograph of de Valera, by now president of the Irish Republic; FitzGerald duly got his apology.[18]

The supposedly glorious, sectarian and insensitive celebrations in 1966 have often been cited as a factor in the outbreak of the Troubles in Northern Ireland, but Roisín Higgins in her book *Transforming 1916* (2012) pours cold water on this theory. Because of the outbreak of the Troubles a few years after the 1966 events, even nearly fifty years later, the commemoration was being recalled mostly in a negative context, as something the likes of which should never happen again, with the assertion that it had created momentum for more extremist republicans.[19] In 1991, Unionist leader David Trimble maintained that the commemorations were 'a significant factor in starting the Troubles'.[20] This, it seemed, became accepted wisdom, but it is not an idea that was interrogated enough, as Higgins makes clear. Although there was undoubtedly little consideration given to the impact the commemorations in the south might have on relations with Northern Ireland, it is clear that as well as genuflecting to an older Ireland, the official commemorations in 1966 were also about 'the presentation of a new reality'.

There was a sidelining of the republican movement in favour of a focus on a prosperous, modernised and not just agricultural but now also industrialised republic. What it amounted to, in essence, was a 'tug between past and future'. As Taoiseach on the last lap of power, Lemass was upfront about this: 'Forget the Island of the Sean Bhean Bhocht [Poor old Woman] and think of Ireland of the technological expert.'[21] He also intervened to acknowledge his and others' guilt in questioning the motives of the Irish who had volunteered for service in the British army in the First World War, though there persisted a denial that some of these had fought for the British Empire. Inevitably, there were different meanings ascribed to 1916, and it was presented as 'an idea, an ideal, an illusion and a delusion: all bitterly fought over'. Commemoration also involved the exclusion of alternative narratives; the labour movement, for example, was subsumed into the broader nationalist story and Minister for Agriculture, Charles Haughey, when opening the Mellows agricultural college in Galway, which was named after Liam Mellows, executed during the civil war, insisted that the Pearse legacy was of central relevance to rural Ireland: 'What finer end could there be for a boy who aspires to become a man according to Pearse's ideal than to follow the calling of the land.'[22]

In relation to the official state commemorations, what is striking are the varying degrees of enthusiasm that existed; the original plan for a two-week celebration was watered down to one week. There was a strong emphasis on education, scholarships, pageants, religious services, parades and lectures and debates, including one in Naas with the title 'Has Pearse turned in his grave?' The GAA provided a ready-made national structure that could be utilised and was keen to use the commemorations to promote its own interests; its president, Alf Murray, referred to the organisation's 'spiritual contribution' to national identity in the years around the rising.[23]

There were alternatives to state commemoration. Many were dissatisfied with contemporary conditions and what was perceived as the betrayal of the ideals of 1916, including Irish language groups, artists and disgruntled republicans. The sisters of Seán MacDiarmada, one of the signatories of the 1916 Proclamation, objected to what they called the 'Free State' army's involvement in commemorative services and instead endorsed the republican National Graves Association and its Golden Jubilee Committee.[24]

Commemoration in Northern Ireland was tense and saw a re-emergence of the UVF. The idea that nationalists were not part of the citizenry of Northern Ireland was implicit in some of the unionist denunciations of the commemoration that witnessed 70,000 parading to Belfast's Casement Park and a rival Ian Paisley parade. But arrests on Easter weekend in 1966 were minimal and some representatives of the RUC encouraged compromise. There was contention over the use of the tricolour, but Easter celebrations were not banned outright as long as they were kept out of view of unionists. Higgins suggests the activities in Northern Ireland cannot be held responsible for the outbreak of the Troubles; they were instead, 'one of a series of events that exacerbated the fault lines within the societies and contributed to the growing sense of division'.[25]

There were also cultural tensions and concerns about RTE's highly ambitious TV drama *Insurrection*, written by Hugh Leonard, which involved 200 extras and 300 members of the defence forces in a reconstruction of the events of Easter week. The idea was to underline the 'heroic drama' of the week for a younger audience while also giving space for the voices of the survivors. At the beginning of the project, Leonard believed 'the entire project seemed as gallant and doomed as the Rising itself'. *Insurrection* was broadcast twice in 1966 and never since, not, it has been maintained, due to the Troubles or political correctness, but because of the cost of repeat fees, an explanation that appears far-fetched. It was a big success, and Higgins suggests it made a valiant attempt to complicate a simplistic narrative of the politics of the Rising by referring to social conditions.[26] Phyllis Bean Uí Cheallaigh, wife of the former president Seán T. O'Kelly, had only one complaint to make about *Insurrection*: 'They made the Volunteers behave like a rabble, untrained, ill assorted, couldn't walk or march or talk and they all looked so gloomy and dismal. And my girlish recollection was that you all looked like Gods, brave, heroic, handsome young men, and, sure enough, 50 years later, I see and know that I was right.'[27]

Memorial sites were also an important aspect of remembrance, including the newly opened Kilmainham jail museum and the Garden of Remembrance in Dublin city. Oisín Kelly, who fashioned the Children of Lir memorial in the garden, referred to the general difficulty of expressing 'the heroic in our time'. The absence of the aged children in the sculpture suggested 'a sense of the nation's lack of completion', underlining two conflicting realties in 1966: the achievement of independence and the failures of freedom. But perhaps the most dramatic development was 'not in monument but in anti-monument', with the blowing up of Nelson's Pillar by a republican splinter group; the pillar, dedicated to British navy hero Horatio Nelson, killed in the Battle of Trafalgar in 1805, had been there since 1808. It was this gesture that effectively provided the iconic moment of the golden jubilee; a measure of the popularity of the toppling of Nelson was reflected in the fact that a song, 'Up Went Nelson', topped the charts for eight consecutive weeks.[28]

Culturally, there were robust challenges to any sense of complacency. For all the emphasis on the notion of the poetic Rising, *Dublin Magazine* maintained, 'if we are prepared to confront realities we must surely admit that from a cultural point of view Ireland is a disgrace'. It was regarded as humiliating that the Northern Ireland Arts Council received double the funding of the Republic's. In relation to artistic endeavour there were 'pockets of ambiguity and ambivalence that tilted at the official message'.

The mission to project modernisation while also preserving the 'folk values' of the past was a difficult balancing act in relation to the commemorations abroad and provided a headache for the Irish tourist board, Bord Fáilte, which got exasperated about Irish stereotypes and the use of the phrase 'the Irish of it' to describe 'all acts of ignorance, clumsiness and shiftlessness'. The government was also concerned about the desire of Breton nationalists to participate in the commemorations, a reminder that for all the desire to take credit for striking a decisive blow against the British Empire in 1916, by the 1960s, the state had 'a vested interest in the promotion of international law and in international stability'.[29]

In relation to British assessments of how the commemorations played out, there were still hints of a sneering snobbery in the use of the phrase 'typically Irish', and other diplomatic communications; for example, reference was made to 'the inordinate length of the celebration and the profusion of anniversaries ... In a strange but typically Irish way it has been noted that, whereas in Belfast rival parades were held with a minimum of disturbance, in Dublin, the parade on 24 April caused a direct clash between the Gardaí and the marchers.'[30] However, Ambassador Tory, in a letter to the Secretary of State for Commonwealth Relations, was much more upbeat and positive: the celebrations were over and 'Anglo-Irish relations are none the worse. I almost think they are better.' Regarding civil war divisions, 'the Irish themselves seem surprised to discover how little bitterness now remains', while in relation to north–south relations 'a note of asperity entered for a moment but this will soon be forgotten'. Regarding the Northern Ireland government, he believed there had been a 'remarkable liberality in their attitude to nationalist demonstrations.'[31]

THIRTY-THREE

COMMEMORATION DURING THE TROUBLES AND THE PEACE PROCESS

Inevitably, the Troubles in Northern Ireland from 1969 onwards changed the approach to commemoration, and led to the abandonment of the military parade to commemorate the 1916 Rising. But Irish political parties still had an appetite for prolonging their civil war legacies. In 1968, Taoiseach Jack Lynch was asked if he would further the momentum provided by President Éamon de Valera who had attended a memorial Mass for Michael Collins, by attending the annual Collins commemoration at Béal na Blá, where Collins had been killed. Lynch replied that as it was organised by Fine Gael, unlike the memorial Mass organised by the Old IRA, the government would not be represented.[1]

There were poisonous exchanges in the Dáil in 1971 about the fiftieth anniversary of the Anglo-Irish Treaty, the culmination of anger about the lack of a sense of communal political commemoration of the Treaty in the decades after its signing. As was noted by the political correspondent of the *Irish Times* newspaper in 1946, at the time of the twenty-fifth anniversary of the Treaty, 'the celebrations must inevitably be of a one sided character', even though 'the fact that the Oireachtas is able to assemble in Leinster House and direct the government of the country stems essentially from the Treaty'. The Fianna Fáil government then in power had no intention of marking the occasion. Fine Gael, in contrast, assembled in the Mansion House to stress that the Treaty admitted Irish sovereignty 'in peace and war'. Fine Gael leader Richard Mulcahy also emphasised that the Treaty

'gave Ireland back her purse', a reference to the concession of fiscal autonomy conceded by the British towards the end of the Treaty negotiations.[2]

The fiftieth anniversary of the Treaty was once again regarded as a
Fine Gael commemoration, although its leader Liam Cosgrave suggested
'it would be far better if commemoration was organised by the state'. Taoiseach Jack Lynch's failure to mark the occasion was referred to as 'pigmy-
minded pettiness' by Fine Gael's Richie Ryan.[3] But earlier that year, Lynch
was praised when he announced that the army would be at Béal na Blá
for that year's fiftieth anniversary Collins commemoration; one contemporary response to this announcement was that, with it, 'the last stitches
of the last deep wounds of the civil war were removed'; but this was an
exaggeration as it was also observed, 'Nor is Jack Lynch yet ready to go to
Cork; softly, softly, he sends the army.'[4]

President Erskine Childers, whose father had been executed during
the civil war, in a private letter to Cosgrave in May 1974, suggested the
need for a new focus on the revolutionary era:

> We do not do half enough to commemorate the lives of those who
> worked for Ireland in the social, political and cultural fields in the
> nineteenth and twentieth centuries to arouse the self-confidence
> of Irish people. When I opened the swimming pool in Tipperary I
> found a museum commemorating the life of Seán Treacy [one of the
> leaders of the IRA in Tipperary during the War of Independence].
> The museum contained nothing but guns. I nearly called you up and
> asked that I be allowed alter the sentence which spoke of St Patrick's
> Day commemorating those who died for Ireland to read 'those who
> worked for and died for Ireland'.[5]

Although UCD hosted an exhibition about Daniel O'Connell for
the bicentenary of his birth in 1775, a speech written by civil servants for
Cosgrave the same year deliberately emphasised O'Connell's legacy in the
context of the need for his rehabilitation, as historians and politicians
'had allowed or even pursued a policy of denigration and, unconsciously
or otherwise, of misrepresentation of O'Connell's life and work'.[6]

The centenary of the birth of 1916 Rising leader Patrick Pearse in
1979 also raised sensitivities. At the end of 1977, all government departments were asked to submit proposals as to how the centenary could be
marked. The view was expressed that 'in the prevailing Northern Ireland

situation such commemoration could raise delicate issues affecting relations between the communities in the North and possibly extending to
Anglo-Irish relations', but that a decision not to mark the occasion 'could
be open to misinterpretation and might leave the field to subversive elements who might seek to capitalise on the situation for their own ends'.[7]
There was a feeling that commemoration should concentrate on 'Pearse's
contribution in the literary, cultural and educational fields'.

As Richard Stokes, a civil servant in the Department of the Taoiseach, saw it, a proposal for a £75,000, thirty-five-foot-high statue of Pearse
in O'Connell Street was outlandish and foolhardy:

> The scope of the project is considerably greater than the profile which
> prudence would suggest for a Pearse commemoration, given the
> implications in regard to the North etc ... would be a major target for
> vandalism and for bomb attacks from certain quarters ... political cor-
> respondents and other commentators with their readiness to apply
> facile labels are likely to describe it as a victory of Hawks over Doves.[8]

As the Troubles in Northern Ireland continued, much of the commemorative focus in the 1980s was centred on the idea of condemning
'senseless violence' and the assertion that 'physical force is out of the
question' to solve the northern crisis. Focus on 1922 was not about dis-
cussing the causes of the civil war but ensuring 'there must never again
be a civil war in our land', as a Fianna Fáil senator put it at a civil war
commemoration in 1980.[9] There were also numerous pleas for a national
day of commemoration under an umbrella of reconciliation, and by the
mid 1980s, the second Sunday of July was chosen as such a day, described
by Una O'Higgins O'Malley, the daughter of Kevin O'Higgins (who
was assassinated by three IRA members acting on their own initiative in
1927) and who was very active in peace and reconciliation groups from
the 1970s, as 'of a rather understated nature'. Her ambition was that the
Irish could be seen as 'a forgiving and a forgiven people'.[10] But there were
also warnings that an all-inclusive day of commemoration would lead to
an ambivalent blurring and confusing of different historic allegiances and
resistances; relatives of those executed in 1916 expressed disappointment
that, for example, the government was seemingly not interested in marking the seventieth anniversary of the Rising in 1986 and that the families
would have to hold their own 'fitting commemorative events'.[11]

By the end of the 1980s and towards the seventy-fifth anniversary commemoration of 1916 in 1991 there was some resentment of what Declan Kiberd termed the 'elephant of revolutionary forgetfulness'.[12] Dermot Ahern, a Fianna Fáil TD, suggested in 1991 that 'the muted commemoration of recent years reflected a desire to let the world know that there was no link between 1916 and the present IRA campaign of violence', a statement that drew criticism from the 'Reclaim the Spirit of 1916 group' for effectively 'giving political expression to the cult of revisionism'. But there seemed little political appetite to respond to the request of the leader of Fine Gael, John Bruton, that the Irish who died in British army uniform should be included in the seventy-fifth anniversary commemoration.[13] Forgetfulness could also give way to ferocious denunciation; by the time of the eighty-fifth anniversary in 2001, Pearse was referred to by one of his most virulent critics as an 'anti-democratic proto-fascist' presiding over a school where Cúchulainn had been an 'almost a silent member of staff', while one of his biographers, Ruth Dudley Edwards, was insistent that the difficulty with the Pearse legacy was compounded because for so long, 'nobody bothered to learn anything about him'.[14]

What was the impact of the peace process from the early 1990s onward on commemoration? There was no shortage of declarations of change, history making, new eras and transformations in April and May 1998 as the Good Friday Agreement (officially known as The Belfast Agreement) was signed and an all-island electorate, 94 per cent in the Irish Republic and 71 per cent in Northern Ireland, endorsed it. Paul Bew noted that in the aftermath of the agreement, the Irish government's approach to commemoration still cultivated the idea of 'two histories, separate and in conflict', while Roy Foster remarked on 'the development of fashionable neo-nationalism in some sections of Irish opinion in the 1990s'.[15] But how true was the contention of Fintan O'Toole that a more assertive ownership by the establishment in the Republic of the War of Independence legacy would give succour to those who believed that the only difference between a patriot and a terrorist was the passage of time?[16] (When she was interviewed in 2013 about her memories of her parents, writer Julia O'Faoláin recalled that her father Seán, who died in 1990, had 'no sympathy' for the new IRA towards the end of his life; he thought them 'brutal, unlike his lot', but as Julia accurately and succinctly remarked, 'His lot must have been somewhat brutal too if you think about it.')[17]

O'Toole's assertion was a reaction to events in 2001, when the bodies of ten IRA Volunteers were disinterred from the grounds of Mountjoy prison in Dublin for reburial with full state honours in Glasnevin cemetery. The best known of them was also the youngest, Kevin Barry, who was condemned to death on 20 October 1920 for murdering three soldiers and was hanged in Mountjoy prison on 1 November 1920.

Some media commentators complained that the state funerals would function as a cynical prolonging of the Fianna Fáil Ard Fheis (annual assembly), but the Taoiseach, Bertie Ahern, was upstaged by Cardinal Cahal Daly, who presided over the state Mass and funeral and delivered an oration in the Pro-Cathedral in Dublin that emphasised the place in the Irish revolution of the aspiration to social justice, by quoting from the 1916 Proclamation and the First Dáil's Democratic Programme of 1919.[18]

Before the hearses left the jail, a private ceremony was held, attended by about a hundred relatives of the men, who acted as pallbearers while prison officers formed a guard of honour. The cortège then proceeded to the Pro-Cathedral through Dame Street, College Green, and past the General Post Office. Pat Traynor-Sheridan, a grandniece of one of the re-interred men, Thomas Traynor, admitted 'we were nervous of disruption, of people coming out in balaclavas'. There was heckling of the Gardaí when the gates were closed to all but the relatives of the men from some outside Glasnevin cemetery. They cheered raucously when the Sinn Féin leaders arrived – the same leaders who, as some observers knew, were in the process of making an unprecedented move to decommission IRA arms.[19] Whatever unpleasantness such cheering caused, it did not outweigh the genuine and spontaneous applause of pride that came from an estimated 30,000 lining the streets as the funeral cortège passed by. These people seemed to welcome being brought closer to their history.

Bertie Ahern in his oration acknowledged that his party did not own Kevin Barry or his legacy. He spoke of Éamon de Valera, but also of Michael Collins, Arthur Griffith and Desmond FitzGerald, whose son Garret, the former Fine Gael Taoiseach, looked on stoically, bringing to mind a poem about Kevin Barry written in the 1940s by Padraic O'Halpin, which included the line 'He gave not to you or I, we do not own him'.[20]

As early as 1922, Michael Collins had suggested that the provisional government of the Irish Free State should move the bodies out of Mountjoy, but the civil war soon intervened. According to Donal O'Donovan, a nephew of Kevin Barry who wrote an account of his life, *Kevin Barry and his Time* (1989), proposals had been made to move the bodies from the prison in the 1930s and 1940s but agreement from the families could not be secured. The Barry family had little time for de Valera or Fianna Fáil, and initially refused to allow Barry's body to be moved from the prison on the grounds that the aim he died for – a thirty-two-county republic – had not been achieved. At the funeral of Kevin Barry's mother in 1953 the family refused to speak to de Valera, who had to content himself with unveiling a new set of headstones in the prison in 1961.[21]

Hostility to the day's events in 2001 came from individual journalists long associated with critiques of the modern IRA and the bloody origins of the state, but was not widespread in the media. The arguments in opposition to the funerals were almost a carbon copy of the reasons offered in 1991 in opposing any celebration of the seventy-fifth anniversary of the 1916 Rising. Most of the critics argued that these men's actions in 1920 and 1921 were foolish and unnecessary, and the state funerals a glorification of murder. In the weeks before the event Fintan O'Toole had suggested the idea of the state funerals bordered on the 'grotesque' in the aftermath of the 11 September atrocities in America.[22] Even allowing for the emotion generated by the attacks on America, this highlighted the danger of reading history backwards. O'Toole's *Irish Times* colleague Kevin Myers also bemoaned the idea of republicans perpetuating the cult of 'single-sided victimhood'.[23]

During a BBC radio discussion on the state funerals, journalist Bruce Arnold recalled that as a student in Trinity College, he participated in a dreadful one-act play called *Kevin Barry* where the stage instructions informed him he was to act like 'a typical British officer'. The play, written by Gerard Westby in 1953, was indicative of the one-dimensional way young people were taught in earlier decades to view the legacy of Barry, but arguably, the state funerals provided an opportunity to point out how much had changed in that regard; at the prison, for example, prayers were offered in memory of those who were the victims of Barry's IRA brigade.[24]

But just how did political communication relate to collective memory in the early twenty-first century in Ireland? This was a theme addressed by communications academic Farrell Corcoran in 2002. What struck him in relation to state-organised memory was that actions 'that are politically designed to create public consensus often result in generating further social divisions'. In referring to the state funerals of 2001, Corcoran identified a dilemma about the response to it by opponents of the government, as it was 'a funeral timed, planned and controlled in every detail by the government', but those involved with other political parties could hardly be seen to oppose it, given the similar origins of their own parties. Another issue was what these events would mean for how a new generation might view the legacy of Kevin Barry in a country where national memory had been, in Corcoran's view, 'cauterised' by 'revisionism and censorship'. What became clear was that 'there was no unanimity within that memory system about the meaning of Kevin Barry in the political environment of 2001'.[25]

There was an official positioning of Barry 'within an interpretative framework that linked him directly to the mainstream consensus that existed between most political parties and the dominant media that supported the Good Friday Agreement'. Cardinal Daly explicitly linked past and present by suggesting the true inheritors of the legacy of the revolutionary period were those 'explicitly and visibly' committed to the Good Friday Agreement. He excluded the idea of the 'unfinished business' of republicanism in the political sense by emphasising the unfinished business of social justice in both the north and south. Bertie Ahern, meanwhile, focused on the idea of a War of Independence mandated by the 1918 general election and placed those who wanted to 'stretch the democratic mandate of 1918 far beyond its natural term' outside of the fold, while also undermining the 'revisionists' by asserting that what Barry had done was 'precisely what Englishmen would be doing under the same circumstances and under the same provocation'. The response of the president of Republican Sinn Féin, Ruairí Ó Brádaigh, was that the Mountjoy Ten's 'memory cannot be hijacked by politicians who are attempting to calm the Irish people into believing that the British occupation of the Six Counties is normal and the National Question has been resolved by means of the unworkable agreement of 1998'. What the funeral meant, according to Corcoran, was 'the opening up of a discursive space that had been under pressure for a long time'.[26]

The emerging electoral success of Sinn Féin in the Republic – it had one TD elected in the general election of 1997 which rose to fourteen by 2011 – also meant commemoration was open to new ways of manipulation. The decision by the government in 2006 to reintroduce the military parade for the ninetieth anniversary of the Rising was instructive in this regard. When President Mary McAleese introduced a conference on 1916 organised by the history department in University College Cork in January 2006 – 'The Long Revolution: The Rising in context' – she did so under the title – '1916 – a view from 2006'. Kevin Myers described her speech as 'triumphalist, imbecilic and fatuous'.[27] McAleese's address referred in glowing terms to the architects of the Rising as progressive internationalists with broad minds, tolerance and vision; a defiant defence of the Rising. Combined with Bertie Ahern's announcement of the reintroduction of the military parade to commemorate the Rising, a practice that had been abandoned during the Troubles, it led to suspicion that any commemoration of 1916 was not going to be about what happened and why, but how a selective use of the events of 1916 could be employed by those wishing to wrap the green flag around themselves, in order to 'out republicanise' their opponents. Others detected in the gestures and words of the president and Taoiseach a long-overdue willingness to confront self-doubts about the origins and worthiness of the Irish state.[28]

Whatever about the motives behind the decision to make a fuss of the commemoration in 2006, scholars also used these opportunities to continue to produce new and challenging work, and the writers and readers of Irish history were afforded an opportunity to significantly advance interpretations of 1916. In the words of historian Gabriel Doherty, McAleese's speech led to a debate that was 'prolonged, extensive and searching'. That debate also served to rebut the presumption that the historical analysis of 1916 was by any means complete.[29] It also facilitated a focus on forgotten promises and the failures of contemporary policy, as was apparent with the regular use by the Labour Party of the phrase 'cherishing the children of the nation equally' from the 1916 Proclamation: 'an annunciation to the world. And so, for us, it can again be a living document ... we still have a long distance to travel before we can claim to be either nurturing or valuing our children equally.'[30] On the evidence of some opinion polls, it also appeared that the new political environment had made people more firm in their expressions of pride in the Rising: 65 per cent of them according to an *Irish Independent* poll in 1991 during the seventy-fifth anniversary of the Rising, but 80 per cent according to a *Sunday Business Post* poll in the run-up to the ninetieth anniversary.[31]

Some of the most striking images from the military parade in 2006 were not the military ones, but the portraits of people with strong personal connections to the Rising reflecting on their loss. Fr Joe Mallin, aged ninety-two, son of Michael and the only surviving child of any of the executed 1916 leaders, was photographed standing outside a cell in

Kilmainham jail, the same cell where he had visited his father on 8 May 1916, the day Michael was executed. Fr Mallin articulated an uncomplicated interpretation of 1916; it was, he said, 'an unselfish act that gave us our freedom', and he insisted his father and his fellow insurgents 'had tremendous concern for the people'.[32]

In 2006, Middle Ireland looked on approvingly. That the crowd attending the official state parade for the ninetieth anniversary was largely composed of the middle classes was one signal of the new respectability afforded by the peace process to the commemoration of the Irish state's bloody birth. They were the same class of people who turned up in October 2001 to line the streets and applaud the Mountjoy Ten at the time of the state funerals.

Another indication of the changed political landscape by 2006 was the presence of the British ambassador, Stewart Eldon, and the fact that there was not a hint of disgruntlement from the opposition party leaders, who all went out of their way to praise the day's efforts. Granted, a few days earlier Fine Gael leader Enda Kenny had accused Fianna Fáil of using the commemoration for party political purposes, and the original announcement of the plans at the Fianna Fáil Ard Fheis had prompted allegations that it was a cynical stunt to pull the green rug from under Sinn Féin's feet. Of course, there was a measure of truth in that, but the accusations did not stick, because as the plans evolved, and as the debate became animated, the commemoration developed a life of its own, independent of any one political party. That was the reason for its success; the 'national conversation', to use Ahern's choice of phrase, was prolonged and inclusive.[33]

THIRTY-FOUR

REMEMBERING THE FIRST WORLD WAR AND WELCOMING THE QUEEN

Such inclusiveness, however, in light of the peace process, also had to extend to remembering Irish soldiers in the British army in the First World War, an issue that had been problematic since the foundation of the two states. An estimated 40,000 Irishmen died during that war, and remembrance of them worked in different ways in both parts of the island. In the north, the focus was on demonstration of loyalty to the UK and in the south it was usually (though not always) characterised at official level by amnesia: in the words of Catríona Crowe, 'both sides effectively froze the war into shapes or absences that served darker purposes to do with foundation myths for societies born in violence'.[1]

Unionists made much, understandably, of their own sufferings and sacrifice, particularly in the context of the Battle of the Somme in 1916, 'after which nothing would ever be the same again', and it was only in Ulster that Protestants outnumbered Catholic volunteers among Irish recruits to the British army.[2] Inevitably, Somme remembrance became an important part of the Ulster Protestant self-image; from 11 November 1919 Armistice Day in Northern Ireland featured broadly religious events in many towns, though the laying of wreaths at the Belfast cenotaph did not include Catholics.

An Ulster tower situated near to where the 36th Ulster Division had been positioned at the Somme was built by public subscription and dedicated in 1921: one part of the process of ensuring historical validation of the Ulster sacrifice that justified the creation of the state of Northern Ireland. In his speech at Thiepval in Belgium to mark this unveiling, the prime minister of Northern Ireland, James Craig, spoke specifically of an Ulster identity. The following year, in unveiling a war memorial in Coleraine, Craig further declared: 'Those who passed away have left behind a great message to all of them to stand firm and to give away none of Ulster's soul.'[3]

But not all Somme commemoration was bombastic; official memorialisation has been described as 'relatively muted', as 'following partition its only role was to symbolise the sacrifice to Britain and otherwise, like much else in Protestant history, it was largely buried by the Protestant state'.[4] July 1 was taken over by the Orange Order as 'little twelfth', but the idea that Ulster Volunteers in the trenches were wearing sashes and roaring about inspiration from 1690, the year of the Battle of the Boyne, part of the Williamite war which confirmed the Protestant dominance of Irish society, was rubbished by one survivor: 'What nonsense is stuck onto the story ... Nothing was further from my mind than the Boyne on the Somme.'[5] Nonetheless, the 'evocation of the battle on gable walls' gave it a visibility and what emerged was 'a ceremonial emphasis on a single soldier as representative of both the division for whom he fought and the community from which he came', which was not possible in relation to Ulstermen in the Second World War as they were dispersed across so many different regiments.[6]

In 2006, at the time of the ninetieth anniversary, the first year it was officially commemorated in the Republic, it was noted that historically, memory of the Somme 'was absorbed into a partial and sectarian exercise in selective memory that was itself a kind of forgetfulness ... in order to remember the battle as a glorious sacrifice (contrasted to the stab-in-the-back of treacherous Catholics in the Easter Rising) it was necessary to forget its essential obscenity' and, indeed, the presence of Catholic nationalist divisions, but in truth, 'nationalist orthodoxy was happy to leave the Somme to the Unionists and to define it as an essentially British concern'.[7] The difficulty was that it was not a specifically 'British' concern; commemorating the Somme may have been used to recall a time when 'the heart of Ulster beat in time with the Empire', but there was also another consciousness relevant; a specific, local Ulster identity underlined by a sense that Protestant memory never lost its 'foundational fear' and was 'tempered by a note of anxiety'.[8]

Such anxiety also had a class dimension and use of the Somme sac-rifice was inevitably affected by tensions within unionism (the idea that working-class Protestants would see themselves as 'puppets no more') and, by the 1960s, the adoption by paramilitaries of its memory. The modern UVF was established in 1966 on the fiftieth anniversary of the Somme and presented itself as historically validated by using the iconography of the Somme, part of a mythologising process that reduced the past to select events, 'primarily sectarian or redolent of Catholic duplicity'.[9] In 1966 prime minister of Northern Ireland Terence O'Neill, after the UVF's first murder, insisted there was no connection between 'men who were ready to die for their country in the fields of France and a sordid conspiracy of criminals prepared to take up arms against unprotected fellow citizens'.[10]

A few days later, O'Neill was in France to mark the fiftieth anniver-sary of the Somme. At least the government in the Irish Republic had one advantage; 1916 Rising survivors did not have too far to travel to the GPO. In contrast, for the Northern Ireland government the logistics of organis-ing a fiftieth anniversary Somme pilgrimage to Thiepval created concern about legal liabilities. The Ministry of Finance was advised by a solicitor: 'If any of the pilgrims died from natural causes while on the Pilgrimage, I do not see how a claim could be brought against the Ministry ... It is more the principle of taking a considerable number of elderly men abroad at government expense which gives rise to certain problems.'[11] Underlining the growing generational gulf, one of those elderly gentlemen's grandsons noted his grandfather 'was an Ulster Volunteer ... before they let all the cowboys in'.[12]

In subsequent decades, the UVF sought to re-characterise the Somme as an unofficial people's history; a part of the Ulster past that 'owes little to Bourgeois official unionism'.[13] This inward focus only served to highlight the continuity of insecurity about identity: trying to convince Britain that Ulster should not be seen as 'less than British' or 'semi-detached', and the struggle to find an Ulster identity 'shorn of paranoia', more difficult when their slaughter in the Somme 'as a down payment for the reciprocal loyalty of the government' did not carry the same weight or faith.[14] The golden jubilee of the Stormont parliament in 1971 was also difficult to commemo-rate because of the onset of the modern Troubles; the government failed to commemorate it as intended, or to secure a royal visit, and 'in its dif-ficulties uniting disparate forces to organise the events and indeed, in its failure to dictate the form the jubilee would take, the Northern Ireland government in effect indicated it was no longer in control of the state'. By 1971 'Northern Ireland's past was as contentious as its present'.[15] The parliament was suspended the following year and direct rule from Westminster reinstituted.

Whatever about these complications, commemorating the First World War across the border was much more problematic. The IRA killed approximately 200 ex-servicemen during the War of Independence, some undoubtedly because of their British army service. The other side of that coin is that some ex-servicemen became very committed and effective IRA men. There was a degree of silence and ambivalence about the southern Irish links to the war to the extent that by 1967, historian F. X. Martin referred to a deliberate 'historical amnesia'.[16] The notion of amnesia about the war can, however, also be exaggerated. Thousands gathered at College Green in Dublin in the early 1920s on remembrance days – 150,000 poppies were sold in Dublin in 1923, and in 1924, 20,000 veterans assembled in Dublin before an audience of 50,000 – and there are war memorials in towns and villages all over southern Ireland. In 1999 archaeologist Seamus Taaffe pointed out

> the panoply of such memorials on this island is considerable. They include public monuments, memorial plaques in institutions, dedicated buildings, stained glass windows and church memorials. What is remarkable about them is how little is known about their existence. A conservative estimate would suggest a total of 1,500 on the island as a whole.[17]

The war, Jane Leonard argues, was not banished from sight or consciousness; an expanding British legion network ensured large armistice parades in the 1930s, but at the same time, interwar Dublin was 'an extremely unnerving and dangerous place to wear service medals or poppies'.[18] Bernadette McAliskey, who rose to prominence as an Irish republican socialist in the late 1960s, also made the point that it was a myth to suggest that Irish soldiers were forgotten in nationalist areas:

> Much has been made of the fact that there's been a shift in the thinking in the south about the Irish participation in the battle of the Somme, and I think that again is a constructed narrative. When you talk about going back to my childhood, I still remember all the songs I learnt

in my own home that related to Suvla Bay, and not simply the Irish songs of the people who didn't go there, but of the people who did. Because in the real communities of real people, real grandfathers and real fathers died there and they were never, ever forgotten. Never forgotten. My mother bought poppies when we were children. We had Easter lilies on Sunday and we bought poppies.[19]

But there is no doubt the idea of official state remembrance was problematic. A war memorial had originally been proposed for Merrion Square, but this was so close to government buildings that Kevin O'Higgins, Minister for Justice in the 1920s, felt it 'would be to give a wrong twist, as it were, a wrong suggestion to the origins of the state'. But he wanted it understood that he spoke 'in no spirit of hostility to ex-servicemen', reminding fellow politicians that his two brothers had fought, with one of them, Michael, killed in France. O'Higgins went on to represent the Irish government at the unveiling of a war memorial tablet in Westminster Abbey in 1926.[20] It was decided to situate the Irish war memorial, by Edwin Lutyens, at the less central location of Islandbridge, outside the city centre, where from 1939 the British Legion held its Armistice Day ceremony; there was a permanent cancellation of the Armistice Parade in 1971 and the memorial lay decrepit and neglected until its restoration by the Office of Public Works in 1988.

At the time of O'Higgins's gestures, Seán O'Casey's play about the First World War, *The Silver Tassie* (1927) was rejected by the Abbey Theatre in Dublin. Yeats and Lady Gregory had previously done much to defend O'Casey and ensure that *The Plough and the Stars* was staged and its denunciators faced down in 1926 but, according to Colm Tóibín, the rejection of *The Silver Tassie* 'and the consequent alienation of O'Casey stands alone in Lady Gregory's career as an example of mismanagement and short-sightedness'. Yeats thought 'there is no dominating character, no dominating action, neither psychological unity nor unity of action'.

O'Casey was livid and would not be silenced: he wrote to Lennox Robinson wondering if Yeats 'thinks that I would practise in my life the prevarication and wretchedness that I laugh at in my plays?'[21] (a production of the play opened in London in 1929). Other prevarications were apparent; the descendants of Thomas Kettle, the nationalist MP killed at the Somme, had proposed a small monument to his memory in St Stephen's Green in Dublin: 'The project was delayed for twenty years (until

1937) because the Commissioners for Public Works would not countenance three simple words: Killed in France.'[22]

As seen earlier, in 1965 and 1966, Taoiseach Seán Lemass made significant interventions to acknowledge the inappropriateness of ambiguity in relation to the sufferings of the Irish who had volunteered for service in the British army in the First World War ('I also was guilty in this respect') and said they had died 'as honourably' as those republicans killed during the War of Independence.[23] Lemass was born in a part of Dublin city that had provided a large batch of recruits for the British army and many of his contemporaries would have served for economic reasons, underlining the disingenuousness of the assertion of Owen Patterson, the Secretary of State for Northern Ireland in 2012, that 'the suggestion that any of these men enlisted for the sake of a job is completely bizarre or that they went with anything but the motive that they were doing the right thing'. Such a naïve and sweeping statement cannot withstand historical scrutiny. As pointed out by well-known Irish priest Fr Brian D'Arcy, 'My grandfather didn't want to fight for anybody. He had no other job.'[24]

Almost sixty years after O'Casey's effort, another Irish playwright, Frank McGuinness, made a considerable impact with his play *Observe the Sons of Ulster Marching towards the Somme*, performed in 1985 at the Abbey Theatre in Dublin. According to a contemporary of his, when he was writing it in the 1980s, one of the refrains was 'we were never told' in relation to how history was taught at schools and the exclusion of an Irish First World War narrative.[25] The play was widely regarded as a powerful exploration 'of the Ulster Protestant psyche', dramatising the relationship among a group of Ulstermen caught up in the slaughter. It was also, according to Terence Brown, 'remarkable for its compassion, expressed in pity for the fate of British soldiers in that terrible war and in understanding of the effect memory of sacrifice had on the Protestant unionist mindset. The play's metaphoric implications were stark for those in the South who had not attempted such acts of empathetic imagining.'[26]

The same decade, General M. J. Costello, chairman of a group that was formed as a direct consequence of the participation of Irish army troops in 1983 Poppy Day ceremonies, called for troops not to be involved in such ceremonies in the future, and instead press for a national day of commemoration that would honour all Irish men and women who died as a result of war, 'irrespective of the causes served', with Irish defence forces participation, under state control. His argument was that the majority of

Irishmen did not join the British army 'out of loyalty to the British crown', but due to 'economic pressure, misguided leadership, sense of adventure etc. It is accordingly, inappropriate that such men be commemorated by the Royal British legion, which is a British institution.' As Taoiseach, however, Garret FitzGerald appeared reluctant to meet Costello's group.[27] Also in the 1980s, Irish governments were still reluctant to embrace the annual Remembrance Day service at Dublin's Church of Ireland (Anglican) St Patrick's Cathedral; President Patrick Hillery received an invitation from the British Legion to attend and was willing to go, but Taoiseach Charles Haughey refused permission. Hillery's successor, Mary Robinson, however, did attend, as did her successors. Alongside these developments, the peace process of the 1990s gave the Islandbridge war memorial a new profile and greater political importance.

Recognition of a shared heritage was also given much momentum by the opening of the Messines Peace Tower in Belgium in 1998; the tower was built to honour the memory of soldiers from the 36th Ulster Division and 16th Irish Division who fought alongside each other in the British army during the battle of Messines in June 1917.[28] President Mary Robinson had also played her part in 1996 at Westminster Cathedral by laying a wreath to commemorate the Irish who died in the First World War; she also lunched with the Queen at Buckingham Palace. Robinson did this in spite of misgivings by some that this was inappropriate or too much too soon. In November 2005, a ceremony was organised by Glenn Barr, a former Loyalist paramilitary, at the Derry cenotaph to honour all those from Ireland who had died at Messines, including fourteen-year-old John Condon from Waterford (one of the youngest allied soldiers to die in the war). His family attended the event and the tricolour was flown at the cenotaph alongside the union flag. Barr, who worked closely with Fine Gael politician Paddy Harte on these initiatives, commented: 'The whole theme of our work is reconciliation through remembrance for all and that was reflected in the service ... It's been a long time coming to have the British and Irish flags flying together at the Cenotaph here in this city, but I always knew this day would come.'[29]

Journalist Kevin Myers also returned repeatedly to the theme of amnesia, referring to the Orangemen 'celebrating their myths' on the anniversary of the Somme, myths also subscribed to 'by default amongst nationalist Ireland'. He also suggested Frank McGuinness's 'well-intentioned' play was something that buttressed myth; the 36th Ulster Division, Myers pointed out, was not just representative of the six counties that became Northern Ireland, but of the nine counties of Ulster and 'Irish Loyalism generally'. He highlighted the sacrifices of volunteers from Cavan, Monaghan and Donegal as 'especially poignant' as they were subsequently excluded from the new state of Northern Ireland. He also pointed out that 'over 140 men of the Dublin and Wicklow Loyal Volunteers had marched to the recruiting office in Dublin to offer their services when war broke out in 1914, and were enlisted in the 9th Inniskilling Fusiliers serving with the Ulsters'.[30]

This is a reminder that part of the process of commemoration was about proper research into the scale of recruitment, volunteering and death. The exact figure of Irish fatalities is not known; a major source to identify dead Irish-born soldiers was *Soldiers died in the Great War, 1914–19* (HMSO, 1921). In using this, Patrick Casey identified over 30,000 Irish-born fatalities.[31] The true figure is undoubtedly higher; county compilations have augmented the traditional records by using other sources, as seen in the work of Tipperary historian Tom Burnell; for his own county, he suggested the true figure for deaths was 1,499, not the 1,050 recorded by the official memorial records. In the case of Cork, Casey records over 2,200 war dead, but 3,700 have been identified in a research project by using a greater variety of sources; the figure includes soldiers who were not Irish-born, but had become Irish residents through marriage, or had been stationed here for a long time prior to the war.[32] Given these kind of findings, it is likely the number of Irish-born war dead was much higher than the official estimate of the Irish Free State registrar general of 27,405 (a figure which excludes officers) or the 30,000 recorded by Casey.[33] Myers has suggested a figure closer to 40,000, and about 40 per cent of 'Irish-Irish' deaths (as opposed to British-born soldiers in Irish regiments) were of Irish-born emigrants recruited in Britain; many deaths also 'escaped a bureaucratic net that quite simply couldn't cope'.[34]

There was also a new peace process emphasis on 'parity of esteem for the war experiences of Catholics and Protestants ... emphatically in the spirit of the times in the new Northern Ireland',[35] which in the Republic involved an unprecedented formal state commemoration of the Battle of the Somme in 2006. There was also renewed focus in 2008 on the 'forgotten soldiers': those 'shot at dawn', as explored by BBC journalist Stephen Walker. Most of the twenty-eight cases he examined involved those who had histories of ill discipline and repeat desertion, though the court martial system in place was inconsistent and flawed and often failed to follow proper procedure, with class and cultural biases at work. A decade previously, Gerald Orman had argued that Irish soldiers were more likely to be condemned to death by field general court martial than any other national group; later, Peter Mulvany, founder of the Shot at Dawn Campaign, brought this issue to government and public attention; ultimately this pressure secured conditional pardons from the UK Ministry of Defence.[36]

In December 2013, Taoiseach Enda Kenny and British prime minister David Cameron spent a few hours together in the fields of Flanders in Belgium, visiting war graves, laying wreaths and paying homage to the dead of the First World War. It was the first joint visit by a Taoiseach and prime minister to honour the British and Irish men killed in that war as soldiers of the British army. When he made the first official state visit of an Irish president to Britain in April 2014, President Higgins also took the opportunity to underline the historic ties that bind the two countries as a result of the war by quoting Tom Kettle, one of the best-known Irish victims of the Battle of the Somme. Higgins suggested Kettle had died 'an Irish patriot, a British soldier and a true European'.[37] Such joint gestures and language marked a complete transformation in the attitude of the Irish state.

The Messines initiative would not have been possible during the Troubles, but by 1998, President McAleese used it to speak of a visit by Queen Elizabeth II to the Irish Republic, the first visit by a British monarch to southern Ireland since 1911, as almost inevitable. The undisturbed playing of 'God Save the Queen' at the Ireland vs England rugby match at Croke Park in 2007 prompted more assertions about the 'normalisation' of relations.[38] The eventual state visit of Queen Elizabeth in May 2011 was frequently referred to as historic, and with much justification. The visit set a new tone in which different aspects of the legacy of the Irish revolution could be framed, marked and reflected on.

The royal visit gave some momentum to a pressure that was already apparent to ensure the commemorations of milestones of the Irish revolution would be more inclusive than previously. There was opposition to the royal visit by republicans on the grounds that 'our' country is still 'occupied' by Britain, and that in the words of Republican Sinn Féin, 'The Queen of England is head of the British state which has brought only starvation, repression and suffering to the Irish people.'[39] These were depicted as the voices of extremism; the preferred contemporary narrative was the one adopted by Bertie Ahern in his speech at the Palace of Westminster in May 2007, when he became the first Irish Taoiseach to address the Houses of Parliament: 'No two nations and no two peoples have closer ties of history and geography and of family and friendship ... We are now in a new era of agreement – of new politics and new realities ... Solidarity has made us stronger. Reconciliation has brought us closer.' There was a lot more of that kind of rhetoric during the royal visit, as the shoulders of various dignitaries felt the hands of history.[40]

The visit was regarded as a resounding success. Its defining image was powerful in its dignity and its simplicity. Head bowed in the Garden of Remembrance in Dublin, Queen Elizabeth did what she had done countless times in many countries at national shrines. But this was different; because of all that had happened in Anglo-Irish affairs in the hundred years since her grandfather, King George V, was in Dublin, and because she was there to pay respect to those who had died fighting against the British Empire, not to be received by loyal subjects as her grandfather was. That it happened was an indication of confidence on the British and Irish sides that both were ready for a gesture of this significance.[41]

There was also the question of the broader framework for the visit. It was obvious that the British political establishment took it very seriously; the presence of prime minister David Cameron and foreign secretary William Hague was testament to that. It also became clear that while Sinn Féin was opposed to the visit, it was a muted opposition; anything louder would have involved Sinn Féin placing itself in the company of those opposed to the peace process and, given the move of Sinn Féin into the constitutional mainstream, north and south, this was not going to happen.

There was some far-fetched speculation about the possibility of an apology during the Queen's speech at a state banquet in Dublin Castle, ignoring the fact that the monarchy does not anymore intervene directly in politics. The visits that the Queen made, including her presence on the hallowed nationalist turf of Croke Park, the site of the Bloody Sunday massacre during the War of Independence, and her visit to the Islandbridge war memorial, were silent but highly charged confrontations with the difficult past and did not require explanatory royal speeches. What the Queen did instead, when she did speak, was to maintain that it is 'impossible to ignore the weight of history' and she acknowledged, 'with the benefit of historical hindsight we can all see things which we would wish had been done differently or not at all'.[42]

The speech of President McAleese was inevitably framed in the context of the peace process; it was the ultimate exercise in the bridge building she championed from 1997, but there was also acknowledgment of, in McAleese's words, 'Ireland's difficult journey to national sovereignty' and pride in 'how we have used our independence to build a republic'. This was about diplomatic equality; that the Queen was received in the historic centre of British rule in Ireland by the president of the Irish Republic underlined that emphatically.[43]

The process of the massaging or symbolic burying of differences was given further weight by a handshake between Queen Elizabeth and Martin McGuinness, Sinn Féin's deputy first minister in Northern Ireland in June 2012 in Belfast, described on the front page of the *Independent* as 'a miracle of reconciliation' and 'a gesture that would have been unthinkable a decade ago'.[44] Once again the word 'historic' was used liberally, but in this case a more cynical assessment was that this was another illustration of what Ed Moloney had once referred to as 'exercises in management towards already decided outcomes',[45] and was about Sinn Féin seeking to recover from its loss of profile and opportunities in order to stress their leadership and maturity, something that had taken a blow when it chose not to embrace the Queen's visit the previous year.

THIRTY-FIVE

INVOKING REVOLUTIONARY GHOSTS AS THE CELTIC TIGER DIES AND FIANNA FÁIL COLLAPSES

The positive peace process mood music, however, was not going to neatly solve all commemoration dilemmas, and alongside the sense of a new respect for diverse historical narratives and multiple identities, alternative reflections on the revolutionary decade were prompted by the loss of sovereignty and the economic and political crisis that engulfed the Irish Republic from 2008. As a consequence, the revolutionary past and its ghosts were invoked for very different reasons, and too often crudely and simplistically. When a new essay was added in 2011 to the seminal edited collection of T. W. Moody and F. X. Martin first published in 1967, *The Course of Irish History*, it sought to bring the book right up to date, and its conclusion about the Irish economic crisis and the catalogue of depressing developments from 2008, including national bankruptcy and a bailout from the ECB/EC/IMF 'Troika' as well as smaller loans, including from the UK, was that the choice before contemporary political leaders was either continued undermining of competent governance or a 'return to the idealism of the founding generation of the state and restoring Ireland to a position of dignity internationally and its rightful place among the nations of the world',[1] which, arguably, made the assumption that such idealism was noble, clear-cut and uncompromised from 1916–23.

There was much of this hankering after the ghosts of the past going on in the context of the crisis, perhaps most memorably in an emotional *Irish Times* editorial in November 2010 as the Troika arrived, under the heading 'Was it for this?' The despondency and humiliation was palpable, as the editorial invoked the ghosts of the 1916 Rising: 'A bailout from the German chancellor with a few shillings of sympathy from the British chancellor on the side. There is the shame of it all. Having obtained our political independence from Britain to be the masters of our own affairs, we have now surrendered our sovereignty to the European Commission, the European Central Bank, and the International Monetary Fund.'[2]

Much was made of the description 'loss of sovereignty' in the context of that bailout being imposed in 2010. The sentiments expressed in this regard were not necessarily marked by a refusal to recognise that real sovereignty had been steadily diminished over previous decades, especially in light of Ireland's forty years of EU membership. They were framed in the context of a longer history; pride in the achievement of independence and disgust that the impulses that drove the revolutionary generation had, it appeared, been so compromised. The *Irish Times* editorial articulated 'the shame of it all' because 'the desire to be a sovereign people runs like a seam through all the struggles of the last 200 years'.[3] But with the constant assertion of the significance of sovereignty – and a 2014 documentary by veteran Irish film-maker Seán O'Mordha on the history of the revolutionary period was entitled *A Sovereign People* – there was also a convenient sidestepping of the fact that notions of sovereignty were sometimes dismissed in Ireland in 1922; it was, according to Michael Collins, the case that 'our ideal of nationality was distorted in hair splitting over the meaning of "sovereignty" and other "foreign words"'.[4] Perhaps of more relevance to the dire straits the Republic found itself in nearly ninety years after his death, was the fact that Collins's warning in 1922 for the future was not heeded: 'We must not have state departments headed by a politician whose only qualification is that he has climbed to a certain rung on the political ladder.'[5]

The general election in 2011 swept Fianna Fáil from power and new Taoiseach, Fine Gael's Enda Kenny, and the Labour Party Tánaiste (deputy prime minister) Éamon Gilmore sought to depict themselves, in the words of Irish author and journalist Gene Kerrigan as 'The New Liberators'; with a constant reiteration of the notion of winning back sovereignty and 'waving goodbye to the IMF'. In tandem, the cult of Collins was particularly invoked by Fine Gael. In August 2012 Kenny told the annual Béal na Blá gathering:

We are again, as Collins did, having to build, to rebuild, our economy and restructure our institutions [there was little restructuring of Irish institutions in the 1920s] ... In keeping with Collins's ambition, mental force and high ideals ... the government is approaching our task of national recovery with the passion and determination and zeal that Collins would have applied.[6]

Kerrigan argued that this 'juvenile posing' was more about seeking to finish Fianna Fáil off than having a coherent economic strategy for dealing with the crisis, given the craven submission in relation to the burning of bondholders – those who had speculated by buying Irish government bonds and whose investments were guaranteed. Instead 'it [was] a political strategy based on party advancement' but indicated no wider strategy beyond hoping that austerity would balance the books.[7]

The invoking of Collins was not just a reaction to the economic crisis; in the early twenty-first century, dramatic claims and exaggerated conclusions abounded at Béal na Blá, involving a misty-eyed, romantic and selective indulgence for the most part, simplifying what was a complex life and overlooking the anger and confusion of Ireland in the early 1920s. This had been the case even during the Celtic Tiger economic boom. During his oration in 2001, the leader of Fine Gael, Michael Noonan, suggested that, 'Collins had placed a heavy emphasis on the maintenance of public order, the security of life, personal liberty and property.' Presumably that was not a reference to his time as director of intelligence for the IRA, an indication of the tendency to be highly selective when dwelling on his career. In his 2006 oration, for example, Enda Kenny spoke of 'the brilliant west Cork boy, the military genius, and the one-man revolution who made Ireland ungovernable, forcing the British Empire not just to a truce but to its knees'. In 2012 Minister for Agriculture Simon Coveney entered the fray as a warm-up act for Kenny, then preparing for another Béal na Blá address, by asserting in Cork City Hall, that what impressed him most about Collins was 'his mind as a modernist', his championing of exports and competitiveness and his vision of Ireland 'as a place of economic excellence, willing and able to compete in international markets'.[8]

Senior Fine Gael figures continued to find the Collins they wanted in order to address their contemporary priorities, as they had repeatedly done in the past. When making the case for the Collins 22 Society, who were seeking to have a statue of Collins erected outside Leinster House to mark the centenary of his death, Gerry O'Connell, as vice president of Fine Gael, insisted Collins would 'find common ground with the first-time house buyer, the young married couple that have the ground swept from under them under a barrage of stealth taxes and rip-off practices. Michael Collins would find common ground with the people who use our public health services.'[9] There is much truth in the assertion made by British film producer Lord David Puttnam, in his address at Béal na Blá in 2007, that Collins was an example of a life suspended somewhere between history and myth. Puttnam also said he would go to his grave believing that, had Collins lived, he would have forged his own place alongside the likes of Nelson Mandela and Mahatma Gandhi, 'men who, having freed their own people from the shackles of oppression, became icons for peace and reconciliation everywhere'.[10]

That last assertion was fanciful, particularly when the depth of feeling that caused the Irish civil war is considered, and the fact that neither Collins nor his contemporaries had any idea how to free their fellow nationalists in the north of Ireland from 'the shackles of oppression'. Puttnam, however, was hardly going to be measured in his comments. In the late 1980s he played a role in bringing to fruition what became the 1996 Neil Jordan film *Michael Collins*, by commissioning Jordan to write the original screenplay. The film did much to promote the myth of Collins at the expense of others, most notably Éamon de Valera, and the film was almost cartoonish in its depiction of heroes and villains. Historian Michael Hopkinson was accurate in suggesting that Collins can still be seen as 'the essential man in the winning of a large measure of Irish independence'. But to present him as a progressive, left-leaning social democrat, and a champion of a caring welfare state, or an early twentieth-century version of the early twenty-first-century consumer champion, or, indeed, the great modernist advocate of the international markets, was both ahistorical and completely unnecessary.[11] In 2013, Tim Pat Coogan embraced the chance to elevate Collins even further, under the heading 'Michael Collins's expertise could have prevented economic meltdown', to mark the ninety-first anniversary of his death: 'Firstly, it should be said, he would not have allowed the crisis to happen; he was skilled in financial matters ... He organised a superbly efficient Dáil loan and had a banking inspector who attempted to interfere with it, Alan Bell, shot dead.'[12]

But some of the invoking of the glorious Irish patriots was even more ludicrous. When it came to a decision as to whether to publish photographs of Britain's Prince Harry cavorting naked during a game of strip poker in Las Vegas in August 2012, most in both the UK and Irish media were circumspect and decided not to publish them. The *Irish Star* tabloid newspaper, however, had no such reticence; it not only published them but castigated others for not doing so:

> The *Star* is the only newspaper that had the guts yesterday to defy the wishes of Britain's Queen Elizabeth and publish the pictures of Prince Harry in the nude. The other so-called Irish tabloids bent the knee to the British monarchy ... for God's sake, was it for this that the men and women of 1916 fought and died for Ireland's independence?

Gene Kerrigan noted wryly that these words reconfigured the definition of the struggle for Irish independence: 'Our freedom is now defined by our right to publish snapshots of a foreign prince's arse.'[13]

Many who were organising conferences, summer schools and think tanks of various hues also began to look to the past. At the MacGill summer school in 2010, for example, an annual gathering to commemorate the life and work of Patrick MacGill, the writer from Donegal who authored strong social critiques in the early twentieth century, one of the central themes was 'Building a Republic that reflects the ideals and ambitions of its founders'.[14] A simplistic version of the revolution and the impulses that drove it was attractive in austerity Ireland, but so too was the broadly accurate idea that what had been achieved in the revolution was about the active participation and sacrifices of many, and that, it was suggested, was a reminder that if there was a desire to build a republic reflecting the ideals of this earlier period there was a need for a return to genuine public service, which had been sullied so much in recent times by the pursuit of personal profit. This was not just about politicians leading; it was also about challenging the apathy of the general public that was often apparent in subsequent decades in relation to fundamental wrongs, an apathy that endured, as was suggested by Garret FitzGerald in March 2008 when he observed that 'what is quite striking about our society ... is the extreme passivity of public opinion in the face of maladministration by weak politicians'.[15]

The publication of tribunal reports revealing corruption in Irish politics and payments to politicians also invited reflection on the gulf between past and present, particularly because of the findings of the Moriarty

Tribunal. This included investigations into payments to Charles Haughey, leader of Fianna Fáil from 1979 to 1992, and its report concluded that the very incidence and scale of payments to Haughey – he received over £9 million from businessmen between 1979 and 1996 – 'particularly during difficult economic times nationally, can only be said to have devalued the quality of a national democracy'.[16] The report underlined the gulf that existed between Haughey and the civil war generation of Taoisigh (prime ministers) in terms of their perception of public service and the dignity of their office; in 1991 alone, Haughey spent £16,000 on handmade shirts from the Paris luxury supplier Charvet, and had insisted it was appropriate that a statesman should receive financial assistance from admirers. Both Haughey's parents were War of Independence veterans who lived in reduced circumstances in the 1930s when Haughey was a child in Dublin. He was also the son-in-law of former Taoiseach Seán Lemass, whose estate when he died consisted of a modest dwelling in a Dublin suburb.

The Mahon Tribunal's report, as a result of inquiries that lasted from 1997 to 2012, was on another level and served to highlight the dysfunction of a whole political culture. It looked in great detail at corrupt payments for planning in particular, and concluded that corruption

> continued because nobody was prepared to do enough to stop it. This is perhaps inevitable when corruption ceases to become an isolated event and becomes so entrenched that it is transformed into an acknowledged way of doing business. Specifically, because corruption affected every level of Irish political life, those with the power to stop it were frequently implicated in it.[17]

Taking the long view, perhaps the very impulses that created stability and consensus in the earlier decades of independence also facilitated a fundamental neglect of civic morality and citizenship. This neglect ultimately allowed the sort of 'systemic and endemic' corruption exposed by the Mahon Report. Nor was the revolutionary generation free from culpability; some of the revolution's consequences included a dearth of debate about policy, ideology or the consequences of a ruthless centralisation and authoritarianism. As Tom Garvin observed, in 1922, whatever about devotion to national politics, 'these unenthusiastic democrats were qualified in their attachment to democratic ideas and were not prepared to trust people with the power to run local affairs'.[18] This point about trust was vital; in the absence of meaningful local autonomy and owing to an abuse of centralisation, other ways of getting things done were sought, and with that the likelihood of corruption increased. While there were valiant attempts from the 1920s to clean up malpractice in local government, in the long run local authorities were stripped of most of their powers and the few that they were left with, including the power to rezone land, were abused.

Nonetheless, in 1997, at the time of the seventy-fifth anniversary of the foundation of the state, Garvin penned a robust defence of politicians' performances in the context of their success in establishing the legitimacy of the state and its democratic institutions, particularly during times when other countries in Europe failed lamentably to do that. 'Despite their mistakes and sins', he wrote, 'the Irish revolutionaries-turned-politicians got it more right than wrong.'[19] It appeared quite a convincing argument, underlining the achievements of the civil war generation in overcoming the divisions of the early 1920s in order to create stability during difficult times. But the cumulative effect of various tribunal reports, especially Mahon, and the disastrous political leadership, lack of regulation and the ability of bankers and speculators to cause public indebtedness on an unprecedented scale that resulted in the economic collapse, suggested historians and political scientists needed to question or qualify some of their earlier assumptions about the achievements of independence.

The same could be argued about revelations concerning the institutionalisation and abuse of children over many decades. Historically, all societies have gone through fits of 'moral panic' and have sought to condemn, hide and punish those they regarded as socially unacceptable. The Irish moral panic appeared to be particularly pronounced and enduring. The preferred solution – to rely increasingly on incarceration without supervision, when such an approach was being abandoned elsewhere – suited far too many who were obsessed with the visibility of those whose behaviour or existence challenged the notion of the Irish as more chaste, pious and respectable than people elsewhere. The Ryan Report in 2009, which was the result of a commission of inquiry into abuse in state funded, religious run institutions, and contains devastating personal accounts of abuse, deals with 216 institutions, an astonishing number given the Irish Republic's small size.[20] The existence of so many institutions was particularly ironic, given the social aims of the Irish War of Independence. Rhetoric based on improving the manner in which children were treated was an important part of the revolution, with Sinn Féin promising it would make amends for the harshness of Victorian British oppressors. But many of this revolutionary generation betrayed this piety even before independence had been achieved, as seen in Part II of this book.

In terms of national politics, Fianna Fáil and Fine Gael were born of civil war divisions, rather than having competing visions about how to shape society. After the laying of the state's foundations, the practice of politics became about the spoils of the system rather than engagement with ideas about the nature of citizenship. It was about management rather than vision. It was also about, in a society so homogeneously Catholic, abrogating responsibility to the Catholic Church in too many crucial areas, including education and welfare, with a resultant narrow focus on what constituted immorality.

In the last few years of his life Garret FitzGerald occasionally broached the issue of corruption in Irish politics, suggesting in 2010 that the civil war generation through its 'unselfish patriotism' provided a barrier 'to the spread to politics of the socially inadequate value system that we, as a people, had inherited from our colonial past'.[21] This may be too sweeping an assertion, but there is some truth in it. There was more of a premium in that era placed on integrity and dignity in public life and the very fact that some of the founding generation of Fianna Fáil, including Frank Aiken, Seán MacEntee and de Valera, expressed strong reservations about the probity of the Fianna Fáil generation coming behind them suggests that they knew priorities had changed and that quality leadership was threatened. There is a danger here, however, of assuming that the civil war generation was lily-white in this regard, which it was not. The network of alliances, powerful vested interests and pressure groups that was built up and facilitated corruption did not just emerge in recent decades. They thrived initially in a small, protected economy and in a society that was snobbish and hierarchical.

As the Republic edged towards the centenary of the events that comprised the revolution of the early twentieth century it faced stark conclusions: it was bereft of meaningful sovereignty due to bankruptcy, with a governing culture that had been exposed as rotten, and a once dominant Catholic Church some of whose members had been revealed as responsible for a catalogue of horrific abuse.[22] In facing these failings, some commentators returned to the Democratic Programme of the first Dáil in 1919, which was forgotten almost as soon as it was enunciated.

But what distinguished this programme, Fintan O'Toole argued, was the way it defined a republic by what it does, not by what it is ('it shall be the first duty of the Government of the Republic to make provision for the physical, mental and spiritual well-being of the children, to ensure that no child shall endure hunger or cold from lack of food, clothing or shelter'). The late historian Tony Judt was also cited; he made the point in relation to the global economic crisis of which the Irish Republic was one of the most spectacular victims, that 'we have substituted endless commerce for public purpose and expect no higher aspirations from our leaders'.[23]

Veteran Irish political correspondent James Downey was also vocal about a return to the text of another key document of the revolution, the 1916 Proclamation, in the context of a crisis-ridden Republic:

> It's tempting to say that our ancestors won it and that our own gener-
> ation threw it away. Not only tempting but in important respects true.
> Undoubtedly we have lost our economic independence and will take
> a very long time to regain it. But some of the aspirations of the 1916
> Proclamation were never feasible anyway. No country, even the biggest
> and most powerful, has 'unfettered' control of its destinies. Inde-
> pendent Irish governments did not set out to make Ireland either a
> Marxist paradise or a dreamy medieval vision on the de Valera model.
> They set out to make it a normal liberal-democratic capitalist state. To
> a considerable extent they succeeded ... where they went wrong was
> not so much in the excesses of the Tiger years – although these have
> brought us and will continue to bring us much suffering – as in the
> failure and worse than failure, to curb corruption and what we like
> to call gombeenism ... it was endemic before independence. It is still
> endemic ... who thinks the Fine Gael–Labour coalition will eradicate
> the cronyism that tarnished its predecessors? We won't find answers
> to such sad questions in commemorations. We have to seek them in
> the here and now.[24]

But if there was a growing sense that there might be little to cheer about in 2016, in any case, what was the notion of 'Towards 1916' about? In addressing this, some politicians undoubtedly used the revolutionary ghosts to simplify history and serve current affairs. This was encapsulated most effectively in an interview with the deputy leader of Sinn Féin, Mary Lou McDonald, in 2012, when she asserted, in a manner as sweeping as it was erroneous, that the 1916 Rising was not about 'physical force confrontation involving weapons'; it was about 'the men and women of Ireland, the children of Ireland, about political concepts, about good governance, about the sense of the collective, the marshalling of common resources, the distribution of wealth – things that really matter'.[25] It would be hard to find a more contrived reading of the past in order to hoist the Rising on to a contemporary agenda.

NEW COMMEMORATIVE PRIORITIES, SACRED COWS AND THE STATUS OF HISTORY

The revisionism of Mary Lou McDonald that closed the preceding chapter was, of course, a mere continuance of what had always been the case in relation to commemorating the revolutionary period; remembrance of the revolution from the outset had been influenced by contemporary politics and coloured by who was in power and who was seeking power. But another aspect of commemoration has involved historians highlighting new perspectives and new sources, and discouraging the simplification or distortion of history by politicians and propagandists who can contrive a selective approach to the past that is more useful or palatable than the messy historical realities. The peace process and the focus on improved Anglo-Irish relations were also relevant here. In 2013 Cork historian Tom Dunne observed: 'When the event commemorated has clear implications for ongoing conflict and attempts at reconciliation, historians can come under intense pressure to prioritise contemporary political concerns over their primary duty to engage critically with the sources.' He was writing in relation to his experience of the 1798 rebellion bicentenary commemorations in 1998, when the complexity of the period was too often ignored in favour of embracing a 'United Irish Revolution' in order to trumpet the significance of 'shared history' to add momentum to the peace process.[1]

In her address to the Burren Law School in Clare in May 2012, archivist Catríona Crowe, credited the same year as someone 'who has helped revolutionise access to public records',[2] noted that the decade of commemorations

> is capable of all kinds of uses, abuses, interpretations, misinterpret-
> ations, illuminations, mischiefs, sublime new understandings and
> ancient bad tempers ... While the events of 1912–23 are largely seen
> in political terms, conventional, reformist and revolutionary, there are
> many other currents lying in wait for exploration which should have
> equal billing with the big public issues of the decade.[3]

That decade, she noted, was marked by many things, but principally by death. As befitting her role in Irish academic and public life, she observed simply, 'History, if it is to be in any way accurate, depends on good primary sources'; what was needed was 'a new understanding, well supported by good archival evidence with no concession to sacred cows'.[4]

There was also the issue of a new generation asking new questions prompted by the transformed Ireland they lived in, which had also been a feature of previous commemorations. Wayne Jordan, a young theatre director, had little or no historical education before he came to direct Seán O'Casey's *The Plough and the Stars* at the Abbey Theatre in 2010. As someone who grew up gay in Ireland, he found himself with scant sympathy or unable to personally relate to those who fought for Irish nationalism as he 'didn't feel part of that Irishness'. He spoke to the literary director of the theatre 'and she said that these men imagined a different Ireland to what was available to them. And they went out and made it happen. They all sat round and said "This world could be different to how it is now". And I thought, that's really interesting.'[5] But this did not mean Jordan was seduced by a romantic notion of a Celtic new dawn; what he was really interested in was the needs of women. For him *The Plough and the Stars* was about 'impotent men and very potent women, and those potent women's agency being decimated by the romantic nationalism that the men become addicted to in lieu of actually providing for the communities in which they live. I think that's deeply political.'[6]

Measured anger and sadness also seemed to be a part of remembrance as various centenaries loomed. Poet Theo Dorgan, for example, during a TG4 (Irish language) television series on the civil war executions, said:

> I had never given concentrated thought to those reprisal executions,

but the more I think of it the more horrified I become at the idea of reprisals against prisoners. I have always thought the anti-Treaty forces were tactically, strategically and morally wrong not to have made their struggle a purely political one. I find myself equally horrified that our state, at its inception, was so brutally prepared to step outside legality, to fight terror with terror.[7]

Others focused on the idea of rescuing the revolution's forgotten victims from silence. Approximately forty children were killed during the 1916 Rising; historian Ann Matthews maintained the children had not been commemorated due to class; they 'lived and died in the city', were from 'working class backgrounds' and 'are still not considered worthy of a commemorative plaque'. One of the stories she uncovered was of a two-year-old child being shot in the head; almost a hundred years after the event, Matthews maintained that there 'is still a resounding silence about the impact the rebellion had on the lives of men, women and children who for six days lived within a heartbeat of death'.[8] The role of the RIC also received prominence in debates about neglect and amnesia. In August 2012, two retired Gardaí organised a remembrance event in Glasnevin cemetery to commemorate the disbandment of the RIC in 1922 and the DMP in 1925. But for some the fact that the organisers sought official recognition for their gesture was 'bordering on the unbelievable', as critics of the RIC accused it of 'thuggery and brutality' in its policing and its association with the Black and Tans and the B Specials. Others responded that failure to acknowledge them was to perpetuate a denial of remembrance 'of the fallen'; they were another group of victims.[9]

The ceremony went ahead at Glasnevin at a communal grave site where more than 100 RIC members are buried; about 150 attended – many more than the organisers were expecting – to, in the words of the organisers 'pray for the souls of the approximately 549 members of the RIC [some bodies were never recovered] and the 14 members of the DMP who were killed between Easter Monday 1916 and the disbandment of the RIC in August 1922'. They acknowledged that some RIC members 'did behave disgracefully and dishonoured the uniform, but that is not to denigrate the vast majority who joined'. The organisers had hoped theirs would be an official commemoration, but having 'sniffed around' they discovered that this was not going to happen 'so we said we would do it ourselves'. Also present were representatives of the Royal Ulster Constabulary and the Northern Ireland

Retired Police Organisation alongside retired Gardaí whose fathers had been members of the RIC. A 'small group' of republican protestors turned up 'but left after a short burst of heckling'. When the organisers were asked about those who objected due to the RIC's association with the Black and Tans and Auxiliaries they responded: 'We move on. If the Queen can shake hands with Martin McGuiness, it's time we moved on, isn't it?'[10]

One correspondent from London suggested 'it is ironic the only church memorial to the disbanded force is the RIC chapel in Westminster Cathedral' in London, as the majority of the force were Irish Catholics; another pointed out that support for the essential 'decency' of the force was provided in the memoir of Tom Barry.[11] Another correspondent from England wrote simply:

> When my grandmother was being brought up, her own maternal grandfather was never mentioned in the house, so she came to suspect there must have been some great shame in the past. Years later she discovered what that 'shame' was; her grandfather had been a member of the RIC ... when we try to ignore the complexities of history we discover, like my grandmother, that we have lost part of who we are.[12]

The Oscar-nominated Irish actor Michael Fassbender also pointed out that as well as being related to Michael Collins he had a great-grandfather who joined the RIC 'and was disowned by his family'.[13]

The work of Sebastian Barry also made a powerful impact during this era; he used his own family's history for the content of his books, including *On Canaan's Side*, which was longlisted for the Man Booker Prize in 2011. Barry was 'openly obsessed' with the period of Irish history 1914–22, and particularly interested in the middle-class Catholics who stayed loyal to the Crown and then found themselves marginalised. One of his own grandfathers had been a British army major and the other an Irish republican who nonetheless married the daughter of a policeman he regarded as an agent of imperialism. Barry summed up his approach:

> I am trying to rescue my characters from the cold hand of history and from the silences that surround certain turbulent periods in our past ... Ireland's history is so much more rich, exciting, varied and complicated than we had realised. What I'm trying to do is gather in as much as I can – it's not to accuse but just to state that it is so.[14]

Barry's play the *Steward of Christendom* (1995) was based on his great-grandfather, the last chief superintendent of the DMP and the difficulties he then encountered in an independent southern Ireland in which he was ostracised. In *A Long Long Way* (2005) the same man's son fights in the Royal Dublin Fusiliers in the First World War before returning home on leave and getting caught up in the Easter Rising. In speaking about his writing, Barry also elaborated on his views in relation to the Irish in the First World War:

> To be followed by silence, total silence, for a generation, or even longer, ignored, forgotten and left to their horrible wounds and hideous asylums. These men deserved a most wonderful thanks for their ordinary, divine courage. That they were not thanked when they came home was a profound indictment of a state that could not find it in its narrowing heart – though in its own way a brave narrowing heart – to include them.[15]

Eloquent as this is, it is also misleading. These men did not come back to a state, but a country on the cusp of revolution and it could equally be contended that its heart was anything but narrowing.

There were also assertions that the events being commemorated were about the history of one Ireland, the need for a 'radical inclusivity that starts with the notion that there are not two histories but one history with many strands. All the events have to be commemorated as part of the same package, not least because they are utterly intertwined.'[16] And therein lay an interesting dilemma: was that history about one history and one Ireland, or one history and two Irelands? A draft document from the Community Relations Council (CRC) in Northern Ireland in 2011 emphasised that the decade of commemorations 'provide some of the most important opportunities to develop our understanding of how commemoration should be fostered in the public space and arenas. The principles that could underpin this should aim for deepening understanding and respect as well as welcome for difference, complexity and debate.' One of the warnings was that 'if the outcome entails developing or augmenting more destructive patterns of relating, then the action or event can be judged to be sectarian', with 'hardening of boundaries between groups, overlooking others, belittling or demonising others, justifying or collaborating in the domination of others, physically attacking or intimidating others'. It also included a phrase – which could be intensely annoying to historians – 'Remembering the future'.[17]

Gerry Moriarty, writing in the *Irish Times* in January 2012, also warned of the dangers of commemorations being divisive; the need to navigate around the 'icebergs that are the coming decade of sensitive centenaries'. The contemporary rhetoric was around the notion of a 'shared society', but if politicians were to 'play to the baser emotions they will cause trouble'; better it seemed, to 'agree to disagree', with a working group of Belfast City Council, for example, drawing up a model with the title 'Shared history, differing allegiances', including exhibitions, civic receptions, lectures and drama.[18] One of Moriarty's southern-based colleagues, Stephen Collins, continually returned to the subject of the neglect of the constitutional tradition and the role of constitutional nationalism in the creation of 'an independent Ireland'.[19]

The centenary of the introduction of the Third Home Rule Bill in April 2012 was also a chance to rehabilitate the reputation of John Redmond; former Taoiseach John Bruton took issue with an *Irish Times* editorial in April 2012 that had praised his 'moment of triumph' with the introduction of the Third Home Rule Bill, but criticised his 'disastrous miscalculation' of urging Irishmen to join the British army during the First World War, which, Bruton believed,

> underestimates what Redmond achieved and overstates his responsi-
> bility for the Irish casualties in the Great War ... Redmond's position
> was more enlightened than that of the Republicans of Easter Week
> 1916, who explicitly invoked, in their Proclamation, their 'gallant allies'
> in Europe. These allies were imperial Germany, the Austro-Hungarian
> Empire and the Ottoman Empire. The morality of this alliance has yet
> to be seriously questioned, but it should be.

Redmond's risk of calling the Irish to British arms was taken, Bruton argues, because he was trying to vindicate Belgian neutrality and persuade Ulster unionists to come voluntarily into a home rule Ireland (which ignores the extent to which it was justifiable for so many to be slaughtered to achieve that). There was, Bruton insists, no 'better plan'; no one knew how long that war was going to last and in any case, so many Irish would have volunteered regardless: 'Redmond was a realist. Unfortunately some of his successors were not.'[20]

This was, according to one critic of Bruton's analysis, a 'laughable distortion of history' and he suggested Bruton

> might think on the anecdote told by the Republican activist George Gilmore, a Protestant in Dublin who spent his holidays in County Down where his family originated. Gilmore explained that when his train left Dublin he could see a poster urging young men to join the army and fight to 'Defend Catholic Belgium'. But when he arrived in Portadown the poster there read 'Join the army and fight Catholic Austria'. You don't need to be a man of John Bruton's intellect to see that both sets of Irishmen were being manipulated and duped.[21]

While the CRC in Northern Ireland was drafting its documents, an advisory group was appointed by the Irish government to advise the state on its approach to commemorations; its mission statement asserted the need 'to ensure that significant events are commemorated accurately, proportionately and appropriately in tone', that 'there should be no attempt to contrive an ahistorical or retrospective consensus about the contemporary impact and legacy of divisive events', and that 'the state cannot be expected to be neutral about the events that led to its formation'. Gearóid Ó Tuathaigh, a member of the group, suggested the sense of context

> may best be achieved by encouraging the study/exploration of the historical evidence for the social history of Irish people – in their families, communities and associational worlds – during the decisive decade. In effect, this would encourage individuals, schools, and dedicated societies/organisations, to investigate the historical evidence for what was actually happening in their own families, communities, and localities during the decade 1912–23. Rather than seeking, mechanically, to identify the 'impact' of 1913, 1916 etc. on 'my' community/locality, the interesting historical questions would be, 'What issues preoccupied my community, what was happening in it?' during this momentous decade. Thus, the *leitmotiv* of widespread public engagement in the decade of commemoration would be, 'exploring the lived experience of communities in Ireland during the decade of revolution 1912–23'.[22]

This was an approach that would also be facilitated by the revolution in the accessibility of online source material.

There were also warnings about the militarisation of commemorations; James Connolly Heron, the great grandson of James Connolly, suggested 'while it would be absurd to dismiss the reality that our freedom was won through a military uprising' it was necessary to highlight the cultural angle: 'Pádraig Pearse himself said that without Conradh na Gaeilge [the Gaelic League], there would not have been a Rising'; the leaders were lecturers, poets, artists and writers and it was for that reason he and others were calling on the Moore Street site, the last stand of the retreating 1916 leaders, to be 'developed as a cultural quarter' to honour them; this too would contribute through tourism, to 'a crucial way out of recession'.[23] There was also an argument that commemoration could involve silence; that 'there are silent remembering places deep in the Irish psyche that require no flag waving or soldiers marching'.[24] Bernadette McAliskey went further, by suggesting that 'to assemble in the street simply to claim the past is to my mind a tyranny, because the past cannot belong to the present'.[25]

It was also reasonable to assert that any government insisting it was prioritising commemoration and historical understanding deserved charges of hypocrisy if it was prepared to authorise, sanction or encourage the downgrading of the status or study of history. In June 2011, in launching a multi-volume History of Ireland series at the National Library in Dublin, Taoiseach Enda Kenny asserted that

> as we move into the decade of commemorations that stretch before us ... it is imperative that the social, cultural, economic, administrative and political environments that shaped these events be understood ... Reflect for a moment upon our understanding of history. All of us here are of an age where we can remember events that are currently being taught in our schools as modern history – but do we know the facts? ... Subliminally our initial opinion was shaped by how we grew up and what we heard. Many of us went on to benefit from a great education system and solid historical research and made up our own minds ... Interest in history has never been as great as it is now – think of the rise of the History Channels on television.[26]

While Kenny was lauding such projects and the study of history, a curriculum assessment unit was at work with plans to no longer have history as a core compulsory subject at Junior Cert level, the main state exam for those midway through their secondary education. The centrality of history in the curriculum had also been a controversial issue in the UK. Historian and Labour MP Tristram Hunt, for example, pointed to 'far too few students' receiving the vivid history teaching he had enjoyed; there was not just a fall in the numbers taking GCSE history, 'but ... the study of the past is becoming the preserve of the private sector. Our national story is being privatised, with 48 per cent of independent pupils taking the subject compared with 30 per cent of state school entrants. The elimination of the past is nothing short of a national tragedy.' He quoted, approvingly, Eric Hobsbawm: 'Most young men and women at the [twentieth] century's end grow up in a sort of permanent present lacking any organic relation to the public past of the times they live in.'[27]

In 2010 Niall Ferguson – irritatingly, in his view, labelled a 'right-wing' historian – also echoed criticisms made by Raphael Samuel, often labelled a left-wing historian, twenty years previously about history being 'banalised and marginalised' in the school curriculum. The context for Ferguson's probing was the recent global financial meltdown and he invoked the insistence of the Oxford philosopher R. G. Collingwood that the real meaning of history comes from the juxtaposition of past and present. Ferguson offered a robust defence of studying very broad narratives of history in order to understand practical problems of our time rather than focusing on too many unconnected fragments of history. Many, after all, who in the past developed a passion for history, got their interest from grand sweeping narratives that whetted the appetite, prompted debate and disagreement but ultimately stimulated and encouraged inquiring and often provocative minds.[28]

As enunciated by the *Guardian*'s Martin Kettle, the weakness of the British curriculum was that 'Britain lacks a strong enough common culture to support the sustainable teaching of a common history', a problem common internationally in an era of multicultural globalisation.[29] What was also worrying in the UK was the number of schools, estimated at one-third, that merged together history, geography and religious education to create more time to teach 'general learning skills'.[30]

Meanwhile, in the Irish Senate in 2010, the Minister for Social and Family Affairs, Éamon Ó Cuív, a grandson of Éamon de Valera, praised the Irish history curriculum, in the context of a Council of Europe recommendation on history teaching in conflict and post-conflict areas to contribute to greater understanding and tolerance, discussed briefly by Ministers for Education north and south in the context of the Good

Friday Agreement, as a means to 'develop an appreciation of the other'. He added: 'It must be acknowledged that the teaching of history has changed dramatically in our schools. The history programmes at primary, junior cycle and Leaving Certificate now place a key focus on the skills of working as a historian, using evidence from a variety of sources, appreciating cause and effect and developing empathy,' while emphasising that evidence may be open to more than one interpretation.[31]

Concerns about the Irish curriculum were nothing new; in 1995 the Labour Minister for Education Niamh Bhreathnach published a White Paper on Education, 'Charting our Education Future', and there was no mention of history and geography, included in the core curriculum for secondary (though not vocational or comprehensive) schools since the foundation of the state. A campaign launched by the History Teachers' Association of Ireland highlighted the possibility that history might disappear as a compulsory core subject and the pressure exerted worked temporarily, but the commitment given about history in response was not watertight – it was maintained that it would remain a part of the core curriculum, not that it would continue to be a core subject, but rather fitted into some interdisciplinary framework. In autumn 1996 in *History Ireland*, Pauric Travers pointed out that this approach to history had already been tried in the primary schools, and it did not work.[32]

In response to these concerns in 1996, Garret FitzGerald excoriated the 'insidious form of Thatcherism' that had taken over the Irish educational system; a bias towards supposedly 'useful' subjects (that is, economically productive), arguing that if the government was serious about the question of history at secondary level, it should not get 'bogged down in the irrelevant issue of what has come to be called "revisionism" in Irish history', the teaching of which was no longer 'a matter of chauvinist myth-making', suggesting the recurrent controversy over commemorating 1916, and 'the studied avoidance five years ago [in 1991] of any serious commemoration of the 75th anniversary of that event showed that we have not yet come to terms with our history'.[33]

By 'we' he meant his generation; indeed, the first article he wrote for the *Irish Times* when he returned as a contributor after retiring from politics in 1991, was on the 1916 Rising and the inability 'to come to terms' with modern Irish history. He then made the interesting observation that, 'as one of the last of the children of our revolutionaries to be writing about public affairs it is, perhaps, easier for me than for others in public life to address these issues'. He then referred to his 'pride' in his parents' role in 1916 and went on to 'repudiate the right of a tiny minority' to pursue the legacy of 1916 against their fellow countrymen in defiance of the majority. To counteract the argument that this still involved a convenient overlooking of the lack of a mandate for the 1916 Rising, he pleaded for an appreciation of context, pointing out that the 1916 insurgents rose when violence in Europe and war was glorified and seen as noble; there was idealism and courage 'in Flanders as much as in Dublin ... but today? No, for we live in a quite different world ... The truth is that it is only through the study of history that we learn to understand and empathise with a very different past.'[34]

But concerns about the curriculum in 2011 and beyond were particularly timely in the context of the centenary of the revolution, and it was argued that an attack on historical literacy was also an attack on those 'already on the outside' and 'on the idea of citizenship'. The emphasis on historical method 'provides some protection against the manipulation of emotions by distorted and selective histories ... It would be a lovely Irish irony, though, if we were to enter our decade of commemorations with the first generation of children not to have been given a basic sense of their history.'[35]

Nonetheless, the changes to the Junior Cert programme proposed by a national curriculum assessment unit, with the aim of improving literacy and numeracy, were unveiled and endorsed in October 2012, and described as radical and seismic under the banner title 'Towards a Framework for Junior Cycle'. History and geography were no longer to be compulsory subjects; instead, history was alluded to under a statement of learning to the effect that a student would value 'local, national and international heritage, understand the importance of the relationship between past and current events and the forces that drive change' by means of an optional 'short course' or 'learning experience' which could also be fulfilled by a range of other subjects, including Chinese or religious education.[36] History, it was clear, was not going to be taught under this curriculum in a systematic, thorough or meaningful way and could be ignored if that was the choice of the school. This led to a suggestion that 'this would be one of the worst acts of cultural vandalism that could be imagined in our current circumstances'; if students did not have a good grasp of the subject at Junior Cert level they would hardly take it up at Leaving Cert level. According to the State Examinations Commission, the number taking history at Leaving Cert level, out of roughly 54,000 sitting the Leaving Cert exams, was 11,910 in 2010, rising to 12,100 in 2011.[37]

The Labour Minister for Education until mid 2014, Ruairí Quinn, preferred to absolve the state from responsibility to support history, suggesting instead that 'good and enthusiastic teachers in history and geography have the opportunity to inspire a real interest in their subject and so ensure that pupils will want to sit the exam', failing to address the significance of history's blatant downgrading to an optional, ill-defined fragment in the new curriculum.[38] The state was more focused, it seemed, on the perceived need to 're-imagine our future', a phrase used in the government's draft programme for commemorating the centenary of the 1916 Rising, than ensuring that young Irish citizens would have a good knowledge of what happened in 1916 and why.

NOTES

Introduction

1. National Archives of Ireland (hereafter NAI), Department of Foreign Affairs (DFA), Provisional Government, 37/1–2, Report of George Gavan Duffy, April 1922.
2. Public Record Office of Northern Ireland (hereafter PRONI), Papers of Robert Daniel, T2782/31, Cecilia H. Daniel to I. Lett, 3 December 1918.
3. Clara Cullen (ed.), *The World Upturning: Elsie Henry's Irish Wartime Diaries, 1913–19* (Dublin, 2013), pp. 200–201, entry for 21 April 1918.
4. Colm Tóibín, *Lady Gregory's Toothbrush* (Dublin, 2002), p. 88.
5. Conor McCabe, '"Your only god is profit": Irish class relations and the 1913 Lockout', in David Convery (ed.), *Locked Out: A Century of Irish Working-Class Life* (Dublin, 2013), pp. 9–23.
6. Brian Barton, *From Behind a Closed Door: Secret Court Martial Records of the 1916 Rising* (Belfast, 2002), p. 81.
7. Ibid.
8. R. F. Foster, *Vivid Faces: The Revolutionary Generation in Ireland, 1890–1923* (London, 2014), p. 314.
9. Ibid., p. xvii.
10. Colm Tóibín (ed.), *The Penguin Book of Irish Fiction* (London, 2000), p. ix.
11. Michael Laffan, '"Labour must wait": Ireland's conservative revolution', in P. J. Corish (ed.), *Radicals, Rebels and Establishments: Historical Studies XV* (Belfast, 1985), p. 203.
12. Quoted in Margaret O'Callaghan, 'Language, nationality and cultural identity in the Irish Free State, 1922–7', *Irish Historical Studies*, vol. 24, no. 94 (November 1984), p. 228.
13. Foster, *Vivid Faces*, p. 14.
14. George Rudé, *The Crowd in History: A Study of Popular Disturbances in France and England, 1730–1848* (London, 1964); George Rudé, 'The changing face of the crowd', in Ed Harvey and J. Kaye (eds), *The Face of the Crowd: Selected Essays of George Rudé* (Exeter, 1988), pp. 56–72.
15. Ibid.

16. Peter Jupp and Eoin Magennis (eds), *Crowds in Ireland, 1720–1920* (London, 2000), p. 2.

17. C. S. Andrews, *Dublin Made Me: An Autobiography* (Dublin, 1979), p. 208.

18. Dermot Meleady, *John Redmond: The National Leader* (Dublin, 2014), pp. 453–4.

19. Foster, *Vivid Faces*, p. 1.

20. Jupp and Magennis, *Crowds in Ireland*, p. 261.

21. Henry Pelling, *Popular Politics and Society in Late Victorian Britain* (London, 1979), pp. 81–107.

22. Ibid.

23. William Murphy, 'Alice Sophia Amelia Stopford Green', in James McGuire and James Quinn (eds), *A Dictionary of Irish Biography, from the Earliest Times to the Year 2002* (9 volumes, Cambridge, 2009) (hereafter *DOIB*), vol. 4, pp. 232–4.

24. Diarmaid Ferriter, *The Transformation of Ireland* (London, 2004), pp. 123–5.

25. Richard English, *Radicals and the Republic: Socialist Republicanism in the Irish Free State, 1925–1937* (Oxford, 1994), p. 48.

26. Stephen J. Brown, 'What is a nation?', *Studies*, vol. 1, no. 3 (September 1912), pp. 496–511.

27. Ibid.

28. Nicholas Mansergh, *The Irish Question, 1840–1921*, 3rd edn (London, 1975 [1965]), p. 23.

29. James Connolly, *Labour in Irish History* (Dublin, 1910), pp. 139–68.

30. Foster, *Vivid Faces*, p. 146.

31. Patrick Maume, *The Long Gestation: Irish Nationalist Life, 1891–1918* (Dublin, 1999).

32. Charles Townshend, *The Republic: The Fight for Irish Independence* (London, 2013), p. 55; Mansergh, *The Irish Question*, p. 27.

33. Tom Garvin, *1922: The Birth of Irish Democracy* (Dublin, 1996), p. 144.

34. Mansergh, *The Irish Question*, p. 29.

35. Joost Augusteijn, *From Public Defiance to Guerrilla Warfare: The Experience of Ordinary Volunteers in the Irish War of Independence, 1916–1923* (Dublin, 1996); Marie Coleman, *County Longford and the Irish Revolution, 1910–1923* (Dublin, 2003); Michael Farry, *The Aftermath of Revolution: Sligo, 1921–23* (Dublin, 2000); Peter Hart, *The IRA and Its Enemies: Violence and Community in Cork, 1916–23* (Oxford, 1998); John O'Callaghan, *Revolutionary Limerick: The Republican Campaign for Independence in Limerick, 1913–21* (Dublin, 2010).

36. Peter Hart, 'The social structure of the IRA, 1916–23', *Historical Journal*, vol. 42, no. 1 (March 1999), pp. 207–31.

37. Peter Hart, 'Definition: defining the Irish revolution', in Joost Augusteijn (ed.), *The Irish Revolution, 1913–23* (Basingstoke, 2002), p. 30.

38. Louise Ryan, '"In the line of fire": representations of women and war (1919–1923) through the writings of republican men', in Louise Ryan and Margaret Ward (eds), *Irish Women and Nationalism: Soldiers, New Women and Wicked Hags* (Dublin, 2004), p. 46.

39. Brian Ó Conchubhair (ed.), *Kerry's Fighting Story, 1916–21: Told by the Men Who Made It* (Cork, 2010). Introduction by Joe Lee, p. 10.

40. NAI, 3/495/25, Committee on Claims of British Ex-servicemen, 1927–8, box 1, evidence given in Dublin by the Dublin Municipal ex-Servicemen and Dependants Association, 31 March 1928.

41. Catherine Morris, *Alice Milligan and the Irish Cultural Revival* (Dublin, 2012).

42. Foster, *Vivid Faces*, p. 323.

43. Peter Murtagh, 'History of the Rising in our own words', *Irish Times*, 2 November 2013 and http://dh.tcd.ie/letters1916

1 **Opening the Witness Accounts**

1. O'Callaghan, *Revolutionary Limerick*, p. 7.
2. University College Dublin Archives (hereafter UCDA), Papers of Robert Dudley Edwards, LA22/333(141), Bureau of Military History, R. J. Hayes to Robert Dudley Edwards, 14 February 1958.
3. Gerard O'Brien, *Irish Governments and the Guardianship of Historical Records, 1922–1972* (Dublin, 2004), pp. 140–47.
4. UCDA, LA22/333(34), Papers of Robert Dudley Edwards, Dudley Edwards note of 21 July 1951.
5. Ibid., LA22/333, R. J. Hayes to Robert Dudley Edwards, 22 February 1958.
6. Ronan Fanning, 'Richard Mulcahy', *DOIB*, vol. 6, pp. 746–52.
7. See, for example, Cormac K. H. O'Malley and Cormac Ó Comhraí, *The Men Will Talk to Me: Galway Interviews by Ernie O'Malley* (Cork, 2013), p. 7; Foster, *Vivid Faces*, p. 310.
8. Irish Military Archives, Cathal Brugha Barracks, Dublin (hereafter IMA), Bureau of Military History (hereafter BMH), Witness Statement (hereafter WS) 632, Elizabeth Bloxham and WS450, Bridget O'Mullane.
9. Catríona Crowe (ed.), *Guide to the Military Service (1916–1923) Pensions Collection* (Dublin, 2012).
10. Ibid., p. 67.
11. Ibid., p. 71.
12. Ibid., p. 124.
13. IMA, Military Service Pensions Collection (hereafter MSPC), ID178: James Connolly, Nora Connolly O'Brien to 'Seamus', 9 July 1941.
14. IMA, MSPC, MSP34, REF57456, Thomas Barry: Tom Barry to Registration Board, 29 January 1940.

2 **Who Owned the Revolution?**

1. Ernie O'Malley, *The Singing Flame* (Dublin, 1978), pp. 278–9.
2. NAI, Papers of George Gavan Duffy, 1125/15, 'Voice recording made for the Bureau by the Hon. George Gavan Duffy, President of the High Court', 20 January 1951.
3. *Irish Times*, 9 April 2014 and *Sunday Business Post*, 13 April 2014.
4. Jude Collins (ed.), *Whose Past Is It Anyway?* (Dublin, 2012), p. 112.
5. Kevin O'Higgins, *Three Years' Hard Labour: An Address Delivered to the Irish Society At Oxford University* (1924), p. 7 University College Dublin Library Special Collections (hereafter UCDLSC).
6. Ibid., p. 8.
7. Ibid.
8. George Russell, 'Lessons of Revolution', *Studies*, vol. 12, no. 45 (March 1923), pp. 1–6.
9. Diarmaid Ferriter, 'Beyond the Beyonds', in *The Plough and the Stars* (Abbey Theatre, Dublin, 2010), pp. 6–8.
10. Seán O'Casey, *Three Dublin Plays*, introduced by Christopher Murray (Dublin, 1998).
11. Ferriter, 'Beyond the Beyonds'.
12. Fintan O'Toole, 'Rising to the challenge', *Irish Times*, 23 April 2011.
13. Máire Nic Shiubhlaigh, *The Splendid Years* (Dublin, 1955), p. xvi.

3   The History Wars

1. UCDA, P80/302, Papers of Desmond and Mabel FitzGerald, 18–20 August 1922.
2. Michael Laffan, 'Arthur Griffith', *DOIB*, vol. 4, pp. 277–86. An Irish Language biography of Griffith was published in 1953, Seán O'Luing's *Art Ó Griofa* (Dublin, 1953). See also Richard Davis, *Arthur Griffith and Non-Violent Sinn Féin* (Dublin, 1974), p. xiii.
3. W. A. Phillips, *The Revolution in Ireland, 1906–23*, 2nd edn (London, 1926), p. v.
4. Ibid., p. vii.
5. Ibid., p. 177.
6. 'Recent Irish History', *Irish Times*, 5 March 1926.
7. *Irish Times*, 16 November 1923.
8. NAI, Department of Taoiseach (hereafter DT), S13081A, Irish History Research, Bureau of Military History, 7 December 1933.
9. Ibid., Tomás Derrig to Minister for Defence.
10. Eileen McGough, *Diarmuid Lynch: A Forgotten Irish Patriot* (Cork, 2013), p. 9.
11. *Irish Times* display advertisement, 1 August 1924.
12. *Irish Times*, 17 October 1927.
13. Dan Breen, *My Fight for Irish Freedom* (Dublin, 1924), pp. 38–59.
14. Peadar O'Donnell, *The Gates Flew Open: An Irish Civil War Prison Diary* (Cork, 2013), p. 3.
15. Desmond Greaves, *Liam Mellows and the Irish Revolution* (London, 1971), p. 365.
16. UCDA, P17/A18, Papers of Ernie O'Malley, 17 September 1922.
17. Michael Laffan, *The Resurrection of Ireland: The Sinn Féin Party, 1916–1923* (Cambridge, 1999), p. 423.
18. Patrick Murray, 'Obsessive historian: Éamon de Valera and the policing of his reputation', *Proceedings of the Royal Irish Academy*, 101 C (2001), pp. 37–65.
19. Ibid.
20. Deirdre McMahon, '"A worthy monument to a great man": Piaras Béaslaí's life of Michael Collins', *Bullán*, vol. 2 (Winter/Spring 1996), pp. 55–67.
21. Ibid.
22. P. S. O'Hegarty, *The Victory of Sinn Féin* (Dublin, 1924), p. 66.
23. UCDA, P152/193, George Gavan Duffy Papers, Gavan Duffy to Mary Childers, 16 July 1935.
24. UCDA, P155/13, Kathleen O'Connell Papers, Éamon de Valera to Kathleen O'Connell, 19 January 1924.
25. Cormac K. H. O'Malley, 'Publication History of *On Another Man's Wound*', *New Hibernia Review*, vol. 7, no. 3 (Autumn 2003), pp. 136–9.
26. Ibid.
27. John McGahern, 'Return of the Revolutionary', *Irish Times*, 8 June 2002.
28. Richard English, *Ernie O'Malley: IRA Intellectual* (Oxford, 1998).
29. Ibid.
30. UCDA, P155, Kathleen O'Connell Papers, Éamon de Valera to Kathleen O'Connell, 23 September 1935.
31. Risteard Mulcahy, *Richard Mulcahy (1886–1971): A Family Memoir* (Dublin, 1999), p. 94.
32. Desmond Ryan, *The Man Called Pearse* (Dublin, 1919), p. 3.
33. UCDA, LA10/J, Papers of Desmond Ryan, copy book entries for 24–30 June 1917 and 25–27 July.
34. Ibid., entries for 25–27 July 1917, pp. 47–57.

35. Kathleen Kirwan, *Towards Irish Nationalism: A Tract: Offered in Awe and Reverence to the Sublime Patience and Agonised Endurance of the Exploited People of Ireland* (Dublin, 1938).

4   The Fighting Stories

1. Brian Ó Conchubhair (ed.), *Dublin's Fighting Story, 1916–21: Told by the Men Who Made It* (Cork, 2009 [1948]), p. 9.
2. Ibid., p. 7.
3. Ibid., p. 10.
4. Ó Conchubhair (ed.), *Dublin's Fighting Story*, pp. 426–34.
5. Ibid., p. 19.
6. Tom Garvin, *Preventing the Future: Why Was Ireland so Poor for so Long?* (Dublin, 2004), p. 309.
7. Diarmuid Breathnach, 'Rock and hedge', *Capuchin Annual* (1952), p. 114.
8. Seán O'Faoláin, '1916–41: tradition and creation', *The Bell*, vol. 2, no. 1 (April 1941), pp. 5–13.
9. *Father Matthew Record*, vol. 36, no. 2 (February 1943), p. 5.
10. Fr Henry Anglin, 'Reamhrá', *Capuchin Annual* (1966), p. 152.
11. Seán O'Faoláin, 'One world', *The Bell*, vol. 8, no. 6 (September 1944), pp. 461–72; Seán O'Faoláin, 'The Gaelic Cult', *The Bell*, vol. 9, no. 3 (December 1944), pp. 185–96.
12. F. X. Martin, '1916 – myth, fact and mystery', *Studia Hibernica*, no. 7 (1967), pp. 7–127.
13. Alvin Jackson, 'Unionist history', *Irish Review*, vol. 1, no. 1 (Spring 1993), pp. 58–67.
14. Bridget Hourican, 'Roland McNeill', *DOIB*, vol. 6, pp. 163–4.
15. Henry Maxwell, *Ulster Was Right* (London, 1934), p. 233.
16. Henry Harrison, *Ulster and the British Empire: Help or Hindrance?* (London, 1939), p. 28.
17. Hugh Shearman, *Not an Inch: A Study of Northern Ireland and Lord Craigavon* (London, 1942), p. 80.
18. Review of Shearman's *Not an Inch* by R. M. Henry, *Irish Historical Studies*, vol. 4, no. 15 (March 1945), pp. 282–3.
19. Linde Lunny, 'James Armour', *DOIB*, vol. 1, pp. 153–4.
20. Jackson, 'Unionist histories', p. 65 and Martin, '1916 – myth, fact and mystery'.
21. Alvin Jackson, 'Unionist myths, 1912–85', *Past and Present*, no. 136 (August 1992), pp. 164–85.

5   Closing Young Minds?

1. Seán Farren, *The Politics of Irish Education, 1920–1965* (Belfast, 1995), p. 133.
2. Brian Walker, *Past and Present: History, Identity and Politics in Ireland* (Belfast, 2000), p. 105.
3. Peter Collins, 'History teaching in Northern Ireland', *History Ireland*, vol. 3, no. 1 (1995), p. 48.
4. *Report of National Programme Conference* (Dublin, 1922), p. 5; Francis T. Holohan, 'History teaching in the Irish Free State, 1922–35', *History Ireland*, vol. 2, no. 4 (Winter 1994), pp. 53–5.
5. David Fitzpatrick, 'The futility of history: a failed experiment in Irish education', in Ciaran Brady (ed.), *Ideology and the Historians* (Dublin, 1991), pp. 168–87.
6. Ibid.

7. Gabriel Doherty, 'National identity and the study of Irish history', *English Historical Review*, vol. III, no. 441 (April 1996), pp. 324–49.

8. Lawrence W. McBride, 'Young readers and the learning and teaching of Irish history, 1870–1922', in Lawrence W. McBride (ed.), *Reading Irish Histories: Texts, Contexts and Memory in Modern Ireland* (Dublin, 2003), pp. 80–118, and pp. 101–2.

9. Mary Hayden and George Moonan, *A Short History of the Irish People, Part II, 1603–1924* (Dublin, 1927), p. iii.

10. Ibid., pp. 556–69.

11. Diarmaid Ferriter, 'Mary Teresa Hayden', *DOIB*, vol. 4, pp. 531–2.

12. C. J. Woods, 'James Carty', *DOIB*, vol. 2, pp. 398–9.

13. Eileen F. Webster, 'History in our schools', *The Bell*, vol. 7, no. 3 (December 1943), pp. 192–200.

14. R. F. Foster, 'History and the Irish question', in Ciaran Brady (ed.), *Interpreting Irish History: The Debate on Historical Revisionism, 1938–1994* (Dublin, 1994), pp. 122–46.

15. PRONI, Home Office (hereafter HO), 5/47, 'Teaching of history in Irish republican schools', memorandum by G. D. Anderson, 6 August 1958.

16. Ibid., J. Chadwick to T. Green, 14 August 1958.

17. *Irish Times*, 30 October 1957.

18. Tom Garvin, *News from a New Republic: Ireland in the 1950s* (Dublin, 2010), p. 11.

19. Gene Kerrigan, *Another Country: Growing Up in 1950s Ireland* (Dublin, 1998), pp. 163–7.

20. Mark Tierney and Margaret Mac Curtain, *The Birth of Modern Ireland* (Dublin, 1969), p. 188.

21. Margaret Mac Curtain et al., 'The Teaching of History in Irish Schools', *Administration*, no. 15, vol. 4 (1967), pp. 268–85.

22. Ibid.

23. Elma Collins, 'The origin and early years of the History Teachers' Association of Ireland', *Stair*, Journal of the HTAI (2013), p. 11.

24. Ibid.

25. Ibid.

26. *Irish Times*, 8 September 1973.

6   Keepers of the Revolutionary Flame

1. UCDA, P53/297–308 and 315, Papers of Michael Hayes, 1965–74.

2. UCDA, P53/319, October 1964.

3. UCDA, P53/325, November 1965.

4. *Irish Times*, 1 March 1975.

5. UCDA, P24/1266, Papers of Ernest Blythe, Basil Chubb to Blythe, 16 April 1960, P24/1216, Blythe to Hector Legge, 6 December 1949; P24/1225, Michael Rooney to Blythe, 21 December 1966; P24/1253–4, John E. Sayers to Blythe, January 1963.

6. UCDA, P24/1249, Ernest Blythe to the editor of the *Irish Independent*, 17 April 1968.

7. *Irish Times*, 17 July 1962; *Irish Independent*, 17 July 1962; *Irish Press*, 19 July 1962; Maurice Gorham, *Forty Years of Irish Broadcasting* (Dublin, 1967); Michael Hopkinson, *Green Against Green: The Irish Civil War* (Dublin, 1988); Garvin, *1922*.

8. 'Blythe on the Treaty', *Irish Times*, 4 October 1965.

9. Ibid.

10. UCDA, P24/1455, Papers of Ernest Blythe, Seán MacEoin to Blythe, 4 October 1965.

11. Ibid., J. J. McElligott to Ernest Blythe, 4 October 1965.

12. *Irish Times*, 12–15 July 1966.
13. Ibid., 14 July 1966.
14. Ibid., 15 July 1966.
15. Ibid.
16. Leon O'Broin, 'The Fenians and after', *Irish Times*, 4 January 1969.
17. Ibid.
18. Calton Younger, *Ireland's Civil War* (London, 1979 [1968]), p. 87.
19. Obituary of Calton Younger, *Telegraph*, 3 February 2014.
20. Michael Hayes, 'Dáil Éireann and the Irish civil war', *Studies*, vol. 58, no. 229 (Spring, 1969), pp. 1–23.
21. *Dáil Éireann Debates*, 6 January 1922.
22. Gerard O'Brien, 'The record of the first Dáil debates', *Irish Historical Studies*, vol. 28, no. 111 (May 1993), pp. 306–9.
23. Hayes, 'Dáil Éireann and the Irish civil war'.
24. Maryann Gialanella Valiulis, 'The man they could never forgive: the view of the opposition: Éamon de Valera and the civil war', in J. P. O'Carroll and John A. Murphy (eds), *De Valera and His Times* (Cork, 1986), pp. 92–102.

7 **Broadening the Interpretations and the Sources**

1. R. F. Foster, 'Francis Stewart Leland Lyons', *DOIB*, vol. 5, pp. 667–8.
2. Deirdre McMahon, 'The 1926 Imperial Conference and Kevin O'Higgins's proposals for a dual monarchy', *Analecta Hibernica*, no. 44 (2013), pp. 99–121.
3. Terence de Vere White, 'A pride of lions', *Irish Times*, 1 May 1971.
4. R. F. Foster, *The Irish Story: Telling Tales and Making It Up in Ireland* (London, 2001), pp. 37–58.
5. Mansergh, *The Irish Question*, p. 19.
6. Michael Laffan, 'New variations on an old theme: recent works on Irish history, 1914–1922', *Stair*, Journal of the HTAI, vol. 2 (1979), pp. 11–13.
7. Ibid.
8. Stephen Gwynn, *John Redmond's Last Years* (London, 1919), p. 325.
9. Paul Bew, *John Redmond* (Dundalk, 1996), p. 5; Denis Gwynn, *The Life of John Redmond* (London, 1932).
10. Maurice Moynihan (ed.), *Speeches and Statements of Éamon de Valera, 1917–1973* (Dublin, 1980), pp. 576–8.
11. Jackson, 'Unionist history', p. 63.
12. Ibid., p. 65.
13. Henry Patterson, *Class, Conflict and Sectarianism: The Protestant Working Class and the Belfast Labour Movement, 1868–1920* (Belfast, 1980), pp. 84–5.
14. Patrick Buckland, *James Craig* (Dublin, 1980), p. 98.
15. Alvin Jackson, 'James Camlin Beckett', *DOIB*, vol. 1, pp. 401–3.
16. J. C. Beckett, *The Anglo-Irish Tradition* (London, 1976), pp. 94ff.
17. O'Brien, *Guardianship of Historical Records*, pp. 87–94.
18. Ibid., p. 99.
19. United Kingdom National Archives, Kew (hereafter UKNA), DO, 160/6, C. W. Dixon, PRO, to A. Woods, Cabinet Office, 14 February 1963.
20. Ibid., J. D. Woods to Charles Dixon, 21 February 1963.
21. Ibid., C. D. Overton to Costley, 5 November 1963.
22. O'Brien, *Guardianship of Historical Records*, p. 108.

23. Diarmaid Ferriter, *Ambiguous Republic: Ireland in the 1970s* (London, 2012), pp. 231–43.

24. Alisa C. Holland, 'Anecdote on anarchy: the foundation years of the ISA', *Irish Archives*, vol. 17 (2010), pp. 4–16.

25. Ibid.

26. O'Brien, *Guardianship of Historical Records*, pp. 1–14.

27. Deirdre McMahon and Michael Kennedy, *Reconstructing Ireland's Past: A History of the Irish Manuscripts Commission* (Dublin, 2009), pp. 46–82.

28. NAI, DT, 2006/133/520, 'State Paper Office: transfer of files to', Department of Taoiseach memorandum, 15 April 1976 and notes for the Taoiseach, 13 January 1971.

29. Ibid., Jack Lynch to Liam Cosgrave, 9 February 1971 and *Irish Independent*, 28 January 1971.

30. NAI, DT, 2008/148/356, 'State Paper Office: transfer of files to', Dan O'Sullivan to O'Riordáin, 5 September 1977.

31. Editor, 'Robert Walter Dudley Edwards', *Irish Archives* 1 (1989), pp. 8–9.

32. Deirdre McMahon, 'Robert Dudley Edwards (1909–1988) and Irish Archives', *Irish Archives*, vol. 17, no. 21 (2010), pp. 1–14.

33. Foster, *Vivid Faces*, pp. 1–11. Foster draws extensively on the National Library collections in this book.

8   New Scepticisms, New Revisions and the Shadow of the Troubles

1. Roland Tormley, 'The construction of national identity through primary school history: the Irish case', *British Journal of Sociology*, vol. 27, no. 3 (July 2006), pp. 311–24.

2. Ibid.

3. Ibid.

4. David Harkness, *History and the Irish* (Belfast, 1976), pp. 1–15.

5. Karin Fischer, 'University historians and their role in the development of a "shared" history in Northern Ireland schools, 1960s–1980s', *History of Education*, vol. 40, no. 2 (March 2011), pp. 241–53.

6. Ibid.

7. Martin, '1916: myth, fact and mystery'.

8. Patrick Maume, 'Francis Shaw', online entry to *DOIB*, added December 2013, http://dib.cambridge.org

9. Francis Shaw, 'The canon of Irish history: a challenge', *Studies*, vol. 61, no. 242 (Summer 1972), pp. 117–51.

10. Seán O'Faoláin, 'A portrait of the artist as an old man', *Irish University Review*, vol. 6, no. 1 (Spring 1976), pp. 10–19.

11. *Irish Times*, 12 and 15 November 1979.

12. Michael Laffan, 'Insular attitudes: the revisionists and their critics', in Máirín Ní Dhonnchadha and Theo Dorgan (eds), *Revising the Rising* (Dublin, 1991), pp. 106–22.

13. John M. Regan, *Myth and the Irish State* (Dublin, 2014).

14. David Fitzpatrick, 'Dr Regan and Mr Snide', *History Ireland*, vol. 20, no. 3 (May 2012), pp. 12–13 and NAI, DT, S1031A, Memorandum from Irish Committee of Historical Sciences (January 1943), Robert Dudley Edwards to Florrie O'Donoghue, 9 April 1946.

15. F. S. L. Lyons, 'The dilemma of the Irish contemporary historian', *Hermathena*, no. 115 (Summer 1973), pp. 45–57.

16. Fitzpatrick, 'Dr Regan and Mr Snide'.

17. Eamon O'Flaherty, 'Michael Laffan: portrait of a historian', in Susannah Riordan and Diarmaid Ferriter (eds), *The Irish Revolution: Essays in Honour of Michael Laffan* (Dublin, 2015), pp. 19–34.

18. John Bowman, *De Valera and the Ulster Question, 1917–73* (Oxford, 1982), pp. 35–89 and p. 308.

19. Michael Hopkinson, *The Irish War of Independence* (Dublin, 2000), pp. 198–204.

20. R. F. Foster, *Modern Ireland, 1600–1972* (London, 1988), pp. 494–515.

21. Arthur Mitchell, *Revolutionary Government in Ireland: Dáil Éireann, 1919–22* (Dublin, 1995), pp. x, 334–41; Mary Kotsonouris, *Retreat from Revolution: The Dáil Courts, 1920–24* (Dublin, 1994).

22. Terence Brown, *Ireland: A Social and Cultural History, 1922–2002* (London, 2004), p. 277.

23. Liam Harte and Yvonne Whelan (eds), *Ireland Beyond Boundaries: Mapping Irish Studies in the Twenty-first Century* (Dublin, 2007), p. 95.

24. Tom Garvin, 'The Rising and Irish democracy', in Ní Dhonnchadha and Dorgan (eds), *Revising the Rising*, pp. 21–9.

25. Alvin Jackson, 'What if home rule had been enacted in 1912?', in Niall Ferguson (ed.), *Virtual History* (London, 1997), pp. 175–228.

26. Ronan Fanning, 'The great enchantment: uses and abuses of modern Irish history', in James Dooge (ed.), *Ireland in the Contemporary World* (Dublin, 1986), pp. 131–48.

27. Ibid.

28. Ibid.

29. Ronan Fanning, 'The British dimension', *The Crane Bag*, vol. 8, no. 1 (1984), pp. 41–52.

30. Brendan Bradshaw, 'Nationalism and historical scholarship in modern Ireland', *Irish Historical Studies*, vol. 26, no. 104 (November 1989), p. 333.

31. Ibid., pp. 341–2.

32. Interview with Brendan Bradshaw, *History Ireland*, vol. 1, no. 1 (Spring 1993), pp. 53–5.

33. Thomas Bartlett, *Ireland: A History* (Cambridge, 2010), p. 443.

34. Hugh Kearney, 'The Irish and their history', *History Workshop*, no. 31 (Spring 1991), pp. 149–55.

35. Garvin, *1922*; Tom Garvin, 'Revolutionaries turned politicians: a painful, confusing metamorphosis', *Irish Times*, 6 December 1997.

36. Regan, *Myth and the Irish State*, pp. 39–45.

37. Ciaran Brady, 'Constructive and instrumental: the dilemma of Ireland's first new historians', in Brady (ed.), *Interpreting Irish History*, pp. 3–35.

9   Labour, Gender and the Social Perspective

1. Roisín Higgins, *Transforming 1916: Meaning, Memory and the Fiftieth Anniversary of the Easter Rising* (Cork, 2012), p. 176.

2. Anthony Coughlan, 'Desmond Greaves, 1913–1988: an obituary essay', *Saothar*, vol. 14 (1989), pp. 5–17.

3. Ibid.

4. UCDA, P29/C7, De Courcey Ireland Papers, Wolfe Tone Society, 1969.

5. Ibid., P29/C10, Anti-imperialist festival, July–August 1974.

6. Ibid., P29/G63, John de Courcey Ireland to David Thornley, c. 1973.

7. Arthur Mitchell, 'William O'Brien (1881–1968) and the Irish labour movement', *Studies*, vol. 60, nos 239–40 (Autumn/Winter, 1971), pp. 311–31.

8. Emmet O'Connor, 'An age of agitation', *Saothar*, vol. 9 (1983), pp. 64–7.

9. Ibid.

10. Arthur Mitchell, *Labour in Irish Politics, 1890–1930: The Irish Labour Movement in an Age of Revolution* (Dublin, 1974).

11. Emmet O'Connor, 'A historiography of Irish labour', *Labour History Review*, vol. 60, no. 1 (Spring 1995), pp. 21–34.

12. Ibid.

13. Liam Cahill, *Forgotten Revolution: The Limerick Soviet, 1919 – A Threat to British Power in Ireland* (Dublin, 1990), pp. 105–32.

14. O'Connor, 'Historiography of Irish labour'.

15. Ibid.

16. Arthur Mitchell, 'The course of Irish labour history', *Saothar*, vol. 22 (1997), pp. 101–7.

17. Donal Nevin, *James Connolly: A Full Life* (Dublin, 2005).

18. Ibid., p. 157.

19. Ibid., p. 218.

20. Emmet O'Connor, 'James Larkin', *DOIB*, vol. 5, pp. 318–22.

21. 'A supreme storyteller whose life remained true to trade unionism', *Irish Times* obituary of James Plunkett, 31 May 2003; Godeleine Carpentier, 'Dublin and the drama of Larkinism: James Plunkett's *Strumpet City*', in Patrick Rafroidi and Maurice Harmon (eds), *The Irish Novel in Our Time* (Lille, 1975), p. 213.

22. Pádraig Yeates, *Lockout: Dublin, 1913* (Dublin, 2000), pp. x and xxviii.

23. Emmet O'Connor, *James Larkin* (Cork, 2002).

24. Tom Garvin, 'The anatomy of a nationalist revolution: Ireland, 1858–1928', *Comparative Studies in Society and History*, vol. 28, no. 3 (July 1986), pp. 468–501.

25. Ibid.

26. Ernie O'Malley, *On Another Man's Wound* (Dublin, 1979), p. 144.

27. John Borgonovo, *The Dynamics of War and Revolution: Cork City, 1916–18* (Cork, 2013), pp. 38, 80 and 141.

28. Fergus Campbell, *Land and Revolution: Nationalist Politics in the West of Ireland, 1891–1921* (Oxford, 2005).

29. Coleman, *Longford and the Irish Revolution*, pp. 149–79.

30. O'Callaghan, *Revolutionary Limerick*, pp. 54–8.

31. Pádraig Yeates, *A City in Wartime: Dublin, 1914–18* (Dublin, 2011).

32. Margaret Mac Curtain, *Ariadne's Thread: Writing Women into Irish History* (Dublin, 2008), pp. 13–41.

33. Cited in Ruth Taillon, *When History Was Made: The Women of 1916* (Belfast, 1996), p. ii.

34. Margaret Ward, *Unmanageable Revolutionaries: Women and Irish Nationalism* (London, 1995), p. 2.

35. Joan Hoff, 'The impact and implications of women's history', in Maryann Gialanella Valiulis and Mary O'Dowd (eds), *Women and Irish History* (Dublin, 1997), pp. 15–38.

36. Brendan Kelly, *Ada English: Patriot and Psychiatrist* (Dublin, 2014).

37. Margaret Ó hÒgartaigh, *Kathleen Lynn: Irishwoman, Patriot, Doctor* (Dublin, 2006); Marie Mulholland, *The Politics and Relationships of Kathleen Lynn* (Dublin, 2002).

38. Sonja Tiernan, *Eva Gore Booth: An Image of Such Politics* (Manchester, 2012), pp. 196–232.

39. Leeann Lane, *Rosamund Jacob: Third Person Singular* (Dublin, 2010), pp. 1–11.

40. Annie Ryan, *Witnesses: Inside the Easter Rising* (Dublin, 2005), p. 106; Annie Ryan, *Comrades: Inside the War of Independence* (Dublin, 2008), pp. i–iii; IMA, BMH, WS1754, Leslie Price.

41. Angela Bourke et al. (eds), *The Field Day Anthology of Irish Women's Writing*, vols 4 & 5 (Cork, 2002).

42. Catríona Crowe, 'Testimony to a flowering', *Dublin Review*, no. 10 (Spring 2003), pp. 42–69.

43. Borgonovo, *Dynamics of War and Revolution*, pp. xi and xv.

44. Foster, *Vivid Faces*, p. 166; Morris, *Alice Milligan and the Irish Cultural Revival*.

45. Senia Paseta, *Irish Nationalist Women, 1900–1918* (Cambridge, 2014), p. 1.

10 The Politics of Peace and the Twenty-first-Century Perspective

1. John Horne (ed.), *Our War: Ireland and the Great War* (Dublin, 2008); David Fitzpatrick (ed.), *Ireland and the First World War* (Dublin, 1988).

2. Horne, *Our War*, pp. 1–15.

3. John Horne and Edward Madigan (eds), *Towards Commemoration: Ireland in War and Revolution, 1912–23* (Dublin, 2013), pp. 1–5.

4. William Mulligan, 'Violence and war in Europe and Ireland, 1911–14', in Horne and Madigan (eds), *Towards Commemoration*, p. 18; Robert Wohl, *The Generation of 1914* (London, 1980).

5. David Miller, *Church, State and Nation in Ireland, 1898–1921* (Dublin, 1973), p. 208.

6. Jérôme aan de Wiel, *The Catholic Church in Ireland, 1914–18: War and Politics* (Dublin, 2003), p. 41.

7. Enda McDonagh, 'Church State relations', *Irish Press*, 26 May 1976, supplement: 'Fianna Fáil golden jubilee'.

8. NAI, Dáil Éireann files (DE), 2/85, Draft letter to cardinal and bishops regarding recognition of the Dáil, 21 December 1920.

9. Michael McCabe, *For God and Ireland: The Fight for Moral Superiority in Ireland, 1922–1932* (Dublin, 2013).

10. Ronan Fanning, Michael Kennedy, Eunan O'Halpin and Dermot Keogh (eds), *Documents on Irish Foreign Policy*, vol. 1: *1919–22* (Dublin, 1998).

11. Laffan, *Resurrection of Ireland*, p. 465.

12. Anne Dolan, 'Divisions and divisions and divisions: who to commemorate', in Horne and Madigan (eds), *Towards Commemoration*, pp. 145–54.

13. 'Peter Hart and his enemies', *History Ireland*, vol. 13, no. 4 (July/August 2005), p. 16.

14. Hart, *The IRA and Its Enemies*.

15. Paul Bew, *Ireland: The Politics of Enmity, 1789–2006* (Oxford, 2007), pp. 393–444.

16. Meleady, *John Redmond*, p. 9.

17. Ronan Fanning, *Fatal Path: British Government and Irish Revolution, 1910–1922* (London, 2013), pp. 133–7; 143–80.

18. Michael Laffan, 'John Edward Redmond', *DOIB*, vol. 8, pp. 411–18.

19. Peter Hart, *Mick: The Real Michael Collins* (London, 2007), p. 117.

20. Ibid., p. 264.

21. Ibid., p. 292; Townshend, *The Republic*, pp. 48–55.

22. Hart, *Mick*, pp. 422–6.

23. Denis Lenihan (ed.), *The Path to Freedom: Speeches by Michael Collins* (Dublin 2010), p. vi.

24. Napoli McKenna, 'In London with the Treaty delegates', *Capuchin Annual* (1971), p. 330.

25. Margery Forester, *Michael Collins: Lost Leader* (London, 1971), p. 347.

26. John Regan's description, *Irish Times*, 24 July 2000, supplement: 'Michael Collins'.

27. Michael Hopkinson, 'Michael Collins', *DOIB*, vol. 2, pp. 678–82.

28. T. P. O'Neill and Lord Longford, *Éamon de Valera* (Dublin, 1970), p. 463.

29. Tim Pat Coogan, *De Valera, Long Fellow, Long Shadow* (London, 1993), pp. 693–705.

30. Diarmaid Ferriter, *Judging Dev: A Reassessment of the Life and Legacy of Éamon de Valera* (Dublin, 2007), pp. 361–73.

31. Gerard MacAtasney, *Tom Clarke: Life, Liberty and Revolution* (Dublin, 2013).

32. The contention of former Fianna Fáil minister Mary O'Rourke, *Sunday Tribune*, 22 August 2010.

33. McGough, *Diarmuid Lynch*, pp. 9–11.

34. Kieran Glennon, *From Pogrom to Civil War: Tom Glennon and the Belfast IRA* (Cork, 2013), p. 11.

35. Jack White, *Misfit: A Revolutionary Life* (Dublin, 2005), review by Derrick White, accompanied with press release from Livewire publications, 17 June 2005; *Irish Times*, 24 January 2014.

36. Sineád Joy, *The IRA in Kerry, 1916–21* (Cork, 2005), p. 3.

37. Ibid., p. 124.

38. O'Callaghan, *Revolutionary Limerick*, p. 7.

39. Dominic Price, *The Flame and the Candle: War in Mayo, 1919–24* (Dublin, 2012), p. x.

40. Micheál Ó Súilleabháin, *Where Mountainy Men Have Sown* (Cork, 2013 [1965]), p. 312.

41. Eoin Neeson, 'There are no conquerors or winners in a civil war', *Irish Times*, 24 May 2003.

42. Eoin Neeson, *Birth of a Republic* (Dublin, 1998), p. 275.

43. Fearghal McGarry, *Rebels: Voices from the Easter Rising* (London, 2011), foreword; Fearghal McGarry, '1916 and Irish republicanism: between myth and history', in Horne and Madigan (eds), *Towards Commemoration*, pp. 46–54.

44. Anne Dolan, 'The War of Independence', *Irish Independent*, 28 April 2010, supplement: 'Birth of a nation, part 2'.

45. Ibid.

46. O'Faoláin, 'Portrait of the artist as an old man'; Ernie O'Malley quoted in R. F. Foster, 'Historian who clears a path through the fog of war', *Irish Times*, 28 September 2013.

47. Regan, *Myth and the Irish State*, pp. 1–18.

48. Seán O'Faoláin's editorial in *The Bell*, vol. 1, no. 1 (October 1940), p. 5; Marc Bloch, *The Historian's Craft* (Manchester, 1954), pp. 48–79 (this book was written from 1940 to 1944, the year Bloch was executed by the Nazis, and published in 1954).

49. Collins (ed.), *Whose Past Is It Anyway?*, pp. 132–42.

50. Cited in *New York Times*, 19 September 1964.

11   An Evolving Nationalism

1. David Fitzpatrick, *Politics and Irish Life: Provincial Experience of War and Revolution* (Dublin, 1977), p. 217.

2. IMA, BMH, WS1365, Bulmer Hobson.

3. McBride, 'Young readers'.

4. Mary Colum, *Life and the Dream* (Dublin, 1966 [New York, 1958]), pp. 95–102.

5. Donal McCartney, *UCD – A National Idea: The History of University College, Dublin* (Dublin, 1999) pp. 40 ff.

6. Martin Maguire, *The Civil Service and the Revolution in Ireland, 1912–1938* (Manchester, 2008), p. 86.

7. L. M. Cullen, *An Economic History of Ireland Since 1660* (London, 1987), p. 166; Mary E. Daly, *Social and Economic History of Ireland Since 1800* (Dublin, 1981), p. 111.

8. Caitríona Clear, *Nuns in Nineteenth Century Ireland* (Dublin, 1987), pp. xvi–xix.

9. Cullen, *An Economic History of Ireland*, pp. 138–43; L. P. Curtis, 'Ireland in 1914', in W. E. Vaughan (ed.), *A New History of Ireland*, vol. 6: *Ireland Under the Union II, 1870–1921* (Oxford, 1996), pp. 145–88.

10. Dan Bradley, *Farm Labourers: Irish Struggle, 1900–1976* (Belfast, 1988).

11. Cormac O'Gráda, *Ireland: A New Economic History, 1780–1939* (Oxford, 1994), p. 264.

12. Bradley, *Farm Labourers*, p. 13.

13. Cullen, *An Economic History of Ireland*, p. 168.

14. *Irish Citizen*, 8 June 1912.

15. *Irish Citizen*, 28 December 1912.

16. IMA, BMH, WS391, Helena Molony.

17. Ibid.

18. Hanna Sheehy-Skeffington, 'Reminiscences of an Irish suffragette', in Rosemary Cullen Owens (ed.), *Votes for Women: Irish Women's Struggle for the Vote* (Dublin, 1975), pp. 4–18.

19. IMA, BMH, WS919, Ina Heron; IMA, BMH, WS418, Una Stack.

20. Lambert McKenna, *The Church and Working Women* (Dublin, 1913).

21. Mona Hearn, *Below Stairs: Domestic Service Remembered in Dublin and Beyond, 1880–1922* (Dublin, 1993), pp. 43–60.

22. Catríona Crowe (ed.), *Dublin, 1911* (Dublin, 2011), pp. 152ff. See also www.census. nationalarchives.ie

23. Mary E. Daly, 'Two centuries of Irish social life', in Brendan Rooney (ed.), *A Time and a Place: Two Centuries of Irish Social Life* (Dublin, 2006), pp. 3–12.

24. Crowe (ed.), *Dublin, 1911*, p. 88.

25. IMA, BMH, WS1770, Kevin O'Shiel.

26. D. A. Chart, 'The housing of the labouring class in Dublin', *Journal of the Statistical and Social Inquiry Society of Ireland*, part 94, vol. 13 (December 1914), pp. 160–76.

27. Jacinta Prunty, *Dublin Slums, 1800–1925: A Study in Urban Geography* (Dublin, 1999), p. 153.

28. Patrick MacGill, *Children of the Dead End: The Autobiography of an Irish Navvy* (London, 1914), pp. 36–7.

29. Neal Garnham, 'Accounting for the early success of the Gaelic Athletic Association', *Irish Historical Studies*, vol. 34, no. 133 (May 2004), pp. 65–78.

30. Andrews, *Dublin Made Me*, pp. 9–63.

31. IMA, BMH, WS391, Helena Molony.

32. S. J. Connolly (ed.), *The Oxford Companion to Irish History* (Oxford, 1998), p. 381.

33. IMA, BMH, WS111, Denis McCullough.

34. Arthur Clery, 'The Gaelic League, 1893–1919', *Studies*, vol. 8, no. 31 (September 1919), pp. 398–408.

35. IMA, BMH, WS841, Patrick Sarsfield O'Hegarty.

36. Cited in Clery, 'The Gaelic League'.

37. Joe Nugent, 'The sword and the prayerbook: the ideal of authentic Irish manliness', *Victorian Studies*, vol. 50, no. 4 (Summer 2008), pp. 587–613.

38. Ibid.

39. Ibid.

40. Owen McGee, '"God Save Ireland": Manchester-Martyr demonstrations in Dublin, 1867–1916', *Eire-Ireland*, vol. 36, nos 3–4 (Fall/Winter 2001), pp. 39–66.

41. Ibid., p. 65.

42. Thomas J. Brophy, 'On Church grounds: political funerals and the contest to lead Catholic Ireland', *Catholic Historical Review*, vol. 95, no. 3 (July 2009), pp. 491–514.

43. Ibid.

44. Patrick Maume, 'Patrick Augustine Sheehan', *DOIB*, vol. 8, pp. 882–4.

45. UCDA, P48/B374, Papers of Terence MacSwiney, P. S. O'Hegarty to MacSwiney, 15 July 1904.

46. Peter Hart, 'The geography of revolution in Ireland, 1917–1923', *Past and Present*, no. 155 (May 1997), p. 171; McBride, 'Young readers'.

47. McBride, 'Young readers'; Fitzpatrick, 'The futility of history', p. 174.

48. Ibid.

49. Ibid.

50. Andrews, *Dublin Made Me*, pp. 4, 90–95.

51. IMA, BMH, WS371, Robert Holland; Foster, *Vivid Faces*, p. 145.

52. Revd E. Gaynor, 'Our musical tradition', *The Leader*, vol. 22, no. 8 (8 April 1911).

53. Liam Deasy, *Towards Ireland Free* (Cork, 1992), pp. 1–2.

54. English, *Ernie O'Malley*, p. 118; Andrews, *Dublin Made Me*, pp. 58–9.

55. C. R. L. Fletcher and Rudyard Kipling, *A School History of England* (London, 1911), pp. 209, 241–8.

56. Maume, *Long Gestation*, pp. 5–9.

57. Marie Louise Legg, *Newspapers and Nationalism: The Irish Provincial Press, 1850–1892* (Dublin, 1999), p. 3.

58. Foster, *Vivid Faces*, pp. 145–59.

59. Felix M. Larkin, '"A great daily organ": The Freeman's Journal 1763–1924', *History Ireland*, vol. 14, no. 3 (May/June 2006), pp. 44–50.

60. McGee, '"God Save Ireland"'.

61. Ibid., p. 51.

62. Fergus Campbell, 'Emigrant responses to war and revolution, 1914–21: Irish opinion in the United States and Australia', *Irish Historical Studies*, vol. 32, no. 125 (May 2000), p. 75.

63. Marnie Hay, 'The foundation and development of Na Fianna Éireann, 1909–16', *Irish Historical Studies*, vol. 36, no. 141 (May 2008), p. 53.

64. Robert Lynch, *Radical Politics in Modern Ireland: The Irish Socialist Republican Party, 1896–1904* (Dublin, 2005), p. v.

65. Ibid.

66. Michael Laffan, 'In the shadow of the national question', in Paul Daly, Rónán O'Brien and Paul Rouse (eds), *Making the Difference? The Irish Labour Party, 1912–2012* (Dublin, 2012), pp. 32–43.

67. Mitchell, *Labour in Irish Politics*, pp. 25–47.

68. Ibid., p. 57.

69. Ibid., pp. 83ff.

70. James Loughlin, 'Joseph Devlin', *DOIB*, vol. 3, pp. 241–3.

71. Philip Cambray, *Irish Affairs and the Home Rule Question* (London, 1911), p. 117.

72. *Irish Independent*, 14 May 1909.

73. William O'Brien, *An Olive Branch in Ireland and Its History* (London, 1910), p. 89.

74. Maume, *Long Gestation*, p. 19.

75. Donal Murphy, *Blazing Tar Barrels and Standing Orders: Tipperary North's First County and District Councils, 1899–1902* (Tipperary, 1999), p. 18.

76. Curtis, 'Ireland in 1914', p. 185; Maume, *Long Gestation*, pp. 77–90.

77. UCDA, P48/B377, P. S. O'Hegarty to Terence MacSwiney, 27 September 1907.

78. Deirdre McMahon, *The Moynihan Brothers in Peace and War, 1909–1918: Their New Ireland* (Dublin, 2004), pp. 36–95, Letter of 9 November 1912.

79. Ibid., Letter of 17 November 1913.

80. McGarry, *Rebels*, p. 240.

81. Fergus Campbell, *The Irish Establishment, 1879–1914* (Oxford, 2009).

82. Senia Paseta, *Before the Revolution: Nationalism, Social Change and Ireland's Catholic Elite, 1879–1922* (Cork 1999), p. 84.

83. James Meenan, *George O'Brien: A Biographical Memoir* (Dublin, 1980).

12 Ulster Prepared with One Voice? 1910–14

1. Timothy Bowman, *Carson's Army: The Ulster Volunteer Force, 1910–1922* (Manchester, 2007).

2. Ferriter, *The Transformation of Ireland*, p. 114.

3. J. C. Beckett (ed.), *Belfast: The Making of the City, 1800–1914* (Belfast, 1983), pp. 174–89.

4. Ruth Dudley Edwards, *The Faithful Tribe: An Intimate Portrait of the Loyal Institutions* (London, 1999), p. 183.

5. Reginald Lucas, *Colonel Saunderson MP: A Memoir* (London, 1908).

6. Peter Murray, 'Radical way forward or sectarian cul-de-sac: Lindsay Crawford and Independent Orangeism reassessed', *Saothar*, vol. 27 (2002), pp. 31–43.

7. K. T. Hoppen, *Ireland Since 1800: Conflict and Conformity* (London, 1989), pp. 126–7.

8. Lucas, *Colonel Saunderson*.

9. Ibid.

10. Dudley Edwards, *Faithful Tribe*, p. 241.

11. Alvin Jackson, 'Edward Henry Carson', *DOIB*, vol. 2, pp. 383–8.

12. James Quinn, 'Frederick Hugh Crawford', *DOIB*, vol. 2, pp. 966–8.

13. R. B. McDowell, *The Church of Ireland, 1869–1969* (London, 1975), p. 104.

14. UKNA, CO, 904/27, Fermanagh, 20 April 1911 and 1 March 1912.

15. UKNA, CO, 904/23, Chief Secretary's Office to undersecretary, 23 February 1912.

16. UKNA, CO, 904/27, Memorandum from Attorney General, 7 February 1913.

17. IMA, BMH, WS492, John McCoy.

18. Bowman, *Carson's Army*, pp. 54–5; Geoffrey Lewis, *Carson: The Man Who Divided Ireland* (London, 2005), p. 143.

19. A. T. Q. Stewart, *The Narrow Ground: Patterns of Ulster History* (Belfast, 1986), p. 67.

20. UKNA, CO, 904/27, 'City of Belfast', memorandum of Joseph Edwards, 26 April 1913.

21. Ibid., 'Unionist movement versus home rule: weekly reports', 28 March 1914.

22. Bourke et al. (eds), *Field Day Anthology of Irish Women's Writing*, vol. 5, p. 69.

23. PRONI, D1098/1/3, Ulster Women's Unionist Council, Exec Committee minutes, 28 January 1919.

24. David Fitzpatrick, *The Two Irelands: 1912–1939* (Oxford, 1998), p. 36.

25. Ibid., pp. 96–9.

26. A. C. Hepburn, *Catholic Belfast and Nationalist Ireland in the Era of Joe Devlin, 1871–1934* (Oxford, 2008), pp. 5–6.

27. PRONI, D1327/1/1, Unionist Club Council minute books, 19 May 1996.

28. Ibid., 11 January 1911 and 5 April 1911.

29. Ibid.
30. J. J. Lee, *Ireland, 1912–1985: Politics and Society* (Cambridge, 1989), p. 39.
31. PRONI, D1327/1/1, Unionist Club Council minute books, 29 February 1912.
32. Ibid., Executive Committee minutes, 19 May 1914.
33. Ibid., 23 August 1912.
34. Fitzpatrick, *Two Irelands*, p. 49.
35. Paul Bew, Peter Gibbon and Henry Patterson, *Northern Ireland, 1921–1994: Political Forces and Social Classes* (London, 1995), p. 23.
36. John Gray, 'The 1907 Belfast Dock Strike', in Alan Parkinson and Eamon Phoenix (eds), *Conflicts in the North of Ireland, 1900–2000* (Dublin, 2010), pp. 15–27.
37. Owen Dudley Edwards, *The Sins of Our Fathers* (Dublin, 1970), pp. 170–72.
38. John Biggs-Davison, *The Hand Is Red* (London, 1973), pp. 72–5.
39. Bew, Gibbon and Patterson, *Northern Ireland*, p. 24.
40. PRONI, MS, T3580, Memoirs of Frederick B. McGinley.
41. UKNA, CO, 904/21, Chief Secretary's Office, Colville Barclay to Edward Grey, 20 July 1914.
42. Alvin Jackson, 'James Craig', *DOIB*, vol. 2, pp. 953–7.
43. Buckland, *James Craig*, pp. 35–52.
44. Michael Foy, 'Ulster unionist propaganda against home rule, 1912–14', *History Ireland*, vol. 4, no. 1 (Spring 1996), pp. 49–53.
45. PRONI, D1327/18A/8, Ulster Unionist Council correspondence, 1912–13.
46. Patrick Buckland, 'The southern Irish unionists, the Irish question and British politics, 1906–14', *Irish Historical Studies*, vol. 15, no. 59 (March 1967), pp. 228–55.
47. Ibid.; Patrick Buckland, *Irish Unionism I: The Anglo-Irish and the New Ireland, 1885–1922* (Dublin, 1972).
48. Michael Laffan, *The Partition of Ireland, 1911–1925* (Dundalk, 1987), pp. 19–49.
49. Lennox Robinson, *Bryan Cooper* (London, 1931).
50. Ian d'Alton, 'A vestigial population? Perspectives on southern Irish Protestantism in the twentieth century', *Eire-Ireland*, vol. 44, nos 3–4 (Fall/Winter 2009), pp. 9–42.
51. Buckland, *Irish Unionism I*; Pádraig Yeates, *A City in Turmoil: Dublin, 1919–21* (Dublin, 2012), p. 254.
52. Thomas C. Kennedy, '"The gravest situation of our lives": Conservatives, Ulster and the home rule crisis, 1911–14', *Eire-Ireland*, vol. 36, nos 3–4 (Fall/Winter 2001), pp. 67–82.
53. Ibid.
54. M. L. Connelly, 'The army, the press and the "Curragh Incident", March 1914', *Historical Research*, vol. 84, no. 225 (August 2011), pp. 535–57.
55. Ibid.
56. Charles Townshend, 'Military force and civil authority in the United Kingdom, 1914–1921', *Journal of British Studies*, vol. 28, no. 3 (July 1989), pp. 262–92; Thomas C. Kennedy, 'Troubled Tories: dissent and confusion concerning the party's Ulster policy, 1910–1914', *Journal of British Studies*, vol. 46, no. 3 (July 2007), pp. 570–93.
57. Florence O'Donoghue, Review of A. P. Ryan, *Mutiny at the Curragh* (London, 1956), *Irish Historical Studies*, vol. 10, no. 38 (September 1956), pp. 243–6.
58. PRONI, D1700/5/17/2/1, Diary of Major Fred Crawford, 26 March 1914 and 7 April 1914.
59. Jérôme aan de Wiel, 'Austria-Hungary, France, Germany and the Irish crisis from 1899 to the outbreak of the First World War', *Intelligence and National Security*, vol. 21 (2006), pp. 237–57.

60. PRONI, D1327/2/12, UUC, Agenda for special meeting in Belfast, 24 September 1913.
61. UKNA, CO, 904/27, Report on private meeting in Belfast, 24 July 1913.
62. PRONI, D1327/2/12, UUC, Edward Carson to George Richardson, 19 May 1915.
63. Thomas Johnson, *A Handbook for Rebels: A Guide to Successful Defiance of the British Government* (Dublin, 1918); UCDLSC, 1.V.8/8.

13 Labour, Nationalism and War: 1913–16

1. Connolly, *Labour in Irish History* (1917 edn); introduction by Robert Lynd, p. iii.
2. F. X. Martin (ed.), *The Irish Volunteers, 1913–1915: Recollections and Documents* (Dublin, 1963).
3. Ibid.
4. Emmet O'Connor, 'Larkin's road to revolution', *Irish Times*, 11 September 1913, supplement: 'Locked out: the story of the 1913 Dublin Lockout'.
5. James McConnel, 'The Irish Parliamentary Party, industrial relations and the 1913 Dublin Lockout', *Saothar*, vol. 28 (2003), pp. 25–36.
6. Ibid., p. 36.
7. *Irish Worker*, 1 November 1913.
8. T. M. Healy, *Dublin Strikes 1913: Facts Regarding the Labour Disputes Contained in Speech by Mr. T. M. Healy MP At Court of Inquiry in Dublin Castle, 1 October 1913* (Dublin, 1913); UCDLSC, 34.S.7/1.
9. James Larkin, *Larkin's Scathing Indictment of Dublin Sweaters* (Manchester and London, 1913), UCDLSC, 39.E.2/18.
10. John Newsinger, 'Reporting the Lockout', *Saothar*, vol. 28 (2003), p. 125.
11. Dermot Keogh, *The Rise of the Irish Working Class* (Dublin, 1982), pp. 245–50.
12. James Curry, 'Delia Larkin: "More harm to the Big Fellow than any of the employers"', *Saothar*, vol. 36 (2013), p. 22.
13. Mary Jones, *These Obstreperous Lassies: A History of the IWWU* (Dublin, 1988), p. 5.
14. Arnold Wright, *Disturbed Dublin: The Story of the Great Strike* (London, 1914), pp. 141–2.
15. IMA, BMH, WS919, Ina Heron.
16. UKNA, CO, 904/158, 'Dublin Labour Troubles Report', 1913.
17. *Irish Independent*, 3 September 1913; see also www.rte.ie/centuryireland
18. Priscilla Metscher, *Republicanism and Socialism in Ireland* (Frankfurt, 1986), p. 406.
19. Seán O' Casey, *Drums Under the Windows* (London, 1973), pp. 265–6.
20. *Irish Worker*, 16 September 1913.
21. *Irish Worker*, 6 September 1913.
22. *Sinn Féin*, 30 September 1911.
23. *Irish Freedom*, December 1911.
24. Samuel Levenson, *Maud Gonne* (London, 1977), p. 84.
25. Larkin, *Larkin's Scathing Indictment*.
26. Wright, *Disturbed Dublin*, p. 183.
27. Nicholas Mansergh, 'Eoin MacNeill – a reappraisal', *Studies*, vol. 63, no. 250 (Summer 1974), pp. 133–40.
28. 'Manifesto of the Irish Volunteers', *Irish Review*, vol. 3, no. 34 (December 1913), pp. 503–5.
29. Mulligan, 'Violence and war in Europe and Ireland, 1911–14', p. 18.
30. Ciara Breathnach, *The Congested Districts Board, 1891–1923: Poverty and Development in the West of Ireland* (Dublin, 2005).

31. *Tuam Herald*, 6 and 27 March 1915.
32. UKNA, CO, 904/21, RIC Crime Department Special Branch, November 1916, Waterford.
33. Irish Reconstruction Association, *The Scope of Reconstruction in Ireland* (Dublin, 1921), p. 10; UCDLSC, 35.E.2/1.
34. Yeates, *A City in Wartime*, pp. 30–48.
35. Ibid.
36. Lionel Smith-Gordon and Cruise O'Brien, *Starvation in Dublin* (Dublin, 1917), pp. 17–21, UCDLSC, 4.S.13/12.
37. *Irish Times*, 7 April 1915.
38. Keith Jeffery, *Ireland and the Great War* (Cambridge, 2000), p. 21.
39. Kevin Johnston, *Home or Away: The Great War and the Irish Revolution* (Dublin, 2010), pp. 46–7; John Morrissey, 'Ireland's Great War: representation, public space and the place of dissonant heritages', *Journal of the Galway Archaeological and Historical Society*, vol. 58 (2006), pp. 98–113; Michael MacDonagh, *The Irish at the Front* (London, 1916).
40. Johnston, *Home or Away*, pp. 46–7.
41. Fitzpatrick, *Ireland and the First World War*, p. 19.
42. Horne, *Our War*, pp. 1–35, 63.
43. *Kildare Observer*, February 1916, cited in *Irish Times*, 27 June 2006, supplement: 'The Somme, 90th anniversary'.
44. Ibid.
45. www.livesofthefirstworldwar.org, accessed 13 May 2014.
46. Ibid.
47. *Irish Independent*, 10 May 2014, supplement: 'Ireland at war'.
48. *Irish Times*, 22 May 2013, supplement: 'Stories of the Irish revolution'.
49. Catriona Pennell, *A Kingdom United: Popular Responses to the Outbreak of War in Britain and Ireland* (Oxford, 2012), p. 172.
50. Deirdre McMahon, 'Ireland and the Empire-Commonwealth, 1886–1972', in Kevin Kenny (ed.), *Ireland and the British Empire* (Oxford, 2004), pp. 182–220.
51. IMA, BMH, WS713, Denis Dwyer.
52. IMA, BMH, WS1355, John Riordan.
53. Lar Joye, 'The Mauser Model 71 rifle', *History Ireland*, vol. 19, no. 1 (January/February 2011), p. 49.
54. Jeffery, *Ireland and the Great War*, p. 47.
55. Horne (ed.), *Our War*, p. 105; John S. Ellis, 'The degenerate and the martyr: nationalist propaganda and the contestation of Irishness, 1914–1918', *Eire-Ireland*, vol. 35, nos 3–4 (Fall/Winter 2000), pp. 7–34.

14   1916: An Idea 'Essentially Spiritual'?

1. Martin, '1916 – myth, fact and mystery'.
2. J. J. Horgan, *Parnell to Pearse* (Dublin, 1948), p. 285.
3. Francis Shaw, 'Eoin MacNeill, the Person', *Studies*, vol. 62, no. 246 (Summer 1973), pp. 154–64.
4. UCDA, LA1/G120, Papers of Eoin MacNeill, Statement by Thomas MacDonagh, 23 April 1916.
5. UCDA, LA1/G121, June 1916.
6. F. S. L. Lyons, 'The Rising and after', in Vaughan, (ed.), *A New History of Ireland*, vol. 6, pp. 207–22.

7. Ruth Dudley Edwards, *Patrick Pearse: The Triumph of Failure* (London, 1977), p. 233.
8. UCDA, P88/1, Papers of James Ryan, copy of *Irish War News*, 25 April 1916.
9. Lynd, introduction to Connolly, *Labour in Irish History*.
10. IMA, BMH, WS1766, William O'Brien.
11. John Horne, 'James Connolly and the Great Divide: Ireland, Europe and the First World War', *Saothar*, vol. 31 (2006), p. 75.
12. Martin, '1916 – myth, fact and mystery', p. 66.
13. UKNA, CO, 904/21, Crime Department Special Branch to undersecretary, 'Précis of reports relative to secret societies in DMP district furnished on 1 January 1915'.
14. UKNA, CO, 904/23, 'SF Activities: meetings in 1916', report from 'Chalk', 22 April 1916 and 'Granite', 7 April 1916.
15. Ibid., from Detective Department, 16 and 27 March 1916.
16. UKNA, CO, 904/23, 17 March 1916, 'SF parades', 'Strength of Sinn Féiners'.
17. IMA, BMH, WS1766, William O'Brien.
18. IMA, BMH, WS399, Mary Mulcahy (Min Ryan).
19. IMA, BMH, WS1343, James Cullen.
20. IMA, BMH, WS705, Christopher Brady.
21. *Proclamation of the Republic of Ireland*, National Museum of Ireland.
22. http://dh.tcd.ie/letters1916, Gerald O'Driscoll, accessed 14 May 2014.
23. Charles Townshend, *Easter 1916: The Irish Rebellion* (London, 2006), p. 250.
24. Stephen Ferguson, *GPO Staff in 1916: Business as Usual* (Cork, 2012), pp. 41–54.
25. Ibid., p. 101.
26. Ibid.
27. Una Newell, 'The Rising of the Moon: Galway 1916', *Journal of the Galway Archaeological and Historical Society*, vol. 58 (2006), pp. 114–35.
28. *Tuam Herald*, 13 May 1916.
29. IMA, BMH, WS1776, William O'Brien.
30. Fitzpatrick (ed.), *Terror in Ireland, 1916–1923* (Dublin, 2012), p. 51.
31. McGarry, *Rebels*, p. 168.
32. IMA, BMH, WS399, Mary Mulcahy (Min Ryan), and WS391, Helena Molony.
33. UCDA, P151/111, Papers of Kathleen O'Connell, Padraig O'Shea to O'Connell, 31 May 1916.
34. McGarry, *Rebels*, p. 64.
35. Ibid., p. 207.
36. IMA, BMH, WS371, Robert Holland.
37. Ibid., pp. 142–3.
38. Máire Nic Shiubhlaigh, *The Splendid Years* (Dublin, 1955), pp. 140–87.
39. O'Callaghan, *Revolutionary Limerick*, pp. 44–5.
40. Ibid.
41. IMA, BMH, WS1754, Mrs Tom Barry (Leslie Price).
42. IMA, BMH, WS551, Thomas Duggan.
43. McGarry, *Rebels*, p. 293.
44. G. A. Hayes McCoy, *The Irish at War* (Cork, 1964), p. 94.
45. Aodh de Blácam, *Towards the Republic: A Study of New Ireland's Social and Political Aims* (Dublin 1919), p. 109.

15 The Perfect Patriots

1. Townshend, *Easter 1916*, pp. 269ff.

2. Martin, '1916 – myth, fact and mystery', p. 32.
3. A. Newman, *What Emmet Means in 1915: A Tract for the Times* (Dublin, 1915), p. 6; UCDLSC, 39.D.3/2.
4. Robert Kee, *Ourselves Alone* (London, 1972), p. 4.
5. IMA, BMH, WS993, Cahir Davitt.
6. Frederic W. Pim, *The Sinn Féin Rising: A Narrative and Some Reflections* (Dublin, 1916), p. 14, UCDLSC, 4.S.14/12.
7. Jason Knirck, 'Women's political rhetoric and the Irish revolution', in Thomas E. Hachey (ed.), *Turning Points in Twentieth-Century Irish History* (Dublin, 2011), p. 43.
8. Yeates, *A City in Wartime*, p. 121.
9. UCDA, P88/2, Sean T. O' Kelly to James Ryan, 12 June 1916.
10. UCDA, P88/4, Ryan's letter from Wandsworth prison, c. June 1916.
11. UCDA, P88/19–23, Madge Calnan, letters to James Ryan, June 1916.
12. IMA, BMH, WS587, Jenny Wyse Power.
13. Ward, *Unmanageable Revolutionaries*, p. 121.
14. Sineád McCoole, *No Ordinary Women: Irish Female Activists in the Revolutionary Years, 1900–1923* (Dublin, 2003), pp. 62–4.
15. UKNA, CO, 904/26, Hugh O'Hehir and Robert Rooney, 'Civil servants in sympathy with Sinn Féin', 5 May 1916.
16. UKNA, CO, 904/26, Lord Lieutenant to W. Connolly, Secretary GPO, 11 December 1918.
17. UKNA, CO, 904/26, Mary Byrne to CSO and reply of E. O. Farrell, 18 May 1916, and statements of Patrick, Francis and James Byrne.
18. UKNA, CO, 904/26, list of postal officials who came under notice for 'SF sympathies', 16 December 1914 and memorandum from post office, 7 July 1916.
19. Ibid., memorandum of J. Fagan, detective sergeant, 27 May 1916.
20. Eason and Son, *The Rebellion in Dublin, April 1916* (Dublin, 1916); UCDLSC, 1.V.13/9.
21. INAVDF, *Aftermath of Dublin Week, Published for the Benefit of the Irish National Aid and Volunteers' Dependants Fund* (Dublin, 1917); UCDLSC, 1.V.6/10.
22. *The Sinn Féin Leaders: With Numerous Illustrations and Complete Lists of Deportees, Casualties Etc* (Dublin 1917); UCDLSC, 39.N.8/7.
23. T. W. Murphy, *Dublin After the Six Days Insurrection: Thirty-One Pictures from the Camera of Mr T. W. Murphy* (Dublin, 1916–17) UCDLSC, 1.V.13/8.
24. Eason and Son, *The Rebellion in Dublin*.
25. Martin, '1916 – myth, fact and mystery', p. 127.
26. James Stephens, *The Insurrection in Dublin* (Dublin, 1916), p. ix.
27. *Royal Commission on the Rebellion in Ireland: Report of Commission* (London, 1916), pp. 3–6.
28. Ibid., pp. 10–12.
29. Foster, *Vivid Faces*, p. 217.
30. Deirdre McMahon, 'The Irish settlement meeting of the Unionist Party, 7 July 1916', *Analecta Hibernica*, no. 41 (2009), pp. 201–70.
31. Peter Hart, 'What did the Easter Rising really change?', in Hachey (ed.), *Turning Points*, pp. 7–21.
32. Ibid.

16 1917–18: Bonfires and Ballots

1. UKNA, CO, 904/23, Sir John Maxwell to Duke, 29 September 1916.

2. *The Kerryman*, 24 June 1917.
3. Ferriter, *Judging Dev*, pp. 28–9.
4. UKNA, CO, 904/21, RIC Office, Dublin Castle, Crime Department Special Branch, 'United Irish League, Meetings etc'.
5. Ibid., Downpatrick, September 1917; Longford, 26 August 1917.
6. Ibid., Longford, 25 November 1917 and 2 December 1917.
7. Ibid., 17 March 1918.
8. Ibid., County Donegal, 16 March 1919.
9. Ibid., Carrickmacross, County Monaghan, 11 May 1919.
10. Terence Dooley, 'IRA veterans and land division in independent Ireland', in Fearghal McGarry (ed.), *Republicanism in Modern Ireland* (Dublin, 2003), pp. 86–108.
11. UKNA, CO, 904/193, David O'Driscoll to Board of National Education, 6 November 1917.
12. Ibid., Letter of Aileen Barry, 1 November 1917.
13. IMA, BMH, WS1316, John Flanagan, and WS939, Ernest Blythe.
14. *Irish Citizen*, November 1917.
15. Garvin, *1922*, p. 95.
16. 'Conscription in Ireland', *House of Commons Debates* (Hansard), vol. 104, cols 1361–2, 9 April 1918.
17. UKNA, CO, 906/34, James O'Mahony to Edward O'Farrell, May 1918.
18. *The Kerryman*, 20 April 1918.
19. Moynihan, *Speeches and Statements of Éamon de Valera*, p. 12.
20. *Irish Independent*, 13 April 1918.
21. *Freeman's Journal*, 24 April 1918.
22. Moynihan, *Speeches and Statements*, p. 12.
23. Mansion House Committee, *No Conscription! Ireland's Case Restated: Address to the President of the USA from the Mansion House Conference* (Dublin, 1918); UCDLSC, 34.K.2/15.
24. Mansion House Committee, *Memorandum to Local Defence Committees, Issued by the Mansion House Committee* (Dublin, 1918); UCDLSC, 39.E.3/11.
25. IMA, BMH, WS518, James Sullivan.
26. *'Eamon De Valera States His Case', Interview Reprinted from the 'Christian Science Monitor', Boston, 15 May 1918, Republished by Sinn Féin* (Dublin, 1918), UCDLSC, 34.Va.4/19.
27. IMA, BMH, WS1336, Patrick Lennon; WS1393, Edmond McGrath; WS721, Nicholas Smyth; WS687, Michael Curran.
28. IMA, BMH, WS687, Michael Curran.
29. F. S. L. Lyons, *John Dillon, a Biography* (London, 1968), p. 434.
30. *Northern Whig*, 7 March 1918.
31. *Irish Independent*, 7 March 1918.
32. W. B. Wells, *John Redmond* (London, 1919), p. 192.
33. Gwynn, *John Redmond's Last Years*, p. 25.
34. *Northern Whig*, 7 March 1918.
35. UCDA, P197, Papers of Kevin O'Higgins, O'Higgins to Mrs Sheridan, 20 October 1918.
36. *Dundalk Democrat*, 26 January 1918.
37. *Frontier Sentinel*, 26 January 1918.
38. UKNA, CO, 906/34, James O'Mahony to Edward O'Farrell, 18 May 1918.
39. UKNA, CO, 904/23, Sinn Féin activities: SF funds, 1917–18, c. December 1918.

40. Peter Hart, *The IRA at War: 1916–23* (Oxford, 2003); Ó Súilleabháin, *Where Mountainy Men Have Sown*.

41. Coleman, *Longford and the Irish Revolution*, p. 148.

42. Hart, *The IRA and Its Enemies*, p. 164; Augusteijn, *From Public Defiance to Guerrilla Warfare*.

43. Townshend, *The Republic*, p. 43.

44. Augusteijn, *From Public Defiance to Guerrilla Warfare*, p. 260.

45. Hart, *The IRA and Its Enemies*, p. 135.

46. Laffan, *Resurrection of Ireland*, p. 44.

47. English, *Ernie O'Malley*, p. 121.

48. Quoted in Laffan, *Resurrection of Ireland*, p. 190.

49. IMA, BMH, WS1279, Seán Clifford.

50. Fitzpatrick, *Politics and Irish Life* (1998 edn), p. 6.

51. *Wexford People*, 2 January 1918.

52. John Borgonovo, 'A Soviet in embryo: Cork's food crisis and the People's Food Committee', *Saothar*, vol. 34 (2009), pp. 21–38.

53. Ibid.

54. Ibid.

55. Ibid.

56. Robert Brennan, *Allegiance* (Dublin, 1950), pp. 163–4.

57. *Nationality*, 5 January 1918.

58. *Wexford People*, 4 December 1918; *Irish Independent*, 11 December 1918.

59. 'A Western Priest', *The Two Policies: Sinn Féin or Parliamentarianism* (Dublin, 1918) UCDLSC, 35.E.4/31.

60. Sinn Féin, *The Policy of Abstention* (Dublin 1918); Revd J. Clancy, *The Failure of Parliamentarianism* (Clare, 1917), UCDLSC, 4.S.13/7.

61. Sinn Féin, *Mr Dillon Wants to See Poland, Finland, Bohemia ... Absolutely Independent* [election leaflet of Patrick J. Little] (Dublin 1918), UCDLSC, 34.Va.4/12; Sinn Féin, *The Conscriptionists* (Dublin, 1918), UCDLSC, 35.E.4/31, 'A Western Priest', *The Two Policies*; Sinn Féin, *Parliamentarianism in a Nut Shell* (Dublin, 1918), UCDLSC, 1.I.3/9; Sinn Féin, *Farmers! Your Turn Now* (Dublin, 1918), UCDLSC, 35.E.2/3.

62. Sinn Féin, *Did You Ever Think of This?* (Dublin 1918), UCDLSC, 1.I/3/13.

63. Darrell Figgis, *The Economic Case for Irish Independence* (Dublin, 1920), pp. 78–9 UCDLSC, 39.K.24.

64. Sinn Féin, *An Appeal to the Women of Ireland* (Dublin, 1918), UCDLSC, 34.Va.4/57.

65. Ibid.

66. J. R. White, *The Significance of Sinn Féin: Psychological, Political and Economic* (Dublin 1919); P. S. O'Hegarty, *Sinn Féin: An Illumination* (London, 1919).

67. Selma Sigerson, *Sinn Féin and Socialism* (Dublin, 1919); foreword by Aodh de Blácam.

68. Spálpín, *Sinn Féin and the Labour Movement* (Dublin 1918).

69. Michael Wheatley, *Nationalism and the Irish Party: Provincial Ireland, 1910–1916* (Oxford, 2005), p. 266.

70. McGarry, '1916 and Irish republicanism', p. 49.

71. Ernest Augustus Boyd, *The Worked-Out Ward: A Sinn Féin Allegory in One Act* (Dublin 1918), UCDLSC, 1.V.6/4.

72. Lyons, *John Dillon*, p. 439.

73. Ibid.

74. Ibid.

75. Wheatley, *Nationalism and the Irish Party*, pp. 250–66.
76. *Derry Journal*, 1 January 1919.
77. Ibid.
78. UCDA, P48/B12, Nan MacSwiney to Terence MacSwiney, 5 December 1918.
79. William Maloney, *The Irish Issue* (New York, 1919), p. 31 UCDLSC, 35.M.22/12.

17 **War of Independence (1) 1919–20: Catching the Waves**
1. Diarmaid Fleming, 'Last man standing: Dan Keating', *History Ireland*, vol. 16, no. 3 (May/June 2008), pp. 38–41.
2. Dolan, 'The War of Independence'.
3. Ibid.
4. Ibid.
5. NAI, Land Settlement Commission (LSC), Misc. 2A/13, Memorandum of Art O'Connor, c. July 1921.
6. Michael Hopkinson, 'Daniel Breen', *DOIB*, vol. 1, pp. 796–7.
7. Joost Augusteijn, 'Why was Tipperary so active in the War of Independence?' *Tipperary Historical Journal 2006* (Tipperary, 2006), pp. 207–21; Joost Augusteijn, 'Accounting for the emergence of violent activism among Irish revolutionaries, 1916–21', *Irish Historical Studies*, vol. 35, no. 139 (May 2007), pp. 327–44.
8. *Freeman's Journal*, 22 January 1919.
9. *Tipperary Star*, 25 January 1919.
10. *Freeman's Journal*, 23 January 1919.
11. *Tipperary Star*, 1 February 1919.
12. *History Ireland*, vol. 15, no. 3 (May/June 2007), pp. 56–7.
13. J. A. Kensit, *Rome Behind Sinn Féin* (London, 1920).
14. IMA, BMH, WS271, Michael Fogarty.
15. Maryann Gialanella Valiulis, *Portrait of a Revolutionary: General Richard Mulcahy and the Founding of the Irish Free State* (Dublin, 1992), p. 47.
16. UKNA, CO, 941/193, A. M. Sullivan to Lord Lieutenant, October 1919.
17. Lee, *Ireland*, p. 42.
18. Quoted in English, *Radicals and the Republic*, p. 29.
19. Laffan, *Resurrection of Ireland*, p. 295.
20. Tom Garvin, *Nationalist Revolutionaries in Ireland, 1858–1928* (Oxford, 1987), p. 109.
21. Seán O'Faoláin, *Vive Moi!* (Boston, 1964), p. 146.
22. D. G. Boyce, *Nationalism in Ireland* (London, 1995), p. 318.
23. J. Anthony Gaughan, *Thomas Johnson* (Dublin, 1980), pp. 155–7.
24. Cahill, *Forgotten Revolution*, p. 8.
25. Ibid., pp. 79–87.
26. Ibid., p. 143.
27. Breen, *My Fight*, p. 34.
28. Fearghal McGarry, 'Keeping an eye on the usual suspects: Dublin Castle's "Personality Files", 1899–1921', *History Ireland*, vol. 14, no. 6 (November/December 2006), pp. 44–9.
29. IMA, BMH, WS509, J. J. McConnell.
30. IMA, BMH, WS580, John Duffy; WS467, Eugene Bratton.
31. NAI, DE, 2/172–243, Diarmuid O'Hegarty to SF executive, 24 April 1919.
32. W. J. Lowe, 'The war against the RIC, 1919–21', *Eire-Ireland*, vol. 37, nos 3–4 (Fall/Winter 2002), pp. 79–117.

33. Joost Augusteijn (ed.), *The Memoirs of John M. Regan* (Dublin, 2007); Lowe, 'The war against the RIC'.
34. Lowe, 'The war against the RIC'.
35. Ibid.
36. UKNA, CO, 904/139, RIC reports, County Cork, 28 April 1920.
37. Ibid., County Mayo 29 April 1920.
38. Ibid., County Wicklow, 28 April 1920.
39. UKNA, CO, 906/19, County Clare, 21 April 1921.
40. NAI, 1125/20, Papers of George Gavan Duffy, Michael Collins to Gavan Duffy, 18 June 1921.
41. NAI, DE, 2/269, Ministry of Foreign Affairs, report of 10 June 1921.
42. Michael Kennedy, 'Robert Brennan', *DOIB*, vol. 1, pp. 814–15.
43. Ronan Fanning et al. (eds), *Documents on Irish Foreign Policy*, vol. 1, p. xii.
44. NAI, DE, 210, Desmond FitzGerald's report of 1 January 1920.
45. Mitchell, *Revolutionary Government*, p. 106.
46. NAI, DE, 2/269, Michael Collins to undersecretary at Foreign Affairs enclosing letter from Art O'Brien, 1 August 1921.
47. NAI, DE, 2/269, Report of Foreign Affairs ministry, January 1921.
48. Sinn Féin, *Sinn Féin, America and Ireland* (Dublin, 1918); UCDLSC, I.1.3/14.
49. Dave Hannigan, *De Valera in America: The Rebel President and the Making of Irish Independence* (New York, 2010), chapters 3 and 4.
50. UCDA, P150/727, Papers of Éamon de Valera, Arthur Griffith to Daniel Cohalan and John Devoy, 23 June 1920.
51. Laffan, *Resurrection of Ireland*, p. 308.
52. McGarry, 'Keeping an eye on the usual suspects'.
53. Ibid., p. 45.
54. Seán O'Casey, *Autobiographies: Volume 2* (London, 1980), pp. 40–41.
55. W. J. Lowe, 'Who were the Black and Tans?', *History Ireland*, vol. 12, no. 3 (Autumn 2004), pp. 47–51.
56. D. M. Leeson, *The Black and Tans: British Police and Auxiliaries in the Irish War of Independence, 1920–21* (Oxford, 2011).
57. Ibid., pp. 68–82.
58. Fitzpatrick (ed.), *Terror in Ireland*, pp. 59–66.
59. Gabriel Doherty and John Borgonovo, 'Smoking gun? RIC reprisals, summer 1920' *History Ireland*, vol. 17, no. 2 (March/April 2009), pp. 36–8.
60. Seán O'Riordan, 'Culprit who led burning of Cork finally identified', *Irish Examiner*, 11 December 2010.
61. Dolan, 'The War of Independence'.
62. Richard English, '"The inborn hate of things English": Ernie O'Malley and the Irish Revolution, 1916–23', *Past and Present*, no. 151 (May 1996), pp. 174–99.

18   The Chivalrous Soldier and the Cruel Killer

1. Francis J. Costello, *Enduring the Most: The Life and Death of Terence MacSwiney* (Dingle, 1996), p. 9.
2. Ibid., p. 245.
3. Ibid., p. 139.
4. UCDA, P48/B43–85, Terence MacSwiney to Muriel MacSwiney, 24 June 1918.
5. Ibid., 18 July, 4 September and 13 December 1918.

6. UCDA, P48/B416, Terence MacSwiney to Cathal Brugha, 30 September 1920.

7. Ibid., P48/B417, 8 September 1920.

8. M. A. Doherty, 'Kevin Barry and the Anglo-Irish propaganda war', *Irish Historical Studies*, vol. 32, no. 126 (November 2000), pp. 217–31.

9. Ibid., p. 231.

10. Hopkinson, *Irish War of Independence*, pp. 88–91.

11. Peter Hart (ed.), *British Intelligence in Ireland: The Final Reports* (Cork, 2002); Hart, *Mick*, pp. 242–68; Townshend, *The Republic*, p. 205.

12. Hopkinson, 'Michael Collins'.

13. Ibid.

14. Hopkinson, *Irish War of Independence*, p. 97.

15. UCDA, P152/151, Papers of George Gavan Duffy, Michael Collins to Gavan Duffy, 18 May 1920.

16. Charles Townshend, 'The IRA and the development of guerrilla warfare', *English Historical Review*, vol. 94, no. 371 (1979), pp. 318–45.

17. Arthur Mitchell, 'Alternative government: exit Britannia', in Augusteijn (ed.), *The Irish Revolution*, p. 84.

18. Richard Abbott, *Police Casualties in Ireland, 1919–22* (Dublin, 2000), p. 170.

19. Hopkinson, *Irish War of Independence*, p. 177.

20. *New Statesman*, 30 November 1920; IMA, BMH, WS379, Jeremiah Mee, and WS1449, Patrick J. Whelan.

21. William Sheehan, *British Voices from the Irish War of Independence, 1918–1921* (Cork, 2005), pp. 94–130 and, pp. 151–228.

22. IMA, BMH, WS423, Vincent Byrne.

23. Anne Dolan, 'Ending war in a "sportsmanlike manner": the milestone of revolution', in Hachey (ed.), *Turning Points*, pp. 21–38.

24. William Murphy, 'The GAA in Dublin during the Irish Revolution, 1913–23', talk given to the Sport and City Seminar, Dublin City Library, 11 September 2010.

25. Ibid.

26. Richard McElligott, *Forging a Kingdom: The GAA in Kerry, 1884–1934* (Cork, 2013).

27. Michael Hopkinson, 'Thomas Barry', *DOIB*, vol. 1, pp. 349–51.

28. IMA, BMH, WS1017, Patrick Cassidy, and WS830, Patrick Cannon.

29. IMA, BMH, WS1713, James L. O'Donovan.

30. NAI, DE, 2/244, Arthur Griffith to Éamon de Valera, 1 September 1921.

31. UKNA, CO, 906/19, County Cork, 3 October 1921.

32. Brian Hanley, *The IRA: A Documentary History, 1916–2005* (Dublin, 2010), pp. 1–39.

33. Dolan, 'Ending war in a "sportsmanlike manner"'.

34. Ibid.

35. Louise Ryan, '"Drunken Tans": representation of sex and violence in the Anglo-Irish War, 1919–21', *Feminist Review*, no. 66 (Autumn 2000), pp. 73–95.

36. Ibid.

37. Ibid.

38. IMA, BMH, WS1737, Séamus Fitzgerald.

39. IMA, BMH, WS821, Frank Henderson.

40. Aideen Sheehan, 'Cumann na mBan: policies and activities', in David Fitzpatrick (ed.), *Revolution? Ireland, 1917–1923* (Dublin, 1990), pp. 88–97.

41. Fitzpatrick, *Politics and Irish Life*, p. 183; Ryan, *Comrades*, p. 228.

42. Margaret Ward, 'Gendering the Irish revolution', in Augusteijn (ed.), *The Irish Revolution*, p. 182; Eve Morrison, 'Bureau of Military History and female republican activism, 1913–23', in Maryann Valiulis (ed.), *Gender and Power in Irish History* (Dublin, 2007), pp. 59–84.

43. McCabe, *For God and Ireland*, p. 36; Senia Paseta, 'Constance Georgine Markievicz', *DOIB*, vol. 5, pp. 363–6.

44. UCDA, P48/A9, Mary MacSwiney papers, Máirín de Daiblat to MacSwiney, April 1921.

45. Ibid.

46. IMA, BMH, WS450, Bridget O'Mullane.

47. Sineád McCoole, *Guns and Chiffon: Women Revolutionaries and Kilmainham Gaol, 1916–1923* (Dublin, 1997), pp. 37–8.

48. McCoole, *No Ordinary Women*, p. 77.

49. William Murphy, *Political Imprisonment and the Irish, 1912–1921* (Oxford, 2014), pp. 231–2.

50. Ivy Bannister, 'Images of Constance Markievicz', in Marie Heaney (ed.), *Sunday Miscellany: A Selection from 1995–2000* (Dublin 2000), pp. 133–4.

51. PRONI, D41311K/7/10, Constance Markievicz prison letters, Markievicz to Eva Gore Booth, 26 September 1917 and c. July 1921.

52. Joanne Hayden, 'The Life of Julia', *Sunday Business Post* magazine, 17 March 2013, speaking about her book *Trespassers: A Memoir* (London, 2013).

53. *Cuala News*, 11 January 1920; UCDLSC34.QQ.5/3.

19   Governing, Social Realities and Justice

1. Coleman, *Longford and the Irish Revolution*, p. 329.

2. Diarmaid Ferriter, *Lovers of Liberty? Local Government in Twentieth Century Ireland* (Dublin, 2001), p. 54.

3. IMA, BMH, WS449, William T. Cosgrave.

4. Quoted in Conor Kostick, *Revolution in Ireland: Popular Militancy, 1917–1923* (London, 1996), pp. 54, 182.

5. NAI, DE, 2/54, Report of the Ministry of the National Language, August 1921.

6. NAI, DE, 2/58, File on lines of communication, William T. Cosgrave to Diarmuid O'Hegarty, 5 October 1920, and Kevin O'Higgins to O'Hegarty, 12 October 1920.

7. NAI, DE, 2/51, Diarmuid O'Hegarty to each government department, 31 May 1921.

8. NAI, DE, 2/58, Secretary, Department of Labour to Diarmuid O'Hegarty, 13 October 1920.

9. NAI, D362, Ministerial appointments, extract from private session of Dáil proceedings, 6 August 1920.

10. James O'Mara and Francis Carroll, *Money for Ireland: Finance, Diplomacy, Politics and the First Dáil Éireann Loans, 1919–1936* (Westport, 2002).

11. Mitchell, *Revolutionary Government*, pp. 57–65.

12. NAI, DE, 2/450, report of Joseph Connolly, 12 December 1921.

13. NAI, DE, 2/7, First National Loan, September 1920.

14. NAI, DE, 2/160, 8 March 1921.

15. NAI, DE, 2/357, Irish Republican Government Loan in Argentina, 3 February 1922.

16. NAI, DFA, early files, box 17, Foreign consuls, 27 May 1922.

17. NAI, files of Dáil Éireann's Department of Local Government (DELG), 17/15, Limerick, Thomas Meaney, ITGWU Monroe, to Department of Labour, 5 September 1921.

18. NAI, DELG, 17/15, Constance Markievicz to Limerick County Council, 8 September 1920.

19. Conor McCabe, 'The Irish Labour Party and the 1920 local elections', *Saothar*, vol. 35 (2010), pp. 7–23.

20. UKNA, CO, 904/158, Crime Department Special Branch, ITGWU strikes, 1920–21 c. April 1920.

21. Ibid., Dublin, Drogheda and Cork, August 1920.

22. NAI, DE, 2/50, Secretary, Department of Labour to Diarmuid O'Hegarty, 10 December 1920.

23. NAI, DE, 2/48:, 'Railway strike after incident at Mallow', Michael Collins to Art O'Brien, 17 February 1921; O'Brien to Collins, 11 and 26 February 1921.

24. NAI, DE, 2/51, Report of Ministry for Home Affairs, 6 December 1921.

25. NAI, DE, 2/102, Standing committee of Irish Farmers Union to Éamon de Valera, 7 April 1921, and de Valera's reply transmitted through O'Hegarty, 9 April 1921.

26. *Freeman's Journal*, 2 August 1921.

27. *The Voice of Labour*, 29 October 1921.

28. *The Voice of Labour*, 21 January 1922.

29. *Freeman's Journal*, 13 September 1921.

30. 'Help the Irish White Cross', *Freeman's Journal*, 26 November 1921.

31. *Freeman's Journal*, 15 September 1921.

32. NAI, DE, 2/405, Vaccination laws, 1922.

33. Guy Beiner, Patricia March and Ida Milne, 'Greatest killer of the twentieth century: the Great Flu of 1918–19', *History Ireland*, vol. 17, no. 2 (March/April 2009), pp. 40–43.

34. Ibid.

35. NAI, DELG, 9/18, Dublin County Council, 15 May 1921.

36. Ibid., 21 November 1921.

37. NAI, DELG, 17/4, Limerick, Report of outbreak of dysentery in Limerick District Asylum, 29 September 1921.

38. *Freeman's Journal*, 28 and 15 September 1921.

39. NAI, DE, 2/416, anti-profiteering decrees, November 1921.

40. NAI, DE, 2/100, Trade and commerce, general, 25 April 1922.

41. NAI, DELG, 5/2, Ballyvaughan Union Board of Guardians, c. April 1921.

42. NAI, DELG, 25/11, Roscommon County Council, Misc. papers: Memorandum on amalgamation, 9 March 1922.

43. NAI, DELG, 21/19, Mayo County Council, 25 November 1921.

44. NAI, DELG, 26/9, Sligo Workhouse, October 1921.

45. NAI, DELG, 17/4, Visit to Limerick Union, 5 November 1921.

46. Garvin, *1922*, p. 86.

47. Laffan, *Resurrection of Ireland*, p. 330.

48. NAI, DE, 84, William T. Cosgrave to Austin Stack, 3 May 1921.

49. *Irish Times*, 13 July 1921.

50. PRONI, D41311K, Constance Markievicz prison letters; Markievicz to Eva Gore Booth, n.d., c. September 1917.

51. Yeates, *City in Turmoil*, p. 215.

52. NAI, DELG, 26/9, James Gilligan to William T. Cosgrave, 14 October 1921.

53. NAI, DELG, 26/9, Listowel, William T. Cosgrave to clerk of Listowel Rural District Council, 11 October 1921, and DELG, 12/10, Listowel RDC, June 1921.

54. NAI, DELG, 21/19, Report of Belmullet, 25 November 1921.

55. NAI, DELG, 9/18, Dublin County Council, 25 August 1921.
56. NAI, DE, 14/72, October 1921.
57. IMA, BMH, WS708, Conor A. Maguire.
58. Claremorris Community Radio, *The People's Courts: Ireland's Dáil Courts, 1920–24* (Mayo, 2013), p. 5.
59. Ibid., p. 16.
60. Ibid.
61. *Irish Times*, 2 June 1920.
62. IMA, BMH, WS1516, P. H. Doherty.
63. Kotsonouris, *Retreat from Revolution*, p. 12.
64. NAI, DE, 27/1, Circular from Ministry for Home Affairs, 19 August 1919.
65. NAI, DE, 25/1, Ministry for Home Affairs, Reports, June 1920.
66. Ibid.
67. Kotsonouris, *Retreat from Revolution*, pp. 31–2.
68. NAI, DE, 25/1, Report of Ministry for Home Affairs, 16 August 1921.
69. NAI, DE, 27/1, Report of Ministry for Home Affairs, 24 November 1921.
70. NAI, DE, 25/1, Report of Ministry for Home Affairs, April 1922.
71. NAI, DE, 16/4–7, Registrars' reports, November 1921–February 1922.
72. Kotsonouris, *Retreat from Revolution*, p. 134.

20   Land for the People?

1. Kotsonouris, *Retreat from Revolution*, p. 134.
2. Heather Laird, *Subversive Law in Ireland, 1879–1920: From 'Unwritten Law' to the Dáil Courts* (Dublin 2005), pp. 123–8.
3. NAI, DE, 25/1, Report of Ministry for Home Affairs, 16 August 1921.
4. NAI, LSC, Misc. 26, LSC work, September 1921.
5. NAI, DE, 2/45, Nenagh Housing Scheme, 22 July and 18 August 1920.
6. NAI, LSC, Tipperary 109, Cork 102 and Misc. 25, no dates, c. 1920–21.
7. UKNA, CO, 904/139, RIC: Summary of police reports sent by RIC Dublin Castle to undersecretary, 1 May 1920.
8. UKNA, CO, 904/139, RIC reports, Clare, 10 May 1920.
9. NAI, LSC, Offaly 119, August 1921.
10. Pat Feeley, *The Gralton Affair: The Story of the Deportation of Jim Gralton, a Leitrim Socialist* (Dublin, 1986).
11. Luke Gibbons, 'Labour and local history: the case of Jim Gralton, 1886–1945', *Saothar*, vol. 14 (1989), pp. 85–93.
12. Ibid.
13. Ibid.
14. Hart, 'Definition: defining the Irish Revolution', p. 30.
15. Campbell, *Land and Revolution*, p. 220.
16. Garvin, *Nationalist Revolutionaries in Ireland*, p. 90.
17. *Irish Bulletin*, vol. 5, no. 46 (4 August 1921), copy in NAI, LSC, Misc. 12.
18. Fergus Campbell, 'The last Land War? Kevin O'Shiel's memoir of the Irish Revolution, 1916–21', *Archivium Hibernicum*, vol. 57 (2003), pp. 155–200.
19. NAI, LSC, Misc. 2A12–13, Art O'Connor report to Dáil, 21 May 1920.
20. Ibid.
21. NAI, LSC, Misc., Report of Patrick Hogan, Minister for Agriculture on work of department January 1922–April 1922.

22. NAI, LSC, 2A13, Clare, Dineen Farm, June 1922.
23. Ibid., Colonel W. F. Spaight, Ardataggle, 1922.
24. NAI, LSC, Misc., Mayo, 8 March 1922.
25. Campbell, 'The last Land War?'
26. NAI, LSC, Limerick 41, IRA chief of staff to Minister for Defence, 23 June 1921, and note of IRA warning, 29 June 1921.
27. NAI, LSC, Limerick 41, Frank Roche to Robert Barton, 4 September 1921.
28. Ibid., Seán O'Fogarty to Robert Barton, 9 January 1922.
29. NAI, LSC, Laois 190, Land agitation in Queen's County and E. Richardson to Heavey, 18 December 1922.
30. NAI, LSC, Misc., Michael Collins to William T. Cosgrave, 21 September 1921.
31. Dooley, 'IRA veterans and land division', p. 86.
32. NAI, LSC, Kerry 150, Ardfert village tenants petition, March 1922.

21 **War of Independence (2) 1921–2: The Juggernaut of Politics**

1. UCDA, P197/2, Kevin O'Higgins to Brigid Cole, 29 May 1920.
2. Ibid., 24 June 1920 and 22 November 1920.
3. UCDA, P197/62, Kevin O'Higgins to Brigid Cole, March 1921.
4. Ibid.
5. Ibid., 17 April 1921.
6. Ibid.
7. NAI, DE, 2/51, Ministry for Home Affairs May 1921, and 2/483, report from Ministry for Labour, c. July 1921.
8. NAI, LSC, Misc. 1, Boyle, Roscommon, August 1921.
9. Michael Parsons, 'Nuns asked for sniper to kill crows', *Irish Times*, 11 April 2012.
10. NAI, DELG, 17/15, Limerick County Council, Patrick Kenneally, Askeaton, 23 December 1921.
11. IMA, BMH, WS505, Seán Moylan.
12. UCDA, P80/129, Papers of Desmond FitzGerald 142 and 158, Michael Staines, 10 November 1921, and anonymous prisoner, 5 April 1921.
13. Murphy, *Political Imprisonment and the Irish*, pp. 2–10.
14. David Fitzpatrick, 'Militarism in Ireland, 1900–1922', in Tom Bartlett and Keith Jeffery (eds), *A Military History of Ireland* (Cambridge, 1996), p. 406.
15. T. Ryle Dwyer, *The Squad and the Intelligence Operations of Michael Collins* (Dublin, 2005), p. 252.
16. Charles Townshend, *The British Campaign in Ireland: The Development of Political and Military Policies* (Oxford, 1975), pp. 170 ff.
17. McMahon, 'Ireland and the Empire-Commonwealth'.
18. NAI, DE, 2/10, Report of propaganda department, 18 January 1921.
19. Coogan, *De Valera*, p. 198.
20. NAI, DE, 2/448, Éamon de Valera to Michael Collins 18 January 1921.
21. UKNA, CO, 906/19, Correspondence/telegrams into Irish Office, County Kerry, 14 June 1921.
22. Ibid. , County Cork, June 1921.
23. Ibid., King's County, 25 September 1921.
24. Ibid., Nenagh, 23 September 1921.
25. Piaras Béaslaí, *Michael Collins and the Making of a New Ireland* (Dublin, 1926), p. 99.
26. James Quinn, 'Cathal Brugha', *DOIB*, vol. 1, pp. 951–4.

27. Frank P. Crozier, *Impressions and Recollections* (London, 1930), p. 254.

28. Townshend, *British Campaign in Ireland*.

29. Yeates, *City in Turmoil*, pp. 272–3.

30. Ibid., p. 275.

31. Dolan, 'Ending war in a "sportsmanlike manner"'.

32. Sheehan, *British Voices*, p. 45.

33. Dolan, 'The War of Independence'.

34. NAI, 1125/20, Gavan Duffy Papers, Michael Collins to Gavan Duffy, 18 June 1921.

22   Truce and Treaty

1. Richard English, *Armed Struggle: The History of the IRA* (London, 2003), p. 21.

2. Eunan O'Halpin, 'Counting terror: Bloody Sunday and the dead of the Irish revolution', in Fitzpatrick (ed.), *Terror in Ireland*, pp. 141–58.

3. Charles Townshend, 'The Irish War of Independence: context and meaning', in Crowe (ed.), *Guide to the Military Service Pensions Collection*, p. 110.

4. Leeson, *The Black and Tans*, pp. 192–223.

5. Townshend, 'The Irish War of Independence: context and meaning'.

6. Frank O'Connor, *The Big Fellow: A Life of Michael Collins* (London, 1937), p. 156.

7. NAI, DE, 2/244, Michael Collins to Éamon de Valera, 16 July 1921.

8. UCDA, P7/B28, Mulcahy Papers, October 1921.

9. UKNA, WO, 35/182A, Report of divisional inspector commanding Auxiliary division, Dunmanway, 13 October 1921.

10. McMahon, 'Ireland and the Empire-Commonwealth'.

11. NAI, DE, 2/262, Jan Smuts to Éamon de Valera, 4 August 1921.

12. Laffan, *Resurrection of Ireland*, p. 346.

13. NAI, DE, 2/304, Éamon de Valera to Michael Collins, 19 July 1921.

14. Ferriter, *Judging Dev*, pp. 61–99.

15. Hart, *Mick*, pp. 264–306.

16. Valiulis, *Portrait of a Revolutionary*, p. 101.

17. UCDA, P122/119, Typescript copy of a letter from Éamon de Valera to Frank Pakenham, 24 February 1963, p. 3.

18. Laffan, *Resurrection of Ireland*, pp. 346–86.

19. Ibid.

20. IMA, BMH, WS979, Robert C. Barton.

21. *Freeman's Journal*, 8 October 1921.

22. *Freeman's Journal*, 11 October 1921.

23. In Desmond Williams (ed.), *The Irish Struggle, 1916–26* (London, 1966), p. 112.

24. McMahon, 'Ireland and the Empire-Commonwealth'.

25. Laffan, 'Arthur Griffith'.

26. Thomas Jones, *Whitehall Diary*, vol. 3: *Ireland, 1918–25* (Oxford, 1971), pp. 110–55.

27. Pauric J. Dempsey and Shaun Boylan, 'Robert Childers Barton', *DOIB*, vol. 1, pp. 361–3.

28. Ibid.

29. Kevin Matthews, *Fatal Influence: The Impact of Ireland on British Politics, 1920–1925* (Dublin, 2004) p. 41.

30. Frank Pakenham, *Peace by Ordeal: The Negotiation of the Anglo-Irish Treaty, 1921* (London, 1992 [1935]).

31. Matthews, *Fatal Influence*, pp. 46–50.

32. NAI, DE, 2/304(1), Letter from combined delegation to Éamon de Valera, 26 October 1921.
33. Keith Middlemas (ed.), *Thomas Jones Whitehall Diary*, vol. 1: *1916–25* (London, 1969), p. 174.
34. IMA, BMH, WS979, Robert C. Barton.
35. Pakenham, *Peace by Ordeal*, p. 201.
36. Jones, *Whitehall Diary*, vol. 3.
37. Ibid., p. 183.
38. *Dáil Éireann Debates*, 14 December 1921.
39. Michael Laffan, 'The emergence of the two Irelands, 1912–25', *History Ireland*, vol. 12, no. 4 (Winter 2004), pp. 40–44.
40. Hopkinson, *Green Against Green*, p. 34.
41. *Freeman's Journal*, 14 December 1921.
42. *Freeman's Journal*, 20 December 1921.
43. *Dáil Éireann Debates*, 19 December 1921.
44. *Freeman's Journal*, 23 and 27 December 1921.
45. *Freeman's Journal*, 5 January 1922.
46. Laffan, *The Partition of Ireland*, p. 80.
47. Hopkinson, *Green Against Green*, p. 36.
48. UCDA, P80/298, Papers of Desmond FitzGerald, Anti Treaty Document by Liam Mellows, c. February–May 1922.
49. *Freeman's Journal*, 6 and 22 December 1921.
50. UCDA, P80/258, 13 January 1922, and P80/274.
51. *Freeman's Journal*, 8 December 1921.
52. UKNA, HO, 144/4645, Memorandum on the release on Irish prisoners, 11 February 1922; Memorandum from Home Office, 28 March 1922.
53. *An tOglách*, 9 and 16 December 1921.
54. *An tOglách*, 30 December 1921 and 13 January 1922.
55. Peter Hart, 'Paramilitary politics and the Irish revolution', in McGarry (ed.), *Republicanism in Modern Ireland*, pp. 23–42.
56. Townshend, *The Republic*, pp. 358–62.
57. Hart, 'Paramilitary politics'.
58. UCDA, P7/B153, Papers of Richard Mulcahy, Numbers in the IRA, December 1921, Éamon Price to Eoin O'Duffy, November 1921.

23 The Drift to Civil War

1. David Fitzpatrick, *Harry Boland's Irish Revolution* (Cork, 2003), p. 327.
2. UCDA, P53/27, Papers of Michael Hayes, January 1922.
3. UKNA, WO, 35/182A, 'Peace', December 1921–January 1922, report from Curragh, 30 December 1921.
4. Ibid., 'Precautionary measures, April–May 1922' and 'Handing over of barracks to Free State troops', 1 April, 5 April, 15 February and 10 April 1922.
5. *The Worker's Republic*, 18 February 1922.
6. Florence O'Donoghue, *No Other Law* (Dublin, 1954), p. 231.
7. Garvin, *1922*, p. 43.
8. Oliver Coogan, *Politics and War in Meath, 1913–23* (Dublin, 1983), p. 288.
9. *Seán O'Casey's Juno and the Paycock, Souvenir Programme* (Abbey Theatre, Dublin, 1979), p. 7.

10. NAI, DE, 2/514, S. T. O'Kelly to Michael Collins, 28 April, and reply 1 May 1922; O'Kelly to Collins, 6 May, and reply, 15 May 1922.

11. *Freeman's Journal*, 22 December 1921.

12. NAI, DT, S1322, Winston Churchill to Michael Collins, 12 April 1922.

13. UCDA, P197/87, Kevin O'Higgins to Brigid Cole, 22 June 1922.

14. Fitzpatrick, *Harry Boland's Irish Revolution*, pp. 264–85.

15. UCDA, P104/1237–48, Papers of Frank Aiken, Aiken to Richard Mulcahy, 6 and 30 July 1922.

16. Donnchadh Ó Corráin, *James Hogan: Revolutionary, Historian and Political Scientist* (Dublin, 2001), p. 50.

17. Bill Kissane, '"From the outside in": the international dimension to the Irish civil war', *History Ireland*, vol. 15, no. 2 (March/April 2007), pp. 36–41.

18. Michael Gallagher, 'The pact general election of 1922', *Irish Historical Studies*, vol. 21, no. 84 (September 1979), pp. 404–21.

19. English, *Armed Struggle*, pp. 33–4.

20. See Deirdre McMahon's review of Bill Kissane's *The Politics of the Irish Civil War* (Oxford, 2005) in *Irish Economic and Social History*, vol. 34 (2007), pp. 130–31.

21. Kissane, *The Politics of the Irish Civil War*, pp. 151–77.

22. Ibid., p. 8 and Farry, *The Aftermath of Revolution*.

23. NAI, Seán Mac Caoilte Papers, 1019, Mac Caoilte to Brigid Mac Caoilte, 1 and 9 May 1922.

24. Ibid., 7 May 1922.

25. *Irish Labour Party and TUC Annual Report*, August 1921.

26. Ciara Meehan, 'Labour and Dáil Éireann, 1922–32', in Daly, O'Brien and Rouse (eds), *Making the Difference?*, pp. 43–6.

27. Brian Hanley, 'The Irish Citizen Army after 1916', *Saothar*, vol. 28 (2003), p. 40.

28. Cullen, *An Economic History of Ireland*, pp. 138–43.

29. NAI, DE, 14/1–27, Ministry of Home Affairs, Letter from court organiser in Corofin, Clare, 8 June 1922.

30. *Irish Independent*, 30 January 1922.

31. *Irish Independent*, 24 February 1922.

32. *Dáil Éireann Debates*, 11 September 1922.

33. Ibid., 5 October 1922.

34. Ibid., 10 January 1922.

35. Ibid., 10 May and 11 September 1922.

36. Quoted in Kostick, *Revolution in Ireland*, p. 162.

37. UCDA, P197/139, O'Higgins election speech, June 1922.

38. Alfred O'Rahilly, *The Case for the Treaty* (Dublin, 1922).

39. George Russell, *Ireland and the Empire: At the Court of Conscience* (Dublin, 1921).

40. UCDA, P80/318 and 325, 'Government and civil war: pamphlets, leaflets, handbills', 1922.

41. Kevin O'Higgins, *Civil War and the Events Which Led to It* (Dublin, 1922), pp. 29–42.

42. Garvin, *1922*, p. 62.

43. Ciara Meehan, *The Cosgrave Party: A History of Cumann na nGaedheal, 1923–33* (Dublin, 2010), pp. 1–23.

44. Joseph M. Curran, *The Birth of the Irish Free State, 1921–1923* (Alabama, 1980) and Terence de Vere White, *Kevin O'Higgins* (London, 1948), p. 83.

24 **Civil War**

1. Prionnsias Ó Gallchobhair, *By What Authority?* (Dublin, 1922).
2. O'Malley, *The Singing Flame*, pp. 197–8.
3. Greaves, *Liam Mellows*, pp. 257–8.
4. UCDA, P7A/175, Mary MacSwiney to Richard Mulcahy, 24 April 1922.
5. Owen Dudley Edwards, *Éamon de Valera* (Cardiff, 1987), pp. 110–18.
6. UCDA, P150/1657, Éamon de Valera to Mary MacSwiney, 11 September 1922.
7. UCDA, P88/73, 'A diary from the Four Courts' by Fr Albert, 28 June 1922.
8. *Irish Times*, 25 November 1922.
9. UCDA, P151/140, Kathleen O'Connell diaries, 7 July 1922.
10. Eve Morrison, 'One woman's war', *Irish Times*, 22 May 2013, supplement: 'Stories of the Irish revolution'.
11. Regan, *Myth and the Irish State*, pp. 113–21.
12. UCDA, P7/B50, July 1922.
13. NAI, DT, S1302, Michael Collins to Arthur Griffith, 12 July 1922.
14. UCDA, P88/81, Memorandum by Éamon de Valera, c. June 1922.
15. Ronan Fanning, *The Irish Department of Finance, 1922–1958* (Dublin, 1978), pp. 50–55.
16. Curran, *Birth of the Irish Free State*, pp. 274–6.
17. UCDA, P53/285, George Russell to Michael Hayes, 17 April 1923.
18. NAI, DFA, early years, box 21, Accounts, 1 January 1922 to 10 April 1922.
19. Ibid.
20. *The Fifty-fifth Report of the Deputy Keeper of the Public Records and Keeper of the State Papers in Ireland, 1922–23* (Dublin, 1924), p. 17.
21. *Irish Independent*, 14 April 1922.
22. UCDA, P53/290, Éamon O'Neill to Michael Hayes, 6 June 1923.
23. UCDA, P7/B28, Collins's notes during the civil war, c. July 1922.
24. UCDA, P152/274, George Gavan Duffy to Richard Mulcahy, 30 August 1922.
25. Forester, *Michael Collins: Lost Leader*, p. 347.
26. O'Hegarty, *The Victory of Sinn Féin*, pp. 103–4.
27. Patrick Maume, 'Seán Thomas O'Kelly', *DOIB*, vol. 7, pp. 615–19.
28. *An Saorstát*, 1 April 1922.
29. UCDA, P53/335, Desmond Williams to Michael Hayes, 17 May 1958.
30. UCDA, P88/82, Notice from Éamon de Valera, 22 November 1922.
31. Laffan, 'Arthur Griffith'; 'Poltroons' remark made in Dáil, May 1922.
32. Ibid.
33. *Dáil Éireann Debates*, 7 January 1922.
34. UCDA, P152/197–209, George Gavan Duffy to Michael Collins, 10 March and 26 May 1922; Gavan Duffy to Arthur Griffith, 14 June 1922.
35. UCDA, P152/251 and 261, George Gavan Duffy to William T. Cosgrave, 16 July 1922; Gavan Duffy to Michael Collins, 24 July 1922.
36. UCDA, P152/261–74, George Gavan Duffy to 'Fr H', 15 March 1922.
37. Lee, *Ireland*, p. 63.
38. *Irish Times*, 24 August 1922.
39. Ibid.
40. Rex Taylor, *Michael Collins* (London, 1958), p. 255.
41. *Freeman's Journal*, 30 August 1922.
42. *Cork Examiner*, 24 August 1922.
43. *Cork Examiner*, 22 and 23 August 1922.

44. *Northern Whig*, 24 August 1922.
45. *Boston Daily Globe*, 24 August 1922.
46. NAI, DT, 5750/18, Lionel Curtis to William T. Cosgrave, 24 August 1922.

25   Stone Hearts

1. John Regan, *The Irish Counter-Revolution, 1921–36* (Dublin, 1999), p. 179.
2. Eunan O'Halpin, 'William Thomas Cosgrave', *DOIB*, vol. 2, pp. 880–85.
3. *Dáil Éireann Debates*, 6 December 1922.
4. UCDA, P53/47, Papers of Michael Hayes, Liam Lynch to Michael Hayes, 28 November 1922.
5. UCDA, P53/48, George Gavan Duffy to Michael Hayes, 2 December 1922.
6. UCDA, P152/239, Papers of George Gavan Duffy, 12–16 January 1922.
7. UCDA, P151/141, Kathleen O'Connell diaries, 8 December 1922.
8. John Horgan, *The Irish Media: A Critical History Since 1922* (London, 2001), p. 10.
9. *Dáil Éireann Debates*, 8 December 1922.
10. Hopkinson, *Green Against Green*, p. 188.
11. Garvin, *1922*, p. 163.
12. Ferriter, *The Transformation of Ireland*, p. 263.
13. UCDA, P91/85, Papers of Todd Andrews, Free State Army HQ to various commands, 18–27 January 1923.
14. O'Hegarty, *The Victory of Sinn Féin*, p. 104.
15. McCabe, *For God and Ireland*, p. 169.
16. Knirck, 'Women's political rhetoric'.
17. Ibid.
18. Patrick Murray, *Oracles of God: The Roman Catholic Church and Irish Politics, 1922–1937* (Dublin, 2000), p. 85.
19. McCabe, *For God and Ireland*, p. 8.
20. Ibid., pp. 78–95.
21. Ibid., pp. 114–19.
22. Murray, *Oracles of God*, p. 49.
23. McCabe, *For God and Ireland*, p. 119.
24. Ibid., pp. 123–32.
25. Dermot Keogh, *Ireland and the Vatican: The Diplomacy of Church–State Relations, 1922–60* (Cork, 1995), p. 28.
26. Murray, *Oracles of God*, p. 182.
27. NAI, DT, S1369, 'Civil war prisoners: imprisonment and hunger strike of Mary MacSwiney', Archbishop Byrne to Mary MacSwiney, 8 November 1922.
28. Murray, *Oracles of God*, p. 89.
29. Prionnsias Ó Gallchobhair, *The Bishop's Pastoral: A Prisoner's Letter to His Grace the Archbishop of Dublin* (Dublin and Glasgow, 1922); UCDLSC, 34.N.1/2.
30. *Irish Times*, 20 November 1922.
31. NAI, DT, S1369, E. Skeffington-Thompson to William T. Cosgrave, 21 November 1922.
32. Ibid., Edward Byrne to William T. Cosgrave, 24 November 1922.
33. Ibid., Edward Byrne to Mary MacSwiney, 8 November 1922.
34. Ibid., G. A. Lyons to William T. Cosgrave, 24 November 1922.
35. UCDA, P88/97, Letter from Mary MacSwiney to supporters in America, 18 November 1922.

36. UCDA, P88/78, Phyllis Ryan to James Ryan, 21 November 1923; IMA, BMH, WS1741, Michael O'Donoghue.

37. UCDA, P88/100, circular letter from Sinn Féin to Roman Catholic bishops, 24 October 1923.

38. UCDA, P91/1, Todd Andrews to his mother, 5 April 1923.

39. Francis Stuart, *Things to Live For: Notes for an Autobiography* (New York, 1938), pp. 36–43.

40. IMA, BMH, WS1741, Michael O'Donoghue.

41. UCDA, P7/B178, Mulcahy Papers, 12 February 1923.

42. Valiulis, *Portrait of a Revolutionary*, pp. 172–82.

43. Dorothy Macardle, *Tragedies of Kerry* (Dublin, 1924), p. 24.

44. IMA, MSPC, MSPF 34 REF6759, Stephen Fuller, 25 September 1933.

45. IMA, MSPC, MSPF WP66, Joseph O'Brien: Telegram of 13 March 1923 to Annie O'Brien, recommendation of Pensions Board 3 June 1924; Annie O'Brien to Department of Defence, 20 March and 11 August 1925; Letter of John O'Brien, 22 September 1925.

46. IMA, MSPC, MSPF 24 SP1124, Thomas Roche: Thomas Roche to Gearóid O'Sullivan, 23 April 1925.

47. Lennox Robinson (ed.), *Lady Gregory's Journals, 1916–30* (London, 1946), p. 166.

48. *Dáil Éireann Debates*, 1 March 1923.

49. Ibid.; *Irish Independent*, 2 March 1923.

50. Dooley, 'IRA veterans and land division', p. 87.

51. NAI, LSC, Misc. 24, T. Killeen to Patrick Hogan, 22 May 1922.

52. Andy Bielenberg, 'Exodus: the emigration of southern Irish Protestants during the Irish War of Independence and civil war', *Past and Present*, no. 218 (February 2013), p. 209.

53. Ibid.

54. Fitzpatrick (ed.), *Terror in Ireland*, p. 13.

55. D'Alton, "A vestigial population?".

56. Ibid., p. 20.

57. Ibid., p. 25.

58. Ibid., p. 30, and Nicholas Perry, 'The Irish landed class and the British Army, 1850–1950', *War in History*, vol. 18, no. 3 (2011), pp. 304–32.

59. Terence Dooley, *The Decline of the Big House in Ireland: A Study of Irish Landed Families, 1860–1960* (Dublin, 2001) pp. 171ff.

60. Bielenberg, 'Exodus: the emigration of southern Irish Protestants', p. 232.

61. Ibid.

62. Charles Townshend, 'Historiography', in Augusteijn (ed.), *The Irish Revolution*, pp. 1–16.

63. UCDA, P7/B171, 25 July 1923.

64. *Irish Times*, 18 August 1923.

65. Laffan, *Resurrection of Ireland*, p. 437.

66. UCDA, P150/1818, Item 10, 31 May 1923.

67. UCDA, P150/1826, 19 May 1923.

68. *Irish Times*, 30 March 1940.

26 Ulster's Wounded Self-Love

1. Lewis, *Carson*, pp. 163–4.

2. Albert White, *Ireland: A Study in Facts* (London, 1920), p. 9; UCDLSC, 34.S.3/8.

3. PRONI, D640/7/11–16, James Craig to Fred Crawford, 16 June 1919.

4. Ibid., Fred Crawford to James Craig, 2 June 1920.
5. Fitzpatrick, *Two Irelands*, p. 97.
6. Austen Morgan, *Labour and Partition: The Belfast Working Class, 1905–1923* (London, 1991).
7. Bew, Gibbon and Patterson, *Northern Ireland*, p. 27.
8. Fitzpatrick, *Two Irelands*, p. 98.
9. PRONI, D640, Diary of Fred Crawford, 27 September 1920.
10. *Irish Times*, 22 and 26 June 1920.
11. PRONI, D640/7/11–16, Carson Correspondence, James Craig to Fred Crawford, 6 September 1921.
12. PRONI, D640/11/2–3, Diary of Fred Crawford, 21 July 1920.
13. Ibid., 27 August 1920.
14. Ibid., 1 September 1920.
15. Ibid., 6 and 11 September 1920.
16. Ibid., 27 September 1920.
17. PRONI, D1415/B/39, Diary of Lady Craigavon, 1918–20, 14 October 1920.
18. NAI, DE, 2/492, Joseph Campbell to Arthur Griffith, 13 November 1921.
19. NAI, DE, 2/110, Belfast Boycott, 20 January 1921.
20. NAI, DE, 2/110, Joseph MacDiarmada to cabinet, 3 December 1921.
21. NAI, DE, 10, Propaganda department: activities, 1920–21, 14 February 1920 and 2/89, 5 May 1920, 2/103, April 1921 and 2/110, Belfast Boycott, December 1921.
22. Fitzpatrick, *Two Irelands*, p. 97.
23. NAI, DE, 2/266–91, Michael Collins to Arthur Griffith, 26 January 1921.
24. NAI, DELG, 8/6, Kilkeel Poor Law Union, Co. Down, Peter Murray to William T. Cosgrave, 3 November 1921.
25. Derry City Council Archives (DCCA), Minute book, 1906–13, 20 May 1909, 16 October and 7 November 1911, 18 August 1913.
26. DCCA, Minute books, Rural District Council, 1908–20, 6 May 1911, 19 April 1914, 23 April 1915.
27. Ronan Gallagher, *Violence and Nationalist Politics in Derry City, 1920–23* (Dublin, 2003).
28. UKNA, CO, 906/19, Londonderry, 11 June 1921.
29. Andrew Gailey, 'King Carson: an essay on the invention of leadership', *Irish Historical Studies*, vol. 30, no. 117 (May 1996), pp. 66–87.
30. Ibid., p. 76.
31. PRONI, D640/7/11–16, Carson correspondence, Fred Crawford to Edward Carson, 2 May 1921.
32. Gailey, 'King Carson', p. 80.
33. PRONI, D1327/18/36, UUC, T. N. Watts to Dawson Bates, 19 January 1921; W. Coote to Dawson Bates, 22 January 1921; account of meeting with Carson in London.
34. Ibid.
35. PRONI, D1327/18/36, UUC, Duchess of Abercorn to Dawson Bates, 31 January 1921.
36. Emmet O' Connor and Trevor Parkhill (eds), *Loyalism and Labour in Belfast: The Autobiography of Robert McElborough, 1884–1952* (Cork, 2002).
37. Fitzpatrick, *Two Irelands*, p. 101.
38. *Freeman's Journal*, 1 June 1921.
39. NAI, DE, 2/304(1), Arthur Griffith to Éamon de Valera, 5 November 1921.
40. Fitzpatrick, *Two Irelands*, p. 101.

41. NAI, DE, 2/304/8, Treaty negotiations: Memorandum of meeting at Churchill's house, 30 October 1921.
42. PRONI, D640/7/11–16, Edward Carson to Fred Crawford, 12 November 1921.
43. NAI, DE, 2/304/1, James Craig to David Lloyd George, 14 December 1921.
44. NAI, DE, 2/304/1, Arthur Griffith to Éamon de Valera, 27 October 1921.
45. NAI, DE, 2/473, memorandum by Diarmaid Fawsitt on economic relations, 14 December 1921.
46. R. B. McDowell, *Historical Essays, 1938–2001* (Dublin, 2003), p. 206.
47. NAI, DE, 2/247, Truce: July 1921, Michael Collins to Éamon de Valera, 6 July 1921.
48. Robert Lynch, *The Northern IRA and the Early Years of Partition, 1920–22* (Dublin, 2006).
49. Ibid., p. 4.
50. Ibid., p. 207.
51. PRONI, CAB, 9A/4/1, James Craig to Chancellor of the Exchequer, 8 November 1921.
52. Ibid., James Craig to Hamar Greenwood, 9 January 1922.
53. PRONI, CAB, 9A/4/1, Finance Correspondence, 9 February 1922.
54. Ibid.
55. Ibid., Neville Chamberlain to James Craig, 4 October 1923.

27 The Tyranny of the 'Special'

1. UCDA, P7/A26, Commandant, 2nd Northern Division, to Richard Mulcahy, 15 October 1921.
2. *Freeman's Journal*, 28 February 1922.
3. PRONI, HA, 5/956A, Internee: Cahir Healy: Healy to Kevin O'Shiel, 31 July 1922.
4. Ibid., Healy to the *Argenta* Governor, 3 October and 28 November 1922 and 19 January 1923.
5. NAI, DT, S5462, 'Outrages in Northern Ireland', February 1922.
6. Patrick Riddell, *Fire Over Ulster* (London, 1970), p. 50.
7. NAI, DT, S5462, 'Outrages in Northern Ireland', Michael Collins to Winston Churchill, 16 February 1922.
8. Ibid., Michael Collins to Desmond FitzGerald, 6 March 1922.
9. Ibid., Winston Churchill to Michael Collins, 14 March 1922.
10. Ibid., Statement by Mrs Bunting, 203 Argyle Street, n/d, c. March 1922.
11. PRONI, HA, 32/1/28, Outrages in Belfast: Complaint of Michael Collins, Collins to Winston Churchill, 6 March 1922.
12. Ibid., Wilfrid Spender to Home Affairs, 8 and 11 March 1922 and RIC Commissioner's Office, 10 March 1922.
13. UKNA, CO, 906/30, Belfast reports: June 1920–July 1922, 15 July 1922.
14. Ibid., 'Note on the situation in NI June 1922'.
15. Ibid., Stephen Tallents to James Masterson Smith, 15 July 1922.
16. PRONI, CAB, 6/46, James Craig to Dawson Bates, 10 June 1922.
17. David Fitzpatrick, 'The Orange Order and the border', *Irish Historical Studies*, vol. 33, no. 129 (May 2002), pp. 52–67.
18. Richard English, review of J. Bowyer Bell's *The Irish Troubles: A Generation of Violence, 1967–1992* (Dublin, 1993) *Irish Historical Studies*, vol. 29, no. 116 (November 1995), pp. 619–20.
19. Bew, Gibbon and Patterson, *Northern Ireland*, p. 50.

20. Ibid., pp. 10, p. 345; Denis Kennedy, *The Widening Gulf: Northern Attitudes to the Independent Irish State, 1919–1949* (Belfast, 1988).

21. PRONI, CAB, 9C/21/1, J. A. Dale to W. Spender, 14 October 1922.

22. PRONI, CAB, 9C/1/1, Unemployment Insurance Fund, Wilfrid Spender to Minister for Labour, 21 December 1921.

23. Ibid., Andrews to Craig, 27 April 1922.

24. Ibid., Memorandum of E. Clark, 28 August 1923.

25. Mary Harris, *The Catholic Church and the Foundation of the Northern Ireland State* (Cork, 1993).

26. Ibid., pp. 196–256.

27. John Privilege, *Michael Logue and the Catholic Church in Ireland, 1879–1925* (Manchester, 2009), p. 198.

28. Brendan Lynn, 'Joseph Mac Rory', *DOIB*, vol. 6, pp. 182–3.

29. PRONI, D4089/4/1/1, Parliamentary Elections, West Belfast, Harry Midgley, 6 December 1923, Election to Imperial Parliament.

30. PRONI, CAB, 9B/137/1, Outdoor Relief, G. Corcoran to James Craig, 5 February 1924.

31. Ibid., Thompson Donald to James Craig 5 January 1924.

32. Ibid., Cabinet Secretary to James Muckian, 28 February 1924.

33. Paul Murray, *The Irish Boundary Commission and Its Origins, 1886–1925* (Dublin, 2011) pp. 304ff.

34. Ibid.

35. Ibid., pp. 129–30.

36. Ibid., pp. 105–7.

37. Hopkinson, *Green Against Green*, p. 250.

38. Ibid.

39. Murray, *Boundary Commission*, pp. 110–29.

40. Fitzpatrick, 'The Orange Order and the border'; Harris, *The Catholic Church*, pp. 53–65.

41. Cahir Healy to editor of *Irish Independent*, 30 November 1925, cited in Eamon Phoenix, 'Cahir Healy', *DOIB*, vol. 4, pp. 555–8.

42. NAI, DT, S11209, 'Deputation from Northern Ireland to the provisional government', 11 October 1922.

43. NAI, DT, S5750/2, 25 January 1923.

28   'In danger of finding myself with nothing at all'

1. Hopkinson, 'Thomas Barry'.

2. IMA, MSPC, MSP34, REF57456, Thomas Barry: Tom Barry to Registration Board, 29 January 1940.

3. Ibid., Bill Quirke to Military Service Pensions Board, 2 February 1940 and F. Begley to Military Service Pensions Board, 18 April 1940 and Office of Revenue Commissioners to Tom Barry, 15 January 1974.

4. P. S. O'Hegarty, writing in 1945, cited in Marie Coleman, 'Military service pensions for veterans of the Irish revolution, 1916–23', *War in History*, vol. 20, no. 2 (2013), pp. 201–21.

5. Ibid., p. 221.

6. IMA, MSPC, MSPF/ID315, Michael Malone: Mary Malone to Minister for Defence, 5 May 1925.

7. Ibid., Secretary, Department of Defence to Col. M. Costello, 11 May 1925.

8. Hopkinson, 'Daniel Breen'.

9. IMA, MSPC, MSPF/ID315, Michael Malone: M. Costello to Secretary, Department of Defence, 20 May 1925.
10. IMA, MSPC, MSPF/ID178, James Connolly: William O'Brien to Richard Mulcahy, 6 February 1924.
11. Ibid., Secretary, Department of Defence to Army Finance Office, 8 February 1924.
12. Ibid., Account of interview conducted with Lily O'Connor by Sergeant James Murphy, 15 February 1924.
13. Ibid., Kathleen Clarke to Judge Thomas O'Donnell, 20 May 1941.
14. Ibid., Assessment Board to Nora Connolly O'Brien, 19 October 1941.
15. IMA, MSPC, WMSP34, REF53667, Grace Plunkett: Application form 7 July 1937, advisory committee note, 18 November 1941, and summary of sworn evidence given before the interviewing officer, 19 January 1942.
16. Anne Dolan, *Commemorating the Irish Civil War: History and Memory, 1923–2000* (Cambridge, 2003), pp. 114–19.
17. IMA, MSPC, MSPF DP9900, Cornelius Colbert: Donnchadh O'Briain to Oscar Traynor, 11 August 1953 and Brigid Colbert to Éamon de Valera, 15 July 1953.
18. Ibid., Sr Mary Columba to Oscar Traynor, 24 August 1953.
19. Ibid., Brigid Colbert to Éamon de Valera, 15 July 1953.
20. IMA, MSPC, MSPF DP1909, Patrick Pearse: Margaret Pearse to Mark Hilliard, 30 June 1967.
21. IMA, MSPC, MSPF/ID341, Thomas MacDonagh: C. Gifford Wilson to T. Hennessy TD, 21 June 1930.
22. Ibid., Donagh MacDonagh to Department of Defence, 26 October 1936.
23. Ibid., Donagh MacDonagh to Éamon de Valera, 16 January 1936.
24. Ibid., Fr 'A' to Seán MacEntee, 10 February 1937.
25. Bridget Hourican, 'Donagh MacDonagh', *DOIB*, vol. 5, pp. 916–17.

29 'For the life of my heroic son'

1. IMA, MSPC, WID134, Thomas Traynor: Elizabeth Traynor to Minister for Defence, 9 February 1951 and reply, 23 February 1951.
2. Ibid., Peadar Cowan to Seán MacEoin, 13 March 1951.
3. Ibid., 2 September 1953.
4. Ibid., Note from Department of Defence to Finance Officer, 18 June 1951.
5. Ibid., Memorandum of 'allowances being paid under the Army Pensions Acts to relatives of men executed in the period from 1916 onwards'.
6. IMA, MSPC, WDP9900, Cornelius Colbert: Donnchadh O'Briain to Oscar Traynor, 27 December 1953.
7. IMA, MSPC, WID458, Seán Treacy: Brigid Treacy to J. J. Walsh, 19 October 1925 and Brigid Treacy to Army Finance Office, 13 January 1926.
8. IMA, MSPC, WDP10200, Liam Mellows: Sarah Mellows to Éamon de Valera, 3 December 1935, Sarah Mellows to Department of Defence, 25 January 1940, and memorandum of 18 May 1948.
9. IMA, MSPC, MSP34, REF1985, James Hogan: James Hogan to Assessment Board, 15 March 1944.
10. Ibid., Oscar Traynor to Secretary, Department of Defence, 4 May 1945.
11. Ibid., Assessment Board to James Hogan, 19 September 1945.
12. IMA, MSPC, MSP34, REF23572, William Maher: Annie Maher to Assessment Board, 17 November 1937.

13. Ibid., Note for advisory committee, 21 January 1942.
14. Ibid., Secretary, Department of Defence to William Maher, 9 April 1942.
15. Ibid., John Maher to Office of the Referee, 22 October 1956.
16. Ibid., Office of Referee; note of 11 September 1957.
17. Ibid., John Maher to Office of the Referee, 24 June 1958, and reply of 16 July 1958.
18. Ibid., John Maher to Secretary, Department of Defence, 22 August 1958.
19. Ibid., Secretary, Department of Defence to John Maher, 6 September 1958.
20. IMA, MSPC, MSP34, REF24224, Denis Doran: L. M. FitzGerald, Department of Finance, to J. O'Connell, Army Finance Office, Department of Defence, 20 May 1942.
21. Ibid., Denis Doran to R. Corish TD, Mayor of Wexford, January 1942.
22. Ibid., Attorney General to Secretary, Department of Defence, 2 February 1940.
23. Ibid., L. M. FitzGerald to J. O'Connell, 20 May 1942.
24. IMA, MSPC, MSP34, REF56199, Patrick Wade: Wade to Department of Finance, 25 October 1946.
25. IMA, MSPC, MSP34, REF63404, John Guiney: Unsigned note of 4 April 1940.
26. IMA, MSPC, MSP34, REF25857, Katie Walsh: Katie Walsh to Office of the Referee, 25 October 1940.
27. Ibid., note of Advisory Committee, 16 October 1941.
28. IMA, MSPC, MSP34, REF463, John Joseph Scollan: Sworn evidence of Scollan made before the Advisory Committee on 22 October 1935; Scollan to Office of Referee, 30 November 1936 and 29 May 1938.
29. IMA, MSPC, Departmental Records/8262, John Murphy: Margaret Murphy to Secretary, Department of Defence, 28 January 1933.
30. Ibid., Report on John Murphy by Thomas Mackham, 2 May 1933.
31. IMA, MSPC, MSP24/4055, Patrick Byrne: Lucy Byrne to Secretary, Department of Defence, 10 May 1946.
32. IMA, MSPC, MSP 34 REF178, James Butler: Letters of John Dowling, 22 August 1935, and J. V. Joyce, 4 September 1935.
33. Ibid., James Butler to Army Pensions Board, undated (c. October 1935) and 18 November 1937.
34. Ibid., Medical Officer, Army Pensions Board to Butler, 9 August 1934.
35. Ibid., R. Betterberry to Army Pensions Board, 12 January 1950.
36. IMA, MSPC, WIP724 and W34D1990, Margaret Skinnider: Nora Connolly O'Brien to Military Service Pensions Board, 14 February 1938 and Army Finance Officer, E. Fahy, to Treasury Solicitor, 16 February 1925.
37. Ibid., P. Coll to E. Fahy, 18 March 1925.
38. IMA, MSPC, MSP34, REF1176, Bridget O'Mullane: Sworn evidence given 30 June 1937; Capt. Seán Budds to Military Service Pensions Board, 10 May 1936.
39. Ibid., Margaret Leo Kennedy to Military Service Pensions Board, 16 March 1936.
40. Ibid., Bridget O'Mullane to Éamon de Burca, 5 May 1938.

30 Homes Fit for Heroes?

1. NAI, Committee on Claims of British Ex-servicemen (CCBE), 1927–8, 3/495/25, box 1, Statement of Baltinglass men, 22 February 1928 and evidence given by J. R. Dagg, ex-clerk of Baltinglass District Council, 31 March 1928.
2. Ibid.
3. Eunan O'Halpin, *Decline of the Union: British Government in Ireland, 1892–1920* (Dublin, 1987), p. 121.

4. NAI, DE, 2/243, 15 February 1921.

5. NAI, CCBE, Transcript of evidence of the sitting of the Committee in Cork City Courthouse, 22 March 1928; British Legion, Cork Branch, to CCBE, 22 March 1928.

6. Ibid., Ernest Wolfe to CCBE, 23 February 1928.

7. Ibid., R. Power to CCBE, 28 March 1928.

8. Ibid., Philip Smith to CCBE, 27 January 1928.

9. Ibid., W. D. M. Lean, British Legion, Dublin, to CCBE, 3 May 1928.

10. Ibid., memorandum by A. P. Connolly, British Legion, Dublin, 9 January 1928.

11. Ibid.

12. Fergus D'Arcy, *Remembering the War Dead: British Commonwealth and International War Graves in Ireland Since 1914* (Dublin, 2007), p. 17.

13. NAI, CCBE, Brian Clarke and N. G. Nates to CCBE, 16 January 1928.

14. Ibid., box 2, Evidence of Thomas Long, Cork British Legion, 22 March 1928.

15. Ibid., box 1, Report of the Committee.

16. Ibid., 3/495/26, box 2, W. A. Redmond to J. Berry, January 1928.

17. Ibid., 3/495/27, box 3, William Callan to Secretary, CCBE, 16 December 1927.

18. Ibid., Martin O'Connor to CCBE, 23 December 1927.

19. Ibid., Daniel Slyne to CCBE, 27 January 1928; John A. O'Brien to CCBE, 27 January 1928; P. Hickey to CCBE, 3 February 1928.

20. Ibid., Patrick Nead to CCBE, 9 January 1928.

21. Ibid., box 1, Report of the Committee.

22. According to historian of the First World War, Edward Madigan on the programme *The Forgotten War: Ireland and the First World War*, broadcast on RTE One television, 5 August 2014.

23. Niamh Brennan, 'A political minefield: southern loyalists, the Irish Grants Committee and the British government, 1922–31', *Irish Historical Studies*, vol. 30, no. 119 (May 1997), pp. 406–19.

24. UKNA, DO, 35/1/99, Irish Grants Committee Claims (Irish Distress Committee), Richard Abbott to Winston Churchill, 1 February 1943.

25. Brennan, 'A political minefield'.

26. Ibid.

27. UKNA, DO, 35/1/99, Memorandum of 13 July 1945.

28. UKNA, CO, 762/1, Irish Grants Committee, Replacement grants memorandum, 11 April 1927.

29. Ibid., Edward Troup to Arthur Henderson, Secretary of State for Home Affairs, 26 February 1924.

30. Ibid., Robert Sanders to Major A. R. Jamieson, 28 October 1926; H. Franks to Major White, 13 January 1927.

31. UKNA, CO, 762/1, Irish Grants Committee, 1928–9, Note of interview between Churchill and Sir Alexander Wood Renton, 12 December 1927.

32. Brennan, 'A political minefield'.

31 Scrambling for the Bones of the Patriot Dead

1. NAI, DT, S3670, Terence MacSwiney anniversary in Cork, 1 November 1924.

2. David Fitzpatrick, 'Commemoration in the Irish Free State: a chronicle of embarrassment', in Ian McBride (ed.), *History and Memory in Modern Ireland* (Cambridge University Press, 2001), pp. 184–204.

3. Dolan, *Commemorating the Irish Civil War*, pp. 1–6.

4. Ibid.
5. Fitzpatrick, 'Commemoration in the Irish Free State'.
6. Ibid.
7. Ibid.
8. NAI, DT, S9815A, Easter Week Commemorations, 25 April 1925.
9. *Irish Times*, 5 April 1926.
10. *Irish Press*, 28 March 1932.
11. *Irish Press*, 23 April 1932.
12. NAI, DT, S59815A, 10 May 1933.
13. *Irish Press*, 8 March 1933.
14. NAI, DT, S6405A/1, 10 August 1934.
15. NAI, DT, S6405A/1, 30 May 1934; *Dáil Éireann Debates*, 10 August 1934; *Irish Press*, 8 March 1933.
16. NAI, DT, S6405B, '1916 Memorial GPO, Unveiling ceremony, Easter 1935', 23 March 1935.
17. Ibid., *Irish Press*, 1 April 1935.
18. NAI, DT, S6405B, 9 April 1935.
19. *Irish Press*, 10 April 1935; *Sunday Independent* 14 April 1935; *Irish Times*, 15 April 1935.
20. *Irish Times*, 15 April 1935.
21. NAI, DT, S6405B; *Irish Press*, 18 April 1935.
22. Brian Walker, *Dancing to History's Tune: History, Myth and Politics in Ireland* (Belfast, 1996), pp. 87–91.
23. NAI, DT, S11409, 1 February 1940.
24. Ibid., Department of Defence memo, May 1940.
25. Ibid., 25 October 1940.
26. *Irish Independent*, 14 April 1941.
27. *Irish Press*, 14 April 1941.
28. Broadcast on 24 March 1940, quoted in Shauna Gilligan, 'Image of a patriot: the popular and scholarly portrayal of Patrick Pearse, 1916–1991', unpublished MA thesis, UCD, 1995, p. 44.
29. NAI, DT, S2818, 12 March 1945.
30. Adrian Keane, 'Who fears to speak of Easter Week?', unpublished MA thesis, UCD, 1996, p. 18.
31. NAI, DT, S14440, Éamon de Valera to John A. Costello, 7 April 1949.
32. *Irish Press*, 18 April 1949.
33. Walker, *Dancing to History's Tune*, pp. 90–91.
34. NAI, DT, S9815, E/62, Easter Week commemoration, Frank Casey and Peter Nolan to Lemass, 7 June 1962.

32 'He knew as much about commanding as my dog'

1. *Irish Times Annual Review 1965* (Dublin, 1965), p. 5 and *Irish Times*, 11 January 1966.
2. NAI, DT, S97/6/469, 'First President of the Republic 1916', Kathleen Clarke to Seán Lemass, 11 May 1965 and 29 March 1965.
3. NAI, DT, S97/6/469, Seán Lemass to Kathleen Clarke, 14 May 1965; Comment by Lemass's secretary, 12 June 1965; Jack Lynch to Lemass, 20 May 1965.
4. Eunan O'Halpin, 'Lemass's silent anguish', *Irish Times*, 20 July 2013.
5. NAI, DT, 97/6/532, 1916 GPO flag, Seán Lemass to Prime Minister Harold Wilson, 31 March 1966.

6. 'Suggestions came from all directions for celebrating Easter Rising in 1966', *Irish Times*, 2 January 1997.

7. Ibid.

8. NAI, DT, 98/6/495, Report of interview with British ambassador, 12 October 1965.

9. UKNA, DO, 130/125, 1916 Rising: 50th Anniversary celebrations, G. A. Lovitt to I. Watt, Commonwealth Relations Office (CRO), 7 December 1965; satirical letter addressed to Fred Mulley MP, Minister for Defence, 12 February 1965.

10. Ibid., Secretary, Commonwealth Relations Office to Director General, Imperial War Museum, 2 February 1966.

11. Ibid., Denis Cleary, CRO, to P. A. Carter, Dublin, and reply, 28 February 1966.

12. Ibid., Cleary to Carter, 1 March 1966.

13. Ibid., Ambassador Geoffrey Tory to Robert Flower, CRO, 2 March 1966; J. B. Johnston to Tory, 25 March 1966.

14. Ibid., Johnston to Tory 31 March 1966.

15. Ibid., Lord Tyron to Saville Garner, 25 March 1966 and reply, 29 March 1966.

16. Editor, 'Current comment: 1966 and after', *Studies*, vol. 55, no. 217 (Spring 1966), pp. 1–4.

17. Ibid., David Thornley, 'Patrick Pearse' (pp. 10–20) and Garret FitzGerald, 'The Significance of 1916' (pp. 29–37).

18. Garret FitzGerald, *All in a Life: An Autobiography* (Dublin, 1991), p. 81.

19. Higgins, *Transforming 1916*, p. 1.

20. *Irish Times*, 5 April 1991.

21. Higgins, *Transforming 1916*, pp. 21–7.

22. Martin Mansergh (ed.), *Spirit of the Nation: The Speeches and Statements of Charles J. Haughey, 1957–1986* (Dublin, 1986), p. 63.

23. Higgins, *Transforming 1916*, pp. 52–3.

24. Ibid., p. 107.

25. Ibid., pp. 86–113.

26. Ibid., pp. 124–32.

27. 'Suggestions came from all directions for celebrating Easter Rising in 1966', *Irish Times*, 2 January 1997.

28. Higgins, *Transforming 1916*, pp. 132–57.

29. Ibid., pp. 183–204.

30. UKNA, DO, 130/125, 1916 Rising: 50th anniversary celebrations: notes for dispatch, n.d., c. May 1966.

31. Ibid., Geoffrey Tory to Arthur Bottomley MP, 16 May 1966.

33 Commemoration During the Troubles and the Peace Process

1. *Irish Times*, 11 July 1968.

2. 'Anglo-Irish Treaty "gave Ireland back her purse"', *Irish Times*, 6 December 1946.

3. *Irish Independent*, 7 December 1972.

4. *Irish Times*, 31 May 1972.

5. NAI, DT, 2005/7/605, Erskine Childers to Liam Cosgrave, 13 May 1974.

6. Ibid., Speech of Liam Cosgrave, 15 August 1975.

7. NAI, DT, 2008/148/443, Padraig Pearse: centenary of Birth, N. McMahon, Department of Tourism to Dan O'Suillabháin, 23 December 1977.

8. Ibid., 16 and 21 February 1979.

9. *Irish Times*, 15 September 1980.

10. *Irish Times*, 25 August 1989 and 21 December 2005.

11. *Irish Times*, 28 September 1984 and 8 March 1986.

12. Declan Kiberd, 'The elephant of revolutionary forgetfulness', in Ní Dhonnchadha and Dorgan (eds), *Revising the Rising*, pp. 1–21.

13. Joe Carroll, '1916 commemoration opens up a Pandora's box', *Irish Times*, 9 March 1991.

14. *True Lives* programme broadcast on RTE, 9 April 2001.

15. Bew, *Ireland: The Politics of Enmity*, p. 581 and R. F. Foster, *Luck and the Irish: A Brief History of Change, 1970–2000* (London, 2007), p. 101.

16. Fintan O'Toole, 'A grotesque denial of bloodshed', *Irish Times*, 2 October 2001.

17. Hayden, 'The Life of Julia'.

18. Diarmaid Ferriter, 'On the state funerals', *Dublin Review*, no. 5 (Winter 2001/2), pp. 5–15.

19. *Irish Times*, 15 October 2001.

20. Ferriter, 'On the state funerals'.

21. Donal O'Donovan, *Kevin Barry and His Time* (Dublin, 1989), p. 189.

22. O'Toole, 'A grotesque denial'.

23. Kevin Myers, 'An Irishman's diary', *Irish Times*, 3 October 2001.

24. Gerard Westby, *Kevin Barry: A Play in One Act*, 3rd edn (Dublin, 1971).

25. Farrell Corcoran, 'The political instrumentality of cultural memory: a case study of Ireland', *The Public*, vol. 9, no. 3 (2002), pp. 49–64.

26. Ibid.

27. Cited in Diarmaid Ferriter, 'Rising to the challenge', *Irish Times*, 21 April 2007.

28. Gabriel Doherty, 'The commemoration of the ninetieth anniversary of the Easter Rising', in Dermot Keogh and Gabriel Doherty (eds), *1916: The Long Revolution* (Cork, 2007), pp. 376–408.

29. Ibid.

30. Pádraig Yeates (ed.), *Liberty: 1916–2006* (Dublin, 2006), pp. 3–6.

31. *Sunday Business Post*, 2 April 2006.

32. Diarmaid Ferriter, 'So what will they do for an encore to 1916 Rising event?', *Irish Independent*, 18 April 2006.

33. Doherty, 'The commemoration of the Easter Rising', pp. 377–87.

34   Remembering the First World War and Welcoming the Queen

1. Catríona Crowe, 'Remembrance and forgetting', *Irish Times* Weekend Review, 29 September 2012.

2. Jeffery, *Ireland and the Great War*, p. 58.

3. Keith Jeffery, 'The Great War in modern Irish memory', in T. G. Fraser and Keith Jeffery (eds), *Men, Women and War* (Dublin, 1993), p. 124.

4. B. Graham and P. Shirlow, 'The Battle of the Somme in Ulster memory and identity', *Political Geography*, vol. 21 (2002), pp. 881–904.

5. Ibid.

6. David Officer, 'For God and for Ulster: the Ulsterman on the Somme', in McBride (ed.), *History and Memory in Modern Ireland*, pp. 160–84.

7. *Irish Times*, 27 June 2006, supplement: 'The Somme, 90th anniversary'.

8. Ian McBride, 'Memory and national identity', in McBride (ed.), *History and Memory in Modern Ireland*, p. 19.

9. Walker, *Dancing to History's Tune*.

10. Graham and Shirlow, 'The Battle of the Somme'.

11. PRONI, FIN/18/46/16, Battle of the Somme Commemoration (July 1966), 18 January 1966.
12. Geoffrey Beattie, *We Are the People: Journeys Through the Heart of Protestant Ulster* (London, 1992), p. 115.
13. Graham and Shirlow, 'The Battle of the Somme'.
14. David Officer and Graham Walker, 'Protestant Ulster: ethno-history, memory and contemporary prospects', *National Identities*, vol. 2, no. 3 (2000), pp. 292–307; Gillian McIntosh, *The Force of Culture: Unionist Identities in Contemporary Ireland* (Cork, 1999).
15. Gillian McIntosh, 'Stormont's ill-timed jubilee: the Ulster 71 Exhibition', *New Hibernia Review*, vol. 11, no. 2 (Summer 2007), pp. 17–39.
16. Martin, '1916 – myth, fact and mystery'.
17. Seamus Taafe, 'Commemorating the fallen: public memorials to the Irish dead of the Great War', *Archaeology Ireland*, vol. 13, no. 3 (Autumn 1999), pp. 18–22.
18. Jane Leonard, 'The twinge of memory: Armistice Day and Remembrance Sunday in Dublin since 1919', in McBride (ed.), *History and Memory in Modern Ireland*, pp. 99–115.
19. Collins (ed.), *Whose Past Is It Anyway?*, p. 189.
20. Jeffery, *Ireland and the Great War*, pp. 114–15.
21. Tóibín, *Lady Gregory's Toothbrush*, pp. 114–15.
22. Fintan O'Toole, 'Why we remember', *Irish Times*, 27 June 2006, supplement: 'The Somme, 90th anniversary'.
23. Higgins, *Transforming 1916*, p. 165.
24. Collins (ed.), *Whose Past Is It Anyway?*, pp. 102, 170.
25. Myles Dungan, 'Fighting amnesia', *Irish Times*, 27 June 2006, supplement 'The Somme, 90th anniversary'.
26. Brown, *Ireland: A Social and Cultural History*, p. 352.
27. 'Costello urges national day for war dead', *Irish Times*, 1 August 1984.
28. Diarmaid Ferriter, 'We must unlock these stories to learn about ourselves', *Irish Independent*, 10 May 2014, supplement: 'Ireland at war'.
29. Brian Walker, *A Political History of the Two Irelands: From Partition to Peace* (Basingstoke, 2012), pp. 163, x–xiv.
30. Kevin Myers, *From the Irish Times Column 'An Irishman's Diary'* (Dublin, 2000), pp. 33–5.
31. Patrick Casey, 'Irish casualties in the First World War', *Irish Sword*, vol. 20 (1996–7), pp. 193–207.
32. Gerry White and Brendan O'Shea (eds), *A Great Sacrifice: Cork Servicemen Who Died in the Great War* (Cork, 2010).
33. *Census of Population, 1926, General Report*, vol. x (Dublin, 1934), p. 12.
34. Kevin Myers, 'Crunching the numbers and bursting myths', *History Ireland*, vol. 22, no. 4 (July/August 2014), pp. 40–42.
35. Richard Grayson, *Belfast Boys: How Unionists and Nationalists Fought and Died Together in the First World War* (London, 2009).
36. Stephen Walker, *Forgotten Soldiers: The Irishmen Shot At Dawn* (Dublin, 2007), pp. 168–79; Gerald Oram, *Worthless Men* (London, 1998).
37. *Irish Times* and *Irish Independent*, 9 April 2014.
38. Owen Bowcott, 'God Save Croke Park', *Guardian*, 23 February 2007.
39. 'No to British Queen's Visit', leaflet issued by Republican Sinn Féin, Dublin, May 2011.

40. Bertie Ahern, 'This is what Ireland can give to the world', Speech at Palace of Westminster, 15 May 2007, in Richard Aldous (ed.), *Great Irish Speeches* (Dublin, 2007), pp. 214–19.

41. Diarmaid Ferriter, 'Visit marks sheer effort to overcome our troubles', *Irish Independent*, 21 May 2011.

42. Ibid.

43. Ibid.

44. *Independent*, 28 June 2012.

45. Ed Moloney, *A Secret History of the IRA* (London, 2002), pp. 375–480.

35   Invoking Revolutionary Ghosts as the Celtic Tiger Dies and Fianna Fáil Collapses

1. Patrick Kelly and Dermot Keogh, 'Turning corners: Ireland 2002–11', in T. W. Moody and F. X. Martin (eds), *The Course of Irish History*, new edn (Cork 2011), pp. 358–98.

2. *Irish Times* editorial, 'Was it for this? The state of the nation', *Irish Times*, 19 November 2010.

3. Ibid.

4. Michael Collins, *The Path to Freedom* (Dublin, 1922), p. 14.

5. Ibid., p. 123.

6. Gene Kerrigan, *The Big Lie: Who Profits from Ireland's Austerity?* (London, 2012), pp. 127–8.

7. Ibid., pp. 128–9.

8. *Irish Times*, 13 August 2012; Diarmaid Ferriter, 'Collins: history and myth', *Irish Times*, 18 August 2012.

9. www.generalmichaelcollins.com

10. *Irish Examiner*, 20 August 2007.

11. Ferriter, 'Collins: history and myth'; Hopkinson, 'Michael Collins'; Hart, *Mick*.

12. *Irish Examiner*, 22 August 2013.

13. Kerrigan, *The Big Lie*, p. 125.

14. Joe Mulholland (ed.), *Reforming the Republic: The MacGill Report 2010* (Tipperary, 2010).

15. Garret FitzGerald, 'Public services make a shabby contrast with national wealth', *Irish Times*, 22 March 2008.

16. Diarmaid Ferriter, 'State now morally as well as economically bankrupt', *Irish Times*, 26 March 2012.

17. *Irish Times, Irish Examiner, Irish Independent*, 22 March 2012.

18. Garvin, 'Revolutionaries turned politicians'; Garvin, *1922*.

19. Garvin, 'Revolutionaries turned politicians'.

20. Diarmaid Ferriter, *Occasions of Sin: Sex and Society in Modern Ireland* (London, 2009), pp. 332–3.

21. Garret FitzGerald, 'Apocalypse may yet spark the rebirth of civic morality', *Irish Times*, 16 October 2010.

22. Ferriter, 'State now morally as well as economically bankrupt'.

23. Fintan O'Toole (ed.), *Up the Republic! Towards a New Ireland* (London, 2012); Tony Judt, *The Memory Chalet* (London, 2010), pp. 1–33.

24. James Downey, 'Gombeenism thrives long after it should have been eradicated', *Irish Independent*, 14 April 2012.

25. Collins (ed.), *Whose Past Is It Anyway?*, p. 155.

36   New Commemorative Priorities, Sacred Cows and the Status of History

1. Tom Dunne, 'Commemoration and "shared history": a different role for historians?', *History Ireland*, vol. 21, no. 1 (January 2013), pp. 10–13.

2. Yeates, *City in Turmoil*, p. ix.

3. Catríona Crowe, unpublished address to the Burren Law School, Newtown Castle, Ballyvaughan, 6 May 2012.

4. Report of Burren Law School proceedings, *Irish Times*, 7 May 2012.

5. Kate Butler, 'Coming out for some air', *Sunday Times* Magazine, 5 August 2012.

6. Ibid.

7. *Sunday Times*, 22 July 2012.

8. Genevieve Carbery, 'Call to remember 28 children who died in the Rising', *Irish Times*, 17 August 2011; Ann Marie Hourihane, 'Children of the revolution', *Irish Times*, 22 March 2014.

9. See letters page of *Irish Times*, 25 August 2012.

10. Deaglán de Bréadún, 'Ceremony commemorates forgotten policemen of War of Independence', *Irish Times*, 27 August 2012.

11. *Irish Times*, 5 August 2011.

12. *Irish Times*, 6 August 2011.

13. *Sunday Business Post*, 18 September 2011.

14. Andrew Lynch, 'Prize writer', profile of Sebastian Barry, *Sunday Business Post*, 31 July 2011.

15. Ibid.

16. Fintan O'Toole, 'Rules of engagement for a decade of centenaries', *Irish Times*, 17 September 2012.

17. See www.creativecentenaries.org

18. Gerry Moriarty, 'North's politicians must strike right tone during emotionally charged anniversaries', *Irish Times*, 6 January 2012.

19. Stephen Collins, 'Celebrating momentous events that shaped the course of Irish history a century ago', *Irish Times*, 5 January 2012.

20. John Bruton, 'Redmond was a realist – some successors were not', *Irish Times*, 13 April 2012.

21. Letter of Eoin Ó Murchú, *Irish Times*, 14 April 2012.

22. Gearóid Ó Tuathaigh, personal correspondence with the author, 5 July 2012.

23. *Irish Times*, 26 July 2011.

24. Tom McGurk, 'Observe the Amnesiacs marching towards the Somme', *Sunday Business Post*, 2 July 2006.

25. Collins (ed.), *Whose Past Is It Anyway?*, pp. 182–91.

26. Press release of speech by Enda Kenny at the launch of two books of the multi-volume History of Ireland series, National Library of Ireland, 8 June 2011.

27. Tristram Hunt, 'If we have no history, we have no future', *Observer*, 28 August 2011.

28. Niall Ferguson, *Civilisation: The West and the Rest* (London, 2010).

29. Martin Kettle, 'With no common culture, a common history is elusive', *Guardian*, 3 June 2010.

30. *Daily Telegraph*, 25 June 2009.

31. *Seanad Éireann Debates*, vol. 201, no. 11, 24 March 2010.

32. Pauric Travers, 'History in primary school: a future for our past?', *History Ireland*, vol. 4, no. 3 (Autumn 1996), pp. 13–16.

33. Garret FitzGerald, 'Past plays a crucial role in moulding future lives', *Irish Times*, 20 April 1996.
34. Ibid.
35. Fintan O'Toole, 'History matters in Ireland', *Irish Times*, 10 September 2011.
36. Department of Education and Skills, 'A framework for junior cycle' (Dublin, 2012), pp. 5–30; available at ncca.ie/framework/doc/NCCA-Junior-Cycle.pdf.
37. *Irish Examiner*, 1 September 2011.
38. *Irish Times*, 8 October 2012; *Irish Independent*, 13 April 2013.

BIBLIOGRAPHY

Archives

Irish Military Archives Collections, Dublin
Bureau of Military History Witness Statements and Contemporary Documents
Military Service Pensions

National Archives of Ireland Collections, Dublin
Committee on Claims of British
  Ex-Servicemen
Dáil Éireann
Department of Foreign Affairs
Department of the Taoiseach
Department of Local Government
George Gavan Duffy Papers
Land Settlement Commission
Provisional Government
Seán Mac Caoilte Papers

Public Record Office of Northern Ireland Collections, Belfast
Cabinet
Craigavon Papers
Edward Carson Papers
Major Fred Crawford Papers
Robert Daniel Papers
Finance
Home Affairs
Constance Markievicz Papers
Harry Midgley Papers
Frederick B. McGinley Papers
Unionist Club Council
Ulster Unionist Council
Ulster Women's Unionist Council

United Kingdom National Archives Collections, Kew
Cabinet
Colonial Office
Dominions Office
Home Office
War Office

University College Dublin Archives Collections, Dublin

Frank Aiken

Todd Andrews

Ernest Blythe

Michael Collins

John de Courcey Ireland

Éamon de Valera

Robert Dudley Edwards

Desmond and Mabel FitzGerald

George Gavan Duffy

Michael Hayes

Seán MacEntee

Eoin MacNeill

Mary MacSwiney

Terence MacSwiney

Richard Mulcahy

Kevin O'Higgins

Ernie O'Malley

Desmond Ryan

James Ryan

Maurice Twomey

Official Publications

Dáil Éireann Debates

Seanad Éireann Debates

House of Commons Debates (Hansard)

Royal Commission on the Rebellion in Ireland: Report of Commission (London, 1916)

Report of National Programme Conference (Dublin, 1922)

The Fifty-fifth Report of the Deputy Keeper of the Public Records and Keeper of the State Papers in Ireland, 1922–23 (Dublin, 1924)

Census of Population, 1926, General Report (Dublin, 1934)

Contemporaneous published material (1908–1924)

Anon., *The Sinn Féin Leaders: With Numerous Illustrations and Complete Lists of Deportees, Casualties Etc* (Dublin 1917)

Augustus Boyd, Ernest, *The Worked-Out Ward: A Sinn Féin Allegory in One Act* (Dublin, 1918)

Breen, Dan, *My Fight for Irish Freedom* (Dublin, 1924)

Brown, Stephen J., 'What is a nation?', *Studies*, vol. 1, no. 3 (September 1912), pp. 496–511

Cambray, Philip, *Irish Affairs and the Home Rule Question* (London, 1911)

Chart, D. A., 'The housing of the labouring class in Dublin', *Journal of the Statistical and Social Inquiry Society of Ireland*, part 94, vol. 13 (December 1914), pp. 160–76

Clancy, Revd J., *The Failure of Parliamentarianism* (Clare, 1917)

Clery, Arthur, 'The Gaelic League, 1893–1919', *Studies*, vol. 8, no. 31 (September 1919), pp. 398–408

Collins, Michael, *The Path to Freedom* (Dublin, 1922)

Connolly, James, *Labour in Irish History* (Dublin, 1910)

de Blácam, Aodh, *Towards the Republic: A Study of New Ireland's Social and Political Aims* (Dublin, 1919)

Eason and Son, *The Rebellion in Dublin, April 1916* (Dublin, 1916)

Figgis, Darrell, *The Economic Case for Irish Independence* (Dublin, 1920)

Fletcher, C. R. L., and Rudyard Kipling, *A School History of England* (London, 1911)

Gaynor, Revd E., 'Our musical tradition', *The Leader*, vol. 22, no. 8 (8 April 1911)

Gwynn, Stephen, *John Redmond's Last Years* (London, 1919)

Healy, T. M., *Dublin Strikes, 1913: Facts Regarding the Labour Disputes Contained in Speech by Mr. T. M. Healy MP at Court of Inquiry in Dublin Castle, 1 October 1913* (Dublin, 1913)

INAVDF, *Aftermath of Dublin Week, Published for the Benefit of the Irish National Aid and Volunteers' Dependants Fund* (Dublin, 1917)

Irish Reconstruction Association, *The Scope of Reconstruction in Ireland* (Dublin, 1921)

Johnson, Thomas, *A Handbook for Rebels: A Guide to Successful Defiance of the British Government* (Dublin, 1918)

Kensit, J. A., *Rome Behind Sinn Féin* (London, 1920)

Larkin, James, *Larkin's Scathing Indictment of Dublin Sweaters* (Manchester and London, 1913)

Lucas, Reginald, *Colonel Saunderson MP: A Memoir* (London, 1908)

Macardle, Dorothy, *Tragedies of Kerry* (Dublin, 1924)

MacDonagh, Michael, *The Irish at the Front* (London, 1916)

Maloney, William, *The Irish Issue* (New York, 1919)

Mansion House Committee, *Memorandum to Local Defence Committees, Issued by the Mansion House Committee* (Dublin, 1918)

Mansion House Committee, *No Conscription! Ireland's Case Restated: Address to the President of the USA from the Mansion House Conference* (Dublin, 1918)

McKenna, Lambert, *The Church and Working Women* (Dublin, 1913)

Murphy, T. W., *Dublin After the Six Days Insurrection: Thirty-One Pictures from the Camera of Mr T. W. Murphy* (Dublin 1916–17)

Newman, A., *What Emmet Means in 1915: A Tract for the Times* (Dublin, 1915)

O'Brien, William, *An Olive Branch in Ireland and Its History* (London, 1910)

Ó Gallchobhair, Prionnsias, *The Bishop's Pastoral: A Prisoner's Letter to His Grace the Archbishop of Dublin* (Dublin and Glasgow, 1922)

Ó Gallchobhair, Prionnsias, *By What Authority?* (Dublin, 1922)

O'Hegarty, P. S., *Sinn Féin: An Illumination* (London, 1919)

O'Hegarty, P. S., *The Victory of Sinn Féin* (Dublin, 1924)

O'Higgins, Kevin, *Civil War and the Events Which Led to It* (Dublin, 1922)

O'Higgins, Kevin, *Three Years' Hard Labour: An Address Delivered to the Irish Society at Oxford University* (Oxford, 1924)

O'Rahilly, Alfred, *The Case for the Treaty* (Dublin, 1922)

Pim, Frederick W., *The Sinn Féin Rising: A Narrative and Some Reflections* (Dublin, 1916)

Russell, George, *Ireland and the Empire: At the Court of Conscience* (Dublin, 1921)

Russell, George, 'Lessons of Revolution', *Studies*, vol. 12, no. 45 (March 1923), pp. 1–6

Ryan, Desmond, *The Man Called Pearse* (Dublin, 1919)

Smith-Gordon, Lionel, and Cruise O'Brien, *Starvation in Dublin* (Dublin, 1917)

Sigerson, Selma, *Sinn Féin and Socialism* (Dublin, 1919)

Sinn Féin, *An Appeal to the Women of Ireland* (Dublin, 1918)

Sinn Féin, *The Conscriptionists* (Dublin, 1918)

Sinn Féin, *Did You Ever Think of This?* (Dublin, 1918)

Sinn Féin, *Farmers! Your Turn Now* (Dublin, 1918)

Sinn Féin, *Mr Dillon Wants to See Poland, Finland, Bohemia ... Absolutely Independent* (Dublin, 1918)

Sinn Féin, *Parliamentarianism in a Nut Shell* (Dublin, 1918)

Sinn Féin, *The Policy of Abstention* (Dublin, 1918)

Sinn Féin, *Sinn Féin, America and Ireland* (Dublin, 1918)

Spálpín, *Sinn Féin and the Labour Movement* (Dublin, 1918)

Stephens, James, *The Insurrection in Dublin* (Dublin, 1916)

Wells, W. B., *John Redmond* (London, 1919)

'A Western Priest', *The Two Policies: Sinn Féin or Parliamentarianism* (Dublin, 1918)

White, Albert, *Ireland: A Study in Facts* (London, 1920)

White, J. R., *The Significance of Sinn Féin: Psychological, Political and Economic* (Dublin, 1919)

Wright, Arnold, *Disturbed Dublin: The Story of the Great Strike* (London, 1914)

Newspapers

Belfast News-Letter
Connaught Telegraph
Cork Examiner
Derry Journal
Dundalk Democrat
Freeman's Journal
Frontier Sentinel
Guardian
The Kerryman
Irish Citizen
Irish Examiner
Irish Freedom
Irish Independent
Irish Press
Irish Times
Irish Worker
Leader

Manchester Guardian
Nationality
New Statesman
Northern Whig
Observer
An Saorstát [Free State]
Sinn Féin
Sunday Business Post
Sunday Times
Sunday Tribune
Times
Tipperary Star
An tÓglách
Tuam Herald
Voice of Labour
Wexford People
Worker's Republic

Periodicals, magazines and journals

Analecta Hibernica
Bullán
Capuchin Annual
Crane Bag
Dublin Review
Eire-Ireland
Father Matthew Record
Feminist Review
History
History of Education
History Ireland
Irish Historical Studies
Irish Monthly
Irish Review
Irish Sword

Irish University Review
Journal of British Studies
Journal of the Statistical and Social Inquiry Society of Ireland
New Hibernia Review
Past and Present
Proceedings of the Royal Irish Academy
Saothar
Stair
Studia Hibernica
Studies
Tipperary Historical Journal
Victorian Studies
War in History

Reference works

James McGuire and James Quinn (eds), *A Dictionary of Irish Biography: From the Earliest Times to the Year 2002*, 9 vols (Cambridge, 2009)

Websites

www.bureauofmilitaryhistory.ie
www.census.nationalarchives.ie
www.creativecentenaries.org

http://dh.tcd.ie/letters1916
http://dib.cambridge.org
www.generalmichaelcollins.com

www.livesofthefirstworldwar.org www.rte.ie/centuryireland
www.militaryarchives.ie

Books, articles, chapters and biographical dictionary entries

aan de Wiel, Jérôme, *The Catholic Church in Ireland, 1914–18: War and Politics* (Dublin, 2003)

aan de Wiel, Jérôme, 'Austria-Hungary, France, Germany and the Irish crisis from 1899 to the outbreak of the First World War', *Intelligence and National Security*, vol. 21 (2006), pp. 237–57

Abbott, Richard, *Police Casualties in Ireland, 1919–22* (Dublin, 2000)

Ahern, Bertie, 'This is what Ireland can give to the world', Speech at Palace of Westminster, 15 May 2007, in Aldous (ed.), *Great Irish Speeches*, pp. 214–19

Aldous, Richard (ed.), *Great Irish Speeches* (Dublin, 2007)

Andrews, C. S., *Dublin Made Me: An Autobiography* (Dublin, 1979)

Anglin, Fr Henry, 'Reamhrá', *Capuchin Annual* (1966), p. 152

Augusteijn, Joost, *From Public Defiance to Guerrilla Warfare: The Experience of Ordinary Volunteers in the Irish War of Independence, 1916–1923* (Dublin, 1996)

Augusteijn, Joost, 'Why was Tipperary so active in the War of Independence?', *Tipperary Historical Journal 2006* (Tipperary, 2006), pp. 207–21

Augusteijn, Joost, 'Accounting for the emergence of violent activism among Irish revolutionaries, 1916–21', *Irish Historical Studies*, vol. 35, no. 139 (May 2007), pp. 327–44

Augusteijn, Joost (ed.), *The Irish Revolution, 1913–23* (Basingstoke, 2002)

Augusteijn, Joost (ed.), *The Memoirs of John M. Regan* (Dublin, 2007)

Bannister, Ivy, 'Images of Constance Markievicz', in Heaney (ed.), *Sunday Miscellany: A Selection from 1995–2000*, pp. 133–4

Bartlett, Thomas, *Ireland: A History* (Cambridge, 2010)

Bartlett, Thomas, and Keith Jeffery (eds), *A Military History of Ireland* (Cambridge, 1996)

Barton, Brian, *From Behind a Closed Door: Secret Court Martial Records of the 1916 Rising* (Belfast, 2002)

Béaslaí, Piaras, *Michael Collins and the Making of a New Ireland* (Dublin, 1926)

Beattie, Geoffrey, *We Are the People: Journeys Through the Heart of Protestant Ulster* (London, 1992)

Beckett, J. C., *The Anglo-Irish Tradition* (London, 1976)

Beckett, J. C. (ed.), *Belfast: The Making of the City, 1800–1914* (Belfast, 1983)

Beiner, Guy, Patricia March and Ida Milne 'Greatest Killer of the twentieth century: the Great Flu of 1918–19', *History Ireland*, vol. 17, no. 2 (March/April 2009), pp. 40–43

Bew, Paul, *John Redmond* (Dundalk, 1996)

Bew, Paul, *Ireland: The Politics of Enmity, 1789–2006* (Oxford, 2007)

Bew, Paul, Peter Gibbon and Henry Patterson, *Northern Ireland, 1921–1994: Political Forces and Social Classes* (London, 1995)

Breathnach, Diarmuid, 'Rock and hedge', *Capuchin Annual* (1952), p. 114

Bielenberg, Andy, 'Exodus: the emigration of southern Irish Protestants during the Irish War of Independence and civil war', *Past and Present*, no. 218 (February 2013), pp. 199–233

Biggs-Davison, John, *The Hand Is Red* (London, 1973)

Bloch, Marc, *The Historian's Craft* (Manchester, 1954)

Borgonovo, John, *The Dynamics of War and Revolution: Cork City, 1916–18* (Cork, 2013)

Borgonovo, John, 'A Soviet in embryo: Cork's food crisis and the People's Food Committee', *Saothar*, vol. 34 (2009), pp. 21–38

Bourke, Angela et al. (eds), *The Field Day Anthology of Irish Women's Writing*, vols 4 & 5 (Cork, 2002)

Bowcott, Owen, 'God Save Croke Park', *Guardian*, 23 February 2007

Bowman, John, *De Valera and the Ulster Question, 1917–73* (Oxford, 1982)

Bowman, Timothy, *Carson's Army: The Ulster Volunteer Force, 1910–1922* (Manchester, 2007)

Bowyer Bell, J., *The Irish Troubles: A Generation of Violence, 1967–1992* (Dublin, 1993)

Boyce, D. G., *Nationalism in Ireland* (London, 1995)

Bradley, Dan, *Farm Labourers: Irish Struggle, 1900–1976* (Belfast, 1988)

Bradshaw, Brendan, 'Nationalism and historical scholarship in modern Ireland', *Irish Historical Studies*, vol. 26, no. 104 (November 1989), pp. 329–51

Brady, Ciaran, 'Constructive and instrumental: the dilemma of Ireland's first new historians', in Brady (ed.), *Interpreting Irish History: The Debate on Historical Revisionism, 1938–1994*, pp. 3–35

Brady, Ciaran (ed.), *Ideology and the Historians* (Dublin, 1991)

Brady, Ciaran (ed.), *Interpreting Irish History: The Debate on Historical Revisionism, 1938–1994* (Dublin, 1994)

Breathnach, Ciara, *The Congested Districts Board, 1891–1923: Poverty and Development in the West of Ireland* (Dublin, 2005)

Brennan, Niamh, 'A political minefield: southern loyalists, the Irish Grants Committee and the British government, 1922–31', *Irish Historical Studies*, vol. 30, no. 119 (May 1997), pp. 406–19

Brennan, Robert, *Allegiance* (Dublin, 1950)

Brophy, Thomas, J., 'On Church grounds: political funerals and the contest to lead Catholic Ireland', *Catholic Historical Review*, vol. 95, no. 3 (July 2009), pp. 491–514

Brown, Terence, *Ireland: A Social and Cultural History, 1922–2002* (London, 2004)

Bruton, John, 'Redmond was a realist – some successors were not', *Irish Times* 13 April 2012

Buckland, Patrick, 'The southern Irish unionists, the Irish question and British politics, 1906–14', *Irish Historical Studies*, vol. 15, no. 59 (March 1967), pp. 228–55

Buckland, Patrick, *James Craig* (Dublin, 1980)

Buckland, Patrick, *Irish Unionism I: The Anglo-Irish and the New Ireland, 1885–1922* (Dublin, 1972)

Butler, Kate, 'Coming out for some air', *Sunday Times* Magazine, 5 August 2012

Cahill, Liam, *Forgotten Revolution: The Limerick Soviet, 1919 – A Threat to British Power in Ireland* (Dublin, 1990)

Campbell, Fergus, 'Emigrant responses to war and revolution, 1914–21: Irish opinion in the United States and Australia', *Irish Historical Studies*, vol. 32, no. 125 (May 2000), pp. 75–92

Campbell, Fergus, 'The last Land War? Kevin O'Shiel's memoir of the Irish Revolution, 1916–21', *Archivium Hibernicum*, vol. 57 (2003), pp. 155–200

Campbell, Fergus, *Land and Revolution: Nationalist Politics in the West of Ireland, 1891–1921* (Oxford, 2005)

Campbell, Fergus, *The Irish Establishment, 1879–1914* (Oxford, 2009)

Carbery, Genevieve, 'Call to remember 28 children who died in the Rising', *Irish Times*, 17 August 2011

Carpentier, Godeleine, 'Dublin and the drama of Larkinsim: James Plunkett's *Strumpet City*', in Rafroidi and Harmon (eds), *The Irish Novel in Our Time*, pp. 209–17

Casey, Patrick, 'Irish casualties in the First World War', *Irish Sword*, vol. 20 (1996–7), pp. 193–207

Claremorris Community Radio, *The People's Courts: Ireland's Dáil Courts, 1920–24* (Mayo, 2013)

Clear, Caitríona, *Nuns in Nineteenth Century Ireland* (Dublin, 1987)

Coleman, Marie, *County Longford and the Irish Revolution, 1910–1923* (Dublin, 2003)

Coleman, Marie, 'Military service pensions for veterans of the Irish revolution, 1916–23', *War in History*, vol. 20, no. 2 (2013), pp. 201–21

Collins, Elma, 'The origin and early years of the History Teachers' Association of Ireland', *Stair*, Journal of the HTAI (2013), pp. 10–18

Collins, Jude (ed.), *Whose Past Is It Anyway?* (Dublin, 2012)

Collins, Peter, 'History teaching in Northern Ireland', *History Ireland*, vol. 3, no. 1 (Spring 1995), pp. 48–51

Collins, Stephen, 'Celebrating momentous events that shaped the course of Irish history a century ago', *Irish Times* 5 January 2012

Colum, Mary, *Life and the Dream* (Dublin, 1966 [New York, 1958])

Connelly, M. L., 'The army, the press and the "Curragh Incident", March 1914', *Historical Research*, vol. 84, no. 225 (August 2011), pp. 535–57

Connolly, S. J. (ed.), *The Oxford Companion to Irish History* (Oxford, 1998)

Convery, David (ed.), *Locked Out: A Century of Irish Working-Class Life* (Dublin, 2013)

Coogan, Oliver, *Politics and War in Meath, 1913–23* (Dublin, 1983)

Coogan, Tim Pat, *De Valera, Long Fellow, Long Shadow* (London, 1993)

Corcoran, Farrell, 'The political instrumentality of cultural memory: a case study of Ireland', *The Public*, vol. 9, no. 3 (2002), pp. 49–64

Corish, P. J. (ed.), *Radicals, Rebels and Establishments: Historical Studies XV* (Belfast, 1985)

Costello, Francis J. *Enduring the Most: The Life and Death of Terence MacSwiney* (Dingle, 1996)

Coughlan, Anthony, 'Desmond Greaves, 1913–1988: an obituary essay', *Saothar*, vol. 14 (1989), pp. 5–17

Crozier, Frank P., *Impressions and Recollections* (London, 1930)

Crowe, Catríona, 'Testimony to a flowering', *Dublin Review*, no. 10 (Spring 2003), pp. 42–69

Crowe, Catríona, 'Remembrance and forgetting', *Irish Times* Weekend Review, 29 September 2012

Crowe, Catríona (ed.), *Dublin, 1911* (Dublin, 2011)

Crowe, Catríona (ed.), *Guide to the Military Service (1916–1923) Pensions Collection* (Dublin, 2012)

Cullen, Clara (ed.), *The World Upturning: Elsie Henry's Irish Wartime Diaries, 1913–19* (Dublin, 2013)

Cullen, L. M., *An Economic History of Ireland Since 1660* (London, 1987)

Curran, Joseph M., *The Birth of the Irish Free State, 1921–1923* (Alabama, 1980)

Curry, James, 'Delia Larkin: "More harm to the Big Fellow than any of the employers"', *Saothar*, vol. 36 (2013), pp. 22–34

Curtis, L. P., 'Ireland in 1914', in Vaughan (ed.), *A New History of Ireland*, vol. 6, pp. 145–88

d'Alton, Ian, 'A vestigial population? Perspectives on southern Irish Protestantism in the twentieth century', *Eire-Ireland*, vol. 44, nos 3–4 (Fall/Winter 2009), pp. 9–42

Daly, Mary. E., *Social and Economic History of Ireland Since 1800* (Dublin, 1981)

Daly, Mary E., 'Two centuries of Irish social life', in Rooney (ed.), *A Time and a Place*, pp. 3–12

Daly, Paul, Rónán O'Brien and Paul Rouse (eds), *Making the Difference? The Irish Labour Party, 1912–2012* (Dublin, 2012)

D'Arcy, Fergus, *Remembering the War Dead: British Commonwealth and International War Graves in Ireland Since 1914* (Dublin, 2007)

Davis, Richard, *Arthur Griffith and Non-Violent Sinn Féin* (Dublin, 1974)

de Bréadún, Deaglán, 'Ceremony commemorates forgotten policemen of War of Independence', *Irish Times*, 27 August 2012

de Vere White, Terence, *Kevin O'Higgins* (London, 1948)

de Vere White, Terence, 'A pride of lions', *Irish Times*, 1 May 1971

Deasy, Liam, *Towards Ireland Free* (Cork, 1992)

Dempsey, Pauric J. and Shaun Boylan, 'Robert Childers Barton', in McGuire and Quinn (eds), *Dictionary of Irish Biography*, vol. 1, pp. 361–3

Department of Education and Skills, 'A framework for junior cycle' (Dublin, 2012), available at ncca.ie/framework/doc/NCCA-Junior-Cycle.pdf

Doherty, Gabriel, 'National identity and the study of Irish history', *English Historical Review*, vol. 111, no. 441 (April 1996), pp. 324–49

Doherty, Gabriel, 'Kevin Barry and the Anglo-Irish propaganda war', *Irish Historical Studies*, vol. 32, no. 126 (November 2000), pp. 217–31

Doherty, Gabriel, 'The commemoration of the ninetieth anniversary of the Easter Rising', in Keogh and Doherty (eds), *1916: The Long Revolution*, pp. 376–408

Doherty, Gabriel, and John Borgonovo, 'Smoking gun? RIC reprisals, summer 1920', *History Ireland*, vol. 17, no. 2 (March/April 2009), pp. 36–8

Dolan, Anne, *Commemorating the Irish Civil War: History and Memory, 1923–2000* (Cambridge, 2003)

Dolan, Anne, 'The War of Independence', *Irish Independent*, 28 April 2010, supplement: 'Birth of a nation, part 2'

Dolan, Anne, 'Ending war in a "sportsmanlike manner": the milestone of revolution', in Hachey (ed.), *Turning Points in Twentieth-Century Irish History*, pp. 21–38

Dolan, Anne, 'Divisions and divisions and divisions: who to commemorate', in Horne and Madigan (eds), *Towards Commemoration*, pp. 145–54

Dooge, James (ed.), *Ireland in the Contemporary World* (Dublin, 1986)

Dooley, Terence, *The Decline of the Big House in Ireland: A Study of Irish Landed Families, 1860–1960* (Dublin, 2001)

Dooley, Terence, 'IRA veterans and land division in independent Ireland', in McGarry (ed.), *Republicanism in Modern Ireland*, pp. 86–108

Downey, James, 'Gombeenism thrives long after it should have been eradicated', *Irish Independent*, 14 April 2012

Dudley Edwards, Owen, *The Sins of Our Fathers* (Dublin, 1970)

Dudley Edwards, Owen, *Éamon de Valera* (Cardiff, 1987)

Dudley Edwards, Ruth, *Patrick Pearse: The Triumph of Failure* (London, 1977)

Dudley Edwards, Ruth, *The Faithful Tribe: An Intimate Portrait of the Loyal Institutions* (London, 1999)

Dungan, Myles, 'Fighting amnesia', *Irish Times*, 27 June 2006, supplement: 'The Somme, 90th anniversary'

Dunne, Tom, 'Commemoration and "shared history": a different role for historians?', *History Ireland*, vol. 21, no. 1 (January 2013), pp. 10–13

Ellis, John, S., 'The degenerate and the martyr: nationalist propaganda and the contestation of Irishness, 1914–1918', *Eire-Ireland*, vol. 35, nos 3–4 (Fall/Winter 2000), pp. 7–34

English, Richard, *Radicals and the Republic: Socialist Republicanism in the Irish Free State, 1925–1937* (Oxford, 1994)

English, Richard, '"The inborn hate of things English": Ernie O'Malley and the Irish Revolution, 1916–23', *Past and Present*, no. 151 (May 1996), pp. 174–99

English, Richard, *Ernie O'Malley: IRA Intellectual* (Oxford, 1998)

English, Richard, *Armed Struggle: The History of the IRA* (London, 2003)

Ervine, St John, *Craigavon: Ulsterman* (London, 1949)

Fanning, Ronan, *The Irish Department of Finance, 1922–1958* (Dublin, 1978)

Fanning, Ronan, 'The British dimension', *The Crane Bag*, vol. 8, no. 1 (1984), pp. 41–52

Fanning, Ronan, 'The Great enchantment: uses and abuses of modern Irish history', in Dooge (ed.), *Ireland in the Contemporary World*, pp. 131–48

Fanning, Ronan, 'Richard Mulcahy', in McGuire and Quinn (eds), *Dictionary of Irish Biography*, vol. 6, pp. 746–52

Fanning, Ronan, *Fatal Path: British Government and Irish Revolution, 1910–1922* (London, 2013)

Fanning, Ronan, Michael Kennedy, Eunan O'Halpin and Dermot Keogh (eds), *Documents on Irish Foreign Policy*, vol. 1: *1919–22* (Dublin, 1998)

Farren, Seán, *The Politics of Irish Education, 1920–1965* (Belfast, 1995)

Farry, Michael, *The Aftermath of Revolution: Sligo, 1921–23* (Dublin, 2000)

Feeley, Pat, *The Gralton Affair: The Story of the Deportation of Jim Gralton, a Leitrim Socialist* (Dublin, 1986)

Ferguson, Niall, *Civilisation: The West and the Rest* (London, 2010)

Ferguson, Niall (ed.), *Virtual History* (London, 1997)

Ferguson, Stephen, *GPO Staff in 1916: Business as Usual* (Cork, 2012)

Ferriter, Diarmaid, *Lovers of Liberty? Local Government in Twentieth Century Ireland* (Dublin, 2001)

Ferriter, Diarmaid, 'On the state funerals', *Dublin Review*, no. 5 (Winter 2001/2), pp. 5–15

Ferriter, Diarmaid, *The Transformation of Ireland* (London, 2004)

Ferriter, Diarmaid, 'So what will they do for an encore to 1916 Rising event?', *Irish Independent*, 18 April 2006

Ferriter, Diarmaid, *Judging Dev: A Reassessment of the Life and Legacy of Éamon de Valera* (Dublin, 2007)

Ferriter, Diarmaid, 'Rising to the challenge', *Irish Times*, 21 April 2007

Ferriter, Diarmaid, 'Mary Teresa Hayden', in McGuire and Quinn (eds), *Dictionary of Irish Biography*, vol. 4, pp. 531–2

Ferriter, Diarmaid, *Occasions of Sin: Sex and Society in Modern Ireland* (London, 2009)

Ferriter, Diarmaid, 'Beyond the Beyonds', in *The Plough and the Stars* (Abbey Theatre, Dublin, 2010), pp. 6–8

Ferriter, Diarmaid, 'Visit marks sheer effort to overcome our troubles', *Irish Independent*, 21 May 2011

Ferriter, Diarmaid, *Ambiguous Republic: Ireland in the 1970s* (London, 2012)

Ferriter, Diarmaid, 'State now morally as well as economically bankrupt', *Irish Times*, 26 March 2012

Ferriter, Diarmaid, 'Collins: history and myth', *Irish Times*, 18 August 2012

Ferriter, Diarmaid, 'We must unlock these stories to learn about ourselves', *Irish Independent*, 10 May 2014, supplement: 'Ireland at war'

Fischer, Karin, 'University historians and their role in the development of a "shared" history in Northern Ireland schools, 1960s–1980s', *History of Education*, vol. 40, no. 2 (March 2011), pp. 241–53

FitzGerald, Garret, 'The Significance of 1916', *Studies*, vol. 55, no. 217 (Spring 1966), pp. 29–37

FitzGerald, Garret, *All in a Life: An Autobiography* (Dublin, 1991)

FitzGerald, Garret, 'Past plays a crucial role in moulding future lives', *Irish Times*, 20 April 1996

FitzGerald, Garret, 'Public services make a shabby contrast with national wealth', *Irish Times*, 22 March 2008

FitzGerald, Garret, 'Apocalypse may yet spark the rebirth of civic morality', *Irish Times*, 16 October 2010

Fitzpatrick, David, *Politics and Irish Life: Provincial Experience of War and Revolution* (Dublin, 1977)

Fitzpatrick, David, 'The futility of history: a failed experiment in Irish education', in Brady (ed.), *Ideology and the Historians*, pp. 168–87

Fitzpatrick, David, 'Militarism in Ireland, 1900–1922', in Bartlett and Jeffery (eds), *A Military History of Ireland*, pp. 379–406

Fitzpatrick, David, *The Two Irelands: 1912–1939* (Oxford, 1998)

Fitzpatrick, David, 'Commemoration in the Irish Free State: a chronicle of embarrassment', in McBride (ed.), *History and Memory in Modern Ireland*, pp. 184–203

Fitzpatrick, David, 'The Orange Order and the border', *Irish Historical Studies*, vol. 33, no. 129 (May 2002), pp. 52–67

Fitzpatrick, David, *Harry Boland's Irish Revolution* (Cork, 2003)

Fitzpatrick, David, 'Dr Regan and Mr Snide', *History Ireland*, vol. 20, no. 3 (May 2012), pp. 12–13

Fitzpatrick, David (ed.), *Ireland and the First World War* (Dublin, 1988)

Fitzpatrick, David (ed.), *Revolution? Ireland, 1917–1923* (Dublin, 1990)

Fitzpatrick, David (ed.), *Terror in Ireland, 1916–1923* (Dublin, 2012)

Fleming, Diarmaid, 'Last man standing: Dan Keating', *History Ireland*, vol. 16, no. 3 (May/June 2008), pp. 38–41

Forester, Margery, *Michael Collins: Lost Leader* (London, 1971)

Foster, R. F., *Modern Ireland, 1600–1972* (London, 1988)

Foster, R. F., 'History and the Irish question', in Brady (ed.), *Interpreting Irish History: The Debate on Historical Revisionism, 1938–1994*, pp. 122–46

Foster, R. F., *The Irish Story: Telling Tales and Making It Up in Ireland* (London, 2001)

Foster, R. F., *Luck and the Irish: A Brief History of Change, 1970–2000* (London, 2007)

Foster, R. F., 'Francis Stewart Leland Lyons', in McGuire and Quinn (eds), *Dictionary of Irish Biography*, vol. 5, pp. 667–8

Foster, R. F., 'Historian who clears a path through the fog of war', *Irish Times*, 28 September 2013

Foster, R. F., *Vivid Faces: The Revolutionary Generation in Ireland, 1890–1923* (London, 2014)

Foy, Michael, 'Ulster unionist propaganda against home rule, 1912–14', *History Ireland*, vol. 4, no. 1 (Spring 1996), pp. 49–53

Fraser, T. G. and Keith Jeffery (eds), *Men, Women and War* (Dublin, 1993)

Gailey, Andrew, 'King Carson: an essay on the invention of leadership', *Irish Historical Studies*, vol. 30, no. 117 (May 1996), pp. 66–87

Gallagher, Michael, 'The pact general election of 1922', *Irish Historical Studies*, vol. 21, no. 84 (September 1979), pp. 404–21

Gallagher, Ronan, *Violence and Nationalist Politics in Derry City, 1920–23* (Dublin, 2003)

Garnham, Neal, 'Accounting for the early success of the Gaelic Athletic Association', *Irish Historical Studies*, vol. 34, no. 133 (May 2004), pp. 65–78

Garvin, Tom, 'The anatomy of a nationalist revolution: Ireland, 1858–1928', *Comparative Studies in Society and History*, vol. 28, no. 3 (July 1986), pp. 468–501

Garvin, Tom, *Nationalist Revolutionaries in Ireland, 1858–1928* (Oxford, 1987)

Garvin, Tom, 'The Rising and Irish democracy', in Ní Dhonnchadha and Dorgan (eds), *Revising the Rising*, pp. 21–9

Garvin, Tom, *1922: The Birth of Irish Democracy* (Dublin, 1996)

Garvin, Tom, 'Revolutionaries turned politicians: a painful, confusing metamorphosis', *Irish Times*, 6 December 1997

Garvin, Tom, *Preventing the Future: Why Was Ireland So Poor for So Long?* (Dublin, 2004)

Garvin, Tom, *News from a New Republic: Ireland in the 1950s* (Dublin, 2010)

Gaughan, J. Anthony, *Thomas Johnson* (Dublin, 1980)

Gibbons, Luke, 'Labour and local history: the case of Jim Gralton, 1886–1945', *Saothar*, vol. 14 (1989), pp. 85–93

Gilligan, Shauna, 'Image of a patriot: the popular and scholarly portrayal of Patrick Pearse, 1916–1991', unpublished MA thesis, UCD (1995)

Glennon, Kieran, *From Pogrom to Civil War: Tom Glennon and the Belfast IRA* (Cork, 2013)

Gorham, Maurice, *Forty Years of Irish Broadcasting* (Dublin, 1967)

Graham, B., and P. Shirlow, 'The Battle of the Somme in Ulster memory and identity', *Political Geography*, vol. 21 (2002), pp. 881–904

Gray, John, 'The 1907 Belfast Dock Strike', in Parkinson and Phoenix (eds), *Conflicts in the North of Ireland, 1900–2000*, pp. 15–27

Grayson, Richard, *Belfast Boys: How Unionists and Nationalists Fought and Died Together in the First World War* (London, 2009)

Greaves, Desmond, *Liam Mellows and the Irish Revolution* (London, 1971)

Gwynn, Denis, *The Life of John Redmond* (London, 1932)

Hachey, Thomas, E. (ed.), *Turning Points in Twentieth-Century Irish History* (Dublin, 2011)

Hanley, Brian, 'The Irish Citizen Army after 1916', *Saothar*, vol. 28 (2003), pp. 37–49

Hanley, Brian, *The IRA: A Documentary History, 1916–2005* (Dublin, 2010)

Hannigan, Dave, *De Valera in America: The Rebel President and the Making of Irish Independence* (New York, 2010)

Harkness, David, *History and the Irish* (Belfast, 1976)

Harris, Mary, *The Catholic Church and the Foundation of the Northern Ireland State* (Cork, 1993)

Harrison, Henry, *Ulster and the British Empire: Help or Hindrance?* (London, 1939)

Hart, Peter, 'The geography of revolution in Ireland, 1917–1923', *Past and Present*, no. 155 (May 1997), pp. 142–76

Hart, Peter, *The IRA and Its Enemies: Violence and Community in Cork, 1916–23* (Oxford, 1998)

Hart, Peter, 'The social structure of the IRA, 1916–23', *Historical Journal*, vol. 42, no. 1 (March 1999), pp. 207–31

Hart, Peter, 'Definition: defining the Irish revolution', in Augusteijn (ed.), *The Irish Revolution, 1913–23*, pp. 17–34

Hart, Peter, *The IRA at War: 1916–23* (Oxford, 2003)

Hart, Peter, 'Paramilitary politics and the Irish revolution', in McGarry (ed.), *Republicanism in Modern Ireland*, pp. 23–42

Hart, Peter, *Mick: The Real Michael Collins* (London, 2007)

Hart, Peter, 'What did the Easter Rising really change?', in Hachey (ed.), *Turning Points in Twentieth-Century Irish History*, pp. 7–21

Hart, Peter (ed.), *British Intelligence in Ireland: The Final Reports* (Cork, 2002)

Harte, Liam, and Yvonne Whelan (eds), *Ireland Beyond Boundaries: Mapping Irish Studies in the Twenty-first Century* (Dublin, 2007)

Harvey, Ed, and J. Kaye (eds), *The Face of the Crowd: Selected Essays of George Rudé* (Exeter, 1988)

Hay, Marnie, 'The foundation and development of Na Fianna Éireann, 1909–16', *Irish Historical Studies*, vol. 36, no. 141 (May 2008), pp. 53–71

Hayden, Joanne, 'The life of Julia', *Sunday Business Post* magazine, 17 March 2013

Hayden, Mary, and George Moonan, *A Short History of the Irish People, Part II, 1603–1924* (Dublin, 1927)

Hayes McCoy, G. A., *The Irish at War* (Cork, 1964)

Hayes, Michael, 'Dáil Éireann and the Irish civil war', *Studies*, vol. 58, no. 229 (Spring 1969), pp. 1–23

Heaney, Marie (ed.), *Sunday Miscellany: A Selection from 1995–2000* (Dublin, 2000)

Hearn, Mona, *Below Stairs: Domestic Service Remembered in Dublin and Beyond, 1880–1922* (Dublin, 1993)

Hepburn, A. C., *Catholic Belfast and Nationalist Ireland in the Era of Joe Devlin, 1871–1934* (Oxford, 2008)

Higgins, Roisín, *Transforming 1916: Meaning, Memory and the Fiftieth Anniversary of the Easter Rising* (Cork, 2012)

Hoff, Joan, 'The impact and implications of women's history', in Valiulis and O'Dowd (eds), *Women and Irish History*, pp. 15–38

Holland, Alisa, C., 'Anecdote on anarchy: the foundation years of the ISA', *Irish Archives*, vol. 17 (2010), pp. 4–16

Holohan, Francis, T., 'History teaching in the Irish Free State, 1922–35', *History Ireland*, vol. 2, no. 4 (Winter 1994), pp. 53–5

Hoppen, K. T., *Ireland Since 1800: Conflict and Conformity* (London, 1989)

Hopkinson, Michael, *Green Against Green: The Irish Civil War* (Dublin, 1988)

Hopkinson, Michael, *The Irish War of Independence* (Dublin, 2000)

Hopkinson, Michael, 'Thomas Barry', in McGuire and Quinn (eds), *Dictionary of Irish Biography*, vol. 1, pp. 349–51

Hopkinson, Michael, 'Daniel Breen', in McGuire and Quinn (eds), *Dictionary of Irish Biography*, vol. 1, pp. 796–7

Hopkinson, Michael, 'Michael Collins', in McGuire and Quinn (eds), *Dictionary of Irish Biography*, vol. 2, pp. 678–82

Horgan, J. J., *Parnell to Pearse* (Dublin, 1948)

Horgan, John, *The Irish Media: A Critical History Since 1922* (London, 2001)

Horne, John, 'James Connolly and the Great Divide: Ireland, Europe and the First World War', *Saothar*, vol. 31 (2006), pp. 75–84

Horne, John (ed.), *Our War: Ireland and the Great War* (Dublin, 2008)

Horne, John, and Edward Madigan (eds), *Towards Commemoration: Ireland in War and Revolution, 1912–23* (Dublin, 2013)

Hourican, Bridget, 'Donagh MacDonagh', in McGuire and Quinn (eds), *Dictionary of Irish Biography*, vol. 5, pp. 916–17

Hourican, Bridget, 'Roland McNeill', in McGuire and Quinn (eds), *Dictionary of Irish Biography*, vol. 6, pp. 163–4

Hourihane, Ann Marie, 'Children of the revolution', *Irish Times*, 22 March 2014

Hunt, Tristram, 'If we have no history, we have no future', *Observer*, 28 August 2011

Jackson, Alvin, 'Unionist myths, 1912–85', *Past and Present*, no. 136 (August 1992), pp. 164–85

Jackson, Alvin, 'Unionist history', *Irish Review*, vol. 1, no. 1 (Spring 1993), pp. 58–67

Jackson, Alvin, 'What if home rule had been enacted in 1912?', in Ferguson (ed.), *Virtual History*, pp. 175–228

Jackson, Alvin, 'James Camlin Beckett', in McGuire and Quinn (eds), *Dictionary of Irish Biography*, vol. 1, pp. 401–3

Jackson, Alvin, 'Edward Henry Carson', in McGuire and Quinn (eds), *Dictionary of Irish Biography*, vol. 2, pp. 383–8

Jackson, Alvin, 'James Craig', in McGuire and Quinn (eds), *Dictionary of Irish Biography*, vol. 2, pp. 953–7

Jeffery, Keith, 'The Great War in modern Irish memory', in Fraser and Jeffrey (eds), *Men, Women and War*, pp. 136–58

Jeffery, Keith, *Ireland and the Great War* (Cambridge, 2000)

Johnston, Kevin, *Home or Away: The Great War and the Irish Revolution* (Dublin, 2010)

Jones, Mary, *These Obstreperous Lassies: A History of the IWWU* (Dublin, 1988)

Jones, Thomas, *Whitehall Diary*, vol. 3: *Ireland, 1918–25* (Oxford, 1971)

Joy, Sineád, *The IRA in Kerry, 1916–21* (Cork, 2005)

Joye, Lar, 'The Mauser Model 71 rifle', *History Ireland*, vol. 19, no. 1 (January/February 2011), p. 49

Judt, Tony, *The Memory Chalet* (London, 2010)

Jupp, Peter and Eoin Magennis (eds), *Crowds in Ireland, 1720–1920* (London, 2000)

Keane, Adrian, 'Who fears to speak of Easter Week?', unpublished MA thesis, UCD (1996)

Kearney, Hugh, 'The Irish and their history', *History Workshop*, no. 31 (Spring 1991), pp. 149–55

Kee, Robert, *Ourselves Alone* (London, 1972)

Kelly, Brendan, *Ada English: Patriot and Psychiatrist* (Dublin, 2014)

Kelly, Patrick, and Dermot Keogh, 'Turning corners: Ireland 2002–11', in Moody and Martin (eds), *The Course of Irish History*, pp. 358–98

Kennedy, Denis, *The Widening Gulf: Northern Attitudes to the Independent Irish State, 1919–1949* (Belfast, 1988)

Kennedy, Michael, 'Robert Brennan', in McGuire and Quinn (eds), *Dictionary of Irish Biography*, vol. 1, pp. 814–15

Kennedy, Thomas, C., '"The gravest situation of our lives": Conservatives, Ulster and the home rule crisis, 1911–14', *Eire-Ireland*, vol. 36, nos 3–4 (Fall/Winter 2001), pp. 67–82

Kennedy, Thomas, C., 'Troubled Tories: dissent and confusion concerning the party's Ulster policy, 1910–1914', *Journal of British Studies*, vol. 46, no. 3 (July 2007), pp. 570–93

Keogh, Dermot, *The Rise of the Irish Working Class* (Dublin, 1982)

Keogh, Dermot, *Ireland and the Vatican: The Diplomacy of Church–State Relations, 1922–60* (Cork, 1995)

Keogh, Dermot, and Gabriel Doherty (eds), *1916: The Long Revolution* (Cork, 2007)

Kerrigan, Gene, *Another Country: Growing Up in 1950s Ireland* (Dublin, 1998)

Kerrigan, Gene, *The Big Lie: Who Profits from Ireland's Austerity?* (London, 2012)

Kettle, Martin, 'With no common culture, a common history is elusive', *Guardian*, 3 June 2010

Kiberd, Declan, 'The elephant of revolutionary forgetfulness', in Ní Dhonnchadha and Dorgan (eds), *Revising the Rising*, pp. 1–21

Kirwan, Kathleen, *Towards Irish Nationalism: A Tract: Offered in Awe and Reverence to the Sublime Patience and Agonised Endurance of the Exploited People of Ireland* (Dublin, 1938)

Kissane, Bill, *The Politics of the Irish Civil War* (Oxford, 2005)

Kissane, Bill, '"From the outside in": the international dimension to the Irish civil war', *History Ireland*, vol. 15, no. 2 (March/April 2007), pp. 36–41

Knirck, Jason, 'Women's political rhetoric and the Irish revolution', in Hachey (ed.), *Turning Points in Twentieth-Century Irish History*, pp. 39–57

Kostick, Conor, *Revolution in Ireland: Popular Militancy, 1917–1923* (London, 1996)

Kotsonouris, Mary, *Retreat from Revolution: The Dáil Courts, 1920–24* (Dublin, 1994)

Laffan, Michael, 'New variations on an old theme: recent works on Irish history, 1914–1922', *Stair*, Journal of the HTAI, vol. 2 (1979), pp. 11–13

Laffan, Michael, '"Labour must wait": Ireland's conservative revolution', in Corish (ed.), *Radicals, Rebels and Establishments*, pp. 203–27

Laffan, Michael, *The Partition of Ireland, 1911–1925* (Dundalk, 1987)

Laffan, Michael, 'Insular attitudes: the revisionists and their critics', in Ní Dhonnchadha and Dorgan (eds), *Revising the Rising*, pp. 106–22

Laffan, Michael, *The Resurrection of Ireland: The Sinn Féin Party, 1916–1923* (Cambridge, 1999)

Laffan, Michael, 'The emergence of the two Irelands, 1912–25', *History Ireland*, vol. 12, no. 4 (Winter 2004), pp. 40–44

Laffan, Michael, 'Arthur Griffith', in McGuire and Quinn (eds), *Dictionary of Irish Biography*, vol. 4, pp. 277–86

Laffan, Michael, 'John Edward Redmond', in McGuire and Quinn (eds), *Dictionary of Irish Biography*, vol. 8, pp. 411–18

Laffan, Michael, 'In the shadow of the national question', in Daly, O'Brien and Rouse (eds), *Making the Difference?*, pp. 32–43

Laird, Heather, *Subversive Law in Ireland, 1879–1920: From 'Unwritten Law' to the Dáil Courts* (Dublin, 2005)

Lane, Leeann, *Rosamund Jacob: Third Person Singular* (Dublin, 2010)

Larkin, Felix, M., '"A great daily organ": The Freeman's Journal 1763–1924, *History Ireland*, vol. 14, no. 3 (May/June 2006), pp. 44–50

Lee, J. J., *Ireland, 1912–1985: Politics and Society* (Cambridge, 1989)

Leeson, D. M., *The Black and Tans: British Police and Auxiliaries in the Irish War of Independence, 1920–21* (Oxford, 2011)

Legg, Marie Louise, *Newspapers and Nationalism: The Irish Provincial Press, 1850–1892* (Dublin, 1999)

Lenihan, Denis (ed.), *The Path to Freedom: Speeches by Michael Collins* (Dublin, 2010)

Leonard, Jane, 'The twinge of memory: Armistice Day and Remembrance Sunday in Dublin since 1919', in McBride (ed.), *History and Memory in Modern Ireland*, pp. 99–115

Levenson, Samuel, *Maud Gonne* (London, 1977)

Lewis, Geoffrey, *Carson: The Man Who Divided Ireland* (London, 2005)

Loughlin, James, 'Joseph Devlin', in McGuire and Quinn (eds), *Dictionary of Irish Biography*, vol. 3, pp. 241–3

Lowe, W. J., 'The war against the RIC, 1919–21' *Eire-Ireland*, vol. 37, nos 3–4 (Fall/Winter 2002), pp. 79–117

Lowe, W. J., 'Who were the Black and Tans?', *History Ireland*, vol. 12, no. 3 (Autumn 2004), pp. 47–51

Lunny, Linde, 'James Armour', McGuire and Quinn (eds), *Dictionary of Irish Biography*, vol. 1, pp. 153–4

Lynch, Andrew, 'Prize writer', profile of Sebastian Barry, *Sunday Business Post*, 31 July 2011

Lynch, Robert, *Radical Politics in Modern Ireland: The Irish Socialist Republican Party, 1896–1904* (Dublin, 2005)

Lynch, Robert, *The Northern IRA and the Early Years of Partition, 1920–22* (Dublin, 2006)

Lynn, Brendan, 'Joseph Mac Rory', in McGuire and Quinn (eds), *Dictionary of Irish Biography*, vol. 6, pp. 182–3

Lyons, F. S. L., *John Dillon, a Biography* (London, 1968)

Lyons, F. S. L., 'The dilemma of the Irish contemporary historian', *Hermathena*, no. 115 (Summer 1973), pp. 45–57

Lyons, F. S. L., 'The Rising and after', in Vaughan (ed.), *A New History of Ireland*, vol. 6, pp. 207–22

MacAtasney, Gerard, *Tom Clarke: Life, Liberty and Revolution* (Dublin, 2013)

Mac Curtain, Margaret, *Ariadne's Thread: Writing Women into Irish History* (Dublin, 2008)

Mac Curtain, Margaret et al., 'The Teaching of History in Irish Schools', *Administration*, no. 15, vol. 4 (1967), pp. 268–85

Maguire, Martin, *The Civil Service and the Revolution in Ireland, 1912–1938* (Manchester, 2008)

Mansergh, Martin (ed.), *Spirit of the Nation: The Speeches and Statements of Charles J. Haughey, 1957–1986* (Dublin, 1986)

Mansergh, Nicholas, *The Irish Question, 1840–1921*, 3rd edn (London, 1975 [1965])

Mansergh, Nicholas, 'Eoin MacNeill – a reappraisal', *Studies*, vol. 63, no. 250 (Summer 1974), pp. 133–40

Martin, F. X., '1916 – myth, fact and mystery', *Studia Hibernica*, no. 7 (1967), pp. 7–127

Martin, F. X. (ed.), *The Irish Volunteers, 1913–1915: Recollections and Documents* (Dublin, 1963)

Matthews, Kevin, *Fatal Influence: The Impact of Ireland on British Politics, 1920–1925* (Dublin, 2004)

Maxwell, Henry, *Ulster Was Right* (London, 1934)

Maume, Patrick, *The Long Gestation: Irish Nationalist Life, 1891–1918* (Dublin, 1999)

Maume, Patrick, 'Seán Thomas O'Kelly', in McGuire and Quinn (eds), *Dictionary of Irish Biography*, vol. 7, pp. 615–19

Maume, Patrick, 'Patrick Augustine Sheehan', in McGuire and Quinn (eds), *Dictionary of Irish Biography*, vol. 8, pp. 882–4

McBride, Ian, 'Memory and national identity', in McBride (ed.), *History and Memory in Modern Ireland*, pp. 1–43

McBride, Ian (ed.), *History and Memory in Modern Ireland* (Cambridge University Press, 2001)

McBride, Lawrence W., 'Young readers and the learning and teaching of Irish history, 1870–1922', in McBride (ed.), *Reading Irish Histories: Texts, Contexts and Memory in Modern Ireland*, pp. 80–118

McBride, Lawrence, W. (ed.), *Reading Irish Histories: Texts, Contexts and Memory in Modern Ireland* (Dublin, 2003)

McCabe, Conor, 'The Irish Labour Party and the 1920 local elections', *Saothar*, vol. 35 (2010), pp. 7–23

McCabe, Conor, '"Your only god is profit": Irish class relations and the 1913 Lockout', in Convery (ed.), *Locked Out: A Century of Irish Working-Class Life*, pp. 9–23

McCabe, Michael, *For God and Ireland: The Fight for Moral Superiority in Ireland, 1922–1932* (Dublin, 2013)

McCartney, Donal, *UCD – A National Idea: The History of University College, Dublin* (Dublin, 1999)

McConnel, James, 'The Irish Parliamentary Party, industrial relations and the 1913 Dublin Lockout', *Saothar*, vol. 28 (2003), pp. 25–36

McCoole, Sinéad, *Guns and Chiffon: Women Revolutionaries and Kilmainham Gaol, 1916–1923* (Dublin, 1997)

McCoole, Sinéad, *No Ordinary Women: Irish Female Activists in the Revolutionary Years, 1900–1923* (Dublin, 2003)

McDonagh, Enda, 'Church State relations', *Irish Press*, 26 May 1976, supplement: 'Fianna Fáil golden jubilee'

McDowell, R. B., *The Church of Ireland, 1869–1969* (London, 1975)

McDowell, R. B., *Historical Essays, 1938–2001* (Dublin, 2003)

McElligott, Richard, *Forging a Kingdom: The GAA in Kerry, 1884–1934* (Cork, 2013)

McGahern, John, 'Return of the revolutionary', *Irish Times*, 8 June 2002

McGarry, Fearghal, 'Keeping an eye on the usual suspects: Dublin Castle's "Personality Files", 1899–1921', *History Ireland*, vol. 14, no. 6 (November/December 2006), pp. 44–9

McGarry, Fearghal, *Rebels: Voices from the Easter Rising* (London, 2011)

McGarry, Fearghal, '1916 and Irish republicanism: between myth and history', in Horne and Madigan (eds), *Towards Commemoration*, pp. 46–54

McGarry, Fearghal (ed.), *Republicanism in Modern Ireland* (Dublin, 2003)

McGee, Owen, '"God Save Ireland": Manchester-Martyr demonstrations in Dublin, 1867–1916', *Eire-Ireland*, vol. 36, nos 3–4 (Fall/Winter 2001), pp. 39–66

MacGill, Patrick, *Children of the Dead End: The Autobiography of an Irish Navvy* (London, 1914)

McGough, Eileen, *Diarmuid Lynch: A Forgotten Irish Patriot* (Cork, 2013)

McGurk, Tom, 'Observe the Amnesiacs marching towards the Somme', *Sunday Business Post*, 2 July 2006

McIntosh, Gillian, *The Force of Culture: Unionist Identities in Contemporary Ireland* (Cork, 1999)

McIntosh, Gillian, 'Stormont's ill-timed jubilee: the Ulster 71 Exhibition', *New Hibernia Review*, vol. 11, no. 2 (Summer 2007), pp. 17–39

McKenna, Napoli, 'In London with the Treaty delegates', *Capuchin Annual* (1971), pp. 330–38

McMahon, Deirdre, '"A worthy monument to a great man": Piaras Béaslaí's life of Michael Collins', *Bullán*, vol. 2 (Winter/Spring 1996), pp. 55–67

McMahon, Deirdre, 'Ireland and the Empire-Commonwealth, 1886–1972', in Kevin Kenny (ed.), *Ireland and the British Empire* (Oxford, 2004), pp. 182–220

McMahon, Deirdre, *The Moynihan Brothers in Peace and War, 1909–1918: Their New Ireland* (Dublin, 2004)

McMahon, Deirdre, 'The Irish settlement meeting of the Unionist Party, 7 July 1916', *Analecta Hibernica*, no. 41 (2009), pp. 201–70

McMahon, Deirdre, 'Robert Dudley Edwards (1909–1988) and Irish Archives', *Irish Archives*, vol. 17, no. 21 (2010), pp. 1–14

McMahon, Deirdre, 'The 1926 Imperial Conference and Kevin O'Higgins's proposals for a dual monarchy', *Analecta Hibernica*, no. 44 (2013), pp. 99–121

McMahon, Deirdre, and Michael Kennedy, *Reconstructing Ireland's Past: A History of the Irish Manuscripts Commission* (Dublin, 2009)

Meehan, Ciara, *The Cosgrave Party: A History of Cumann na nGaedheal, 1923–33* (Dublin, 2010)

Meehan, Ciara, 'Labour and Dáil Éireann, 1922–32', in Daly, O'Brien and Rouse (eds), *Making the Difference?*, pp. 43–6

Meenan, James, *George O'Brien: A Biographical Memoir* (Dublin, 1980)

Meleady, Dermot, *John Redmond: The National Leader* (Dublin, 2014)

Metscher, Priscilla, *Republicanism and Socialism in Ireland* (Frankfurt, 1986)

Middlemas, Keith (ed.), *Thomas Jones Whitehall Diary*, vol. 1: *1916–25* (London, 1969)

Miller, David, *Church, State and Nation in Ireland, 1898–1921* (Dublin, 1973)

Mitchell, Arthur, 'William O'Brien (1881–1968) and the Irish labour movement', *Studies*, vol. 60, nos 239–40 (Autumn/Winter, 1971), pp. 311–31

Mitchell, Arthur, *Labour in Irish Politics, 1890–1930: The Irish Labour Movement in an Age of Revolution* (Dublin, 1974)

Mitchell, Arthur, *Revolutionary Government in Ireland: Dáil Éireann, 1919–22* (Dublin, 1995)

Mitchell, Arthur, 'The course of Irish labour history', *Saothar*, vol. 22 (1997), pp. 101–7

Mitchell, Arthur, 'Alternative government: exit Britannia', in Augusteijn (ed.), *The Irish Revolution, 1913–23*

Moody, T. W., and F. X. Martin (eds), *The Course of Irish History*, new edn (Cork, 2011)

Moloney, Ed, *A Secret History of the IRA* (London, 2002)

Morgan, Austen, *Labour and Partition: The Belfast Working Class, 1905–1923* (London, 1991)

Moriarty, Gerry, 'North's politicians must strike right tone during emotionally charged anniversaries', *Irish Times*, 6 January 2012

Morris, Catherine, *Alice Milligan and the Irish Cultural Revival* (Dublin, 2012)

Morrison, Eve, 'Bureau of Military History and female republican activism, 1913–23', in Valiulis (ed.), *Gender and Power in Irish History*, pp. 59–84

Morrison, Eve, 'One woman's war', *Irish Times*, 22 May 2013, supplement: 'Stories of the revolution'

Morrissey, John, 'Ireland's Great War: representation, public space and the place of dissonant heritages', *Journal of the Galway Archaeological and Historical Society*, vol. 58 (2006), pp. 98–113

Moynihan, Maurice, *Speeches and Statements of Éamon de Valera, 1917–1973* (Dublin and New York, 1980)

Mulcahy, Risteard, *Richard Mulcahy (1886–1971): A Family Memoir* (Dublin, 1999)

Mulholland, Joe (ed.), *Reforming the Republic: The MacGill Report 2010* (Tipperary, 2010)

Mulholland, Marie, *The Politics and Relationships of Kathleen Lynn* (Dublin, 2002)

Mulligan, William, 'Violence and war in Europe and Ireland, 1911–14', in Horne and Madigan (eds), *Towards Commemoration*, pp. 13–21

Murphy, Donal, *Blazing Tar Barrels and Standing Orders: Tipperary North's First County and District Councils, 1899–1902* (Tipperary, 1999)

Murphy, William, 'Alice Sophia Amelia Stopford Green', in McGuire and Quinn (eds), *Dictionary of Irish Biography*, vol. 4, pp. 232–4

Murphy, William, *Political Imprisonment and the Irish, 1912–1921* (Oxford, 2014)

Murray, Patrick, *Oracles of God: The Roman Catholic Church and Irish Politics, 1922–1937* (Dublin, 2000)

Murray, Patrick, 'Obsessive historian: Éamon de Valera and the policing of his reputation', *Proceedings of the Royal Irish Academy*, 101 C (2001), pp. 37–65

Murray, Paul, *The Irish Boundary Commission and Its Origins, 1886–1925* (Dublin, 2011)

Murray, Peter, 'Radical way forward or sectarian cul-de-sac: Lindsay Crawford and Independent Orangeism reassessed', *Saothar*, vol. 27 (2002), pp. 31–43

Murtagh, Peter, 'History of the Rising in our own words', *Irish Times*, 2 November 2013

Myers, Kevin, *From the Irish Times Column 'An Irishman's Diary'* (Dublin, 2000)

Myers, Kevin, 'An Irishman's diary', *Irish Times*, 3 October 2001

Myers, Kevin, 'Crunching the numbers and bursting myths', *History Ireland*, vol. 22, no. 4 (July/August 2014), pp. 40–42

Neeson, Eoin, *Birth of a Republic* (Dublin, 1998)

Neeson, Eoin, 'There are no conquerors or winners in a civil war', *Irish Times*, 24 May 2003

Newell, Una, 'The Rising of the Moon: Galway 1916', *Journal of the Galway Archaeological and Historical Society*, vol. 58 (2006), pp. 114–35

Newsinger, John, 'Reporting the Lockout', *Saothar*, vol. 28 (2003), pp. 125–33

Nevin, Donal, *James Connolly: A Full Life* (Dublin, 2005)

Ní Dhonnchadha, Máirín and Theo Dorgan (eds), *Revising the Rising* (Dublin, 1991)

Nic Shiubhlaigh, Máire, *The Splendid Years* (Dublin, 1955)

Nugent, Joe, 'The sword and the prayerbook: the ideal of authentic Irish manliness', *Victorian Studies*, vol. 50, no. 4 (Summer 2008), pp. 587–613

O'Brien, Gerard, 'The record of the first Dáil debates', *Irish Historical Studies*, vol. 28, no. 111 (May 1993), pp. 306–9

O'Brien, Gerard, *Irish Governments and the Guardianship of Historical Records, 1922–1972* (Dublin, 2004)

O'Broin, Leon, 'The Fenians and after', *Irish Times*, 4 January 1969

O'Callaghan, John, *Revolutionary Limerick: The Republican Campaign for Independence in Limerick, 1913–21* (Dublin, 2010)

O'Callaghan, Margaret, 'Language, nationality and cultural identity in the Irish Free State, 1922–7', *Irish Historical Studies*, vol. 24, no. 94 (November 1984), pp. 226–45

O'Carroll, J. P., and John A. Murphy (eds), *De Valera and His Times* (Cork, 1986)

O'Casey, Seán, *Drums Under the Windows* (London, 1973)

O'Casey, Seán, *Three Dublin Plays*, introduced by Christopher Murray (Dublin, 1998)

O'Casey, Seán, *Autobiographies: Volume 2* (London, 1980)

Ó Conchubhair, Brian (ed.), *Dublin's Fighting Story, 1916–21: Told by the Men Who Made It*, new edn (Cork, 2009 [1948])

Ó Conchubhair, Brian (ed.), *Kerry's Fighting Story, 1916–21: Told by the Men Who Made It* (Cork, 2010 [1947])

O'Connor, Emmet, 'An age of agitation', *Saothar*, vol. 9 (1983), pp. 64–7

O'Connor, Emmet, 'A Historiography of Irish Labour' *Labour History Review*, vol. 60, no. 1, Spring 1995, pp. 21–34

O'Connor, Emmet, *James Larkin* (Cork, 2002)

O'Connor, Emmet, 'James Larkin', in McGuire and Quinn (eds), *Dictionary of Irish Biography*, vol. 5, pp. 318–22

O'Connor, Emmet, 'Larkin's road to revolution', *Irish Times*, 11 September 1913, supplement: 'Locked out: the story of the 1913 Dublin Lockout'

O'Connor, Emmet, and Trevor Parkhill (eds), *Loyalism and Labour in Belfast: The Autobiography of Robert McElborough, 1884–1952* (Cork, 2002)

O'Connor, Frank, *The Big Fellow: A Life of Michael Collins* (London, 1937)

Ó Corráin, Donnchadh, *James Hogan: Revolutionary, Historian and Political Scientist* (Dublin, 2001)

O'Donnell, Peadar, *The Gates Flew Open: An Irish Civil War Prison Diary* (Cork, 2013)

O'Donoghue, Florence, *No Other Law* (Dublin, 1954)

O'Donovan, Donal, *Kevin Barry and His Time* (Dublin, 1989)

O'Faoláin, Julia, *Trespassers: A Memoir* (London, 2013)

O'Faoláin, Seán, '1916–41: tradition and creation', *The Bell*, vol. 2, no. 1 (April 1941), pp. 5–13

O'Faoláin, Seán, 'One world', *The Bell*, vol. 8, no. 6 (September 1944), pp. 461–72

O'Faoláin, Seán, 'The Gaelic Cult', *The Bell*, vol. 9, no. 3 (December 1944), pp. 185–96

O'Faoláin, Seán, *Vive Moi!* (Boston, 1964)

O'Faoláin, Seán, 'A portrait of the artist as an old man', *Irish University Review*, vol. 6, no. 1 (Spring 1976), pp. 10–19

Officer, David, 'For God and for Ulster: the Ulsterman on the Somme', in McBride (ed.), *History and Memory in Modern Ireland*, pp. 160–84

Officer, David, and Graham Walker, 'Protestant Ulster: ethno-history, memory and contemporary prospects', *National Identities*, vol. 2, no. 3 (2000), pp. 292–307

O'Flaherty, Eamon, 'Michael Laffan: portrait of a historian', in Susannah Riordan and Diarmaid Ferriter (eds), *The Irish Revolution, 1910–23: Essays in Honour of Michael Laffan* (Dublin, 2015), pp. 19–34

O'Gráda, Cormac, *Ireland: A New Economic History, 1780–1939* (Oxford, 1994)

O'Halpin, Eunan, *Decline of the Union: British Government in Ireland, 1892–1920* (Dublin, 1987)

O'Halpin, Eunan, 'William Thomas Cosgrave', in McGuire and Quinn (eds), *Dictionary of Irish Biography*, vol. 2, pp. 880–85

O'Halpin, Eunan, 'Counting terror: Bloody Sunday and the dead of the Irish revolution', in Fitzpatrick (ed.), *Terror in Ireland*, pp. 141–58

O'Halpin, Eunan, 'Lemass's silent anguish', *Irish Times*, 20 July 2013

Ó hÓgartaigh, Margaret, *Kathleen Lynn: Irishwoman, Patriot, Doctor* (Dublin, 2006)

O'Luing, Seán, *Art Ó Griofa* (Dublin, 1953)

O'Malley, Cormac, K. H., 'Publication History of *On Another Man's Wound*', *New Hibernia Review*, vol. 7, no. 3 (Autumn 2003), pp. 136–9

O'Malley, Cormac K. H., and Cormac Ó Comhraí, *The Men Will Talk to Me: Galway Interviews by Ernie O'Malley* (Cork, 2013)

O'Malley, Ernie, *The Singing Flame* (Dublin, 1978)

O'Malley, Ernie, *On Another Man's Wound* (Dublin, 1979)

O'Mara, James, and Francis Carroll, *Money for Ireland: Finance, Diplomacy, Politics and the First Dáil Éireann Loans, 1919–1936* (Westport, 2002)

O'Neill, T. P., and Lord Longford, *Éamon de Valera* (Dublin, 1970)

O'Riordan, Seán, 'Culprit who led burning of Cork finally identified', *Irish Examiner*, 11 December 2010

Ó Súilleabháin, Micheál, *Where Mountainy Men Have Sown* (Cork, 2013 [1965])

O'Toole, Fintan, 'A grotesque denial of bloodshed', *Irish Times*, 2 October 2001

O'Toole, Fintan, 'Why we remember', *Irish Times*, 27 June 2006, supplement: 'The Somme, 90th anniversary'

O'Toole, Fintan, 'Rising to the challenge', *Irish Times*, 23 April 2011

O'Toole, Fintan, 'History matters in Ireland', *Irish Times*, 10 September 2011

O'Toole, Fintan, 'Rules of engagement for a decade of centenaries', *Irish Times* 17 September 2012

O'Toole, Fintan (ed.), *Up the Republic! Towards a New Ireland* (London, 2012)

Oram, Gerald, *Worthless Men* (London, 1998)

Owens, Rosemary Cullen (ed.), *Votes for Women: Irish Women's Struggle for the Vote* (Dublin, 1975)

Pakenham, Frank, *Peace by Ordeal: The Negotiation of the Anglo-Irish Treaty, 1921* (London, 1992 [1935])

Parkinson, Alan, and Eamon Phoenix (eds), *Conflicts in the North of Ireland, 1900–2000* (Dublin, 2010)

Parsons, Michael, 'Nuns asked for sniper to kill crows', *Irish Times*, 11 April 2012

Paseta, Senia, *Before the Revolution: Nationalism, Social Change and Ireland's Catholic Elite, 1879–1922* (Cork, 1999)

Paseta, Senia, 'Constance Georgine Markievicz', in McGuire and Quinn (eds), *Dictionary of Irish Biography*, vol. 5, pp. 363–6

Paseta, Senia, *Irish Nationalist Women, 1900–1918* (Cambridge, 2014)

Patterson, Henry, *Class, Conflict and Sectarianism: The Protestant Working Class and the Belfast Labour Movement, 1868–1920* (Belfast, 1980)

Pelling, Henry, *Popular Politics and Society in Late Victorian Britain* (London, 1979)

Pennell, Catriona, *A Kingdom United: Popular Responses to the Outbreak of War in Britain and Ireland* (Oxford, 2012)

Perry, Nicholas, 'The Irish landed class and the British Army, 1850–1950', *War in History*, vol. 18, no. 3 (2011), pp. 304–32

Phillips, W. A., *The Revolution in Ireland, 1906–23*, 2nd edn (London, 1926)

Phoenix, Eamon, 'Cahir Healy', in McGuire and Quinn (eds), *Dictionary of Irish Biography*, vol. 4, pp. 555–8

Price, Dominic, *The Flame and the Candle: War in Mayo, 1919–24* (Dublin, 2012)

Privilege, John, *Michael Logue and the Catholic Church in Ireland, 1879–1925* (Manchester, 2009)

Prunty, Jacinta, *Dublin Slums, 1800–1925: A Study in Urban Geography* (Dublin, 1999)

Quinn, James, 'Frederick Hugh Crawford', in McGuire and Quinn (eds), *Dictionary of Irish Biography*, vol. 2, pp. 966–8

Quinn, James, 'Cathal Brugha', in McGuire and Quinn (eds), *Dictionary of Irish Biography*, vol. 1, pp. 951–4

Rafroidi, Patrick, and Maurice Harmon (eds), *The Irish Novel in Our Time* (Lille, 1975)

Regan, John M., *The Irish Counter-Revolution, 1921–36* (Dublin, 1999)

Regan, John M., *Myth and the Irish State* (Dublin, 2014)

Riddell, Patrick, *Fire Over Ulster* (London, 1970)

Robinson, Lennox, *Bryan Cooper* (London, 1931)

Robinson, Lennox (ed.), *Lady Gregory's Journals, 1916–30* (London, 1946)

Rooney, Brendan (ed.), *A Time and a Place: Two Centuries of Irish Social Life* (Dublin, 2006)

Rudé, George, *The Crowd in History: A Study of Popular Disturbances in France and England, 1730–1848* (London, 1964)

Rudé, George, 'The changing face of the crowd', in Harvey and Kaye (eds), *The Face of the Crowd: Selected Essays of George Rudé*, pp. 56–72

Ryan, Annie, *Witnesses: Inside the Easter Rising* (Dublin, 2005)

Ryan, Annie, *Comrades: Inside the War of Independence* (Dublin, 2008)

Ryan, Louise, '"Drunken Tans": representation of sex and violence in the Anglo-Irish War, 1919–21', *Feminist Review*, no. 66 (Autumn 2000), pp. 73–95

Ryan, Louise, '"In the line of fire": representations of women and war (1919–1923) through the writings of republican men', in Ryan and Ward (eds), *Irish Women and Nationalism*, pp. 45–61

Ryan, Louise, and Margaret Ward (eds), *Irish Women and Nationalism: Soldiers, New Women and Wicked Hags* (Dublin, 2004)

Ryle Dwyer, T., *The Squad and the Intelligence Operations of Michael Collins* (Dublin, 2005)

Shaw, Francis, 'The canon of Irish history: a challenge', *Studies*, vol. 61, no. 242 (Summer 1972), pp. 117–51

Shaw, Francis, 'Eoin MacNeill, the Person', *Studies*, vol. 62, no. 246 (Summer 1973), pp. 154–64

Shearman, Hugh, *Not an Inch: A Study of Northern Ireland and Lord Craigavon* (London, 1942)

Sheehan, Aideen, 'Cumann na mBan: policies and activities', in Fitzpatrick (ed.), *Revolutions? Ireland, 1917–1923*, pp. 88–97

Sheehan, William, *British Voices from the Irish War of Independence, 1918–1921* (Cork, 2005)

Sheehy-Skeffington, Hanna, 'Reminiscences of an Irish suffragette', in Owens (ed.), *Votes for Women*, pp. 4–18

Stewart, A. T. Q., *The Narrow Ground: Patterns of Ulster History* (Belfast, 1986)

Stuart, Francis, *Things to Live For: Notes for an Autobiography* (New York, 1938)

Taafe, Seamus, 'Commemorating the fallen: public memorials to the Irish dead of the Great War', *Archaeology Ireland*, vol. 13, no. 3 (Autumn 1999), pp. 18–22

Taillon, Ruth, *When History Was Made: The Women of 1916* (Belfast, 1996)

Taylor, Rex, *Michael Collins* (London, 1958)

Thornley, David, 'Patrick Pearse', *Studies*, vol. 55, no. 217 (Spring 1966), pp. 10–20

Tiernan, Sonja, *Eva Gore Booth: An Image of Such Politics* (Manchester, 2012)

Tierney, Mark, and Margaret Mac Curtain, *The Birth of Modern Ireland* (Dublin, 1969)

Tóibín, Colm, *Lady Gregory's Toothbrush* (Dublin, 2002)

Tóibín, Colm (ed.), *The Penguin Book of Irish Fiction* (London, 2000)

Tormley, Roland, 'The construction of national identity through primary school history: the Irish case', *British Journal of Sociology*, vol. 27, no. 3 (July 2006), pp. 311–24

Townshend, Charles, *The British Campaign in Ireland: The Development of Political and Military Policies* (Oxford, 1975)

Townshend, Charles, 'The IRA and the development of guerrilla warfare', *English Historical Review*, vol. 94, no. 371 (1979), pp. 318–45

Townshend, Charles, 'Military force and civil authority in the United Kingdom, 1914–1921', *Journal of British Studies*, vol. 28, no. 3 (July 1989), pp. 262–92

Townshend, Charles, 'Historiography', in Augusteijn (ed.), *The Irish Revolution*, pp. 1–16

Townshend, Charles, *Easter 1916: The Irish Rebellion* (London, 2006)

Townshend, Charles, 'The Irish War of Independence: context and meaning', in Crowe (ed.), *Guide to the Military Service Pensions Collection*, pp. 110–24

Townshend, Charles, *The Republic: The Fight for Irish Independence* (London, 2013)

Travers, Pauric, 'History in primary school: a future for our past?', *History Ireland*, vol. 4, no. 3 (Autumn 1996), pp. 13–16

Valiulis, Maryann Gialanella, 'The man they could never forgive: the view of the opposition: Éamon de Valera and the civil war', in O'Carroll and Murphy (eds), *De Valera and His Times*, pp. 92–102

Valiulis, Maryann Gialanella, *Portrait of a Revolutionary: General Richard Mulcahy and the Founding of the Irish Free State* (Dublin, 1992)

Valiulis, Maryann Gialanella (ed.), *Gender and Power in Irish History* (Dublin, 2007)

Valiulis, Maryann Gialanella and Mary O'Dowd (eds), *Women and Irish History* (Dublin, 1997)

Vaughan, W. E. (ed.), *A New History of Ireland*, vol. 6: *Ireland Under the Union II, 1870–1921* (Oxford, 1996)

Walker, Brian, *Dancing to History's Tune: History, Myth and Politics in Ireland* (Belfast, 1996)

Walker, Brian, *Past and Present: History, Identity and Politics in Ireland* (Belfast, 2000)

Walker, Brian, *A Political History of the Two Irelands: From Partition to Peace* (Basingstoke, 2012)

Walker, Stephen, *Forgotten Soldiers: The Irishmen Shot at Dawn* (Dublin, 2007)

Ward, Margaret, *In Their Own Voice: Women and Irish Nationalism* (London, 1995)

Ward, Margaret, *Unmanageable Revolutionaries: Women and Irish Nationalism*, new edn (London, 1995)

Ward, Margaret, 'Gendering the Irish revolution', in Augusteijn (ed.), *The Irish Revolution*, pp. 168–86

Webster, Eileen, 'History in our schools', *The Bell*, vol. 7, no. 3 (December 1943), pp. 192–200

Westby, Gerard, *Kevin Barry: A Play in One Act*, 3rd edn (Dublin, 1971)

Wheatley, Michael, *Nationalism and the Irish Party: Provincial Ireland, 1910–1916* (Oxford, 2005)

White, Gerry, and Brendan O'Shea (eds), *A Great Sacrifice: Cork Servicemen Who Died in the Great War* (Cork, 2010)

White, Jack, *Misfit: A Revolutionary Life* (Dublin, 2005)

Williams, Desmond (ed.), *The Irish Struggle, 1916–26* (London, 1966)

Wohl, Robert, *The Generation of 1914* (London, 1980)

Woods, C. J., 'James Carty', in McGuire and Quinn (eds), *Dictionary of Irish Biography*, vol. 2, pp. 398–9

Yeates, Pádraig, *Lockout: Dublin, 1913* (Dublin, 2000)

Yeates, Pádraig, *A City in Wartime: Dublin, 1914–18* (Dublin, 2011)

Yeates, Pádraig, *A City in Turmoil: Dublin, 1919–21* (Dublin, 2012)

Yeates, Pádraig (ed.), *Liberty: 1916–2006* (Dublin, 2006)

Younger, Calton, *Ireland's Civil War* (London, 1979 [1968])

INDEX